CW01391116

'A compelling study of women's words in witchcraft trials across many countries located around the North Sea, it provides different methodological approaches and a transnational regard, giving valuable insight into the field of mentalities. Not only the voices of the accused come alive, but also those of the judges, the scribes, the witnesses, and all those involved in a large number of trials carefully chosen by the author.'

Marina Montesano, *University of Messina*, Italy

'The volume offers a useful model for using classical narratology in history and the history of witchcraft in general, backed up by a variety of sample analysis from various parts of Europe. The methodology is used to analyse questions of gender and agency, but it will be useful for scholars of various other perspectives on the history of witchcraft, too, including topics such as transfer of knowledge, creation of opinions, controlling of emotion and deconstruction of persecutions.'

Raisa Maria Toivo, *Tampere University*, Finland

THE VOICES OF WOMEN IN WITCHCRAFT TRIALS

Women come to the fore in witchcraft trials as accused persons or as witnesses, and this book is a study of women's voices in these trials in eight countries around the North Sea: Spanish Netherlands, Northern Germany, Denmark, Scotland, England, Norway, Sweden, and Finland.

From each country, three trials are chosen for close reading of courtroom discourse, and the narratological approach enables various individuals to speak. Throughout the study, a choir of 24 voices of accused women are heard which reveal valuable insight into the field of mentalities and display both the individual experience of witchcraft accusation and the development of the trial. Particular attention is drawn to the accused women's confessions, which are interpreted as enforced narratives. The analyses of individual trials are also contextualized nationally and internationally by a frame of historical elements, and a systematic comparison between the countries shows strong similarities regarding the impact of specific ideas about witchcraft, use of pressure and torture, the turning point of the trial, and the verdict and sentence.

This volume is an essential resource for all students and scholars interested in the history of witchcraft, witchcraft trials, transnationality, cultural exchanges, and gender in Early Modern Northern Europe.

Liv Helene Willumsen is Professor Emerita of History, University of Tromsø (UiT—The Arctic University of Norway), with a Ph.D. in history (Edinburgh, 2008) and a Ph.D. in literature (Bergen, 2003). Her books include *Witches of the North: Scotland and Finnmark* (Leiden, 2013). She has written the exhibition texts of Steilneset Memorial, Vardø, Norway. She was awarded the Norwegian King's Medal of Merit in 2019.

Routledge Studies in the History of Witchcraft, Demonology and Magic

The Science of Demons
Early Modern Authors Facing Witchcraft and the Devil
Edited by Jan Machielsen

Demonology and Witch-Hunting in Early Modern Europe
Edited by Julian Goodare, Rita Voltmer, and Liv Helene Willumsen

Folklore, Magic, and Witchcraft
Cultural Exchanges from the Twelfth to Eighteenth Century
Edited by Marina Montesano

The Voices of Women in Witchcraft Trials
Northern Europe
Liv Helene Willumsen

Magic, Witchcraft, and Ghosts in the Enlightenment
Edited by Michael R. Lynn

For more information about this series, please visit: www.routledge.com/Routledge-Studies-in-the-History-of-Witchcraft-Demonology-and-Magic/book-series/RSHWDM

THE VOICES OF WOMEN IN WITCHCRAFT TRIALS

Northern Europe

Liv Helene Willumsen

Routledge
Taylor & Francis Group

LONDON AND NEW YORK

Witches' Gathering, 1607 (detail). Frans Francken II (1581–1642)
© Yogi Black/Alamy Stock Photo

First published 2022
by Routledge
4 Park Square, Milton Park, Abingdon, Oxon OX14 4RN

and by Routledge
605 Third Avenue, New York, NY 10158

Routledge is an imprint of the Taylor & Francis Group, an informa business

British Library Cataloguing-in-Publication Data
A catalogue record for this book is available from the British Library

Library of Congress Cataloging-in-Publication Data
Names: Willumsen, Liv Helene, 1948– author.
Title: The voices of women in witchcraft trials : Northern Europe /
   Liv Helene Willumsen.
Description: Abingdon, Oxon [UK] ; New York, NY : Routledge, 2022. |
   Series: Routledge studies in the history of witchcraft, demonology and
   magic | Includes bibliographical references and index.
Identifiers: LCCN 2021046934 (print) | LCCN 2021046935 (ebook)
Subjects: LCSH: Trials (Witchcraft)—Europe, Northern—History. |
   Witchcraft and sex—Europe, Northern—History. | Witches—Legal
   status, laws, etc.—Europe, Northern—History. | Women—Legal status,
   laws, etc.—Europe, Northern—History. | Demonology—Europe,
   Northern—History.
Classification: LCC KJ985.W58 W55 2022 (print) | LCC KJ985.W58
   (ebook) | DDC 345.4/0288—dc23/eng/20211220

ISBN: 978-1-032-18616-0 (hbk)
ISBN: 978-1-032-18617-7 (pbk)
ISBN: 978-1-003-25540-6 (ebk)

DOI: 10.4324/9781003255406

Typeset in Bembo
by Apex CoVantage, LLC

To Tomas and Johannes

CONTENTS

ACKNOWLEDGEMENTS

The work on this book has led me to archival institutions and universities in several Northern European countries and to interesting archives and beautiful places. It has convinced me of the value of transnational studies. During my research stays, I encountered a professional attitude and great friendliness everywhere. I have many people to thank for their help, assistance, and encouragement. The work on this book has taken me twelve years. Reading original court records in different languages was challenging, and I am deeply grateful that so many of my colleagues employed at universities in the former Spanish Netherlands, Northern Germany, Denmark, Scotland, England, Norway, Sweden, and Finland have generously shared their knowledge and time in order to help me read and understand the sources.

Most of the work is based on close readings of original court records from witchcraft trials. The choice of three individual trials from each country established the text corpus to be analysed in this book, which mainly looks at the accused persons' voices. However, I also needed to obtain knowledge about the historical background and judicial conditions of each of the countries, so that the original records could be contextualized. For this, witchcraft scholars across Northern Europe were of enormous help, as they are experts on national or international levels. I am immensely grateful for this support and collegiality.

Starting with the chapter on Spanish Netherlands, I would like to thank Dries Vanysacker for letting me use the transcriptions of the original court records made by Jos Monballyu, and for helpful explanations of difficult words and expressions in the sources. My interactions with Dries Vanysacker were the starting point for the study of records from this area. As I do not speak Dutch, I was dependent on scholars who could help me interpret these records. Alinda Damsma has been of tremendous assistance. I would like to thank her for translating the Dutch sources into English and for coming to see me during one of my research stays in Edinburgh.

I would also like to thank Marieke Krijnen for good help with complementary translations from Dutch into English and for help with editing the entire book. Because my mother tongue is Norwegian, another good helper entered the picture: Synnøve des Bouvrie, who lives in Norway. Having Dutch as her mother tongue, she translated the Dutch sources into Norwegian for me. I would like to thank her for the work and for her respect for research based on original historical documents. Thus, to interpret the Dutch records, several languages were activated.

Moving on to Northern Germany, I am grateful to Rolf Schulte for advice regarding the selection of trials and for answering questions related to the content of the court records. His comprehensive knowledge of witchcraft trials in Schleswig-Holstein was of great help, and his solid published works were an inspiration during my research. During my work with the original court records, I completed several stays in Schleswig, working in the beautiful Prinzenpalais of the Landesarchiv Schleswig-Holstein. I would like to thank Malte Bischoff for good conversations about the archives. I would also like to thank Frau Haase and Frau Seiter for their efficiency and friendliness. Moreover, I am grateful that I was able to use the book collection of Dagmar Unverhau, kept in the library of the Landesarchiv Schleswig-Holstein. In addition, I would like to thank Klaus Struve for help with transcribing the court records from Northern Germany.

For Denmark, I am grateful for the help and guidance of Jens Chr. V. Johansen, whom I met several times during my research stays in Copenhagen. Johansen was a productive witchcraft scholar from the 1970s until his death in 2017, and his comprehensive knowledge of Danish witchcraft trials and perspectives on witchcraft research were important in shaping my interest in the study of witchcraft trials. Another Danish witchcraft scholar whose work has meant a lot to me is Merete Birkelund, who in the 1980s published a study on Danish witchcraft trials. I would also like to thank Louise Nyholm Kallestrup for her contribution to witchcraft research, which inspired my work. In addition, the work of Gustav Henningsen on Danish witchcraft trials has been of great interest. I enjoyed being able to work in the National Archives of Denmark in Copenhagen. I was always met by professional staff, and the hours spent in the reading room gave me memorable moments of archival joy, not least when valuable sources unexpectedly appeared. I would like to thank the Foundation for Danish-Norwegian Cooperation for financial support in 2016 and 2017, when I was stipendiat at Schæffergaarden. My study of Danish witchcraft trials also brought me to the town of Viborg, one of the oldest towns in Jutland, where the regional archives of Northern Jutland are kept in a wonderful old building. I am grateful for the assistance I received there.

Scotland has been important to my research since I started my Ph.D. in history at the University of Edinburgh in 2003. Several individuals have enriched my studies. I would first like to thank Julian Goodare for good cooperation over many years, for his inspiring publications on witchcraft trials, and for his willingness to share Scottish source material with an international audience. I would also like to thank Goodare for the work he has put in as director of the Survey of Scottish Witchcraft, a comprehensive database of importance to me and many other scholars. Next, I would like to thank Arne Kruse for his genuine interest in the magic language of witchcraft court records, and for embarking on a quest to East Lothian in search of traces of alleged witches' meetings. I would also like to thank Diane Baptie for help with the transcription of the Scottish court records, and Rob and Diane Baptie for travelling with me to the home villages of alleged witches from East Lothian. For interesting studies on Scottish witchcraft trials, I would like to thank Anna Cordey, Laura Paterson, Michelle Brock, Sierra Dye, and Brian Levack. I would like to thank the University of Edinburgh, School of History, Classics and Archaeology for inviting me as a visiting scholar in 2015. With regard to financial support, I would like to thank the Institute of Advanced Studies in the Humanities, University of Edinburgh, for hosting me as a visiting fellow in 2017. I would also like to thank the staff at the National Record Office and the National Library of Scotland in Edinburgh for good help.

Going to England, I would first like to thank Malcolm Gaskill for generously lending me his transcriptions of English court records, which enabled me to per- form close readings of the trials included in this book. Also, it was interesting to read Gaskill's publications on witchcraft trials and mentalities, as well as his in-depth study of the Essex witch-hunt. Among other scholars studying English witchcraft documents, I would like to thank Marion Gibson for her contributions based on a linguistic approach. This research was tremendously inspiring and eye- opening for my analyses of courtroom discourse. I also found James Sharpe's studies of English witchcraft trials thought-provoking with regard to new perspectives. In addition, Charlotte-Rose Millar's study on a particular English demonic creature, the familiar, was of interest.

In Norway, my home country, I began studying the Finnmark witchcraft trials from Northern Norway in 1980, when I started work on my master's thesis. Since then, I have expanded the geographical area of my research to include Scotland and Northern Europe, and I have reached out to an international audience by publish- ing the sources from Finnmark in English. From among the witchcraft scholars in Norway, I would first like to thank the Grand Old Man, Hans Eyvind Næss, for good conversations over the years and for his pioneering study on Norwegian witchcraft trials. His Ph.D. from 1981 made him the nestor of Norwegian witch- craft research, and I am grateful for what I have learned from his work. Next, I am grateful to Bente Gullveig Alver, who died in 2020, for her profound studies on witchcraft beliefs and seventeenth-century mentalities in Norway. Also inspiring were the studies of Rune Blix Hagen on men accused of witchcraft in Finnmark, those of Gunnar Knutsen on witchcraft trials in Eastern Norway, those of Ellen Alm on witchcraft trials in Trondheim, and those of Jørn Øyrehagen Sunde on judicial perspectives and legal history. I would like to thank my colleague Randi Rønning Balsvik for her encouragement of and interest in my research. I would also like to thank my colleague Randi Hege Skjelmo for enjoyable hours we spent working together.

The work with Swedish court records brought me to the beautiful, old archi- val buildings in Vadstena. In Sweden, I received good assistance from Per Sörlin in refining and correcting my transcriptions of Swedish court records. I am also grateful for his help with the introductory part of the Sweden chapter. In addition, Sörlin's research on Swedish witchcraft trials was informative and inspiring for my work. Witchcraft research in Sweden has flourished since the early 1970s, when Bengt Ankarloo's Ph.D. paved the ground for research on Swedish witchcraft trials. From among the Swedish studies published later on, it was interesting to read Linda Oja and Marie Lennersand's work on the life cycle of women acquitted during witchcraft trials, Mikael Häll and Per-Anders Östling's studies of folkloric beliefs related to witchcraft, Jacqueline van Gent's study of magical practices connected to the body, and not least Åsa Bergenheim's study on the connection between witchcraft trials, gender, and demonology.

For Finland, the help I received from Raisa Maria Toivo was of great significance. Her patience and encouragement when it came to working with the source material from Finland were immensely important, and I am deeply grateful for this. Also, Toivo's broad range of witchcraft studies, not least her works on witchcraft and gender, were an inspiration to me. Likewise, the research of another Finnish scholar, Jari Eilola, inspired me, particularly his studies on courtroom discourse in trials involving children as witnesses. I would also like to thank Marko Lamberg for his interesting work on women accused of witchcraft. In addition, Marko Nenonen contributed to the field of witchcraft research with original perspectives, which I found noteworthy.

During the years that I worked on this book, Edinburgh became a special place for me. Throughout my research stays there, I encountered knowledge as well as hospitality and warmth. For this I would like to thank Julian Goodare and Jackie Gulland, Arne Kruse and Brigitte Guénier, Rob and Diane Baptie, and Duncan and Elaine Stewart. Friends and family in Norway also gave me continuous support, and I would like to thank my friend Torild Meyer Levlin and my niece Gøril Brox for the care they have shown. I would also like to thank my husband Terje and my sons Tomas and Johannes for being the ground crew.

Tromsø, July 2021
Liv Helene Willumsen

ABBREVIATIONS

ÅD	Ålands Domsaga [Åland court records]
ASSI	Home Circuit Assize Records
BL	British Library, London
CUL	Cambridge University Library
DK	Danske Kancelli [Danish Chancellery]
EDR	Ely District Records
GH	Göta Hovrätt [Göta High Court]
KAH	Kansallisarkisto, Helsinki [National Archives of Finland, Helsinki (NAFH)]
KAT	Kansallisarkisto, Turku [National Archives of Finland, Turku (NAFT)]
KO	Kokkola
LAN	Landsarkivet for Nørrejylland [Regional State Archives of Northern Jutland]
LF	Lagtingsprotokoll for Nordland and Finnmark [Court records of the Court of Appeal for Nordland and Finnmark]
LHAK	Landeshauptarchiv Koblenz [State Archives of Koblenz]
LSH	Landesarchiv Schleswig-Holstein [State Archives of Schleswig-Holstein]
NAL	National Archives of Britain, London
NLS	National Library of Scotland, Edinburgh
NRS	National Records of Scotland, Edinburgh
OSA	Oud Stadsarchief [Old City Archives]
PPRT	Pohjois Pohjanmaan renovoidut tuomiokirjat/Northern Ostrobothnia domböker [District Court records (sent to the Court of Appeal) from Northern Ostrobothnia]
PRO	Public Record Office [became the National Archives of Britain in 2003]

RA   Riksarkivet Norge, Oslo [National Archives of Norway, Oslo]
RAB   Rijksarchief Brugge [State Archives of Bruges], Stad Brugge [City of Bruges]
RAD   Rigsarkivet Danmark, Copenhagen [National Archives of Denmark, Copenhagen]
RAS   Riksarkivet Sverige, Stockholm [National Archives of Sweden, Stockholm]
SABrugge   Stadsarchief Brugge [City Archives of Bruges]
SAT   Statsarkivet i Trondheim [Regional State Archives of Trondheim]
SATØ   Statsarkivet i Tromsø [Regional State Archives of Tromsø]
SF   Sorenskriveren i Finnmarks arkiv [Archives of the Finnmark District Magistrate]
SJT   Sjællandske Tegnelser [Records from Zealand]
SPD   State Papers Denmark
SSW   Survey of Scottish Witchcraft
ST   Stadtarchiv Trier [City Archives of Trier]
UG   Universiteitsbibliotheek Gent [University Library Ghent]
UU   Uppsala universitetsbibliotek [University Library Uppsala]
VL   Viborg Landsting [Viborg District Court]
VLA   Vadstena Landsarkiv [Swedish National Archives in Vadstena]

1

INTRODUCTION

'I listen to the dead with my eyes'.

Francisco Gomez de Quevedo y Villegas[1]

The Topic

'Reading is listening to the dead with your eyes'. Roger Chartier paraphrases a line by Spanish poet Francisco de Quevedo in his inaugural lecture of a chair devoted to the roles of the written word in European cultures between the end of the Middle Ages and the present day.[2] The same line appropriately describes the work I set out to undertake in this book, as the act of listening out for voices in written texts forms the core of my study. Chartier maintains:

> Only in rare documents, and in spite of the betrayals by the transcriptions of scribes, judges, or lettered men, can historians hear the words of the dead who were moved to tell of their beliefs and their deeds, recall their actions, or recount their lives.[3]

The historian's desire is to find such rare documents—sources which can tell us about the life, imagination, and destiny of people who lived before us. In my view, recorded proceedings from witchcraft trials could be documents of this kind, as they contain voices of individuals that can be listened out for.

This book has to do with voices, witchcraft trials, and gender. It is a contribution to research on courtroom discourse in witchcraft trials and on the history of mentalities in Early Modern Europe. It deals with the question of how accused women made their voices heard in witchcraft trials while under severe persecution. The witchcraft trials in Europe took place in the period 1450–1750, and

DOI: 10.4324/9781003255406-1

around 50,000 people were executed.[4] Through a detailed study of individual trial records from eight countries in Northern Europe, this book sheds new light on how voices of women came to the fore in the courtroom in Spanish Netherlands, Northern Germany, Denmark, Scotland, England, Norway, Sweden, and Finland. In addition to presenting the findings on a national level, I carry out a comparison between the countries. The study has significant implications for understanding Early Modern European witchcraft trials, because it is the first comparison of voices in witchcraft trials based on close readings of source material in the original languages of eight countries.

My thesis is that the voices of women as they appear in the court records of witchcraft trials may contribute to new and important knowledge about the ideas and abilities that ordinary women possessed and about courtroom discourse in a wider and more general sense. The strength of the study is its closeness to the language of the court records: it departs from the trials of individually accused women and the words these women uttered in the courtroom. Most often, the interrogation of a woman accused of witchcraft ended in a confession. I argue that these confessions are vital to elucidating the court records of witchcraft trials. These are multilayered, complex texts, with a rich potential for interpretation. In the confessions, it is possible to listen out for *what* the voices of women expressed as well as *how* this was expressed. It is further possible to uncover layers of meaning related to the development of the trial: positions taken by the accused women and the stages that each woman went through. The voices of women as they appear when listened out for in the recorded text tell about agony, despair, disillusion, strength, and hope. These voices are the theme of this book.

The following research questions constitute the backbone of my study: What were the witches' words? What characterized the voices of accused women? What influenced the voices of women? What was the judicial response to witches' voices? Can we find differences between various areas of Northern Europe? Can we find differences between the early and late period of witchcraft persecution in Northern Europe? The answers are manifold. The women protested, argued, told stories, and finally gave in. Their destinies lay in the hands of powerful men. However, even in this dark picture, in the most hopeless of situations, these women were left with a fragile thread of self-presentation, namely expressing themselves through enforced narratives—often with the Evil One as the main protagonist.

The confessions are particularly valuable parts of the records, as they provide insight into the mentalities of ordinary people in the seventeenth century. In addition, women's voices emerged during interrogation of the accused as well as in testimonies given by witnesses. On the one hand, the voices of women that are audible in the sources let us hear people who were in distress, having been exposed to severe pressure in a legal trial that accused them of a crime they could never have committed. On the other hand, the voices provide a glimpse of a world of beliefs and stories, tales learned via oral tradition, and ideas acquired from learned men in court or from the preaching of the church. As learned ideas were steadily assimilated into ordinary people's mental realm, the court records represent a rare possibility to encounter ideas that common people had about witchcraft, and to understand how these ideas were narrated in a courtroom.

The Sources

The main sources used to analyse the witchcraft trials from all over Europe are court records, as these trials were held mainly in secular courts. The proceedings of the trials were recorded by a scribe, and these records form the main objects of analysis. In addition, sources like accounts of expenses as well as adjacent judiciary documents shed light on witchcraft trials.

The court records analysed in this book are mostly unpublished sources, preserved in handwritten minute books or as loose documents in archival boxes. They were important documents in the legal field in a period when state bureaucracy was expanding, as they served to both document the trials and make it possible to pass the trial on to a Court of Appeal. While working on this book, I travelled to archives in person and read archival sources from all countries in the original language used by the scribe, except for court records from the Netherlands, where I needed professional assistance as I do not speak Dutch.[5]

The choice of which witchcraft trials to use for this study depended on several factors. The style used in the recording of the sources strongly influences the possibility to listen out for and conduct an analysis of the voices of women. The court records had to be written in a style that lets individual discourses, the speech of women, come to the fore. This means that it had to be possible to decipher the voices on an individual level and understand who was the speaker or whose words were rendered in a certain passage. It was also important to grasp the questions posed to the accused. In Northern Germany and Spanish Netherlands, questionnaires were used during interrogation, and the questions were written out. Sometimes, questions were denoted in the sources from the other countries, through insertions such as 'Being asked' or 'When asked'. Other times, it was possible to use the technique of 'shadow questions', which scrutinizes the answer given to uncover the question posed. For most of the analysed court records, the questions posed during interrogation could be reconstructed.

Next, the richness of the records' language mattered in the choice of trials to analyse, as a fruitful close reading of court records relies on these characteristics. The sources to be analysed had to be able to demonstrate the voices of women in great detail. Thus, the trial documents used in this study were chosen on linguistic grounds, as their style and linguistic richness made them particularly suitable for close reading with the intention of listening out for female voices. The recording of what was said in the courtroom provides shades and nuances to the trial document, and makes it possible to discern voices of all those who were active during the trial in one way or another.

I also aimed at achieving a balance between the different types of trials. Women accused of witchcraft were brought before the courts in two types of trials: single trials or witchcraft panics. These two types of trials were connected to different legal systems: the accusatorial or the inquisitorial system. A single trial most often followed an accusatory system, while a witchcraft panic most often was conducted according to an inquisitorial system. In a single trial, one individual at a time was brought before the court and accused of having performed witchcraft. In a witchcraft panic, one trial led to another in rapid succession during a short period of time due to denunciation of other suspects by the first accused person.

According to the accusatorial system,

> a criminal action was both initiated and prosecuted by a private person, who was usually the injured party or his kin. The accusation was a formal, public, sworn statement that resulted in the trial of the accused before a judge. If the accused admitted his guilt, or if the private accused could provide certain proof, then the judge would decide against the defendant.[6]

If there was any doubt, the court would appeal to God for signs of guilt or innocence. In witchcraft trials, the prosecutor called on his witnesses and other evidence to establish guilt. Witnesses' testimonies became important evidence. The content of these trials was traditional harmful witchcraft, or *maleficium*.[7]

In an inquisitorial system, 'the accuser was no longer responsible for the actual prosecution of the case (. . .) the new procedure allowed the inhabitants of a community to denounce a suspected criminal before the judicial authorities'.[8] This system allowed an officer of the court to cite a criminal on the basis of rumours or information he had obtained himself. In witchcraft trials, a judicial official usually interrogated the accused person. No witnesses were summoned. However, denunciations from other people accused in the same witchcraft panic carried great weight. Several trials would be linked, and they escalated rapidly due to the idea of participation in witches' gatherings and performance of collective witchcraft.[9] The content of these trials was related to a learned European doctrine: demonology.

However, the two legal principles did not always exist as two distinct systems. Dagmar Unverhau has argued that accusatorial trials often turned into inquisitional trials during witchcraft persecution.[10] This argument is supported by several of the analyses in this book, where it becomes clear that such a change took place during interrogation.

My choice of sources was also influenced by which ideas about witchcraft came to the fore. Two concepts of witchcraft existed in Early Modern Europe, and both are represented in the sources chosen for analysis: the concept of *maleficium* and the concept of demonological witchcraft. In a *maleficium* trial, the first part of the interrogation often dealt with spells that had been cast, causing sickness and death of people and animals, and with the stealing of milk and divination. In a demonological witchcraft trial, the interrogation focused on the demonic: the devil's pact, witches' gatherings, and the performance of collective witchcraft.

The sources chosen for analysis include a range of ideas about witchcraft and are able to throw light on courtroom discourse and court practice. The way the trials were recorded makes it possible to distinguish women's voices in several places, whether in women's speech rendered in third-person imperfect or past tense narration, in inserted sentences or monologues in first-person narration, or in witnesses' testimonies. And the way the documents are recorded enables a close reading, which is fruitful in the analysis of courtroom discourse. It makes it possible to catch and utilize the interplay between different voices in the analysis, and explore oral features surfacing in the accused individuals' confessions, as orality features are a strong indicator of accurate work of the scribe.

Demonology, *Maleficium*, Healing

My analyses will pay close attention to the wide range of ideas about witchcraft that appear in the trial records. The confessions in particular hold this valuable information, which connects to the field of imagination and beliefs.[11] These ideas are partly related to the learned doctrine of demonology and partly to the traditional performance of witchcraft, *maleficium*. In addition, several of the women accused of witchcraft were performers of healing, and ideas related to healing will be mentioned in some of the analyses.

The scholarly doctrine of demonology spread throughout Europe from the late 1400s through the first half of the seventeenth century, following the publication of a number of demonological treatises.[12] The core elements of this doctrine were a pact with the devil, witches' gatherings, and the performance of collective witchcraft. According to demonological ideas, a person who entered into a pact with the devil received the power to perform witchcraft in return. There was a ritual connected with entering the devil's pact. The witches' gathering, or sabbath, was a meeting at which the devil was worshipped. It usually took place in a field or on a mountain top. The trip to the witches' gathering and the activities there—dancing, drinking, eating, and even board games—created exciting stories that were narrated as part of confessions.[13] The main aim of the demonological doctrine was to describe the work of demons and their powers and to identify the devil's secret accomplices on earth. To this end, its teachings centred around how to recognize these accomplices and learn what they could achieve. These ideas had an impact on legislation and church affairs. Their collective aspect, which was implicit in the confessions to witches' gatherings, led to the swift accusation of numerous people within a brief time span, which we see demonstrated in witchcraft panics. These people were brought before the court, indicted for witchcraft, interrogated, convicted, sentenced to loss of life at the stake, and finally burned. Learned judicial officials introduced demonological ideas—entering into a pact with the devil, participating in witches' gatherings, and performing collective witchcraft—into witchcraft trials. These ideas were transmitted to the populace as a narrative that included the basic demonological elements. The confessions in witchcraft trials analysed in this study display various versions of this narrative, always with the main demonological elements preserved.

Performance of *maleficium*, traditional harmful witchcraft, is known from early times. The power some people have to manipulate forces in order to cause harm is known from old legends and in most communities. Even today, it is a living notion.

In the seventeenth century, it was believed that a few people simply had this power, and others did not. Those who had the ability to cast spells that caused sickness and death of humans and animals were gossiped about and feared. The entire community would know about their powers. In witchcraft trials, neighbours and local people appeared in courtrooms with accusations of malefice that had resulted in dead cattle, sick individuals, or shipwrecks. There had to be a reason for accidents that were otherwise impossible to explain. The answer was witchcraft. Witness testimonies exhibit the fear of witchcraft but also the intricate ways in which maleficent witchcraft could be performed, with the use of objects and formulas. As long as a local community experienced envy and a desire for revenge, there was a market for the performance of *maleficium*. The trials analysed will show the ways and means of malefice, and the eagerness and accuracy with which accusations based on hate and envy were expressed before the court.

Malevolent witchcraft was often combined with healing, as it was believed that the same woman who could cast a spell could also take away illness and heal someone. In this way, the ideas of *maleficium* and healing were interrelated: if healing went wrong, it was assumed that malefice had taken place; if spells had been cast, a person with power might be asked to 'unwitch'[14] someone and take the illness away. Bente Alver states that in the Early Modern period, conceptions of magical practice and witchcraft had become integrated into the world views of the intellectual elite and those of ordinary people in different ways.[15] The elite regarded the common man's magical practice as destructive and the performance of magic as evil. This stood in contradiction to the attitudes of ordinary people: 'Within the framework of folk belief, magical acts were not, as in a clerical context, related to the devil and his darkest sources of power'.[16] What emerges in the confessions is that a cunning woman with a reputation as a practitioner was a respected woman. She was the one who people in the village turned to in difficult situations. Bente Alver says: 'The cunning person was seen as a medium between "powers" and humans, and her skills were a power reservoir that could be used *for good and for bad*'.[17] [Original's italics.] This competence of the cunning woman goes in two directions, and this is why the ideas of *maleficium* and healing are intertwined in some trials.

Methodological Approach

The Importance of Language

The methodology chosen for this study is narratology. This methodology may be used in analyses of factual documents, non-fiction, and fiction. Marked attention is paid to language. My study is based on factual trial documents, in particular witchcraft confessions. My aim is to examine how these documents were crafted and how meaning is emphasized through narrative structures and expressed through the voices of the accused women. The manner in which a narrative is expressed impacts the contents.[18]

The importance of language has impacted the work of witchcraft scholars. Stuart Clark emphasizes the necessity of beginning with language if one is to make any kind of sense of the witchcraft beliefs of the past.[19] He underlines that historians are interpreters, 'and that historical understanding is achieved by approaching the past in much the same manner as a reader confronts a text—that is, by exploring patterns of meaning rather than causal relationships'.[20] This view is prevailing in Stuart Clark's comprehensive study *Thinking with Demons*, and in the anthology *Languages of Witchcraft* that he edited.[21] Clark's *Thinking with Demons* contains close readings of a number of demonological treaties. In his review of the book, Quentin Skinner says: 'But the truly novel character of his work stems from his demonstration of the multifarious ways in which demonological beliefs entered into the scientific as well as the religious and political assumptions of early-modern Europe'.[22] Clark assesses the construction of demonological texts and evaluates them on their own terms. He maintains:

> Paying attention to the way witchcraft was constructed, imagined, and represented, to its ability to carry meanings, and to its political, moral, and psychological significance in the lives of individuals and communities might be a different way of approaching it from that adopted in the past, but this approach itself owes much to theoretical assumptions about the relationships between belief and behaviour, language and reality, and the historian and the past.[23]

A collection of articles elaborating on Clark's work has been edited by Jan Machielsen, *The Science of Demons: Early Modern Authors Facing Witchcraft and the Devil*.[24] Another work using a linguistic approach which has influenced the field of witchcraft research is Marion Gibson's pioneering study *Reading Witchcraft*.[25] Her clear structuring of arguments and refined readings of texts have inspired my study of witchcraft trials, motivating me to listen out for voices in witchcraft court records and study narrative structures in accused people's confessions.[26] Also Gibson's study *Witchcraft: The Basics*, which crosses the borders of disciplines, pays tribute to the role of language in creating and shaping the concept of witchcraft.[27] Gibson's work has had an impact on adjacent research, characterized as it is by interdisciplinarity and linguistics. An emphasis on language in witchcraft documents is also seen in Sierra Dye's Ph.D. thesis *Devilishe Wordis*, where verbal performances are seen as key features in utterances that brought alleged witches to the attention of the kirk and the community.[28]

Narratology

My methodological approach is mainly based on Gérard Genette's influential study *Discours du récit* (Paris, 1972).[29] Genette's two subsequent works, *Nouveaux discours du récit* (Paris, 1983) and *Fiction et diction* (Paris, 1991) expand his original narratological framework and discuss the boundaries between fictional and factual narratives.[30] Narratology deals with the study of structures in narrative texts; an exploration of the narrator's function.[31] The narrator is seen as an absolutely necessary textual device in a narrative text. He possesses the highest authority in the text universe.

Genette's methodology fathoms fiction and non-fiction. He uses the terms 'diction' and 'factual narratives' for non-fictional texts, stating that because of research requirements, '[narratology] is unlikely to exempt us from having to undertake a specific study of factual narrative (. . .) Such a study would require a large-scale inquiry into discursive practices such as those of *history*, biography, personal diaries, newspaper accounts, police reports, *judicial narratives*'.[32] [My italics.] For factual narratives, Genette underlines the necessity to interpret them in their historical contexts. This is related to the fundamental difference between factual narratives and fictional narratives.[33] As Lubomír Doležel states, 'historical worlds are subject to restrictions that are not imposed on fictional worlds'.[34] In factual narratives, there is a textual layer of reference to historical events that does not occur in fiction.

Court records, the main documents analysed in this study, are interesting in two ways from a narratological angle. First, the entire document can be analysed as a narrative, with the function of the scribe similar to the function of the narrator, structuring and compiling the text.[35] Second, the narrator can delegate voice to a person taking part in the trial, letting her or him tell a story. Such a story will structurally function as an embedded narrative within the larger narrative of the full trial.

Genette operates with five categories in his analysis of narrative discourse: order, speed, frequency, focalization, and voice.[36] As a narratologist, Genette is particularly known for his handling of the category of voice.[37] The category of voice incorporate the narrator's voice and the person's voice. The narrator's voice is overall and leading, setting the scene, presenting the events, bringing the story forwards. The narrator may appear in first person, audible as an 'I' or 'we', being one of the characters in the story. The story may also be told in third person, the narrator using the pronouns 'he', she', or 'them' about the characters. In this case, there is a distance between the narrator and the characters or persons. The person's voice is heard when one of the persons participating in the story appears as a narrator in her or his own right.[38] This is the most common sort of narration.

In a witchcraft trial, a confession given by an accused woman is an example of a narrative where a person's voice is heard. Most often rendered in indirect discourse, the confession is written down as a coherent story about the learning and performing of witchcraft. The narrative structure lifts forth and strengthens the content of the confession. This type of narrative will primarily be analysed in the following.

The choice of narratology as methodology has to do with the overall structure of my study. I have chosen to study three trials from each country, and carry out close readings of a few trials instead of superficial readings of multiple trials. My aim has been to get close to individual persons accused and interrogated. To this end, narratology's category of voice offers an appropriate methodological tool because in a careful way it allows access to individualized discourse. My desire is to get hold of the personalized voices of women, as they can be discerned in court records. Extensive case analysis will in a pragmatic and tangible manner demonstrate how narratology can be used.

Although my topic is the voices of women, additional voices will resonate in them and influence the interpretation. Therefore, my task is to interpret various types of speech, among them the rendered speech from various persons participating in the trials. These voices are not easily revealed. They are subtle and entangled in different layers of the text. Examples are the voice of the law and the voice of the scribe. Still, these modulations are implicit in the records and can be reached through textual interpretation.

The use of narratology to open up historical documents draws on several disciplines. A narratological analysis pays careful attention to a record's language and the way stories are told, thus giving access to shades of meaning that would otherwise be overlooked. It provides extra insight through offering an understanding of how specific qualities characterize the voices that appear in the text. Singling out and getting close to the various voices in this way makes it possible to broaden the understanding of the discourse at stake and the verbal interaction in the courtroom. My textual interpretation has aimed at reaching intertwined levels of motivation and intention present in women's utterances in court.

A narratological approach connects closely with the abstract 'voices' that emerge separately in court records, whether it is the voice of the accused, the scribe, or the law, or the voices of the witnesses.[39] This approach gets close to the spectrum of meanings that are generated by a complex situation, as it attempts to uncover individual narrative strategies on different textual levels.

Comparison

The voices of women in witchcraft trials have many accents. On the one hand, these voices serve to bring the individual accused woman to the forefront by displaying her personal language and ways of expression. On the other hand, the voices of women contribute to uncovering the development of witchcraft trials as legal processes. The analyses pay attention to the various accents of women's voices, emphasizing that court records are multilayered texts. Although the women are the protagonists of this study, the voices of other participants in the trials will serve to deepen the contextual understanding of women's voices and throw light on the sequentiality and development of the trials.

Eight countries and twenty-four trials are included in the study. I chose three trials from each country: one from the early period of the country's witchcraft persecution, one from the middle period, and one from the late period. Each trial is described and explained as a particular case study, establishing a focal point of persecution on a national level—an illustrative case. By discussing the trials chronologically, a timeline is established, which makes it possible to see the development of the content of trials over the years for each country. The geographical distribution of the case studies offers a number of comparative points of view and an understanding of how legal systems and social structures influence phenomena such as witchcraft and witch trials.

Distinguishing the voices of women in court records of Early Modern witchcraft trials from eight different countries of Northern Europe enables a comparison based on certain factors. I have defined a contextual analytical framework consisting of factors found in all eight countries. I argue that a comparison of trials from the countries in question makes it possible to find patterns in the development of witchcraft trials in which women were accused. Ten factors are examined: confessions, witnesses' testimonies, narrative structures, orality features, interrogation, torture and pressure, enforced narratives, the voice of the law, the voice of the scribe, and transnational transfer. These factors create a framework around the main object, making it possible to compare the countries in terms of similar conditions. The analytical framework includes major factors characterizing the voices of women and provides insight into courtroom discourse, court practice, and the way of thinking of accused individuals, witnesses, and judicial officials.

Naturally, it has to be taken into account that some common institutions may have performed different functions in different societies or at different times, Still, it is possible to find general similarities in a number of fields and to see patterns when investigating witchcraft trials on a more general basis.[40] One can draw general conclusions and look for regularities. Attention to the details of individual cases can contribute to ongoing witchcraft research. I will attempt to formulate some generalizations through parallel descriptions and analyses of common features in the eight countries.

The first point of comparison consists of the confession of the accused woman. This is a very important factor, which will be studied in detail. In the confessions, a broad range of ideas about witchcraft emerges, as do narrative structures and orality features. Here, the voices of women distinctly come to the fore. The confessions are complex texts that can be approached from various angles. They also show how an enforced narrative is created and clarify the turning point of the trial.

The study of the confessions uncovers the questions posed and the answers given during interrogation, which can then be interpreted in the context of the trial. The questions are either rendered in the court records or can be detected by establishing 'shadow questions', traced in the formulation of the women's answers. The uncovering of these questions will provide knowledge about which ideas were given weight during the interrogation, and thus signal the main ideas of the interrogators.

My methodological approach in working with confessions and women's voices is narratology. As most accused women lived in oral societies, the mastering of storytelling was a key element in how they expressed and presented themselves. The confessions are stories that are structured according to the basic rules of a narrative, and these structuring lines usually steer the confession. The analysis of the confessions makes it possible to decipher different modes of women's voices and fathom the complexity and range of interpretative possibilities. The content of the confessions shows what spectrum of ideas about witchcraft the women possessed. The confessions also show the woman's strategy for getting through the trial.

The second point of comparison consists of the witnesses' testimonies, where women's as well as men's voices are heard in the rendering of witchcraft. These testimonies deal with malevolent witchcraft: the performance of *maleficium*. The testimonies were given by people who wanted to provide the court with evidence of performed witchcraft. As the notion of witchcraft is old and was known in most societies and on all continents, the testimonies reflect well-known knowledge among the populace.

The third point of comparison is formed by narrative structures. The linguistic form in which stories were told was crucial in the process of the transference of ideas about witchcraft. This is because the way in which stories were told was already known by the villagers and made the content easy to adopt. It is likely that narrative structures surfaced in the demonological confessions because the story about entering the devil's pact and the witches' gatherings was easy to retell orally.

The fourth point of comparison consists of orality features. Orality features play an important role in the analysis, as they are vital in establishing the personalized and individualized language of the accused woman. Studying orality features is crucial for getting to know the personal language expression of each accused woman. Orality markers in the confessions strengthen the scribe's effort to preserve the words each accused person said as precisely as he could. Elizabeth S. Cohen has pointed to the special position of court records, situated as they are between oral and written discourse: 'Sharing an intermediate textual zone that has attracted increasing scholarly attention in early modern cultural studies, these several sorts of non-literary sources invite a comparative analysis and double modes of reading'.[41] Cohen suggests an approach to court records as documents based on oral utterances given in a courtroom.[42]

The fifth point of comparison is interrogation, which in witchcraft trials was conducted by men alone: the district governor, the bailie, the deputy bailie, the magistrate, or the executioner. The voices of women can be heard when they answer questions. Interrogation was one of the stages of a witchcraft trial that gave access to the ideas directing the development of the trial.

The sixth point of comparison is torture and pressure. To understand the development of witchcraft trials, it is important to bear in mind that the confession had to come from the accused person's own mouth, as witchcraft was a crime that could not be proved by the ordinary burden of proof. This is where the use of torture and pressure came in. Expressing demonological ideas was considered dangerous, and torture or pressure were often used to force a confession. The stages of a witchcraft trial frequently followed a line from resistance to surrender, and the gradual way in which an accused person was broken down through exposure to pressure and torture becomes evident from a close reading of the court records.

The seventh point of comparison is enforced narrative. The accused delivered their confessions as narratives. These stories affected trial outcomes. Gunvor Simonsen, commenting on courtroom practice in Danish West Indian courts, says that 'inclusive procedures and repressive verdicts went hand in hand and enabled slaves to tell their stories while simultaneously allowing judges to sentence them harshly afterwards'.[43] This has a parallel in witchcraft trials. The accused would not have confessed without the use of coercion. Still, the confessions are formed as narratives. Leading questions often directed a confession towards demonology. However, it should be noted that the women responded in a more expanded way than merely 'Yes' or 'No' to a question posed. This points to the competence these women possessed with regard to ideas about witchcraft held before coming to the courtroom. Analyses of enforced narratives provide input to understand emotions that surfaced. The recorded words of an accused woman provide a powerful means of grasping feelings represented in historical documents.

The eighth point of comparison is the voice of the law, which in this study mainly comes to the fore in the wording of the verdict and sentence. The application of torture signals the voice of the law as well. The crime of witchcraft included the performance of demonological witchcraft and of *maleficium*, traditional harmful witchcraft. Also, being an accomplice in the performance of witchcraft and in performing and receiving healing led to accusations in witchcraft trials. The sentences in witchcraft trials varied, but demonological witchcraft as well as *maleficium* were severely punished in all countries analysed in this study. They were the result of a development in the European legal field governed by the state and implemented in the laws and courts; a development in which borrowing between countries was important.[44]

The ninth point of comparison is the voice of the scribe. In Northern Europe, the scribe was a professional person who aimed at providing a broad description of what was said in the courtroom and of the development of the trial. He recorded the various phases of the trial and documented the arguments used to decide on the verdict and sentence, particularly important because the court records could be sent onwards to the Court of Appeal.

The tenth point of comparison relates to transnational transfer, or transnational and transcultural findings related to ideas about witchcraft. The analyses will investigate how ideas travelled and expanded, both within one country and across borders. Related motifs might be found in several countries, and the route of transference can sometimes be discovered. Demonological ideas probably entered Northern Europe from the south. I argue that there was an increase in witchcraft trials in Europe around 1585-1590 due to the circulation of demonological ideas, which occurred via Denmark between three countries: Germany, Scotland, and Norway.[45] The transfer of demonological ideas appears within a 'witchcraft triangle' constituted by borders drawn between Trier in Western Germany, North Berwick in South-Eastern Scotland, and Vardø in Northern Norway. The choice of places has to do with the appearance of demonological ideas in witchcraft trials in these places with only thirty years between them: 1585–89, 1590–91, and 1620. Two of these places, North Berwick in 1590–91 and Vardø in 1620, were pristine areas with regard to demonological ideas.

The Context

Witchcraft trials did not exist in a vacuum. A close reading of the court records requires contextualization, as the context of persecution influenced the words of alleged witches. This study takes the context of trials into account throughout the analyses of court records. Each country is introduced by a short overview of national persecution and judiciary conditions. In this way, the voices of women as they are heard echo discursive features not only from within but also beyond the courtroom.

In Early Modern Europe, lay as well as learned people believed that witchcraft could be performed and that some people possessed this ability. Common people were influenced by the traditional ideas of maleficent witchcraft. By using their power, alleged witches might perform effective witchcraft that could result in a catastrophe or an accident affecting a local community. This belief formed part of the mentality of the populace. The learned way of thinking, on the other hand, was influenced by ideas related to the doctrine of demonology. The written words of learned demonological treaties travelled across Europe and had an impact on the functioning of the state, the laws, the mental luggage of the judiciary, and the preaching of the church. The oral statements of alleged witches as they come to light, particularly in their confessions, were often a mixture of traditional knowledge and new learned ideas. However, the court records reveal that the voices of women in witchcraft trials were much more complex than what could be expected from traditional knowledge alone *or* the sole influence of leading questions during the interrogation based on the judiciary's learned ideas. There are several intermediate levels at which assimilations and transmittance might have taken place. The confessions are a composite of various mentalities activated during the trial. The aim of this study is to try to interpret and understand what is heard in these recorded utterances.

Geographical Scope: Northern Europe

The geographical scope of this book is Northern Europe. Areas included in the study are Spanish Netherlands, Northern Germany, England, Scotland, Denmark, Norway, Sweden, and Finland. For Northern Germany, I have focused on Schleswig-Holstein. For the Nordic countries, I have chosen to treat Denmark and Norway separately because, even if they were united in the period of witchcraft trials, each country had a legal system of its own. Similarly, I have treated Finland and Sweden as separate countries, even though Finland did not exist as an independent country in the Early Modern period. Swedish laws were used at the time in the areas which belong to the country of Finland today.[46] The Finnish cases in this book belong to today's Finland.

There are several reasons for the focus on Northern Europe. The most important one is the way the sources are written. There is a difference between Northern Europe and areas of South-Western Europe when it comes to the style and completeness of written legal records. While court records from witchcraft trials in the Nordic countries, the Schleswig-Holstein area, the Spanish Netherlands, England, and Scotland are very rich and aim at providing an accurate description of what was said and what happened in the courtroom, some court records from South-Western Germany are rewritten and shortened. They contain only a brief summary of the trial, with the verdict and sentence shortened and summarized by the scribe. These records are correct with regard to some points of the trial—such as the name of the accused, the date, location, and type of trial, the verdict, and the sentence—but abbreviated compared to court records from many other areas when it comes to the utterances in the courtroom. This makes the sources unsuitable for discourse analysis.[47] A condensed type of source material is seen in the Trier area, where a register with names of executed people has been preserved, documenting severe persecution.[48] However, trial records related to the individuals named in this register vary considerably, and unfortunately many records have been lost.

To perform a discourse analysis, it is crucial to have sources of great detail that cover what happened during the trial. Such records are found in the Schleswig-Holstein area, as shown by Rolf Schulte and Dagmar Unverhau.[49] Also another complete collection of records from a witchcraft trial in Germany, which has been translated into English, is published.[50] For English witness testimonies, I have worked with source editions, such as the two volumes by L'Estrange Ewen, as well as transcriptions of documents and studies by Malcolm Gaskill.[51] Likewise, rich sources are found in Normand and Roberts's sourcebook about the North Berwick trials.[52] The same is demonstrated in my sourcebook about the Finnmark trials in Norway.[53] I argue that the court records from Northern Europe are very suitable for performing analyses of courtroom discourse, taking into account all necessary text-critical reservations related to the role of the scribe and his potential influence on the records. The suitability of the records has to do with their linguistic richness and completeness and with the scribe's effort to render what was said in the courtroom.

Another reason for the geographic choice of Northern Europe is the impact of the Protestant Reformation. Through religious texts promoted for use in churches, the state had a firm hand in what the church preached on the topic of witches.[54] All countries included in my study, with the exception of Spanish Netherlands, were Protestant countries. This had an impact on the ideas about the devil and his power that surfaced in sermons. In addition, demonological treaties published in Northern Europe and Scandinavia throughout the sixteenth and seventeenth centuries exhibited several similar features in the post-Reformation period.[55] All in all, most of Northern Europe had several ideas in common when it came to religious thought. These came to influence the mentalities of the common people as well as the learned elite. The role of the church was strongly interwoven with the role of the state, and this greatly affected the initiation of witchcraft trials and their continuation. Thus, countries in the geographical area I have chosen to concentrate on were characterized by a religious background influenced by the Reformation and a similar urge by the state to discipline people into following the correct faith.

Northern Europe was also chosen because of similarities in legal practice. In the countries included in this study, accusatorial as well as inquisitorial principles influenced legal practice in the courtrooms during witchcraft trials. Similarities within the field of law will ease a comparative study, while respective differences also have to be taken into account.

A final reason for choosing Northern Europe is its closeness to the sea. People travelled frequently by ship at the time, and boats were the primary communication link between the countries included in this study. Particularly the North Sea was important for routes between the Continent, the British Isles, and the Nordic countries.

Order of Chapters

With eight countries represented in this book, I would like to clarify the choice of the order of the chapters. This order was chosen partly because of geographical closeness and partly because of the transmission of witchcraft ideas. I have, where possible, tried to follow the transmission of witchcraft motives from one country to another. Therefore, a combination of connecting links via cultural transfer and geographical proximity steered the choice of the order of chapters.

The witchcraft trials analysed in this book cover the time span 1584–1685: the last decades of the sixteenth century and most of the seventeenth century. In Southern Europe, particularly Switzerland and Germany, witchcraft persecution had taken place from around 1450. Thus, the witch-hunt spread northwards in Europe. Books related to demonology spread accordingly, helped by Gutenberg's printing press, and towards the end of the sixteenth century, these ideas were well known in northern part of Europe. The famous demonological treatise *Malleus Maleficarum* by Heinrich Kramer, published in Speyer in 1486, made an impact on witchcraft persecution all over Europe through twenty editions published between 1486 and 1520, and another sixteen editions between 1574 and 1669. The Cologne edition was published in 1520.[56] Another influential tract was written by Peter Binsfeld—the suffragan bishop of Trier—titled *Tractatus de confessionibus maleficorum et sagarum*, published in Latin in 1589, in two German translations in Trier in 1590, and twice in Munich in 1591/1592.[57] In addition, a well-known demonological treatise was Jean Bodin's *De la démonomanie des sorciers*, published in Antwerp in 1586, after first having been published in Paris in 1580. By 1604, Bodin's work had been published ten times.[58]

I start this book with the Spanish Netherlands and Northern Germany because these countries played an important role in the process of transmitting demonological witchcraft ideas from South-Western Germany to Denmark at an early stage of the Northern European witch-hunt. This route of transference passed through Cologne and Antwerp before reaching Copenhagen. However, in the Low Countries—the Spanish Netherlands and the Dutch Republic—the intensity of the witch-hunt differed between the northern and the southern parts. The Spanish Netherlands experienced the most severe witchcraft trials. Contrary to the Dutch Republic, which had only three demonological trials before 1590, Flanders and Brabant witnessed a large-scale witch-hunt after 1585.[59]

In the Trier region, including the Prince Abbey of St Maximin, severe witch-hunts strongly influenced by demonological ideas began around 1585.[60] The cases from the city of Trier and the St Maximin district are notorious, due to the huge numbers of executed people, and helped establish a paradigm for a new type of persecution that influenced Northern Europe.[61] Witchcraft scholars emphasize the spread of ideas through the media, including tracts and pamphlets.[62] A tract containing information about the ongoing witchcraft trials in Trier, St Maximin, and Western Germany was translated from German into Dutch in 1589 and printed in Cologne.[63] The tract appeared during a tense period in terms of witchcraft persecution. Its content had probably reached Denmark by 1589, due to the close contact between Denmark and Northern Germany.[64] The tract was published in Copenhagen in 1591 under the title *En Forskreckelig oc sand bescriffuelse, om mange Troldfolck*.[65] In Schleswig-Holstein, the persecution of witches notably increased from 1580 onwards. Rolf Schulte has called this a 'Europe-wide pressure to persecute'.[66] Thus, the chapters on Spanish Netherlands and Northern Germany appear first in the order of this book because these countries influenced Danish witchcraft persecution and also the Scottish witch-hunt.

The two following chapters deal with Denmark and Scotland. As shown above, a considerable amount of demonological witchcraft literature was known in Denmark's neighbouring countries by 1590. These ideas must have influenced Danish witchcraft trials, which began in Copenhagen in the summer of 1590 and which activated demonological ideas. The printing of the tract containing news about the Trier, St Maximin, and Western German witchcraft trials fuelled the Copenhagen 1590 trials. Further, the Copenhagen trials had clear links to the first demonological Scottish trials, the North Berwick trials, which started at the end of 1590 and continued in 1591.

The next two chapters deal with England and Norway. The choice of placing England after Scotland was made because of geographical closeness as well as relations in the political, religious, and legal fields, a complexity studied by Brian P. Levack.[67] However, I also considered discussing Norway directly after Scotland, as there is a direct link of transference of demonological ideas between Scotland and the county of Finnmark in Northern Norway. This transmission of ideas was performed by a Scotsman, John Cunningham, who was in the service of the Danish king and appointed district governor of Finnmark in 1619, an office he kept until 1651.[68] Cunningham knew demonological ideas and activated them during interrogations in Finnmark witchcraft trials. This link can be traced by comparing similarities in words and concepts in the court records of Scotland and Finnmark.[69]

The last two chapters deal with Sweden and Finland. Sweden is placed after Norway due to both geographical closeness and the similarity of a specific motif: a witchcraft gathering place called Blåkulla. In Sweden, the Blåkulla motif is well known in numerous witchcraft trials from the last half of the seventeenth century. However, it is also activated earlier in witchcraft court records from both Norway and Sweden. The Blåkulla motif also creates a bridge between Sweden and Finland, as Blåkulla trials are found in both areas. Close ties between Sweden and Finland are found in the political, religious, and legal fields, as Finland at this time was a part of Sweden. Among other commonalities, the two countries had the same laws and shared a language in some areas (Finnish in some parts, and Swedish in others). These connections between Sweden and Finland come clearly to the fore in the analyses of witchcraft trials. The witchcraft trials in Finland started relatively late compared to the other countries in the study; therefore, it was natural to place the country last.

The links between the eight countries represented in the study show that ideas about witchcraft travelled rapidly in Northern Europe. Similarities as well as differences within states and courts influenced the development of witchcraft persecution, as will become clear in the analyses.

The Role of the Scribe

Several witchcraft scholars have studied the scribe's possible influence on court records. It is an interesting but also difficult aspect to determine, because there are uncertain factors involved. Different countries had different styles of recording, which influenced—among other things—how the confessions were rendered. In the Nordic countries, the confessions were usually written down in past tense, third-person narration, with direct speech inserted as monologues and dialogues. The English court records were written down in the same way, as were the court records from the Spanish Netherlands. In Scotland, the court records combine past tense, third-person narration, and an indictment in which the accused person is addressed as 'You' and the points of accusation are numbered. In Northern Germany, there is a combination of past tense, third-person narration as a brief, initial description of the trial and a confession in numbered points, addressed to a 'You', which the accused person had to confirm. A greater difference, however, is that in some areas of Germany, as mentioned above, the original court records were rewritten and shortened by the scribe. In such documents, women's voices can hardly be traced.

All scholars working with legal documents use texts as their research object. Their interpretation of sources will differ, dependent on their methodology, way of reading, and type of material. There is consensus among scholars that court records were influenced by the scribe in terms of precision, errors, shortcuts, and possible changes introduced by interventions.[70] However, opinions differ on the extent to which a scribe influenced the semantic content of the sources. German scholars have argued that in some areas, the scribe's mark on the records is strong, as shown in Jürgen Macha and co-authors' studies of interrogation minutes,[71] Eva Topalovic's study of interrogation minutes from the district of Westfalen,[72] and Macha and Herborn's sourcebook mentioned above.[73] Rita Voltmer argues that judicial reframing was pronounced in confessions and depositions in witchcraft trials: in search of individual voices in the courtroom, scholars are in danger of labelling as local folklore what is really the lore of the judges and the scribes.[74] Peter Rushton maintains that the type of narrative we hear in witnesses' testimonies in English witchcraft cases is determined by a number of shared understandings that are all intended to be convincing about signs of the diabolical, and that these tenets tend to create a pattern. Rushton argues that 'bewitchment' is constituted in the depositions themselves; we cannot go behind the testimonies to find another source.[75] Such a text-immanent position renders the voices of historical actors inaudible.

Alison Rowlands presents a view that relies more on what historical documents may reveal. In an analysis of the Rothenburg witchcraft trials, she argues that in testimonies' recorded speech, one can find 'perceptions of honour; experiences of motherhood, childhood, marriage, illness and war, and beliefs about magic and religion'.[76] The same view is presented by Barbara Kryk-Kastovsky and Kathleen L. Doty, who have analysed historical courtroom discourse in a variety of documents, including indictments and church minutes. They maintain that courtroom records more faithfully reflect the spoken language in a given historical period than other sources, depending on the degree of orality, and that these sources also provide historical information.[77] This displays trust in historical documents' ability to convey knowledge about factual events.

Malcolm Gaskill, who has been studying depositions, argues that the way these texts were structured provides access to the mental and psychological worlds of the people who spoke these words, not just the expectations of those who demanded them or wrote them down.[78] Gaskill maintains that the historical importance of depositions is not only what they tell us about crime and the law, but also 'how they can help us to recover popular mentalities in general'.[79] This is an understanding of historical documents as complex texts which convey meaning, with possibilities for a broad interpretational approach. I share this understanding. Confessions in witchcraft trials constitute glimpses of a mentality that are otherwise hard to find in seventeenth-century historical sources.

A scribe recording witchcraft trials had to deal with form as well as content. The influence of legal conventions on the scribe's rendering of courtroom discourse is a formal feature. However, rules and conventions did not dictate what a person said.[80] With regard to the content of the witchcraft confessions, the knowledge of the accused person is decisive. When the accused person delivered a confession, it probably reflected ideas and notions known in the villages through oral transfer and assimilation. In my view, it is problematic to argue that the scribe constructed the content of the confessions.

The Gender Perspective

This book is a contribution to gendered witchcraft research. I take a clear gender approach in my choice to study women's voices in particular. My reason for doing so is simple: women were predominant in Early Modern witchcraft trials.[81] It is a well-known fact that women formed the majority—about 80% on average—of those accused and sentenced during European witchcraft persecution.

The topic of women in court involves many complexities. In this study, I focus on representations of women's voices drawn from legal records. The scene is a trial in a courtroom, and thus the backdrop to women's voices as they are revealed in this study is coloured by the judicial apparatus. In the courtroom, the power situation was clear and gendered. The judicial officials had all the power to decide on judicial practice, interrogation, the use of pressure, the verdict, and the sentence.

The judicial officials were individuals: learned people influenced by contemporary ideas. They carried out the interrogation with a subjective understanding of witchcraft and with a certain determination towards this particular part of their work, namely the trying of alleged witches. They might have been acquainted with learned demonological ideas about witchcraft, but the extent to which such ideas had been received and interpreted on an intellectual level probably varied widely. Further, the judicial officials might or might not have had knowledge of traditional beliefs in the local communities. When the interrogation of a suspected witch began, questions had to be of such a nature that they would result in the alleged witch's confession, be that a demonological confession to a pact with the devil or a confession to *maleficium*. The way in which such an interrogation was carried out was influenced by the mental luggage of the interrogator as well as court practice and the letters of the law. In the courtroom, women's voices were heard as responses to such questioning, and the development and outcome of the trial was apparently linked to the judiciary's leading questions. The judicial officials were always men, so the gender context of interrogations was a given.

However, as will be seen in the analyses that follow, the arena of the courtroom was also a place where women acted on their own behalf and where they shared their culture of popular beliefs. A study of the voices of women in witchcraft trials will bring us close to understanding the entanglement of traditional knowledge about witchcraft and Early Modern learned ideas found in the mental realm.

Research on Narrative Discourse, Gender, and Witchcraft

Narrative Discourse

Discourse studies and studies of narrative structures related to court records represent an ongoing field of research. Two examples are Laura Gowing's study on narratives of slander litigation in Early Modern London[82] and Garthine Walker's study of narratives of violence in Early Modern Cheshire.[83] Both studies focus on narrative conventions used by women in the legal courtroom. Gowing and Walker concentrate on the narrative skills that characterize the discourse of a group of women.

Also, interesting research has been performed by Barbara Kryk-Kastovsky, Kathleen L. Doty, and Risto Hiltunen. They have conducted research on general methodological questions and analysed the Salem documents from a linguistic point of view.[84] In addition, another scholar focusing on the linguistic complexity of legal documents and to how legal documents can be read in multiple ways has had an impact on my research, namely Elizabeth S. Cohen, mentioned above. Her analyses of historical legal documents pay particular attention paid to the linguistic interplay coming to the fore in the voices of the accused individuals in the courtroom.[85]

Also, Gunvor Simonsen's *Slave Stories*, mentioned above, has profoundly inspired my close readings.[86] Although Simonsen studies court records from the West Indies, her methodological approach closely resembles mine, as the aim of the study is to interpret the voices of individuals that can be discerned in the court records. Simonsen's explanation of methodological questions sets the example, admirably clear. Another interesting book is Miles Ogborn's *The Freedom of Speech*, a study of speech and slavery in the Anglo-Caribbean world. It relates to my study particularly in its focus on evidence of speech and orality features possible to trace in archival documents, 'where the speech of the enslaved is recorded only under particular circumstances'.[87]

Another close reading of a historical witchcraft narrative is Emma Wilby's *The Visions of Isobel Gowdie*, in which she tried to reconstruct in great detail the interrogation and confessions during a Scottish witchcraft trial while analysing shamanistic and demonological elements.[88] However, methodologically, Wilby's study differs from a narratological approach, particularly because it draws on a wide range of knowledge from different subject fields instead of treating the document text as the object of analysis. In the latter approach, the discourse interaction in itself is of great importance. That said, I would like to underline that when analysing historical source material, the principle of the autonomy of the text—making the text itself the sole object of analysis—is not satisfactory. It is also necessary to bring in the historical context in order to understand the meaning of the text and take its contemporary historical background into account.

There are a few examples in which a narrative perspective attracted the attention of historians. Alison Rowland's study of German witchcraft trials mentioned above and Natalie Zemon Davis's study *Fiction in the Archives* come to mind.[89] Davis especially focuses on the interests of the narrator and the audience in a storytelling event, and she emphasizes the importance of a cultural framework when undertaking historical interpretation. She is also concerned with the

> 'structures' existing prior to that event in the minds and lives of the sixteenth-century participants: possible story lines determined by the constraints of the law and approaches to narrative learned in past listening to and telling of stories derived from other cultural constructions.[90]

This is an important point, especially when investigating the opportunities for demonological ideas to take hold in the oral world of local communities. In addition, Davis has some interesting perspectives on the textual analysis of historical documents, stating that her focus is not on the formal mechanics of a literary structure but rather on how sixteenth-century people told stories and 'how their stories varied according to teller and listener and how the rules for plot in these judicial tales of violence and grace interacted with wider contemporary habits of explanation, description, and evaluation'.[91] The approach suggested by Davis is exemplary, as it takes into consideration the archival text as well as the wider cultural context.

I would also like to mention a Norwegian interdisciplinary study by Petter Aaslestad, *Pasienten som tekst*,[92] in which the author uses Gérard Genette's methodological approach to study patient journals from a mental hospital. I myself have contributed to the studies of court records based on Genette's narratology, particularly the category of voice, carrying out discourse analysis of separate court records in my doctoral thesis in history and in my book *Witches of the North*, in addition to a number of articles.[93]

Gender and Witchcraft

The gender perspective has resulted in witchcraft studies published either as monographs or as articles, whereof a few are included in survey works on witchcraft. In the two most comprehensive works on witchcraft, Richard M. Golden's *Encyclopedia of Witchcraft* and Brian P. Levack's *Oxford Handbook of Witchcraft*, the aspect of gender is treated among other aspects of witchcraft. Both works have specific articles on gender.[94]

Of in-depth studies dealing with gender and witchcraft in particular, I would first like to mention Raisa Maria Toivo's book *Witchcraft and Gender in Early Modern Society*,[95] which is a careful study of witchcraft persecution in Finland. Toivo performs a close reading of a case of a woman in Finland, Agata Pekantytär, who was accused of witchcraft and acquitted. She also follows Agata's life story after the end of the trial and pays attention to the healing process in the local community, which once more accepted Agata as a full member. In addition, the book looks at European witchcraft trials from a gender perspective. Toivo has also discussed the gender question in articles.[96] Jari Eilola takes up the question of witchcraft and the domestic sphere in Finland in an article.[97] Further monographs from the Nordic countries focusing on gender and witchcraft are the Swedish studies by Marie Lennersand and Linda Oja, who look at the life stories of women who were accused of witchcraft and acquitted.[98] A study by Jacqueline van Gent titled *Magic, Body and the Self in Eighteenth-Century Sweden* focuses on the psychological and emotional aspects of magical performance.[99] Another Swedish scholar, Åsa Bergenheim, has written *Den liderliga häxan*, with a focus on the connection between women accused of witchcraft and demonological ideas.[100] From Denmark, Merete Birkelund's book *Troldkvinden og hendes anklagere*[101] is an early contribution to the gender approach to witchcraft studies, and Louise Kallestrup's book *I Pagt med Djævelen* integrates gender questions throughout.[102] Regarding Norway, Ellen Alm has conducted a case study of a trial against a woman in Trondheim in the 1670s.[103] My M.A. thesis *Trollkvinne i nord*[104] is an early gender and interdisciplinary study of witchcraft in Europe's northern periphery. The question of gender also runs through my later publications.[105] I would furthermore like to mention the proceedings from a Nordic gender conference that deal with witchcraft, among other topics.[106]

From the Continent, a few studies on German witch trials take a gender approach. An early witchcraft scholar using this lens was Dagmar Unverhau, who worked with sources from Schleswig.[107] Another study based on German source material is Lyndal Roper's *Witch Craze*.[108] Using a psychoanalytical perspective in her analyses of several witchcraft trials, she opens up new perspectives on studies of historical documents. Laura Kounine's *Imagining the Witch* is a study of witchcraft trials in Württemberg.[109] The book takes a gender approach and tries to identify, on an individual and communal level, the feelings that were involved in witchcraft trials, contributing to the history of emotions.

As for England and Scotland, several volumes using a gender approach to witchcraft have appeared in the last twenty-five years. From England, several interdisciplinary studies have shed new light on gendered witchcraft research. Marion Gibson has written several books that cross the boundaries between literature and history, including *Early Modern Witches*[110] and *Witchcraft Myths in American Culture*, contributing to a broad understanding of the image of the witch.[111] In her study *The Witch in History*, Diane Purkiss uses historical documents and literature. She draws attention to textuality, narration, and genre, and she approaches her topic from a feminist and gender perspective, highlighting the workings of ideology in discourse.[112]

Witchcraft trials in England with female accused, like the Pendle witch trials of 1612, have caught the interest of several authors. So have the Essex witch trials from the 1640s.[113] Malcolm Gaskill has studied the trial of a female witch in a volume on crime and gender edited by Jenny Kermode and Garthine Walker, *Women, Crime and the Courts in Early Modern England*.[114] In the same book, James Sharpe has a chapter on women, witchcraft, and the legal process.[115] With regard to Scotland, Christina Larner has published an article on witch-hunting and discusses the gender question.[116] Julian Goodare has written about women as well as men accused of witchcraft in Scotland.[117] Lauren Martin has published a chapter about women and the domestic, using Scottish material.[118]

Witchcraft studies with a gender approach also include men. About one-fifth of those accused and convicted of witchcraft during the European witch-hunt were men. Geographical variations are present. In some European areas—Finland, Switzerland, Burgundy, Normandy, Estonia, and Iceland—a large percentage of men were accused and convicted of witchcraft.[119] In Iceland, men were in the absolute majority, as twenty-one men and one woman were burnt at the stake during the seventeenth-century witch-hunt.[120] Several interesting studies of male witches have been published. Lara Apps and Andrew Colin Gow have written *Male Witches in Early Modern Europe*.[121] Alison Rowlands has edited the volume *Witchcraft and Masculinities in Early Modern Europe*.[122] Rolf Schulte has published two monographs on men accused of witchcraft in Central Europe.[123] Rune Blix Hagen has published several articles on Sami men accused of witchcraft in Northern Norway.[124] The research on male witches is valuable in a gender context. Trials against male witches differed from trials against female witches when it comes to content and court procedure. They were seldom related to demonological ideas and were most often single trials.

European Witchcraft Research

Above, I have presented a number of studies on narrative discourse, gender, and witchcraft. In the following, I would like to take a historiographical look at the field of European witchcraft research, a field which has flourished during the last thirty years. I will mention overview works encompassing all of Europe, but the emphasis will be on Northern Europe. It is not my aim here to provide a complete overview of all research carried out on the eight countries in this study, but a number of important works will be discussed, in particular those which have been valuable to my study. The historiographical survey is conducted in general terms, as I later will engage in greater detail with the content of relevant literature in the analyses in each chapter and in the discussion in the concluding chapter.

Below, I will first reference some international overview works. Furthermore, I will mention some monographs covering witchcraft persecution in all of Europe, as well as studies dealing with particular aspects of witchcraft trials. Then, a few relevant source editions will be mentioned. Finally, I would like to present some works related to the geographical scope of this book: a selection of works covering the eight countries dealt with in my study.

Published in the course of the last decades, Golden's and Levack's overview works on witchcraft mentioned above have taken into account the whole of Europe and colonial America. These works contain contributions from witchcraft researchers worldwide and create a solid foundation for future witchcraft research. Another survey is provided by *The Cambridge History of Magic and Witchcraft in the West*, edited by David J. Collins,[125] a collection of twenty chapters that also covers the ancient Near East.

A few authors have written monographs that provide an overview of all of Europe. I would like to mention Julian Goodare's *The European Witch-Hunt*, which covers the whole of Europe. It includes a gender approach in a chapter on 'Women, Men, and Witchcraft'.[126] The book has a useful section with suggestions for further reading. Next, Brian P. Levack's *The Witch-Hunt in Early Modern Europe* should be mentioned, a book published in several editions.[127] I would also like to reference Wolfgang Behringer's *Witches and Witch-Hunts* and a corresponding article, which includes contexts outside Europe and looks at climatic conditions as a possible factor in the European witch-hunt.[128] These books, covering many countries and many aspects of the European witch-hunt, contain a huge amount of knowledge and are valuable to all studies of European witchcraft persecution.

As witchcraft trials were criminal cases, studies focusing on judicial conditions have been of interest to me. An example is Laura Stoke, *Demons of Urban Reform*, which focuses on the very first period of European witchcraft trials.[129] Of a more general character when it comes to the courts' work is *People Meet the Law*, edited by Eva Österberg and Sølvi Sogner.[130] Gregory Durston's *Witchcraft and Witch Trials* deals with legal perspectives throughout the entire period of witchcraft trials in England.[131] Also, works on judicial torture have been useful for my research, such as John H. Langbein's *Torture and the Law of Proof*,[132] *The Origins of Adversary Criminal Trial*,[133] and Björn Åstrand's *Tortyr och pinlig förhör*.[134] Jørgen C. Jacobsen's *Danske Domme i Trolddomssager i øverste Instans*[135] is interesting both as a presentation of Danish cases and as a judicial study. Also, Poul J. Jørgensen's legal history on the development of Danish Law from the Reformation until 1683 has a chapter on witchcraft, which provides useful perspectives.[136] Jørn Øyrehagen Sunde's *Speculum legale—rettsspegelen* offers noteworthy judicial perspectives on the study of witchcraft trials.[137]

Folkloric belief and witchcraft are related. Traditional witchcraft has always been seen as something that people used to try to control their environment; a part of the supernatural. To this end, charms and spells were often used. There are several studies on this aspect of witchcraft. In Norway, Bente Alver was one of the first scholars to publish a book on witchcraft belief and witchcraft in 1971, using a folkloristic approach.[138] She continued her research and in 2008 published a book based on close readings of witchcraft trials related to magic.[139] The broad spectre of folkloric motifs also comes to the fore in a collection of articles about the supernatural in Scotland, edited by Julian Goodare and Martha McGill. This book has increased my knowledge about supernatural phenomena and the way they relate to the understanding of witchcraft.[140] Furthermore, Euan Cameron's work about superstition and invisible forces in the minds of late medieval and Early Modern people provides glimpses of an exciting mental universe.[141]

Several collections of essays on witchcraft in Europe have been published. One example is *The Damned Art*, which shows the growing interest in studying witchcraft in the 1970s, with contributions by, among others, Christina Larner, Stuart Clark, Alan MacFarlane, and Peter Burke.[142] I should also mention *Early Modern Witchcraft: Centres and Peripheries*, a collection of papers from a 1984 Stockholm conference, edited by Bengt Ankarloo and Gustav Henningsen.[143] The volume focuses on the themes of witchcraft, law, and theology; origins of the witches' sabbath; and the ideas of geographical centres and peripheries. All Nordic countries are included. An early period of witchcraft research in Scandinavia saw the publication of some historiographical articles, for instance 'Tavshed er guld' [Silence is Gold] by Jens Chr. V. Johansen, covering research from Europe and America, 1966–81.[144] Other collections are *The Witchcraft Reader*, edited by Darren Oldridge;[145] *Witchcraft in Europe, 400–1700*, edited by Alan C. Kors and Edward Peters;[146] *Witchcraft in Early Modern Europe*, edited by Jonathan Barry;[147] *Beyond the Witch Trials*, edited by Owen Davies and Willem de Blécourt;[148] and *Cultures of Witchcraft from the Middle Ages to the Present*, edited by Jonathan Barry, Owen Davies, and Cornelie Usborne.[149] On the 1700s and 1800s, Marijke Gijswijt-Hofstra, Brian P. Levack, and Roy Porter have written *Witchcraft and Magic in Europe*.[150] All these books have been useful for me in terms of new knowledge and new perspectives.

Good source editions contribute enormously to novel witchcraft research. A number of good source editions have contributed to making witchcraft sources available to an international readership, such as *Witchcraft in Europe 400–1700*, cited above. This volume contains medieval texts, demonological theory, and trial records from the seventeenth century, and discusses the scepticism of the eighteenth century.[151] I will also mention Brian P. Levack's *The Witchcraft Sourcebook*[152] and, for England and New England, Marion Gibson's *Witchcraft and Society in England and America, 1550–1750*.[153] Other good source editions on England include the works of J. S. Cockburn[154] and C. L'Estrange Ewen.[155] Peter Morton's text-critical edition *The Trial of Tempel Anneke*[156] and Jürgen Macha and Wolfgang Herborn's sourcebook with records from Cologne[157] provide good insight into cases from Germany. The exhibition catalogue '*Wider Hexerey und Teufelswerk . . .*' contains an article by Rolf Schulte that presents a witchcraft trial against a child.[158] My research has also been inspired by Scottish case studies and text-critical editions, including *Witchcraft in Early Modern Scotland*, edited by Lawrence Normand and Gareth Roberts,[159] in addition to a number of transcription of Scottish cases in the series of the Scottish History Society and other historical associations.[160] From Denmark, good source editions have been published on the witchcraft trials in Ribe.[161] Furthermore, *Malmø tingbøker* contains witchcraft trials from an area of Sweden bordering Denmark.[162] In Finnmark, the northernmost county of Norway, a document was written by regional governor Hans H. Lilienskiold at the end of the seventeenth century and edited by Rune B. Hagen and Per E. Sparboe. Lilienskiold copied a number of sentences in witchcraft trials. This source complements the court records.[163] Also, my work *The Witchcraft Trials in Finnmark, Northern Norway* contains transcriptions of all witchcraft trials that occurred in Finnmark. It has shown me the value and richness of court records.[164] Finally, I would like to mention a sourcebook dealing with Northern France that has inspired me: *The Arras Witch Treatises*, edited and translated by Andrew Colin Gow, Robert B. Desjardins, and François V. Pageau—a solid and pedagogical edition.[165]

Within the geographical scope of the eight countries in my study, a number of works have been published, either on regions or on separate countries, in the form of surveys, general monographs, and edited collections. I will start with the Netherlands,[166] a country that was divided into a southern and a northern part. Witchcraft trials took place in the north as well as in the south, but developed differently with regard to chronology. For the Northern Netherlands, research on witchcraft trials has been conducted by Hans de Waardt, Willem de Blécourt, and Marijke Gijswijt-Hofstra.[167] For the southern part, the Spanish Netherlands, Dries Vanysacker has published articles and a study including both women and men accused of witchcraft in Bruges.[168]

The witchcraft trials in Northern Germany have been studied by Karen Lambrecht, Rolf Schulte, Dagmar Unverhau, and Eva Labouvie. They have been active scholars since the 1980s.[169] Gisela Wilbertz, Gerd Schwerhoff, and Jürgen Scheffler have edited a collection on regional witch-hunts in Lippe in North-Western Germany.[170] Other collections have focused on the Northern areas of Europe, such as *Hexenprozesse, Deutsche und skandinavische Beiträge*, edited by Christian Degn, Hartmut Lehmann, and Dagmar Unverhau.[171] At an early stage of witchcraft research on Northern Germany, Dagmar Unverhau was a productive scholar. She was based in the archives of Schleswig and had a large number of primary sources at hand. She took an interest in several aspects of witchcraft persecution: legal conditions[172] in addition to gender and ideas about witchcraft.[173] Rolf Schulte has published the book *Hexenverfolgung in Schleswig-Holstein 16.–18. Jahrhundert*, a solid study of witchcraft persecution in Schleswig-Holstein.[174] He has also approached witchcraft trials from a gender perspective in his book *Man as Witch*. Among others, this book contains a chapter on male witches in Holstein and on the persecution of men for being werewolves.[175] The gender perspective is also incorporated in Schulte's *Hexenmeister*.[176] Studies covering all of Germany, such as Wolfgang Behringer's book

Hexen und Hexenprozesse in Deutschland, include the Northern area. The same is the case for Sönke Lorenz and Jürgen Schmidt's *Wider alle Hexerei und Teufelswerk: Die Europäische Hexenverfolgung*.[177] Behringer has also studied the Shaman of Oberstdorf and witchcraft persecutions in Bavaria.[178]

In Denmark, Henrik Carl Bering Liisberg published *Vesten for Sø og østen for Hav* in 1909.[179] The book deals with alleged witchcraft against the fleet of the Danish king in 1589 and the trials that followed in Copenhagen and Edinburgh. It was interesting for me to read because its narrative stays very close to the original court records, and it has motivated me to write articles on the topic.[180] Research on witchcraft trials in Denmark received increased interest in the 1980s with Gustav Henningsen's pioneering study on Spain, his doctoral thesis *The Witches' Advocate*, published in 1980.[181] During the 1980s and 1990s, both Merete Birkelund and Jens Chr. V. Johansen published books and articles on Danish witchcraft persecution.[182] Recent research on Danish witchcraft trials is conducted by Louise Nyholm Kallestrup. She attained her Ph.D. in 2007 with a thesis that compared witchcraft trials in Denmark and Northern Italy, published as a book in 2009, and also published *Heksejagt* in 2020.[183] Kallestrup has written articles on witchcraft and co-edited a collection of essays.[184] Thyge Krogh wrote a study dealing with the magical and punishments in the first half of the eighteenth century.[185] Karsten Sejr Jensen's book *Trolddom i Danmark 1500–1588* focuses on social and psychological aspects of witchcraft persecution.[186]

In Scotland, active research on witchcraft trials has been conducted since the 1960s. Cristina Larner attained her Ph.D. in 1962 on the topic of Scottish demonology and its theological background.[187] She published *Enemies of God: The Witch-Hunt in Scotland*[188] and wrote several articles on witchcraft and gender.[189] Since 2000, Julian Goodare has edited several collections of articles related to Scottish witchcraft trials.[190] Goodare was the director of The Survey of Scottish Witchcraft, a comprehensive database completed in 2003, documenting all known Scottish witchcraft trials.[191] Goodare has written numerous articles on witchcraft persecution in Scotland.[192] Moreover, Louise Yeoman, Lauren Martin, and Joyce Miller—who worked on the project The Survey of Scottish Witchcraft—have published articles on the topic. Martin and Miller also wrote their Ph.D. theses on this subject. Also, Sierra Dye and Michelle D. Brock have written their Ph.D. theses on topics related to Scottish witchcraft trials, with Dye focusing on the relationship between speech acts, reputation, and judicial evidence in Scotland's witch-hunts, and Brock focusing on images of the devil in post-Reformation Scotland, a study published as a book.[193] Furthermore, Scottish historians Peter G. Maxwell-Stuart, Stuart Macdonald, and Jenny Wormald have published on Scottish witchcraft persecution or related topics.[194] Anna Cordey and Laura Paterson have written theses and published articles: Cordey on witchcraft trials in the area of Dalkeith and Paterson on witches' gatherings and the execution of Scottish witches.[195] A study by Brian P. Levack, *Witch-Hunting in Scotland*, compares Scotland and England.[196] I myself attained a Ph.D. from the University of Edinburgh in 2008 with the thesis *Seventeenth-Century Witchcraft*

Trials in Scotland and Northern Norway.[197] In 2013, I published *Witches of the North: Scotland and Finnmark.*[198] I have also published articles on Scottish witchcraft trials and on the Scotsman John Cunningham, who became district governor in Finnmark.[199]

In England, scholars have over the years taken various approaches to researching witchcraft trials. Due in part to the influential theories of Alan Macfarlane and Keith Thomas in the 1970s, which were inspired by anthropological studies, research on English witchcraft trials came to focus on the connection between witchcraft accusations and socio-economic change.[200] James Sharpe has countered these arguments, both in *Instruments of Darkness*, a book which contains a valuable survey of legal records documenting English witchcraft trials,[201] and his book *Witchcraft in Early Modern England.*[202] Sharpe has also studied popular versions of the demonic in witchcraft pamphlets.[203] Also, Marion Gibson has conducted considerable research on English witchcraft pamphlets, analysing pamphlets based on a linguistic approach as well as published text-critical editions.[204] Malcolm Gaskill has published works on crime and mentalities,[205] overview articles and articles on witnesses' depositions,[206] and studies on the Essex witchcraft trials of the 1640s.[207] Jonathan Barry has performed an in-depth reading of cases from south-west England and has published a historiographical work with Owen Davies.[208] Ronald Hutton has published research from an anthropological angle.[209] In England, witches often owned a special animal, the familiar, often a cat. Charlotte-Rose Miller has connected this to the diabolical in several books and articles.[210]

In Norway, Hans Eyvind Næss is the pioneer of witchcraft research. He published his doctoral thesis on Norwegian witchcraft trials in 1982[211] and has written a number of books and articles that focus on the legal and social factors of witchcraft.[212] Gunnar W. Knutsen started his research on witchcraft trials in East Norway in the 1990s and later completed a Ph.D. on Spanish witchcraft trials.[213] He has written several articles on the topic from national and international angles.[214] I myself have conducted research on witchcraft trials from the 1980s onwards, first concentrating on Finnmark in Northern Norway and attaining my aforementioned Ph.D. with a comparative study of Finnmark and Scotland, in which I used the analytical concept of voice in my close readings of witchcraft trials.[215] I have written the exhibition texts for the Steilneset Memorial in Vardø, Finnmark, a memorial to the victims of the Finnmark witchcraft trials that opened in 2011.[216] In addition, I have published several articles on the witchcraft trials in Finnmark, including one co-authored with Arne Kruse on *Ballvollen*, a place for witches' gatherings in Vardø.[217] The Finnmark witchcraft trials have also been studied by Rune Blix Hagen. He began studying witchcraft trials in the 1990s and has particularly focused on Sami shamanism, as there were two shamans among the accused persons in Finnmark.[218] Hagen has published broadly on witchcraft related to popular culture, on European witchcraft trials, and on John Cunningham, district governor in Finnmark.[219] Together with Per Einar Sparboe, Hagen has edited a diary of Christian IV's travel to Finnmark in 1599.[220] Nils Gilje has written about the famous trial of Anne Pedersdatter, which took place in Bergen in the late 1500s.[221] Ellen Alm has paid attention to the role of the state in Norwegian witchcraft trials.[222]

In Sweden, witchcraft trials have been studied throughout most of the 1900s, with Emanuel Linderholm's book *De stora häxprocesserna i Sverige* being one of the first works.[223] Several doctoral theses have been written. Bengt Ankarloo attained his Ph.D. in 1971 with a dissertation titled *Trolldomsprocesserna i Sverige*, later published in 1984.[224] Ankarloo was a pioneer within Swedish witchcraft research. He co-edited *Häxornas Europa*, which was published in English as the volume *Early Modern European Witchcraft*.[225] Per-Anders Östling wrote a dissertation on the Blåkulla trials. Blåkulla refers to a hill or mountain where alleged witches' gatherings took place.[226] Per Sörlin has studied witchcraft trials in Southern Sweden. He attained his Ph.D. at Umeå University with a thesis titled *Trolldoms- och vidskepelseprocesserna i Göta Hovrätt 1635–1754*[227] and later published the book *Wicked Arts* on the same topic.[228] Sörlin has also studied criminality and court system in the Jämtland and Härjedalen areas.[229] Linda Oja has edited *Vägen till Blåkulla*, a collection of articles,[230] and published the study *Varken Gud eller natur*, which focuses on popular beliefs.[231] Karin Granquist has been studying witchcraft trials in the Swedish Sami areas.[232] Maria Lennersand wrote a dissertation[233] and co-authored a chapter on the witnesses in the Swedish witchcraft trials in Dalarne.[234] In Lennersand and Oja's book *Livet går vidare*, they show how women acquitted in witchcraft trials in Dalarne continued their lives in the local communities during the late 1600s.[235] *ARV: Nordic Yearbook of Folklore* has published articles by Per Sörlin and Per-Anders Östling on Swedish persecution.[236] Soili-Maria Olli wrote a dissertation on demonological ideas in court records,[237] and Mikael Häll on erotic figures in folk belief.[238] Both Jacqueline van Gent and Åsa Bergenheim have employed a gender perspective in their research.[239]

In Finland, Raisa Maria Toivo, Jari Eilola, Marko Nenonen, and Marko Lamberg have published on witchcraft trials. Toivo has carried out research from a gender perspective but also worked on courtroom discourse and voices.[240] She has written *Faith and Magic in Early Modern Finland*,[241] and the articles 'Gender, Sex and Cultures of Trouble in Witchcraft Studies'[242] and 'What Did a Witch-Hunter in Finland Know about Demonology?'[243] She has co-edited a collection of essays as well.[244] Nenonen has been the spokesman of a new witchcraft paradigm.[245] Eilola has worked on close readings of documents, among others on the topic of child witnesses' stories in the Blåkulla trials in Sweden.[246] Marko Lamberg has written, among other works, an interesting study of Malin Matsdotter from Österbotten, who was tried for witchcraft.[247]

Outline

The chapters of the book will follow geographical locations. After the introduction, the chapters are organized in this order: Spanish Netherlands, Northern Germany, Denmark, Scotland, England, Norway, Sweden, and Finland. The final chapter of the book, 'Comparison and Conclusion', summarizes the study's findings.

2

SPANISH NETHERLANDS—HOLY WATER, WITCHCRAFT POWDER, AND THE COLLAR

Background

The first voices of women heard in this book are from the Spanish Netherlands: the southern part of the Netherlands, a territory that generally corresponds to present-day Belgium. Together with the northern part of the Netherlands, the Republic of the United Provinces, it was part of the Low Countries in the late Middle Ages and the Early Modern period. Witchcraft trials took place in the Northern as well as the Southern Netherlands but developed differently with regard to chronology. The Republic of the United Provinces is known to be the first European state where witchcraft trials resulting in death sentences came to an end: the last witchcraft execution was in 1608.[1] In the Spanish Netherlands, witchcraft persecution lasted until 1685.

The Spanish Netherlands differs from the other countries in this study in several ways. First, it was Catholic, which had an impact on interrogation and confession in witchcraft trials. Second, its neighbour in the north was the Republic of the United Provinces, where witchcraft trials not only ended very early but were of a milder character, measured by the number of executions *per capita*. Third, the Spanish Netherlands was internally divided by a linguistic frontier, with a Dutch-speaking population[2] to the north and French- and German-speaking populations to the south and east of this border.[3] Witchcraft persecution took part on both sides of this frontier, but with differing intensity.

The three witchcraft trials from the Spanish Netherlands included in this study are from the county of Flanders. The first trial chosen is that of Lynken van Brugghe, which took place in Hondschoote in 1596. The second is the trial of Mayken Karrebrouck, which took place in Bruges in 1634. The final trial is that of Clayse Sereyns from 1657, in Morbecque. The selection of trials from the Spanish Netherlands was influenced by the sources available. The court records from the witchcraft

DOI: 10.4324/9781003255406-2

trials in Flanders have been transcribed and published in full text.[4] This eased my analyses of the trials.[5]

The trials from Flanders which are analysed were partly chosen based on chronology: they date from the early, middle, and relatively late period of witchcraft persecution, with several decades between the cases. In terms of the location of courts, two of the trials took place in city courts, and one in a District Court. This is illustrative of persecution in the Spanish Netherlands, where witchcraft trials were far from a rural phenomenon. As for the richness of sources, the court records chosen are detailed enough to provide insight into courtroom discourse, and substantial enough to give access to the interrogation and the accused person's confession. Furthermore, the choice of trials was influenced by the content of each trial. A range of ideas about witchcraft comes to the fore in the questioning and confessions of the accused people. These ideas are related to notions of *maleficium* as well as notions of demonology.

In addition, the accused individuals are related to the activity of healing: this is why they became the subject of rumours in the first instance and appeared in the judiciary's searchlight for witchcraft. The voices of the confessing women create narratives, in which orality features surface. There is a marked turning point in these trials, a point at which the accused woman's resistance is broken. This turning point has to do with enormous emotional strain during interrogation, which can be traced in the records as either words uttered by the accused woman or descriptions of the accused person's behaviour. The voice of the interrogator is echoed in the rendered questioning, making it possible to gain insight into the judiciary's agenda, the order of the questions posed, and the compulsory points of interrogation. The recorded trials offer a complexity of strategies and ideas, and a glimpse of the legal handling of the cases. Also, the words of the confessing witch give an indication of the mentality of the time. The three witchcraft trials from the Spanish Netherlands constitute a valuable addition to the other Northern European witchcraft trials included in this study. Even if, to a certain extent, they differ from these other trials, they display the common ground underlying all witchcraft persecution in Early Modern Europe: a fear of witchcraft supplanting the religious fundament.

The analyses of the chosen trials will focus on the individualized discourse of the accused person. Various emotions come to the fore in the voices of women as rendered in the court records, and this element will add to the understanding of the experience of each woman during the trial. In addition, the voices of the witnesses will be paid attention to. Further, the voices of the interrogators may be heard in the questions they pose, demonstrating their attitudes to witchcraft. The voice of the law will be discussed as well, as it establishes the frame for the trial and for the accused person's words. The voice of the scribe will be commented upon too, discussing his work in the process of recording courtroom discourse.

Persecution in the Republic of the United Provinces

In order to underline the difference in witchcraft persecution between the Spanish Netherlands and the Republic of the United Provinces, I would like to give a brief overview of the latter. Habsburg Netherlands was the collective name of Holy Roman Empire fiefs in the Low Countries, held by the House of Habsburg and later by the Spanish Empire. The Southern Netherlands was conquered by Spain for the second time in 1556,[6] when its crown was passed to King Philip II of Spain. The Spanish reconquest of the Southern Netherlands caused the region to become overwhelmingly Catholic. After the Dutch Revolt that started in 1568, the northern provinces became an independent confederation: the Republic of the United Provinces.[7] In 1581, a declaration of independence was signed, the Act of Abjuration. While the Northern Netherlands was effectively autonomous from 1585 onwards, the southern part's independence was not formally recognized until 1648, when the Dutch War of Independence (1568–1648) had come to an end.

A short survey of witchcraft persecution in the Republic of the United Provinces is provided in order to note features that diverge from those of the Spanish Netherlands. Witchcraft persecution in the Northern Netherlands started in the 1400s and lasted until 1608. Before 1500, scattered trials took place, but there was little consistency in the way authorities proceeded in witchcraft trials.[8] However, during the final decades of the fifteenth century, witchcraft became a concern of the secular authorities.[9] Local bailiffs and sheriffs[10] tended to interpret complaints against supposed witches as reparation claims, making up for harm, damage, or suffering. From 1500 onwards, witchcraft persecution increased, and several hundreds of trials were conducted in the Northern Netherlands, the majority in rural areas. The population of the Republic was ca. one million around 1500, a number that had doubled by 1560.[11] Witchcraft trials were unevenly distributed over the various provinces. Groningen, Gelderland, and Holland were at the top.[12] In total, witchcraft persecution in the Republic of the United Provinces resulted in at least 164 executed people.[13] The percentage of women sentenced for witchcraft in this territory was very high: 94% of those executed were women.[14]

Persecution in the Spanish Netherlands

In the Spanish Netherlands, witchcraft trials took place from 1450 to 1685, during which period at least 2,564 people were executed.[15] The number of alleged witches executed varied strongly according to the linguistic barrier that divided the territory. Witchcraft persecution in the Spanish Netherlands was much more intense in the area south of the linguistic frontier than in that north of it. However, south of the linguistic border there was variation as well: in the French-speaking areas, at least 250 executions took place, while in the French- and German-speaking Duchy of Luxembourg, between two and three thousand people were executed.[16]

North of the linguistic frontier, the actual witch-hunts began in 1589.[17] Witchcraft persecution in this territory often took place in towns. It began at Arras and spread to many cities, among them Bruges.[18] In total, 314 people were executed, of which two-thirds in the county of Flanders. Only six known cases occurred in Flanders before 1500.[19] Flanders experienced the beginning of the 1500s as relatively calm when it came to witch-hunting, but intensified its prosecution of witches after 1520. In 1532, the first witches were burned, a man and a woman, making the aldermen of the city of Bruges the first in the Dutch-speaking Southern Netherlands to execute witches by fire.[20] There were two waves of prosecutions north of the linguistic frontier: one in the 1590s and one during the period 1630–46. In Flanders, 206 persons were executed before 1660, of which 80% women.[21] The last witch in Flanders was burned in 1684.[22] The most striking characteristic of witchcraft persecution in the county of Flanders is its late ending compared to when persecution ended in the Republic of the United Provinces.

In court records from the year 1532, demonological ideas are documented. In Bruges on 6 July 1532, Ampleunie Coopmans, the wife of Gillis Coopman, was sentenced to be burned in fire at the stake because a few years prior, she had 'submitted herself to the enemy[23] from Hell and denied the crucified God'.[24] This is a description of Coopmans entering into the devil's pact: she renounced God and became a servant of the Evil One. The wording 'the crucified God' indicates a clear religious basis in Christendom. The court records of Ampleunie Coopmans's trial state that she promised to do evil and forsake virtue and thus honoured the aforementioned enemy. Further, the records state that ever since submitting herself to the enemy, Coopmans,

> at various times, had committed certain deeds—thereby receiving the means, advice and aid from the same enemy—which are forbidden, which attack God almighty, and which are in contrast to his commandments and the commandments of the Holy Church.[25]

The wording here displays the view that the 'enemy from Hell' is a threat to God and Christianity. Thus, Ampleunie Coopmans had chosen the wrong master. With the power she had acquired when entering the pact, she had performed evil, and 'by these means she robbed certain people of their earthly possessions and substances'.[26] The records then provide the court's reason for sentencing Ampleunie Coopmans: 'to set an example for others, she was sentenced to death'.[27] The last addition in the court records, after the sentence was passed, emphasizes the accused person's voluntary confession: '[m]oreover, Ampleunie had voluntarily—not under torture—admitted to these crimes'.[28] As it was considered necessary to enter this sentence in the records, it might indicate that torture was used during witchcraft interrogations in Flanders in 1532.

Jurisdiction

In the middle of the fifteenth century, a version of the German law book *Sachsenspiegel*, which was heavily influenced by Roman law, was introduced in the Netherlands. 'This code prescribed death by fire for those found guilty of witchcraft'.[29] During the first half of the sixteenth century, Roman law entered court practice in the Low Countries. In 1554, Flemish jurist Joos de Damhouder published his *Praxis Rerum Criminalium*,[30] which was almost immediately acknowledged as the best manual for judges and lawyers. 'It taught them how to interpret the laws of the *Codex Justinian*,[31] including those regarding witchcraft. Damhouder viewed witchcraft as a form of lèse-majesté'.[32] In medieval law, the accusatory procedure, where the complainant collected the necessary evidence, was used. If the complainant failed to produce enough evidence, he could be sentenced to receive the punishment that would otherwise have been meted out to the defendant. Part of the authority of modern monarchs was to administer justice, and their representatives took the initiative in the prosecution of criminals. In the fifteenth century, there was a change in judicial procedure when the inquisitorial procedure was introduced. The sheriffs and bailiffs were obliged to initiate criminal trials and supervise the execution of sentences, and 'torture was introduced to extract confessions, which in the eyes of jurists was the most reliable form of proof'.[33] Punishment for witchcraft was harsh at the end of the sixteenth century. In 1592, the governor-general of the Spanish Netherlands issued an order 'that judges should "proceed rigorously" against witches "by the most severe and exemplary punishments"; there was a threat that judges who were remiss in this duty would themselves be punished'.[34]

Trials revolving around the pact between a 'cumulative' witch and the devil were central in the Southern Netherlands. The term 'cumulative' implies witchcraft as a cumulation of elements.[35] The trials' ingredients were the devil, the pact with the devil, the sabbath, witches' flight, and shape-shifting.[36] The trials were held before local secular benches of aldermen of feudal courts,

> not before episcopal courts or central bodies like the Council of Flanders or the Council of Brabant. Witchcraft trials followed normal criminal procedure, but the judges, influenced by demonology, accepted the combination of facts and especially the *punctum diabolicum*, the Devil's spot or mark, as indications of guilt, which permitted arrests, torture, and even condemnations.[37]

A death sentence had to be preceded by the suspect's voluntary confession.

In the municipal judicial system in Flanders, the term *schepen* was used. A *schepen* (plural: *schepenen*) was a municipal office in Dutch-speaking countries,[38] which in English is called an alderman, municipal councillor, magistrate, or town councillor.[39] From the post-Roman era until the nineteenth century, the word *schepen* referred to a member of a council of deciders, literally judgement finders,[40] which sat at a mandatory public assembly called a *ding*[41] or *vierschaar*, often a roofless building in which four benches were installed along the four walls. Their judgements originally required ratification by a majority of those present. This requirement was dropped, as was mandatory attendance.[42] Later, the institute of the council of aldermen was named the *schepenbank*. The *schepenen* made laws, ratified treaties, and acted as judges.

Each Flemish municipality had an elected town council. During its first meeting after elections, council members voted by secret ballot to elect the *schepenen*.

An absolute majority—more than half the votes—was required for a *schepen* to be voted in. Once elected, the *schepenen* served with the mayor on an executive board charged with the day-to-day management of town affairs. The executive board is referred to in Dutch as the *college van burgemeester en schepenen*.[43]

The learned city aldermen exercised a considerable influence, and they were well informed about the cumulative concept of witchcraft, which they studied in demonological tracts. While *Malleus Maleficarum* from 1486[44] did not have a strong impact, Martin del Rio's *Six Books on Investigations into Magic* from 1599/1600[45] made a powerful impression in his native region. It should also be mentioned that Jean Bodin's demonology was published in Antwerp in 1586,[46] and a tract with information about witchcraft persecution in South-Western Germany was translated into Dutch in 1589.[47] The learned aldermen probably spread the new demonological ideas throughout Flanders.

Lynken van Brugghe, 1596

The Trial

Lynken van Brugghe was a fifty-eight-year-old woman who lived in Warhem.[48] She was born in Cassele, the daughter of Passchier van Brugghe and the widow of Mahieu Coloos. She was brought before the court in Hondschoote on 29 February 1596.[49] Van Brugghe died as a result of torture during interrogation. Of 206 individuals accused of witchcraft in Flanders, twenty-three died in prison during the trial, of various causes. The court records of Van Brugghe's case include the accusation, the interrogation, her confession, a description of her death under questioning, and the judiciary's evaluation of her final fate. Her confession echoes witnesses' testimonies and her husband's denunciation of her. These statements are used to confirm her guilt. The court records belong to the city archives of Hondschoote and form part of judiciary proceedings.

The court records of Lynken van Brugghe contain contradictory statements with regard to her willingness to confess. It is recorded that from the beginning, she confessed of her own free will. Thus, there is a hint of cooperation in her voice, and it is emphasized that her confession is initially not forced. It is further stated that her guilt was established through other means as well. These other means appear to be a confession given by her husband and testimonies given by her neighbours. The court records are organized into ten points, which deal with the interrogation, the content of Van Brugghe's confession, and the judiciary's argumentation in support of the verdict of guilty.

The first point states that Lynken van Brugghe's husband, Mahieu Coloos, was imprisoned before her and was sentenced for witchcraft, apparently to death. His confession during the trial and during informal questioning implicitly confirmed the guilt and corruption of his wife. The confession given by Lynken van Brugghe's late husband is referred to in the beginning of the trial records of Van Brugghe's case, and the *schepenen* gave it weight.

The second point says that when Lynken van Brugghe visited her husband in prison and learned that he had confessed to his crime, she said to him: 'Mahieu, you had promised me not to do that'.[50] This was in agreement with her pre-trial confession. According to this point, Van Brugghe's husband confessed to witchcraft against his promise to his wife, and she became very upset when she heard this.

The third point states that when she learned that her husband had confessed, she fled from her home in Warhem and left several pieces of furniture behind. First, she fled to the house of teacher[51] Jan Juliaen in Hondschoote. Next, she stayed at the house of Maerten Pelgrem. Afterwards, when she was due to be imprisoned, she fled again with some possessions. She said she had wanted to flee to Dunkirk,[52] although it came to the fore that she had tried to rent a carriage in Ieper,[53] which is in another direction, situated further to the south. She had thrown a pack with a shirt and some bedclothes over the hedge, while leaving a bed behind at home, among other things.[54] The judiciary used the fact that Lynken van Brugghe fled to emphasize that she had something to fear. She tried to escape from a trial—a signal that the judiciary interpreted as increasing the likelihood that she was guilty of witchcraft.

The fourth point deals with *maleficium*: Lynken van Brugghe's milking of her two cows, from which she got an abnormal amount of milk. Her husband confirmed that he had seen it happen. Getting an abnormal amount of milk, most often stealing it from other people's cattle, is an old and traditionally well-known act of witchcraft.

The fifth point is about a large vat[55] Van Brugghe bought from Sanders Stappen in order to bring milk to the market. Stappen asked her what she wanted to do with such a huge vessel, because it was big enough to milk twelve cows and she had only two. She responded: 'What concern is it of yours if you got paid?'[56]

The sixth point has to do with a disagreement Lynken van Brugghe had with the wife of Pieter Stevaert about an amount of butter that Van Brugghe sold to her. The wife of Stevaert was of the opinion that she had received less butter than they had agreed upon.

The seventh point is about a confidential conversation Lynken van Brugghe had during her attempted escape. After she left her home and possessions in Warhem, she told the wife of teacher Jan Juliaen in tears and sighing that she was carrying a secret in her heart that she would not dare to tell anyone for anything in the world.

The eighth point has to do with her denial of knowledge of the Lord's prayer. She repeatedly confessed that she had never heard of the words: 'And lead us not into temptation',[57] although it is recorded that the officials of the law taught her these words.[58]

The ninth point is about objects used to perform malefice. Various pots and jars were found at her home containing a creamy substance with arsenic, together with two long knives that were standing next to each other with their tips facing down. Before she fled, she buried the knives at the eastern side of an orchard at Warhem. She buried them herself, ordered to do so by her husband.

The tenth point deals with the closer interrogation of Lynken van Brugghe. Because there had been more incidents that were not explained in a satisfactory way, Van Brugghe was questioned under torture: first by flogging,[59] then by shaving all the hair off her body, and finally by sleep deprivation.[60] However, she did not confess anything, except—and this is recorded to be 'under no torture'—that in the previous summer on a Tuesday she visited the home of Jacob van der Meulen in Warhem. The wife of Jacob was breastfeeding her child and Van Brugghe said: 'What huge breasts you have, you have the double crown, those are breasts to feed a king'.[61] She then stretched out her hand and cast a spell on her. The next day, Van der Meulen went to Lynken van Brugghe to complain that his wife could not produce any breast milk, saying: 'If I find out who was responsible for this, I would give him his heart in his own hand'.[62] Van Brugghe then responded as follows: 'Don't worry, friend, it will be fine'.[63]

That same day, she instantly broke the spell that she cast, as became clear during the testimony. When Lynken van Brugghe was asked which words or substance she had used to break the spell, she remained quiet and eventually said: 'Wait, I shall say it'.[64] She tried to speak and her mouth moved, but she did not speak. When asked whether she was not able to speak or whether the evil spirit[65] had forbidden her to speak, she quietly mumbled, 'Yes'.[66] Despite being urged to call out to God himself to chase away the evil spirit, she was unable to talk. Whilst she was undressed and beaten with sticks on her naked body, her throat and mouth moved more and more, and she fell onto the floor, twisting and winding like someone possessed. When they called out to her that she had to put her faith in God and forsake Satan, she could not or did not want to speak.[67] Then, above her left eye, a black mark appeared, which sometimes became larger, sometimes smaller; one also appeared on the side of her throat, which started swelling and rising. Her tongue became black and her mouth moved, although she did not speak.

After being urged to say the words: 'O Jesus, Son of David, have mercy on me',[68] she quietly repeated them, but very slowly and so that people could hardly hear them. Then she was forced to drink holy water, and she closed her mouth and chewed on the glass as if it hurt to drink the water.[69] When she was beaten on her body and legs with sticks, she cried out: 'du warinne'.[70] When she was urged to call out to God almighty, she kept on saying: 'du warinne'. When asked whether that was the name of the evil spirit[71] that was controlling her, she mumbled, 'Yes'. Some time passed, during which her mouth and throat moved and her legs and stomach made twisting movements. Around eleven at night, she died, although it is recorded that she had been tortured only by being beaten with sticks, which showed that the evil enemy had aided her quick and sudden death[72] in order to, according to the court records, ensure that the truth about similar incidents would remain hidden.[73] Lynken van Brugghe's body was subsequently buried underneath the gallows. The pots, jars, and knives found in her home were broken and then thrown into a fire. All her belongings were confiscated.

The Voice of Lynken van Brugghe

The court records of the trial of Lynken van Brugghe tell a heartbreaking story. They show her voice and life gradually disappearing. She died under torture in front of judicial officials, a death that was 'helped' along by the evil spirit. From the healthy voice that comes to the fore in the initial phase of the court records, when she still has the energy to reproach her husband for confessing to witchcraft against her will, her voice transforms into a faint whisper at the end.

The scribe's description of what happened during the interrogation of Lynken van Brugghe documents, in a professional scribe's neutral language, a very strong fear among the interrogators. It is a fear beyond reason: the interrogators are not fighting a human being but an abstract evil. They try to remove the grasp that the devil supposedly has over Van Brugghe by shaving her and forcing her to drink holy water. However, they are never reassured that the force of the Evil One is obliterated. They continue to beat it after Van Brugghe's body is crushed and she no longer represents any danger.

Bruce Lincoln has touched upon this type of reaction and behaviour in a broad discussion of festivals and massacres.[74] On the feast of St Bartholomew in Paris in 1572, a ritual massacre of (Protestant) Huguenots took place. Victims were subjected to a fearful degradation, 'corpses were stripped naked and dragged through the streets pelted with dung, and flung into rivers'.[75] With two thousand dead during the first days, the massacre and rioting spread into the provinces, and the total number of casualties is estimated to have been around ten thousand.

This massacre has symbolic overtones. Lincoln refers to contemporary witnesses' interpretations of the sixteenth-century violence of St Bartholomew's night as 'acts of ritual purification'.[76] The killing was interpreted as a cosmic fight: a fight against principles, not against human beings. The corpses were ritually treated with the four classical elements: earth, air, fire, and water. People massacred 'not merely to kill enemies, but to eradicate a pollution and to cleanse society of an infesting evil'.[77] To a certain extent, this is similar to the torture and death of Lynken van Brugghe. The naked body and holy water in Van Brugghe's trial have connotations of a ritual. The motivation for the persecution of witches is to cleanse society of witchcraft. This act of purgation is also how the judiciary explains Van Brugghe's fate.

However, the fight against the Huguenots in Paris and the fight against Lynken van Brugghe are battles against an imagined enemy. A victory over this enormous, limitless, and ungraspable evil is impossible, but the interrogators are beyond any normal sense or feeling. Struck by panic, people of authority continue to perform violent and degrading acts, even if there is nobody there to feel the agony. Evil as an abstraction does not reside in the body of Van Brugghe or the bodies of the Huguenots. It is everywhere: in the space, in the room, in the imagination.

In the trial of Lynken van Brugghe, the interrogators do not call evil 'the devil'. Instead, evil is termed 'the evil ghost' or 'the enemy'. It is the force of this enemy that the judicial officials intend to break at any cost. Thus, the interrogation focuses on the power of the devil, and the strong fear that is echoed in the court records reflects the urgency to overcome this power. This struggle is the foundation of the trial. Van Brugghe's voice and its changes during the development of the trial intertwines with the voices of the interrogators and the witnesses. Other voices heard in the courtroom interfere with Van Brugghe's voice: the voices of the witnesses are audible during the first part of the interrogation, and the voice of the interrogator is markedly present in the second part of the interrogation. This change is also a sign of the shift towards torture, as Lynken van Brugghe's willingness to confess seems to valorize the first part of her confession, while her reluctance to confess to any more comes clearly to the fore when she is asked to reveal her secret words, namely the charm she used when she took away an evil spell. Her resistance to confessing more and her alleged connection to the devil lead to a situation where stronger interrogation methods are considered necessary.

This backdrop, which sketches the fear and attitudes of the judiciary during witchcraft persecution, constitutes a frame for the analysis of Lynken van Brugghe's voice, as it provides insight into the harsh atmosphere that reigned in the courtrooms during witchcraft trials all over Europe. In order to understand the development of a witchcraft trial like the one we see in Van Brugghe's case, it is necessary to know that authorities in witchcraft trials were in a state of fear beyond reason and control. They needed a confession to dangerous witchcraft from the accused person's own mouth.

Several accents are heard in Lynken van Brugghe's voice. One of these comes to the fore in the witnesses' testimonies: the voice of Van Brugghe as an outspoken woman who was gossiped about for managing to get too much milk and butter from her cows, but who countered remarks from her neighbours related to this ability with a sharp tongue, and even with humour. She knew how to answer and to defend herself when critical comments came up. Even if she and her husband were suspected of witchcraft, they had their daily function in the local community, which shows that to a certain extent, people suspected of malevolent deeds were tolerated.

Lynken van Brugghe's first attempt to flee shows that before being imprisoned, she had the energy and courage to try to get away. She lived in Warhem and confessed that she had wanted to flee to Dunkirk, on the coast. However, she was seen in a different place (Ieper). She thus provided contrasting information about her flight. In this early part of the confession, her voice is chiefly reliable, particularly because she mentions the names of the people she stayed with and details about what she brought with her and what she left at home.

After Lynken van Brugghe had come into the searchlight for witchcraft, her escape and flight were signs of resistance on her part. Her husband's confession disappointed her, but she was still able to act. She visited him in prison and expressed what she felt: he had let her down. Her words seem to suggest that she considered the practice performed by both her husband and herself would be judged as harmful witchcraft—malefice—and she feared the judiciary's further treatment.

While imprisoned, Lynken van Brugghe confesses voluntarily from the beginning, in a steady voice, providing narratives of a certain length about her performance of *maleficium*. As long as she is describing methods and objects for casting spells, all related to traditional witchcraft, her speech flows. Then, when she is asked about the charm she used for removing spells, she is reluctant, but promises to tell them. However, she never recites this charm. This is the point where Van Brugghe's voice undergoes a fundamental change due to the application of torture.

The court records render Lynken van Brugghe's words partly as direct, partly as indirect discourse. Direct speech comes to the fore in the first part of her confession: as inserted sentences in third-person narration. Direct discourse is used to make the story livelier, to show Van Brugghe's particular way of speaking, and to show her prompt reactions. She protests against the man from whom she bought the milk vessel. In the incident pertaining to butter, Van Brugghe's direct speech is similarly rather blunt. She stands her ground and repudiates others who try to comment on her art: they can look after their own matters. Her direct speech related to the breastfeeding woman contains the striking image of the breasts with two crowns, which is a word play on female fertility and abundance, probably in short supply among the peasants. The image signals the suspicion that common people felt about too much nourishment. Too much milk might be a sign of something unnatural, and Lynken van Brugghe manages to catch this thought in her description of the woman's breasts. In fact, she expresses a prevailing idea among common people, namely that it is necessary to be aware of what seems contrary to nature, as that might be connected to something evil. Her direct speech in the first part of the trial is easy to remember and retell because her language is pointed and rich, and the images used are striking.

Lynken van Brugghe's direct speech in the last part of the trial is different. After intensified torture, the narrative and fluent mode of her speech has vanished. Her direct speech changes into short and abrupt sentences and words pressed forth to answer the interrogators' questions. The accents of her voice representing narration, coherence, and orality disappear and give way to agony and suppression. Finally, there is only silence.

Lynken van Brugghe's voice is also heard in indirect discourse, in Van Brugghe's confirmation of witnesses' testimonies and her husband's accusations. These are passages where she is the only one who knows what has happened, for instance what her husband instructed her to do.

In indirect discourse, Lynken van Brugghe shows her ability to perform traditional witchcraft, a type of knowledge she freely admits she has. She and her husband were obviously known for casting spells using pots with cream with arsenic and other objects. Her home and its surroundings were searched, and pots, jars, and knives were found. Van Brugghe provides details about where she buried the knives. The casting of a spell is performed through a special gesture, by stretching out her hand, so that the posture of her body becomes important next to charms and objects. This cunning accent of her voice shows knowledge of instruments used to perform sorcery. Van Brugghe reveals that she distinguishes between traditional witchcraft, *maleficium*, and dangerous witchcraft connected to the devil. She easily confesses to traditional witchcraft, but does not voluntarily admit to witchcraft connected to the devil—which is what the interrogators wanted to hear about. She knows which concept is most severely punished. Therefore, she refuses to answer the questions related to the Evil One.

Lynken van Brugghe's voice is individualized. It has preserved a personal touch, showing her to be a unique language user. This individualized accent of her voice is first of all related to her remarks in direct speech, but also to her indirect speech, which is introduced by the use of reporting verbs. It shows not only a brave way of talking but also a language user who managed to find well-chosen expressions. The preservation of a personal way of talking in the records is closely related to orality. Orality features surface in direct as well as indirect discourse and contribute to a personalized language. Markers of orality are frequent: additive sentence structures, redundancy, sequential ordering, and cause-effect relations.[78] Language imagery is used a few times. When the husband of the breastfeeding woman came to Van Brugghe, he used threatening language rendered in direct discourse, saying that if he found the one responsible, he would give that person his heart in his own hand. Upon hearing this, Van Brugghe reassured him that he should not worry, that everything would be fine. What makes these remarks so powerful in direct speech in an oral society is the impact of the images the language evokes: easy to remember, easy to retell. In indirect discourse, orality features are strong as well, for instance in Lynken van Brugghe's description of instruments used for performing witchcraft. These are surely related to the traditional knowledge of peasants, as exemplified by the description of the knives in the pantry and of when they were buried. Particular remarks uttered by Van Brugghe continued to live on orally because they were pointed, conjured good images, and rhymed or possessed rhythmic qualities. Such expressions are easy to repeat and easy for the scribe to write down. When the neighbours provided their testimonies, they were eager to retell stories that showed Van Brugghe's particular mode of speaking.

Lynken van Brugghe's mastering of her own language is a significant feature of the first part of the trial. Up to the point of torture, she is able to respond to questions and express herself in a natural way. However, the formulation that she narrated 'under no torture' must be read with suspicion. The threat of torture was always present during interrogation in a witchcraft trial; this was common knowledge.

The introduction of demonological ideas occurs rather late in the interrogation. The interrogators want a confession that proves Lynken van Brugghe's connection to the devil. They bring up the concept of the evil spirit for the first time after she refuses to recite her charm. The devil is not mentioned as the devil *per se* by the interrogators, but is referred to by synonyms. At this point, Van Brugghe is barely able to speak due to torture. The court's admonishing her and reminding her of the Bible's words about temptation, which she says she has never learned, emphasize her perceived distance from the good Lord. She is being led astray to serve the Evil One.

In the last section of the records, Lynken van Brugghe's voice consists of one-syllable words, a repetition of a forced, one-line biblical phrase, and the inexplicable, repeated utterings of 'du warinne'. This is a voice displaying distress. The only sign of resistance left is her chewing on the rim of the glass with holy water before she drinks. There is a notable emphasis on words denoting pressure in the recorded text: urge, force, beating. The narrative smoothness of Van Brugghe's voice has gone. What is left shows a different linguistic mode: abrupt phrases, short sentences, and the repetition of words provided by the interrogators. When Van Brugghe at last confirms that 'du warinne' is the name of 'the enemy', the one she called out for instead of calling out to God, the interrogators have obtained what they wanted. Lynken van Brugghe has a master other than God, and this master is the one she serves.

The interrogation moves towards a confession to demonic witchcraft. Lynken van Brugghe is exposed to psychological and physical pressure. Torture continues after she falls naked onto the floor with her body twisting, like she is possessed.[79] The rhetoric related to the devil becomes stronger, and the word Satan is now used for the first time.[80] She confirms that it was the evil spirit who controlled her.

Witchcraft is seen as a deviance from God and Christianity. The holy water is supposed to break the power that the devil, her 'evil ghost', had over her. Such holy water was also used in witchcraft trials in the Northern Netherlands and may have contained incense, a piece of a priest's stole, and shavings of an Easter candle—all Catholic ceremonial ingredients.[81] Van Brugghe is forced to repeat words begging the Lord for grace; words that the interrogators put in her mouth. Her final 'Yes' to subordinating herself to the devil comes as a result of continued torture. The interrogators are after a confession to demonological witchcraft, and her refusal to provide this sealed her fate.

A spectrum of emotions is displayed in the first part of Lynken van Brugghe's confession: she reproaches, protests, boasts, and assures. She gives comments and remarks: in her reproach of her husband, who had promised her not to confess; in her countering the man who sold her the vessel; in her words on the size of the breasts of the suckling woman; and in her reassuring the husband of the breastfeeding woman that everything would be fine. These emotions show strength. A rather unusual accent of Van Brugghe's voice comes to the fore in testimony given by the wife of teacher Jan Juliaen. She revealed to this wife that she had a secret she did not want to divulge. We do not know what this secret was, but this emotion shows some of her softer qualities. All in all, it is a self-confident voice we hear in the beginning: a voice that is not submissive, whether she is talking to men or to women. There is a marked contrast with her broken voice at the end of the trial.

The Voices of the Witnesses

The voices of the witnesses come to the fore in testimonies and draw a picture of Lynken van Brugghe as a person performing maleficent witchcraft. Her own husband gives the strongest testimony in that respect. He was himself accused of witchcraft, and during interrogation confirms the guilt of his wife, breaking his promise to her. He says that she managed to get hold of an enormous amount of milk from other people's cattle. The suspicion of stealing milk is repeated by Sanders Stappen. A conflict related to selling butter is recounted by the wife of Pieter Stevaert. These witnesses' voices connect to traditional witchcraft and the importance of milk and butter, which were valuable sources of nourishment. Also, Jacob van der Meulen witnessed a spell Lynken van Brugghe allegedly cast on a breastfeeding woman, and her breaking of the spell. The voices of these witnesses distinctly contribute to establishing an image of a practising maleficent witch, an image reinforced by the finding of pots, jars, and cream at her home. One witness, whose testimony is vaguer, is the wife of teacher Jan Juliaen. In an upset state, Lynken van Brugghe told the wife that she had a secret she did not dare tell anyone; however, she never revealed its contents. This testimony strengthens the feeling that Van Brugghe is hiding something, but it also contributes to showing that she is a sensitive woman. The voices of the witnesses are rendered as reliable; the scribe's attitude indicates that he trusts their testimonies.

The Voice of the Interrogator

The interrogator's voice is heard in the direct questions posed, in shadow questions we can distinguish, and in descriptions of actions performed during interrogation. His voice covers a register of accents related to the various stages of the trial, from a beginning where the aim is said to be obtaining voluntary answers, to a violent interrogation where torture is used to press forth a desired confession.

The interrogator follows up accusations related to *maleficium* and more severe accusations related to her connection with the Evil One. The questions related to *maleficium* are aimed at finding out more about Lynken van Brugghe's knowledge, for instance the words she used to break an evil spell. It seems clear that the interrogator believes that she has maleficent competencies. He is interested in finding out more, but she is unable to speak. However, more importantly, it is the interrogator who connects Van Brugghe's words to stop the spell, her inability to speak, and the suggestion that it was the Evil One who was the reason she could not speak. Thus, it is the interrogator who brings in Satan. He urges her to repeat a call to God in order to chase away the evil spirit, to put her fate in God's hands and forsake Satan, to ask Jesus for mercy, and to call out to God almighty. It is the interrogator who presses the last 'Yes' out of her to confirm that 'du warinne' is the name of the evil spirit that controls her. The interrogator takes the lead in establishing Van Brugghe's connection to the demonic. He is also the one emphasizing the irreconcilable gap between the two masters, God and Satan, offering Van Brugghe to repeat a cry for salvation.

A lack of sensitivity comes to the fore in the exculpation at the end of the records and the officials' participation in murder. The interrogator and his colleagues display a fanatic attitude. In clear text, the interrogator's voice brings in the religious foundation of witchcraft persecution. His voice is imperative in directing the outcome of the trial.

The Voice of the Law

The voice of the law primarily emerges in the court records' ten points, in the graded enforcement of torture, and in the judiciary's reason given for her death. The points accusing her of witchcraft are weak. Her husband's confirmation of her guilt is put as number one, apparently seen as carrying heavy weight. The discovery of objects in her home used for *maleficium* also points to her alleged witchcraft practice. Otherwise, the testimonies from neighbours do not prove anything, Lynken van Brugghe fleeing from her home does not prove witchcraft, and it is unclear how the points about butter and telling someone about the secret in her heart relate to witchcraft. The voice of the law is characterized by accusing a person on very thin grounds, with means establishing guilt that are not convincing. The officials know that the 'proofs' given will not suffice in a trial. The formal argument for using torture is that from the point of view of the judiciary, some incidents had not been explained well enough. A confession from Van Brugghe's own mouth is necessary, and the element of salvation is stressed by the urge to press forth her prayer.

In the Spanish Netherlands, torture was allowed in witchcraft trials. All stages of torture occur in this trial, from flogging to beating with stocks. From a beginning in which a confession is said to be of Lynken van Brugghe's own free will, the trial moves to an escalation in the use of torture methods within one day. The voice of the law is apparent in the steady increase in intensity of the torture, demonstrating the aim of the interrogation. There is never a question about whether torture should be applied, or whether it should be stopped.

The reason provided by the judiciary, that the evil enemy had helped her to a quick death in order for the truth about similar incidents to remain hidden, displays the voice of the law in its most primitive mode. As she had been tortured 'only' by being beaten with sticks, her death was explained as help from the evil enemy, in order to hide the truth about similar incidents. The court records of Lynken van Brugghe's trial provide unique insights into the tremendous fear of witchcraft that existed among judicial officials in Early Modern Europe. The trial is special compared to the rest of the trials discussed in this book because it describes torture that eventually led to the death of Van Brugghe. Such a description is rare and crudely displays the fanaticism that drove witchcraft persecution. At the time, new torture techniques applied by efficient executioners spread throughout the Netherlands, and also in the northern Republic of the United Provinces.[82]

The Voice of the Scribe

The voice of the scribe is that of a professional person who records what happens during the trial. This documentation makes it possible for others within the judiciary to evaluate the court's proceedings. The scribe is responsible for the wording of the introductory, factual parts of the court records, describing the woman accused and making clear that her husband, already sentenced for witchcraft, affirmed her guilt. The scribe's pen keeps the confession together, which consists of several points that are each structured as narratives. He adds coherence to the court records and succeeds in merging the different layers of the text. He manages to describe the situation in the courtroom during Lynken van Brugghe's interrogation, providing a detailed recording of participants' words. His own voice is concealed most of the time. The closest we come to hearing it is in the closing part of the records, where a possible but totally unrealistic reason for Van Brugghe's death is given. By recording this, the scribe reveals the judicial attitude to witchcraft and the eagerness of the judiciaries to absolve themselves of all responsibility. These formulations might reveal his own attitudes towards witchcraft as well, as no distancing devices are used to show that he disagrees with the judiciary's statements about Van Brugghe's death.

The gruesome story of Lynken van Brugghe's last hours, of judicial officials watching a dying woman and explaining it as the devil helping her to a quick death, reveals a fundamental lack of respect for human life. A tortured woman without a voice is a strong image that captures the climate of a witchcraft trial on the coast of the North Sea anno 1596.

Mayken Karrebrouck, 1634

The Trial

In the 1630s and after some decades of relative quiet, an intensive period of witchcraft persecution occurred in Bruges that might have been influenced by crises, unrest, and tension, not least the trials held by local courts. In 1631, the population developed the fear that they would be conquered by an army of thirty thousand men, led by the Prince of Orange. In addition, from 1632 to 1637, a deadly pestilence spread throughout Bruges. The years 1634 and 1635 were particularly disastrous and were interpreted by many as reflecting the wrath of God. The bishop of Bruges admonished the congregation to be strong in their beliefs and resist attacks on the Catholic faith. Other concerns at the time were the destruction of crops and that the pestilence would flare up again. In such crises, the time was ripe for scapegoats. Thus, for the women of Bruges who had a reputation of practising witchcraft, the days were filled with anxiety.

The presentation of Mayken Karrebrouck's trial below is partly based on a retelling of the court records in Rijksarchief Brugge by Dries Vanysacker in *Hekserij in Brugge* and partly on sentences recorded in the Verluydboeck, Stadsarchief Brugge.[83] In 1633, Mayken Karrebrouck was a sixty-five-year-old widow who lived in Bruges with her son Jan. Her maiden name was Van Vassenare. Locally, she was known as 'enchanted Maeye'. Karrebrouck had been a widow since 1625 and had lost two sons to illness: Adriaen and Jooris. She earned a modest living by selling milk and butter. In 1633, her life took a turn for the worse. On 24 June, her neighbours decided to test her for witchcraft. One of her neighbours, school-teacher Marie Padieu, had a daughter who had been ill for some time. The daughter would suddenly fall down, froth at the mouth, and start crying. Despite regular visits from the pastor and two Capuchins,[84] the girl's situation did not improve. Marie stated that the illness always manifested itself when a cat meowed, when Karrebrouck's chickens beat their wings, or when a bird sang, but mostly when Karrebrouck's dog barked. On 24 June, the clerk[85] of Bruges's local court,[86] Mr Van der Woestijne, visited Marie. When Marie Padieu's girl had an attack, he sent the schoolteacher and her maid to Mayken Karrebrouck's house. When they knocked on her door, the girl's attack stopped, only to resume shortly thereafter. Van der Woestijne peeped[87] over the wall, but did not notice anything odd.

However, there was a strong suspicion that Mayken Karrebrouck had bewitched the child. When on Christmas Day 1633 the child had eight to ten attacks within two hours—in the presence of canon[88] Franchoys from the Saint Salvador church, Van der Woestijne, and some neighbours—the limit was reached. A few days later, the clerk visited the girl again, together with pastor[89] Crits, and she once more experienced attacks while Karrebrouck's dog was howling and barking.[90] The court of Bruges immediately launched a preliminary investigation and, on 2 January 1634, issued an arrest warrant against Mayken Karrebrouck and her son Jan Coese. That same day, mayor[91] Heyndrick Anchemant, who was in charge of the police corps, arrested Karrebrouck and her son. Karrebrouck was surprised and asked if the judges had not made a mistake, and whether she and her son were arrested because they had 'Beggars' books'[92] in their possession. When Karreb-rouck's house was searched, a small book with the Gospel of John was found, as well as pieces of paper that Karrebrouck had quickly pulled off her neck when the police arrived, and 'a piece of cloth for women'.[93] The Gospel of John, especially the first chapter, was considered to be a very special text, which could protect people from harm. By reciting it, people could ward off evil. Priests would recite it at the end of Mass to protect people from witchcraft. Just like many other inhabitants of Bruges, Karrebrouck engaged in magical practices. However, to be formally persecuted for witchcraft was very severe. She realized this, because when she arrived at the prison, she said: 'I shall die, I won't get it easy'.[94]

After her arrest, Mayken Karrebrouck was immediately interrogated and, also using the information gathered during the interrogation of her son, the court quickly obtained a clear idea of their reputation. During the interrogation, she denounced other inhabitants of Bruges, and these people would suffer in due course as well. Karrebrouck said that she had received protective pieces of parchment from a man 'who lived in the Lane',[95] and that her son Adriaen had been bewitched and killed by a certain Mayken Sobers Neerynghe. She refused to confess to witchcraft and said that she was not a witch herself. On his part, her son Jan pointed out that the piece of paper with small crosses on it[96] as well as the scripture[97] once belonged to a soldier from the Lane, and that those signs were meant to protect against witchcraft. It turned out that the soldier's name was Simon van der Straete.

A few weeks later, the first witness hearings took place: neighbours and former acquaintances remembered their setbacks[98] of the last years, illnesses, and the deaths of children, and they all suspected that Mayken Karrebrouck had been performing witchcraft. She denied everything, and on 7 March 1634 it was decided that she would be tortured on the rack the next day.[99] The day thereafter, they were about to start the torture when something strange happened. The judges and their assistants must have been obsessed with the idea of a possible presence of the Evil One in the torture chamber. When surgeon and executioner Van de Walle started shaving Karrebrouck's body, a bat suddenly came flying through the open window into the smoking torture cellar,[100] and the torturer cried out: 'There already is a young devil'.[101] Everyone looked at Karrebrouck, who kept quiet, but was shaking and trembling.[102] According to the people present, the bat could be no one but the devil, because when they managed to catch it with a cap and threw it into the fire, there was no burning smell and there were no remnants of the bat. It had literally gone up in smoke. In the meantime, Mayken Karrebrouck became notably stronger. She suddenly became better,[103] and managed to stand on her two feet by herself.[104]

After the incident with the bat, and in the presence of *schepenen* and one Mr Muelenaere, the torture chamber was sprayed with holy water, including the rack, and the instruments. Then, the judicial officials[105] went ahead with the first torturing of Mayken Karrebrouck. They placed her naked on the rack and sprinkled her with holy water, but she stuck to her assertion[106] that she had done nothing wrong and that she was not a witch.[107] She kept on saying, 'I belong to the Almighty God', and that they were mistakenly torturing her.[108] Quite soon, the judges decided to release her from the rack.

A month passed by, and from other testimonials it became clear that Mayken Karrebrouck had been a good friend of Magdalene Waltack, a woman accused of witchcraft who had already passed away. On 6 April, the *schepenen* asked Karrebrouck for the first time about the Evil One,[109] and she denied having ever seen him. After four months, the investigation seemed to have gotten nowhere.

The trial of Mayken Karrebrouck was part of a witchcraft panic. She had named other women during interrogation, and a few days after 6 April 1634, the judges in Bruges started a preliminary investigation against one of these: Mayken Sobers Neerynghe. During this pre-trial investigation, six witnesses testified; among them Mayken Sobers's daughter-in-law, a certain Cathelyne Verplaetse, who used to sell mussels. She declared that Mayken Sobers had had a reputation of being a witch for sixteen years and gave some examples of this. She emphasized that Mayken Sobers had quarrelled with Mayken Karrebrouck. According to Cathelyne Verplaetse, they had repeatedly accused each other of being witches.[110] Moreover, when Verplaetse's mother-in-law heard about the arrest of Mayken Karrebrouck, she tried to flee from Bruges, but her husband prevented that by threatening to hang himself if she went away. Finally, Mayken Sobers's daughter-in-law told the *schepenen* that her mother-in-law had a devil.

On 11 April, the court[111] decided to arrest Mayken Sobers. However, she had fled, and they could not get a hold of her until 20 May. She was then interrogated, and the judges asked her whether it was correct that she was rumoured to be a witch.[112] To this, she answered that even though it was a great lie, this was shouted after her. She denied all facts that were blamed on her. Based on twenty-five testimonies, it had come to the fore that Mayken Sobers and Mayken Karrebrouck had had words with each other, and Karrebrouck had accused Sobers of bewitching her late son Adriaen, both before and after his death. Because of this accusation, Sobers's husband threatened to beat Karrebrouck. On 13 June, the two women were confronted with each other. Karrebrouck denied having ever accused Sobers of bewitching and killing her son. Notably, the judges were interested in the conversation between the two women on 20 May, when Mayken Sobers was taken to prison. The prison chief,[113] Gheerard Bouchaerd, told his colleagues that Karrebrouck said the following to Sobers: 'Mayken, are you there? I won't say anything about you'.[114] Sobers apparently replied: 'And I won't say anything about you'.[115] However, when the latter was tortured with the collar[116] on 16 June from 9 p.m. until 3 a.m. the next day, she completely gave in[117] and confessed, and her confession was closely considered by the judges. She said she would be accountable to God for all the people she had bewitched.[118] Leading questions made her confess to entering into the devil's pact, renouncing her baptism, getting the devil's mark, and having sexual intercourse with the devil. In addition, she confessed to having been to meetings with the devil and other witches, where they danced, and that she met Karrebrouck five or six years ago at those gatherings, six or seven times. She also told interrogators which means she used when she performed witchcraft: namely fruit and powder. Eventually, Mayken Sobers confessed that she had bewitched and killed the child of Mayken Karrebrouck, something the court found odd, and the judges asked her if her friend[119] had agreed to her bewitching the child of another witch.

On 20 June, Mayken Karrebrouck was brought before the judges again, who were now losing their patience. Karrebrouck insisted that she was not a witch, but the judges threatened her by saying that Mayken Sobers had confessed, and now it was her turn. They wanted her to confess that she had been to these dances with the devil, together with Sobers. Karrebrouck kept on denying. In response, she was tortured with the collar. From 9.30 p.m. until 2.45 a.m. the next day, Karrebrouck was tortured and asked questions about her relationship with the devil and other witches. Around midnight, she broke down and confessed to all demonological notions that the judges wanted to hear. She admitted that Magdalene Waltack had taught her the art.[120] She said that her devil was a black man, who never showed up as a dog, she-goat, or he-goat.[121] He sometimes gave her some money: silver coins. And yes, she had attended the dance meetings two or three times, somewhere in an open field. She flew there via the chimney, after having rubbed powder onto her body.[122] Her lover, the devil, had accompanied her on her flight.[123] At the meeting, some danced, and they discussed what evil crimes they would commit.[124]

She had been in a physical relationship[125] with the devil three to four times, although she had resisted at first. The intercourse happened after the dance. It was normal otherwise, except for his semen feeling ice-cold.[126] She did not show him any honours and was often beaten by him because she did not want to cause much harm.[127] Finally, she tried to protect her son Jan and Simon van der Straete, who had been imprisoned in the meantime. She said that she did not teach the art to anyone, and that she had never shown her lover to her son; Jan was completely innocent and did not know anything. The collar was then removed.[128]

The trials of Mayken Karrebrouck and Mayken Sobers in 1634 are characterized by the transition from a traditional concept of witchcraft to a learned concept: during the first hearings of suspects and witnesses, the court deals with popular beliefs only: the suspect is solely accused of performing *maleficium*. Subsequently, however, the court switches to another level, that of the demonological concept of witchcraft, and interprets the cases by using the judiciary's own notions of demonology.

Twenty-four hours after her interrogation, Mayken Karrebrouck confirmed her confession, but said that she had not met any men at those dances other than the devil. She did remember Mayken Sobers and Mayken with the rags. She admitted to having harmed people, but never actually killed any of them. Just like Sobers, she admitted that she had made a pact with the devil. On 22 June 1634 in Bruges, Mayken Karrebrouck and Mayken Sobers were sentenced to be strangled and burned at the stake. The women were executed on 23 June.

The sentence of Mayken Karrebrouck entered into the Verluydboeck, Stadsarchief Brugge, is different with regard to a few elements compared to the court records in the Rijksarchief Brugge. This is interesting, as the Verluydboeck reveals, among other things, the voice of the law at the end of the trial and thus expresses the core of the judicial authorities' formal view on witchcraft. The Verluydboeck has this wording:

> Mayken Karrebrouck, whose maiden name was Vassenare, around 66 years old, confessed—without being under torture—that during several years she has committed the horrible crime of witchcraft. She made a pact with the enemy from hell, who first convinced her to forsake God almighty and Mother Mary. He then made her attend meetings and dances with evil enemies and other witches, during which she committed terrible and despicable deeds, the relating of whose details here would be improper. Mayken also received from the devil some sort of mark on her body. She further received from the devil some materials with which she could bewitch people. She indeed bewitched several people, causing some of them to die and others to fall ill and suffer in great misery. Moreover, she was suspected of having caused even more evil through witchcraft. Because such deeds could not go unpunished in a city of justice, and also to set an example, she was sentenced to be strangled and burned at the stake. The sentence was read aloud.[129]

The sentence of Mayken Karrebrouck clearly has a religious basis: forsaking God and Mother Mary is mentioned. The sentence also states that she confessed without torture, which does not correspond to the court records in the Rijksarchief. An explanation for this is that a voluntary confession was compulsory and was required after a forced confession had been given. The sentence mentions her criminal record in condensed form: witches' meetings, unspeakable relations with the devil, and the devil's mark—all well-known demonological ideas. In addition, the sentence mentions physical objects received from the devil in order to perform evil acts. When these objects are received from the devil, they obtain values other than those of charms used for performing malefice. Both sickness and death are mentioned as results of Mayken Karrebrouck's witchcraft. This contrasts with her confession in the court records in Rijksarchief Brugge, where she says that she harmed people but did not kill anyone. There is a suggestion that she performed more evil than what is mentioned. Thus, the sentence recorded in Verluydboeck comprises several points that are extremely severe, and that do not correspond to Karrebrouck's confession in the court records in Rijksarchief Brugge. The points mentioned in Verluydboeck are arguments for the sentence to follow. In spite of the brevity of the sentence in Verluydboeck, it provides enough reasons for execution.

The sentence passed is not unexpected: execution by fire at the stake, after first being strangled. It was read aloud. Many people present in the courtroom, included those accused, could not read; they were living in predominantly oral societies. When the sentence was read aloud, the two accused women perhaps learned about their final fates for the first time.

The case shows that during interrogation, the accusation transforms from *maleficium* into the learned, demonological concept of witchcraft. A confession to demonological witchcraft would directly lead to execution, and this is what happened in the trial of Mayken Karrebrouck.

The Voice of Mayken Karrebrouck

The voice of Mayken Karrebrouck is heard distinctly in her remarks rendered in direct speech. Although such remarks occur only three times in the court records, they reveal something about her strategies during the initial part of the trial, when she still has the hope that she will survive. First, there is her pessimistic remark when she is imprisoned; second, her insistence that she belongs to the Almighty God; and third, her promise to Mayken Sobers that she would not say anything about her. These remarks reveal her confusion and anxiety. She is afraid of the development of the trial, because the community in 1634 is certainly well aware of the odds of escaping a witchcraft trial. Then, there is a more offensive strategy, namely appearing as a true Christian, which implies a denial of a devilish relation. She absolutely denies witchcraft and emphasizes that she belongs to the right master, namely God almighty. Finally, when Sobers is arrested, she promises that she will not say anything about Karrebrouck, and she gets the same promise in response. This shows that Karrebrouck thinks that there is hope, that it is possible to stop the development of a severe trial. And to a certain extent, she manages to maintain strength and resistance for some time. Still, a witchcraft trial is eventually subjected to its own fixed pathway.

Further accents of Mayken Karrebrouck's voice are heard in witnesses' testimonies and in confessions of other accused individuals. Particularly during the trial of

Mayken Sobers—in which her daughter-in-law, Cathelyne Verplaetse, testifies— we get the impression that both Sobers and Karrebrouck are quarrelsome people, a fact that is reinforced by several other testimonies. They had scolded each other for being witches, which was very dangerous at the time. Verplaetse's testimony shows that both women were rumoured to be witches, and that they used this information in situations of disagreement, which points to a stressed atmosphere in the local community. Karrebrouck believed that Sobers had bewitched her son, Adriaen, and was the cause of his death. She brought this accusation forward before and after her son's death. Thus, Karrebrouck believed that lethal witchcraft was possible. There is a confrontation in court between the two women, at which stage Karrebrouck denies having ever accused Sobers of bewitching and killing her son. Of the two women, Sobers is the first to give in and confess to demonological ideas after torture, and she denounces Karrebrouck as a witch and participant in witches' gatherings. However, Karrebrouck denies this. Up to this point, the latter's voice shows resistance to confession, but also a desire to help and support Sobers.

In addition, Mayken Karrebrouck's voice is rendered in indirect discourse throughout the court records, from the moment she is arrested until the end of her confession. Reporting verbs are used to introduce reported clauses or indirect speech. Sometimes, reported speech consists of answers to questions posed by the interrogator. The basic structures of a narrative keep her confession together; the entirety of answers that she gives to leading questions during interrogation form a version of the demonological grand narrative about the devil's pact and witches' meetings. This personalized version in the confession of Mayken Karrebrouck includes: name of mentor (the one who taught her the art of witchcraft), meeting the devil, the devil's appearance, renouncing baptism, the devil's promises and gifts, the devil's pact, sexual intercourse with the devil, the devil's mark, witchcraft powder, flight accompanied by the devil, witches' meetings and dances with no men present, and denunciation.

Mayken Karrebrouck's voice undergoes profound changes. First, she expresses astonishment and attempts to find logical reasons for her and her son's arrest. Her explanation is their possession of 'Beggars' books'. In a period of religious turbulence and tension between Catholics and Protestants, some scriptures should not be kept in one's home. Expressing surprise at arrest and mentioning these books seems to have been a natural response, and is a response that shows a bit of resistance.

Also, her voice is heard in the comment on receiving protective pieces of parchment. She says she left them at home, presumably hoping these notes would not be discovered. Most likely, she knew that after her arrest she would be examined to determine whether she was carrying objects on her person. Later, the responses of Mayken Karrebrouck and her son during interrogation show that signs and crosses were drawn on the pieces of parchment. These objects were charms, believed to protect against bewitchment; a belief shared by Karrebrouck and her son. Such charms, widely circulated at this time, were believed to be effective. This accent of Karrebrouck's voice shows that she is familiar with magical remedies for protection against witchcraft, and that she willingly admits to possessing the books as well as the pieces of parchment. Her imagination is characterized by a magical world view, wherein objects can be used for protection against illness, and witchcraft can be lethal.

After Mayken Karrebrouck's arrest, her voice has two prevailing accents: an accent of denial and an accent of confession. There is a certain vacillation in her voice during interrogation. As she is accused during a panic, the interrogators apparently have already pressed for the denunciation of others during pre-trial interrogation. At this initial stage she names other inhabitants in the local community. However, at a later stage of the trial, she refuses to denounce others, so she must have realized the severity of naming others and accordingly refused to cooperate.

The accent of denial in Mayken Karrebrouck's voice is strong from the beginning. During the first day of her imprisonment, we hear her voice alternating between surprise at being arrested, pessimism regarding the near future, and finally denial of being guilty of witchcraft. These various accents point to her being in a difficult situation, a bit hopeful and a bit despairing. During her first meeting with the representatives of the law, however, she clings to her strategy of denial regarding witchcraft. She emphasizes that she is not a witch.

This first interrogation seems to have taken place without the use of torture. However, to elucidate some points, two months after her arrest, on 8 March, it was decided that she would be tortured on the rack. During the episode with the bat, thought to be the devil, Mayken Karrebrouck remained quiet, but was trembling and shaking so much that she was unable to stand on her feet, so she must have been in a miserable condition. After purifying the torture chamber and the instruments with holy water, torture is effectuated. Karrebrouck continually insists that she has done nothing wrong, that she is not a witch, that she belongs to the Almighty God, and that they are mistakenly torturing her. Thus, she continues to deny and shows that she is able to resist torture. This is a sign that the interrogators and judges cannot overlook. They decide to release her from the rack.

Mayken Karrebrouck is interrogated again on 6 April, and is asked about the Evil One, whom she denied having seen. It is the interrogators who bring the devil into the questioning. Karrebrouck, at this point, has been imprisoned for three months, interrogated three times, and tortured on the rack once. She still denies, and her voice is stable, even after being exposed to pressure.

A small change in Mayken Karrebrouck's voice might be detected one and a half months later, on 20 May, when Mayken Sobers Neerynghe was imprisoned. A touch of sisterhood can be traced in a conversation allegedly overheard by the prison chief and passed on to his colleagues, where the two suspected women promise to protect each other. This attitude is accentuated when the two women meet each other face-to-face on 13 June. The method of letting accused people confront each other in the courtroom, which is often employed in witchcraft trials to force confessions, was used. Frequently, it leads to intensified accusation. However, instead of accusing Sobers, Karrebrouck withdraws the accusation that Sobers bewitched and killed her son, which can also be interpreted as a hand stretched out to a sister.

Influential for the development of the trial of Mayken Karrebrouck is the inter-rogation and confession of Mayken Sobers. On 16 June, three days after her arrest, Sobers is interrogated under torture, gives in after some hours, and confesses to the entire range of demonological ideas. Karrebrouck and others are denounced. Sobers confesses that she bewitched the child of Karrebrouck, a piece of informa-tion that the court finds very strange. It seems that the judicial officials were of the opinion that witches would protect each other, a reaction which the scribe found worthwhile to record.

Four days later, on 20 June, six months after her imprisonment, Mayken Kar-rebrouck is brought before the court again. She still denies that she is a witch, and she continues to deny this, even after the judicial officials threaten her with the content of Mayken Sobers's confession, saying that it is now Karrebrouck's turn, and that she has attended dances with the devil. Then, the change in Karrebrouck's voice arrives. That day and night, Karrebrouck is tortured until she finally gives in and gives a full demonological confession. The comment that she did not show the devil any honours and was beaten by him can be seen as an attempt to claim extenuating circumstances. Mostly, her voice coming to the fore in her confession is flat and without feelings. However, her attempt at protecting her son, and also Simon van der Straete, must be seen as a strong act and a last sign of emotion at the end of the interrogation under torture.

Several accents of Mayken Karrebrouck's voice show a strong person: a woman who cares about her son, a woman who supports a fellow accused woman, a woman who fears a witchcraft trial. A broad spectre of emotions is heard in her voice: anger, fear, hope, concern, desolation, despair, resignation, and grief. Her knowledge of maleficent witchcraft is broad. She is a competent person when it comes to ideas about witchcraft and magical practices. She knows how to distin-guish between dangerous and harmless witchcraft, speaking easily about *maleficium* and the methods employed but not about the devil and demonological ideas. Mag-ical practices and the art of warding off evil are also part of her knowledge. She is a woman who during the first part of her trial denies knowing witchcraft and man-ages to resist torture for a long time, even when exposed to it. The fact that such a strong voice is broken at last shows that she meets a mighty wall. This wall consists of the physical instruments of torture as well as the fear and ideas inside the heads of the judicial officials, the interrogators. The road from *maleficium* to demonological witchcraft is clear-cut, and its aim is simple. For the interrogators, enough is not enough until a full range of demonological ideas is confessed to. The uttermost fear of the judiciary is the devil and his power.

The Voices of the Witnesses

The voices of a considerable number of witnesses—around twenty-five—are referred to in the cases of Mayken Karrebrouck and Mayken Sobers, who were accused at the same time. The majority of the witnesses were neighbours. A picture is drawn of a Mayken Karrebrouck who threatens others and who is knowledgeable about and practises *maleficium*, mostly casting spells resulting in illness and the death of children. The witnesses' testimonies emphasize that she was rumoured to have been practising witchcraft for many years. Mayken Sobers's confession and denunciation also turn out negatively for Karrebrouck.

The initial accusation against Mayken Karrebrouck was that she had bewitched a girl, the child of a female schoolteacher, who suffered from inexplicable attacks. When the mother of the girl brings forth her accusation, she claims that she noted strange signals from a cat, chickens, a bird, and a dog at the same time as the attacks started. Also, the clerk of the local court testifies that the girl's attacks stopped when her mother and the maid went to knock on Karrebrouck's door. In addition to the clerk, clerics had visited the girl—the Capuchins, the canon, and the pastor of the church, all prominent people in the community. The pastor and two Capuchins were apparently called on to counteract the spell, paying regular visits. The word of God was believed to prevent evil. All witnesses find reasons to suspect Karrebrouck of witchcraft. One was that her dog howled on Christmas Day when the girl had severe attacks. The witnesses accept that strange signs strengthened the suspicion. When Karrebrouck was arrested, among those pressing for an investigation were powerful people. The voices of the witnesses incorporate a clear religious element from the beginning; a trust in God's power. As the trial continues, the witnesses are interested in documenting *maleficium* and not so much focused on religious help.

The Voice of the Interrogator

The voice of the interrogator comes clearly to the fore in the court records. The formulations show that Mayken Karrebrouck's confession was steered by leading questions posed during interrogation. The same is the case with Mayken Sobers's confession. After several decades of witchcraft persecution, there was a standard repertoire of elements which had to be present in a demonological witchcraft confession. The interrogator was increasingly interested in extracting demonological confessions that included the name of the mentor, the devil's pact, promises from the devil, the devil's appearance, sexual intercourse with the devil, witches' flight, and witches' gatherings. Then, there are some details that might be added, like the use of witchcraft powder and the devil's ice-cold semen.

According to shadow questions, Mayken Karrebrouck is asked about who taught her the art, the appearance of the devil (was it like a dog or a goat), whether she attended dance meetings and how many times, who accompanied her on the flight to the meeting, what they did at the meeting, whether she was in a physical relationship with the devil and how many times, whether she had shown the devil any honours, and whether she taught the art to anyone.

The voice of the interrogator is well trained in asking relevant questions and pressing for desired answers. This voice is acquainted with the main elements as well as the possible additions to a demonological narrative. It is characterized by a clear direction towards its goal.

The Voice of the Law

The voice of the law comes to the fore in the determination to carry Mayken Karrebrouck's trial through to the very end, in the decision to use torture, and in the proclamation of Bruges as a city of justice. There is no doubt that witchcraft is considered a serious crime by the law. Karrebrouck's trial is taken up again and again, without the judiciary being able to extract a confession. It is not until after Mayken Sober's confession that the legal apparatus reaches its aim, obtaining grounds for sentencing Karrebrouck.

Due to Mayken Karrebrouck's refusal to confess during several interrogation rounds, one of them under torture, it is not easy for legal officials to extract a confession to witchcraft. They take seriously that she first manages to resist torture on the rack and stop the torture. This means that the law was adhered to. However, the collar used later cannot be endured, and the confession is finally a fact. In carrying out a stepwise increase of torture, following the desire to obtain the needed confession at any price, the voice of the law is merciless. The force of torture is impossible to resist, even for the strong Mayken Karrebrouck.

The sentence recorded in the Verluydboeck emphasizes that Bruges is a city of justice and that therefore, Mayken Karrebrouck's deeds could not remain unpunished. Bruges's judiciary has a particular ambition. Also, the importance of setting an example is mentioned. This is a responsibility of the court: to warn people about the consequences of choosing a wrong master. Thus, the content of the sentence has a preventive function.

The Voice of the Scribe

The scribe who recorded the trial of Mayken Karrebrouck has managed to give a description of the full trial in terms of factual information: the dates of the court sessions, the names of the judicial officials, the development of the trial, the courtroom discourse, and the sentence. Courtroom discourse is taken down as accurately as manageable, which means that attention is paid to what is uttered by the accused person, the witnesses, the interrogators, and the judges expressing the voice of the law. The accused person's attitude towards witchcraft is rendered without any distancing linguistic devices, which conveys that concrete objects as well as unrealistic elements like the witches' flight are accepted usable. The way the voices of the interrogator and the witnesses are rendered in the records, with no distancing attitude to what is told, likewise shows that in their understanding of witchcraft, realistic as well as unrealistic elements are accepted.

In letting the voices of each of the actors come to the fore, the scribe has provided insight into the complex conversation that takes place in court during the trial. He has not omitted vital information, and from what is taken down in the records, it is possible to understand the verdict and sentence given in case the judicial proceedings should be evaluated at another legal level or legal institution. The scribe's own attitude towards what is told does not come to the fore. His role, to professionally record what has happened in the courtroom, is carried out well.

Clayse Sereyns, 1657

The Trial

Clayse Sereyns was a forty-eight-year-old married woman, born and living in Morbecque. She was the daughter of Thomas Sereyns, and her husband was Francoys de Cool.[130] She was brought before the court, the *leenhof*,[131] in Morbecque on 27 February 1657. The court records contain the indictment, ordered in points.[132] The formal accuser was Abraham Hoghelaer, and the indictment is recorded as an 'I' speaking to a 'you'.[133] Clayse Sereyns had been imprisoned for some time, and it is mentioned that she is taken out of prison for interrogation. Torture is not mentioned, but it might well have been used, as this was common and has been documented in the above-mentioned trials.

The indictment is formulated in the following way: around eight years ago, you started following the advice of the devil[134] and got involved in witchcraft at your home.[135] The devil was black and had black horse feet. You made a pact with him and forsook God and the Holy Mother.[136] You also had a physical relationship with him and received his mark on your back, and you also renounced your baptism.[137] Once a month, you had a physical relationship with him, and even three times while being imprisoned. He accompanied you when you were taken for examination[138] and back to the prison, assuring you that he would never leave you.[139]

In accordance with the pact, you received five or six times a year a powder, which had a colour similar to clove. With the powder, you first bewitched the child of Boudewijn Fossaert via your breath, and you also touched the child with your hand while it was in the cradle.[140] The child died shortly thereafter. The devil gave you five cents[141] for the deed. In the same way, you bewitched and killed the child of Mahu Hasebaert, by giving the child a waffle sprinkled with the same powder, and for that the devil rewarded you with a Liege coin.[142]

You also bewitched the brown cow of Pieter de Wale by sprinkling powder in its water trough. Shortly thereafter, the cow started swelling up.[143] You received five-cent pieces[144] for this deed.

Yes, you steadily continued your evil life[145] and bewitched and killed the child of Jacobs Andries by sprinkling powder on its lips, and for this crime you received a double five-cent piece.[146]

Yes, you have bewitched Antone Wallyn and his wife, the woman by sprinkling powder on a waffle of buckwheat and the man with a small amount of liquid.[147] For this reason, the man is still suffering today, and his wife is about to die, so you say. You earned a five-cent piece[148] for bewitching the woman and six coins[149] for bewitching the man.

You have in addition done your duty to bewitch Mahu Hasebaert and Jaene Beniaume in the church of Morbecque by blowing your breath into their necks.[150]

You also tried to bewitch the daughter of Charle de Haese by giving her a saucer of milk in which you had put a small animal, like a frog,[151] which you had received from your devil. But you did not have power over these people, as you say.[152]

You also tried to bewitch Margrite Syns by sprinkling powder in her bowl of porridge, but it was too little to kill Margrite, but enough to torment her, which is still the case.[153] For this you earned ten coins.[154]

Yes, and it is also true that during your improper pact with the devil, at fixed times you attended meetings with other witches, usually once a month and at secret locations, at the crossroads[155] next to Pieter de Pours, and also with the wife of Mahu Hasebaert. And there was dancing with another, and you as an admiral, while your devil would be playing on a small drum, and there was the sound of a flute, but you did not know who played the flute. After the dancing, everyone would eat unsalted butter and unsalted sheep meat, and would drink beer or sometimes water using saucers from the dikes.[156] And you departed from each other, each with your own devil, by whom you were caressed.[157] You were transported to different places by the same devil.[158] For this he had given you a black ointment, which you put on your broomstick, and you flew out of the chimney.[159] Several times the devil came to sleep with you, in the absence of your husband, and you felt that he was different from a normal man because he had claws on his feet.[160]

As this in due form and completely has shown your vices, by your own confession and otherwise,[161] due to all these abominable facts and witchcraft, the men at this court point out and condemn you to death by fire, so that you die and the body thus burns, serving as an example for others.[162] All your earthly possessions will be confiscated and the income taken by those who have the right thereto.[163] The costs and expenses for the trial have been deducted beforehand.[164]

The Voice of Clayse Sereyns

Contrary to the two previous cases, the voice of Clayse Sereyns in direct speech is absent, as it is rendered in indirect speech in the indictment. She has confessed prior to the trial, and the indictment is the judiciary's summing up of the points of her confession in order to provide the reasons for the sentence to be passed. Sereyns does not deny having learned and performed witchcraft. It seems she has willingly told the court about all her acts of witchcraft, but there is no information about what happened before she confessed.

The voice of Clayse Sereyns is interwoven with the voice of the law and the voice of the interrogator, and the judiciary approaches her in second person. Twice, the voice of Sereyns is echoed in the expression 'as you say', which means that she has confessed to this already. In both cases, the expression refers to her own voice, and contributes to increasing the credibility of the indictment. The expression 'as you say' is used for the first time in connection with the bewitchment of Antone Wallyn and his wife, when their state of health is referred to as being very bad, according to what Sereyns has said. The expression 'as you say' then functions as an assurance that the couple's misery is a result of the witchcraft that Sereyns performed. The expression is used a second time in connection with deeds of witchcraft that were unsuccessful: the case of two women in the church, whom Sereyns allegedly tried to bewitch, and the case of the daughter of Charle de Haese, who received a bewitched saucer of milk. Apparently, Sereyns had said that she did not have any power over these people, and thus her witchcraft acts were unsuccessful. The expression 'as you say' in this context functions as a statement that her witchcraft was not successful, but no explanation is given for why she did not have power over these people. Similar situations of the unsuccessful performance of witchcraft are found in confessions in witchcraft cases from Finnmark in Northern Norway. These always state that witchcraft was impossible because those targeted believed too strongly in God or prayed too much.[165]

Otherwise, Clayse Sereyns's voice is echoed in propositions: assertions made based on elements from her previous confession. At an early stage, these focus on the devil's pact and on the renouncing of God, the Holy Mother, and Sereyns's baptism. Likewise, they mention the devil's mark, sexual intercourse with the devil, and the devil's promises not to leave her when she was brought back to prison after having been examined. This emphasizes the importance of demonological ideas at an early stage of this trial. These ideas are compressed, with all of them presented in the first paragraph. This signals that the judiciary is keen to insert them into the initial part of the indictment. An effort is made to expand on the demonological ideas in detail, like the devil's mark, the devil accompanying Sereyns, and the use of witchcraft powder. However, this is not a prevalent feature, which suggests that the judicial officials saw no need to ask for details. The confessing witch seemed to have given information about all points needed. By 1657, demonological ideas were probably well known by lay and learned people in the community of Morbecque. It is likely that Sereyns knew about these ideas before she was imprisoned. A confession to these ideas was considered dangerous.

While the first stage of the confession is very much focused on demonology, the middle stage of the confession turns towards *maleficium*. All acts of witchcraft Clayse Sereyns confesses to are about malefice: using powder, using a small animal, and breathing on people. The way this type of performed witchcraft is rendered shows that Sereyns has a broad knowledge of malefice. However, the devil's pact is woven into the malefice section as well. The section starts with stating that in accordance with the pact, she received powder from the devil in order to perform witchcraft acts.[166] This is unusual in a *maleficium* context, as the witches usually make their own powder. There is also another demonological detail involved in Sereyns's acts of malefice: when she has finished her deeds, the devil pays her for work well done. Thus, the devil is brought into the picture again, this time for giving her a reward. This is also unusual in a *maleficium* context, as the performance of this type of witchcraft usually does not mention the pact and the rewarding devil. When the devil is so strongly involved in the performance of malefice, it shows that the two concepts of witchcraft, *maleficium* and demonology, are not strictly separated at this point in time. The importance of the devil and his work has become included in maleficent witchcraft.

The last point of the indictment again clearly brings up a central demonological idea, namely witches' meetings. The activities of a witches' meeting are described, like dancing, playing on drums and a flute, drinking beer or water, eating unsalted food, and Sereyns being an admiral for the participants. It also mentions her leaving the meeting with a personal devil who was very affectionate towards her, her sexual relations with the devil at home when her husband was absent, and the devil being different from a normal man due to clawed feet. The idea of a witch having a personal devil is known from other Flemish trials and also from Danish and Norwegian trials.[167] In addition, the witch's flight is touched upon: the use of ointment provided by the devil, the smearing of the broom with this ointment, and the flying up the chimney on a broom. Introducing the idea of the witches' meetings could be an attempt to obtain the names of Sereyns's accomplices, as this is often the intention of adding this element at the end of an interrogation in a witchcraft trial. However, in this case, no new names of participants of witches' meetings come up. Instead, the key elements of witches' gatherings appear. Apparently, Sereyns was asked who the flute player was, and she answered that she did not see.[168] This is the only time it clearly comes to the fore that leading questions were used during interrogation, but these were probably used more than once. Contrary to witches' sabbaths further south in Europe, cannibalism is absent: there is no mention of killing babies in order to make ointment, even if ointment is mentioned as what she should put on her broomstick. The entire point is characterized by brevity. It has a compressed stylistic form, like the introductory point about the devil's pact.

The voice of Clayse Sereyns, as it is echoed in this case, shows knowledge of demonological ideas and *maleficium* alike. As a woman who is forty-eight years old, born and bred in Morbecque, she has been living in a community where ideas of *maleficium* were passed on for a long time through oral transmission. In addition, at the time, demonological ideas became integrated into its mentality and merged with the traditional concept of witchcraft. In that respect, Sereyns is representative of many people in Europe around 1660. On the one hand, she exemplifies a conception of witchcraft that some people were believed to have: a place and a role that mediates between human beings and supernatural powers, using individual, nature-given talents. On the other hand, she has learned throughout her life about the devil and his reign, about the possibility of obtaining access to evil power through entering into a pact with him. She also knows about the range of demonological ideas connected to the devil's pact and the witches' meetings. The latter impacted witchcraft trials due to the collective performance of witchcraft, with denunciations and a rapid increase in the number of witchcraft trials as a result. This mixture of two concepts of witchcraft is displayed in her confession and shows how a dangerous witchcraft confession is the result of a crossing of ideas in a complex mental realm. However, as we approach the end of witchcraft persecution, there is also a tone in this confession that is weaker than in the other two confessions from Spanish Netherlands analysed above: almost a listing up of compulsory points for a death sentence to be passed. This might point to the fact that the strong fear of witchcraft loosened its grip on the minds of the judiciary as the decades approached the end of the 1600s.

The Voices of the Witnesses

The voices of the witnesses are indirectly heard in the indictment in the mentioning of all the children who were bewitched and died, of the adult people who were bewitched and grew ill, and of the cow that began swelling up. These incidents were all tragedies, impossible to explain, and could easily be understood as happening due to witchcraft. Clayse Sereyns is accused of having used various methods of malefice to cause these accidents. But there is also mention of people whom Sereyns tried to bewitch unsuccessfully, and one case where the powder used by Sereyns was not enough to kill, only to torment.

The voices of the witnesses show that there is a belief in maleficent witchcraft in the local community, and that death and illness might be accounted for by the use of such means. The understanding that objects and remedies are effective in performing *maleficium* seems to be common, whether these are powder, liquid, or breath used by the witch. The tragedies mentioned in the indictment seem to have come up in retrospect, after the arrest of Clayse Sereyns. The witnesses present suspicions of performed witchcraft that span a period of about eight years. These suspicions might have been dormant for some time but were reactivated when a witchcraft investigation started. Now, the time had come to state the nature of the bad luck. A consistent cause-and-effect logic establishes the pattern of interpretation expressed by the witnesses.

The Voice of the Interrogator

In the same way as the voices of the witnesses, the voice of the interrogator comes indirectly to the fore in the indictment. In fact, what we get, ordered in points, is the result of the interrogation. The interrogator is aware of the importance of a demonological confession, and in that respect manages to get a hold of all main elements needed to secure a death sentence. In addition, he is aware of the many details of a demonological narrative. As for *maleficium*, the interrogator is acquainted with remedies, methods, and alleged effects. He further expresses the notion that the devil paid Sereyns to perform witchcraft.

The priority of content in the indictment signals an interrogator who is experienced in questioning during witchcraft trials. After initially securing a demonological confession, he returns to witches' meetings at the end in order to get denunciations. This is a common strategy in witchcraft trials and shows a conscious manoeuvre to first confirm severe witchcraft and later obtain new names for the panic to continue. In addition, the interrogator repeats cases of death and sickness that have occurred in the community during many years, connects this to maleficent witchcraft, and places the blame on Sereyns. The voice of the interrogator shows the fear of witchcraft in the community and how this fear is channelled into accusations and explanations of witchcraft.

The Voice of the Law

The voice of the law comes to the fore particularly in the way the points of the indictment are ordered, in the demand for a confession from Clayse Sereyns's own mouth, and in the wording of the sentence. The importance of ordering is demonstrated, emphasizing the law's understanding of the graveness of demonology via the content of the first and last points.

A confession from Sereyns's own mouth is given weight in the points dealing with demonological as well as maleficent witchcraft. In the sentence, it is directly stated that it is her 'own confession' which has demonstrated her vices. Even if torture is not mentioned, the voice of the law is echoed in the demand for a personal confession.

In the wording of sentence, 'the men at this court' are the ones who condemn Clayse Sereyns to death by fire. The power of the judiciary is underlined: they have the responsibility to be the voice of the law. The expression 'you die and the body thus burns' might connote a difference between the soul and the body, since in the burning of a witch, there was still hope for the next life according to the understanding of the law. The act of executing witches as part of setting an example for others is also emphasized in the sentence, as this was a major ambition for the handling of crimes in the Early Modern period. Even if the sentence is brief, the main concerns of the law are accounted for.

The Voice of the Scribe

The role of the scribe when composing an indictment is a work of rewriting and joining bits and pieces of the interrogation and confession to a coherent text. The rhetoric shows a formal legal language when it comes to the conclusion, where the letters of the laws are echoed. However, there is also a hint of an informal, personalized language on the part of the accused person. By using minutes from the pre-trial interrogation, the scribe worked to compile the points into a consistent text. As the grammatical form of the indictment is an 'I' speaking to a 'you', it was important for him to insert 'as you say' as a recurring reference to Clayse Sereyns's pre-trial confession, which increased the credibility of the document.

The rendered points vary in length, with the two dealing with demonological ideas being the longest. These are also the points that mention details connected to witchcraft objects and the performance of witchcraft: the powder has a colour like clove; the ointment smeared on the broomstick is black; there is a small drum and the sound of a flute at the dance; they were eating unsalted butter and unsalted sheep meat; the devil was a black man with black horse feet. These details are connected to the oral sphere, and show that the scribe left the orality features intact when writing the indictment. The same is the case with the ordering sequence of the text: it mentions the number of years since Clayse Sereyns entered the devil's pact and points out time markers such as 'once a month' and 'five or six times a year', referring to how often Sereyns received powder from the devil. At the witches' meeting, the ordering of events forms a timeline: 'once a month', 'after the dancing', 'and you departed from'. This resonance of orality signals that the scribe has managed to convey the individuality of Sereyns's language, and this has resulted in points in which detailed demonological notions are recorded.

When it comes to the *maleficium* elements Clayse Sereyns confessed to, we see that each point is formed as a narrative with orality features, however short the text may be. A timeline is established, an additive sentence structure is used, the way witchcraft is performed is explained, and the cause-and-effect argument is carried through. When casting sickness, 'you first bewitched' and 'you also touched'; first, the performance of witchcraft takes place, and 'shortly thereafter', a person or an animal is sick or dead. Witchcraft is performed by touching with a hand, blowing in the neck, mixing witchcraft powder into milk or food, sprinkling witchcraft powder onto the lips of a child or in the water trough of an animal. In relatively short passages, the art of maleficent witchcraft is described in its many shades. The way it is told is neutral; there is no sign of the scribe's own opinion on the matter.

The role of the scribe is professional. His work is to record what was said and argued during the trial. While the voice of the interrogator is only echoed in the points of the indictment where his questions are implied, other voices are more distinct. The courtroom discourse we see in this recorded trial has become so rich—with access to the mood of several participants and the way they see witchcraft—because of the scribe's ambition to get down on paper not only the formalities of the judiciary but also the voices of the actors. Due to the effort of the scribe, it becomes clear that a range of ideas about witchcraft have impacted all those involved in the trial. What was asked, answered, and testified to turns out to be the most valuable footprint that the scribe could leave behind. In addition, the final paragraph, where the voice of the law comes to the fore, is important for understanding the core of this criminal trial.

Conclusion

The voices of women heard in the three trials from the Spanish Netherlands show a remarkably broad knowledge of ideas about witchcraft held by common people at the end of the 1500s and throughout the 1600s. This goes for knowledge of ideas about *maleficium* as well as for demonological ideas. There is, however, a distinction when it comes to the willingness of accused women to confess to witchcraft. While traditional ideas of *maleficium* and the performance of this art are easily confessed to during interrogation in witchcraft trials, even sometimes confessed to with pride, demonological ideas have to be forced out of them by the use of torture. People know that it is very dangerous to confess to demonological ideas like the devil's pact and witches' gatherings, and they deny this type of witchcraft as long as they can manage. With the exception of the trial of Clayse Sereyns in 1657, in which torture is not mentioned, the trials of Lynken van Brugghe in 1596 and Mayken Karrebrouck in 1634 document extreme torture in order to obtain a demonological confession. The urgency with which the interrogators seek to wrangle a confession from the mouth of the accused person is striking.

The study of the three trials also shows that there is a change in intensity from 1596 to 1657. In the first two trials, it is possible to see a turning point caused by the use of severe torture: the rack, beating with sticks, or the collar. At a certain point, the accused woman cannot stand the torture any longer, at which point she gives in and the demonological confession is delivered. In the last trial, it is not possible to trace a turning point, as the entire demonological confession is given before the indictment is written. Still, torture might have been applied. In the trial of Lynken van Brugghe, it is recorded that she confessed to some points without torture. This is a modified truth, as the use of torture in witchcraft trials was commonly known, and there was always a threat of torture if a person did not confess.

The voices of women in witchcraft trials cover a range of accents. Elizabeth Cohen's discussion of double modes of reading is relevant when it comes to the voices of women heard in the trials from the Spanish Netherlands.[169] On the one hand, the voices of women heard in the court records can be interpreted at a straightforward textual level and are easy to read as weak voices. However, a close reading of the court records shows another, and deeper, textual level: that the women argue, resist, protest, defend themselves, and have strategies for dealing with difficult situations. They manage to stick to their own language and turn out to be good narrators. They show an enormous strength in resisting torture. They show emotions and even want to protect their children in situations where they themselves are in a miserable condition. There is an inherent complexity present in these voices. All these qualities show that the women were nuanced individuals and illustrate that it is possible to stand upright in challenging situations by clinging to one's language. Not least, the occurrence of orality features strengthens the personalized approach to, and interpretation of, courtroom discourse.

The voices of the witnesses document a range of ideas about witchcraft and demonstrate their way of understanding the performance of witchcraft, with a clear cause-and-effect logic. The witnesses, most often neighbours and people from the local community, have detailed knowledge of *maleficium* ideas. Peasants seem to have become more aware of ideas on demonological witchcraft as the decades passed by. These originally learned ideas were transmitted orally to peasants in local communities, so that the devil's pact and witches' meetings were well known among common people in 1657.

The voice of the interrogator is heard in the first two trials in the form of questions and shadow questions; in the last trial, it is possible to trace the echo of his questions in the structure of the indictment, which is organized in articles. What appears from the study of these trials is the enormous fear among judicial officials when it comes to the power of the devil over human beings who are in alliance with him. The ways in which Catholic objects and ceremonies are used to destroy the devil's grip on an alleged witch display a desire to purge evil forces from an accused person, which takes on symbolic dimensions. It is not the accused witch herself who represents evil; the interrogators are fighting against an abstraction.

This fear of evil—which overshadows the range of individuals—is one of the factors driving witchcraft persecution and might explain the fanatic behaviour that is seen in the trial of Lynken van Brugghe. To understand the development of witchcraft trials and interpret the sound of women's voices in these trials, the judiciary's fear of a mighty devil must be taken into account. Even when all kinds of religious manoeuvres—such as holy water to sprinkle and drink—and the rack are used, all remedies come up short of fighting this evil. Even the word 'devil' is hard to use: we see the figure described indirectly as 'the enemy from hell', 'the evil ghost', 'the evil spirit', 'the evil friend'. The name 'Satan' is used once, in the trial of Lynken van Brugghe. The judiciary has to decide on how to deal with this enemy in the courtroom, and the interrogators in particular seem to be panic-stricken in the late 1500s.

The voice of the law is heard primarily in the wording of the sentence of Mayken Karrebrouck, in which demonological ideas surface. One reason for the verdict is that such a crime should not go unpunished in 'a city of justice'. In the sentence of Clayse Sereyns, it is mentioned that her deeds were confessed to by herself 'or proved otherwise', an expression very difficult to interpret when it comes to witchcraft trials, as proving witchcraft is an impossible task. In the trial of Lynken van Brugghe, the judiciary tried to wash its hands of the accused woman's death, saying that her evil enemy helped her to a sudden death. Even if this cannot be classified as the voice of the law, it shows an attitude on the part of the legal apparatus that supported the use of lethal torture in order force a confession, which was the best proof in a witchcraft trial.

The voice of the scribe is not easy to detect. The scribe was a professional person, and usually his way of recording was neutral. He tried to document the courtroom discourse and the reasons given for the sentence. In case the trial was going to be passed on to a higher level within the court system, it was of utmost importance to see which arguments were used to prove guilt and pass the sentence. The scribe never emerges as an 'I' in the court records. What might reflect the scribe's opinion is the choice of elements included in the court records. We see this for instance in the trial of Lynken van Brugghe, when the scribe inserted the court's excuse for her death. When it came to recording ideas about witchcraft, there was a change which made itself felt in the slightly more mechanical way in which ideas belonging to the demonological doctrine were recorded in the chapter's last trial. Generally, the scribe seems to have strived for accuracy and reliability.

3

NORTHERN GERMANY— BLOKSBERG, RED RIDER, AND TORTURE 'IN A HUMANE WAY'

The three trials chosen for analysis in this chapter all took place in Northern Germany, in the region Schleswig-Holstein. The choice of trials was based on criteria similar to those of the other countries studied in this book. A chronological line was drawn, and one trial from the early, middle, and late period of witchcraft persecution each was chosen. Trials held at different locations in the region are represented. Relatively long and detailed court records were selected in order to carry out close readings to comprehend linguistics as well as content. Court records that allow access to complex ideas about witchcraft, demonological notions, and ideas of *maleficium* entangled in the confessions were chosen. In addition, the selected records also provide insight into notions related to healing and traditional folkloric motifs.

In the chosen trials, the voices of women mainly come to the fore in accused individuals' confessions and in the testimonies of female witnesses. Both the confessions and the testimonies are narratives and are structured as such. The way these narratives are told matters when it comes to the analysis of courtroom discourse. Through the confessions, the interrogation becomes visible as well, as leading questions and the interrogator's voice may be traced. The accused person's own knowledge of witchcraft ideas surfaces alongside the learned ideas of the judiciary.

The analyses will demonstrate several elements of courtroom discourse. The fact that these accused people lived in oral communities is reflected in the mastery of storytelling that comes to the fore and particularly in orality features, which tend to individualize the language of each accused person.

The chapter aims at shedding light on accents of the female voices. The court records provide insight into the emotional strain on the accused individuals, be that as a result of specific and acute painful experiences such as torture, constant pressure due to imprisonment over time, or disappointment in hopeful strategies that turned out impossible to fulfil. The emotive expressions will also display any change in the voice of the accused person between the beginning and the end of the trial.

DOI: 10.4324/9781003255406-3

The court records on which analyses of the trials are based are written texts produced within a legal frame and are several hundred years old. Thus, the work of the scribe and the accuracy with which he performed his work bridges the Early Modern court records and today's scholarly studies. The rendered discourse, the scribe's effort to express the drama evolving during a witchcraft trial through words on paper, his professionalism and ambition; all this impacts reliability when court records are studied today. However, there will always be a filter to take into consideration when working with historical documents, as text-critical evaluation is an inherent part of analytical work. The scribe's potential influence in the process of recording will therefore also be a factor included in the study of these trials.

The three cases from Northern Germany I have chosen to study are the trials of Kistina Netelers, 1607; Anneke Rickers, 1641; and Anna Spielen, 1669. The trial of Kistina Netelers took place in Flensburg, which belonged to the duchy of Schleswig, which from 1460 until 1864 was in a personal union with the kingdom of Denmark.[1] The trial was held at the town court and ended in a sentence of execution. Torture was applied from the beginning, with an early confession as a result. The trial of Anneke Rickers took place in the district of Bordesholm, in the duchy of Holstein, the northernmost state of the Holy Roman Empire.[2] The court records show the interaction between the duke and the magistrate in the decision to use torture and in the confirmation of the sentence of execution. The trial of Anna Spielen took place in Lübeck, which was an imperial free city in the Holy Roman Empire,[3] one of the cities of the Hanseatic League. The city had immediate superiority[4] in the Holy Roman Empire and was subject only to the authority of the Holy Roman Emperor. Anna Spielen was tried under the jurisdiction of the Lübeck Cathedral Chapter, *Domkapitel*, a forum in which the bishop and the ministers at the cathedral discussed and decided in cases related to religious questions.[5] She was tried during a witchcraft panic and underwent torture to elicit a confession. Her trial ended in a sentence of execution.

For each of the trials, first a description of the trial is given, followed by an analysis of the voice of the accused woman. In addition, comments on the voices of the witnesses, the voice of the interrogator, the voice of the law, and the voice of the scribe are provided. Factors highlighted in the analyses are comparable to those emphasized in the other chapters of this book: courtroom practice, denial of witchcraft, ideas about witchcraft related to demonology and *maleficium* that emerge, notions of healing, orality features, and possible changes in the voices that might reveal a turning point in the trial. In closing, the main findings of the chapter will be summarized.

Background

Persecution

The region of Schleswig-Holstein is of great importance within the range of countries explored in this book, as it is one of the gates through which witchcraft ideas travelled northwards, from Southern Germany to the Nordic countries of Denmark, Norway, and Sweden.[6] Germany is known as the heartland of witchcraft trials. Indeed, '[o]f the estimated 90,000 individuals prosecuted for witchcraft in Europe, at least 30,000 and possibly as many as 45,000 came from the Germanies, roughly encompassed at the time by the Holy Roman Empire and nearby territories'.[7] The population of Europe was around one hundred million in 1600, and approximately two-thirds of legal executions for witchcraft 'were concentrated in the German-speaking lands ("Germany", Austria, and part of Luxemburg and Switzerland), with only one-fifth of the population'.[8] Within Germany, the west and south were areas of intensive persecution, which was particularly intense around the rivers Rhine and Mosel, where the Electorate of Trier and the Imperial Prince-Abbey of St Maximin suffered severe witch-hunts in the period 1585–96, in which around four hundred persons were executed.[9] In other parts of Europe, Switzerland, parts of Luxemburg, Lorraine, and Scotland experienced similarly high rates.[10]

Historically and politically, the southern part of Jutland, *Sønderjylland*, has been important for Denmark because it bordered Germany.[11] The area consisted of the duchy of Schleswig, to the south of which lay the duchy of Holstein. When the last male representative of the Holstein dukes died in 1459, a common policy for Schleswig-Holstein began that was aimed at preserving the unity between the two districts in relation to the Danish throne. This structural organizing started with the Danish king Christian I being elected Duke of Schleswig and Earl of Holstein in 1460 by the Treaty of Ribe. He acknowledged the rights of the Holstein nobles, *stormenn*. Twelve of them would administer the area and were summoned once a year to a council. In 1474, the Holy Roman Emperor Frederick III granted the kings of Denmark Holstein as an imperial fief.[12] He made Danish king Christian I Duke of Holstein. The House of Gottorp was established in 1554 when Danish king Christian III shared the duchies of Schleswig and Holstein with two brothers, Adolf and John the Elder, one of which resided in Gottorp and the other in Haderslev.[13] The king, Adolf, and John the Elder each got one-third. The dukes co-governed Schleswig and Holstein together with the kings of Denmark, and they acted relatively independently.[14] Flensburg belonged to Royal Schleswig-Holstein. Through treaties in 1658 and 1660,[15] Denmark released the Schleswig-Holstein-Gottorp dukes from feudal bonds and recognized their sovereignty.

The persecution of witches in Schleswig-Holstein began in the sixteenth century, with the first witchcraft trial taking place in Kiel in 1530, and continued for nearly two hundred years until 1735.[16] After two initial cases in 1530, there was a steady stream of witchcraft trials from the 1540s onwards, punctuated by three waves of concentrated trials.[17] In total, 846 people were accused of witchcraft in the region during this period. Of the trials in Schleswig, 86% ended in execution; of the trials in Holstein, 77%. Seen in relation to a population of 495,000 at the beginning of the seventeenth century, the intensity of the persecution in Schleswig-Holstein region was average compared with other European countries.[18]

The first wave of persecution in Schleswig-Holstein took place from 1580 to 1590. The second wave—the peak of persecution in this region—occurred between 1600 and 1640, with the decade 1600–1609 counting 68 persons, the two decades from 1610 until 1630 counting 126 and 119 accused individuals, respectively, and the decade 1630–39 totalling 78 accused people.[19] A third wave occurred after 1660, and the last trial that ended in execution took place in Lauenburg in 1689. After 1680, there was a sharp decrease until 1705, after which there were only a few additional cases.[20] The endpoint of witchcraft persecution in Schleswig-Holstein was 1739. To a certain extent it coincided with an intervention by the Danish king, Christian V,[21] who issued a new collection of Danish laws in 1683, the Danish Code, which had an impact on the Danish royal parts of Schleswig-Holstein.[22] These laws tried to bring court practice in witchcraft trials under control and prevent misuse—for example by fining judicial officials and taking their position from them, which had a deterrent effect.[23]

Most witchcraft trials in Schleswig-Holstein were individual trials and small witchcraft panics involving two to five accused persons. Individual trials made up 52.3% of all trials, and small panics encompassing two to five individuals made up 40.2%. Witchcraft trials involving six to ten people accounted for 5% of all trials, while 1.6% involved ten to twenty people and 0.8%, twenty to thirty. These numbers show that individual trials were most common, but also that small witchcraft panics accounted for a substantial part of the accused people as well.[24]

Geographically, witchcraft trials in Schleswig-Holstein were unevenly distributed, even if there was persecution in all duchies. Few trials took place in the western part, such as Eiderstedt. On the east coast, in Ditmarschen and Neustadt, there are no known sentences in witchcraft trials. In Nordfriesland, persecution was mild as well. As a whole, the area of Marschland did not experience severe persecution. Only one-tenth of witchcraft trials took place in the areas towards the north-west.[25] However, other areas of Schleswig-Holstein suffered from a severe witch-hunt. Eighty per cent of all witchcraft trials took place in the eastern part of Holstein, in landscapes where the administration of justice by the nobility was predominant and sovereignty claims were highly fragmented.[26] The island of Fehmarn was strongly affected by the ongoing persecution as well.[27]

The gender distribution in witchcraft trials in Schleswig-Holstein shows a very high percentage of women, 91%.[28] This is 10% above the average European percentage of executed persons in relation to the population of the area. The highest percentage of women in witchcraft trials in Schleswig-Holstein is found in the decade 1590–99: 97%. Also, the decades 1600–1609, 1630–39, and 1640–49 have a very high percentage of women, at 94%, 96%, and 95.5%, respectively. These high percentages were in place during the first two waves of persecution. Of the accused women, 75% were executed in this area, while 50% of the accused men got a death sentence. After 1650, there was an increase in the number of men accused, but it always remained below 30% of all accused. The last death sentences in the area were passed against men.[29]

During the period of witchcraft persecution, Schleswig-Holstein consisted of duchies under the Holy Roman Empire and under the kingdom of Denmark. In most German lands under the Holy Roman Empire, structures of authority were fragile and fragmented. Central control was weak; there were 'lords and other splintered jurisdictions with their own law courts and legal traditions'.[30] The weak institutions of the empire shared authority with prince-electorates, secular principalities, ecclesiastical principalities, independent lordships, imperial abbacies, imperial cities, and imperial knights.[31] This had a strong impact on judicial practice. As for the kingdom of Denmark, the Danish king passed laws in 1547 and 1576 to rein in the persecution of witches.[32] Danish legislation and jurisdiction left its mark on early witchcraft persecution in the Danish royal parts of Schleswig-Holstein, but the *Carolina*—the Imperial Criminal Law Code issued by Kaiser Karl V in 1532[33] with its Roman law tradition—forced its way into the duchy of Schleswig from the beginning of the 1600s onwards. Already around 1550, the scribe in the town of Schleswig referred to the *kaiserlichen* law in witchcraft trials rather than to the Danish law.[34]

Jurisdiction

Even if the Treaty of Ribe of 1460 stated that the two duchies of Schleswig and Holstein were indivisible, the border between them marked two different jurisdictions. In the duchy of Holstein, the *Carolina* was in use. It was supposed to support and complement the existing jurisdiction in the various districts.[35] In the duchy of Schleswig, the Jutland Law, *Jyske Lov*, was in use as a supplementary law code from 1241.[36] Schleswig was a Danish fief and did not formally fall under the jurisdiction of the *Carolina*. However, as mentioned above, court practice varied. Of the three cases I have chosen to study, Flensburg was located in the region of Schleswig and under Danish jurisdiction; Bordesholm in the duchy of Holstein, under *kaiserlichen* law; and Lübeck was an imperial free city, also under the kaiser's—the emperor's—jurisdiction.[37] In the Holstein area, the sixteenth century marked a change in the exercise of power in court practice: whereas previously, a group of peasant assessors, *Holsten*, could judge the accused under the leadership of a regional representative,[38] the influence of centrally appointed legal officials now increased. The district governor, *Amtmann*, was given the authority to imprison individuals suspected of witchcraft and reported by private accusers, interrogate the accused, bring forth witnesses, and provide proof—by for example searching houses and carrying out procedures to obtain circumstantial evidence. The prime period of witchcraft persecution was thus marked by a transition from the old 'folk courts' to increased influence by central authorities on judicial matters due to their ability to appoint people with decisive power. The professionalization of the legal system through the installation of university-educated judges also contributed to this shift.[39]

Jurisdiction in Schleswig and Holstein was based on two distinct legal systems for deciding on guilt or innocence in serious crimes: the customary system and the Roman system. Differences between the two systems included the use of torture and the validity of witnesses' testimonies. Schleswig's legal fundament, the Jutland Law, was based on the customary system.[40] Here, 'the decision on guilt or innocence was made by a jury of the suspect's neighbours. The judge presided over the trial and passed sentence if the jury convicted the suspect, but the actual verdict was the responsibility of the jury'.[41] In Danish law, however, important changes took place in 1547 and 1576. Previously, witnesses' testimonies against an accused person and the decision of a jury of men elected from the local community constituted sufficient proof for a death sentence to be passed—the content of this proof did not have to be verified anew.[42] Two clauses of the Copenhagen Recess of 1547 had an impact. The first decided that 'no statement of evidence from a dishonest person could form the basis of the conviction of a third party, while the other clause ensured that no torture was permissible until after the final sentence'.[43] Thus, persons accused of witchcraft were not allowed to testify in Danish witchcraft trials. In addition, death sentences passed in lower courts—first instance courts—were prevented. The Kalundborg Recess of 1576 stipulated that no person found guilty by the jurors was to be executed before the case had been appealed in the court of second instance—and a final sentence had been pronounced.[44] These laws contributed to limiting the scope of witchcraft persecution in Danish areas.

The Roman system—so called because it was based on the law of the ancient Roman Empire—was inquisitional: there was no jury, and the judge presided over the trial, supervised the investigation into the crime, and decided on the accused's guilt or innocence. The system had strict rules on evidence: 'A suspect could be convicted of a crime only if there were two witnesses to the actual crime, or if the suspect confessed credibly to having committed the crime'.[45] The rule regarding two persons witnessing the crime was almost impossible to fulfil, particularly when it came to witchcraft.[46] Gerhard Schormann states that witchcraft is a special crime: witchcraft trials are criminal proceedings without a criminal act.[47] This means that no criminal act had in fact been performed when a person was accused of witchcraft, and no witness could have seen the performance of witchcraft. It was a *crimen exceptum*, an exceptional crime that could not be proved by ordinary means. It was not like murder, where a corpse could be found. It was not like theft, where stolen goods could be found. The way to prove the crime of witchcraft was to extract a confession from the mouth of the accused person, and this was achieved by the use of torture. Torture was legalized within the frames of a new legal system of proofs as a means of finding the truth. Confession and torture formed 'an unholy alliance'.[48] Julian Goodare states: 'The Roman system placed its emphasis on the suspect's confession, and on torture'.[49] *Carolina* set a common legal standard for witchcraft persecutions throughout the Holy Roman Empire. This code of law was used in the Holstein area.

However, the two systems mentioned above did not exist as two distinct structures. Dagmar Unverhau has argued that during the witchcraft persecution in Schleswig-Holstein, accusatory trials often turned into inquisitional trials.[50] In both cases, torture and circumstantial evidence were used. According to *Carolina*, torture was allowed, 'but magistrates could prescribe it only when a certain weight of evidence pointed to the guilt of the accused'.[51] Because witchcraft was an exceptional crime, a confession was vital for a conviction. The application of torture was graded according to strength and was repeated three times,[52] with each application not to exceed one hour.[53] A prudent, reasonable judge[54] was to authorize the application of torture in witchcraft trials.[55] The use of torture was recorded openly in the court records of witchcraft trials in Germany—in contrast to records from other countries discussed in this book. In Germany, torture was applied early in the course of a witchcraft trial. This had an impact, as torture often marked the turning point in the trial that led to a confession. *Carolina* also decreed death sentences for alleged witches who had not performed harmful witchcraft.[56] However, while by the early 1600s, *Carolina* was widely cited in court, 'the imperial law remained subordinate to territorial and local laws. In practice, many lower courts operated virtually independent of central review and oversight'.[57]

New and learned ideas about demonological witchcraft entered the area of Schleswig-Holstein in the late 1400s. On the other hand, a *Beictspeigel*[58] document, which is a questionnaire used by Lübeck ministers during confessions, dated 1484, shows that widespread magical folk belief was known by the church. The magical activities could be good or evil, but were not unambiguously seen as negative. At this time, the church did not interpret magical activities as being the same as witchcraft.[59] However, change was coming. Fifty years later, the picture was different. In some districts of Schleswig-Holstein in the 1540s—Nordfriesland, Ditmarschen, and Eiderstedt—the devil's pact and witches' conventions were now well-known ideas.[60] In these areas, district laws (*Landesrechten*) issued by the district governors (*Landesherren*) in 1567, 1572, and 1591 stated that the death sentence should be used in trials concerning witchcraft performed after a pact with the devil had been made.[61] However, harmful and non-harmful magic were separated until the Husum town laws of 1608 were issued by the Duke of Gottorp, when such a separation no longer applied.[62]

Demonological ideas had an impact on regional legislation in Schleswig-Holstein in the latter half of the 1500s. This change might have been influenced by treaties on witchcraft published by powerful theologians, like Niels Hemmingsen and Samuel Meiger. Hemmingsen's book was published in 1575 and Samuel Meiger's treaty in 1587.[63] The transition is also reflected in the terms used to characterize the crime and performers of witchcraft: while the words *Toversche* and *Toverer*, *Zauberin* and *Zauberer* were used in Schleswig-Holstein until the late 1500s, the term *Hexe* appeared in 1588,[64] signalling new ideas. Around 1640, *Hexe* was the term applied in all legal documents.[65] At the end of the 1500s, demonological ideas influenced witchcraft laws in Denmark as well. A decree issued in 1617[66] particularly reflected the influence of demonological ideas on Danish laws, stating that 'true' witches[67] were those who were associated with the devil.

Therefore, in spite of differences between the two areas, the laws taken into consideration by courts and the relative number of executions in the two areas of Schleswig and Holstein were to a large extent similar.[68] Rolf Schulte summarizes the judicial aspects of witchcraft trials in Schleswig-Holstein as follows:

> accuser and witnesses are men, but also women; the prosecutor and judicial bodies are willing authorities in the form of a lord, a Protestant *Domkapitel*,

a jury of peasants in a district or a council in a town; the proceedings are a seemingly absurd accusation due to which several people, after sadistic torment, are at the end killed or deprived of their livelihood.[69]

Kistina Netelers, 1607

The Trial

In the Flensburg area, thirteen known witchcraft trials occurred between 1564 and 1607–08, as presented in a source book published by A. Wolff in 1887.[70] The court records of Kistina Netelers's trial are included in this book. This trial is discussed in Rolf Schulte's pioneering study *Hexenverfolgung in Schleswig-Holstein 16.–18. Jahrhundert*.[71] The sources from Flensburg do not use the High German words *Hexe* and *Hexerei*;[72] instead they use *Töverschen* and *Töverei*, which are Low German words.[73]

Kistina Netelers was brought before the court in Flensburg[74] for witchcraft[75] on 27 November 1607. Present were the town bailiff,[76] the Honourable[77] Petri Kalliesen, and city treasurers[78] Jacob von der Wettering and Ritzer Zurbruwer. In addition, four citizens of the *Borgertuegen*—Karsten Kalliesen, Henrici Siferts, Caspari Brandes, and Peter Knutzsen—represented the court.[79] As in many German witchcraft trials, torture was used from the beginning as a means of getting Netelers to confess.[80] She was interrogated under torture[81] in the presence of the above-mentioned officials from the town's administration. She confirmed her confession before the council in the town hall, followed by a vote from the mayor and the council regarding the sentence of execution.[82]

Kistina Netelers had long been rumoured to be a practitioner of witchcraft. During her interrogation, a questionnaire was likely used, as the interrogation records are structured according to numbered points.

The first point deals with her confession to meetings with a lover, who had slept with her when her husband was not at home.[83] This eerie[84] figure, called Niβ, spoke Danish and promised to give her food. This had occurred approximately three and a half[85] years earlier, when her husband Paul had been away in Svendborg on Fyn. Niβ—her 'patron' or 'master'—had come to her in bed, and though his figure was human, he was black and rough,[86] short, thick, and cold. He seduced her with promises that she would always have enough to eat, which was a common promise all over Europe, and had intercourse with her. He also had intercourse with her at other times when her husband was not home. Kistina Netelers said she gave him groats and cabbage to eat in the loft, and that he ate a great deal.[87] She also confessed that he had come to her in her cellar when her husband had been out drinking, and that she had once seen him in her stable in the shape of a one-year-old calf. However, Bernt, the farmhand who worked for her at the time, had not been able to see him. She confessed further that her 'patron' had promised her that her cattle would prosper, and that he had provided food for her domestic animals.

The second point of Kistina Netelers's confession focuses on love magic. She confessed that Nanne Jenses of Achtrup had made two magical objects for her so she could perform love magic on her husband, whom she suspected of being unfaithful. Jenses had made Netelers two crosses out of rye straw with a red woolly thread twined round them.[88] These were to be placed under Kistina Netelers's husband's pillow in order to make him love her again and leave his mistress, Kistine Schwartfrowen.

The third point of Kistina Netelers's confession concerns the stealing of milk. Netelers said that she could practise several kinds of witchcraft and, in particular, that she had milked the cows of Herman Funden and Paul Schoemaker from a distance. When asked how she had accomplished this, she replied that she had struck a block of wood with an axe and milk had emerged—an old, traditional method related to *maleficium*, known across Europe through orally transmitted ideas and illustrations.[89] Kistina Netelers also said that it was good that she had been away from this world for the last three or four years,[90] as she had not performed any evil deeds during that time. While it is somewhat unclear what she means here, a plausible interpretation is that she had been sick during the past three or four years.

The fourth point pertains to a prayer used for healing. Kistina Netelers confessed that she had learned this prayer from a 'cunning woman'[91] named Margaretha ten years earlier. The prayer went as follows: *Jlne Jlakz, Christ Jens, Christ und S. Johans in Namen des Vaders, Sohns und des h. Geistes.* This is a charm that was known in traditional folk belief; the fusing of colloquial and religious language is reflected in the invocation of Christ and St John (Johannes) in combination with the colloquial name Jens. A prayer like this must have been easily and successfully transmitted orally, evidenced by both its rhythmical elements and its use of a standard, well-known church prayer format.

The fifth point focuses on healing through prayer and bringing magical objects to church. Kistina Netelers confessed that she had healed her own horses and cows with the healing prayer she learned from Margaretha, and that two years prior to the trial, she had cured a horse belonging to Hans Forman. Further, she said that she brought a stocking tie[92] with her to church so mass could be read over it; she later put the stocking tie under the stomach of a sick horse, and the animal recovered. At the time, the practice of bringing objects intended to be used for magic and sorcery—whether for good or for evil—to a church service was well known.

The sixth point deals with denunciation. Kistina Netelers, pressed by the interrogators, denounced her alleged instructor, Ellin Herdekuen, who had performed counter-magic[93] against the stealing of butter. Netelers said that Herdekuen had taught her the art of retrieving stolen butter. To perform this magic, she prepared a pot in the name of the Evil One, put milk and metal pieces[94] in it, and, when the milk boiled, threw a stone into the mixture. In this way, she could retrieve butter that had been stolen from her. She explained that she and Herdekuen had performed this act twice in Netelers's cellar, with Herdekuen using a jug of milk and broth one time, and a piece of bread and pork the other.

The seventh and last point also pertains to denunciation. Netelers finalized her confession by saying that she did not know anyone in the town who knew the art of sorcery, except a woman named Katrina v. Tunderen, who did not live at her place of birth but at Nordertor[95] in Flensburg.[96] They searched for this Katrina, but she could not be found.

On 4 December 1607, the confession was read aloud to Kistina Netelers before the council in the town hall. After Netelers confirmed her confession, the mayor and the council unanimously voted that she be sentenced to execution by fire at the stake.[97] Reading the confession aloud in its entirety would have been an effective way of spreading a warning about the dangers of witchcraft, cautioning any listeners against following a similar path.[98]

After the December 1607 trial of Kistina Netelers, town officials prosecuted several more women in Flensburg in the spring of 1608. Four of these accused women were sentenced to death by fire at the stake and were executed before the summer, two of them were banished from the town, and two were acquitted.[99]

The Voice of Kistina Netelers

Most of Kistina Netelers's confession is in the third person, with her speech rendered as indirect speech. Reporting verbs are used to introduce reporting clauses. The only phrase written down in direct speech is the charm, which was rendered *verbatim*. It is likely that a questionnaire was used—as Dagmar Unverhau has argued, confessing to having intercourse with the devil is typical of the contents of questions[100] found in recorded questionnaires. While only a few questions are directly documented in these records, it is possible to trace those posed to Netelers by using the technique of shadow questions, which tries to find the original questions by closely studying the answers the accused provided.

Kistina Netelers had been rumoured to have been a practitioner of witchcraft long before she was brought to trial. She was tortured immediately after the trial began—as torture was allowed according to the *Carolina*, its use was recorded quite openly. Due to the immediate application of torture to elicit a confession, her resistance was broken from the very beginning; the records indicate that she willingly answered the questions posed. The additive structure of the text (new paragraphs starting with 'she also confessed', 'she confessed also', etc.) signals that the interrogators wanted to expand on the previously confessed point, using further questions to extract a more detailed explanation. As such, the point-by-point recorded confession provides clues about the questions that were asked, particularly with regard to the final point, in which Netelers was obviously asked to denounce other people suspected of witchcraft.

The ideas about witchcraft that become apparent in Kistina Netelers's confession include both demonological ideas and *maleficium*. Notions connected to healing and love magic are also activated. The priority seems to have been, however, to get her to confess to demonological elements, seen in the first and the two last points. In the first point of the confession, the questions apparent in the trial records clearly centre on Netelers's association with the devil. The first and most important part of her confession—that she had had a relationship with the devil when her husband was in Svendborg on Fyn—is expanded with information about the devil's appearance and promises. These pieces of information were most likely given as answers to questions posed after her first meeting with the devil was confessed to, according to the ordering of the points. The new answers deal with when she met the devil and where her husband stayed at the time. There is then an addition wherein Netelers says that the devil was with her at other times when her husband was not at home, followed by a new paragraph that describes what she fed the devil, concluding with the information that she met the devil in the cellar when her husband went out drinking. As the confession is shaped as a narrative with an additive sentence structure, the addition of sentences thus expands the point's initial focus: the devil's pact. The expansion contains additional demonological ideas, such as the devil having the shape of a man, being black and rough and cold, and seducing her using promises. There is a clear demonological impact: her relationship with the devil is one that gives Netelers power. Leading questions about the appearance of the devil and his ways of acting are closely connected to demonological thought. The mentioning of exact geographical locations shows the confession's closeness to the content of oral tales, in which it is important to pinpoint date, year, place, and people's names in order to make the tale convincing. Even if the devil is described as being humanlike, he also possesses other qualities: she saw him in the farmhouse while her farmhand did not, which stresses that there is something supernatural about the figure: only special people are able to see him and have contact with him. Kistina Netelers seems to find this plausible, which probably means that in people's imaginations at the time, it was possible to experience supernatural elements.

Maleficent witchcraft enters into the confession in the third point. Given that the interrogator steers the confession, this element seems to have been of less importance to be confessed to than the demonological element. The point related to *maleficium* deals with the stealing of milk. Netelers confesses that she struck a wooden block with an axe when she wanted to steal milk. This practice of stealing milk from afar is clearly a form of sorcery that Netelers is familiar with. No linguistic devices are used to create distance between Netelers—as the narrator—and the story; her narration style signals that she means that she truly is able to milk other people's cows. The idea that some people can milk others' cows remotely using certain objects was a well-known folk belief; it was also believed that this kind of milking could be continued until not milk but blood emerged, at which point the cow would die.

In terms of demonological notions as well as ideas about *maleficium*, Kistina Netelers's confession is detailed and demonstrates comprehensive knowledge. She gets short questions and provides answers that are related to her daily existence and the events she experienced. This goes for the devil's pact as well as for the performance of *maleficium*. Her understanding of demonological ideas is framed by her own life and the people closest to her, first of all her husband. He appears with his first name intact, and the geographical names of the places he was travelling to are rendered in a realistic way. Then there is the idea of a 'patron', a named devil, who is her lover and with whom she has entered into the devil's pact.[101] He has a name, which is somewhat unusual, speaks Danish, and comes to her in her house and in her cellar. In addition, he eats cabbage, which is traditional peasant food. Thus, we see a version—and an understanding—of the devil's pact in which elements of her life are present. Also, the promises of the Evil One pertain to sustenance and having enough to eat for herself and her cattle. Sexual relations with the devil are highlighted and appear in the very first sentence. The kinds of demonological notions that we hear about from Netelers have been adjusted to the minds of common people. One can recognize the idea that the devil is cold as having come from demonology, but the description of the devil that Netelers gives is otherwise well known in folkloric accounts from all over Europe. The demonological ideas that Kistina Netelers confesses to must largely have been part of her own ideas from before she was imprisoned and interrogated. She is asked specific questions and responds to these with a narrative that contains demonological elements with a personal stamp. This means that adjusted versions of the core ideas of the devil's pact were most likely part of the mental realm of common people in Schleswig-Holstein in 1607.

The stealing of milk is similarly confessed to in a familiar manner. Kistina Netelers gives the names of the owners of the cows that she has stolen milk from, and she knows which method to use. She also admits that she knows how to perform many types of witchcraft. This shows that she has a repertoire as a practitioner of witchcraft, and the interrogator clearly wants to know what she actually does, thus acknowledging her knowledge of the art. Lay and learned people alike shared a magical world view at the time, and the judiciary was eager to obtain information about magical practices.

Traditional witchcraft does not only deal with casting sickness on other beings or performing other types of maleficent magic, but also with how to take away witchcraft that has been cast. The art of retrieving stolen butter in the sixth point pertains to such an activity. Kistina Netelers confesses that she practised this act twice in her own cellar with her mentor. Her explanation is detailed and down-to-earth. It displays how common it was to believe in the efficacy of magical objects and charms. This was knowledge that peasants possessed and used in their lives, and the interrogator wanted to hear about its factual performance. All in all, we see in Kistina Netelers's confession how ordinary daily experiences were merged with supernatural elements, which formed a seamless part of daily life.

This magical world view is also demonstrated in the second point, in the part of the confession that deals with love magic, a less serious charge. Netelers had consulted another woman in order to obtain magic objects that would bring her (Netelers) unfaithful husband back to her. These objects were crosses made of rye with a red woollen thread wound around them. The love magic was to occur when her husband was sleeping, as she had placed the crosses under his pillow. Names of persons are accurate—even the name of her husband's mistress—and the number of crosses is mentioned. Closeness to her own lifeworld is marked. This point is clearly taking it as a given that some people were known to be 'cunning' in the art of witch-craft and magic, as Netelers had obtained these objects from a woman who was known to make such items. Netelers expresses no doubt about the effectiveness of such magic. Love magic is a type of magic used in many countries and is mastered as an individual art by specific people who are well known in their local communities.

Performing the art of magic, or manipulating powers, was not believed to be used for evil deeds only. In the trial of Kistina Netelers, beneficent magic was included in her competence as well, since the fourth point of the confession per-tains to a prayer for healing. This is the first time during the trial that Netelers's reputation as a healer is referenced. She had learned a prayer for healing from a woman named Margaretha ten years before the trial. The prayer is short, consist-ing of only seventeen words, and is rendered in its entirety in the court records—it must have been written down according to Netelers's oral recitation. It mentions the names of the Father, the Son, Christ, and the Holy Spirit, but they are used in such a way and in combination with colloquial names that they are not in accord-ance with the church's use.

When healing again comes up in the fifth point, the factual method used for healing is emphasized. This concerns Netelers's use of the charm to heal not only her own horse and cow but also a horse belonging to another person. Further, in addition to the charm, she knew other ways of performing healing by trying to manipulate powers for the purpose of good and using specific objects. The stocking tie taken to church so that mass would be read over it was her method of healing a sick horse. A similar act, using salt, is well known from other countries. The aim here is to connect the power of the Christian word to an object so that it becomes imbued with a healing power or can be used for magical manipulation, an act common in Europe.

Kistina Netelers confesses to the element of healing without any delay or hesita-tion. Apparently, this was knowledge that she was comfortable voicing. She recites the full prayer of healing, states who had taught her the prayer, speaks in detail about the healing of her own cattle and another man's horse by means of the prayer, and says she brought a stocking tie to church to have mass read over it. As she is not asked follow-up questions, the information must have been sufficient. Healing seems to have been considered a positive activity, and the populace clearly used many prayers, charms, and objects for practising this.

Denunciation of other suspect people was compulsory during interrogation in demonological witchcraft trials. If the accused person provided names of accom-plices, the continuation of the trials was secured. So also in Kistina Netelers's con-fession. She is asked whether she knows anyone with knowledge of sorcery. In addition to the name of her mentor, whom she had already denounced, she gives the name of one woman whom she alleges knows witchcraft, and informs the interrogators of where she lives. On the whole, Kistina Netelers seemed to have been rather reluctant to denounce others.

The way Kistina Netelers's confession is told shows that narrative structures form its backbone. The confession displays several narrative strategies. There is a clear, linear format emphasizing the order of events, for example from the first time she met the devil through subsequent meetings. This reinforces the point that the relationship between Kistina and her 'patron' lasted over time. Variation between rapid- and slow-moving parts of the text is reflected in the shifts between 'speedy' passages of the text—often only a few sentences spoken by the narrator—and descriptions and dialogues, which are characterized by a lower speed. This accent of duration provides a feeling of authenticity and shows the similarities between the confession and a story told orally in the community. The strategy of frequency—telling an event more than once—is activated when the use of the prayer for healing is rendered. The reason may be that this prayer is precious to Netelers, as it was taught to her by a cunning mentor and as she herself believes it is efficient and delivers results. The narrator's attitude towards what is told in the rendering of witchcraft beliefs and healing—the narration mood—is seen in the lack of distancing devices. This signals that the narrator thought witchcraft was possible and that healing could be successful. In this way, an important glimpse of the imagination of common people appears through linguistic features. The narrator, Netelers, uses her textual authority to delegate voice to other persons. The rendering of the dialogue with the devil enlivens the narrative about entering a devil's pact and pinpoints the parallels between traditional beliefs and demonological ideas. It reflects the context in which the narrative would traditionally be told, namely an oral context.

In the confession, orality features surface. The use of additive structures is seen in the description of the devil.[102] Then there is the closeness to the human life-world: the devil comes to her when her husband is away; the devil is eating cabbage; the husband is out drinking; she wishes to get the love of her husband back; the devil makes the promise of enough food—these are formulations connected to subsistence needs and basic experiences and emotions. Finally, the rendering of the charm adds a strong oral flavour to the confession. These orality features contribute considerably to an understanding of the living conditions of common people. Netelers's confession constitutes a glimpse of a mentality that is otherwise hard to find in seventeenth-century historical sources.

As for ideas about witchcraft, Netelers displays a broad knowledge of demonological notions as well as *maleficium*. While demonological ideas are to a large extent unrealistic and centre around the devil's pact and sexual intercourse with her 'patron', the notions of *maleficium* are concrete and focus on the actual methods used for performing witchcraft. When Kistina Netelers appears as a narrator, she displays her ability to tell stories and also shows that as early as 1607, there were versions of the demonological narrative about the devil's pact that were adjusted to individual and local conditions in Northern Germany. This means that some demonological ideas were taken up by peasants and were assimilated into the local imagination as an addition to prior notions of *maleficium*. Moreover, healing occupies an important place in Netelers's confession and comes to the fore through vivid descriptions of performance. Her seeming reluctance to denounce others and preparedness to talk about her own knowledge might have been related to her wish to protect her neighbours and acquaintances.

Kistina Netelers's confession does not show much emotion. The recording of her trial starts after the stage in which accents of her voice revealing anger, protest, and denial could be detected, so we do not learn what she felt when she was imprisoned. The only figure she allegedly feels negatively about is the demon. He is described as eerie. When it comes to her competence regarding witchcraft and magic, she reveals almost a kind of pride, saying that she knows several types of witchcraft and displaying details about witchcraft methods. Having performed witchcraft and experienced its results is a distinct factor in her confession.

The Voices of the Witnesses

The voices of the witnesses are not mentioned directly in these court records, but are still echoed in the second, third, fourth, and fifth points, which means all points except those with demonological content. Netelers's confession to maleficent witchcraft and healing—the stealing of milk from cows, the curing of a horse, the performance of counter-magic, the retrieving of butter together with Herdekuen—most likely relates to factual incidents that have taken place. Her performance of love magic, using objects made by Nanne Jenses, likewise. The incidents mentioned in these points relate to named persons or animals of named farmers; probably there has been talk about inexplicable bad luck and ditto good luck in the community. These incidents may have been mentioned in testimonies delivered as part of the trial. Thus the voices of the witnesses, as they are echoed in the records, express belief in efficient witchcraft and give an impression of what has been rumoured locally. The witnesses also must have been willing to connect the rumours to Kistina Netelers's alleged performance of witchcraft in their testimonies.

The Voice of the Interrogator

The sequence of points in Kistina Netelers's confession reveals not only the interests but also the priorities of the interrogators. The order in which questions were asked points to the most desired items for conviction. The first point of the confession, which includes the devil's pact and Netelers's relationship with the devil, is clearly the most important one. In subsequent points, a mixture of *maleficium* and healing magic follows, ending with denunciation as the last element. It is difficult to ascertain how many of these ideas came from the interrogators and were introduced by leading questions during interrogation, and how many were based on the knowledge of the accused person herself. As shown above, shadow questions may be traced. They were used to expand on particular points of the confession. However, it seems clear that a large part of Netelers's confession derived from her own knowledge.[103] The fusion of demonological witchcraft, *maleficium*, and healing magic that we see in these trial records was a common feature of many witchcraft trials. In this context, the courtroom becomes a meeting place between ideas and motifs from folk belief and new, demonological ideas published in learned books, the latter often in amended versions. In the case of Kistina Netelers, the interrogators make sure to include the point critical to securing a sentence of execution (confessing to a devil's pact) and the point crucial to the continuation of witchcraft trials (the denunciation of others) in Kistina Netelers's confession.

The Voice of the Law

The voice of the law is heard in the ordering of the points of the confession, in the carrying through and confirmation of torture, in the search for another suspected witch, in the vote regarding the sentence of execution, and in the reading aloud of the same sentence.

The voice of the law is apparent in the ordering of the points, because demonological ideas are given a place in the initial point and in the two last points of the confession. In between, we find ideas on *maleficium*, counter-magic, healing, and love magic. This ordering demonstrates the law's view that demonology is the severest type of witchcraft and that denunciation of other suspects is a compulsory end of the trial.

The voice of the law influences the confession in particular when it comes to the decision to use torture. In this trial, torture was applied from the very beginning, which was allowed according to *Carolina*. This shows how important the judiciary thought it was to obtain a confession rather quickly. Torture was applied with officials from the town administration present. Moreover, the confirmation of Kistina Netelers's confession took place before the council in the town hall. This open use of torture, with witnesses present, reflects a legal system wherein torture was seen as a natural means to reaching a justified sentence. It was required that a confession given under torture be confirmed afterwards, so court practice follows the law here. Also, court procedure signals that the judicial officials maintained a high standard.

Kistina Netelers denounced another woman and told officials where she lived. The court decided to search for this woman at once, which signals the fear of witches but also the urge to continue the panic after Netelers's trial was finished.

The sentence was passed unanimously by the mayor and the council, and it was read aloud. The voice of the law is heard in the procedure followed, in which the persons voting and those present during the reading of the sentence are recorded. The reading aloud of the sentence was an important element of the legal system, as the people present in the courtroom would be warned not to follow a wrong path.

The Voice of the Scribe

The role of the scribe was to record, in a professional manner, courtroom discourse. He notes the main points of the confession, including some of the questions posed. The voice of the scribe does not come to the fore through his own comments or interpretations, nor does he use any distancing devices to mark his attitude towards what is told. The majority of Kistina Netelers's confession is rendered in indirect speech, using reporting verbs and reported clauses. In addition, there is the prayer, which is rendered in direct speech. The rendering of individualized discourse highlights the accuracy of the scribe's recording of Netelers's speech, whether it was indirect or direct. Not least, the heavy stamp of orality in the confession is a mark that the scribe aspired to rendering personalized speech, thus portraying the accused person as an individual language user. In this respect, it is credible that the records taken down by the scribe are reliable. Even if the entire interrogation took place after the application of torture, there is no description of the method of torture—the scribe focuses entirely on recording the confession, verdict, and sentence.

Anneke Rickers, 1641

The Trial

The trial of Anneke Rickers took place in the district of Bordesholm,[104] where the Neumünster Abbey was situated. The town of Bordesholm formed its centre. Frederick III (1597–1659) was Duke of Schleswig-Holstein-Gottorp at the time of this trial.[105] The chancellor was Anton von Wietersheim.[106] The administrative unit of *Amt* fell under the jurisdiction of a magistrate.[107] He wrote the court records and corresponded with the chancellor on judicial decisions.

Anneke Rickers lived in Buchwald near Bordesholm and worked as a maid. She was accused of witchcraft in 1641. In the year 1641 alone, twenty-four people in this district were led before the court for witchcraft: twenty-two women and two men.[108] Of the accused, twelve were sentenced to execution, two were banished, and four were acquitted. The rest received unknown sentences. Out of the group of accused women, twenty-one were led before the court in linked trials. This suggests that demonological ideas were activated during interrogation, since confessions to witches' meetings led to denunciations and the continuation of trials.[109]

Magistrate Johann Pundt of Bordesholm recorded the trial of Anneke Rickers from beginning to end. As the use of torture in witchcraft trials was allowed according to *Carolina*, the torture of Anneke Rickers was openly recorded. Her case clearly illustrates how an accused person could, over the course of a short period, be pushed from denial to confession, and the role that torture played in this process.[110] Her trial is also illustrative of how the confession, as a text, represents a type of discourse situated between oral and written language: On the one hand, it is a narrative that was created individually, with clear orality features; on the other, it is a document reflecting learned ideas and written laws. Leading questions inserted during the interrogation signal the direction in which the interrogation was moving, reflecting what legal officials considered important for Rickers to confess to.

The dossier of the trial of Anneke Rickers consists of sixteen paginated folio pages.[111] The timeline of the trial and confirmation of her sentence of execution provide important information: it lasted from 14 May to 13 June, which means that

Rickers was tortured, interrogated, sentenced to death, and given a formal confirmation of her death sentence within one month of being accused. The accuser was Jurgen Nefen von Buchwald.[112] The accusation was witchcraft against his cattle. On 22 May, Magistrate Johann Pundt sent a request to the chancellor[113] to apply torture. This was based on the accusation and a witness testimony, but not on a confession. Permission to use torture was granted on 26 May. Torture was applied on 2 June, approximately two weeks after the initial accusation. Anneke Rickers was interrogated and confessed to witchcraft on 5 June. The indictment was read to her on 10 June, and on 11 June, a letter was sent to the chancellor stating that she had confirmed all twenty-five points of the indictment. On 13 June, the chancellor sent a letter which confirmed the execution of Anneke Rickers.

The court session[114] of Anneke Rickers's trial took place in Bordesholm. Jurgen Nefen, who suspected his maid of witchcraft,[115] believed she caused first his horse and then his cattle to die, one after the other. His suspicion was based on the fact that the previous winter, she had shown him a plait of hair, a brass ring, a leather shoelace, and the hoof of a pig.[116] She had found these remedies in the stable of Hans Embke, a farmer,[117] and said that they had been placed there by a woman named Anna Kake.[118] Rickers denied that she had shown Nefen these objects, that she had spoken with Anna Kake, and that she had done anything to Nefen's cattle. Here, we hear the voice of Anneke Rickers for the first time in the records.

The accuser Jurgen Nefen then mentioned that Hans Embke had told him about this event. Embke was called forth as a witness, and testified before the court about the loss of five horses the previous year, one after another, within a short period of time. Shortly afterwards, the accused had come to his house and told him how he could prevent this kind of bad luck from happening again. She had said that he had to remove some objects that were buried under his stable, or the bad luck would continue. She then went to the stable with him, where, with his own eyes, he saw her take the plait of hair and other items from under the floor; she told him that a woman called Anna Kake had put them there. The accused denied that this happened and further denied knowing anything about it.[119] This is the second time Anneke Rickers's voice is rendered in the court records.

The Holsten Court[120] then considered the matter and came to the conclusion that the accused had buried hair and other objects beneath the barn floor herself, and that this had been witnessed by others. They stated that Anneke Rickers had made herself a suspect of witchcraft in this way and was therefore to be exposed to torture, at a time decided on by the court.[121] We see here that torture was requested based solely on the accusation of Jurgen Nefen and the testimony of one witness, Hans Embke, who was brought forward by Nefen.

A document written by Magistrate Johann Pundt, dated 22 May 1641, stated that the accuser, Jurgen Nefen von Buchwald, had at a local court[122] on 14 May the same year formally accused one of his maids, Anneke Rickers, of being responsible for the death of his horse and cattle. This letter, addressed to Chancellor Anton von Wietersheim, was a request for the permission to use torture. It was received by the chancellor on 26 May 1641.[123] The same day, the chancellor commanded that

Anneke Rickers be tortured,[124] albeit in a humane way,[125] because of the *deponiret*—the objects buried under Hans Embke's barn. The letter is addressed to Magistrate Johann Pundt of Bordesholm. The reason for using torture is clearly suspicion of *maleficium*, although at this point—twelve days since she was first accused—Anneke Rickers has not yet confessed to anything.

The next document is dated 5 June 1641.[126] This is the record of Rickers's interrogation. It contains her full confession and some of the questions posed. Torture is recorded to have taken place on 2 June, and the completion of the records took place on 5 June. Interrogation is documented to have taken place both before[127] and after torture was applied, and the beginning of the torture is clearly marked in the records. The first part of the confession pertains to the plait of hair and other objects of witchcraft. Anneke Rickers admitted that she had cut hair from the horses, and said she was to go to a woman called Frau Wickers and ask her to 'think it over' and give her advice on how to perform witchcraft directed at horses. However, she had not gone to Wickers, but instead to Anneke Ratke, old Heinrich Ratke's wife. Anneke Ratke told Rickers that she was to cut the horse's hair, braid it, tie something to the plait, and then go to Hans Embke and tell him that Anna Kake had buried something in his stable. Rickers had done this, and Embke offered her two *thaler*,[128] one of which she was to give to Ratke.

The first question was then posed by the interrogator: Rickers was asked what role she played with regard to Jurgen Nefen's cattle—whether she was to blame for their swift deaths. She confessed that the previous year, about three weeks before Michaelmas, Heinrich Ratke's wife had said to her that, although Rickers was only a poor child, she would like to teach her so much that she would become rich enough and provide her with a suitor who would bring her a lot of money. Rickers had initially refused this.[129] Later, Anneke Ratke asked her again whether she wanted to do this, and Rickers had answered that she very much wanted to.[130] They then went to a barn together,[131] where they left a nest of hair and feathers that they had made. Then, Ratke had taken her by the hand and said the following words, which Rickers was to repeat after her: 'I now walk over the nest, and leave our Lord Jesus Christ'.[132] She had repeated this charm as she walked over the nest.

After this initiation ritual, a rider in red clothes appeared to Rickers, standing next to the cows' field at the farm of a man called Hans Poppen. The rider said to her, 'Anneke, will you make me happy? Then I will have you, and give you a lot of money, but first you must have sexual intercourse with me'.[133] When Rickers replied that she was willing to comply with his wish, he had thrown her on the ground; he then presented the money to her in a black bag, which was too heavy for her to carry, so Anneke Ratke had taken it to the village. The same night, the suitor had come to her bed, and had had intercourse with her, which had been as cold as ice. He then told her that he believed she had to give him something in return.[134] When she asked what that would be, he replied that he wanted to have the calf of Jurgen Nefen, which she then gave to him.[135]

The following morning, Anneke Rickers had gone to Anneke Ratke to claim[136] the bag of money, which Ratke then fetched[137] from the cows' stable. However, there was no money inside; it had become 'horse crap'.[138] Rickers complained about this to Ratke, saying that Ratke had cast evil over it,[139] but Ratke told her that she was content and had given her one *thaler*.

Three weeks later, Anneke Rickers had wanted to go to church, but her idol, who was dressed in black, met her in Eiderbrock Forest[140] and asked where she wanted to go. She had answered that she wanted to go to church, but he had said,[141] 'You serve me, what will you do in church? On Sundays you have to work[142] together with me'. After that, she went back.

Eight days later, he [the idol] appeared to Anneke Rickers in the shape of a black dog[143] in Jurgen Nefen's field. Because she was frightened, he reverted to the shape of a human being and asked her how long she would serve him. She answered that she would not like to do so for very long, whereupon he said: 'You are now mine, and shall also remain mine'.[144] When she was asked during interrogation what this man called himself, she answered: 'He is named Beelzebub, and Ratke's idol is named Kreÿenfues'. All this she confessed to of her own good will, without being tortured, the records state. In addition, she said that Jurgen Nefen's cattle had died innocently, except for the aforementioned calf, which she had given to her lover.

Anneke Rickers was then taken to be tortured. Under 'light' torture, she confessed that Anneke Ratke had made powder for her in a box, which she was to give to the cows of Jurgen Neven. At first, she would not, but then she had prepared herself to do it and had thrown the powder into a kettle full of water, which she had given to the cattle to drink; it was from this that the cattle had died, one after another. The powder had appeared black, like gunpowder, and it had been alive.

Rickers was next asked why she had said that a man called Eggert Resen and his wife, the shepherd woman from Buchwald[145] had caused Jurgen Nefen's wife to be permanently bedridden. To this, she answered that Anneke Ratke had said this to Nefen's wife. At this point, the interrogator questioned whether she had perhaps spoken untruthfully about Ratke.[146] He cautioned her to admit the truth and not denounce innocent people. In response, Rickers confirmed what she had previously confessed to. She stated that, like her earlier confessions, this was true, and that she would live and die on this. She then added that she had nothing else to say, '*as she also was torn to pieces*'.[147] [My italics.]

On the same date, 5 June, a letter was sent from the chancellor to Johann Pundt[148] about Anneke Ratke. The chancellor stated that Ratke had been denounced by Anneke Rickers and that the two women had had a confrontation. He was of the opinion that Ratke should be brought before the court and that the denunciation should be read to her. If she confirmed it, the Holsten Court should decide on a sentence, but she should not be executed. In the meantime, the chancellor decided that Ratke should be kept in custody until her court appointment.

A document dated 10 June states that a court session[149] was held regarding the implicated Anneke Rickers, and that she was asked to answer the articles read to her. This document comprises the court's indictment: twenty-five articles formulated on the basis of what she was accused of and what she confessed to. The document was signed by Johann Pundt, and the twenty-five articles have the form of yes/no questions with a positive orientation (expecting the answer 'yes').[150] Each article begins with the words, 'Is it not true that (. . .)'.[151] The content of the articles was taken from Anneke Rickers's confession, but the personal pronoun and tense are different, as the confession has shifted from third-person narration into yes/no questions with a positive orientation. As such, the main points are emphasized.

When Anneke Rickers was confronted with her confession, she was asked whether she 'voluntarily'[152] still stood by all that she had confessed to in the morning. To this, she replied that everything was just as she had answered, and on this she would live and die. Although it is recorded that she confirmed this without torture, it should be remembered that severe torture had just ceased. Also, she knew that if she refused to confirm her confession, she would be tortured again. This demonstrates the impact of torture. Its influence was effective before, during, and after its occurrence.

Anneke Rickers was first asked to confirm Article 1: that she confessed, both voluntarily and under torture, that she had met Anneke Ratke the year prior, three weeks before Michaelmas, and that Ratke said to her that she was just a poor child, and that she would like to teach her how to become rich. In Article 2, she was asked whether it was not true that she went with Anneke Ratke to a barn, where Ratke showed her a nest made of hair and feathers that she had made, and told Rickers to walk over the nest, saying a formula. In Article 3, it was asked whether it was not true that she, Anneke Rickers, had left God and become an apostate.

In Article 4, Anneke Rickers was asked whether it was not true that she had gone with Anneke Ratke to the cow field of Hans Poppen's enclosure and that a rider in red clothes stood there. Here, some words are written in the margin of the document, signalling that Anneke Rickers corrected this article. It is written that she said before the court that the rider appeared before her at the barn, as in a vision.[153] In Article 5, she was asked whether it was not true that the rider had said to her that he would give her a lot of money if she would make him happy.[154] In Article 6, she was asked whether it was not true that she had agreed to his wish[155] and that they held their arms around each other and that he threw her to the ground. In Article 7, she was asked whether it was not true that she had received money in a black bag—so much of it that she could not carry the bag—and that Ratke took it home. In Article 8, she was asked whether it was not true that the same night, the suitor had come to her bed and slept with her, and that, at his request, she gave him Jurgen Nefen's calf. In Article 9, she was asked whether it was not true that, the following morning, she had claimed the money from Anneke Ratke, who herself fetched the bag from the cow barn and opened it, whereupon Rickers found that the money had become horse manure. In Article 10, she was asked whether it was not true that she thereafter had complained to Ratke, saying that Ratke herself had transformed the money. Ratke said she was satisfied and gave Rickers a one *thaler* coin.[156]

In Article 11, it was asked whether it was not true that her idol called himself Beelzebub and that, one Sunday when she had wanted to go to church, he met her in Eiderbrock Forest in black clothes and asked where she wanted to go; and that, when she answered that she wanted to go to church, he told her that she served him, had to work with him on Sundays, and had to go home, which she did. In Article 12, it was asked whether it was not true that eight days after this instance, her idol had appeared before her again, first in the shape of a black dog at Jurgen Nefen's barn and then in human form, because she was frightened. When he asked her how long she would serve him, she answered that she would rather not do so for very long, to which he replied that she was now his.

In Article 13, it was asked whether it was not true that Ratke had shown her a powder and wanted her to give this to Jurgen Nefen's cattle. In Article 14, it was asked whether it was not true that she had refused at first, and that Ratke gave her sweet milk and wheat bread[157] to eat. In Article 15, it was asked whether it was not true that she had been given the powder by Ratke, had placed it in a kettle full of water, and had given it to the cows to drink. In Article 16, it was asked whether the same powder had not been black to look at, and alive.[158] In Article 17, it was asked whether it was not true that the cows had died thereafter, one after another. In Article 18, it was asked whether it was not true that she had gone to Hans Embke, saying that she would provide him with help for his horses.[159] In Article 19, it was asked whether it was not true that she had cut some hair from one of his horses. In Article 20, it was asked whether it was not true that Ratke had taken the hair, and other things too—such as a leather shoelace, a brass ring, some thread, and an iron nail—and said to Rickers that she should take these to Hans Embke, let him know that they had been buried in his stable by another woman, and then pretend to take them out.[160] In Article 21, it was asked whether she had done this herself, and whether Embke had given her two *thaler*, which she shared with Anneke Ratke. In Article 22, it was asked whether it was not true that she had asked Ratke why the wife of Jurgen Nefen was always sick and bedridden. In Article 23, it was asked whether it was not true that Ratke had replied that she could well answer the question that Anneke Rickers asked (in Article 22).[161] However, she was to tell the wife of Nefen that the wives of Hans Embke and Eggert Resen caused her sickness.[162] In Article 24, it was asked whether it was not true that she had confessed that Anneke Ratke's idol was called Kreÿenfues, and that he came to her [Rickers] in prison, to kill her, so that she would not confess anything about Ratke. In Article 25, it was asked whether it was not true that her [Anneke Rickers's] idol had come to her in prison and said that she should confess to everything.

All Anneke Rickers had to do was confirm the questions. The articles were presented to Rickers in public, and she confirmed each of them by saying 'Yes', that she would live and die on that.[163] She then requested that Ratke, who had seduced her into practising witchcraft, would go down the same road.[164]

The Holsten Court ruled that,[165] under torture, Anneke Rickers had renounced her Christian faith and become an apostate from God, and had also harmed the cattle of her accuser, Jurgen Nefen.[166] The court passed the sentence that she should pay not with money or property, but in flesh and blood. And that the executioner should lead her out and tie her to the ladder alive.

There is an additional document dated 10 June, which was addressed to the chancellor[167] and signed by Johann Pundt, which refers to the session on 5 June.

Here, it is stated that Anneke Rickers heard her indictment and confirmed it. The letter also refers to the impending execution of Rickers, asking how it should be performed. It then discusses how Anneke Ratke should further be dealt with. This document was sent to the chancellor on 11 June.[168] On 13 June, a letter was sent from the chancellor to Pundt confirming Anneke Rickers's sentence of execution on 10 June. However, it adds that prior to the execution, she had to visit ministers and be educated in order to convert. About Anneke Ratke—who had been imprisoned again after she fled—the letter states that if she would not confess of her own good will, she should be brought to torture.

The Voice of Anneke Rickers

The category of voice is a tool for clarifying the individual participant's contribution to courtroom discourse. Of all documents in Anneke Rickers's dossier, the confession is the most important with respect to hearing her voice. While her initial denial is brief, as is the confirmation of her indictment, the confession provides access to Rickers's own voice: an individualized voice that comes to the fore in direct and indirect speech. The recorded interrogation provides information about the questions posed and the use and consequences of torture.

At the beginning of Anneke Rickers's trial, indirect speech is used, rendered in the third person and using reporting verbs and reported clauses. Here, we hear a voice of denial. During the first court meeting on 14 May, she denies the accusation put forward by Jurgen Nefen, saying that she did not show him any objects, did not speak with Anna Kake, and did not do anything to his cattle. The same accent of her voice is heard after the testimony of witness Hans Embke: Rickers denies his assertion that she came to him and offered to help him prevent misfortune from happening to his horses. Even if these denials are brief utterances, this is a firm voice—there are no signs of doubt and there is nothing that signals a desire to confess.

Then, a change occurs. Anneke Rickers's voice is heard again in her confession on 5 June, more than a month after her imprisonment and three days after she had been tortured. The turning point, from denial to confession, seems clearly connected to the use of torture. She gives a colourful confession that consists of several points, some of which are formed as small narratives. The confession is fluent and consistent, with clear orality features, which indicates that we are hearing her own way of talking. The confession has interwoven elements of demonology, *maleficium*, and folklore, which not only convey glimpses of her broad knowledge of ideas about witchcraft but also provide a hint of folk belief.

The beginning of Anneke Rickers's confession deals with maleficent witchcraft. It is a story about traditional sorcery, knowledge of which most common people at this time possessed. An object of witchcraft was used to kill cattle. Several people were allied with Rickers, among them Anneke Ratke. This way of performing witchcraft was well known, and the story is narrated in a detailed manner, revealing the ingredients of the witchcraft object and where it was buried. Rickers is familiar with the ideas, and her storytelling signals that she believes the remedies are working. The belief in efficient witchcraft and methods to undo it is part of daily life in local communities, and also money is involved.

As the confession continues, more ideas about witchcraft emerge. It turns out that small magical objects create a bridge between traditional witchcraft and demonological ideas. When Anneke Ratke first invited Anneke Rickers to learn witchcraft, to become rich and get a suitor, Rickers refused. However, she soon regretted this and consented. After the two women went to the barn and placed a nest of hair and feathers there, Rickers walked over the nest repeating a charm in which she stated both the act of walking and the leaving of the Lord Jesus Christ. In doing this, she left her baptism pact. The question posed during the interrogation regarding Rickers's connection with Jurgen Nefen's cattle thus leads straight into a story about how and from whom she learned witchcraft, and about the ritual she conducted when she renounced her Christian faith. Surrendering to evil witchcraft is symbolically equated with physically crossing a border and at the same time leaving Jesus. The charm does not mention the devil or the devil's pact. However, formulations about renouncing the baptism pact were at this time closely connected to entering into a pact with the devil, a formulation frequently found in verdicts in European witchcraft trials.[169] Thus, the charm contained half the wording of the common formulation connected to entering the devil's pact. The combination of the nest—a traditional witchcraft object for *maleficium*—and the content of the charm, which is related to demonology, shows how intricately these elements are woven together in a Northern German witchcraft confession anno 1641. The two spheres of ideas are not kept apart but are united into an object, a physical movement, and some powerful words—all the ingredients necessary for performing witchcraft. The old-fashioned type of witchcraft is not performed on its own: it has become attached to the idea that the person who is learning witchcraft is leaving the Christian pact. When you leave something, you enter into something else; this is how crossing a border is usually interpreted. The implicit message is: when you leave your faith in God as your master, you surrender yourself to the devil as your master. This point of the confession shows that core demonological ideas were adjusted to local versions of witchcraft performance at the time, and that these new versions were known and used among common people.

The most fascinating part of Anneke Rickers's confession is the story about the red rider, which constitutes a voluminous part of the confession's text. It is a version of the narrative about the devil's pact but in an original frame, influenced by fairy tales and folklore. A rider in red clothes appears, persuades her to comply with his wish, gives her money in a black bag, comes to her bed to have intercourse, and requests Jurgen Nefen's calf in return, which he gets.

The devil in the shape of a red rider invokes fairy tales in which the rider enters the picture as a saviour of a female protagonist and swiftly carries her away on his horse. He represents positive and romantic qualities. This is a motif known from orally transmitted fairy tales that were written down throughout Europe during the Romantic Movement, which occurred after the witchcraft trials had ended.[170]

The mentioning of the red rider in Rickers's confession is thus an early written documentation of Northern German folk tradition; the motif existed at this time in oral folk belief. In Rickers's story, however, the devil disguised as a rider is not a Romantic figure. He is a seducer, one who tempts a weak woman into an alliance with evil forces. This is a women's view echoing the demonological doctrine. The element shows the influence of folk belief on a demonological witchcraft confession, where a motif traditionally believed to represent good is now turned around and represents evil. The red rider is not to be trusted: he is a figure promising money, but it is all a fraud.

Anneke Rickers's next two meetings with her 'suitor' and 'idol' point to demonological ideas. First, on her way to church, she is stopped by the rider and reminded that she now has to serve him and work for him, whereupon she returns home. Second, in Jurgen Nefen's field, her fright at seeing a black dog leads to the devil coming back shaped as a man. When asked, she wants to limit the period she spends serving him, but he maintains that she is his and will remain so. Although Rickers obeys by returning home instead of continuing on her way to church, her voice is not completely subservient: she objects to the idea of remaining his servant for a long time. In this respect, she challenges his power over her. The incident with the black dog that shape-shifts into a man contributes to a portrayal of the rider as a cavalier, showing concern for her feelings. This element in Rickers's story adds positive qualities to the devil's behaviour and strengthens the connection to the Romantic rider image. The figure of the red rider becoming part of the confession of a tortured woman signals a stage in the development of versions of the devil's pact narrative in a local community. Folkloric ideas are merged with demonological ideas. We see a mixture of fairy tales and demonological stories about the devil, which might well have been commonly circulating among provincial folk at the time.

Comparing Anneke Rickers's confession with Jurgen Nefen's accusation and Hans Embke's testimony from 14 May, we see in the confession a personalized story. The idea of becoming rich after leaving God and entering into a relationship with the devil is clearly demonological, as is the renunciation of Rickers's Christendom; the use of a witchcraft object and charm are related to *maleficium*; and the red rider is related to folklore. This means that certain demonological ideas had been part of Anneke Rickers's knowledge before the interrogator began to ask questions. She most likely obtained these ideas from orally transmitted stories, which supports an argument for assimilation: by the 1640s, a range of learned ideas about witchcraft had merged with traditional folklore.

To the interrogator's question about the name of her idol, Anneke Rickers responds with the names of both her own and Ratke's demons. The question certainly shows an interest on the part of the judiciary in obtaining additional information about a field that Rickers mastered but whose content they were not familiar with. The mixture of a biblical name and a colloquial name for the devil is found in descriptions of the devil in witchcraft confessions from many countries.[171] In addition, Rickers remarks that Jurgen Nefen's cattle died innocently, except for the calf, which she had to give to her lover.[172] This statement, which was not an answer to a question, signals her own belief in the effect of witchcraft: it could target innocent and guilty creatures, and in this case, the calf was not innocent. She evidently believed that it was possible to perform witchcraft. The comprehensive part of the confession dealing with maleficent witchcraft and the red rider is reported as having been confessed to of her own good will, without torture. She has apparently answered the questions posed to her without hesitation, and she has provided many details based on her knowledge of several spheres of witchcraft, magic, and folklore. She has displayed her expertise. Apparently, this is not enough.

When Rickers is questioned under torture, two points are taken up. The first adds information about her knowledge of witchcraft. The powder she received from Anneke Ratke, which she used to cast evil on Jurgen Nefen's cows, is the initial issue. Anneke Rickers points to Ratke as the initiator and herself as the accomplice, stating how she (Rickers) gave the cattle the powder in water to drink, that it looked like black gunpowder, and that it had been alive.[173] The information she gives here deals with details on methods of witchcraft. Again, the recorded words seem to signal her belief in effective witchcraft. However, the final part of the interrogation deals with denunciation. This is probably what the judiciary is after, as the next question concerns people Rickers mentioned as practising witchcraft. She is asked why she talked about Eggert Resen and his wife, the shepherd woman as having caused the illness of Jurgen Nefen's wife. To this, Anneke Rickers answers that Ratke told her to make Jurgen Nefen's wife believe this.[174] The blame is placed on Ratke here, and the interrogator follows up critically. He appeals to Rickers's sentiment by urging her to tell the truth about Ratke and not denounce innocent people. In response, she confirms what she has previously confessed to. She adds that she has nothing else to say, even if they tore her to pieces. The last question focuses on eliciting both a denunciation of Ratke and a confirmation of the denunciation. Rickers's statement about being torn to pieces suggests severe torture. Here, there is a pause in the interrogation and the use of torture is suspended. This part shows not only the interrogators' objective of obtaining a confirmation of the confession but also, as is reflected in the question's wording, of safeguarding the element of honesty in the confession. It is clear that at this point, Rickers is in a very bad state. Her cry that she has nothing more to say is a strong signal of exhaustion; she probably would have confessed to anything in order to stop the pain.

The points of the confession conveying ideas about witchcraft display clear narrative structures. Even the indictment's brief articles have room for narrative structuring; the possibility of constructing small narratives within the overall confession has thus been fully exploited. The confession shows interesting features with regard to content and linguistics. Each point of Anneke Rickers's confession contains a timeline, with clear markers of weeks and days. Delegation of voice is effectuated by inserted direct speech, whether uttered by Rickers, Ratke, or the devil. Variations in tempo between passages is seen in the descriptive paragraphs, for instance those about the powder, which temporarily depart from the timeline. Frequency is seen in the repeated mentioning of the red rider, which apparently was an item of importance. The mood of the confession is reflected in numerous examples of Anneke Rickers's attitude to witchcraft: she is a believer in witchcraft and its results. These features show Rickers's competence as a storyteller, and they point to the position that court records occupy between oral and written language.

A multitude of orality features are found in the documents. In the interrogation, orally transmitted fairy tales are echoed in the figure of a rider in red clothes. Additional orality features include an additive sentence structure, pointed wording, and directly rendered speech. The indictment also contains strong orality features, as seen in the precision regarding locations and details about weekdays, colours, and the name of the idol. Closeness to the human lifeworld shines through all stories and events taking place.

The storytelling accent is heard continually until severe torture is applied and Rickers's voice is silenced. The contrast between the narrative flow and her voice at the end of the trial is enormous. The last time the voice of Anneke Rickers is rendered in the records, she says only one word: 'Yes'. This word is uttered to confirm the indictment. Grammatically, the indictment is formed as a list of yes/ no questions with a positive orientation, which are read aloud to her. The effect of this single word—'Yes'—is strong. The case has come to a point where her narrative ability is no longer requested; the judicial officials are interested only in her one-word confirmation.

It is also through her last word that her emotions are most clearly emphasized. Contrary to the shades of her voice—the accents of her language previously so richly displayed—only this one-syllable word is left. The emotions she has shown previously—anger, fear, and hope—have been quieted. She has given in, and with that the range of her emotions, as far as they can be interpreted from the confession taken down by the scribe, has disappeared.

The voice of Anneke Rickers shows a clear change from the beginning to the end of the trial. A voice that is strong and resistant at the beginning is turned, via torture, into a cry to stop the pain and the denunciation of her witchcraft ally. To follow this changing voice through the stages of her trial is like following a distressing experience and its result. The first part of her confession is a demonstration of splendid storytelling influenced by oral tradition. Her voice cracks to signal the transition from denial to confession, which took place under torture. After this turning point, the trial ends in a denunciation out of misery, which is a very human reaction: Rickers says that she will not suffer this sentence alone, that there is another person who is equally skilled in witchcraft and who should suffer the same fate. Thus, Rickers's last words, that another woman should be treated the way she herself was treated, is a bitter ending of her courtroom discourse. We hear a voice that has been subdued at all levels; a woman defeated and only looking towards her death.

The Voices of the Witnesses

There is only one formal witness in this trial, namely Hans Embke. His testimony is related to Jurgen Nefen's accusation: Rickers caused the death of his horse and cows. Embke was called forth as a witness because Rickers had shown Nefen several objects hidden in Embke's stable—objects used to perform maleficent witchcraft. Embke testifies that he holds Rickers responsible for the death of five horses. Also, after this loss, Rickers came to his house and offered help so that this kind of bad luck would not happen again. She only had to remove some objects buried under his stable, which he paid her for. The testimony of Hans Embke supports Nefen's accusation that Anneke Rickers could perform maleficent witchcraft and was to blame for their cattle's deaths.

The voice of the witness is important, as he saw things himself and can thus confirm that Rickers found the objects under his stable. He is also the one who received the offer of counter-magic. The voice of the victim signals belief in efficient witchcraft, particularly against losing valuable cattle. His testimony is given weight by the judicial authorities, as it supports Nefen's main accusation, and the decision to apply torture is based on these two men's statements.

Another accusation that comes up during the trial is the sickness of Jurgen Nefen's wife. This point is introduced during the interrogation of Rickers after torture has been used, and is related to Rickers's denunciation of Ratke and rumours about who caused this sickness. It is possible that Nefen's wife was questioned by the judiciary, but she did not have formal status as a witness. Hans Embke is not mentioned in this context.

The Voice of the Interrogator

The questions posed to Anneke Rickers during interrogation serve to direct the confession from maleficent towards demonological ideas. The questions lead her answers sequentially closer and closer to a very serious confession, ending in denunciation. The first question—concerning the kind of connection she had with the cattle of Jurgen Nefen—leads straight to the story of how she learned witchcraft and from whom, of the suitor and the possibility of becoming rich, and then of the ritual, using an object and a charm, that she carried out when she renounced Christendom. The second question, which asks about the name of her idol, is intended to identify her personal demon. The third question, posed after torture has begun, is about the powder she received from Anneke Ratke, a confession related to the initial accusation on 14 May. The fourth question deals with denunciation: she blames Ratke for making Jurgen Nefen's wife believe that Eggert Resen and his wife had caused her sickness. The last question pertains to truthful denunciation: Rickers is asked to tell the truth about Ratke and cautioned not to denounce innocent people. The questions posed during torture revolve around Anneke Ratke and her participation, signalling the importance of Anneke Rickers's confirmation of the denunciation of Ratke so that the witchcraft trials would continue. Following a plan, the interrogator steers the questioning closer and closer to the naming of other suspects.

Important demonological elements are confessed to before torture is applied, although the threat of torture is there: Anneke Rickers confesses to having renounced her baptism pact, having entered into the devil's pact, and having performed evil deeds with her demon. For the interrogator, certain key elements of a confession are important to elicit from the accused—torture is thus used to obtain the specific answers needed for a sentence to be passed and a subsequent trial to commence.

In the indictment, the voice of the interrogator resembles the voice of an accuser. The aim is to get Rickers to confirm every article. When it comes to prioritizing content, the indictment's articles are ordered in such a way that priority is given to demonological ideas.

The Voice of the Law

The voice of the law appears in the correspondence between the magistrate and the chancellor about important legal decisions to be taken, in the ordering and content of questions during interrogation, in heeding correctness in court practice, and in the wording of the sentence.

The correspondence between the magistrate and the chancellor demonstrates that effectuating the law rests upon communication between different judicial levels. The voice of the law is one; however, administering the legal field is challenging due to scattered judicial authority.

The voice of the law is heard in the judicial legitimation of steps taken during the development of the trial, particularly concerning permission to use torture and the confirmation of sentences of execution. The justification to use torture provided by the court, based only on Nefen's accusation and Embke's testimony, is that Rickers had made herself a witchcraft suspect by burying objects under Embke's stable, an act witnessed by others. This suspicion of witchcraft is sufficient for torture to be applied.

The voice of the law emerges in the accurate way torture is recorded, for instance at what time it started and ended. Also, Rickers's own words—that she was 'torn to pieces' during torture—are recorded. This signals that openness related to torture was common in the recording of witchcraft trials, and that the use of torture was regarded as a natural means of extracting a confession.

When it comes to the order of articles in the indictment, demonological ideas are paid attention to in articles 1–12, maleficent ideas in articles 13–23, and demonological ideas again in articles 24–25. The voice of the law appears in the priority given to demonological ideas, in the detailedness of each article, and in the order of the articles. Maleficent ideas are not given the same attention. According to the law, therefore, demonological witchcraft was severe.

Correctness in court practice is strived for, signalling respect for the law. The necessary permission from the chancellor is requested. Rickers confirms each article of the indictment in public. The use of torture is mentioned in the sentence. The wording of the sentence on the one hand emphasizes religious grounds, on the other the main accusation: Anneke Rickers has renounced her Christian faith and become an apostate, and she has harmed Nefen's cattle. The voice of the law thus makes clear that Rickers's wrong faith and the mischief she performed are reasons for the severe sentence.

The Voice of the Scribe

The scribe took down a detailed account of Anneke Rickers's confession. His way of recording preserves the development of the trial, the turning point, narrative features, orality features, ideas about witchcraft, and emotions. It is possible to hear tones of denial, complaint, protest, begging, confession, and storytelling. Rickers's voice is rendered as strong and consistent, with appropriate answers. The scribe also includes one comment by Anneke Rickers regarding the vision of the red rider, which is a sign of his accuracy. He likewise notes down traditional as well as learned witchcraft ideas related to the demonological doctrine. Even the one word that comes out of Rickers's mouth after she has been tortured for some time is included. Her cry is a strong signal that highlights the turning point from denial to confession in a witchcraft trial. Furthermore, the rendering of her cry in the court records reflects the task of the scribe to record her words in detail—he could otherwise have simply deleted her complaint. This contributes to the understanding that the scribe is a professional person who tries to do his work properly. He follows legal terminology. The part of her confession that she is said to have given willingly must be understood in this context.

When writing the indictment, rules for organizing the text according to a fixed format are followed. The ordering of articles is exploited to highlight demonological ideas. As I see it, the role of the scribe was to create a reliable report of what happened during the trial. Within the frames of writing a text which provides insight into courtroom discourse, he has done his best.

Anna Spielen, 1669

The trial of Anna Spielen in 1669 took place in Lübeck, an imperial free city within the Holy Roman Empire and one of the cities of the Hanseatic League. It is situated in the area of Stockelsdorf in East Holstein. The witchcraft trials in Lübeck started in 1544, and forty-seven trials took place in this town during the 1600s and 1700s. Compared to the surrounding regions, this major Hanseatic town practised a more moderate policy with regard to witchcraft persecution. Fewer persons were accused of witchcraft, and their chances of survival were higher.[175] This restraint can be understood as a response to the high costs of each trial and the fact that those rumoured to be practising witchcraft were often banished to nearby territories.[176] However, it might also have had to do with the contemporary intellectual discussions in the area. Voices critical of witchcraft trials were heard already before 1600. An example is Konrad v. Anten from Lübeck, who published a tractatus in 1590 with sharp criticism of court practice regarding repeated torture, denunciation, defence possibilities for the accused, and the use of the water ordeal as circumstantial evidence.[177] Other critics, like Ericus Mauritius from Itzehoe[178] and Henricus Michaelis, working in Kiel and Lübeck,[179] contributed to the intellectual discussion through works published in 1669 and 1670, even though they were not unambiguously against witchcraft persecution. They frequently quote German Jesuit theologian Friedrich Spee,[180] a strong opponent of the persecution of witches and of the use of torture in witchcraft trials.

The Trial

On 5 October 1669, Anna Spielen, a woman living in the village of Gramsdorf, was brought before the court.[181] She stood accused of witchcraft in a panic that involved six people: five women and one man.[182] When Anna Spielen's trial started, a witchcraft case against Cathrine Hildebrand had just come to an end. Hildebrand had been imprisoned in May 1669 and was burned at the stake.[183] The case of Cathrine Hildebrand was linked to the case of Anna Spielen, as Hildebrand—according to Spielen's confession—was her mentor. Witchcraft trials were expensive to carry through, and the expenses for the trials of Hildebrand and Spielen are recorded in a detailed document.[184]

The trial of Anna Spielen took place under the jurisdiction of the Lübeck Cathedral Chapter (hereinafter Chapter).[185] Spielen had been imprisoned by the Chapter in order to have rumours about her investigated and the holy justice of the place preserved.[186] The deputy head of the Chapter was in charge of the trial.

The trial started when several neighbours in Gramsdorf, which is a town to the south of Hemmelsdorf, wanted Anna Spielen to be tried before the court,[187] as she was said to be evil and rumoured to perform witchcraft. She was then imprisoned, kept in custody, and interrogated about the witchcraft rumours. The Honourable Deputy *Capituli Herren* let Anna Spielen be interrogated first 'in the good', but later under severe torture, which means that she had refused to confess to witchcraft or to answer all questions during the initial interrogation.[188] Once torture had been applied, she spoke out and confessed.[189] An indictment was composed, based on her confession. The indictment is itemized, using numbers to demarcate seven separate points. A questionnaire was most likely used. Her answers are fairly brief but comprehensive enough to constitute a confession on the basis of which a sentence could be passed.

The first point of the indictment contains three elements: a confirmation that Anna Spielen knew witchcraft; information on who had taught her witchcraft; and information on how she had entered into a pact with the devil.[190] The second point of the indictment is also related to the devil. Spielen confessed that, through the use of a stick, she had had contact with her spirit or devil, who was called Paul.[191] The third point elaborates on her personal relationship with the devil, now on an intimate level. She confessed that she had had sexual intercourse with the devil several times.[192] The fourth point of the indictment reflects the expansion of demonological ideas on this topic. She confessed to two elements: that she had been to Bloksberg several times and that she had ridden a male goat.[193] The fifth point is about denunciation. Spielen confessed that she had seen some well-known people at Bloksberg.[194] However, she did not give any names.

While the first five points of the indictment were clearly concerned with well-known demonological ideas, the sixth point is related to *maleficium*. Anna Spielen confessed that she had killed a blue cow that belonged to a milkmaid from Wilmsdorf, now living in Gramsdorf.[195] The last and seventh point of the indictment states that she confessed that during the Holy Communion in church, she had taken the consecrated communion bread from her own mouth and had given it to Satan in a handkerchief.[196] This is a common element in confessions in witchcraft trials, although it has some variations.

The indictment was read aloud for Anna Spielen so she could confirm it, which she did.[197] Then the sentence followed. Spielen was sentenced to death by fire.[198] In the wording of the sentence, the words 'voluntary' as well as 'forced' are mentioned in relation to her confession. The sentence in itself is said to be 'voluntary' and 'lasting'.

The Voice of Anna Spielen

Anna Spielen's voice is heard in the rendering of her confession. The confession of Anna Spielen expresses resistance, as she first denies witchcraft and confesses only under torture. Under interrogation, Spielen answers specific points that the interrogators feel are necessary to have recorded and therefore target. The court records are rather brief, but Anna Spielen's voice can still be heard in her initial denial, in the content of each point, and in the overall tone of her confession.

It is clear that the interrogator poses questions that invite more than an answer of 'Yes' or 'No'. When we read 'confessed that', I interpret this to be a rendering of what she said, using reporting verbs and reported clauses. The interrogator clearly focuses on certain topics, but he has not formulated the answers; Anna Spielen does so herself.

In the first point of her confession, Anna Spielen first admits to knowing witchcraft, which is a dangerous thing to admit to. Second, she confesses to having a personal relationship with a mentor, whose name only Spielen herself could give. Spielen displays a respectful attitude towards her mentor, and in that way shows pride in having learned the art of witchcraft. She talks about how she entered into the devil's pact by grasping a white stick and quoting a charm: 'I grasp this stick, forgive me God, and will hold on to this devil'.[199] The charm contains orality features and is likely rendered in the court records just as it was uttered. Rhyme, rhythm, intonation, and short and pointed wording all signal that the charm was written down *verbatim* by the scribe. These are words from an oral tradition that Anna Spielen was familiar with and that the interrogator probably did not know much about. The charm is formed according to conventions within the oral tradition that people in the local community practised. However, the content of the charm—that she is leaving God and joining the devil[200]—represents a fundamental demonological idea. In this way, a demonological idea takes the shape of a traditional charm: easy to use and easy to remember. Narratives about the devil's pact must have been well known among the peasants at this time, and Spielen is retelling one version of the story in the courtroom. The questions must have been about whether she knew witchcraft, who taught it to her, and how she entered into the devil's pact. They are all answered in a personalized way.

The question answered in the second point must have been about how she performed witchcraft—an expansion of the first question. Here, too, the confession has a personal character. She explains how she used the white stick and what the name of her personal devil was. Again, we hear Anna Spielen's own words, as the interrogator could not have known how she used the stick, nor its colour, nor the name of her devil. The content is personal—she is speaking about her own way of practising witchcraft and describing her personal relationship with the devil.

The third point concerns Anna Spielen's intimate relationship with the devil. The question here could have been whether she had had sexual intercourse with him. Her answer is that she had sexual intercourse with him several times. However, she does not go into details. Sexual intercourse with the devil is a recurrent feature in witchcraft confessions across Europe, although the occurrence of this element varies by country.

The fourth point pertains to witches' meetings. Anna Spielen was likely asked whether she had been to a witches' meeting and possibly how she got there. She confesses that she went to Bloksberg twice and that she rode a male goat to get there. As such, she admits that she went to witches' meetings, states how often she went, and explains how she reached them. Bloksberg was well known in many parts of Europe at that time as a mountain on which witches gathered. According to folk belief, witches assembled there at *Walpurgisnacht*[201] to dance with the devil.[202] The other well-known folkloric element present in this point is Spielen's riding a buck to the witches' meeting. Many persons accused of witchcraft across Europe confessed that they rode animals to reach a witches' gathering. The male goat is often found in witchcraft confessions, and the devil himself often appears in the figure of a goat. The two elements in Spielen's answer display a personal touch and relate to orally transmitted ideas. The way in which the answer is formed seems to indicate that the details related to the witches' meeting are Anna Spielen's original contributions to a response to the interrogator's question.

The fifth point has to do with naming other people. Anna Spielen must have been asked whether she saw any familiar people at the witches' meeting, and she answers that she saw some well-known individuals there. This answer is unsatisfactory for the interrogator, as no names are mentioned. The denunciation of people by name was an important objective of interrogation during a witchcraft trial, as it ensured that the trials would continue.

The sixth point focuses on what kind of witchcraft Spielen performed, related to a question that might have asked about the same. When this point is not further elaborated on by Anna Spielen, it seems that interrogators had no additional questions and were content with a short point stating only that she confessed to the death of a cow. The *maleficium* ideas are thus apparently less interesting to further expand on than the previous points containing demonological ideas. Spielen answers that she killed a cow, and she describes its colour and owner, including where the owner came from and where she lives. The details about the cow and the milkmaid must have been part of Spielen's own knowledge. However, she does not explain exactly how witchcraft was performed nor points to any cause-effect relationship between a spoken charm and the death of the cow.

The seventh point is again a combination of *maleficium* and demonological ideas. It has to do with taking sacramental bread from church. The question might simply have been about additional evil deeds she could confess to. Anna Spielen confesses that she received the Holy Communion in church but took it out of her mouth and gave it to Satan in a handkerchief. The idea of using sacred objects, or objects that were blessed by a minister, to perform evil deeds is connected to traditional sorcery beliefs. It could just as well have been wine or salt; the main requirement is that a minister unknowingly read Christian words over the object, which then becomes an object of power when used to perform evil deeds. The unusual element in Spielen's confession is that she gave the communion bread to Satan. Usually, the object used to perform witchcraft is kept by the witch and used for specific occasions. The idea that Satan would use this object creates a link between *maleficium* and demonology, and this link could only be created by Spielen herself. Giving sacred objects to Satan instead of keeping them herself to perform witchcraft, which was the common belief, signals a version of demonological ideas. Usually, not Satan but the witches performed witchcraft, using powers obtained from Satan when entering the devil's pact. This point about the use of the communion bread is not elaborated on through additional questioning. For the records, it sufficed that Spielen simply confessed to having used sacred communion bread.

In Anna Spielen's confession, her voice comes to the fore through personalized content as well as the use of orality features. We see this in descriptions of people and objects and in the inclusion of content that could only be her own. The interplay between the voice of the interrogator and the voice of Spielen does not portray the accused woman as a person without words. On the contrary, her words can be recognized by personal touches. Anna Spielen's personal knowledge related to ideas, concepts, and practices that were unknown to the interrogator and that could not have been formulated in questions. Instead, most of the questions were of an open kind, inviting Anna Spielen to reveal what she knew.

The direction of the confession is steered in a certain way. First, attention centres on the devil's pact and witches' meetings. Then, it focuses on combined ideas about *maleficium* and demonology. This pattern shows not only what was prioritized in the interrogation, but also that there was no clear separation between the two concepts. The points of the confession that are concerned with *maleficium* are fused with features of demonology. This is the case for the cow that died and for the communion bread taken from church. Spielen's confession shows that she had knowledge of *maleficium* as well as of demonology. As this is a late case, demonological ideas would have been known in local communities in all of Northern Europe. Spielen could give her confession by retelling ideas that had been orally transmitted to her. This goes for content based on ideas connected to learned demonology, and for traditional witchcraft beliefs. The interrogator's questions and the accused person's answers provide a path to a clearer understanding of the range of witchcraft ideas that were told and retold in local communities.

The trial of Anna Spielen was initiated by an accusation from her neighbours, as she was rumoured to have practised witchcraft and was therefore reported to the authorities. When her trial started, however, she was immediately drawn into an ongoing panic. With regard to court practice, we can see how Anna Spielen's trial changed from an individual trial conducted according to accusatorial principles— with witnesses led before the court—to a trial conducted according to inquisitorial principles, which did not require any witnesses. Her own confession was considered valid proof.

In the voice of Anna Spielen, we can hear an individualized confession with a clear, intact narrative structure. A timeline is established that orders events, like the mentioning of the 'first time' she went to Bloksberg and the multiple times she met the devil. Narrative strategies also stand out in terms of duration. For instance, the clauses—added by Spielen on her own part—about the communion bread contain descriptions that contribute to slowing down the narrative speed. The narrator's handling of voices, enlivening the story, is seen in the use of direct speech to quote the charm. Taken together, these narrative strategies required a profound knowledge of storytelling, which appears even in the brief points of the confession. The narrator's attitude towards witchcraft comes clearly to the fore when she speaks about Bloksberg, about the cow, and about the communion bread. The impression is that Anna Spielen believed in witchcraft and in the effectiveness of the witchcraft methods described. In addition to narrative structures, we find the use of oral-style mnemonic practices in Anna Spielen's voice when she quotes the charm. Other orality features found in her confession are additive sentence structures, language images, redundancy of details—like the *blue* cow, a *male* goat, or place names connected to the milkmaid—in addition to a closeness to the human lifeworld throughout.

The Voices of the Witnesses

At the beginning of the records, it is mentioned that several neighbours have reported Anna Spielen to the authorities because she is rumoured to practice witchcraft and they believe she is capable of performing witchcraft. However, we do not get testimonies from individual neighbours; they are presented as a group. The voices of these witnesses signal belief in witchcraft and fear that it may be used in the local community. They want to get rid of an unwanted person.

The Voice of the Interrogator

During the interrogation, which is recorded in the indictment, the voices of Anna Spielen and the interrogator are heard. It is possible to discern these two voices and their interplay. The voice of the interrogator may be traced through shadow questions. As such, attention is drawn to certain topics, primarily those related to demonological ideas, but also to *maleficium*. Spielen then reacts to these questions by giving a full answer in her own words and with her own content. If the interrogator is not satisfied with the answer he receives and wants to know more about a specific topic, he asks follow-up questions.

Looking at the order of questions posed and their content, demonological ideas are clearly manifested in the first four points of the confession, which means that this content was given priority. In a late witchcraft trial like Anna Spielen's, the interrogator knows which questions should be included in the interrogation in order to secure a death sentence, and he works efficiently to reach this goal. Less successful on the part of the interrogator is in Spielen's refusal to give names of other people she had seen at witches' meetings. That the interrogation also included *maleficium* ideas shows the tight bonds between malevolent and demonological witchcraft in this area at this time, and that the performance of both forms was regarded as important to include in a confession to witchcraft.

The Voice of the Law

The voice of the law is heard in the statement on the Chapter's authority, in giving the reason why Anna Spielen is arrested and accused, in the confession's order of points, in the rendering of applied torture, and in the wording of the sentence.

As the trial of Anna Spielen took place before a clerical court, it is stated at the beginning of the records that the Chapter of the high 'Stiffts Lübeck' has the authority from God to investigate the case of Anna Spielen, who is imprisoned and in the custody of the Chapter. In this way, it is emphasized that the court has the full right to hold a trial and pass a sentence. It is also mentioned that the Holy Justice in place in this manner would be preserved.

The justification for Anna Spielen's arrest consists of complaints from neighbours: she is rumoured to practice witchcraft, and the neighbours fear her. According to the law's understanding, she is a suspicious person and likely a threat to her environment. When the court opens an investigation, it is doing what falls within the range of their duties.

Regarding the ordering of points, the initial point dealing with a charm used when Anna Spielen was initiated into witchcraft contains combined content consisting of *maleficium* and demonological ideas. Further, while the largest part of her confession deals with demonology, maleficent witchcraft surfaces again in the last point. The voice of the law thus sees both concepts of witchcraft as severe, and expresses that a fusion between traditional belief in witchcraft and demonological ideas was not only possible, but was in fact common at the time.

There is an accurate rendering in the records about when the confession is given voluntarily and when torture is applied. This is an accent of the voice of the law that provides transparency. Torture is allowed in order to extract a confession, and there is a clear understanding that the application of torture has an effect on the willingness to confess and that this should be recorded properly.

The wording of the sentence includes that her confession is willing as well as forced. The sentence also states that her own confession is why she should be punished and executed by fire from life to death. The voice of the law is steady and firm.

The Voice of the Scribe

Moving to the voice of the scribe, we see professionalism. He has managed to record the trial's different phases. Anna Spielen confesses according to an established sequential pattern in witchcraft interrogation, starting with the devil's pact and proceeding to witches' meetings, denunciation, and finally *maleficium*. However, there is nothing in her confession that indicates that answers were fed to her: she formulates her own answers. This is indicated in the way the confession is recorded. While Spielen's belief in efficient witchcraft is signalled, the situation is different for the scribe. He uses no distancing textual devices that might reveal his own attitude to what is told, or whether he believes what is told.

The scribe must have written down Anna Spielen's answers more or less as he heard them—for example the charm. He took down her words, including orality features. While the grammatical form changes, as he switches from third-person to first-person narration when recording the confession, he preserves the content of Anna Spielen's answers, thus also echoing the interrogator's questions. It is due to the thorough work of the scribe that we can distinguish the voices in this source material. And not least, it is the scribe's accurate work that has made it possible for a scholar to trust the records.

Conclusion

In this chapter, we have encountered the voices of three women from Northern Germany who were accused in witchcraft trials in the period 1607–69. Court records have provided insight into their knowledge about demonological witchcraft and maleficent witchcraft, their folkloric belief, their narrative abilities, and their use of oral language in confessions. The element of healing is not given weight in these trials. Even though the women lived in different places, there are strong similarities in the development of the trials of Kistina Netelers, tried in Flensburg; Anneke Rickers, tried in Bordesholm; and Anna Spielen, tried in Lübeck.

Interrogation was steered according to a fixed pattern and questionnaires were used, all leading to a desired confession. As for ideas about witchcraft, the confessions display a wide range of knowledge. All confessions show a fusion between demonological ideas and ideas related to *maleficium*, with interwoven motifs of folklore. This goes for the chapter's first, middle, and last trial and signals that demonological ideas were adjusted to traditional ideas about witchcraft in each of the three areas dealt with, and that they were known by common people around

1600. The Evil One himself gives promises when the woman enters the pact, sometimes consisting of money that turns out to be manure. A recurring ingredient in the demonological parts of the confessions is that a personal devil is given to the woman when entering the devil's pact. This devil has either a colloquial or a biblical name. In the first two cases, from 1607 and 1641, the devil is not named a 'devil' but is circumscribed as 'idol', 'patron', and 'lover'. In the last case, from 1669, the personal and named devil is called 'spirit' or 'devil', and the Evil One is called Satan. Sexual intercourse with the devil as part of entering the pact is common in these confessions, and the same goes for later meetings with the devil, which are confessed to as having been recurrent. Witches' meetings are sometimes held on mountains, for instance Bloksberg. Transnational transmission related to learned ideas about witchcraft has put a stamp on the confessions.

With regard to maleficent witchcraft, a number of ideas stand out: casting spells on cattle, stealing milk from other people's cows, stealing communion bread from church, making and burying objects of witchcraft, using charms combined with bodily gestures and witchcraft objects, and using love magic. Folkloric motifs are in some cases woven into the confessions. An example is the figure of the red rider.

For all trials, the confessions show adjusted versions of demonological ideas in local communities. The peasants took up some core elements of the demonological doctrine and connected them with traditional beliefs about witchcraft. Thus, various versions of demonological notions can be found in witchcraft confessions in different places in Schleswig-Holstein. However, the core ideas of demonology are always preserved.

Witnesses' testimonies display common people's eagerness to blame persons suspected of witchcraft for inexplicable accidents that have taken place in local society. Social structures influence witchcraft trials. Neighbours and acquaintances testify about tragedies and bad luck, about death and sickness which have struck people and animals. Belief in witchcraft is strong, likewise that some people are to be feared because they have the power to perform witchcraft. The simple logic of cause and effect is underlying all testimonies; a few angry words uttered towards an alleged witch, and an evil return was around the corner. A tragedy's reason could always be witchcraft.

The legal systems that the judiciary operated in were effective. In witchcraft trials, even if resistance and anger emerge in the initial denials of knowing and performing witchcraft, it also becomes clear how this protest was crushed. The laws in Germany allowed the application of torture in witchcraft trials as part of interrogation and before a sentence was passed. The use of torture could thus be freely entered into the records. This provides a good opportunity to observe the relationship between the consistent application of torture and the cracking of a voice as the woman starts to confess to witchcraft. Torture was graded from light to severe. The three trials from Northern Germany underline the impact of graded torture in witchcraft trials: it works according to its aim, namely to force a confession quickly. Even when the label 'in a humane way'[203] is used, the expression signals a forced confession and, in addition, that the use of 'sharp' torture is on its way. Women who were exposed to extensive torture responded with fear and horror.

The clearest turning point from denial to confession in the course of the trial is seen in the case of Anneke Rickers, wherein the change in her voice when she gives up her resistance is documented as being directly connected to torture. In the trials of Kistina Netelers and Anna Spielen, torture was also used, but the indictment does not provide information about the period before torture, namely the start of the interrogation. It seems that torture occurred very early, almost at the same time as interrogation began. However, all women have denied witchcraft initially; otherwise, the use of torture would not have been necessary.

The confessions of the three women were forced, but with narrative structures intact. They are enforced narratives, demonstrating a competence shared by people living in predominantly oral societies. All women were good storytellers with a firm grasp of narrative strategies. Orality features are fluent in the confessions, adding a touch of individuality to their expressions. The occurrence of orality features portrays the accused women as individual language users and is an important marker of the scribe's reliability. The scribe recorded the words that were uttered in the courtroom as they were spoken, and this strengthens the impression that the courtroom discourse rendered in the witchcraft court records is valid.

The analyses of the voices of women show a range of accents that display strength and endurance. Still, the lives of the three women ended in a tragic way. They received death sentences. Today, we can hardly imagine the state of mind and the overwhelming feeling of powerlessness that accompanied an accusation of witchcraft, in Schleswig-Holstein and beyond.

4

DENMARK—WEATHER MAGIC, WITCHES' DANCE, AND PERSONAL DEMONS

Three trials from Denmark are included in this study. The first is from Copenhagen and took place in 1590. It is related to alleged witchcraft against ships of the Danish king, Frederik II, that were to bring his daughter, Princess Anne, to Scotland as the bride of Scottish king James IV. The second witchcraft trial analysed took place in 1618 in Viborg, Northern Jutland, and was related to a witchcraft panic that occurred in Viborg in 1618–19. The third trial is from the district of Ribe and took place in 1652 as the last witchcraft trial in Ribe. This district saw twenty-two witchcraft trials in the period 1572–1652.

These trials provide glimpses of three chronological stages of witchcraft persecution in Denmark. In-depth studies of women's voices as they come to the fore in the trials' discourse will shed light on the demonological element, ideas of *maleficium*, notions of healing, and traditional folkloric notions. In addition, the fact that confessions are enforced narratives—extracted using torture or the threat of torture—will be taken into account. The orality features that become apparent in the confessions will be studied as well. A close reading of the court records makes it possible to catch any change in voice from the beginning to the end of the trial. The confessions play an important part in what emerges in the voices of women and help show various accents coming to the fore. It is possible to listen out for witchcraft ideas, which arise partly as an expression of the accused person's own knowledge and partly as a response to leading questions during interrogation. In the confessions, features of folk tradition are mixed with learned demonological ideas and the impact of judicial legal influence. The confessions enable an understanding of common people's world views.[1] The Copenhagen trials of 1590 are interlinked with the North Berwick trials in Scotland of 1590–91, and thus with the first trial analysed in the chapter on Scotland in this book.[2]

DOI: 10.4324/9781003255406-4

Background

Jurisdiction

The first laws related to witchcraft in Danish law are the Church Law of Skaane, Article 7, and the Church Law of Sjælland, Article 11, both dated to around 1171.[3] An ordeal by walking on hot iron,[4] seen as God's judgement, was used as circumstantial evidence to prove *maleficium*. This ordeal was repealed in 1216 for the area of Skaane, but nothing is said about punishment.[5] The next law decision is the Jutland Law, *Jyske Lov*, which was valid for one geographical area and used before and after the Reformation.[6] Article 69 stated that if a woman was accused of witchcraft and denied, she was to ask a number of people from the parish to swear a compurgation oath for her in court.[7] The Jutland Law was complemented with a number of decrees and recesses. Important is the Copenhagen Recess of 1547,[8] repeated in the Kolding Recess of 1558.[9] Two articles affected witchcraft trials, even if one of them did not deal with witchcraft in particular.[10] First, Article 18 in the Kolding Recess stated that no person without honour[11] was to be believed as a witness in any trial. This had an impact on witchcraft panics, because denunciations made by accused witches were not to be believed and could not result in a sudden increase in witchcraft trials. Second, Article 19 in the Kolding Recess stated that nobody was to be questioned under torture before they were found guilty and sentenced to death. Both these articles had a large impact on Danish witchcraft trials. Article 18 hindered the escalation of witchcraft trials. Article 19 prevented the use of torture at an early stage of a witchcraft trial. In the Kalundborg Recess of 1576—issued by Fredrik II, who was regent from 1559 to 1588—another important article is found, stating that a sentence of execution in a witchcraft trial was to be brought before *Landstinget*, the Danish Court of Appeal. Thus, a Danish lower court's verdict of witchcraft always had to be appealed in a higher provincial court.[12] The first two of these legal statements mentioned were repeated in the Kolding Recess of 1588, issued by Fredrik II: testimonies given by witches denouncing others were not to be believed,[13] and nobody was to be tortured before sentence was passed.[14] The mentioned laws and recesses dealt with *maleficium* and did not include the devil's pact or healing.

A change came with the Witchcraft Decree of 1617,[15] which also strongly impacted witchcraft trials. First, it incorporated a demonological definition of witches into the letter of the law: 'true'[16] witches were those who had associated with the devil or had something to do with him.[17] Second, healing was designated a criminal offence. Third, witches' accomplices were to be tried as well. This decree became the foundation of Danish Code of 1683, when complete national legal unity was reached.[18] The 1683 law prescribed fire at the stake as punishment for those who confessed to the devil's pact. Male witches intentionally causing harm, called 'malefice', were punished by working 'in iron' on Bremerholm[19] for the rest of their lives. Women were sentenced to work in a spinning factory.[20] For white magic, or benevolent magic, the punishment was banishment from the country and loss of goods.[21] Accomplices were punished by public penitence for a first time[22] and fines for a second time.[23] There was an imperative command that death sentences in witchcraft trials conducted in first instance court should be passed on to a higher court for confirmation, and in 1686, a decree was issued stating that sentences in witchcraft trials should not be executed before they had been brought to the highest court.[24]

Persecution

In 1080, Pope Gregory VII wrote to Danish King Harald,[25] warning him against accusing women of causing changes in temperature, creating storms, or inflicting diseases on humans. For the next four hundred years, sorcery was only occasionally mentioned in Danish sources. Cases of sorcery and witchcraft reached Danish courts only in the early sixteenth century.[26] There was a difference between individual witchcraft trials, based on *maleficium* ideas, and witchcraft panics, based on demonological ideas. The *maleficium* trials dealt with individuals' abilities to harm without the agency of the devil. The witchcraft panics involved a pact with the devil or his assistants. Around the mid-1500s, Denmark had become part of the European witchcraft tradition, as evident from church murals from this time, which reveal a close connection between witches and the devil.[27]

In the early witchcraft trials in Denmark, weather magic was known through two catastrophic events, which occurred in 1543 and 1566 and both resulted in the shipwrecks of royal Danish ships. These accidents were allegedly caused by performed witchcraft.[28] The first event, in 1543, occurred when some witches outside Elsinore allegedly bewitched a fleet of twenty-four ships to be used in the ongoing war against Holy Roman Emperor Charles V.[29] The second was in 1566, when witches in Copenhagen outside the coast of Gotland were said to have conjured a storm in which the best ships of the fleet went down. The events led to witchcraft panics, with many accused witches involved. Denunciation played an important part and demonological ideas, like witches' gatherings, surfaced.[30] Witchcraft trials were held in Copenhagen, Elsinore, and Malmø. Hence, during the mid-1500s, witchcraft trials related to weather magic and demonological ideas had obtained a foothold in Denmark, which contributed to the continuation of trials. However, notions of *maleficium* were activated during these trials as well. Thus, early Danish witchcraft trials point to a range of ideas related to demonology as well as *maleficium*, that came to influence subsequent witchcraft persecution in the country.

In 1590, famous witchcraft trials took place in Copenhagen. From the Trier region and the territory of the Imperial Abbey of St Maximin in south-western Germany, where intense demonological witchcraft trials took place from 1585 to 1596, rumours spread northwards.[31] News about these trials reached Denmark. This is seen among others in the tract *Troldfolck*, which mentions the intense trials in Trier and St Maximin. The tract was translated from German into Dutch and printed in Cologne in 1589, and would probably have been known in Denmark from this year onwards.[32] The Trier trials may have fuelled the 1590 witchcraft trials in Copenhagen. Even if the idea of witches conjuring a storm was known in Denmark from before, in two incidents, the Copenhagen 1590 trials were certainly triggered by new demonological notions reaching the country. Ideas from the Copenhagen trials influenced the North Berwick trials in Scotland.[33] After the trials in Copenhagen in 1590, demonological ideas were transferred to Scotland, both by King James VI himself and by travelling persons and diplomatic correspondence.[34] The Copenhagen witchcraft trials in 1590–91 also comprised weather magic and demonological ideas, and other trials followed in Zealand, Malmø, and Funen.[35]

After 1617, the number of witchcraft trials increased. In fact, 60% of Danish witchcraft trials took place between 1617 and 1625, while '[f]rom 1625 until the early 1650s there was a slow but steady trickle of trials'.[36] In the 1680s, a final flare-up occurred, primarily due to the role played by a minor nobleman.[37] The last witchcraft trial ending in execution was the trial of Anne Palles in 1693.[38]

In total, two thousand witchcraft trials are known to have occurred in Denmark between 1536 and 1693. Out of Denmark's population of 570,000 in 1600, approximately four hundred people were executed during these trials.[39] Compared to other European countries—such as Switzerland, parts of Germany, and Scotland—witchcraft persecution in Denmark must be considered as average in its intensity.[40] Most Danish witchcraft trials were related to *maleficium*. However, confessions about entering into a devil's pact did occur, and so did references to witches' gatherings.[41] Jens Chr. V. Johansen says:

> One reason why Danish trials never reached mass proportions must be found in the lack of a widespread and shared notion of the Sabbat and the all-important role of the Devil. An idea existed of an organization among the witches, who met at specific times.[42]

Also, the demonological idea of witches having a personal demon was quite common in Denmark: some female witches were believed to have a demonic helper, who were called as a *dreng*, a servant boy, or Apostle.[43] They obtained this personal demon when they entered into the pact with the devil himself. The demon could shape-shift into a dog or another animal, and was sent out to enter houses, cause shipwrecks, and bewitch victims, often in connection with collective witchcraft-related activities.[44]

The typical Danish witch is described by Johansen as a woman who was married but past childbearing age.[45] Often, she was rumoured to be a witch. The majority of Danish witchcraft trials took place in the countryside, where almost 90% of the population lived at the time. Danish witchcraft accusations centred on two subjects: the death or illness of humans and the death or illness of farm animals.

A few theologians contributed with their writing to the Danish witch-hunt after the Reformation. One of these was Peder Palladius, who studied in Wittenberg under Luther. He was elected bishop in Zealand in 1537 and travelled around in his district in 1538–43, giving sermons that were later collected and published.[46] His preached harshly against witches and emphasized that it was not only the state's responsibility to extinguish them; it was also the duty of each individual. In addition, learned ideas about witchcraft were known partly through the work of a famous theologian, Niels Hemmingsen, who was a professor—first in Greek, later in theology—at the University of Copenhagen. He studied in Wittenberg from 1537 to 1542 under Philip Melanchthon. In 1574, he published *Syntagma institutionum cristianorum*, but was obliged to retract it in 1576 following pressure from Augustin I of Saxony, who considered it to be crypto-Calvinism. In 1575, Hemmingsen published a warning against practising witchcraft, *Admonitia de superstionibus magical vitandis*, an important text on demonology and witchcraft in the sixteenth century. He used a broad definition of witchcraft that included all superstitious and magical behaviour. Hemmingsen maintained that most of the devil's power lay in illusions, and that witches performed physically impossible things only in dreams. He did not believe in shape-shifting, witches' gatherings, or witches' flight. He also claimed that the water ordeal was unreliable since it relied on superstition, which the devil could manipulate. Hemmingsen was dismissed from his professorship because his views—on the holy sacraments, for one—deviated from those of the official Lutheran Church. Even after his dismissal, however, his demonological treatise continued to have an effect among students, both in Denmark and in Northern Germany.

The theological dimension had an impact on jurisdiction, as witchcraft was interpreted as renouncing Christianity. Still, it should be kept in mind that witchcraft trials were judicial operations that were held before the courts, and only the legal apparatus could pronounce a death sentence in Denmark. At the beginning of the eighteenth century, the understanding of the magical element and its importance for the legal field changed to scepticism, influenced by ideas from the Age of Enlightenment. This held true for the entire learned field. The views of the clerics changed as well.[47] Jens Chr. V. Johansen has argued that Danish clerics did little to persecute witches, and that Danish ministers were influenced by the Lutheran Johannes Brenz, among others. He emphasized that suffering came from God and not from the evil deeds of witches. These ideas played a role in the cessation of witchcraft trials in Denmark.[48]

Prelude to the Copenhagen Witchcraft Trials of 1590

On 20 August 1589, at Kronborg Castle in Denmark, Frederic II of Denmark's second daughter, Princess Anne, married James VI *per procura*.[49] A man from the Scottish court—Lord Marischal, George Keith—was standing in for King James. On 1 September 1589, Princess Anne left for Scotland, her ship one of four in a small fleet sent by the Danish king. Admiral Peder Munk was the leader of the fleet, which immediately encountered problems. A storm and leaking ships prevented the fleet's crossing of the North Sea, and it sought harbour at the south-western coast of Norway, in the village of Flekkerø. After several attempts at crossing the North Sea, the fleet turned around on 29 September. One ship brought Princess

Anne to the Norwegian capital Oslo; it was decided that she should stay there for the winter.

In Scotland, King James prepared to receive his bride. The servants of the king's late mother—Mary, Queen of Scots—were busy preparing for the new queen.[50] Then, an accident occurred. Lady Kennedy, Queen Mary's former lady-in-waiting, died when the ferry from Burntisland to Leith capsized in September 1589: 'the vehement storm drave a ship forcibly upon the said boat [the ferry]'.[51]

Admiral Peder Munk wrote about the Danish fleet's turning back: 'We were half way between Scotland and Norway'.[52] Two ships sailed to Copenhagen and arrived there on 14 October. One ship sailed to Edinburgh, where Danish messenger Sten Bille arrived in Leith on 10 October.[53] Bille brought official letters saying that the Danish ships had been 'tresindstyve mile'[54] from the Scottish coast when they turned, which is much more than halfway. He could tell more about the hardships the princess had been exposed to and went straight to King James VI at Craigmillar Castle to have a meeting. Thomas Fowler wrote in a letter from 20 October:

> Steven Beale, a Dane, had arrived with message about the storm; the ships had been *thrown back* and had to seek shelter at the coast of Norway. In his company is a Scottish gentleman of the Earl Marishal's train, Andrew Synk[l]er by name, who says that the princess is in good health, and her company, but sorely beaten with the seas. She put out twice for this coast, but both times *driven back by contrary winds*.[55] [My italics.]

William Ashby, Queen Elizabeth I's ambassador to the Scottish court, wrote to Lord Burghley, Queen Elizabeth I's chief minister, on 'Saturday xj of October 1589', the day after Bille's meeting with the king:

> Be the report of the gentlemen of Scotland quhilk arrived upon the x day in the morning, it is understand that the Quene and all the flete has bene in greit payne and dangier, having at five severall tymes bene drevin bak be storme and contrarious wyndis, sundrie of the schippis being lek, and specialie that quhairin the Quene wes.[56]

These letters, written by people at court, strongly emphasise the storm that prevented Princess Anne from going to Scotland as well as the danger she had been in. State correspondence, especially diplomatic correspondence, repeats that there was a storm on Michaelmas, St Michael's Day, with strong headwinds. While witchcraft was not directly mentioned during the first weeks after the failure to take the future queen across the North Sea, there was a feeling at court that the storms had to do with sorcery and enchantment. And all these bad omens were felt and commented upon at the Scottish court. On 28 November, William Ashby wrote to Michael Throckmorton: 'Doubts not but the storm will be overblown, and hopes to see *those make shipwreck that have by their enchantments raised the tempest*'.[57] [My italics.]

This feeling of uneasiness characterized the voyage from the very beginning, as bad omens turned up from then onwards. The fleet of the Danish king experienced several accidents. First, a gunner was shot dead in Copenhagen on 1 September, just as the ships were about to leave the city. Then, one of the cannons on board the ship got loose and killed several sailors in front of Princess Anne's eyes before it rolled overboard. Then, there were four weeks of continuous storms, culminating in the Michaelmas storm, when they finally had to give up the voyage. One ship got loose from its anchor and crashed into another ship, and two sailors were killed in an effort to keep the ships apart. The date of the Michaelmas storm was important, as the Danish as well as the Scottish witches who were accused later confessed to having raised the storm this day.[58] The idea of witches creating a storm to delay Princess Anne is also commented upon by Patrick Anderson, in a continuation of Hector Boece's history book:

> {written in margin—Tempests raised by magicians} Many there were that thought these tempests were raised by the Sorceries of Magicians and Witches for the winds were more blustering, the seas more rough and loftie, the gusts more schort and frequent then those which proceed of naturall causes; and that the devills the princes of the ayre do raige more licenciousely amongest the Northen Nations which are Barbarously simpell.
>
> And indeed these mens opinions are confirmed by certane Magicians and Witches taken after th[a]t in Scotland, who confessed oppenly at there tryalls, that they had raised these stormes to dryve the Queene frome the coasts of Scotland.[59]

The Leith ferry accident in Scotland, during which Lady Kennedy drowned, was linked to the turning around of the Danish fleet in the North Sea. Just one week after the failure of Princess Anne's fleet, the two accidents—which both affected the Scottish king—were commented upon in court circles. This linking of the accidents was crucial for the development of the witchcraft trials in Copenhagen in 1590 and also came to be important for the North Berwick witchcraft trials in Scotland in 1590–91. On 8 October, William Ashby wrote to Lord Burghley:

> The wind has continued south and south-west since the princess's first embarking, which are flat contrary, and have been so strong as no vessel could come to bring news. This long uncertainty brings fear of some disaster, that is increased by two ominous chances, as they are here interpreted. The [one] upon her embarking a great pe[ce in the] amiralles ship brake in shoting and killed tow o[r thre] of the gonners. Th'other chance hapened h[ere] in the Firth: a boote passing from Bru[nt] Island in Fiffe the 8 of Sept. towardes [Lythe], *in the midwaie being under saile*, and the tempest growing verie great caried th[em] with such force upon a ship under saile as the boote presentlie suncke, and almost a[ll the] passengers drowned; *emongest whom was [Madam] Kenedie, who was with the late Quene in Eng[land]*, and divers gentlewomen

and marcha[nts] of Edenbrowghe, *to the nomber of fourtie that per[ished], with plate and hangings brought hither f[or] the mariage, which was all lost.*[60] [My italics.]

The interpretation that the ferry accident in Scotland was influenced by witches spread in royal circles. King James's brother-in-law, Sir James Melville, wrote in his diary that Scottish witches confessed to having raised a storm and 'drowned the gentlewoman and all the persons, except two'.[61]

The king, full of feelings about these chances, the long delay, and the head-winds, sought refuge in God and commanded public fast and prayer. That autumn, he mostly stayed at Craigmillar Castle, which had been his mother's castle as well. He had difficult decisions to make. On the other side of the North Sea, on 14 October, the two Danish ships from the royal fleet that had been stranded in Norway reached Copenhagen, and the same day, Thomas Tennecker, English ambassador to Denmark, wrote to Walsingham—principal secretary to Elizabeth I from 1573 until his death in 1590—from Copenhagen:[62]

I have no good newes at the present too wryt of (. . .) by contrary wyndes the kings shippes w[i]th the lady anna skotse queen are retorned clld not recover skotland being allso loath too send [*page damaged*] ther great shippes on that dangerous coast so late in the year w[hi]ch must nede be a great greeff on boath syds.[63]

And the king himself wrote just before he left for Norway same autumn:

These reasons, and innumerable others howerlie objected, moved me to hasten the treatie of my mariage: for as to my owne nature, God is my witnesse I could have absteined longer nor the weill of my patrie could have permitted. (. . .) This treatie then beinge perfited, and the Quene my bedfellow cuming on hir journey, how the contrarious windes stayed hir and where she was driven it is more then notorious to all men (. . .) The word then comminge to me that *she was stayed from cuming through the notorious tempestes of windes (. . .) I, upon the instant, yea verie moment, resolved to make possible on my part that which was impossible on hirs (. . .)* The place where I resolved this in was Cragmillar, not one of the whole Counsell being present their. And as I take this resolution onelie of my self, *as I am a trew prince, so advised with my self onelie what way to follow fourth the same.*[64] [My italics.]

On 24 October 1589, King James left the harbour of Leith in Scotland 'in the night', and was driven back by a sudden storm at Pittenweem, where he stayed until the morning of 25 October.[65] He 'arryvitt att Fleckra the 29 of the same', William Hunter writes to William Ashby on 3 November, and he makes it a point that 'The Kingis majestie was never sick'.[66] After the stop in Flekkerø, the same place where the Danish fleet sought shelter, King James went to Oslo to meet Anne, his bride. On 23 November 1589, he ratified the marriage contract. Two days later, on 25 November 1589, there was a solemn wedding ceremony at Old Bishop's Palace in Oslo, at which delegates from Scotland were present.[67] The royal couple did not stay long in Oslo. On 22 December, they left the Norwegian capital and went to Elsinore, where they remained at the court for about four months. During this stay, King James had conversations with two widely known Danes: theologian Niels Hemmingsen and astronomist Tycho Brahe. The conversations with Tycho Brahe must have been exciting for a king who probably related astronomy to a type of magical performance.[68] Born in 1513, Hemmingsen was an old man in 1590, living in the town of Roskilde.[69] It is known that Niels Hemmingsen and King James talked about predestination.[70] It is not known whether they discussed demonological details, but at this time King James was already interested in learned demonology, and he knew several European demonological works. A few years later, in 1597, he became the only monarch in Europe to publish a demonological treatise, *Daemonologie in Forme of a Dialogue*.[71]

On 21 April, a fleet from the Danish king left Copenhagen with the royal couple on board, heading for Scotland nine months after the first attempt with Princess Anne on board. Again, Admiral Peder Munk was the leader of the fleet. They arrived in Leith on 1 May 1590. Anne was crowned Scottish Queen on 17 May 1590, during a magnificent coronation ceremony at which Peder Munk was present as well.[72] Two days later, she arrived in Edinburgh under a grand ceremony.[73]

Witchcraft Trials in Copenhagen, 1590

The original court records from the witchcraft trials in Copenhagen in 1590 have a peculiar prehistory.[74] Although Henrik Carl Bering Liisberg's book *Vesten for Sø og østen for Hav: Trolddom i København og i Edinburgh 1590: et Bidrag til Hekseprocessernes Historie*, published in 1909,[75] contains a narrative about the royal Danish fleet's voyage and the trials, it does not have any exact references to archival sources. Obviously, Liisberg must have seen the original documents. Danish historians have otherwise only briefly mentioned the 1590 witchcraft trials in Copenhagen.[76] The reason for the lack of studies is probably that these court records were archived in an unexpected place in Denmark's National Archive and have therefore not been used by scholars for a long time.[77] I rediscovered these court records by chance in 2016.[78] They are the main sources documenting the Copenhagen witchcraft trials of 1590 and they give new perspectives to the Scottish North Berwick trials.[79] Other preserved records valuable for elucidating these trials are the Court of Appeal records of the trial of Margrete, the wife of Jacob the Scribe.[80]

The trials against these women are remarkable. The witchcraft trials bring us into the royal circles of Denmark and Scotland. Before King James and his bride left Denmark in spring 1590, several women in Copenhagen were accused of witchcraft and tried before the court. Admiral Peder Munk actively brought up these cases. The women were accused of having performed witchcraft to prevent Princess Anne from coming to Scotland in the autumn of 1589.[81] News of these trials spread rapidly in Danish court circles and via diplomatic correspondence. Thus,

King James certainly knew about them and could bring the news back to Scotland with him.

The first woman accused was Ane Koldings, called 'the Devil's mother'. Her case came up in April 1590. She confessed that Jacob the Scribe had asked her whether she and her fellows could bewitch the royal fleet. Demonological ideas were activated during the trial, including witches' gatherings, collective performance of witchcraft, and personal demons. Her Apostle was a personal demon that accompanied her when she was going to perform evil deeds. This is a demonological idea that is also found in other countries.[82] Ane Kolding wanted to use the demon belonging to one of the other women as well as her own Apostle to go with her and see the condition of the people in the royal fleet. When interrogated and exposed to torture, she confessed that she had participated in performing witchcraft that stayed the fleet: '"The Miss"[83] should not come *the first time* to Scotland'. [My italics.] The expression 'the first time'[84] occurs several times in these court records, and refers to the Danish fleet's voyage in the autumn of 1589, in contrast to the voyage of spring 1590. With collective witchcraft being the assumption, Ane denounced nine other women in Copenhagen, of whom six were imprisoned and three were released on bail. Thus, the continuation of the trials was a fact. King James must have known the content of the accusations against Ane Kolding, because of sensational rumours. The accusations of witchcraft against the Danish fleet, with the bride of the Scottish king on board, could also be seen as an attack on royal persons beyond Denmark. It was not only directed towards the Danish King, but might be interpreted as an attack on King James as a political person, which meant treason. Demonological notions were brought to his attention as well. Ane received her death sentence on 20 May, at the city court in Copenhagen.[85] She was burned in the middle of June 1590 in Copenhagen, most likely after Admiral Peder Munk had returned to Denmark from Scotland.[86]

News about the first Danish trial related to witchcraft against the royal ships and Princess Anne travelled to London quickly. This might have had to do with Queen Elisabeth I's eagerness to know what happened to the Scottish king.[87] Only a week after the execution of Ane Koldings, this message was sent to London:

> The xvijth of this moneth thair was an wytch burnt at Copemanhaven convinced to have bewitched the Queenes voyage towards Scotland this last year, and at her death she confessed divers others and some chif women to have ben partakers of this Sorcery, the w[hi]ch be apprehended, and like to be punished.[88]

The court records preserved from these cases show that after Ane Koldings's execution on 15 June, witchcraft trials continued around mid-July 1590, when the other suspected women were brought to trial. There was a tense situation in Copenhagen after Admiral Peder Munk came back from Scotland. He actively accused the alleged witches and was struggling to free himself from the official failure to bring Princess Anne to Scotland in 1589.

In the summer of 1590, nine women were brought before the city court in Copenhagen, with Peder Munk playing an important role. Interrogation took place from 13 to 16 July 1590. All women confessed to witchcraft against the king's ships, and they were burned between 4 September 1590 and 17 February 1591, in less than six months. News about continued Danish witchcraft trials reached Scotland on 23 July through this message that arrived in Edinburgh:

> It is advertised from Denmark, that the admirall there hathe caused five or six witches to be taken in Coupnahaven, upon suspicion that by their witche craft they had staied the Queen of Scottes voiage into Scotland, and sought to have staied likewise the King's retorne.[89]

As the Copenhagen women were first brought before the court on 13 July, the message to Scotland must have been sent immediately. As the Admiral is not mentioned by name in this message, this may either mean that he was a well-known figure in Edinburgh and thus mentioning his name was considered unnecessary, or that his title was more important than his name in this correspondence.

On 13 July, Karen, the wife of the Weaver, was brought before the city court in Copenhagen. She confessed that Kirsten Söndags,[90] Margrete, the wife of Jacob the Scribe, and a farmer's wife had visited Margrete to ask whether she would send her Apostle Langinus[91] together with their Apostles to the king's ships set to sail to Scotland in order to destroy them. However, she said that she herself did not speak with Margrete. Karen further confessed that she had spoken with the farmer's wife and admonished her three times, for the sake of Christ's death and suffering, that she should not harm the king's ships because her husband, son, and son-in-law were on board. She also confessed that Kirsten Söndags took her Apostle from her and put him in an empty beer barrel, and that the same barrel and Apostles were close to the fleet at sea. Thereafter, the same farmer's wife came to Karen and asked her where her Apostle was, and she answered that he was there, next to the fleet. Then Karen answered that if she had known that they would use him for that purpose, she would not have lent him out. She also confessed that the farmer's wife said to her that the Miss[92] should not come to Scotland the first time[93] and that she sent her Apostle, Langinus, to the farmer's wife twice. She said that she admonished the same devil that he should pester the wife with pestilence and sickness[94] so that she would have a quick death and could not harm the king's ships or cause the death of anyone, because she had her husband, son, and son-in-law on board the ships.

Two days later, on 15 July, Maren, the wife of Mads the Brewer, was interrogated before the court. She confessed that she had been with the other women, in council and deed,[95] using pots to perform witchcraft in the house of Karen, the wife of the Weaver. Then she was asked which art they would perform with the pots, and what they meant. She answered that she believed that they would bewitch the ships to prevent them from reaching Scotland, and Maren swore on her soul and salvation[96] that Ane Koldings said to her that it had to do with bewitching the ships.

Here, there is a pause in the interrogation, when possibly the rack was in use, according to Liisberg. This is not entered into the court records, as it was illegal to use torture in Denmark and Norway before the sentence was passed.[97] When the interrogation continues, Maren is very willing to confess and denounce more women than she had before. Even more,[98] Maren confessed that Anne, the wife of Jesper, Kirsten Söndags, Ane Koldings, Karen, the wife of the Weaver, and she were gathered at the same time in the house of Karen, the wife of the Weaver. And they had clay pots on the table, and they wanted to prevent that the ships should come the first time to Scotland,[99] and on this she swore on her soul and salvation.

Maren, the Wife of Mogens, 1590

The Trial

The trial of Maren, the wife of Mogens, is a continuation of the previous trials. She was interrogated on 16 July. She had been rumoured to be engaged in witchcraft for many years and had been tried before, in 1578. That time, however, she was acquitted.[100] During the interrogation on 16 July, she first confessed that Margrete, the wife of Jacob the Scribe, participated in bewitching the king's ships,[101] so that they would not come to Scotland the first time, and that Margrete was as equally skilled in the art of witchcraft as she and the others were.[102] This means that Maren's confession started with a denunciation of Margrete.

Then she confessed that Margrete; Anne, the wife of Jesper; Ane Koldings; Kirsten Söndags; the farmer's wife; Karen, the wife of the Weaver; and she herself were gathered in the house of Karen, the wife of the Weaver,[103] to bewitch the king's ships, which she swore on her soul and salvation to be true, and on this she wanted to go to her death.[104] Further, Maren confessed that Ane Koldings had admitted to her that Jacob the Scribe had asked her [Ane] about bewitching the king's ships.[105] Thus, here we have Maren's own words stating that it was Jacob the Scribe who stood behind the evil act of witchcraft against the king's ships.

Here, they may have paused the interrogation, as the next paragraph starts with '*Item*'.[106] It is possible that the rack had been used in the meantime.[107] As the next point, she was asked about when they were gathered to bewitch the king's ships so that the fleet would not come to Scotland. She answered that it was last year around Michaelmas,[108] which is 29 September. She was very accurate about the date, and for good reasons. This date was of uttermost importance, which will be seen in the further development of the case. This date also created a link to Scotland. Michaelmas was supposed to be one of the days during the year when evil forces were at work. So it was important to have it recorded that the gathering of women in the house of Karen, the wife of the Weaver, took place on this particular day.

Maren, the wife of Mogens, confessed and swore, as true as she intended to become a child of God,[109] that Ane Koldings came to her and asked her if she would let her devil Pilhestskou[110] follow her Apostle Smuck[111] to the king's ships to see how they were doing, according to a request of Jacob the Scribe,[112] because

Jacob had promised her that she would be rewarded for this, which was also the case for the others. Maren confessed that Kirsten Söndags had borrowed the devil Langinus from Karen, the wife of the Weaver. Kirsten had put him in an empty beer barrel and afterwards commanded him to go to the ships, as they were on their voyage, which he also did, and the Apostles arrived at the ships at the same time.[113]

The Danish royal court was fully aware of the ongoing witchcraft trials. On 22 July, the Danish king wrote in a letter that efforts should be made to secure the three women, who were released on bail.[114] The trials continued, focusing on Margrete, the wife of Jacob the Scribe, and also on Jacob the Scribe himself, who was accused as well. Jacob fled from prison but was arrested and brought back to Copenhagen on 22 August. The executions also continued. On 4 September, two alleged witches were burned, possibly Maren, the wife of Mogens, and Karen, the wife of the Weaver.[115]

The Voice of Maren, the Wife of Mogens

The voice of Maren, the wife of Mogens, is one of several voices shaping a collective narrative about the witchcraft against the Danish king's ships. She complements an existing story told in the confessions of those previously interrogated, sticking to the core of the story and following the storyline but providing a few more details. Thus, to a certain extent, she gives the existing narrative an individual touch. However, the confession of Maren is an enforced narrative, in the sense that she knew that torture could be used to extract it. Her confession is clearly directed by leading questions of the interrogators. Still, even as an enforced narrative, her urge to establish narrative structures is predominant, like sticking to a timeline, the delegation of voices to actors, and variation in the narrative's speed.

Maren's voice has various accents. It reveals her knowledge of demonological ideas, traditional performance of witchcraft, *maleficium*, and folkloric ideas known by common people at the time. Maren's confession is a mix of learned notions and common people's understanding of witchcraft, and is a good illustration of the interplay that exists between different spheres of ideas that emerge in witchcraft trials. Her voice echoes the judiciary's thoughts as well as the peasant's traditional ideas.

The interrogators would want to have repeated and strengthened the previous confessions about witchcraft against the king's ships. Sometimes the questions are rendered in the records; sometimes it is possible to trace shadow questions by scrutinizing the answers she gave. Following the direction of the interrogation, the first point is the denunciation of Margrete; the second is the denunciation of the six women, who in addition to Maren, the wife of Mogens allegedly took part in the gathering in the house of Karen, the wife of the Weaver; the third is the involvement of Jacob the Scribe; the fourth is the question about when the witchcraft gathering took place; the fifth is her lending out her Apostle to Ane Koldings to perform witchcraft against the king's ships; and the sixth is about the Apostle of Kirsten Söndags, who was also lent out to perform witchcraft against the kings' ships.

Demonological ideas are brought to the fore partly by questions posed to Maren. These ideas mainly have to do with witches' gatherings, personal demons, and denunciations—all notions that relate to dangerous, demonological witchcraft. Ideas about witches' gatherings and the performance of collective witchcraft are connected to a meeting the women were alleged to have had with the intention to stay the royal fleet in autumn 1589. Personal demons were sent out to help. Within demonological thought, personal demons are supposed to be given to a person entering the devil's pact. Personal demons are thus an implicit marker of the devil's pact. It is an element known in various versions in several European countries.[116]

During witchcraft interrogation, denunciations emerge as a result of the idea of witches' gatherings, at either witchcraft sabbaths or the performance of collective witchcraft. It is the same in Maren's confession: several denunciations occurred, underlining the witches' meeting as well as emphasizing the participation of Margrete, the wife of Jacob the Scribe, who is described as being 'as good as' the rest of them. In addition to the six women denounced, Maren provides the name of Jacob the Scribe as the one who allegedly requested the women to perform witchcraft, promising a reward. This point brings another level of authority into the witchcraft operation, as he was a well-renowned person. That he should be the one behind the witchcraft operation enables an explanation connected to court circles and political motifs. Jacob the Scribe had earlier been *Borgmester*,[117] and he was acquainted with many people at court. He had also had a disagreement with Admiral Peder Munk, and was supposedly hit by him. Widening the circle of suspects to include more than a group of women made it more plausible that the aim of the witchcraft operation was to harm royals. In this respect, the voice of Maren, the wife of Mogens, points to the later connection of these cases to the Scottish North Berwick trials of 1590–91.

Ideas about *maleficium* merge with demonological ideas in Maren's confession. We hear about traditional *maleficium* notions related to the use of objects. At the witches' meeting, the women would have used clay pots, and Maren's Apostle, her demon, was placed in an empty beer barrel and sent out to the fleet in the North Sea. The use of objects, along with the use of charms, was common in traditional witchcraft, whether harmful or beneficent. Maren seamlessly weaving together the use of objects and demonological ideas is a sign of how ideas about witchcraft might root themselves in a society's mental realm and be transformed into a new version of a demonological narrative, adapted to local conditions.

Folkloric notions are echoed in Maren's confession. There is an interest on the part of the interrogator to have the day of the witches' gathering mentioned. Maren's answer is Michaelmas. This is an example of folkloric notions being included in a witchcraft confession, for instance the mentioning of a particular day on which evil forces were known to be out, often forces from the other world. By posing a question about a special day for the witches' meeting, the interrogators signal that they would like to have the coinciding of witchcraft and Michaelmas confirmed.

Orality markers are strong in the confession of Maren, the wife of Mogens. The names of the Apostles are either biblical or connected to folk belief, and are rather humorous or a play on words. Additive sentence structures are common throughout her confession and in particular phrases with alliteration, like she swore 'on her soul and salvation' and *med sott och Siugdomb*.[118] The use of repetition is strong. Examples are the repeated phrase about 'the first time to Scotland' and the repetition of *Kongens skibe*. The scribe recorded the oral features of Maren's discourse, signalling a desire to record the words she uttered during the interrogation as precisely as possible in order to preserve her personal language.

The voice of Maren, the wife of Mogens, is a voice that has given in from the beginning of the trial. In the preceding days, she has seen and heard what happened to the other accused women. There is no denial, no protest, no anger in her voice, and at the other end of the scale there is no hope or optimism. In Maren's voice, there are echoes of sorrow. She has come to an insight about her fate. She is not pitying herself. Her voice is indifferent, flat. Maren's confession does not start with a denial of witchcraft but with a denunciation of Margrete. Usually, the denunciation comes at the end of a witchcraft interrogation, helped by leading questions. Here, it is the opposite. It signals that she has understood that it is best to cooperate. She is forthcoming with her knowledge and her story, but there is no power in her way of telling it. However, a bit of pride can be noticed in her bringing forth ideas of *maleficium* and folklore. Her voice is more or less a voice repeating motifs already heard before the court. When the interrogation comes to an end and she is urged to provide more names of suspects, she does what is expected from her. Even if several names have been mentioned already, it is important to the interrogators to reinforce the previous denunciations.

Although the voice we hear is resigned, the language is coherent and clear. Her voice does not flounder or hesitate, but provides distinctly formulated answers to all questions posed. She is not expressing fear but is formulating a story that she seems to know well. It is a confession leading to her death sentence, but she is still showing her strength as a narrator. Her voice displays knowledge of learned ideas as well as knowledge of traditional beliefs.

Other Female Voices

The voices of women in the Copenhagen court records are blended. The trials continued after the burnings of the women accused in July. One of the voices that indirectly comes to the fore is the voice of Margrete, the wife of Jacob the Scribe. In the confessions given in July, the witchcraft operation was explained as a work ordered by Jacob the Scribe.

The name of Margrete, the wife of Jacob the Scribe, is first mentioned when she is denounced by Karen, the wife of the Weaver, and also by Maren, the wife of Mogens. What is furthermore recorded about Margrete stems partly from the court records of the Copenhagen witchcraft trials in July 1590 and partly from a defence plea written and signed by her brother's son Hans Olsen. The latter was to be used when her case was brought before the Court of Appeal, *Landstinget*, which was obligatory for all death sentences in witchcraft trials in Denmark.[119] To explain why he, being her nephew, writes the defence document, Hans Olsen states that Margrete's husband is imprisoned and that Margrete has very few relatives. He says that, on behalf of Margrete, he cannot understand whether the sixteen men of the jury in the Copenhagen trial had sworn right or false.[120] He repeatedly states that the testimonies have serious weak points and argues that the accusations are not sufficient to sentence Margrete to death.

The trial against Margrete must have started in August 1590, since a letter mentions it in the beginning of September the same year.[121] On 29 September, there was a search in the house of Jacob the Scribe to collect more material against Margrete. On 19 October, Margrete was sentenced to death by fire at the stake, and the case had to be sent to *Landstinget*.[122] Hans Olsen's plea was treated at *Landstinget*. Several witnesses gave their testimonies. However, the appeal to *Landstinget* was not successful; Margrete's death verdict was not altered.[123] Margrete was burned in 1591, while her husband, Jacob the Scribe, did not receive a death sentence. He had all his property sold on 8 July 1591[124] and ended his days in an institution for the poorest.

One of the witnesses recorded in Hans Olsen's document says that Margrete had been rumoured to be a witch for twenty years. In the confessions from the witchcraft trials of July 1590, she is mentioned as one of those who took part in the gathering on Michaelmas 1589. According to Karen, the wife of the Weaver, Margrete's Apostle was called Langinus. The Apostles were allegedly used, together with clay pots and beer barrels, to prevent the king's ships from sailing to Scotland for *the first time*. Margrete's husband, Jacob, the former *Borgmester*, was also accused. When his position is mentioned in English or Scottish letters, he is called 'bailiff', 'bailie', or 'consul'. In news sent over to England, the explanation of the witchcraft operation is that Jacob the Scribe wanted to take revenge on Peder Munk due to a quarrel they had had, and therefore ordered the witches to perform an operation. We see the same explanation in Scotland in the aftermath: in his memoirs, Sir James Melville of Halhill uses Munk hitting Jacob as the reason for these trials. Melville explains the raising of the storm in this way:

> Quhilk storm and wind was alleged to have been raisit by the witches of Denmark, by the confession of sundrie of them, when they were burnt for that cause. What moved them was a cuff, or blow, quhilk the Admiral of Denmark gave to *ane of the baillies of Copenhagen, whose wife being a notable witch*, consulted her cummers, and raised the said storm to be revengit upon the said Admiral. [My italics.][125]

Before Admiral Munk led the fleet to Scotland in April 1590, he had accused *Rentemester*[126] Christoffer Valkendorf of being responsible for the leaking ships in autumn 1589.[127] He claimed that in Valkendorf's position, securing the fleet of the Danish king was a duty. The case against Valkendorf was heard on 27 July and Munk lost on 4 August.

Witchcraft trials were certainly hot stuff, since details related to individuals were described. One of the learned men of Copenhagen, Paul Knibbe, wrote a letter from Kolding, dated 3 September 1590, to Daniel Rogers. It was received on 13 October 1590:

> Christopher Valckendorf was exempted from the position of governor (. . .) Our admiral [Peter Monck] [*sic*] has been made an inquisitor of the depravity of witches. Last year, when we were about to sail to Scotland, several wicked women conspired to drown[128] him, like some of them had freely confessed— having since been burned. But as the entire ship was to be destroyed, and the Queen of Scotland was likewise on board, they were not able to agree amongst themselves for a long time. Yet through the urging on of *the wife of Jakob Skriver* [Jacob the Scribe], consul of Copenhagen, they finally attempted it, and witnessed the powerful hand of God, which kept the most excellent sovereign and all of us in the same ship safe from the snares and follies of the Devil. When the consul, having been returned here [to Kolding] after fleeing, furthermore sought to break his thread of life by a noose in prison— brought about by the most apparent marks of his bad conscience—the nobles sent [him] to Copenhagen, along with his wife, to be examined there more thoroughly and submitted to due punishment. Travelling with them was the admiral—out of hatred for whom the very clear confessions [state] these sorceries to have been prepared—so that he might urge on the delaying magistrates.[129] [My italics.]

Christoffer Valkendorf was still dismissed from his position as governor.[130] In addition, Jacob the Scribe, in despair, tried to commit suicide in prison, something explained by his bad conscience. When the wife of Jacob the Scribe is mentioned in this letter, and also that husband and wife will be interrogated and punished, this is a continuation of the previous witchcraft trials. The letter indicates that the investigation has come closer to catching those who were really behind the witch-craft operation.

The Voices of the Witnesses

Like in other European countries, women in Denmark were allowed to testify in witchcraft trials. Of the witnesses brought before the court at *Landstinget* in the trial of Margrete, three were women: Jngeborg, the wife of Christen Holst; Anne And; and Boeldt, the wife of the Fribytter.[131] Jngeborg and Anne testify that Margrete asked which ship was named *Gideon*, the ship where the Miss was on board.[132] Hans Olsen comments that it did not seem to him that Margrete could be sentenced to death for this question, as no damage or destruction had happened.[133] He maintains that it was very common to ask such questions, particularly about big ships. Boeldt, the wife of the Fribytter, testifies that Margrete bewitched Master Niels Sommer, who was district master of the holy guest house.[134] Hans Olsen states that his opinion is that Margrete could not be sentenced to death based on this testimony. Two other witnesses, one woman and one man, counter Boeldt's testimony and claim that Niels Sommer died suddenly from a *pestelenndtze*.[135] Even Niels Sommer's wife gives Margrete a Christian and honest certificate of character and testimony.[136] The testimonies of the female witnesses do not differ much from the testimonies of male witnesses; all come up with possible accusations against Margrete.

However, there are other female voices indirectly referred to in Hans Olsen's defence document, supporting Olsen's argument that the contents of the testimonies given are not sufficient to support a death sentence for Margrete. Some of these voices come indirectly to the fore when male witnesses render their wives' statements. For instance, there is a testimony against Margrete that she performed witchcraft by measuring with her feet in the house of Hans the Baker.[137] Thereafter, some trolls had come into his boiling kettle, and great misfortune had fallen over him.[138] Hans Olsen states that in his opinion, this testimony could not harm Margrete, because according to Knud [*sic*] the Baker, his wife did not know whether Margrete was to blame for this. And she said that they did not know whom to blame for damage and misfortune without God.[139] Thus, we hear female voices arguing rationally and casting doubt on Margrete's guilt into consideration.

The three female witnesses brought before the court try to throw suspicion on Margrete by saying that she asked about the ship *Gideon* and that she had cast sickness on a man. However, their evidence is not very strong. But voices with different opinions also appear in Hans Olsen's defence writ, namely the voices of the male witnesses' wives. These voices are referred to indirectly but represent more rational explanations. One instance is the case of Hans the Baker's sickness, when Knud the Baker's wife testifies that Margrete was not to blame. Another woman gives Margrete a positive certification of character, saying that she is a good and Christian woman. A third woman argues that the deadly illness Margrete was supposed to have cast on Niels Sommer could just as well have been caused by the plague. Thus, the voices of female witnesses provide testimonies that on the one hand constitute accusations meant to harm Margrete but on the other hand form suggestions that reduce her guilt, with explanations other than witchcraft being the reason for sickness and death.

Collective Narrative

The voices of the accused women in Copenhagen in 1590 each contribute to a story about witchcraft against the king's ships, in which the addition of details and the repetition and reinforcement of events form a coherent collective narrative. The women know each other's names, except for the farmer's woman, who does not have a name. The full story is known to them all, but they promote certain events and fill in details according to their own style of storytelling and version of the story. Elements common to all are that the meeting took place in the house of Karen, the wife of the Weaver, that the participants performed witchcraft by using clay pots to raise a storm against the ships of the Danish king bringing Princess Anne to Scotland, and that the intention of this meeting was to prevent the Miss, in Danish *Frøkenen*, to come to Scotland 'the first time'. The witchcraft operation is said to have occurred around Michaelmas.[140] In addition, common to all is their cooperation when it came to performing evil deeds: they convened and borrowed the Apostles from one another. The idea that this operation was ordered by Jacob the Scribe exists from the beginning. The use of unrealistic features surfaces, like sending an Apostle in an empty beer barrel to the king's fleet in the North Sea.

The voices of the accused women establish a collective confession with narrative structures: a timeline, an order of events, the delegation of voices to the individuals taking part, and a mixture of dialogue and storytelling. Moreover, we have additive structures in abundance, for instance an accumulation of redundant words and embellishing adjectives. In addition, clear markers of orality emphasize the connection between the confessions and an oral society where stories spread easily.

Mette Lauridsdatter Kongens, 1618

The Trial

Mette Lauridsdatter[141] Kongens was a shepherd in Ørting, married to Hans the Shepherd.[142] She was the mother of a small boy, so she was probably in her twenties or thirties. Mette was brought before the court in Viborg on 18 July 1618.[143] She had been denounced by another woman, Maren Alrøds, who was tried in June 1618. Maren was part of a panic in the district of Åkjær in the municipality of Hads, which fell under the jurisdiction of Viborg Landsting. In 1618, eight people were accused of witchcraft in this district, with two more accused in 1619, all due to denunciations.[144] Local police officer[145] Laurids Ebbesen saw to it that the denunciations were followed up by the court. The trials lasted from June 1618 until June 1619. Before the panic of 1618–19, there were witchcraft trials in the Århus district in 1590–91 and in 1612–13.[146] After 1619, there were no more witchcraft trials in this district.

The panic started with the trial of Maren Alrøds. She was an elderly widow, married to Anders. She was first accused by Søren Jensen, who said she had threatened to put a clamp on him so that he would fade away as dew before the sun.[147] Second, Knud Jensen claimed that she had been the reason for a disease that affected his genitals after Maren promised him misfortune because he had beaten her daughter. Third, Simon Jørgensen testified that ten years prior, he chased a cow from the churchyard at the minister's request and threw a stone after it, so that it was hurt. Maren had promised him bad luck for this, and right afterwards he became sick and lost his vigour permanently. Then the brother of Maren testified that if Simon Jørgensen had not beaten his sister's cow, he would have looked better, which is an indirect admission of Maren's blame for his sickness. Next, the sons of Rasmus Pedersen testified that on his sickbed, their father blamed Maren for his disease because she had promised him evil. In addition, the minister and twenty-four men swore that Maren had been rumoured to be a witch since the quarrel with Knud Jensen. Maren defended herself, saying that the sickness on his secret member was due to drunkenness. She refused to confess, but she did not provide witnesses to swear a compurgation oath for her.[148] On 6 June 1618, Viborg Landsting confirmed an oath sworn by the minister and twenty-four men appointed by the church that Maren was rumoured to be a witch.[149] After this, Maren delivered several confessions and denounced ten people, resulting in six trials with five convictions. On 29 August, there is mention of her execution.

One of the elements in Maren's confession was a gathering of witches[150] at which they had all assumed the shape of cats, so that they would not recognize each other. The gathering had taken place on Michaelmas the previous year, and they had danced in order to cast scabies and sickness on human beings, a spell which changed direction and came over the sheep. Mette Kongens,[151] her husband, Hans the Shepherd, and Maren herself performed another evil deed: they ploughed one evening to 'turn the rain', so that the barley was destroyed. However, they were disturbed and did not succeed. Maren also confessed to a witches' dance at Guldhøj on St Valborg's night.[152] In her confession, she also denounced Mette the Baker, saying that Mette was as good at witchcraft as she (Maren) was and that she also had given herself to the devil.[153] This is the closest one can come to the idea of the devil's pact in the witchcraft court records from Northern Jutland.[154]

The trial of Mette Kongens was started by Laurids Ebbesen of Tulstrup, the local police officer who also initiated Maren's trial. Also representing the legal authorities were commander of Skanderborg, Hans Wise Boedt, and bailiff of the same place, Jacob Jensen.[155] Mette Kongens was accused of acts of witchcraft that she allegedly performed.[156] She denied, but confessed to having made the sign of the cross over Brunk Pedersen and having cured cattle in the name of the Holy Trinity. She said she had performed no evil after the king's letter about witchcraft was issued, which included healing as a deed to be punished.[157] However, on 22 June, the local court of Hads swore[158] that she was guilty of witchcraft, and on 18 July *Landstinget* confirmed this oath.[159] In the meantime, she had tried to flee from prison, but was apprehended and brought back to custody.[160] From 22 July until 17 August, she gave eight confessions. They were given after she had been to *Landstinget* and most likely after torture.[161] She denounced no less than twenty-four people, of whom ten were burned. On 29 August, Mette Kongens is first mentioned to have died, but the date of her execution is unknown.

Several witnesses were brought before the court during the trial of Mette Kongens. All testimonies were about her performance of healing, which mostly had a good outcome. However, one of the witnesses testified that his illness had become worse after her healing: Brunk Pedersen from Ørridslev, 15 to 20 kilometres from Ørting. Pedersen gave his testimony about his meeting with Mette Kongens from his sickbed, and it was brought to court by other people, as he could not come to court himself.[162] He testified that a year earlier, he had wanted to go to a barber[163] in order to be treated with cupping glasses.[164] On his way to the barber, his wagon toppled over, and he asked a boy nearby whether there were some people who could help raise the wagon. The boy fetched his mother, Mette Kongens, who had been asleep. She asked him where he lived and where he wanted to drive to. He told her, and she answered that she knew about his illness and had thought several times of going to him to tell him that his disease could not be cured by the barber.[165] In other words, Mette allegedly knew that this man, living a good distance from her, was sick, and she knew what ailed him. She arranged that he first came to her for healing, when he was still able to walk.[166] A few days later, she came to his home, went to his bed, made the sign of the cross over him, recited a prayer, and gave his mother a drink that he was supposed to drink the following Sunday morning before the sun went up. He did. However, the following Tuesday he lost the function of his feet. After that, he never walked.[167]

The other witnesses testified that Mette Kongens had cured sick cattle and predicted the sex of calves. In addition, she had always been suspected of dealing with 'ghost, cross and healing'.[168] One witness, Jens Jensen, testified that there were rumours that a black-billed magpie with holes through both wings jumped behind Mette Kongens, and that this bird allegedly belonged to Maren Alrøds.

In addition, the fate of Mette Kongens's husband was mentioned by one witness, Jens Mikkelsen. He testified that shortly before Mette was imprisoned, her husband was sitting in Jens's house and cried because he was afraid that she would be imprisoned, as people said that his wife had had something to do with Maren Alrøds.[169] He offered to give a cow to the king and a sow to Jens Mikkelsen in order to be left in peace.[170] Jens Kjær from Ørting testified that when Maren Alrøds was brought before *Landstinget*,[171] Hans the Shepherd asked him what would happen with the woman who was brought before the court, and Jens answered nothing other than she would be burned at the stake.[172] Then Hans the Shepherd said that he wished to be out in the blue water, where it was deepest, because he feared that he would be imprisoned the same evening.[173] Jens Kjær answered that it was bad that he wished disaster upon himself. The same evening, Hans the Shepherd disappeared and was not found again.

The Voice of Mette Lauridsdatter Kongens

The voice of Mette Lauridsdatter Kongens comes to the fore partly in her own confession, partly in testimonies provided by the witnesses, and partly in confessions of other people accused of witchcraft. Her voice is rendered primarily in indirect speech, third-person narration, but utterances in first person are heard too. Also, her knowledge is displayed and her voice is heard in a prayer for healing, which is recited in court.

In her own confession, her voice is strong and consistent. First of all, we hear an accent of denial when it comes to the performance of witchcraft. Mette says that she is not guilty of witchcraft.[174] Anger is heard in this denial, which is delivered at a time when she still had the power to protest. She never admits to having performed witchcraft, even if she confessed to healing. The evil deeds Mette ostensibly performed were alleged by witnesses or confessed to by Maren Alrøds during her trial.

Mette Kongens was a professional healer, and this accent comes to the fore in her voice. She clearly believes in her own healing activity and always emphasizes that sick people and cattle became better after she had made the sign of the cross over them.[175] She confesses without hesitation that she had healed and made the sign of the cross over Brunk Pedersen, the same with the drink she made for him with vinegar, which she gave to his mother.[176] She emphasizes that her healing was performed with God's help.[177] The prayer of healing that she read over Brunk, which she recites in court, uses the names of the Virgin Mary and Jesus.[178] She states that she had done nothing evil since the royal letter of 1617 was issued, an act which made healing a criminal offence.[179] This means that she was aware that healing was considered a crime to be persecuted. Fear can be heard when she mentions the royal decree of 1617. However, her healing activity has another side as well: pride can be perceived in her voice when she mentions it, and the recital of charms is also a sign of her knowledge, of which she is proud.

In addition to what Mette Kongens herself confessed before the court, the records contain information about her voice provided by other people. A threatening accent of her voice is heard when, according to a witness, she said to Brunk Pedersen that if she was going to suffer on her body, he would suffer for all eternity.[180] Important here is the confession of Maren Alrøds, which contained the denunciation of Mette. This was a confession to witches' gatherings that Mette allegedly took part in and a confession to witchcraft performed in order to destroy the barley. Maren confessed that Mette said to her that if she would come over one evening, a strange miracle was going to happen.[181] Maren went over to her, and Mette, her husband, a farmhand, and Maren went out to plough the field in the shape of black horses before the barley was sown, in order to destroy the barley and other growth. However, they were disturbed by men from the village, so that they could not achieve their aim.[182] In one of the witnesses' testimonies, the voice of Mette is rendered in first person.[183]

In the confession of Maren Alrøds, love magic is mentioned in connection with Mette Kongens as well. Maren was a widow, and Mette allegedly offered to find a man for her, using magic.[184] In addition, witches' gatherings are mentioned. The participants were organized in districts,[185] and Mette and her husband were said to belong to the same district as Maren. They could take on the shape of cats and perform other devilry, as they had done at Thudsdam around Michaelmas the previous year.[186] Mette was also said to have danced with five other women between Skanderup church and Skanderup three days after Michaelmas in order to perform witchcraft on police officer Laurids Ebbesen, castle bailiff Peder Segemand, and bailiff Jacob Jensen.[187] The most famous story confessed to by Mette was a witches' gathering at Bjerge Lie (Bjerrelide), during which they tried to destroy barley. At this gathering, a man was playing bagpipes, and they had a scribe, Gryder Knud. However, he fell over and their evil deed did not succeed.[188] Mette Kongens denounces several individuals for having participated in this gathering; denunciations that led to new trials.

As a whole, the voice of Mette Kongens is stable. It is strong when it comes to healing, which is a field she masters well and has much knowledge about. The information she provides about her healing activities is down-to-earth and without exaggerations. Most of Mette's confessions revolve around healing and *maleficium*. However, she also has ideas related to demonology. The idea of shape-shifting, which is an unrealistic feature, is activated in connection with the witchcraft operation to destroy barley. Those performing evil took on the shape of black horses. The same idea is connected to witches' gatherings, when participants took on the shape of cats. The idea of witchcraft organization in districts, with twelve witches in each district and a master as a leader—in this case, Gryder Knud—is clearly related to witches' gatherings and the performance of collective witchcraft. The voice of Mette Kongens thus contains accents of healing, *maleficium*, and demonology—a mixture of old folk belief and new and learned ideas about witchcraft.

The Voices of the Witnesses

The witnesses play an important role in providing details to the accusations against Mette and giving information about the fate of her husband. As in many other witchcraft trials, when healing goes wrong, an accusation often surfaces. So also in the case against Mette Kongens, as Brunk Pedersen claims he was worse after her attempted healing and was so ill that he had to rely on others to bring his testimony before the court. Other witnesses testify about Mette's curing of cattle and predicting the sex of calves. One man testifies about rumours about a black-billed magpie belonging to Maren Alrøds who jumps behind Mette Kongens, probably adding to suspicions about the demonic.

Mette Kongens's relation to Maren Alrøds was testified to by a couple of witnesses, thus increasing the fear of Mette's husband that this relation would be a reason for imprisoning him. This fear also ended his life in a tragic way.

The voices of the witnesses support an understanding that witchcraft is possible and that some people are able to perform witchcraft. Furthermore, the understanding is that while healing might go right or wrong, it works. Finally the severity of being accused in a witchcraft trial was commonly known, and likewise the danger of having anything to do with those rumoured to be witches.

The Voice of the Interrogator

In the trial of Mette Kongens, testimonies play a major role. The voice of the interrogator comes mainly to the fore in the weighting of topics discussed, such as witches' gatherings and healing that went wrong. The interrogator has apparently obtained names of new suspects by asking who participated in witches' gatherings, and so the panic can continue. He has also paid particular attention to witnesses' testimonies about the blame assigned to Mette Kongens when her healing did not succeed.

However, opportunities to expand on demonological ideas about activities at the witches' gatherings are not followed up, and ideas about the black magpie are not further investigated by the interrogator, even if this creature might have demonic implications. The devil's pact is not mentioned. The interrogator takes the content of the witnesses' testimonies seriously, but does not perform his questioning according to a clear demonological agenda.

The Voice of the Law

During the panic in the district of Åkjær, from the summer of 1618 until the summer of 1619, accusations by village inhabitants resulted in trials that included denunciations. The legal procedures were closely recorded, so that it is possible to get a good idea of the initial steps of the trial. The local police officer saw to it that the denunciations were followed up by the court. In the first trial in the panic, against Mette Alrøds, the voice of the law comes to the fore in the minister and twenty-four men swearing that she was rumoured to be a witch due to a man accusing her of affecting his genitals. It is interesting that the minister is part of this group, as he is not often mentioned as active in initiating a trial in Nordic countries' records. When Mette Alrøds denied, the court required her to provide witnesses to swear an oath of compurgation for her. When she did not succeed, the local court confirmed the oath sworn about her being rumoured to be a witch. Next, she confessed, denounced many, and was sentenced to death. As it was difficult for an accused person to get people to swear an oath of compurgation, these legal requirements disadvantaged the accused.

The trial of Mette Kongens was started by the local police officer, the commander of Skanderborg Castle, and the bailiff. She denied witchcraft, but confessed to curing cattle in the name of the Holy Trinity. The local court swore to her being guilty of witchcraft, which was later confirmed by *Landstinget*, a second instance court. The interplay between first and second instance court is important, as Mette Kongens's trial was passed on from the local court. After confessions and denunciations, she was sentenced to death. Merete Birkelund argues that she most likely was tortured,[189] but this was not documented. The voice of the law as it is heard in the trial of Mette Kongens shows how fear of witchcraft could escalate within a year in a rural district, and that the likelihood of an accused person managing to free herself from an accusation of witchcraft was low. Even if the decisions of the law were followed, it was difficult to be freed by compurgation.

The Voice of the Scribe

The scribe took down the voice of Mette Kongens in the court records in a trustworthy manner. No linguistic devices were used to create a distance to her voice. The difference between the pride in her voice when she describes healing activities and her unwillingness to confess to witchcraft is particularly poignant and provides important glimpses of the mentality of common people. Further, the entire rendered courtroom discourse gives a reliable impression of what was uttered in the courtroom. Also, decisions related to court procedure are accurately recorded, showing the necessity of cooperation between local court and *Landstinget*.

Anna Bruds, the Wife of Thomas, 1652

The Trial

Anna Bruds was the last person burned during the witchcraft trials in the Jutland town of Ribe, which took place during 1572–1652. During this period, there were twenty-two witch trials. Of the people on trial, eleven were found guilty and burned: the first, Johanne Christensdatter Rygge, was executed in 1572 and the last, Anna Bruds, in 1652. Twelve court records from these witchcraft trials have been transcribed and published, showing the development of witchcraft persecution in Ribe.[190]

The most famous of the Ribe witchcraft trials was the case against Maren Splid, the wife of a wealthy tailor and herself an independent businesswoman. In 1637, one of her husband's business rivals, Didrik the Tailor, accused Maren Splid of witchcraft. Didrik claimed that he had been woken up by three witches, one of whom was Maren, who had blown into his mouth. The following day, after feeling sick, he vomited up an object he believed was moving. Upon showing the object to several ministers and the local bishop, they declared it to be of unnatural origins. The case went to trial in Ribe, but Maren's husband stood by her and managed to get her acquitted. However, Didrik found witnesses to support him and went to the king, Christian IV, who declared the case reopened. In 1640, Maren was asked to find fifteen character witnesses to swear a compurgation oath, which she could not do, and she was thus found guilty in the first instance court. However, the case was passed on to second instance court, which acquitted her of all charges. But this was not the end. The case was then brought before the highest court, presided over by King Christian IV himself. Maren was taken to the Blue Tower in Copenhagen Castle, where she was tortured for days prior to her trial. She eventually confessed, naming six women as part of her coven, after which she was pronounced guilty and transported back to Ribe to be publicly executed in 1641. Among the people she denounced for witchcraft was Anna Thomasdatter, who was tried and executed in 1642.[191] Several of the denunciations made by Maren Splid and Anna Thomasdatter were repeated by Anna Bruds.

Anna Bruds, the wife of Thomas, was first questioned on 3 February 1652 at Korsbrødre Manor,[192] originally a medieval monastery and at the time the bishop's place. On this day, she confessed that she was a witch.[193] Already during this first interrogation, she denounced many other persons for witchcraft, among them Volborg Nielsdatter. After three weeks, on 23 February, her case was brought before the local court in Ribe. On behalf of his master, police master and *lensherre* Mogens Sehested,[194] castle scribe Povel Jensen[195] asked Anna Bruds whether she was a witch, as she had admitted this in the presence of respectable people. Sehested was in charge of the *len* Riberhus in 1651–55. To this she answered in the affirmative, and she said that another woman, Mette Skeies, participated in casting witchcraft on the boy Berthel Thomasen, the son of late Thomas Arild. Afterwards, Anna Bruds had promised, with the help of God, to make him better again if she could. However, she confessed that because she was beaten so that her nose was bleeding, she became angry and could not help him.

The mother of the boy came forth and testified, by laying a hand on Anna Bruds, that Anna cast sickness on her son, who was standing there, by means of witchcraft. This made him dumb and lame. Anna admitted that this accusation was true. She was asked again by Povel Jensen whether she would confirm the accusations, words and speech, which were heard on 3 February in the presence of his master and other respectable individuals. To this she answered, 'Yes', and would explain further.

In addition, Povel Jensen asked her what was the name of her personal helper—her 'servant boy'.[196] She answered that her boy was named Brud, and at present he was not with her. At the time when witchcraft was cast on Berthel Thomasen, her boy Brud was lying in the brewery[197] of Thomas Arild in the shape of a red man. On behalf of his master, Povel Jensen asked the Danes present whether they had anything to say concerning Anna Bruds's life.[198] Then, Niels Sørensen came forward and testified that she had been rumoured to have been a witch for several years. However, he did not know whether she was a witch. This testimony was confirmed by sixteen trustworthy men, the records state.

The day after, on 24 February, she was further questioned about who participated with her in performing witchcraft. She then denounced several people who had previously been denounced by Maren Splid and Anna Thomasdatter, among them Volborg Nielsdatter. Volborg's legal defender, Carsten Sørensen,[199] objected to this denunciation and asked Anna Bruds whether she had been with Volborg performing witchcraft. To this, Anna answered that two years previously, she had been with Volborg in her house, performing witchcraft. Since then, she had had nothing to do with her in evil deeds, even if she had visited her. Then Carsten Sørensen asked her if she knew whether the aforementioned Volborg Michelsdatter[200] had harmed anybody, to which she answered negatively. Povel Jensen asked Anna Bruds whether her confession that Volborg was a witch was true on all points, to which she answered, 'Yes'. Then, Carsten Sørensen protested that this was against the law and recess.

Next, castle scribe Povel Jensen asked Anna Bruds whether Niels Holdensen, whom she had previously denounced on 3 February, was a witch,[201] to which she answered that she did not know. He also asked her whether Maren, the wife of Jelle the Tailor,[202] was a witch, as she had stated on 3 February, to which she answered, 'Yes'. To counter this, Peder Jensen appeared in court on behalf of Maren, the wife of Jelle the Tailor, and appealed to the judges that this denunciation should not cause her any hinder or damage.

In addition, Povel Jensen asked about several other women whom Anna Bruds had denounced at Korsbrødre Manor on 3 February. He asked whether it was God's truth that they were witches, to which Anna answered in the affirmative for Giertrud, the wife of Christen Madsen, Margaretha Schibelunds, and Karen Dynespassens, on whose behalf Peder Jensen protested that she was not a witch, stating that Anna previously denounced her in mendacity. For Maren, the wife of Christen the Furrier[203] and Kirsten Thomasdatter, Anna said they were not witches.

Moreover, Povel Jensen asked Anna Bruds whether Mette Skeies, who was standing next to her before the court, was a witch and had dealt with the art of witchcraft, as she previously had denounced her at Korsbrødre Manor. Anna answered in the affirmative, but Mette loudly denied. Anna also confessed that Mette was with her when casting witchcraft on the boy Berthel in his mother's brewery,[204] and that he would not have been treated so badly if Mette had not been present. Anna repeated that Mette was a notorious witch and had used witchcraft in the same way as she herself had. She also confessed that Mette had been with her at St Peder's Churchyard, and that Margaretha Schibelunds and the wife of Jelle the Tailor, named Maren, and Volborg Michelsdatter were there at the same time, last Valborg's Eve. And the farmhand of Mette Skeies fetched a pitcher of beer in town, and that same farmhand was called Nies [sic] Puge.

On 1 March 1652, Povel Jensen asked Anna Bruds on behalf of his master before the court whether Anna, the wife of Niels, living at the Southern Gate, was a witch, as she previously had been denounced at Korsbrødre Manor in the presence of his master and other trustworthy men. Anna answered that yes, she was a notorious witch, raised her fingers, and asked God for help. To counter this, Anna, the wife of Niels, met with her son Jens Nielsen and denied this denunciation under the highest of oaths. Likewise, Povel Jensen asked Anna Bruds whether Anna, the wife of Hans the Smith, was a notorious witch, as she had denounced her at Korsbrødre Manor before many trustworthy people. She answered that she did not know whether the wife of Hans the Smith, who was present, was a witch, nor did she know her or her name, and she did not know anything to accuse her of.

On 8 March, on behalf of his master, castle scribe Povel Jensen asked Niels the Baker, citizen at the same place, whether he in any way suspected Anna Bruds of being responsible for the sickness that had come over him in the last eighteen weeks, which kept him to his sickbed in great pain,[205] according to the supplication from his wife to the police officer that was dated 26 February 1652 in Ribe and read to the court the same day. Niels the Baker confirmed, swearing with raised fingers, that the supplication was true on all points. Anna Bruds answered that it was not all true.

On 15 March, before the court, Volborg Michelsdatter asked Anna Bruds whether she ever had had anything to do with her regarding witchcraft or had seen her at illegal places, to which Anna answered negatively. Povel Jensen asked Anna why she had previously accused Volborg of witchcraft and now, before the court, withdrew her previous confession. To this she answered that she did not dare to stand by her confession in the presence of Volborg Michelsdatter.

In addition, Povel Jensen asked Anna Bruds, after all the documents and confessions were read aloud to her, whether they were truthful. To this she answered that all her previous confessions were true.

Then Thomas Jacobsen, the chairman of the fifteen trustworthy men, came forward and said that since they were legally appointed, and according to the documents, as well as Anna Bruds's own confession, he swore with raised fingers by the Holy Gospel that he accused Anna Bruds of witchcraft, and therefore that she should suffer as the court would decide. This oath was confirmed by the other men, and they asked God for help so that they would swear right and not wrong. On 26 March, this oath was confirmed in Ribe's council house.[206] According to Anna Bruds's own confession and accusation and testimonies in the case, the court did not come up with anything against the fifteen men's oath, and confirmed it should be maintained.[207]

The trial was still not finished, however. On 5 April, in the city hall, Anna Bruds was tortured in the presence of four Danish men at the request of Povel Jensen on his master Mogens Sehested's behalf.[208] She confessed that after she had cast witchcraft on the son of Thomas Arild, she wanted to make him better. She confessed moreover that she was a notorious witch and had learned from an old woman named Anna, the wife of Jens, who lived at the Southern Gate and was dead. She said in addition that all that she had previously admitted was God's truth, nothing was untrue, that she had forsworn her baptism and Christendom about four years prior, and that it happened at a house in Hundegaten.[209] In addition, she confessed that Maren, the wife of Jelle the Tailor, was a witch, as were Mette Skeies, Anna, the wife of Niels, and Giertrud, the wife of Christen Madsen. She also confessed that Margaretha, the wife of Christen the Furrier, was a witch. This means that some denunciations that she had withdrawn were now made anew. She also repeated that her boy was called Brud.

On 7 April 1652, after torture and confessions, the town bailiff with the *Borgmester* and the council passed the sentence that she would suffer as a notorious witch.[210]

The Voice of Anna Bruds

The voice of Anna Bruds has several accents. On the one hand, there is a willing and accommodating voice, eager to answer questions posed in an affirmative way. On the other hand, there is an unstable voice, vacillating between several answers. The examination of Anna Bruds is based on a previous confession at Korsbrødre Manor on 3 February, and many of the questions they ask her have to do with confirming the denunciations from that date. In addition, she was examined on 23 and 24 February and 1, 8, and 15 March, and questioned about previous denunciations every time. The last time she was examined was on 5 April, when torture was applied, and she repeated many denunciations.

Anna Bruds's willing voice comes to the fore during the early examinations. When she is asked, on 23 February, whether she is a witch and whether she cast witchcraft on a boy called Berthel Thomasen, she immediately answers in the affirmative. The same is the case when Berthel's mother appears in court, places her hand on Anna Bruds and accuses her of being responsible for the sickness affecting

Berthel. She also answers in the affirmative when it comes to questions about a number of denounced women. She answers directly and without hesitation that the denounced people were notorious witches.

In addition, she occasionally adds a short narrative to her answer. This goes for the confirmation of the denunciation of Mette Skeies: a brief story about witches gathered in a churchyard on Valborg's Eve and partying afterwards, with beer fetched for them. A short story is also inserted when the denunciation of Margaretha Schibelunds is confirmed: Anna Bruds says that Margaretha sent the devil after her on the street in the shape of a pig, and the pig knocked her down and made her sick for six weeks. A devil in disguise is mentioned, demonstrating that the figure of the devil is activated in the notions circulating about witchcraft. The stories show Anna Bruds as a skilled narrator.

However, she vacillates between stating that some people are witches and stating that they are not. A few times, she says that she does not know whether they were witches or that she does not know them: for instance Anna, the wife of the Smith, and Niels Holdensen. Sometimes, her response is that the suspected person is no witch at all, for instance Kirsten Thomasdatter and Maren, the wife of the Furrier. Anna Bruds is also hesitant about the supplication brought forward by the wife of Niels the Baker, responding that it is not all true. Until the torture, she answers either in the affirmative or in the negative, not always as expected by the interrogators. She is mostly in control of her own voice and of what she confesses. Her ability to stand her ground during the many interrogations, except for the last one, shows strength. She is giving answers according to her knowledge and conviction; however, she changes back and forth with regard to denunciations. This vacillation may indicate pressure.

Then, during the last interrogation on 5 April, when Anna Bruds is tortured, her voice changes. There is no resistance or independence in her discourse any longer. Torture is a turning point. She confirms that all her previous confessions are true. This shows that denunciations, and with them the possibility of continued trials, were a central point for the interrogators. Obtaining denunciations was also a reason to use torture. In addition, considerably new ideas are heard after torture was applied. She confirms that she learned witchcraft from an old woman and has 'has forsworn baptism and Christendom'.[211] This wording is very close to the first part of a confessed devil's pact, heard in witchcraft trials all over Europe. This is clearly a demonological idea. During examinations under torture, more dangerous notions of witchcraft than previously confessed to appear. The voice of Anna Bruds, as it develops throughout the trial, provides clear signs of the effect of torture. Torture takes away the last possibilities of judgement and action on one's own. Most questions posed during torture are answered with words that the interrogator wants to hear. After several weeks under pressure, Anna Bruds has lost her strength and her power to resist. The change in her voice when she is exposed to torture is a change towards resignation.

What is lacking in this Danish confession is the complete demonological narrative, namely the entering of the devil's pact after having renounced the Christian pact; however, the first part is definitely present. Either Anna Bruds herself knows about the formulation of leaving her baptism and Christendom when she enters into company with the devil, or the idea has been introduced to her during interrogation. It is interesting to note that in Denmark in 1652, one finds half a devil's pact confession, while the devil himself is not mentioned. Instead, Anna confesses that she has a personal demon called Brud. So in fact we have a Danish version of the demonological narrative in Anna's confession, which includes renouncing baptism but places her personal demon in the role that is frequently reserved for the devil himself in witchcraft confessions. This version seems to be frequent in the Nordic countries as well as in England.

The Voices of the Witnesses

Male as well as female witnesses are heard in the trial of Anna Bruds. One male witness is Niels Sørensen, who testifies on behalf of sixteen men that she was rumoured to be a witch. Another male witness is Niels the Baker, who sends a supplication about his sickness, which he suspected Anna Bruds caused. These male voices deal with the local community, inexplicable sickness, rumours about an alleged witch, and the decisive power a body of men had to confirm a suspected person's guilt.

In addition, female voices are heard when women appear in court to counter or confirm accusations and denunciations. They strengthen their testimonies by placing a hand on Anna Bruds. This is the case for Inger, wife of Thomas and mother of Berthel, the boy who was allegedly bewitched by Anna Bruds. With her hand on Anna, she accuses her of having cast witchcraft on her son. Anna accepts this accusation. Likewise, Anna, the wife of Niels, appears in court accompanied by her son to counter the denunciation made by Anna Bruds. She swears that the denunciation is untrue. However, the most remarkable entry of a woman before the court during this trial is the appearance of Volborg Michelsdatter. Volborg must have been denounced on 3 February, since her defender Carsten Sørensen protests against the denunciation on 23 February on behalf of Volborg. He asks Anna whether she knows if Volborg Michelsdatter harmed anybody, which Anna denies. However, afterwards, when asked whether Volborg Michelsdatter is a witch, Anna Bruds answers in the affirmative. Then, on 15 March, Anna appears before the court and is asked whether she ever had anything to do with Volborg regarding witchcraft. Anna answers in the negative. When Povel Jensen asks her why she previously denounced Volborg Michelsdatter for witchcraft and then withdrew her denunciation, she answers that she did not dare to stand by her denunciation in the presence of Volborg.[212] With this explanation, Anna shows that when the person denounced was standing in the courtroom, it affected the perpetuation of the denunciation. Maybe, when seeing Volborg in person, the severity of a denunciation became clearer in Anna's mind. But notable is that when torture was applied, all restraint with regard to denunciations vanished, and Anna Bruds confirmed her previous denunciation of Volborg and also added new ones.

The voices of the witnesses in Anna Bruds's trial echo a local community where rumours about witchcraft were frequent and where fear of witchcraft was strong. People in Ribe had lived with witchcraft persecution for nearly a hundred years. They knew the danger of a denunciation and the odds against an accused person in a witchcraft trial. The female voices are heard denying and arguing during confrontations with the accused woman in court, showing uncertainty about their own fates. The male voices are determinate, well aware of the power of their words and decisions.

The Voice of the Interrogator

Castle scribe Povel Jensen is the interrogator. He is after denunciations from the beginning of Anna Bruds's trial. From among existing ideas about witchcraft, he chooses to focus on her confession to being a witch, her accomplices in performing witchcraft, the name of Anna Bruds's servant boy, the discrepancies between her denunciations and the denials of the denounced persons, at what time and from whom she has learned witchcraft. The interrogation under torture brings forth notions related to demonology. The interrogator is firm in his voice, and his questioning is directed towards specific ends: to obtain sufficient points in the confession for a death sentence to be passed and to get new names for the witchcraft trials to continue. The interrogator knows that a confrontation in the courtroom between the accused and the denounced is a fruitful method. As an experienced legal official, he has good knowledge of efficient methods to bring the trial to a desired end.

The Voice of the Law

The voice of the law comes to the fore mainly through diligent questioning, correct court procedure, and the use of legal advisers. Correct court procedure is followed among others in the requirement of fifteen character witnesses to swear an oath of compurgation in order for her to clear herself of suspicion, the use of fifteen trustworthy men to swear an oath that they accused Anna Bruds of witchcraft and that she should suffer as the court would decide, and the court's confirmation of this oath, the requirement that witnesses be present during the application of torture, keeping the required numbers of court meetings, and the formalities related to the passing of the sentence.[213] The legal advisers protest when the letter of the law is not adhered to. The trial records show judicial officials aware of their responsibility.

The Voice of the Scribe

In the court records of Anna Bruds's trial, the voice of the scribe comes to the fore in the records' correctness, the covering of legal details as well as contents of confessions, and a strong weight placed on denunciations. The scribe accurately recorded the dates of the various trials and the names of those participating in the trials, be those the names of the judiciary, the accused, the men confirming that Anna Bruds was rumoured to be a witch, the men present during torture, the witnesses, and the denounced persons. This accuracy enabled other court instances to follow the development of the trial closely and evaluate court practice and the evidence presented for the sentence to be passed. The covering of legal details is particularly interesting because of the defender's protestation, as according to the law, an accused person's testimony was deemed unreliable. The content of the confessions is recounted, especially the denunciations. The courtroom discourse describing the confrontation between the accused and the denounced is rendered with dialogues intact, and the movements of the witnesses and the denounced persons are related. The wording of the sentence is given, and the names of the judicial officials responsible. The records are written by a very professional scribe.

Conclusion

The voices of women heard in three Danish trials display a range of accents when it comes to ideas about witchcraft, traditional folklore, narration, orality, and changes in voice during the trial. These accents emerge in particular in the confessions, where elements from various spheres are intertwined: learned demonological ideas, *maleficium*, healing, and traces of folkloric knowledge, related in a narrative spiced with orality features.

The Danish trials distinctly show that there is a marked change in the voices of women, which occurs when torture is applied. This is documented in two of the trials discussed above. Mette Kongens and Anna Bruds showed resistance from the beginning: they denied witchcraft. A change in the development of the trial of Mette Kongens came when *Landstinget*, the second instance court, confirmed the verdict of the local court, namely that she was guilty of witchcraft. The same is the case for Maren Alrøds, who denounced Mette Kongens. After the confirmation of the verdict at *Landstinget*, the women knew that all hope was lost. Mette Kongens most likely delivered her confession after torture. In the trial of Anna Bruds, the change came after torture as well. These women managed to deny witchcraft for a while. However, after pressure and the use of torture, they finally confessed. Maren, the wife of Mogens, did not deny, but from the beginning answered the interrogators' questions according to their wishes. However, she was one of the last accused in linked trials in which torture was used, so her situation was hopeless throughout the trial. Torture had the effect of breaking people down and making them confess. After torture, the voices of the women became flat and without power or colour. It seems that torture made emotions disappear.

Fear is a keyword in witchcraft records everywhere. In the Danish trials, it can be traced in Mette Kongens's denial of witchcraft and seen in her desperate flight from prison. Anna Bruds showed fear in a way in her effort to answer all questions willingly from the beginning of the interrogation. Fear is connected to anger, which can be heard in the voices of the denying witches. Sometimes, the accused women felt that they had been wronged when accused of witchcraft, as they rather wanted to promote their competence in a benevolent field: Mette Kongens confessed to healing but denied witchcraft.

The Danish witchcraft trials are often described as dealing predominantly with *maleficium*. It is therefore interesting to see that the demonological element was also important in Denmark: it is present in the voices of all trials analysed above. Variations on the grand demonological narrative appear: personal devils given to those who renounced their baptism or who gave themselves to the wrong master, witches' gatherings, the performance of collective witchcraft, and the denunciation of suspects. While learned demonological ideas must in first instance have been transferred to Denmark from further south in Europe via various channels, a kind of adjustment has occurred that provided these ideas with a foothold in local society.

In the range of demonological notions heard in the confessions, the devil himself does not appear vividly. Instead, the witch has a personal demon, called an Apostle or a servant boy, as a helper. Maren, the wife of Mogens, mentions named Apostles who helped destroy the royal Danish fleet. The same goes for her accomplices, who even borrow Apostles from one another when needed. In the trial of Mette Kongens, the person who denounced her—Maren Alrøds—testified that a black-billed magpie with holes through both wings jumped after Mette. This bird allegedly belonged to Maren Alrøds. Even if the devil's pact is not explicitly mentioned in the cases above, something that comes very close is expressed in the trial of Maren Alrøds. She said that Mette had given herself to the devil, which clearly resonates with the devil's pact. In the trial of Anna Bruds, she confessed that she had a servant boy called Brud. He was human-like, lying in the shape of a red man in the brewery.[214] She denounced Margaretha Schibelunds for attempting to harm her with a devil. These examples all have to do with appearances of the devil's helpers, in the shapes of either humans or animals. Evidence is provided that accused persons possessed knowledge of demonological ideas. For instance, shape-shifting is mentioned: Mette Kongens and accomplices shape-shifted to black horses when they went out into the fields to 'turn the rain'. Maren Alrøds confessed to a witches' gathering at which they had all assumed the shape of cats.

Additional demonological ideas that surface in the Danish witchcraft confessions are witches' gatherings and the performance of collective witchcraft. This is a major aspect of the witchcraft allegedly performed to create a storm against the royal fleet in 1589, during which the alleged witches met in the house of one of them. It was a major element in the confession of Maren Alrøds and in her denunciation of Mette Kongens. In addition, the idea of many witches gathering came appears in the trial of Mette Kongens, in which they were organized in districts, with twelve in each district and a leader. The confession of Anna Bruds mentions a witches' convention at St Peder's Churchyard, and the numerous denunciations characterize witchcraft as a collective performance.

As seen in the witnesses' testimonies, the peasants were aware not only of demonological ideas but also of the judiciary's decisions on demonology. In her trial, Mette Kongens said that she had performed no evil after the king's letter on witchcraft was issued in 1617. In the wording of the confession of Anna Bruds, she mentioned that she renounced her baptism and Christendom, which is frequently found as the first point of a verdict in witchcraft trials. This may have been influenced by the interrogator or may have been a formulation that she knew herself. The versions of demonological notions coming to the fore in these trials show that throughout the entire period of witchcraft persecution, learned ideas were received and adjusted to local culture in Denmark. At the end of the 1500s, aspects of the demonological doctrine had become part of local society's imagination and storytelling.

Folkloric ideas made their way into the confessions. One connection between demonological notions and traditional folklore is the mentioning of quarter days in connection with witches' gatherings. We hear about Michaelmas and Valborg's Eve. Also, love magic is mentioned in the trial of Mette Kongens, who had the means to find a man for a woman. An echo of folk tradition surfaces in the confessions, such as the special days of the year when evil was supposed to happen. Such a meeting point between demonological notions and traditional folk knowledge signals that the stories we hear in the confessions were told over and over again in the local communities.

Maleficium is mentioned in all trials, in the form of harmful witchcraft cast on humans and animals, often with physical objects and charms used as help. In the trial of Maren, the wife of Mogens, the women used clay pots to raise a storm against the royal ships. In the trial of Mette Kongens, ploughs were used to perform the miracle of turning the rain. There was an understanding that there are forces in the world that people cannot see, and that it was possible to manipulate these forces.

Healing plays a role in the trials of Mette Kongens and Anna Bruds. Mette was proud to be a healer and said that her healing was performed with God's help. She signed with the cross, read a prayer, and gave a sick person a drink. She was willing to recite prayers in court, as this was part of her professional knowledge. Healing was also confessed to in the trial of Anna Bruds. She confessed to having performed healing and to the signs she used and the prayers she recited. As is often seen in witchcraft trials, when healing went in the wrong direction, sickness became worse, which paved the way for witnesses' complaints. Healing seems to have been a respected activity at the time of the witchcraft trials, and every community had one or more individuals who performed healing.

The accents we hear in the confessions of these accused women clearly show how different notions are mixed: learned demonological notions, *maleficium*, healing, and folkloric ideas. The women bring some of their own knowledge and their own understanding of ways of manipulating forces into the confession.

The confessions in witchcraft trials are narratives. In all trials in question, it is clear that the confessing women were also good storytellers. They lived in predominantly oral societies, knew narrative structures from experience and training, and knew how to use orality features. Even if the confessions are enforced narratives due to the threat of torture, the mastery of storytelling shines through. Also, a rich array of orality features is activated. The voice of each individual comes to the fore, with its own touch. This personalized language does not only provide a glimpse of this person's way of speaking but is also the strongest indicator of a professional scribe at work.

The scribe, as he appears in the court records, wrote down the words expressed by the women. These are not standardized confessions, but individualized ones. The scribe accurately recorded the discourse as he heard it in the courtroom. It becomes evident what the accused person was asked about and also—by looking at the range of questions—what the priorities on the part of the interrogators were: which questions came first and which came last. The interrogation was of the uttermost importance. However, the women also brought in something of their own ideas and knowledge. They contributed to the courtroom discourse with their words and imagination, coloured by their own language and their own understanding of the world. Obviously, the scribe was in a position to delete or add words and sentences in the court records. But his professional attitude supports a correct recording. The role of the interrogator was more important than the role of the scribe. The interrogator was a person who, through leading questions, was able to direct the interrogation towards dangerous or less serious witchcraft.

5

SCOTLAND—DEVIL'S PACT, GATHERINGS, AND SLEEP DEPRIVATION

The choice of three trials from Scotland is based on the same criteria as the choice of trials from the other countries: one trial from the early, middle, and late period of witchcraft persecution each; trials held in local and central courts; different locations of trials; detailed court records; and complex ideas about witchcraft entangled in the confessions. In focusing on the voices of women, demonological notions as well as ideas about *maleficium* surface. In addition, healing and traditional folkloric motifs will be paid attention to. As the confessions are narratives, narrative structures are prominent in the way the confessions are formed, as are orality features. The court records provide insight into the development of the trial from beginning to end and offer an opportunity to note any changes in the voices of the women. Witchcraft trials put enormous emotional strain on the accused individuals, which can occasionally be caught in the recorded text: in the expressions of the accused women and in the interpretation of accused women's behaviour. Several other voices can be heard as well. The voice of the interrogator poses the questions during examination and is in a position to influence the content of the confession. The same is the case for the voices of the witnesses and the voice of the law. The way the scribe performs his work as a recorder is closely related to the analysis of women's voices. Taken together, in merging a range of ideas and various linguistic layers, the courtroom discourse provides a glimpse of the world view of the accused individual and the other actors of the trial, and also of the mentality of the time.

The first trial analysed in this chapter is the trial of Agnes Sampson from Keith, which was part of the North Berwick trials of 1590–91, named after a place of an alleged witches' convention. These trials are interlinked with the Copenhagen trials of 1590, and thus with the first trial analysed in the chapter on Denmark in this book. The formal trial of Agnes Sampson took place in the central court in Edinburgh in 1591. The second trial analysed is the one of Helene Clerk from

DOI: 10.4324/9781003255406-5

Newhaven, 1643–45. This was a combined local and central trial, and trial documents exist from both the local and the central courts. Finally, there is the trial of Isobell Eliot from Peaston—held in 1678, at a time when the number of witchcraft trials in Scotland was decreasing. For each of the trials, first a description of the trial will be given, followed by an analysis of the voice of the woman accused.[1] Like in the other chapters, the analysis will focus on the elements of demonology, *maleficium*, healing, narrative structures, and orality features, in addition to changes in the voices throughout the trial. Attention will also be paid to the voices of the witnesses, the interrogator, the law, and the scribe.

Background

Persecution

The documentation of the Scottish witchcraft trials is well known due to a comprehensive database, the Survey of Scottish Witchcraft.[2] Most trials were authorized centrally. Trial records from the High Court of Justiciary in Edinburgh have survived well, but those from local trials are more patchy.[3] Scotland experienced intense witchcraft persecution from 1561 to 1727,[4] during which period 3,837 people were suspected of witchcraft, and 3,413 accused of witchcraft.[5] Of those accused, 84% were women, which is above the European average of 80%.[6] The intensity of the witch-hunt in Scotland was extreme, and Scotland's execution rate of accused witches per capita is among the highest in Europe.[7] Both *maleficium* trials and demonological trials took place, and the bulk of accusations and executions occurred during witchcraft panics, with continuous trials happening in a relatively short period of time.[8] In the North Berwick witchcraft trials of 1590–91, demonological ideas are documented for the first time during Scottish witch-hunts, focusing on the pact with the devil and witches' conventions.[9] Christina Larner argues that in Scotland, the crime of being a witch was usually related to the demonic: 'the primary act of witchcraft was the demonic pact, and (. . .) all witches were part of a Satanic conspiracy'.[10] This view is supported by Michelle D. Brock, who maintains that Satan instilled 'an urgency' in witchcraft trials.[11]

After 1590, an increasing number of trials took place. The largest panics occurred in 1590–91, 1597, 1628–31, 1649–50, and 1661–62.[12] Women were more prone to be accused in panic years than in non-panic years, and there is a relatively higher frequency of execution in panic years than in non-panic years.[13] The frequency of demonic pact confessions followed the upsurge in panics. Women were treated differently during witchcraft trials in panic years than in non-panic years and were clearly more frequently tortured than men. There is also a significant correlation between local trials and panic years for women: women were over-represented in local trials whereas men were over-represented in central trials.[14]

The most intense persecution took place in the south-eastern part of the country, particularly in East Lothian, Fife, Dumfries, and Aberdeen. However, witchcraft trials also occurred in the south-west of Scotland, on the West Coast, and on the Northern Isles, albeit on a smaller scale. After 1662, a protracted decline set in, and the last execution was in 1727.[15]

Jurisdiction

Julian Goodare states that witchcraft was a relatively rare offence, '[b]ut when it occurred, its punishment was so dramatic that it must have done a great deal to colour people's attitude towards the religion that the authorities were imposing on them'.[16] Goodare emphasizes that '[w]itch-hunting in Scotland was a Protestant business. The witchcraft statute was passed in 1563, just three years after the Reformation'.[17] Christina Larner has also pointed to the role played by religion in witchcraft persecution, with the dominant idea in seventeenth-century Scotland being 'that of the godly state in which it was the duty of the secular arm to impose the will of God upon the people'.[18] The church often played an active role in starting prosecution for witchcraft in Scotland. Different levels of church organization could urge the interrogation of a suspected person.[19] The church was organized with a Church Session (Kirk Session) in every parish consisting of the ministers and elders. The presbytery was a grouping of several parishes, and the Synod was a grouping of several presbyteries.[20]

A witchcraft accusation in Scotland passed through several stages.[21] In the legal system, six different types of courts could be involved in the witch-hunt: local church[22] courts (Church Sessions and presbyteries), the Privy Council of Scotland (or sometimes parliamentary or estate committees), the High Court of Justiciary, circuit courts, regular local courts, and local criminal courts held under commissions of justiciary.[23] The local church courts had no criminal jurisdiction. The Privy Council of Scotland issued commissions of justiciary authorizing the convening of trials, but the council did not hold trials itself. The High Court of Justiciary was the highest criminal court and was usually held in Edinburgh.[24] One-tenth of trials were held in the central justiciary court, while nine-tenths were mostly held in local courts.[25] Circuit courts were travelling versions of the central court that occasionally visited the regions. These periodic travelling courts were also called 'justice ayres'.[26] The Survey of Scottish Witchcraft distinguishes between central, local, and mixed central-local trials, with the last category understood as an umbrella term covering several different patterns.[27] Brian P. Levack argues that, as there were more procedural options in Scotland than in England, it was much easier to start a witchcraft case in the former.[28] There were two types of local courts: sheriff courts and burgh courts. These courts did not normally try witches, as witchcraft was considered a serious crime that was beyond their jurisdiction. Most Scottish persons accused of witchcraft were tried in ad hoc courts convened to try witches, which were local criminal courts held under commissions of justiciary.[29] In all Scottish courts, there was an assize (jury) of local propertied men who delivered a verdict. If they convicted, the sentence was usually for the alleged witch to be strangled at a stake and have her or his body burned.[30]

The local church and presbytery courts were powerful bodies. Even if they could not execute anyone, they could summon suspects and witnesses, interrogate them, and compile dossiers of evidence, which were passed on to the judiciary.[31] The courts were also of uttermost importance. The relative degree of central and local control during the Scottish witch-hunt has been debated by Christina Larner, Julian Goodare, and Brian P. Levack. While Larner argued that there was a strong role for the central government,[32] Levack stressed that the original impetus for prosecution came from the localities rather than from the centre, and that most Scottish trials were held by local lairds using commissions of justiciary, who were not centrally accountable for their decisions.[33] To this, Goodare responded that commissions to try witches were set up centrally by the Privy Council, which demanded a detailed written case against the suspect: it 'was not surprising that most local trials ended in convictions, because local trials only occurred once a central body had decided to authorize them'.[34] Goodare and Levack agreed that authorizing local elites to hold trials represented a lower degree of central control than holding trials in courts directly organized by the centre.[35] In my view, the state played a decisive role in the witch-hunt by authorizing witchcraft trials held in local courts, where the bulk of the trials took place, in addition to its impact on circuit courts and trials held in central courts.

Goodare underlines that the role of the state is related to legal procedure, whereas the debate has focused on torture.[36] There is no doubt that torture was used extensively to extract confessions during witchcraft prosecutions in Scotland, in particular demonological confessions. The suspicion of Satanic conspiracy was used to justify torture as a means to obtain the names of accomplices. The types of torture used in Scotland were sleep deprivation, burning feet, 'thrawing' (twisting/distorting) the head with ropes, hanging by the thumbs, whipping, and the stocks.[37] In my research, I have shown that a range of torture methods were performed, that torture was used in pre-trial interrogations and mostly in local trials, that it affected mostly women, and that there was a connection between the use of torture and panic years with a high execution rate, which points to trials with devil's pact confessions and denunciations.[38] The use of torture played a decisive role in the escalation of Scottish witchcraft trials during panic years. Documentation of torture in witchcraft trials is found in primary and secondary sources and has been discussed by, among others, R. D. Melville, Christina Larner, Brian P. Levack, Stuart Macdonald, P. G. Maxwell-Stuart, Julian Goodare, and me.[39]

Levack and Goodare have debated the issue of torture in Scottish witchcraft trials, with Levack arguing that a warrant from the Privy Council was necessary for torture to be performed legally in witchcraft trials.[40] The Privy Council issued such warrants 'when they considered information from the accused to be vital to the state'.[41] These applied to crimes of a political nature, but to witchcraft as well. Therefore, Levack contends that torture was in fact illegal, because it was authorized on an exceptional basis only. Goodare questions this argument, asking why so little effort was made to stop torture. Levack answers that the local elites who were administering torture were largely autonomous. Goodare, however, maintains that central authorities were important, documented by among other things the Privy Council's intervention in some irregular cases.[42] I agree with this point of view, as

I interpret witchcraft trials as governmental operations. In 1708, an Act of British Parliament prohibited torture in Scotland.

The repeal of the 1563 Witchcraft Act came in 1736.[43] It was the result of an initiative from England, not Scotland: three burghers from southern England proposed to repeal the English Witchcraft Acts, and the Scottish Act was included through a House of Lords amendment. Indeed, 'they were replaced by the Witchcraft Act 1735 which admitted only the crime of pretended witchcraft and which prescribed for a conviction a maximum of a year's imprisonment and pillorying on quarter days'.[44] A few prosecutions took place under its provisions in Scotland.[45]

Agnes Sampson, 1590–91

Agnes Sampson was a widow from Nether Keith in East Lothian and was one of the first persons to be imprisoned, interrogated, and executed during the North Berwick trials of 1590–91. A text-critical edition of the court records of these trials, including depositions from pre-trial interrogations, has been published.[46] These trials have attracted attention from historians as new, demonological ideas about witchcraft—including the devil's pact—surfaced in Scotland. The trials have been discussed by, among others, Christina Larner, P. G. Maxwell-Stuart, Laura Paterson, Jenny Wormald, Brian P. Levack, Julian Goodare, Thomas Riis, and me.[47] King James's role in bringing demonological ideas from Denmark to Scotland was central in this debate. In 1961, Christina Larner (née Ross) maintained that King James VI brought the idea of the devil's pact with him.[48] Larner's thesis has been countered by Maxwell-Stuart and Jenny Wormald, who claim that demonological ideas of witchcraft existed in Scotland pre-1590.[49] Contrary to this, Laura Paterson argues that the accused individuals in North Berwick did not have any pre-existing belief in the witches' sabbath.[50] Riis maintains that since witchcraft accusations in Denmark were largely based on maleficent witchcraft in villages, Denmark was an unlikely source for the demonic pact.[51] Regarding knowledge of demonological ideas in Scotland before 1590, Julian Goodare has argued that the Protestant Minister John Knox, leader of Scotland's Reformation 1560, was aware of the demonic pact.[52] As for legal procedure, Goodare has shown that the general commission for trying witches from 1591 until 1597, assumed first by Larner, and later by Norman, Roberts, and Wormald, was illusory: no such commission had existed. Procedures for trying witches remained constant throughout the Scottish witch-hunt, with trials kept either in the justiciary court in Edinburgh or in the locality by the authority of a commission of justiciary.[53] Further, Goodare disagrees with Wormald, who argues that King James became a 'sceptic' before or during the 1597 panic, and that King James' doubts were evident in his treatise *Daemonologie* (1597). Goodare states that the order of August 1597, which revoked recent witchcraft trial commissions, was not only a 'sceptical' measure but could also be supported by witch-hunting enthusiasts. There was evidence in September 1597 of the king's keenness to prosecute witches, something the genuine 'sceptics' criticized him for. In addition, Goodare maintains that it was not credible to suggest that *Daemonologie* was a 'sceptical' work.[54] Goodare and Levack agree that the most important aspect of

King James's involvement in 1590–91 was that it politicized Scottish witchcraft.[55] My argument is that King James was the carrier of demonological ideas about witchcraft from the Copenhagen witchcraft trials to Scotland, particularly the notion of witches' gatherings. The Copenhagen trials started before he left Denmark, and of which he knew. The accusations against the suspected women included witches' gatherings and witchcraft against the royal Danish ships that were to bring Princess Anne to Scotland in autumn 1589, ideas that influenced the North Berwick trials.[56] From the content of the pre-trial interrogations during the North Berwick trials, in which King James participated, it is clear that King James VI knew about the notion of witches conjuring a storm.[57] He is also most likely the one who suggested that Danish witches cooperated with Scottish witches, a point opening the recorded pre-trial interrogation of the accused North Berwick witches. The king knew from his stay in Denmark about the rumours of such a cooperation.[58]

The North Berwick convention was alleged to have taken place in the local kirk on All Hallows Eve 1590, as confessed to during the trials.[59] I have studied the published as well as unpublished court records for the analysis of Agnes Sampson's trial.[60] Regarding the first pre-trial interrogation, the pages of the records are partly damaged, so that part of the text is missing. From the formal trial, a *verbatim* transcription of the primary sources, the dittay or indictment, was used for my analysis.[61] Dittays have been preserved for four individuals.[62] In addition, Agnes Sampson's trial is reported on in detail in the pamphlet *Newes from Scotland*, published in London in 1591, and in David M. Robertsen's sourcebook on East Lothian Witchcraft, *Goodnight My Servants All*.[63]

The Trial

Agnes Sampson was called 'The Wise Wife of Keith'.[64] She was a practising healer and had many clients in the East Lothian area. As early as spring 1589, she was pursued by church courts for witchcraft. In the beginning of April 1589, the Synod of Lothian and Tweedale received a complaint against the presbytery of Haddington for not calling Agnes Sampson before them, as she was suspected of witchcraft. Haddington was the nearest town to Agnes's place of residence. The presbytery answered that they did not find any grounds to accuse her, but they were still ordered to call her before them. Any information about her dealings with witchcraft or about people who had had dealings with her had to be provided within fifteen days.[65] This did not happen. Then, in September 1589, the presbytery of Haddington was again ordered by the Lothian Synod to call Agnes Sampson before them and see to it that she was questioned. This was repeated by the Synodal Assembly in Edinburgh in September 1590.[66] On 7 October 1590, the Synod recorded that the brethren of the presbytery of Haddington answered that they had started on Agnes Sampson. It appears from the court records that she was imprisoned in Haddington. Thus, Agnes was in the searchlight for witchcraft due to her practising of healing, before the alleged witchcraft operations in the North Sea in autumn 1589.[67] This shows that witchcraft persecution on a small scale took place in East Lothian and Haddington as early as in spring 1589.

Next, she was brought to Edinburgh, where by 11 November, several persons accused of witchcraft had been arrested and placed in the Edinburgh Tolbooth.[68] The first one questioned was Geillis Duncan. She was a maid at David Seton's place, and her employer suspected her of witchcraft because she often stayed out at night. Seton questioned her under torture and pressed forth a witchcraft confession in which she implicated Agnes.[69] The first questioning of Agnes Sampson took place just before December 1590, when she was interrogated together with Geillis Duncan.[70] The record is undated and the names of the interrogators are not recorded. It is most likely that King James VI was present and was one of the interrogators. The king was the only person in the circle of potential interrogators who possessed the idea of cooperation between Scottish and Danish witches, that was initially brought up.[71] The second questioning—when Agnes was definitely examined by King James VI—occurred on 4 and 5 December 1590, and the third interrogation in January 1591.

The dittay is dated 27 January 1591, the day of Agnes's formal trial.[72] A dittay, or an indictment, is a legal accusation, a compilation of the points confessed to. Agnes Sampson's dittay consists of fifty-one articles, each highlighting what she has been accused of. It is compiled from the confessions in the pre-trial documents[73] and summarizes the accusations. At the end, she was sentenced to be 'tane to the Castell of Ed[inbu]r[gh] and their bind to ane staik and wirreit q[uhi]ll sche wes deid and th[air]eftir hir body to be brunt in assis and all hir movable guidis to be escheat and imbrocht to o[u]r soverane lordis use'.[74] Agnes Sampson was executed on Castle Hill in Edinburgh on 28 January 1591, the day after her trial.[75]

Three pre-trial documents provide a clear impression of Agnes Sampson's voice. The first interrogation must have taken place before 4 December, as the 4 December examination follows the first one in the records. It opens with Geillis Duncan's confession to a meeting between Scottish and Danish witches 'in the midst of the firth'.[76] This is the first point that has been considered important enough to record. Surprisingly, this is a continuation of the narrative that appeared in the confessions of the Danish witches during the Copenhagen trials of summer 1590. As we have seen in the chapter on Denmark, Danish witches were accused of conjuring a storm on Michaelmas in 1589 to prevent Danish Princess Anne from arriving in Scotland 'the first time'.[77] Now, as the opening point in the interrogation of the North Berwick witches, Scottish and Danish witches were *together* suspected of this operation, which means that the idea of a witchcraft bridge between Denmark and Scotland is established. The transfer of ideas about witchcraft confessed to by Danish witches took place during the spring and summer of 1590.[78] At the centre of this transmission was King James VI himself, who was in a position to redefine and expand the Danish narrative about witches raising storm as a joint Danish-Scottish enterprise when the North Berwick trials started.

In the first pre-trial document, part of the page is damaged, which makes the text incomplete and several sentences fragmentary. The voices of Geillis and Agnes clearly emerge in their answers to the questions posed to them: 'Geillis confesses' or 'Agnes confesses'. Their words are rendered in the third person. Geillis Duncan was questioned first, but the questioning of Agnes Sampson took over, occupying around four-fifths of the document. King James knew from Danish court circles about the turning point of the Danish fleet 'in the middle' of the North Sea at Michaelmas 1589 and, through diplomatic correspondence, about the Scottish ferry accident 'in the midway' between Burntisland and Leith; two incidents that are definitely parallel to the expression 'in the middle of the firth'.[79] This first interrogation's mentioning of the meeting with a witch from Copenhagen, the connection between witchcraft operations in the two countries, the idea of witches' meetings, the idea of witches raising a storm by performing collective witchcraft, and the mentioning in both countries of the storm being conjured to prevent the queen's coming home support Larner's view that the North Berwick trials were a turning point for witch theory in Scotland. For the first time, demonological ideas emerged during examinations and in confessions. However, in my opinion it was not directly the devil's pact that was brought from Denmark, as Larner argues, but demonological ideas like witches' gatherings and the collective performance of witchcraft. In addition, the idea about personal demons provided to the witches when they entered into the devil's pact, found in the Danish trials, implicitly includes the devil's pact.

The devil was a central figure in Agnes's confession. She confessed to having seen the devil, whom she sometimes called 'the Sprite'. She said that as early as when she was imprisoned in Haddington Tolbooth, a fire came down, and the devil appeared as a long, black thing at the end of the fire. She confessed to the devil's promises: among others, he had told her that he would save her from being taken.[80] Agnes said that when she called upon 'Eloa', the devil appeared. The conception of the devil as a physical being is common in witchcraft trials.[81]

During the first interrogation, Agnes's answers seem to jump from one issue to another. Although her answers were rather abrupt and confusing, the questions posed to her can be detected. They form the backbone of a narrative that is expanded during later interrogations. She referred to the North Berwick convention, to an operation to destroy a ship in North Berwick, and to a letter that was written 'to raise the storm for staying the queen's coming home'.[82] These items are blurred and entangled in Agnes's first confession, but gradually unfold and are clarified during subsequent interrogations.

Agnes confesses to each witchcraft operation in an ad hoc way, which partly is due to damaged records. However, when it comes to the destruction of the ship in North Berwick, the bits and pieces of information rendered make it possible to establish a timeline. First, several people shipped in at North Berwick, and some women rowed with oars.[83] The devil brought wine out of the ship's hold and gave it 'out of his hands to them'.[84] Agnes confessed that she had been given some silver and that she gave twenty shillings to a participant of the operation called 'Grey Meal'. She mentioned the ship again when she confessed that they were all cross because Robert Grierson had gotten the wreck of the ship and the rest nothing.[85] It is also mentioned twice that there were several persons in a ship with an uncouth woman. In addition, it is said that there was an Irish tailor present on the same occasion. Next, the people gathered came out (of the ship) and the devil remained and raised the storm immediately. The name of the ship that was to be destroyed is not provided here, but given later: *The Grace of God*.

Next, there is the North Berwick convention. Agnes mentioned the North Berwick kirk, where they had been 'in like manner' together, and that she had alighted before she came to the kirk, which means that she rode to the place. She mentioned a large law head, a large hill,[86] probably the North Berwick Law. She also described how the participants worshipped the devil in the church[87] and gave the names of ten people, including herself, who had been gathered in George Mott's house. This was certainly in response to a question.[88] This gathering was probably related to the letter mentioned above, as a note in the document's margin suggests. Agnes confessed to the delivery of a letter, a bill, out of her own hand.[89] This letter contained information on the storm to be conjured. Thus, the Michaelmas tempest appears several times in this very first and brief interrogation, which means that the topic must have been emphasized and put forward by the interrogator. Agnes's confession was primarily related to demonological ideas. However, amidst the demonological items in her confession, she touched upon her practice as a healer: for example, she confessed that she had mastered the art of removing sickness from a man or creature and casting that same illness on another being.

The next examination of Agnes is said to have taken place on 'Saturday before noon'; however, no date is given.[90] In the beginning, the form of the transcribed confession is repetitive, with eight consecutive sentences starting with the phrase, 'She confesses (. . .)'. Two sentences introduce a paragraph; the rest stands alone. This part is followed by two longer texts: the first is about a collective endeavour to destroy David Seton through witchcraft, which is a new theme.[91] The second text is about another new theme: the devil's pact. It consists of a consecutive account of the six times the devil appeared to Agnes. This was clearly an attempt by the interrogators to examine Agnes's relationship with the devil in more depth. The pact between Agnes and the devil is described, including their sexual relations, her receipt of the devil's mark, and the promise made to her by the Evil One that she should 'never want'—a very Scottish expression of the promise that the devil gave to a person entering the pact. It is repeatedly stated that the devil asked the participants at every convention if they had kept their promise to him, and that he desired them to be true to him.

Another new item coming up during this second interrogation is Agnes's saying that 'she was out of Scotland oft enough on the sea',[92] and that they were 'eight and forty hours on the sea in the boat which flew like a swallow'.[93] These descriptions are clearly unrealistic, with connotations of the witches' flight. Another new item is Agnes saying that it would be hard for the king to come home, and that the queen would never come except if the king fetched her.[94] Yet another new item is Agnes asking the devil to foretell whether the king would have lads or lasses, and that he answered that 'he should have lads and then lasses'.[95] In addition, another item Agnes confessed to on this day is that the devil said that 'the ministers would destroy the king and all Scotland, and if he would use his counsel he should destroy them'.[96] This expressed a serious threat against the king, and it is possible to see the connection to the storm raised to stay Princess Anne's arrival to Scotland. All these new items recurred with slight variations in subsequent examinations of Agnes.

Then, some items from the previous interrogation are repeated. This interrogation does not pay attention to the North Berwick convention, but it mentions other witches' gatherings at which the devil gave orders to his servants. The theme of the Michaelmas storm comes up again; in fact it is the devil foretelling Agnes about this storm. Also, the theme of the ship in North Berwick that the witches allegedly destroyed is repeated, with a few variations. This time, Agnes said that they drank wine from a great cup, that she remained in the boat in which they shipped in to North Berwick, and that she did not enter the large ship. She now said that the devil vanished before they landed in North Berwick.

This second pre-trial document records the questioning of Agnes Sampson as taking place on 4 and 5 December 1590, probably in Holyrood Palace in Edinburgh. There were three examinations in all.[97] What was 'demanded' of her or 'inquired' is stated three times.[98] The king is the interrogator. That the king of Scotland himself, a European monarch, was examining an alleged witch was extraordinary.[99] Storms in the North Sea had been raised twice in the first pre-trial interrogation, allegedly to hamper his queen's arrival to Scotland. The North Berwick trials might partly be seen as an attempt to find scapegoats for the storms. In contrast to the first pre-trial document, Agnes now denied many of the charges. Following questions pertaining to her healing practice, which includes prayers, it is recorded that 'the king's Majesty' insisted upon knowing more about some 'contraries gathered upon her words'.[100]

In the beginning, King James doubted Agnes's confession. According to *Newes from Scotland*, the king became convinced that Agnes's words were true when 'she took his Majesty a little aside, she declared unto him the very words which passed between the king's Majesty and his queen at Upslo[101] in Norway the first night of their marriage, with their answer each to other'.[102] Indeed, now 'his Majesty charged straitly to confess the truth', which Agnes did, in a long and coherent confession. At one point, it seems that the king broke in with an extra question, with her being 'demanded' how she began to serve the devil.[103] Her confession started Friday before noon, continued Friday afternoon, and then again Saturday afternoon. After Agnes confessed to her entering into the devil's service, she said that had it not been for the present occasion which forced her,

> she would never have left him, and that when she was 'taine first she had vowed not confess anything, and was that same day resolved never to confess, were not his Majesty's speeches that had moved her, whereof she praised God that had wrought a repentance in her and a sense of feeling of her sins.[104]

The questioning of Agnes Sampson included the use and effects of a prayer for life and death—a prayer and a skill Agnes confessed to having learned from her father. She explained that when the prayer stopped once, the person she was praying for was bewitched; if the prayer stopped twice, there was no remedy: the person would die. Agnes denied several charges related to her healing practice during the examination Friday before noon. The first was about the use of eggs as an ingredient in a remedy for a disease; Agnes denied knowledge about this. However, afterwards, she confessed that she did in fact know how the eggs should be used in this context, so she was evidently asked about the same thing again. She denied sending any of her sons, daughters, or goddaughters to clients, and denied having received clothes from anyone to be used for healing. She denied the healing of some individuals but confessed to healing others 'by her prayer alone. This she granted with difficulty'. This 'difficulty' was probably because Agnes knew that it was very serious to confess to having performed a cure that could not be classed as 'natural'.[105] It suggests that Agnes, in early December, was afraid of the outcome of the trial.

Agnes also denied that Geillis Duncan was ever in her company or that she even knew her. And she denied that 'she knew anything about the boat that perished betwixt the Burntisland[106] and Leith but that she heard mean made for it'.[107] This is a reference to the ferry accident of 1589 and indicates rumours in the local communities about witchcraft related to this incident.[108] These rumours had been known in court circles for several months, as diplomatic correspondence and state papers show.[109] And King James himself knew about these rumours.

The king is eager to know about Agnes's pact with the devil, which was a dangerous element to confess to, with Agnes '*being demanded* how she began to serve the devil'.[110] [My italics.] One denial is recorded regarding a specific meeting with the devil: 'She *denies* that after he [the devil] had appeared she put him away again with any sacrifice, but charged him on the law that he lived on to pass away'.[111] [My italics.] Notably, in each of her descriptions of situations involving the devil, she ends up being in charge, with the devil having to obey her. For example, when she tells the devil in the guise of a dog to go away, he does—howling as he leaves. This contrasts with the common understanding elsewhere about the devil–witch relationship, in which the devil is in charge and is the one who gives commands.

The entire confession before the king is rich and detailed, with reference to the times of day when events happened, such as 'she was sent for that day in the morning',[112] and, connected to an incident at Patrick Edminston's house in Newtown, when the devil came out of a well in the shape of a black dog: 'Betwixt five and six at even she passed to the garden herself to devise upon her prayer', and 'Fra this time while after supper he [the devil] remained in the well'.[113] A timeline is constructed, and the credibility of the narrative increases. It also underlines closeness to the human world as well as the experience of the actual event.

The devil's appearance and his ability to see into the future are recurring themes. With regard to the latter, Agnes explained that she 'had to ask the devil what would happen to people', as 'he was the one with the answers'. She also stated that it was the devil who had conjured the storm, not the witches—this is a divergence from traditional beliefs about witches and weather magic in Scotland at the time.[114] The images of the devil portrayed in Agnes Sampson's confession are unusual.[115] In addition to the devil appearing as a black dog—a common notion at the time—Agnes said he took the shape of smoke, a stag, or a bundle of hay.[116] She further described several witches' conventions in Bara, Acheson's Haven, Newton, Garvet, Keith, Foulstruther, Ormiston, and between Cousland and Carberry. Next comes the large North Berwick convention, in which more than one hundred people, six men and the rest women, participated. Here, the devil appeared in a black gown and a black hat in the North Berwick kirk, where they had been digging up corpses from the churchyard outside so they could make 'powder from their joints' to be used for magic; he called their names from the pulpit and asked them if they had been good servants. Before they departed, they 'kissed all his arse'.[117] All this Agnes related fluently, and there was no need for the king to ask follow-up questions.

The next day, Saturday afternoon, the examination continued—first with a focus on the destruction of David Seton, followed by a round of questions concerning Agnes being at sea and staying for forty-eight hours, sometimes longer, sometimes shorter, 'upon ships on uncouth coasts'.[118] This information about how long she was at sea had not yet been touched upon during the interrogation, so it might well have been an answer to a question. Then, Agnes repeated her previous confession regarding the devil foretelling the Michaelmas storm and the 'bill' delivered to Geillis Duncan, about how the king 'should hardly come home' and the queen 'should never come home except the king fetched her', about the king's children, 'first lads, then lasses' and that 'the ministers would destroy the king and all Scotland'.[119] There are several repetitions, not only of answers given in previous examinations but also of those within this same interrogation, and there is no clear line in the structure of the text. If this is a confession that was developed through leading questions, then these questions appear to have been haphazard. However, Agnes could also have been exhausted and simply have been repeating the same things she had said before.

At the end of the interrogation, the ship *The Grace of God*, which had perished at North Berwick, became the focus. Agnes said that they went out to the ship 'in a boat like a chimney'—an unusual image—and that the devil passed before them like 'a rack of hay', another unusual image, taking them to a party on board the ship. The witches were invisible: the mariners did not see them, and they did not see the mariners. This can be interpreted as a type of shape-shifting.[120] When they returned, the devil remained under the ship's hold and raised a storm, so that the ship perished.

The third and final pre-trial examination of Agnes Sampson occurred in January 1591 and, while the exact date is unknown, it must have taken place before the date of her trial on 27 January. Thus, this pre-trial examination occurred four to six weeks after the preceding one. She had not been examined in the morning on this day. The questioning took place before John Gedde, the Master of Work—the official in charge of the king's buildings.[121] It opens with a confession in six articles related to demonological ideas, consisting of Agnes's confirmation of when the devil first appeared to her, followed by the confirmation that she conjured the devil in the form of a black dog, received the devil's mark, attended the conventions at Bara and Carberry, and conjured an image of Mr John Moscrop using wax. Also, she confessed that a woman named Janet Drummond had come to her for consultation about an illness.

Then, surprisingly, Agnes denied four items: the collective effort at Foulstruther to destroy David Seton,[122] sending the bill, sailing on the sea, and the convention at North Berwick—but she ultimately 'confesses this *again*'. [My italics.] This suggests that Agnes was pressed by the interrogator, at which point she clearly vacillated, ending with a confirmation of her previous confession. Her denials here might have been influenced by her long imprisonment. It is likely that, by now, Agnes knew that she was in a hopeless situation. But she probably also knew that she had the option to withdraw her previous confession to avoid conviction. And maybe this is what she tried to do. However, it appears that, in this moment, Agnes was too weak to stand her ground; for instance, she gave up on denying North Berwick. This could have had to do with a fear of torture, as *Newes from Scotland* says explicitly that Agnes Sampson was tortured.[123] The records show a woman in distress.

The first part of the examination is very brief—only fourteen lines in total. The sentences are compressed and bare; her replies apparently responses to leading questions. The form of her answers indicates that she simply confirmed or responded negatively to the interrogator's question. Then, the examination shifts to a new item: Agnes's three meetings with a woman named Barbara Napier, who was an important accused individual in the North Berwick trials.[124] One meeting was in Dalkeith and two took place in Cameron. Agnes confessed that Barbara had asked her to use a picture made from wax to destroy a man named Archie, who was thought to damage Barbara's husband, as they were not friends and the husband feared enemies. Barbara had also given Agnes her ring to read a prayer over, so that Barbara could obtain the favour of a woman named Lady Angus.[125] At this point in the interrogation, it had evidently become important to collect information about Barbara Napier, as her trial was the next in line. Thus, at the end, after Agnes confessed to acts related to core demonological ideas, the questioning focused on denunciation. Moreover, Agnes confessed that she had put mould under the foot of the bed of a woman called Euphame MacCalzean to help her give birth.[126] The interrogation closes with Agnes being accused of having dealings with Barbara Napier and Euphame MacCalzean.

In the dittay, most of Agnes's words from the interrogation are repeated. There is no new information in this final trial document, as all items contained within it had been covered in pre-trial examinations. However, the content is structured into fifty-three articles and is ordered in a coherent manner, and the language is fluent, with complete sentence structures. As such, when it comes to the stylistic devices of grammar and language fluency, the editing hand of a scribe is therefore more visible in this document than in the pre-trial depositions.

The articles of which Agnes was 'fylit and convict' correspond to the articles in the dittay.[127] Articles 1 through 12 focus on her practice as a healer, her 'devilish art of witchcraft in curing' and her 'devilish prayers'.[128] Many of her healing activities are described as related to the devil. Article 13 deals with the devil's foretelling of the Michaelmas storm and Article 14 with the devil's saying that the queen would never come home unless the king fetched her. Then, Articles 15 to 25 deal with her father as mentor and with her as a practising healer. Article 26 indicates a more dangerous practice, linking her healing activities to demonological ideas through the digging up of bones in a cemetery in order to make them into powder. The following articles, 27 through 32, again pertain to Agnes's healing activities. In Article 32, her prayer for her patients' life or death is rendered *verbatim*. From Article 33 through 42, there is a change in the style of the records, as the articles become longer and more like narratives. Their content is linked to demonological ideas about becoming the servant of the devil—including renouncing one's Christian baptism, being made promises by the devil, receiving the devil's mark, shape-shifting, performing collective witch-craft, participating in witches' gatherings, digging up corpses from the grave-yard, performing witchcraft using a wax image, and using witchcraft powder made from the joints of corpses. Articles 43 and 44 again concern the healing of people, with her prayer for healing rendered in full. Articles 45 and 46 pertain to the charming of cattle. Then, articles 47 through 50 focus once again on demonological ideas, this time in the form of witchcraft conventions. The apex is arguably the confession in Article 50, in which Agnes Sampson 'confest before his maiesteisis':[129] a dramatic account of the convention at the North Berwick kirk. Article 51 concerns the deal between Agnes Sampson and Barbara Napier to take revenge on a man named Archie, for which purpose they had used a wax picture in the name of the devil. Article 52 details Agnes's performance of gain-ing favour through the use of a ring that belonged to Barbara Napier. Finally, Article 53 states: 'Item for ane co[m]moun notorious witch and usar of sorcerie and inchantmentis w[i]th the Invocatioun of the devill hir maister abusing the puir simple people th[air]w[i]th drawing thame fra the levi[n]g to the (. . .) of god and to beleve in the support of the devill'.[130] Her entire confession confirms that she could perform evil witchcraft helped by the devil.[131]

It is quite clear that Agnes had a reputation in the district not only as some-one who could heal but also as someone who could take away any illness that had been cast on one person by another. She was believed to have been able to predict 'by her witchcraft' whether a sick person would recover and whether someone was going to die. She was apparently an outspoken woman, saying that by her witchcraft, William Mackestoun was a dead man,[132] or that 'she being send for to the lady Rosleine quha wes seik sche knew be hir develisch prayer that the said lady wes nocht hable to recover and thairfore sche wald nocht cu[m] to hir'.[133] Agnes was also able to see if an illness was caused by an 'elfshot'—cast by fairies.[134] She was accused of the unsuccessful healing of a man who became 'a crepill'.[135] Then there is the evil side of Agnes's activities: she was accused of having gone 'to Natoun kirk at night together with the witch of Carbarrie and others' and having dug up buried corpses and taken the joints to make powder for witchcraft. This act was a well-known feature of Continental witchcraft trials.[136]

The Voice of Agnes Sampson

The voice of Agnes Sampson, as it comes to the fore during the first examinations, is to a certain extent reserved. Leading questions move the interrogation along, as Agnes herself only gives brief answers to the questions posed. However, as the examination continues, she begins giving longer answers that resemble small narratives. A sentence starting with 'She confesses (. . .)' is linked to a similar sentence and, little by little, a detailed picture of an event emerges. Agnes Sampson's voice becomes more prominent when her confession turns into a telling of narratives of a certain length.

The pre-trial transcriptions are fragmented, with many unfinished sentences due to damaged court records. Still, we can perceive the voice of Agnes Sampson in the content of the interrogation: she is the one bringing knowledge that only she possesses into the discourse. She voices a narrative about becoming the devil's servant, the North Berwick convention, and other witches' gatherings. She denounces other people as having been participants in conventions. She describes specific motifs, such as the devil's physical appearance. She refers to the devil foretelling the king's bairns.[137] She describes her six meetings with the devil, the first one consisting of carnal relations, and her receipt of the devil's mark. By putting bits and pieces together, Agnes's story about the conjuring of the storm and the North Berwick convention is developed into a narrative with a marked timeline and a clear cause-and-effect argumentation. This narrative is detailed and there are clear orality features, such as recounting the foretelling of the devil.

In the voice of Agnes Sampson, as it is rendered in the pre-trial documents, we hear several accents. We hear the accent of a healer with knowledge about benevolent remedies for diseases and a prayer for taking them away. In fact, Agnes used two prayers: one prayer for healing the sick and one for divination. We hear the accent of a storyteller who knows the traditional oral tales about elfshots and evil blasts—a kind of whirlwind—from fairies. We also hear the accent of a malevolent witch. We hear the accent of a woman in a pact with the devil, participating in evil witchcraft conventions. And we hear the accent of a denouncing witch, naming other suspects who allegedly took part in collective witchcraft endeavours.

Characteristic of Agnes Sampson's voice is the range of her talent for storytelling, willingly demonstrated in rich and colourful language:

> umq[uhi]le Ro[ber]t Kers in Dalkeyth quha wes havelie tormentit w[i]th wichcraft and diseis laid on him be ane westla[n]e warlaoch quhen he wes in Du[m]freis quhilk[138] seiknes sche tuik upoun hir selff and kepit the sam[yn] w[i]th grit grou[n]ings and torment q[uhi]ll the morne at q[uhi]lk tyme thair wes ane gritt dyn hard in the hous quhilk seiknes sche caist of hir selff in the clois to the effect ane catt or doge mycht haif gottin the sam[yn] and nocht w[i]thstanding the sam[yn] wes laid upoun Alexr Douglas in Dalkeyth quha[139] dwynit and deit th[ai]rw[i]th and the said umq[uhi]le Ro[ber]t Kers wes maid haill.[140]

Also, we hear a reluctant voice emerging only under duress: 'confesseth the first appearing of the devil. [S]he confesseth the mark. The first meeting at Bara, he being in visible form'.[141] These two accents constitute extremes on a discursive scale, representing completely different expressions.

There are clear features of orality in Agnes's speech, and the sentence structure is additive, with the frequent use of conjunctions: for example, 'then' at the start of sentences, followed by phrases like 'she said' and 'he answered'. Agnes's confession comprises a fleshed-out narrative.

Agnes knows how to develop stories and build lively narratives, with all essential structures intact. She knows how to develop plots, how to weave different threads of a story together:

> Bot the said David being stayit to cum that day as thay thocht sould haif
> done the wrak lichtit in the hyndis//and his dochter quha evir since hes
> bene heavelie vexit w[i]th terrible vissiounes and apparitiounes and hir body
> tormentit w[i]th ane evill spreit q[uahi]rw[i]th sche hes beine possest maist
> petiefullie.[142]

Agnes knows how to switch between plain passages, where she as the narrator has the authority, and rendered dialogues between herself and the devil. For instance, she inserts a conversation with the devil, 'Eloa'.[143] She knows how to change the speed of the narrative, shifting between rapid sequences with a lot of action and passages that stand still. She paints images with words, such as the ones she uses to describe the North Berwick convention. This compelling aspect is the voice we hear when she gives her confession before the king. At this point in the confession, she is still able to form vital and coherent stories.

Then, a change occurs during the examination on 5 December, on a Saturday afternoon. During this examination, not a single denial is heard from Agnes, unlike in her examination the day before. It seems that all her resistance has vanished. Furthermore, her answers do not bring many new things. Her vitality as a storyteller is lacking—the language as well as the content is reduced.

Likewise, we hear a compressed and suppressed voice in the final pre-trial examination, which took place before the Master of Work John Gedde, in January. This voice is barely audible: there is pain that can be traced in its lack of vitality. It is a voice that has been stripped. While Agnes confesses to something of her own when she speaks about her meetings with Barbara Napier, the rest of the examination consists of very few of her own words. This is a voice in despair that tries to deny several acts previously confessed to. This attempt, however, is quickly replaced by a repeated confession. Her cry of protest is rapidly silenced. The vacillation between confessing, denying, and confessing again certainly indicates pressure and torture. Furthermore, her trial date is fast approaching, and at this point she would have known that the outcome would not be in her favour.

Agnes's responses in the pre-trial documents provide some clues about the questions she was asked. The records indicate that the interrogators were most interested in obtaining information about the conjuring of the storm against the royal ships and about the North Berwick convention. Another element of apparent interest was the particular knowledge that Agnes had as a practising healer.

In the dittay, by comparison, Agnes Sampson's words are rendered in third-person indirect speech. This type of courtroom discourse has been discussed by several scholars, each of whom emphasizes the connection between rendered indirect speech in court records and orality features.[144] The court records of the Agnes Sampson trial confirm this argument, as we see a text composed according to legal rules and regulations and a professional scribe who has tried to record the reasons for the verdict and sentence in the records. In the dittay, the style is consistent, as the scribe always follows the same structure in each article. A cause-and-effect argumentation is articulated throughout: after practising witchcraft or magic, a consequence ensues. Agnes Sampson's voice is rendered in the court records by the introductory conjunction 'that', for instance: 'Item fylit and convict *that* W[ilia]m Blakeis sone sark being send to hir scho be hir witchcraft declarit that the seiknes th[a]t he had was ane elf schot'.[145] [My italics.] The dittay consists of itemized accusations that are based on Agnes's previous confessions. Parallel phrases and word repetitions show that it was composed according to fixed principles and structures and that it was influenced by legal conventions with regard to style.

The confession expressed in Agnes Sampson's voice is a mixture of traditional tales and knowledge of benevolent magic, malevolent witchcraft, and demonological ideas. The interrogation proceeds along leading questions, whether these were posed by the king, the Master of Work, or other interrogators. With regard to the repetition of questions and the focus on specific items, it is clear that Agnes was regarded a dangerous witch the moment when she revealed her pact with the devil. The questions' steady circling around the appearance of the devil, the conjuring of the storm, the conventions, and the devil's prescience about the king's children-to-be points towards the fear of witches. The interrogator wants to obtain the knowledge he assumes Agnes has. The king even protests when he feels that the different versions of her confession conflict.

However, while the king and the other interrogators might have influenced the type of questions posed and the content of the answers, much of the information that surfaces in Agnes Sampson's confession can only have come from her—for example, the names of the other participants in the conventions. Laura Paterson, Michelle D. Brock, and Sierra Dye underline that accused persons confessed according to their beliefs and knowledge.[146] It is not clear how much the peasants, people in rural areas, or the interrogators themselves knew about demonological ideas at this time. As for King James himself, in his early published works, 'references to Satan and to the Devil are plentiful',[147] which reflects learned Europeans' demonologies. King James's own book collection shows that he owned books by Jean Bodin, Niels Hemmingsen, and Agrippa.[148] The clearest indication that the king knew about demonological ideas around 1590 is his participation in interrogation during the North Berwick trials. Also, in his demonological treatise, which he might have started writing at the time of the North Berwick trials,[149] the king mentions several European intellectuals who were related to demonology.[150] However, King James had certainly heard of the key demonological notion of witches' gatherings, which receives particular attention during the North Berwick trials, in Denmark early in 1590. He carried this home as part of his mental bagage

The Voices of the Witnesses

As this was a trial based on denunciation, witnesses were not brought before the court. Agnes Samson was implicated by Geillis Duncan. There were likely witnesses at the very first stage of her trial, when she was brought before the presbytery of Haddington, but this was before the North Berwick trials started.

The Voice of the Interrogator

In this trial, the rare situation occurs that the voice of one of the interrogators is a royal voice. In the pre-trial interrogation at the beginning of December, King James VI is documented to be questioning Agnes Sampson; his ideas and knowledge have an impact on the content and progression of the interrogation. However, other interrogators take part as well.

With regard to interrogation, an important question is: to what extent does the interrogator place words in Agnes's mouth, such that she simply repeats or confirms his question? Judging from the length of her answers, this could have been the case for about 5%–10% of the questions. When her answers are recorded as, 'She confesses the delivery of the bill out of her own hand' or 'She confesses the bill was to raise the storm for staying the queen's coming home',[151] these could have been repetitions of questions posed. The scribe preserved the answers' brevity and recorded the sentences as Agnes spoke. Some of the pre-trial documents contain answers that are longer and more fluent—paragraphs with a clear narrative structure. This reflects the obvious interest in the North Berwick convention, the alliance with the devil, the appearance of the devil, and the witches' performance of evil—especially the conjuring of the storm. In these passages, the interrogator probably introduced the topic, but he could not have provided the entire content of the answer, nor could he even have known the content of the answers, as they had to do with specific events related to the North Berwick convention and Agnes's practice of healing. Therefore, in parts of the interrogation, the interrogator might have steered the course of the interrogation and the topics covered through leading questions, but the content of the answers came from Agnes Sampson herself.

Judging from the pre-trial records, it seems that Agnes Sampson might have had a deal of knowledge about the North Berwick convention before the interrogation started. She might have learned about these ideas during her imprisonment or perhaps before she was imprisoned, as such content might have been spread in the local communities via oral narratives. In addition, Agnes gave details about practising benevolent magic, and the interrogator clearly believed that she had the ability of divination. The interrogator was eager to get hold of knowledge about her art.

The Voice of the Law

The voice of the law is primarily heard in the eagerness to extract confessions. As this is the first time demonological ideas are heard in Scottish witchcraft trials, the voice of the law seems competent in such ideas. However, interest in *maleficium* and healing is also marked. In the dittay, Latin is used in the introduction, and the voice of the law comes to the fore by the rendered names of the advocates and the assize, the terminology and rhetoric used, the ordering of the particular points, and the wording of the sentence. The voice of the law echoes legal competence.

The Voice of the Scribe

The voice of the scribe is neutral. He does not give any comments of his own, and there are no traces of distancing devices to cast doubt on the content of Agnes's confession. The scribe has recorded the discourse as he heard it during the interrogation, however fragmented. The structure of these documents reflects the scribe's awareness that the content of the confession, related in Agnes Sampson's own words, was important, with profound implications regarding her life or death. When recording the pre-trial documents, he clearly aimed to get the discourse written down as carefully as possible.

The pre-trial documents focus on the questions posed and consist of itemized confessions. The first document opens with what seem to be reminders for the interrogator, denoting the subjects to deal with during the interrogation: 'to be speered concerning', 'concerning them that wer[e]', 'concerning the ring', 'memorandum to speer concerning (. . .) dall (. . .)'.[152] The text follows the questioning step by step, giving indications of what Agnes has been asked about by the frequently recurring phrase 'she confesses (. . .)'. This phrase is repeated twenty times over the course of five pages, so it was clearly important to note what Agnes said. The force of repetition is very strong in each of the four pre-trial documents, becoming a prominent textual feature, with the repetitive phrases and words working almost like a spell.

It is important for the scribe to record Agnes's words, particularly when the interrogation changes from healing to demonological witchcraft. In the dittay, benevolent and malevolent witchcraft are rendered in the articles in rather brief, stereotypical, and repetitive language. However, the language shifts when Agnes starts confessing about the devil. Demonological ideas present in Agnes Sampson's confession are the devil's pact, the devil's mark, the devil's appearance, witches making themselves invisible, collective witchcraft operations, and witches' conventions. Shape-shifting is not directly mentioned in relation to the North Berwick convention, as the alleged participants appeared to have attended in their own human bodies.[153] However, the alleged witches were said to be invisible when they were at sea.[154]

The intention and ambition of the scribe is professional: his job is to record the proceedings accurately enough to provide readers with an understanding of what went on during interrogation and in the courtroom, and to show that judicial practice was performed according to the correct procedures. This also holds true for the legal reasons and arguments leading up to the passing of the verdict and sentence.

Helene Clerk, 1643–45

The Trial

On 16 October 1643, Helene Clerk, a fisherman's wife from Newhaven, was questioned at the North Leith Kirk in Edinburgh. The dossier of her trial consists of loose documents from the examination before the moderator and minister of North Leith Kirk, as well as court records from the central court in Edinburgh. Helene was suspected of witchcraft, and on 22 December of the same year, she was formally accused by the central court: by Sir Thomas Hope of Craighall and two parishioners of North Leith, Robert Robiesone, and William Dunkiesone:

> for thame selffis & in name & behalf the remanent sessioun of the said kirk informeris to o[u]r advocat in the mater underwrittin Upoun helene clerk spous to George boyle fischer in Newheavin that q[uhai]r albeit be the devyne law of almytie god mentionat and set doun in his sacred word all userie & practizerie of witchcraft sorcerie charming suithsaying and inchanting ar ordanit to be puneist to the daith.[155]

The accusation refers to the Witchcraft Act: 'diverse actis of parliament of this our kingdome Speciallie be the 73 act of the Nynth parliament of o[u][r darest goodame queane marie of good and nevir deing memorie'.[156] This was the beginning of more than one year in the Edinburgh Tolbooth for Helene Clerk. The trial started with her examination by the minister of North Leith Kirk, Minister Andrew Fairfull. The bailie of Newhaven, George Crawford, and the Reader at the same kirk, Mr Alexander Wardrop, took part as well.[157] In addition to these three men, three other men verified the confession of Helene Clerk: George Cunningham, John Cunningham, and Jealis Hunter.

The documents of this trial are extraordinary, because it is possible to trace the linguistic development in one document after another, and because there is a petition wherein we can hear Helene Clerk's own words. The entire dossier enables us to gain insight into the various steps of the trial.

In chronological order, the dossier of the trial comprises an entry dated 18 November 1643, which states that she was 'pricked' by a 'witch-pricker'; an entry that records two pre-trial examinations that were sent from the moderator of the presbytery to the Lord Advocate on 23 November 1643; the dittay, dated 22 December 1643, Edinburgh; a document probably written by the Lord Advocate, summing up six articles in the dittay and two eiks,[158] inserting an evaluation of the articles that were repelled by Helene Clerk, describing what is not relevant and what is not witchcraft, and a last addition saying: 'The Last article anent the devillis m[ar]k & hir birnt of witchcraft findis it may be conjoinet w[i]th ony of the articles fund relevant per se';[159] a continuation of the trial on 10 and 11 March 1645, when forty-three citizens from North Leith and five citizens from Newhaven, in addition to twelve female witnesses, were summoned to an inquest of 'helen clerk under the paines contenit';[160] a document dated 14 March 1645 with additional witnesses' testimonies against Helene Clerk;[161] and, finally, a petition from Helene Clerk to 'My lord Justice and his ma[jes]ties advocat', asking for a delay of the trial. These sources show the development of the trial as well as Helene Clerk's own voice, both in the petition and rendered in the witnesses' testimonies.[162] We do not know the verdict or sentence.

The trial of Helene Clerk provides many pieces of information about the mentalities at the time, of lay as well as learned persons. The style and fluency of the different documents vary a great deal. While the minutes from the pre-trial examinations are relatively short and focus on the content of diverse events, the dittay is more voluminous, with a strong legal stamp on the language. The minutes from the pre-trial examinations record what Helene Clerk related about learning witchcraft, for example being washed with charmed water by 'Ellspeth the spae wyff quha wes brunt in south Leith for witchecraft'.[163] They also render in full the content of the witnesses' testimonies. In the dittay, the core content from the pre-trial examination is preserved, but legal rhetoric and voluminous legal phrases are poignant. The 73rd Act of the 9th Parliament is mentioned, which is the Scottish Witchcraft Act of 1563.[164] The wording of the document closely resembles the wording of the Witchcraft Act itself, as it covers all benevolent and malevolent witchcraft and sorcery practices: its key terms are witchcraft, sorcery, and necromancy.[165] It is emphasized that these crimes are to be punished by death.

Helene Clerk swore an oath before she started her confession. She said that when she was sick twenty years ago, Elspeth, the 'spae wife', who was burned for witchcraft in South Leith, was sent for in order to wash Helene. Elspeth put a pair of sheets[166] around the tub so that the water would not splash onto the floor. When the washing was finished, Elspeth 'commanded that the water be emptied'[167] in a 'private place where there was no basin'.[168] She asked the servants to drain the water, and they transported it to the seaside and emptied the tub there. After the servant returned home, they declared that the water had been 'cast in the sea', 'and thereafter there arose a great storm of weather and took away ane yole of newhavin and wes never seen th[air]efter And be the storme four houssis in newheavin war blowin doun'.[169]

Then the witnesses were brought forth. First, Jeane and Christiane Thomsone, who swore before the men, in the presence of Helene Clerk, that they were 'reputt to be of gude lyff and conversa[tio]un w[i]thin the parochin'.[170] They testified that,[171] after the accused person was washed by the spae wife, she had acquired the art of witchcraft herself.[172]

Afterwards, to verify the accusation of witchcraft against Helene Clerk, two of her neighbours, Euphamia Randell and Janet MacKinlay, swore that there had been a conflict between Helene and James Bissett involving Helene's son, and that she had threatened him and said that he would never sail another year, after which he fell ill and died.[173]

Another witness came forward, named Jonet Annieson, who testified that on Easter Monday, Helene Clerk came to her home, where the husband of Jonet, James Bisset, lay sick and dying. Helene wanted to give twenty shillings from the neighbours for the necessities of the sick husband. Helene and James Bissett had not spoken to each other for a long time, due to a controversy. Now, she looked him in the face and said that she wished it was undone, what was done. Jonet said that she once had come to Helene's house and said to Helene's god-daughter that she had provided much salt, whereupon Helene answered that there was more salt provided than would be wanted that year, whereupon it followed that there was no catch of herring that year.[174]

Margaret Boyle, inhabitant[175] of Leith, was brought forth as the next witness. She swore and testified that there had been an argument between Helene Clerk and herself, after which she had become sick for eighteen weeks. She recovered her health when, on Shrove Tuesday,[176] Helene gave her a mackerel that had been sent by Helene Sword, a woman who was dead, commanding that Margaret 'eat of it'.[177]

Another witness, Barbara Purves from Leith, came forward and swore her oath, and testified that, several years prior, Helene Clerk and her husband had owed her seven pounds. When Barbara went to Helene and asked for the money, Helene told her to go home, and that 'she should go worse home than when she came'. When Barbara arrived home, her child was 'taken out of a boiling kettle', probably a big pan used for cooking which the child had fallen into. The child died.[178]

The last witness was Helene Thomsone, the wife of William Craige in Newhaven. She swore her oath and testified that John Smith had come to her house and said that Helene Clerk 'would cause his death' because he had not married her daughter. He 'got a sickness' and suspected Helene Clerk 'to be the occasion thereof'. He went to Helene Clerk's house and 'craved his health', and sent her a pint of ale. Helene then gave him two eggs, which he ate. But when he said to Helene that 'he would go to a doctor to mend his back', she said that he could not, and a short time afterwards, he died.[179]

After these eight female witnesses had testified,[180] the examination was over. However, there are two additions to the documents, showing that the examination had an addendum. The first addition is an entry signed by a moderator of the kirk, Mr William Dalgleish. On 18 November in Leith, one month after her first examination, a witch-pricker—William Scobie from the nearby village of Musselburgh—came to Helene. A witch-pricker was an officially employed person who pricked suspected witches on the body with a big needle in order to find an insensitive spot which did not bleed. He examined Helene Clerk after she had taken off her clothes.[181] On her left arm,

> thair wes fund thair upon ane mark Q[uhi]lk the said williame persaving thrust ane prene being ane insche and ane half of lenth thairin quhairof the

said helene wes nowayes sensible nor no blood followit efter the preine wes taikin out haveing remaynit ane half hour within hir airme.[182]

The mark did not bleed and did not hurt when it was pricked: proof that this was a devil's mark. He showed this mark to the examiners and the parishioners. Present were Mr Andrew Fairfull, bailie George Crawford, Reader Alexander Wardrop, and some of the *fronderis*[183] of the kirk.

The entry is signed by William Dalgleish, only five days before the recorded examination reached the Lord Advocate in Edinburgh—this might indicate that the men considered the finding of the mark to be very grave, and that they wanted the trial to proceed as soon as possible. In light of the fact that the pre-trial document does not make mention of demonological ideas, the idea of searching for a devil's mark on Helene through pricking must have arisen between 6 October and 8 November. This was clearly a step towards switching from a *maleficium* trial to a demonological trial. The same minister, bailie, and moderator who were present during the examination on 16 October witnessed the finding of the mark.

The procedure of searching Helene Clerk for the devil's mark is also described in the dittay, and here it becomes clear that on 18 November she was asked, by the same men who had examined her in October, whether she had a devil's mark. She denied having one:

> And demanit *gif schoe had the devillische mark upone hir q[uhi]lk schoe denyet* w[illia]m stobie in Mussilbrut being p[rese]nt haveing sightit the said helene and hir claithes tane aff hir *thair was thane fund upone hir left airme the said mark* q[uhi]lk the said w[illia]m stobie knawing & perseaveing for tryell and cleiring th[ai]rof thrust in ane lang great preine being ane insche and ane halff of lenthe in the said mark q[uhai]rof the said helene was noways sensible q[uhi]lk preyne remanit th[ai]rin the space of halff ane hour and eftir drawin furthe th[ai]rof na blood followit.[184] [My italics.]

The word count of the pre-trial document and the dittay is approximately the same, and the content of the witch-pricking event is similar, except for the addition in the dittay that Helene Clerk was asked whether she had the devil's mark, and her denial. By 1643, demonological ideas about the devil's mark and the impact of this mark were known among common people across mainland Scotland and the Northern Isles, as was the work of witch-prickers.[185] In Helene's case, the witch-pricker lived in a nearby village. The fact that Helene denied having a devil's mark suggests that she knew that having one would send the trial in a much more serious direction.

The last entry of this document is a short note stating that the minutes from the pre-trial examination in North Leith had been sent to Edinburgh. At the very end of the document, in the same handwriting as the signature of the document stating the examination of the mark, William Dalgleish wrote: 'At Edinburgh the 23 of November Recommends to the Lord advocat to peruse thir depositions and to report his judgement thereanent'.[186] This indicates that the recorded pre-trial examination by the minister of the North Leith Kirk had been sent to Edinburgh after the discovery of the mark on Helene Clerk's arm, and that one and a half months later, the Lord Advocate was asked to use this document to prepare for a trial in the central court of Edinburgh. The dittay states that Helene's husband was summoned to come to Edinburgh on 12 January 1644, which was supposed to be the date for her trial:

> Our will is heirfoir and we chairge yow straitlie co[m]mandis that incontinent thir o[u]r L[ett]res sene ye pas and in o[u]r name [*rest of line damaged*] co[m]mitter of the cryme abonespe[cife]it in maner foirsaid *and the said george boyle fischer in newheavin hir spous for his entreis to co[m]peir befoir o[u]r Justice & his deputtis And underly o[u]r lawis for the samyn In o[u]r tolbuithe of Ed[inbu]r[gh] the twelff day of Januar nixtocum* in the hour of caus to the effect that upone hir tryell and convictione of the said crymes schoe may be puneist in hir persone & guidis conforme to the lawis of this realme.[187] [My italics.]

However, this intended trial never took place, and Helene Clerk was kept in the tolbooth until March 1645, while a new trial was prepared. We do not know the reason for this change. It might have been caused by political turbulence, but it could also have been cancelled because the Lord Advocate did not find the trial against Helene to be strong enough. There is a sheet of paper in the bundle related to Helene's trial that seems to be the Lord Advocate's evaluation of the points in the dittay. He approved of four articles but found the others to be irrelevant for a witchcraft trial. The articles that he did find relevant were the following: First, an article about the death of James Bisset, '*releva[n]t in the first member th[ai]rof* & nocht of the secund';[188] second, an article noting that Helene had been sick twenty years before, '*releva[n]t the persewar condiscending how long scho was seik & q[uhe]n sho deceissit*';[189] third, an article referring to Margaret Boyle's illness and the mackerel cure, 'the Inchantit mccrell *fund relevant* w[i]th this caveat that the assyse tak heid to the probatioun';[190] and finally, the article about the finding of the devil's mark, 'The Last article anent the devillis m[ar]k & hir birnt of witchcraft findis it may be conjoinet w[i]th ony of the articles *fund relevant per se*'.[191] [My italics.] The rest of the articles were dismissed as being irrelevant to the trial. For example, the Lord Advocate stated that it could not be proved that the child falling into a kettle with boiling water or John Smith's sickness and death were due to witchcraft. Moreover, the claim that Helene had been washed with charmed water was not considered to be related to witchcraft.

The separate sheets of paper that follow the trial contain information that was included in the trial document. Therefore, this information must have been recorded after the first examination on 6 October and after the date of the trial. One document is the undated 'Addition to Helene clerk hir dittay'. Here, three episodes are brought forth to strengthen the accusation against Helene. The first pertains to the sale of oysters: 'Ye the said helene haveing sauld to margaret runsieman than servant to Lucres alias Luse Cokburne indweller in [*blank*] ane laid gallone full of oisteris'.[192] When Helene brought the 'leid gallone' to Luse Cockburne's house, she asked Luse's servant, Margaret Runsieman, to 'toome the leid gallone', to empty the lead[193] gallon. This led to a dispute between Helene and Margaret, who told Helene that she could empty it herself, whereupon Margaret took the gallon and threw it away with such force that one of the 'girthes'[194] broke. Next, Helene threatened her, and the same night, Margaret burned her leg.[195]

The next recorded episode was more serious, as it concerned the death of a man. Helene Clerk had come to William Oswald—a shoemaker in South Leith—in search of a pair of good boots, 'thraitini[n]g him at that tyme gif the buittis war nocht guid & sufficient he sould nevir make ane uth[i]r pair to ony in Newheavin th[air]of'.[196] Uttering these words became dangerous for her, because William became seriously ill and died:[197] 'And sua was crewallie murdreist and slane by yo[u]r sorcerie and witchcraft laid be yow upone him as said is'.[198]

A third addition is related to John Smith, who accused Helene Clerk of making him ill because he had not married her daughter—this illness ultimately led to his death. The sister of John Smith verified as a witness 'that she hard hir brother upone his deid bed leave his daith and causis th[air]of upone the said helene clerk be hir sorcerie & witchcraft'.[199] Helene felt that John Smith should have married her daughter because she 'bore a child to him'. About fifteen days before his death, he claimed that Helene Clerk was 'the reason of his death, and that he was troubled with her in the night, and three other women with her'.[200]

The accusation related to the oysters is rendered on a separate sheet and includes the quarrel between Helene Clerk and the servant woman, Helene's threat and its result, and the servant's burned leg.[201]

Next, there is a document related to James Bisset and an incident pertaining to the sale of a boat. Hew Boyle, the son of Helene, was involved in the sale. A dispute occurred and, according to Helene,

> Hee James bisset boucht the halff of that coble he sall nevir goe to dumbar in hir for[202] my sone boucht the uth[e]r halff of hir And he sall have hir all And depones upone hir great oathe schoe said farder he will pyne away lyk ane head hair.[203]

Fifteen days later, James Bisset retired to his bed and 'lay in pain with sickness'—'sweating out' up to three shirts a day—for twenty-nine weeks, at which point he died.[204] James's neighbours helped him during his illness, having gathered and contributed resources among themselves to supply the necessities:

> q[uhi]lk contributione the said helene clerk ressavit brocht in to the said James bisset his hous and sit doun befoir his bedsyd And lookit in his face he being than sweating And utterit thir speaches to him Hows me gossop gif it war to be do that is done[205] to q[uho]m James replyet Lord tak me ath[e]r aft

this warald or els grant me my healthe unto q[uho]m the said helene replyet Ill warand gossop yo[u]r days not be long now And in effect the sa[i]d James bisset w[i]thin aucht days th[ai]reftir deceissit.[206]

The start of the dittay refers to the laws pertaining to witchcraft. Thereafter, the document contains the total of all information given in the witnesses' testimonies. It begins with Helene's alleged sickness twenty years earlier, along with the bewitched water she washed herself[207] with: charmed water made by the 'notorious witch', Elspeth, who had already been burned at the stake for witchcraft. Further, it is stated that when this water was thrown into the sea, a 'terrible storm arose', which destroyed several boats and several houses in Newhaven.

For the most part, the dittay follows the wording of the document recording the minister's questioning. The same itemization is followed, relating one testimony after another to focus on a particular event. The information contained in the two additional dittays is included in the trial document, as is the rendering of Helene Clerk's own words. However, the sentence is more detailed. A difference in style compared to the pre-trial documents can be traced, particularly the frequent mentioning of 'devil' and 'devilish'. These words are often repeated in the dittay, but are not found in the pre-trial documents.

In the dittay, a few points were added to the examination by the minister, among them a point regarding the death of the husband of Margaret Burges in Wairdie, who was allegedly bewitched by Helene Clerk: 'And sua be hir sorcerie and witchcraft was crewallie murdreist & slane'.[208]

Throughout the testimonies, there is a clear cause-and-effect argumentation, as all the witnesses argue that there was first a dispute involving Helene Clerk, followed shortly by the sickness and death of the individual involved in the dispute.

The Voice of Helene Clerk

The voice of Helene Clerk comes to the fore in the minutes of the pre-trial examination, in the dittay, and in several of the witnesses' testimonies. In addition, her voice is heard in the petition. In the witnesses' testimonies, her voice is rendered in the third person, while in the petition, her own words—addressed to the Lord Advocate—are in the first person. Formally, the rendering of Helene Clerk's voice changes between the pre-trial documents and the dittay. In the pre-trial documents, her voice is rendered as reported speech introduced by 'sayd' or another reporting verb. In the dittay, her voice is depicted in various ways. Sometimes a reporting verb is kept as an introduction to a reported clause, and sometimes it is deleted—in the latter case, Helene's utterance has been validated as a proposition, a statement. However, the pre-trial discourse was most likely followed in the dittay, as there are strong linguistic similarities between the two in terms of content, strings of words, word order, and orality features.

In Helene Clerk's voice, there is an accent of her belief in witchcraft. When she became ill, she sought help in the wrong place,

> schoe for hir cure and releiff th[ai]rof expres againe the lawis of almytie god and o[u]r actis of parliament preferring the cure & help of the devill and his devillische & wicked instrumentis witcheis & sorceris befoir the help & cure of the omnipotent and almytie god and the ordiner meanes appoyntit be his sacred word'.[209] [My italics.]

This help would ultimately prove fatal to her, as the conspicuous alleged event during which she is washed with charmed water by the well-known witch Elspeth is seen as an initiation into witchcraft. I interpret Helene Clerk's confession to Mr Faithfull as stating that Elspeth knew that the water she had washed Helene with possessed strong powers, and that she wanted to have it emptied in 'sume privat place quhair no repair wes', because the water might cause an accident.[210] Helene believes she possesses the same power to cure. When neighbours asked how she was feeling after the washing, the minutes from the pre-trial examination contain the following wording: '*hir reply wes* scho will be weill for they neidit not to send for hir seing thair wes nothing that wes done bot the pairtie accused could doe the samyn hirselff'.[211] [My italics.] The dittay states, '*schoe for answer th[ai]rto declairit that schee wald be weill* aneughe for thai neidit not to ask at hir sic questiones becaus all that was doun for cureing of hir could have bene alsweill practeizet and doun be the said helen hirselff as be the said spay wyfe'. [My italics.] The content in both versions is that healing could be practised by Elspeth as well as Helene.

Helene Clerk's voice also has a personal touch. In the minutes from the first examination by the minister, Helene's voice is rendered in reported speech, but with reference to her words: 'she deponed that (. . .)'. In this way, Helene's voice carries the narrative—we see this, for instance, in the story about the charmed water. Helene refers to herself in the third person: 'when *she* was sick'; 'Elspeth did wash *hir*'. [My italics.] The voice of Elspeth is also heard: she was careful with the charmed water, so 'nothing should be spilt' and *she* [Elspeth] 'gave streit cumand to tome the water in a private place'. [My italics.] In the dittay, however, Helene's voice—and Elspeth's voice, too—have become somewhat subdued. In the rendering of the story of the charmed water, there is no referring verb like 'deponed' or 'said' connecting certain utterances to Helene. The voices of Helene and Elspeth have thus been turned into a plain, past-tense narrative:

> Addressit hir selff *and consultit* w[i]th ane Notorious witche callit Elspethe the spay wyfe quha was convict and brunt for witchcraft be quhus devillische directiones the said helene *did wesche hirselff* with water charmet & inchantit be the said spay wyfe in the practeizeing q[uhai]rof ane pair of scheittis was put about the tub in the q[uhi]lk the water was put that nane of the charmit water sould spill or ryn over w[i]th this express injunctione gevin be the said witch that eftir the said helene hir wascheing th[ai]rwith *the said charmet or inchantit*

water sould be careit to some private place quhair na repair of people was and th[ai]r to be cassing furth and tumed Bot sa it is that the said inchantit water being transpoirtit & careit to the sea syde and castin in the sea be the carey-ers th[ai]rof Be that occasione and be the sorcerie and witchcraft of the spay wyfe & of the said helene clerk q[uhi]lk was cured th[ai]rby.[212] [My italics.]

When we compare the content of the pre-trial records with that of the dittay, we see that the dittay does not add new items to the pre-trial examination minutes. However, the grammatical structure of the sentences has changed, as the verb that introduces the person speaking has been deleted in some places. Thus, in the dittay, the person speaking loses some characteristic features of her own, as well as some authority. The narrator is now the one deciding how to delegate a voice to whomever is speaking. A statement given by Helene is thus transformed into a proposition: the washing event is not only something *she said she was doing*; it was something *she was doing*. Thus the sentence is transformed into a more general statement than one belonging to Helene Clerk's voice alone.

Helene Clerk's belief in the connection between the charmed water, 'by accident toomed in the sea', and the storm in Newhaven is clearly expressed in the examination by the minister: 'Quhairupon[213] the pairtie accused with the spae wyff *sayd* that they war grieved and th[air]efter thair arose ane gritt storme of wether'.[214] [My italics.] In the dittay, the referring verb 'sayd' has disappeared, and the text has become more voluminous. In particular, the repetition of nouns, adjectives used as epithets to strengthen a specific feature, and verbs with identical meaning contribute to an expansion of the text:

> *Be that occasione and be the sorcerie and witchcraft* of the spay wyfe & of the said helene clerk q[uhi]lk was cured th[ai]rby *Ane horrible & grivous storme & tempest of wind & wether* arrais q[uhi]lk tuik away ane bot or yole out of the harburie of newheavin q[uhi]lk nevir was sene agane As also four severall houssis w[i]thin the said toun war *blawin doun & distroyit to the ground* to the greit loss of *the albueris [sic]*[215] *and heritouris*[216] t[hai]rof eftir the practeizeing of the q[uhi]lk *devilissche cure* upone the said helene clerk in maner foirsaid. [My italics.]

The utterance about the storm is now a statement authored by the narrator. Still, the main content is the same: the deed was performed by devilish means.

Helene's voice is also heard in the witnesses' testimonies. Sometimes, as in the example below, it is a threatening voice. The story about James Bisset illustrates the differences between how Helene's voice is displayed in the testimonies versus how it appears in the dittay. James Bisset and Helene Clerk had a dispute about Helene's son. In the testimony, it is stated that the witness

> *depones* that the said heleine pairtie accused *affirmit* to James bissett (thair being ane contraversie betuixt hir and him anent hir sones sailling with the

said James for bying of ane pairt of ane boit that hir sone has ane mynd to) that *the said James sould nevir saill ane uther yeir thairefter* Quhairupon the said James bissett imediatlie th[air]efter took seiknes dwynet and died. [My italics.]

The introductory verb 'depones' relates to the witness, while the verb 'affirmit' introduces the personal voice of Helene, along with her threatening words. In this story, the dittay has kept the referring verb with regard to Helene's voice:

tha[i]rof *threatnit* maist maliciouslie *the said James bisset that he sould nevir prosper not saill ane uth[e]r yeir th[ai]reftir* According to the q[uhi]lk devillische threatning and be the said helene clerk hir devillische sorcerie and witchcraft he immediatlie th[ai]reftir contractit ane seiknes q[uhai]rin he remanit bedfast w[i]th contenuall sweiting ane lang space th[ai]reftir And in end deceissit.²¹⁷ [My italics.]

In this citation, adverbs are used to emphasize meaning: 'threatnit' is underlined by 'maist maliciouslie'; an additional verb is used with an emphasizing purpose: 'nevir saill' is expanded to 'nevir prosper not saill'. A lively accent in Helene's voice is heard when the wife of James Bisset '*depones*' that Helene came with money, even if there had been a controversy between Helene and James:²¹⁸

And *beholding him in the face said* that *scho wissit that it war undone that is done* Lykeas the deponer depones that haveing cumet in to the pairtie accuset hir hous and scho haveing sayd to Jonet cunynghame the pairtie accused guid dochter that scho had provydit meikill salt *The pairtie accused replyit Tuty tuty thair wes more salt provydit nor wald be watt this yeir* whairupon followit that their wes no tak of heiring this year.²¹⁹ [My italics.]

In the dittay, this text has been expanded, but the context is maintained.²²⁰ To make the event even livelier, Helene's statement has been rendered in first-person present tense:

And *behalding* the said James bisset being in bedfast and *looking in his face* utterit thir words to the said Jonet his spous *I wische that war undone that is done* declairing th[ai]rby that he was bewitchit be hir and be hir devilrie & witchcraft casin upone him that feirfull seiknes q[uhai]rof he deceissit as said is And siclyk schortlie th[ai]reftir the said Jonet anisone haveing come to the said helene clerk hir hous and forgaddering w[i]th Jonet cuninghame dochter to the said helene declairit to hir that schoe had provydit meikle salt meaneing for the herring at dumbar drave Q[uhai]runto the said helen *replyet in thir wordis* in maist threatning and bitter maner *Tuty tattie th[ai]r is mair salt provydit nor will be wat this yeir* Q[uhair]upone and according to the said helen hir devillische predictione and be the sorcerie and witchcraft practeizet be hir and hir devillische assosiattie thair was no tak of herring that year.²²¹ [My italics.]

Here, we see that the dittay preserves the content, the string of words rendered in direct speech—for instance, 'I wische that war undone that is done'—and the initiating verb denoting indirect, reported speech from the testimony. In addition, a threatening phrase with clear orality features, 'Tuty tuty' (. . .) vs 'Tuty tattie (. . .)' was likewise kept with almost identical wording and spelling of the initial words. We see how the devices such as alliteration on the letter *t* and also rhythm, created by the stress on the first syllable, are maintained in the two orthographic solutions.

As seen above, the voice of Helene Clerk is characterized by features of orality, particularly in her threats. The use of strong and daring expressions makes her words easy to remember and retell. Features like repetition and rhyme also make the sentences easy to remember. The utterances are displayed almost identically in both the pre-trial examination minutes and in the formal dittay. When Helene sent Barbara Purves, to whom she owed money, home without payment, the pre-trial documents are worded as follows: '*the pairtie accused sayd go home go home, tho sould go worse home nor scho cam afeild*'.[222] [My italics.] In the dittay, it reads, '*The said helene* in great wreathe and anger brak furthe in thir wordis *Saying to hir goe hame goe hame thow sall goe wars hame than thow hes cume a field*'.[223] [My italics.] The referring verbs 'sayd' and 'brak furthe' introduce Helene's speech. Helene's voice here is determined and confident. In Barbara's accusation, Helene's threat is used to construct a cause-and-effect argument after an accident, as Barbara had returned home to find her child dead.

The threatening tone of Helene Clerk's voice occurs in a variety of situations. She must have been an outspoken woman, perhaps even a bit ill-tempered. She sold fish, carrying it around in baskets.[224] Indeed, one of the accusations against Helene Clerk concerned the sale of seafood, and is related above. Margaret Runsieman testified before four men, one of them Alexander Wardrop, Reader at the North Kirk in Leith, who had also been present at the first examination of Helene.[225] Helene supposedly came to Margaret Runsieman, who was then a servant, and asked her to 'toom a gallon of oisters'. They fell out, and Helene scolded Margaret:

> ye than *said* to the said servand woman, *hes thow done this I sall gar the rew and repent the same* Accordingly to the q[uhi]lk *malicious thraitini[n]g sua utterit be yow* the said m[ar]garet runsieman the same verie nycht be yo[u]r sorcerie & witchcraft laid be yow upoun hir hir leg was brunt. Quhilk sho hes affirmit to be of veritie.[226] [My italics.]

Helene's threatening words above are rendered as a quote, in first-person narration. Similar threats, using words like 'repent' and 'rew', are also rendered in plain, third-person past tense. In the story about Margaret Boyle and the 'makrell' cure, the threatening words are introduced by the referring verb 'saying':

> The said helene out of ane devillische dispositione and mad humo[u]r threatnit w[i]th cursed speiches the said margaret [Boyle] *saying to hir thir wordis that schoe sould repent and rew it* or it war lang according to the q[uhi]lk wiked and

devillische threattning ane grevous seiknes was laid upone the said Margaret boyle be the said helene clerk hir sorcerie and witchcraft q[uhai]rin schoe lay dwneing in great dollo[u]r & payne the space of auchtene oulkis[227] th[ai] reftir or th[ai]rby.[228]

However, Helene Clerk was also rumoured to have the power to take away illness and, in this case, the neighbours asked her for help.

Q[uhai]rupone the said helen being upbraidit be hir nychtboris quha affirmit that be hir devillische meanes sorcerie and witchcraft the said margaret boyle was sua paynet & tormentit the said helen for cure & help of the said margaret be hir [*word unreadable*] witchcraft & charmeing sent in to the said margaret boyle ane inchantit or charmet makrell q[uhi]lk was careyit be [*word unreadable*] favord new dead w[i]th the (dis)creit injunctione and directione that the said margaret sould [*word unreadable*] owt th[ai]rof that nycht *under the payne of hir lyfe* According to the q[uhi]lk injunctione and be the said helene clerk hir charmeing sorcerie & witchcraft abonewrittin the said margaret boyle was cured of hir said deseis.[229] [My italics.]

In the story above, narrative structures are prevalent, echoing the way confessions and testimonies are formulated. Linguistic devices, such as the cause-and-effect argumentation that creates a reason for Margaret's sickness and her healing, the timeline of the narrative, additive sentence constructions, and orality features are all preserved in the records. The same is seen in the testimony given by a witness about how Helene Sword brought the mackerel to Margaret Boyle, and where a ritual is included in the eating of the mackerel:

depones that (. . .) the pairtie accused haveing sent in ane mccrell about fasterence evin w[i]th helene sword now deid scho then recoverit heir health and became weill, and *when the said helene brocht in the mcrell scho gave the deponer ane strait comand that scho sould under the paine of hir lyff eit of it yit micht bot to eit it the morne neirest hir hairt.*[230] [My italics.]

When Helene Sword, who was now dead, brought in the mackerel, she ordered the witness,[231] Margaret Boyle, to eat the mackerel in the morning, holding it close to her heart. A story with a different outcome was related in a testimony about witchcraft allegedly cast on John Smith by Helene Clerk. The reason given for this incident was, as stated above, that he did not want to marry Helene's daughter:

[John Smith] contractit seiknes and *suspecting the said helene clark pairtie accused* to be the occasioner thairof went to the pairtie accuset at the dwelling house of the deponer so craved his healthe and send about ane pynt of aill to the quhilk pairtie accused gave him tua eggis quhilk he eitit and quhan he wes telling the pairtie accused that he wald go to ane doctor to mend his bak *scho sayd that he could not doe it and ane schort tyme th[air]efter he died.*[232] [My italics.]

John Smith suspected Helene of causing his illness, and he wanted her to take it away. In response, she had given him two eggs to eat—which had apparently not cured him—and then told him that a doctor could not help him. In the dittay, the text has been expanded, but the core of the story—the words spoken by Helene— conveys the same content:

> Item the said *helene clerk haveing consavit ane deadlie heatret malice and evill will aganes Jon Smyth* (. . .) the said helene in revenge th[ai]rof and be hir sor- cerie & witchcraft laid ane heavie & greavous seiknes upone the said Johnne smyth (. . .) the said helene clerk for his cure and releiff gave to him tua eggis q[uhi]lk he than eattit at hir desyre Eftir his eatting of the q[uhi]lkis eggis the said Johnne smyth finding him selff no better come bak agane to the said helene and said to hir that he behouvet to goe to some doctor of phisick to be cured *To the q[uhi]lk the said helene replyet and affirmet that th[ai]r was na doc- tor could mend him th[ai]rof* sua that w[i]thin few dayis th[ai]reftir he deceissit of the said seiknes And sua the said Johnne smyth was crewallie murdreist & slane be the said helene hir sorcerie and witchcraft practeizet be hir upone him at the tyme foirsaid.[233] [My italics.]

Described here is *maleficium* related to revenge. We again see a cause-and-effect argumentation when there is a need to explain a person's death: a link is con- structed between threats made by the accused and some kind of misfortune befall- ing the person threatened. The verb connected to Helene Clerk's voice is preserved in both documents; Helene 'sayd' or 'replyet'. The increased length of the formal document is due to the doubling of adjectives and the insertion of phrases from legal rhetoric, which was influenced by the Witchcraft Act, among others.[234]

Helene Clerk's voice is a voice of consistent resistance, as she never confessed to witchcraft. It clearly surfaces in her petition, in which she requests a delay of her March 1645 trial because her procurator[235] is absent. Her voice is humble, but still strongly declaims her innocence: 'I am incarcerat keipit and detenit in waird within the tolbuith of this burgh of ed[inbu]r[gh] *be the space of this yeir bygane* for *allegit* being airt and pairt of the cryme of witchcraft *quhairof I am most innocent*'.[236] [My italics.] She emphasizes her innocence, after having been incarcerated in the tolbooth for a long time. The expression 'this yeir bygane' probably means that she had been imprisoned continuously since her trial on 22 December 1643, which means more than a year. She must have been exhausted when she formulated her petition, but there is still power in her words as she protests against unjust accusa- tions and treatment. The wording of the petition might also have been influenced by the notary whom she employed.

In her petition, Helene Clerk specifically mentions the name of the minister 'Mr Andrew Fairfull', but also those of other examiners, whom she feared would take advantage of the situation when her procurator was away. With the witch-pricking in mind, she knows her '*dilatoris*[237] *and accuseris*' can increase her pain.[238] What also comes to the fore is that Helene fears for her life, as the trial has taken a dangerous turn. The finding of the devil's mark on her arm would certainly have signalled to her the peril she was in. Further, Helene does not expect to be treated fairly without her procurator present; 'no uther will compeir for me *insistis most maliciuslie and crullie agains me for suteing of my Lyfe* he haveing defendit me in tyme bygane and knawing the haill secreitis of the caus'.[239] [My italics.]

At the end of her petition, Helene's voice is both insistent and full of despair: she knows that her enemies are powerful. This is her only chance at being defended by a professional:

> I will most humelie intreat yow for the favor of god to grant me ane contine-watioun for the space of xv dayis and I sall caus my pro[curato]r be heir to attend upoun the defending of me and I shall sute no forder continewatioun but sall pray for yow.[240]

The formulaic ending shows in addition a professional notary's influence on the text. It is clear that the same minister who began her examination in 1643, and who was present during the witch-pricking, is still the person she considers her prime accuser. Helene Clerk would likely have been apprehensive about her second time before the court.

In Helene's voice, we hear a tough woman who was able to articulate her anger and frustration. Her voice could be threatening at times, and people may therefore have been afraid of her. However, in her petition we hear a humble, but sceptical voice. We can also trace vulnerability in this voice.

The Voices of the Witnesses

Those testifying against Helene are all women: neighbours and residents of Leith. Their voices are persuasive as they attempt to show, through examples, that there is reason to believe that Helene Clerk has practised witchcraft. They argue that Helene caused several accidents that affected the local community. Their testimonies are narratives: They describe the scene, actors, dates, and places of specific incidents; they then relate the words Helene said at the time—which she often uttered in a state of anger; and, finally, they detail the results that occurred shortly afterwards. The voices of the witnesses are clearly dominated by orality features, such as the quoting of phrases spoken by Helene and others in their narratives. The witnesses often use dramatic devices to make their stories lively, for instance recounting things that other people heard, not what they heard themselves. The common denominator between all testimonies is the construction of a link between a specific accident and Helene's angry words, thus providing an explanation for inexplicable events like people falling ill or dying, or ships and houses being damaged by bad weather.

The Voice of the Interrogator

In the records of Helene Clerk's trial, the emphasis is on Helene's and the witnesses' answers, not on the questions posed to them. The voice of the interrogator, Mr Fairfull, comes to the fore once in the pre-trial documents: when the devil's mark is brought up. In the dittay, it is recorded that Helene was asked whether she had the devil's mark on her, which she denied. However, it is clear that the trial is steered in the direction of demonological ideas, as the devil's mark comes up rather late in the course of the pre-trial examination. Thus, the minister, who is the main interrogator, the bailie of Newhaven, the Reader of the kirk, and some of the parishioners who are present during Helene's pricking press for a development of the trial towards demonological witchcraft. The interrogator would be central in this pressure. Therefore, his voice is influential.

The Voice of the Law

In Helene Clerk's trial, the voice of the law surfaces most clearly in the final trial document, in the dittay, and in the Lord Advocate's evaluation of the articles in the dittay. If one wants to determine what kind of ideas the lawyers and judges had about witchcraft, the dittay is a good place to start, as it shows that the devil and all that is devilish was emphasized. The judges and lawyers at the central court in Edinburgh obviously knew the contemporary rhetoric of law, but they also knew both learned demonological ideas and the wording of the Witchcraft Act. These ideas had entered into the lawyers' language and way of arguing their cases before the courts. All these accents—the linguistic features—were inserted into the language of the final trial document, thus polishing the surface of the text with a legal terminology. The voice of the law is spiced with expressions related to witchcraft and sorcery, to the practice of witchcraft, to malicious and deplorable art, and to evil and devilish deeds. This voice thus portrays Helene Clerk as a dangerous woman; a person who has renounced God and is serving the devil. Also, in the evaluation of Helene Clerk's dittay, which was most likely written by the Lord Advocate, the content of each article is carefully judged as to whether or not it is relevant to the trial. Here, judicial arguments are the only ones deemed acceptable—if an action or event could not be proven to have been witchcraft-related, the article was to be repelled.

The Voice of the Scribe

In all documents related to Helene Clerk's trial, the scribe has been very professional. He has written down what he heard and what will be the basis for evaluation. Even when the pre-trial documents at the central court in Edinburgh were reworked into a dittay, the scribe's accuracy was maintained: we see his diligent work down to the smallest detail, among other vernacular words, because the original content was kept and no new content added. The only additions made by the scribe are certain legal and stylistic devices—hence, he has done his job well. However, the way Helene Clerk's voice is presented differs between the pre-trial documents and the dittay, as the individuality of her voice decreases in the dittay and her statements are transformed into a more general form.

The voice of the scribe provides no indication of his own part in the trial, but accurately records what happened and what was said, without any description of the attributes of the accused person or the witnesses. He gives no signs as to whether or not he believes that witchcraft is possible.

Isobell Eliot, 1678

Isobell Eliot was one of ten women from Peaston who were accused, tried, and executed for witchcraft in 1678. In addition to the court records of the trial, the register of the Privy Council of Scotland has information on what happened before and during the trial, and on the execution of the women.[241] Eight women were interrogated and gave their confessions to the local authorities in Peaston in the beginning of July 1678.[242] Shortly after, court messenger David Chalmer went to Edinburgh with the confessions of the accused women and presented a bill for the Privy Council to get a commission—a warrant—to try the alleged witches at home. He delivered these documents to the clerks of the Privy Council and their servants, whom he paid, and he also 'had other expenses that week', amounting to 18 lb. 3s. 4d.[243]

The Privy Council actually refused the commission, and later the 'Lairde' went to Edinburgh himself.[244] He presented them with a second bill for a commission and gave the clerk of the council 'three rex dollors'.[245] This must have helped, for commissions were now written out.[246] 'As the number of witches incressed, he gave him 2 dollors'.[247] The same amount was also given to the macers[248] of the council at two different times when the bills were presented. In addition, the Lord Advocate, George MacKenzie, got 85 lb. 12s.[249] Thus, considerable amounts of money were involved in the Peaston trials from an early stage. More money had to be paid for the trial to continue: several clerks and servants were paid, horses were rented, people were sent to Edinburgh to obtain indictments and warrants, and people had to be paid for the convictions after. At the end, 'According to the number of the witches that wer indyted the expenses of every one of them will be 47lb.15s. 2d'.[250]

The entire dossier of the Peaston witches consists of two stages of confessions. The first stage comprises those confessions brought to Edinburgh to convince the Privy Council to issue commissions so the accused could be tried. These documents have been lost. However, we can see by the record of payment to the central court's clerks that these confessions were rewritten in the dittay, which has been preserved. The second stage consists of the confessions that the accused women gave before the assize during the formal trial. In these confessions, the women confirm the content of the dittay, and also add some details. This confirmation was crucial with regard to the passing of a sentence.

The Trial

Isobell Eliot was brought before the central court in Edinburgh on 13 September 1678. The Master of the Court was Gilbert Mair, and the commissioners of justiciary were Sir James Foulis[251] of Colintoun, Robert[252] Nairne from Strathurd, John[253] Lockhart from Castlehill, David Balfour from Forret,[254] and David Falconar from Newtoun. The accused women were Isobell Eliot, Marion Veitch, Margaret Dods, Helen Laying, Margaret Lowis, Isobel Shank, Margaret Douglas, Helen Forrester, Margaret Smaill, and Christian Hogger. The records do not mention the duration of their imprisonment or whether torture or other types of pressure were used.

The records open with a reference to the Scottish Witchcraft Act, followed by 'the Cryme of Witchcraft is declaired to be ane horrid abomina[tio]n and Capitall Cryme punishable with the paines of death and confisca[tio]n of movables Neverthelesse the haill fornamed persons have committed and are guiltie of the said Cryme'.[255] The suspects were then brought before the court. Isobell Eliot was the first accused, and her dittay, which mentions several of the other accused, reads:

> [A]bout tuo years since the said Isobell Eliot being then servant to Helen Laying in Peastoun ane witch *ye at her desyre* stayed at home from the kirk *and wes present* at a meiting with the divill the s[ai]d Helen Laying and Marion Campbell witches in the said Helens house wher *the divill kissed you and offered to lye with you and caused you renunce your baptisme and baptised you* upon the face with ane waff[256] of his hand like a dewing[257] *calling you Jean and ye being then with child the divill did forbear to lye with you but efter ye wer kirked the divill hade carnall copulation with you* and since that time *ye have hade severall meitings with the divill* and severall witches *and hes hade many tymes carnall copulation* with him and sicklyke *ye were present* with Katharin Halyday Helen Laying Sarah Cranstoun and severall other witches at the contryving of the death of [blank] Hair daughter to the s[ai]d Katharin Halyday and William Hair her husband.[258] [My italics.]

Next, dittays against the other women accused of witchcraft were read. In addition to Isobell, dittays were written separately for Marion Veitch, Margaret Dods, and Helen Laying. A collective dittay was written and read for the remaining six. They were all accused of having been the devil's servants for several years; Marion for twenty-seven years. They allegedly met the devil, renounced their baptism, entered into a pact with the devil, attended dance meetings with the devil in Ormiston wood and Murraisburne on a 'black haugh',[259] with a piper present, and had carnal copulation with the devil.[260] Marion received the new name 'Broad Back'. Helen Laying was also accused of participating in the murder of her husband, William Laying, 'committed in the moneth of [blank] imvic [blank] by sorcerie witchcraft & necromancie and of severall other malefices'.[261] The elements mentioned in these three dittays are similar; it seems almost as though the judiciary was simply filling in a form, asking each of the accused the same range of questions.[262]

Isobell Eliot was accused of many meetings with the devil, 'and particularlie ye wer present as a witch with the said Helen Laying *when she and Isobell Eliot her servant did kill and murder William Laying spouse to the said Helen'*.[263] [My italics.] She might also be included among the 'other witches' who killed the daughter of William Thomson. The collective dittay interweaves their stories, with the strings of words resembling one another. A certain number of elements mentioned are used as proof of guilt. Each of the accused

> are guiltie of the said Cryme of Witchcraft in suae fare as *ye have entered in paction with the divill* the enemie of your salvation and have *renunced our blissed Lord & Saviour* and your baptizmes and *have given your selves both soulls & bodie to the divill* by useing the abominable & detestable solemnitie of putting on of your hands upon the crown of your head and the other upon the sole of your feet and *have bein at severall meitings with the divill and sundrie other witches* and par[ticular]lie of late at the Barliehill and woodhead [*Woodhead*]of Crightoun wher ther wer *great danceing & playing with pypes* Wherthrowe the *persons above compleaned upon and ilk ane of them have committed and are guiltie of the s[ai]d horrid and abominable cryme of witchcraft* and are airt and part of the samen the whilk being found be ane assyse they *ought to be punished with the paines of death* & confisca[tio]n of movables to the terror & example of others to committ the like hereafter.[264] [My italics.]

By 1678, key demonological ideas were influential: entering into a devil's pact, renouncing one's baptism, participating in a ritual to enter into a pact with the devil, receiving a new name, having sexual intercourse with the devil, and participating in witches' gatherings with the devil present. After this collective dittay was read, the Lords affirmed it and the trial was passed on to the assize.[265] However, the number of accused was reduced to nine, as the dittay of one of the suspects was repelled: 'The Lords with consent of his Majesties advocat deserts the dyet as to Christian Hoger'.[266]

After this first stage of the trial, when the dittays were read aloud to the women, the next stage was to have the content of the dittays confirmed before the assize. This implied a new round of interrogation. The assize consisted of fifteen men, living in various villages and working in a variety of professions: merchant, tailor, skinner, hammerman,[267] whitironman,[268] and baxter.[269] There were four merchants, two of whom were from Edinburgh.[270] The assize examined the accused one by one to extract confessions. Isobell Eliot confessed to having entered into a devil's pact as well as to her dealings with the devil, participating in witches' meetings, and practising witchcraft when she and Marion Veitch assumed the shape of bees and Marion later shifted into the shape of a corbie.

> Isobell Eliot in Templehall *declaires* that tuo years since the divill appeared to her in Helen Layings house in Peastoun sitting betwixt the said Helen Laying and Marion Campbell and the divill laid hands on her and made her

renunce her baptizme and give her self over to him by laying on[e] of her hands on the crown of her head and the other on the sole of her foot and *declaires* therefter the divill hade carnall copula[tio]n with her *declaires* she wes at many meitings with the divill and particularlie at Crightoun wher ther wer many witches present & a flaming fyre and *declaires* the divill gave them a kind of sacrament and preached amongst them and blasphemed God and *declaires* she wes present at the poysouning of William Thomsons child who wes poysouned by Marion Veatch and the childs grand mother and *declaires* that she and the s[ai]d Marion Veatch wer in the shape of Bume bees when the child wes poysouned and that Marion Veatch caryed the poyson in her cleuchs wings and mouth *declaires* she left her bodie in Pencaitland kirk and went in the shape of a corbie to Leswade Loanhead to see a child which she nursed to William Ramsay ther *declaires* she cannot wreitt.[271] [My italics.]

The confession is detailed with regard to places, names, and collaborators, and many demonological ideas are represented. Isobell Eliot's entry into a pact with the devil allegedly took place in Helene Laying's house, with Marion Campbell and Helene Laying present. The rendering of Isobell's meeting with the devil and the ritual is identical in both her dittay and in her confession before the assize. However, certain points included in the dittay—for example, that she had stayed away from church and that she had been with child—were not mentioned in the confession before the assize, nor were the new name given to her by the devil or the devil's offer to lie with her, which could only happen after she was 'kirked'.[272] The witches' meetings were a focal point of the confessions before the assize. The 'Crightown'[273] gathering is mentioned, with a 'flaming fyre' and 'playing with pypes'.[274] The devil gave them a sacrament, preached among them, and blasphemed God. This is an echo of the witches' gathering in the North Berwick Kirk nearly ninety years previously. Interesting is the attention paid to the poisoning of William Thomson's child by Isobell and Marion Veitch—the child's grandmother[275]—and the shape-shifting into bees and corbies.[276] Isobell said she had left her body in Pencaitland Kirk and travelled in the shape of a corbie to Leswade Loanhead.[277] She also stated that she shifted into a corbie in the kirk, which signifies that this was a deed mocking God and the Christian faith. It is difficult to say whether she had been asked questions that motivated her to augment her previous confession with these motifs. We do not know what the accused women talked about with one another. We do know, however, that the motifs Isobell added were a well-known part of the folklore of many countries. Shape-shifting into a corbie, a raven, for example, is mentioned in Scottish witchcraft trials in Alloa.[278]

At the end of Isobell's confession, it is noted that she could not write and was thus unable to sign the confirmation of her confession—this was the case for all the accused.

The women confirm their meetings with the devil. Margaret Douglas confessed that the devil had come to her thirteen years earlier, after she had a disagreement with her daughter. He promised her revenge on her daughter, so she renounced her baptism and entered into a pact with him. Margaret Lowis confessed that she met a man who she believed was an Englishman 'that cured diseases in the countrey'.[279] Margaret Smaill said that

> having come to the house of Jannet Borthwick in Crightoun she sawe a Gentleman sitting with her and they desyred her to sitt doun and having sitten doun the gentleman drank to her and she drank to him and therefter the said Jannet Borthwick told her that Gentleman wes the divill.[280]

Isobell Eliot was the fourth woman to confirm her previous confession. The minutes of her examination are short. However, she brought new motifs into her confession before the assize, which suggests that the members of the assize took an interest in her knowledge.

The dossier has a clear demonological profile, and it is likely that the women on trial were steered towards demonological confessions via leading questions. Some of the motifs and images appearing in the women's discourse most likely belong to their own traditional beliefs, such as shape-shifting into bees and corbies. However, this range of traditional ideas seems to have merged with demonological ideas, so the confessions are a mixture of local folklore and ideas from abroad.[281] For example, the piper at the witches' meeting is a motif known from German witchcraft trials, and other Scottish occurrences exist.[282] Also, the entire narrative about entering the devil's pact occur in several individual variations related by the accused women. Nevertheless, this document gives the impression that it was written hastily. The accused women are quickly examined by the assize, one after another; processed speedily through a mill to obtain confirmations so sentences could be passed.

On 11 September 1678, when the assize was lawfully sworn and no objections had been made, His Majesty's Advocate produced 'judiciall Confessions underwritten'.[283] The verdict was then recorded:

> Efter leading and adduceing of the whole proba[tio]n the persons of assyse abovenamed removed altogither furth of court to the assyse house wher having reasoned & voted upon the points & articles of the dittay & proba[tio]n abovewritten and being therwith well and ryplie advised they reentered againe in court and returned ther verdict in presence of the saids Lords wherof the tenor followes The assyse all in on voice be the mouth of James Paterson ther Chancelar find[284] Margaret Douglas in Crightoun Margaret Lowis Margaret Smell Isobell Eliot Helen Veatch spouse to George Thomson in Keith Helen Laying in Peastoun Margaret Dods Isobel Shanks in Crightoun Helen Forrester[285] *ther pannalls all guiltie of the Cryme of witchcraft in respect they have all confest paction with the divill and renunceing ther baptism* Sic subscrivitur James Paterson chancelar.[286] [My italics.]

Finally, 'the doom'—the death sentence—is recorded. Five of the women were to be taken to the Gallowlee of Edinburgh.[287] The last four women to be executed, among them Isobell Eliot, were to be taken to Peaston Muir to be burned:

> And alse be the mouth of the said Adam Auld dempster decerned & adjudged the saids Isobell Eliot Marion Veatch Margaret Dods and Helen Laying to be taken to Paistoun muir upon Fryday[288] nixt the twentie day of this instant betwixt tuo and four aclock in the efternoon and ther to be strangled at ane stake till they be dead and therefter ther bodies to be burnt to ashes and all ther movable goods and gear to be escheat and imbrought to his Majesties use as being found guilty by ane assyse of the Cryme of witchcraft ment[ioned] in ther dittays which wes pron[u]nced for doom.[289]

On 13 September 1678, it was decided that two men should see to it that the execution was carried out: the women 'putt to dewe execution'.[290] These two men were Sir Robert Hepburn of Keith and John Pringle of Woodhead, both of them among the investigators following the entire trial. The execution took place on 20 September 1678, after which fourteen men testified to the burning:

> [W]e, the fornamed persons, under subscrivers, do testifie that we wer all present at and did see and were witnesses to the putting of the forsaid sentence and doome to death to due execution upon the bodies of the four witches above named at tyme, day and place abovementioned and conforme to the forsaid doome and sentence of doome abovementioned in all poynts.[291]

The expenses of the burning of the four witches were considerable. Money to 'give back their plaids',[292] dempster,[293] hangman, legal officials, carts of coal, trees and nails to the gallows and scaffold, four tar barrels, wright,[294] tows and rope—all these expenses to burn four women amounted to 38 pounds and 3 shillings.[295]

The Voice of Isobell Eliot

The voice of Isobell Eliot is heard in the dittay and in her confession before the assize. When the dittay was written, Isobell had confessed to a first meeting with the devil and to entering the devil's pact. She emphasizes that she had been with child and that she had obeyed her mistress, Helen Laying, who had asked her to stay home from the kirk in order to take part in the meeting with the devil. She further states that she, being pregnant, prevented the devil from lying with her at first, but that after she had been 'kirked', she had sexual intercourse with him. This emphasis on her own condition gives her voice a personal touch, and her relationship with the devil is highlighted. Her confession about attending the witches' gatherings is also important, as this is where the denunciation of other suspects occurred: she gives the names of four other women. As the dittay is grammatically addressed to the accused, the pronouns 'you', 'your', and 'ye' are significant with regard to what Isobell has confessed to, which is now turned against her as accusations. The content of each of these articles concerns her serving and worshipping the devil and practising witchcraft. There is no sign of resistance in this voice, nor is there a specific turning point in the trial. From the very beginning, Isobell seems to have confirmed all points, willingly providing the answers desired by the judiciary.

In Isobell Eliot's confirmation given in front of the assize, the verb 'declaires' is mentioned eight times. This probably means that she was given eight points to confirm and was responding to these. We do not know what physical or emotional state she was in at this stage in the trial, but the content of her declaration is largely related to core demonological ideas, with some details inserted, for instance the 'flaming fyres' at the witches' gathering. The names of places and descriptions of situations are more detailed than in the dittay. The denunciation is an important and compulsory point. Isobell seems to be cooperative, likely due to exhaustion. Several weeks had passed since her first confession.

The parts of the dossier directly related to Isobell Eliot, which include both the dittay and her confession before the assize, show that the most important items are the demonological notions: renouncing one's baptism, entering into a pact with the devil, participating in the 'hand and foot' ritual when entering into the devil's pact, receiving a new name, having carnal relations with the devil, participating in witches' meetings, denouncing others, and practising witchcraft.

The Voices of the Witnesses

As the trial of Isobell Eliot was part of a witchcraft panic and initiated by denunciation, no witnesses were brought before the court. Information about her witchcraft—participation in witches' meetings and performance of evil deeds— came from the confessions of other accused women. However, at the beginning of the trial, the parents of a child who died, Katharin Halyday and William Hair, probably have testified about this tragedy. They are named in Isobell Eliot's dittay. The child allegedly died due to witchcraft performed by Isobell and three other accused women. Thus, the panic was related to death in the local community which could not be explained, and where witchcraft is believed to be the reason.

The Voice of the Interrogator

The voice of the interrogator is most frequently heard in 'shadow questions'. For instance, the verb 'declaires' is repeated eight times in Isobell Eliot's confession before the assize, which denotes pointwise organizing through questions posed to her. These questions reveal the elements that were activated and point to what was considered relevant. Clearly, in Isobell's trial, the interrogator managed to steer the confession towards particular demonological notions. Isobell's confession also shows, through the details provided, where follow-up questions were posed. Moreover, the denunciation of others at the end of the interrogation was the result of the interrogator's intervention. Thus, both the structure and the content of Isobell's confession echo the voice of the interrogator.

The Voice of the Law

The voice of the law is echoed in the type of questions asked and the points focused on. Further, this voice becomes particularly recognizable through specific repetitions of word strings from the Witchcraft Act, such as 'sorcery witchcraft & necromancy'. In addition, the phrases 'renounce the baptism' and 'blaspheme God' are frequent expressions in Scottish witchcraft trials at the time. Furthermore, the use of certain adverbs and adjectives characterizes the rhetoric of the judiciary—for example, 'horrid and abominable cryme of witchcraft'. The understanding of this crime in the 1670s no doubt had a demonological focus. Nevertheless, the voice of the law in this trial seems a bit more lifeless than thirty years earlier, in the trial of Helene Clerk. The trials were recorded in a brief and hasty way, with blanks where names of months and years should have been filled in, among other indicators—a sign that there had been many such trials over the years.

The Voice of the Scribe

The role of the scribe in the trial of Isobell Eliot was to record the first interrogation in Peaston, write the dittay for the central trial, record the confirmation of the confession before the assize, and record the verdict and sentence. The scribe ensured that the judicial arguments used were taken down correctly and clarified the connections to the Witchcraft Act and the reasons for the verdict. Likewise, he recorded the voices of the interrogators and accused to provide a correct impression of courtroom discourse and courtroom practice. At the end of the trial, the written verdict and sentence would echo the voice of the law and prove the correct judicial handling of the case. In addition, as one who knew the legal terminology and mastered the art of writing formal documents, the scribe ensured linguistic fluency when joining the separate elements into a consistent document. In short, he kept the records together.

Several clerks took part in the process of writing the records. Even if they had the opportunity to influence the documents with regard to language and content, this is not what we see. A close reading of the records with an emphasis on the accused individuals' voices shows an attempt at accurate recording: we see reporting verbs used as introduction to reported clauses, so that indirect speech can easily be detected. The same goes for direct speech. Even if text-critical considerations are taken into account, features of original pronounced speech may be traced in the court records. The predominance of orality features in the accused persons' reported speech is in my view proof that the scribe did not distort what was originally said, but tried to stick to the words uttered. When it comes to the rendering of the interrogation and references to witchcraft laws, the same aspiration to correctness comes to the fore. We see a kind of professionalism that signals reliability.

Even if several scribes were involved in developing the dossier, they all shared the common objective of ensuring that the main points of the dittay were written down in a clear way. They also shared a mastery of stylistic devices and the rhetoric that guaranteed uniformity in the process of recording.

Conclusion

This chapter has provided insight into the voices of three women. The demonological element is present in all trials. The interrogation clearly leads in the direction of the devil's pact and witches' gatherings. The devil's mark was found on all three women. In addition, *maleficium* as well as healing are factors present in all trials. Two of the women, Agnes Sampson and Isobell Eliot, were known for being healers in their local communities, but also for performing maleficent witchcraft. The third, Helene Clerk, was known for being able to cause sickness and take it away. The voices of all three change during the trials. They are unable to uphold the strategies they used in the beginning.

Agnes Sampson had been suspected of witchcraft for more than a year before the trial, and was, after repeated orders from the Synod, questioned by the presbytery of Haddington in October 1590 and imprisoned in Haddington. Later that same autumn, she was imprisoned and interrogated pre-trial in Edinburgh and tried in a central trial in January 1591. Agnes vacillated between confession and denial. Because of torture during the pre-trial interrogation, she withdrew her confession, only to confess again later. The items confessed to were demonological witchcraft, maleficent witchcraft, and healing. The dittay, consisting of points from the pre-trial interrogation, reveals accents of her voice. First, resistance is heard, then resignation. Finally, we hear the voice of a denouncing witch. Torture seems to have been a turning point in her trial. She was executed shortly after her formal trial.

Helene Clerk was first examined before ministers of North Leith Kirk in 1643, with the local bailie present. Later, she was tried before the central court in Edinburgh. She confessed pre-trial to having been washed with charmed water by a renowned witch in order to be cured of an illness. The charmed water allegedly gave Helene the power to cast sickness upon people, and also to take it away. Eight witnesses testified against her, all of them giving examples of Helene's threats against others; threats that were realized in the form of illness and death. Helene was kept in prison until 1645. She never confessed to witchcraft but maintained her innocence. At the end, she delivered a petition to the central legal authorities. The sentence and verdict of this trial remain unknown.

Isobell Eliot was accused in a witchcraft panic in Peaston in 1678 and questioned locally. Her pre-trial confession contained demonological as well as maleficent notions. The same was the case for several other suspected women. Later, Isobell and the other alleged witches were tried in a central trial in Edinburgh, in which a collective dittay emphasized key demonological notions. Isobell confirmed her confession before an assize. The content was centred around demonological ideas, and there was a demand for the key notions to be pronounced. The alliance with the devil was central to the performance of witchcraft. Isobell Eliot was sentenced to be burned at the stake.

For the three trials, orality features are fluent in the confessions, particularly in rendered direct speech in dialogues but also in indirect speech. Reporting verbs and reported clauses give access to accents of each woman's voice. This personification of the accused person's language makes it possible to glimpse how these women experienced the trial. We can hear anger, resistance, despair, and surrender. Only Helene Clerk never gave in.

6

ENGLAND—FAMILIARS, TEATS, AND WITCHFINDERS

The court records from England chosen for analysis are the trials of Thomasine Read, Haddenham, 1647, and of Isabel Atcheson and Jane Simpson, Newcastle, 1664.[1] The records used for Thomasine Read are preserved in the Cambridge University Library[2] and those for Isabel Atcheson and Jane Simpson in the National Archives, Kew, London.[3] The original sources are written in the secretary hand.

The survival of court records which can document witchcraft trials in England varies from county to county and from decade to decade of the witch-hunting period. The most valuable sources for the study of English witchcraft trials are the Home Circuit assize records from South-Eastern England.[4] Assize courts were 'travelling courts that went on "circuit" round groups of counties'.[5] They were county courts presided over by judges from the central law courts.[6] In addition, a few other records from secular legal courts and ecclesiastical courts have been preserved.[7] These sources provide valuable information about witchcraft persecution in England, but they do not offer complete documentation of witchcraft trials throughout the period of the witch-hunt. Due to gaps in relevant court archives, it is difficult to paint a comprehensive picture of English witchcraft trials.[8] However, witchcraft pamphlets, of which a rich number have been preserved, constitute an interesting type of sources in addition to court records. Witchcraft pamphlets have been thoroughly analysed by witchcraft scholars, providing important information about the English witch-hunt.[9]

Like in the rest of this book, the voices of women uncover many aspects of courtroom discourse and court practice. Analysis of courtroom discourse provides a glimpse of words uttered and meanings conveyed by the accused persons and the witnesses, as well as an echo of the voices of the interrogator, the law, and the scribe. When it comes to court practice, it is interesting to see to what extent circumstantial evidence was used during the trials. One thread that runs through this study is the goal to obtain knowledge of ideas about witchcraft as they existed

DOI: 10.4324/9781003255406-6

among people at the time of witchcraft persecution. In English witchcraft trials, accusations of witchcraft based on *maleficium* as well as on learned ideas about demonology are found. The trials chosen for analysis will contribute to shedding light on both these concepts of witchcraft.[10] Indictments brought to the assizes show that *maleficium*, doing harm by witchcraft to humans and animals, was at stake most often.[11] *Maleficium* figured in 94% of all indictments for witchcraft tried by the Home Circuit.[12] In addition, a mass hunt in 1645–47 put its stamp on English witchcraft persecution through its intensity and by bringing demonological ideas to the fore.[13] A particular element in English witchcraft trials related to demonology were familiars: demonic domestic animals kept by alleged witches. They were often mentioned in witchcraft interrogations, witnesses' depositions, and accused individuals' confessions. The notion of familiars will be paid attention to when it comes to interpreting the ideas about witchcraft that emerge.[14]

In the trials analysed in this chapter, the voices of women are rendered in direct and indirect speech, in the witnesses' depositions as well as in their own confessions. In the witnesses' testimonies, the voices of the accused are dominated by angry words: threats which happen to come true. In the accused's confessions, a register of notions provides a glimpse of villagers' mentality at the time. Through a close reading of the confessions, the chapter will discuss the factual interrogation of the accused person and also reflect on court discourse in a wider sense, in which voices of several participants are important.

The confessions are studied as narratives, in which the accused person's competence in the field of narrative structures forms the backbone. Of particular interest are orality features, as these substantiate the individualization of language users. This aspect invites a discussion of the scribe's work.

For each of the trials analysed, first a description of the development of the trial is given, followed by an analysis of the voice of the accused woman. Various ideas about witchcraft will be investigated, as will narrative strategies and orality features. Resistance and denial on the part of the accused person will be emphasized, and a potential turning point of the trial will be discussed. Then, the voices of the witnesses will be examined, followed by a brief discussion of the voice of the interrogator, the voice of the law, and the voice of the scribe. The chapter concludes with a summary of its main findings.

Background

Persecution

The witch-hunt in England was moderate compared to the one in Scotland, its neighbouring country to the north, where persecution was extreme. However, the English witch-hunt was more severe than the one in France, which persecution is characterized as mild.[15] In England, the period of witchcraft persecution lasted from 1542 to 1736, starting with the passing of the first witchcraft statute, which was in force by 1560, and ending with the repeal of all witchcraft statutes in 1736.[16]

In this period, of a population of 4,400,000 in England, 500 persons were executed for witchcraft.[17] It is difficult to say how many persons in total were accused of witchcraft, but it is documented that around 1,000 men and women were tried in English secular courts.[18]

A great deal of original legal records documenting witchcraft trials in England have been published in text-critical editions, and it is useful to take a closer look at these in order to get an impression of the persecution. C. L'Estrange Ewen's source-book of 1929 contains 790 witchcraft indictments from 1,373 Home Circuit assizes. The book includes the official records of the trials. These contain actual charges and sentences, which indicate that the primary method of execution in English witchcraft trials was hanging. Ewen's data show that during the period 1558–1607, 187 people were indicted in Essex, 13 in Sussex, 25 in Kent, 29 in Hertford, and 35 in Surrey.[19] Prosecution levels in Essex were thus higher than in the neighbouring counties.[20] Around the end of the sixteenth century, there was a drop in witchcraft prosecutions in England. Between 1598 and 1627, 91 people were indicted on the Home Circuit—60% fewer than in the three preceding decades. The conviction rate remained constant, however, at between 23 and 28%.[21] Pendle, in Lancashire, experienced a more serious episode in 1612, when 16 alleged witches were tried and 10 were executed.[22] These trials have attracted much attention, not least due to a pamphlet by Thomas Potts, *The Wonderfvll Discoverie of Witches in the Covntie of Lancaster*, which was published in London in 1613.[23] In the decade from 1628 to 1637, there were only 11 Home Circuit prosecutions: 5 in Essex, 4 in Kent, and 2 in Surrey. None of these resulted in a sentence of execution.[24] In 1634, a witch panic broke out—again in Pendle, Lancashire—during which the accusers were sent to London to be questioned and the king ordered his physician to examine their bodies. The accused were cleared and the accusers censured.[25] In Essex, 45 people were tried for witchcraft between 1638 and 1647, with the most intense period of persecution occurring between 1645 and 1647. This was England's biggest witchcraft panic. It occurred in the later stages of the English Civil War, when the assize courts had been suspended, and the territory instead established a special court that could persecute witches without the usual restraints.[26] Like the Lancashire trials of 1612, these trials inspired several pamphlets on witchcraft.[27] The witch-hunt of 1645, which accounted for most of the prosecutions, was part of a wider eastern outbreak, in which 300 people were interrogated and one-third of these hanged.[28] In the 1640s, the conviction rate increased to between 42% and 46%. In the 1650s, however, the conviction rate fell,[29] and after 1660, almost all cases resulted in acquittals.[30] The last definitive execution took place in 1682, in Exeter, and the last recorded guilty verdict was from a trial in Taunton, in 1689.[31] The last person convicted of witchcraft in England was Jane Wenham, in 1736.[32]

The last phase of witchcraft persecution in England took place in the eighteenth century.[33] As late as 1751, a mob attack killed a couple who were suspected of being witches.[34] Jonathan Barry's book *Witchcraft and Demonology in South-West England, 1640–1789* explores six cases from south-western England. The final case he discusses is a late case from Bristol, which took place from 1787 to 1788 and dealt with devil possession and exorcism.[35] Other late witchcraft trials in England have been studied as well.[36]

C. L'Estrange Ewen's second comprehensive book on witchcraft, published in 1933, consists of about 330 items and brings together narratives about the alleged acts of accused witches.[37] Ewen's work was groundbreaking and has been used in recent research.[38]

Due in part to the influential theories of Alan Macfarlane and Keith Thomas in the 1970s, which were influenced by anthropological studies, English witchcraft accusations were for a period mainly explained as being part of a pattern of quarrels followed by misfortune, in which witchcraft functioned as an explanation.[39] This thesis has been influential and led to an England/Continent dichotomy stating that English witch-hunting came 'from below'. Accusations of witchcraft and being a witch in England were long thought to be different from those on the Continent.[40] However, Julian Goodare points out that Macfarlane and Thomas made clear that their work covered England only, and that the acceptance of the England/Continent dichotomy by witchcraft scholars on both geographical sides has been unhelpful.[41] The notion that witchcraft accusations in England differed from those on the Continent has also been challenged by James Sharpe, both in his study *Instruments of Darkness*[42] and in *Witchcraft in Early Modern England*:

> English trials were free of some of the more bizarre elements which are to be found in witchcraft trials in some parts of continental Europe: there is little by way of the sabbat, of night-flying, or of sexual intercourse with incubi or succubi, while even the idea of sexual intercourse between witch and devil came relatively late and uncertainly to England. The English also experienced little by way of officially-directed mass trials of witches. But it is now clear that the English experience of witchcraft and witch-hunting was not unique, but rather that it was a variation of a number of themes which can be found throughout Europe (. . .) The 'English' pattern of a low intensity of witch-trials, of isolated accusations against the individual witch or small batches of three or four suspects, was to be found in many other European regions.[43]

An additional point put forward by Macfarlane and Thomas's works has been discussed by Sharpe, namely that their approach to witchcraft concentrated on ideas about witchcraft on a popular level, and concentrated on the connections between witchcraft accusations and socio-economic change. Sharpe maintains that despite its undoubted importance, this approach had the effect of marginalizing witchcraft as an intellectual, theological, and indeed political issue.[44]

Several studies have been conducted after Macfarlane and Thomas's books, giving weight to studying witchcraft 'from above' and to the importance of the role of the state and legal institutions in the persecution of witches. Among others, Christina Larner, Brian P. Levack, and Julian Goodare have contributed with solid studies taking this approach. However, the studies of these scholars also comprise witchcraft beliefs and mentalities.[45] The 'refusal-guilt syndrome', which was identified in English witchcraft trials by Thomas and Macfarlane and explained the casting of evil spells by village quarrels, was argued to be linked to the English development of organized poor relief in the late sixteenth century. This has been opposed by Goodare, who states that the syndrome was not unique to England nor new in the late sixteenth century. This syndrome is found in many Continental cases, from the fifteenth century onwards, and must be understood as a 'notable type of the quarrelsome interaction that was likely to lead to witchcraft accusations'.[46]

My view, which this volume bears witness to throughout, is that the role of the state in the legal persecution of witches was imperative, and that intellectual ideas about witchcraft were a powerful factor in the initiation and continuation of witchcraft trials and in the passing of the verdict and sentence. The carrying through of trials and the conviction of witches took place in secular legal courts, in which witchcraft accusations 'from below' as well as 'from above' were heard and judged. However, the trials were governmental operations.

Jurisdiction

At the time of witchcraft persecution, England had experienced an expansion of state authority into the village. The country 'saw a long-term shift in local office-holding from officers representing the community to officers representing the king or central state'.[47] That the state gained more of a foothold in the village had an impact on the development of witchcraft trials, because legal representatives from central authorities participated in trials in local courts.

Jurisdiction in England differed on several points from jurisdiction in Scotland with regard to witchcraft. Brian P. Levack has compared the witch-hunts in England and Scotland in terms of law, politics, and religion. He argues that '[t]he English central government never relinquished its control of local witchcraft trials in the way the Scottish government often did'.[48] The English government had a mechanism for ensuring central judicial supervision of local trials. There was a jury system, in which assizes decided on guilt or innocence. Almost all English trials for witchcraft took place at the assizes. In most cases, 'the supervision of the judicial process by professional judges provided greater assurances that accused witches would receive the benefit of whatever procedural safeguards the law allowed than if the judicial process were left in the hands of local amateurs'.[49] The professional judges could assist the jury in evaluating whether there was sufficient proof for conviction in a witchcraft case.[50]

English laws on witchcraft differed not only from those of Scotland, but also from those of many other European countries, not least due to the fact that torture was not allowed during trials. Two witchcraft statutes were published: the Elizabethan Witchcraft Act of 1563 and the Jacobean Witchcraft Act of 1604.[51] The Act of 1563 condemned those who practised invoking and conjuring evil and wicked spirits, and also those who used witchcraft, enchantments, charms, and sorcery to destroy persons and goods of their neighbours and other subjects of the realm.[52] 'It prescribed death for any person who killed another through witchcraft or evil spirits and (. . .) a one-year prison sentence for anyone who harmed but did not kill a person through witchcraft or for anyone who damages somebody's goods'.[53] This prison sentence applied only to the first offence; for subsequent offences, the death penalty was imposed. The Act of 1604 reinforced the formulations anent evil spirits: it was made illegal to keep, feed, or reward these spirits. Thus, a woman could now be prosecuted for witchcraft if a witness claimed that she was keeping evil spirits; it was not necessary to claim that she had used the spirits to harm others.[54] The Act of 1604 also contained provisions against necromancy, the use of dead bodies in magic.[55] The words 'diabolical' or 'devilish' are not mentioned in the witchcraft statutes of 1563 and 1604.[56] The stricter formulations of the Jacobean Witchcraft Act did not lead to any increase in witchcraft trials, however, as these declined from the 1580s until the 1640s. The Witchcraft Acts of 1563 and 1604 were the legal basis of England's witchcraft persecution. The repeal of the Witchcraft Act occurred in 1736.[57]

Torture is a point on which England differs from the other countries in this study:

> The extraction of evidence and confession by the infliction of bodily torture was practiced in England up to the Commonwealth period, but there is no evidence to shew that it was ever applied to facilitate the examination of suspected female witches. Such practices were, in fact, contrary to the common law, and only lawful as an act of royal prerogative which was probably never exercised in the case of women.[58]

This important aspect of English judicial practice likely had an effect on those being interrogated, as they did not have to fear torture, and on the development of the interrogations, as interrogators knew they could not use torture to obtain confessions. This certainly led to a more humane experience for the accused in England than for those accused in many other European countries. However, Goodare points to the fact that because English juries could convict a suspect on indirect or hearsay evidence, this was in fact less evidence than what would allow a court within the Roman system to authorise torture.[59]

As for conviction in capital cases, confessions were not needed in England. Levack states that there is a close correlation throughout Europe between the freedom courts had to torture people accused of a capital crime and the number of convictions in witchcraft cases. He maintains that the strict prohibition of torture explains why the conviction rate in England 'was lower than in almost all European countries'.[60] Also, English law required proof of specifically magical harm, which among other things resulted in the witches' sabbath rarely being mentioned in trials, as evidence of attending a sabbath was useless in court.[61] During the last decades of the 1600s, the criteria for a witchcraft indictment became stricter than before. Clive Holmes states that after 1660, many lawyers and magistrates refused to frame an indictment unless *maleficium* had resulted in the death of the victim or the accused was directly involved in diabolical practices.[62]

Circumstantial evidence in witchcraft trials was allowed in England, for example witch-pricking, which entailed searching for a spot on the body that was neither sensitive nor would bleed when pricked with a needle—such a spot was believed to be a sign of the devil's pact. Witch-pricking could lead to confessions, as these marks were seen as evidence; indeed, '[e]vidence that a mark had been found on a witch's body was thus an empirical indication of supernatural intervention in the world'.[63] In the early decades of persecution in England, the notion of the devil's mark received little attention in the trials. In the 1640s, however, a more intense witch-hunt began, and the search for the devil's mark became a common element of English witchcraft trials.[64] A particular kind of devil's mark, 'found mainly in England and its colonies, was a teat that witches were believed to use to suckle their animal familiars'.[65] This notion of having a bodily mark or 'teat' related to a familiar—a demonic creature—was specific to England.

Another type of circumstantial evidence common in English witchcraft trials was the water ordeal, during which suspects were dropped into water to see whether they floated: 'it was usually carried out as an informal pre-trial procedure, but its evidence could be used in court'.[66] The water ordeal was commonly used in several of the countries analysed in this study, particularly in Finnmark, Norway, and was usually witnessed by people from the local community. It often led to confessions, as the accused's resistance rapidly broke down after floating. It should be noted that most people who underwent the water ordeal did indeed float.

Thomasine Read, 1647

The Trial

Thomasine Read belonged to a group of people in the Isle of Ely district who were accused of witchcraft in the 1640s. The cases are related to the work of witchfinders Matthew Hopkins and John Stearne.[67] Thomasine was born in Cottenham, where she lived in a poor district. In the confession she gave during her witchcraft trial, she complained about a difficult life. She said that 'dissatisfaction with her living conditions and anger at people all around' had led to her 'inviting the devil into her heart'.[68] This allegedly was at the beginning of the 1630s, and the death of her husband in 1632 had 'deepened her despair'.[69] She later moved to Haddenham and settled on the north side of the village, in a one-room cottage.[70] People like Thomasine Read experienced a huge contrast between their own housing and the principal farmsteads in Haddenham. These were situated along Hill Row, where families embodied a new kind of social power: 'They were parvenus who feared God, worked hard, paid their taxes and ran the parish'.[71]

Many people suspected of performing witchcraft were 'pricked' by witchfinders in search of a devil's mark, which was believed to indicate a pact with the devil.[72] A number of peasants from the villages were accused of witchcraft during this witch-hunt, the majority of whom were women, and the conviction rate of those accused was relatively high.[73] Thomasine Read was arrested and searched for the devil's mark on 26 May 1647, three days before she was brought before the court and witnesses gave their testimonies. On 29 May, Thomasine was taken to the house of the magistrate, Thomas Castell Esquire—one of the king's justices of the peace for the Isle of Ely—accompanied by John Stearne and the witnesses. The latter included a boy named Robert Miller, son of John Miller of Hill Row, who had allegedly been bewitched by Thomasine. The same day, five witnesses gave their testimonies—one woman and four men.

The witnesses' testimonies were given 'upon oath' before Thomas Castell and the rest of the judiciary. The search for the devil's mark was conducted by several people, among them Ellen Pope. She had apparently been trained as a witch-pricker, and she used assistants for the pricking. Finding a devil's mark was crucial to the development of a witchcraft trial, as it signalled a relationship between a suspected witch and the devil. Most women accused of witchcraft in Essex in 1646–47 were searched for devil's marks—the searches were carried out by other women, even if a man was directing the search. In most of these cases, devil's marks were found.

Then the witnesses were brought forth. The first witness was Edward Mason, who restated what Thomasine had told him, namely

> that the divell appeared to hir in the likness of a Muse and demanded of hir the life of hir Child w[hi]ch the said Tommison would not agree unto, then the divell demanded of hir some of hir blood w[hi]ch she consented & yeald unto w[hi]ch was noe soner granted, but the divell comming to the said Tomison to know what he should doe for hir, *she said unto hime send my spirit to bewitch the Child of John Miller of Hillrow* all w[hi]ch was spedily p[er]formed by hir spirit cald Muse & the said Child hath ever since been most grevosly tormented & being by this Informant asked if she could not unwitch the Child agayne she answered she Could not for if she could she would & further this Informant saith not.[74] [Italics in original.]

In this retelling of Thomasine Read's own words, the point of the pact has been kept, as has Thomasine's refusal to sacrifice her own child, her agreeing to give blood to the devil, the devil's offer to do something for her, the bewitchment of Robert Miller, and finally Edward Mason's request that she 'unwitch' the child and her answer that she could not, as she would have done so otherwise. The bewitchment of Robert Miller is the main focus of the narrative, but the devil also plays a prominent role. Clear demonological notions emerge, like the appearance of the devil in the form of an animal and the devil's demand that Thomasine give him some of her blood. Thomasine shows a position of authority towards the devil when she refuses him the life of her child, decides who should be bewitched, and commands the devil to use her personal demon to perform the bewitchment—and Edward mentions that the bewitchment was speedily performed after the command was given. However, her power is restricted, at least in Edward's rendering of Thomasine's own words, in that she cannot 'unwitch' the bewitched.

The second witness to testify was Ellen Pope, the wife of Oliver Pope and the only female witness. Ellen Pope was taken 'upon oath' before Thomas Castell, whereupon she had said that 'Tommison Read being in this Informantes howse after she was apprehended & searcht & by the searches fownd to have Teates & marks of a witch'.[75] Ellen Pope related that Thomasine had told her the following:

> that when she lived att Cottenham w[hi]ch is about 16 years since the divell appeared to hir in the liknes of a muse and prickt hir in the thygh & so for a tyme left hir afterwardes she comming to live at Haddenham the divell appeared the second tyme & demanded of hir Child or els hir blood & presently the divell gave the said Tomison a prick or nip upon the breast & the spirit mus suckt hir blood & *she comanded hir spirit mus to goe and bewitch & tutch the Child* of John Miller which was spedily p[er]formed & the s[ai]d Child handled in a most greavus & tormenting Manner & further she told this Inform[an]t that *she commanded hir other spirit Catt to bewitch to death the sheepe of Tho. Woodbridg [and] of Tho. Gray* both of hillrow w[hi]ch was forthw[i]th p[er]formed & 8 of the sheep of woodbridg & Tho. Gray did die & further this Inform[an]t saith not.[76] [Italics in original.]

Ellen Pope and Thomasine Read were apparently acquainted, as Thomasine had come to Ellen's house. Most of the testimony is a retelling of Thomasine's own words. Compared with the testimony of Edward Mason, Ellen Pope's testimony contains the additional point of Thomasine bewitching not just Robert Miller but also the sheep. In addition, we hear that the devil allegedly came to Thomasine twice, although we do not know the interval between these two visits. The first time was when he, in the likeness of a mouse, gave her his mark on her thigh as a sign of their pact. The second time was after she had moved to Haddenham, when he had given her a nip on her breast and a spirit mouse had sucked her blood.

In this narrative, like in the testimony of Edward Mason, the devil demanded either her child or her blood. In Thomasine's speech, as rendered by Ellen Pope in her testimony, Thomasine herself ordered the mouse and the cat to perform evil deeds—in Mason's testimony, by contrast, Thomasine asked the devil to send her personal demon to bewitch the child. In both versions, Thomasine is the one with the authority and power to perform evil deeds. Ellen Pope also mentioned that the bewitchment was speedily performed after Thomasine commanded it, and she added that the effect was severe. In Ellen Pope's testimony, the act of 'touching' is emphasized: the devil *touched* Thomasine on the thigh and on the breast, and the spirit mouse had to *touch* Robert Miller to cast sickness on him. Ellen, in her rendering of Thomasine's words, thus paid attention to bodily places explicitly related to women, such as the breasts, and her doubling of words with the same meaning—such as 'a prick or nip upon the breast'—also served to highlight the devil's mark on the breast. Ellen Pope used epithets to strengthen specific expressions, for example 'grievous & tormenting manner', but tried to be precise when she told of the bewitchment of the sheep, stating for instance that eight sheep had died. In Ellen's testimony, compared with Edward Mason's, additional elements have increased the word count.

Following Ellen Pope, the third witness was Robert Miller, the boy who had allegedly been bewitched by Thomasine Read. He declared that John Read, Thomasine's son, had come to him one day and

> desired hime to goe w[i]th hime to the howse of his mother w[hi]ch this Informant did & being there Tomenson Read gave this Informant a white Root to eate which this Inform[an]t did eate & in a short tyme after had his first tormenting fitt & hath to this present been in great payne & miserie.[77]

Robert thus created a story with a clear parallel to the timeline of the alleged bewitchment: First, Thomasine's son John came to Robert, asking him to accompany him to Thomasine's house; next, Robert was given a root to eat; a short time later, he had his first 'tormenting fitt', and he had been 'in great pain and misery' since. The conclusion of Robert's testimony clearly shows that he invented the links in this story himself: 'all which this Inform[an]t doth veryly beleave was done by Tomenson Reade'.[78] His own belief about Thomasine was the only 'proof' he had. The cause-and-effect aspect was strong, but the evidence, as it stood, was weak.

Next, the fourth witness gave his sworn testimony, which shifted the focus from Robert Miller's sickness to the bewitched sheep. The witness, Thomas Woodbridge, was one of the owners of these sheep, and 'saith that in Aprill 1647 this Inform[an]t had died out of his flocke 12 sheepe w[hi]ch sheepe died in a strang mannor & in a very short tyme'.[79] Thomas's testimony is just a short statement to the effect that, in only a short span of time, many of his sheep died in a 'strange manner'. Thomasine Read is not mentioned, nor is there any reference to Thomasine casting evil on the sheep. This testimony simply functions as a statement about an event that the owner of the sheep found peculiar.

The final witness to testify was Robert Gray. He was the co-owner of the sheep that had died, and he was also the master of Thomasine Read's son, who had been working at his farm as a farmhand but whose job had been given to another boy. Robert Gray

> saith that having the sone of Tomenson Reade to drive his plow, this Inform[an]t Changed the s[ai]d sone of Tomenson & tooke another boy that was more stronger, w[hi]ch the s[ai]d Tomenson hearing said hath this Roug Gray taken another Boy if I live Ile be even w[i]th hime for so doing.[80]

These threatening words allegedly spoken by Thomasine would turn out to be dangerous for her, as

> presently after this Informant had two of his sheep died within an hower[s] space, w[hi]ch att that tyme this Informant said unto the shepheard that he

did veryly beleave was bewitcht By the s[ai]d Tomenson Read.[81] [Italics in original.]

Again we see that the witness created a story about revenge, in which there is a link between Robert Gray's decision to replace Thomasine's son with another farmhand and the loss of two of his sheep shortly afterwards. In this testimony, nothing can be proved—Thomasine is connected to the loss of sheep only through her relation to the dismissed farmhand and her threatening words when he lost his job. Robert Gray draws attention to the near-immediate effect of her threatening words, as the sheep died within an hour of Thomasine's threat. As with Robert Miller's testimony, the evidence here is very weak, as it is based on suspicion only.

Thomasine Read gave her confession before the same individuals that heard the witnesses' testimonies later that day, on 29 May 1647. In her confession, all points mentioned in the witnesses' testimonies are activated. The content of Thomasine Read's confession is a mixture of demonological ideas and traditional folkloric ideas, and the overall structure follows a common pattern for demonological witchcraft confessions. First, the confession targets Thomasine's pact with the devil, followed by her personal demons, and then her practice of witchcraft. What is lacking in Thomasine's confession, compared with what we see in many other demonological witchcraft confessions, is the witches' gathering and thus the subsequent denunciation of other participants. Thomasine's performance of witchcraft must therefore be characterized as an individual practice of witchcraft based on *maleficium* as well as demonological elements.

Thomasine Read confessed

that about 7 yeares since there appeared unto this ex[amine]th a great muse & gave hir a prick upon the Thygh & hath suckt upon hir body every [day] since untill wednesday last being the 26 of May 1647 & after this ex[amine]th had made hir Contract w[i]th the divell.[82]

The most striking information in this first part of her confession is her mention of a 'Contract' with the devil, a clear reference to the devil's pact, which is similar to a number of confessions in the Essex witchcraft trials between 1645 and 1647.[83] By 1645, witches were commonly believed to have entered into 'a solemn league' with the devil.[84] The idea of an animal sucking blood from witches' bodies is specific to witchcraft cases in England and is not found in court records from the other countries in this study. Thomasine said that she was sucked on by a spirit mouse for seven years. The English witches were believed to have a familiar, most often a cat. Thomasine's 'great muse' may have been such a familiar.[85] In England, the devil's mark was a teat, a spot created by the demonic animals for suckling; in Scotland, the devil's mark was a mark on the body that was impervious to pain and resulted from the devil's touch. In most countries, the devil's mark was believed to be a result of the ritual of entering into the pact, not a mark made beforehand. In Thomasine's confession, it seems to be implied that, before one enters into the devil's pact, one would already have had a relationship with an imp or another demonic creature.

Thomasine Read then confessed that the devil had asked her to sacrifice her own child and that she refused:

> the first thinge that the divell askt of hir was to make away her Child w[hi]ch this ex[amine]th refused but Commanded hir spirit Muse to goe touch & bewitch Rob[er]t Miller the sone of John Miller which as this ex[amine]th Confesseth was presently p[er]formed by hir spirit mus & the Child ever since to this xxix of May [is] in great torment.[86]

Thomasine's refusal to give the devil her child shows autonomy vis-à-vis the devil, and such a reaction on the part of a mother has many similarities with witchcraft cases in other countries: the mother most often wants to protect her child.[87] However, the demonological notion of mothers sacrificing their children to the devil and mothers teaching their eldest daughters witchcraft is seen in source material from other countries.[88] Children accused of witchcraft, for instance in Finnmark in Norway, confessed that they had learned witchcraft from their mother or aunt.[89]

The confession of Thomasine Read includes the idea of the transference of illness. Thomasine Read saved her own child, but the illness was cast on another child instead. This is an old folkloric idea, known in many countries and seen in witchcraft confessions in, among others, Shetland, Scotland, and Norway.[90] Transferring sickness from one person to another—as well as removing sickness from a person who has been bewitched—was a common element in witchcraft cases, and part of either healing practices or malevolent witchcraft.[91] It was most often related to *maleficium*, and the practising witch usually used charms and remedies to perform the act of casting and removing evil spells.

In many European countries at this time, 'cunning people' were believed to have the ability to remove sickness. From Thomasine Read's confession, it emerges that her power in this respect was limited:

> this ex[amine]th being asked if shee could not command hir spirit muse to forsake the Child she answered she Could not for if it was in hir power she would but further said that old Hitch of Aldre Could unwitch Millers Child.[92]

As women generally knew who in the area could take away sickness, Thomasine recommended a 'cunning man' in Aldreth. Thus, she signalled that, even if she believed that she herself had mastered the art of bewitchment, she believed that her own power to remove illness was limited.

Thomasine Read's confession shows that she had not one but two familiars: a mouse and a cat. They would suck blood from her and perform evil deeds:

> further this ex[amine]th saith that she had another spirit in the liknes of a Catt w[hi]ch she gave suck unto w[hi]ch Catt she Commanded to goe to the

fold of tho[mas] woodbridg & Rob[er]t Gray & worrie 12 of there sheepe because thay would not have hir Boy noe longer to blow [*sic*] but tooke anothe[r] Boy.[93]

The cat had killed the sheep at her command because she wanted revenge against the sheep farmers, who had given her son's position to another boy. Again, the confession includes an item of *maleficium*, casting sickness on animals, which in this case resulted in economic loss for the farmers.

The final point of Thomasine Read's confession concerns the practice of witchcraft. She declared that she was in command of both her spirits, the mouse and the cat, and that she could order them to do evil deeds. Indeed,

> being asked when hir spirits suckt upon hir body this ex[amine]th saith that thay both Came in a great wynd the last night betweene 12 & on[e] of the Clocke & that as sone as thay had done sucking of hir she Commanded hir muse spirit to goe in to the body of Rob[er]t Miller & hir Catt spirit she Commanded to goe & destroy the Corne that Groeth in Hillrow field.[94]

The spirits came to suck on her at midnight, and they arrived via a 'great wynd'. This may be related to the whirlwind of the fairies, known from Scotland, a wind in which the fairies were believed to travel. There is, however, a difference, as the fairies' whirlwind would often result in the death of the person hit by it, which did not occur in this case.[95] In this last part of Thomasine's confession, a new point emerges, namely the destruction of a cornfield—a recurring element in many European witchcraft trials, particularly in Central Europe, but also in Denmark.[96] At the very end of her confession, Thomasine declared that she could not write; she therefore put her mark under her confession, unlike the witnesses, who had written out their names.

In the case of Thomasine Read, we see in her confession a combination of ideas related to demonology and malevolent witchcraft. The content encompasses the devil's pact; the suckling spirits, who are under her command with regard to performing evil; and the practice of malevolent witchcraft, such as the casting and transferring of sickness and the destruction of a cornfield. To a large extent, the content is similar to that of confessions in other European countries, and the elements confessed to seem to serve a scapegoat function related to disasters that hit the local community. The suckling animals and the teats, however, likely remain England-specific variants.

The outcome of the trial is unknown. In essence, the records of Thomasine Read's case are brief, with unconvincing evidence against her.

The Voice of Thomasine Read

In the legal documents, the voice of Thomasine Read appears directly, in her confession, and indirectly, in the references to and rendering of her words in the witnesses' testimonies. Concerning the latter, we hear differences in the way Thomasine's voice is rendered by the various witnesses.

In Edward Mason's depiction of Thomasine Read's voice, her utterances are down-to-earth and rather short. Apparently, she spoke these words to him in person. The main points regarding her entering the devil's pact and her performance of sorcery are there, but the language is not expansive. Edward apparently believed that Thomasine could 'unwitch' as well as bewitch, but she explained to him that this was not the case. The content of Edward's testimony is slightly different from that of Thomasine's own confession, specifically as regards the balance of power between the devil and Thomasine. In Edward Mason's story, the devil is the one with the power to perform evil, not Thomasine. It was the devil who came to her to ask what he could do for her after she allowed him to suck her blood, and it was the devil who sent out the spirit mouse to cast sickness on Robert Miller. In Edward's view, the devil is the more powerful figure of the two, and this colours his narration. In her own version of this narrative, Thomasine herself is the one who sends out the spirit mouse and the demon cat to perform witchcraft.

When Ellen Pope renders the voice of Thomasine Read, the latter's speech is drawn more towards the female sphere. This comes to the fore in the choice of words and in additive sentence structures that are more 'embroidered' by the use of epithets, with a stronger highlighting of female body parts and more details about the individuals related to Thomasine's deeds. In short, Ellen's rendering of Thomasine's voice shows a Thomasine with a more extensive vocabulary.

The only rendering of Thomasine Read's voice in the testimony of Robert Gray is her threat: 'hath this Roug Gray taken another Boy if I live Ile be even w[i]th hime for so doing'. Thomasine threatens Robert because he did not employ her son as his farmhand. This is a serious threat, but words many might speak in anger. However, this time the witness can link these words to the loss of his sheep and thus raise suspicion about Thomasine, since the two events occurred not too far apart and because the cause-and-effect aspects are convincing.

Thomasine Read's confession is formed as a narrative with a clear timeline. We find a detailed representation of years, dates, and times of day: the devil came to her '7 yeares since'; 'hath suckt upon hir body every [day] since untill wedensday last being the 26 of May 1647'; '& after this ex[amine]th'; 'the first thinge that the divell askt of hir'; 'the sone of John Miller which as this ex[amine]th Confesseth *was presently p[er]formed* by hir spirit mus & the Child *ever since to this xxix of May* [is] in great torment'; 'but *further* said'; '*further* this ex[amine]th saith'; 'the *last night* betweene 12 & on[e] of the Clocke'; '*as sone as* thay had done sucking of hir'. [My italics.] The words denoting the time and chronological order of events support the reliability of the text and make it easier for the reader and listener to follow. The order of events is unmistakable.

The confession of Thomasine Read is characterized by the repetition of certain words: 'spirit' is mentioned six times, 'muse' five times, 'suckle' four times, and 'divill' twice—all words that, in this context, are related to the diabolic. Spread out evenly across a relatively short text, the string of these closely related terms influences the style and content of the confession. Sometimes, these words are uttered in response to specific questions: it is clear that the interrogator wants to know more about Thomasine's knowledge of this particular demonological field.

There is movement related to speed in the confession: it has a rather slow pace in the beginning, with Thomasine Read's description of the spirit mouse and the devil's pact, which steadily increases until the brisk listing of her evil deeds, one after another, at the end. It seems as if the interrogator, having obtained the answers he wanted, has no need to go deeper into exploring her witchcraft practice in detail. There is a very abrupt end to the confession, almost as though it was cut short.

The confession was written down by the scribe, recording Thomasine Read's oral speech. Thomasine could not write and probably could not read either. However, she could tell stories and knew the narrative structures of those stories. The most conspicuous orality feature in her confession is the additive sentence structure. This sentence and language structure is emphasized visually and orthographically by the scribe's use of an ampersand (&) to combine additive sentences and sentence fragments. Another orality feature is the insertion of traditional folkloric motifs, like the whirlwind.

The narration of the confession is coherent. There are no contradictions, and the same narrative thread is followed throughout. Nor is there any trace of denial in Thomasine Read's voice concerning the main points she is confessing to—the only denial we hear is her refusal to give the devil her own child. She seems to confess willingly to all that she is asked about, not denying that she knows witchcraft and has practised malevolent witchcraft, that she has entered into a pact with the devil, and that demonic animals have suckled on her. If there is a turning point in this case, it would be the day she was searched for the mark. In her own confession, this is when she began to send out her demonic animals, familiars, to perform evil. There are no signs in the records that torture was applied.

The question remains as to why Thomasine Read, in her own confession and thus in her own voice, did not give a more detailed account of the various aspects of witchcraft that she was believed to have performed. Could it be that she was so exhausted after the search for the mark and her time in the dungeon that she did not have the strength to voice a more vigorous narrative? Or could it be that the interrogator, David Chalmer, thought he had enough for a sentence once she had confessed to the critical points, namely the devil's pact, the demonic animals, and the performance of specific acts of malevolent witchcraft? One thing we do know for certain is that, had witches' gatherings been included in the witnesses' testimonies or in Thomasine's own confession, the trials would have taken on a much larger dimension.[97]

The Voices of the Witnesses

In the same way that the distinct timeline is drawn, a clear cause-and-effect argumentation is employed throughout Thomasine Read's confession and the witnesses' testimonies. The effect of the mouse and the cat suckling on her was her entry into the devil's pact; the effect of her contract with the devil was the power to command her two spirits; the effect of her commanding them was that the cat destroyed the sheep and the corn, and that the mouse harmed Robert Miller. This link between cause and effect proved very effective in terms of casting suspicion on Thomasine. It suggests a shared understanding among all involved that there was a direct relationship between Thomasine's actions and the results of those actions. This relationship was constructed after the event to explain the illness and accidents that were otherwise difficult to explain. Such a narrative was necessary to establish the image of a dangerous witch—this type of post hoc rationalization made her into a powerful and frightening figure. This is a common feature in witchcraft confessions, and it helped steer the confession in the direction intended by the interrogator through the use of testimonies as 'proof' that the suspected person really was the cause of unexplained illness, death, or catastrophes. This type of argumentation infused logic into the narrative and exploited the witnesses' testimonies as plausible 'proofs' for the suspected witch's evil deeds.

When looking at the witnesses' testimonies, however, there are some contradictions in the rendering of Thomasine Read's voice. Interestingly, these concern the devil and the range of Thomasine's power. While Edward Mason allows Thomasine's rendered voice to state that the devil was the one with the power to perform evil, Ellen Pope gives this authority to Thomasine, in accordance with Thomasine's own confession. This is an important point, because the power to perform evil is a decisive factor for being considered a witch. The clearest connection between the sucking of blood and the demonic animals being sent out is found in Ellen Pope's testimony: it seems that this bloodsucking was a preparatory act for the performance of evil. It should also be noted that Edward Mason included the point about Thomasine's helplessness when it came to the 'unwitching' of Roger Miller. The sole female witness, Ellen Pope, was probably the only witness who had substantial knowledge about the field of witchcraft, and thus the only one with insight into how witchcraft was performed. If we understand this knowledge as having been shared primarily among women, Ellen was a good spokeswoman. Her knowledge about witchcraft was most likely part of an oral tradition passed from one person to another in the local village. These types of stories were passed on like news and would have been retold before the assize during a testimony.

The Voice of the Interrogator

In the recorded discourse of Thomasine Read's confession, we can hear the voice of the interrogator as well as Thomasine's own voice. To a certain extent, it is possible to trace the kinds of questions she was asked. At the beginning of her confession, we just find the words 'whoe saith that', which means that a question must have started the interrogation. She is likely asked when she entered into the pact with the devil, as this is the content of the answer she then gives. Next, she is asked about the range of her power: 'this ex[amine]th *being asked* if shee could not command hir spirit muse'.[98] [My italics.] This means that the interrogator wants to know whether

her power is strong enough to perform a range of evil deeds, which she answers in the negative. She is then asked when the spirits had come to suck on her: '& *being asked* when hir spirits suckt upon hir body'.[99] [My italics.] In response, she describes in strong and definite sentences how she practised her 'evil power' and states the exact time when the familiars came to her. In the records, the phrase 'being asked' is inserted twice before her responses, which indicates that these questions pertained to Thomasine commanding her spirits and the exact time they came to her: these were thus questions with demonological impact. The procedure for entering into the devil's pact, as it is described in Thomasine's confession—entailing first being suckled on by an animal and then entering into a contract with the devil—is not found in any of the other countries in this study. In Scotland, by comparison, there were long and detailed rituals involved in a witch's entry into the devil's pact.

Evil in the form of familiar spirits is mentioned in the two main statutes of witch-craft published in England. Several scholars on English witchcraft have pointed to the change in formulations from the Elizabethan Witchcraft Act of 1563, which condemned those who used evil spirits to harm others, to King James's Witchcraft Act of 1604, which made it a capital offence to 'consult, covenant with, employ, feed or reward any evil or wicked spirit to or for any intent or purpose'.[100] The conjuring of spirits was punished with the death penalty.[101] Charlotte-Rose Millar argues that the familiar spirit added a diabolic element to English witchcraft belief.[102] Based on a study of pamphlets, she maintains that the devil—often in the form of a familiar spirit—played a crucial role in English witchcraft belief prior to the 1640s.[103]

I agree with the basic understanding of the familiar as a demonic creature. It is interesting that the familiar has parallels in other countries. There is a clear resemblance between familiars as witches' helpers in England and the Apostles as witches' helpers in Denmark and Norway. The Apostles are creatures given to an alleged witch when she entered into a pact with the devil, and they were used when the witch performed evil.

The Voice of the Law

The voice of the law comes to the fore in these records through the questions posed by the judiciary, which clearly lead in a demonological direction. The judiciary apparently is acquainted with demonological ideas, including the notion of a witch's familiar. The letter of the law is echoed in the court procedure, when the witnesses swear an oath, in the rhetoric highlighting the name of the devil and other expressions related to witchcraft legislation, and in the use of witch-pricking to obtain circumstantial evidence. Furthermore, torture is not applied, which is a characteristic feature of the English legal system.

The Voice of the Scribe

The scribe was a professional whose job was to write down what he heard—both the questions and the answers. There is no sign that he added his own opinion to the recorded text. It is more likely that we hear the voice of the interrogator, who, during the interrogation, may have influenced the records through the repetition of certain central words and expressions and by asking leading questions centred on demonological notions.

Isabel Atcheson and Jane Simpson, 1664

The Trial

The trial of Isabel Atcheson took place alongside the trial of Jane Simpson in July 1664 in Newcastle upon Tyne before the mayor of the town, Sir James Clavering Barrt. Isabel and Jane were accused of having cast sickness on Dorothy Heron, a sudden disease that struck her. She was the wife of Anthony Heron, baker and brewer in Newcastle. Isabel was a married woman, the wife of Ralph Atcheson in Newcastle, and Jane Simpson was a widow. Both women were imprisoned in the tolbooth of Newcastle, where they were interrogated. Dorothy's husband, Anthony Heron, gave his sworn testimony on 20 July 1664, stating that

> aboute five weekes agoe one Jane Simpson huckster haveing Chirryes to sell: Dorothy wife to this Informer bought of her one pounde of Chirryes and payd her for ye same viii d and ye s[ai]d Dorothy reproveing ye s[ai]d Jane for exacting and takeing more of her then she did of others: p[er] 2 d in ye pound: ye s[ai]d Jane Gave ye s[ai]d Dorothy very scurrellous and threat[en]ing words: And w[i]thin a ffewe dayes after ye s[ai]d Dorothy tooke sicknes.[104]

This is the beginning of a story of revenge: Dorothy Heron said that Jane Simpson asked a higher price for her cherries when she sold them to Dorothy than she asked of others, and Dorothy had reproached her for this. Jane had answered her with threatening words, and a few days later, Dorothy had fallen ill. The narrative about the cherries was constructed after the illness occurred; two events that did not necessarily have anything to do with one another were linked to provide a reason for Dorothy's illness. The words that Jane Simpson was said to have uttered, and which were overheard by a member of the Heron family, thus became dangerous for Jane: she was tried as a witch because of them, fuelling an after-the-fact, cause-and-effect narrative.

One of the reasons this case ended in an interrogation before the Newcastle mayor was probably that Dorothy Heron had been gravely ill for a while, with fits and dramatic changes in mood; she had been 'most strangly and wonderfully handled' and the doctors could not determine what was wrong with her, nor could they help her. She was confined to bed for twenty days

> and did in the s[ai]d tyme take most sad and Lamentable: fitts[105] to ye admiration and astonishm[en]t of all spectators: being sometymes in her sicknes rageing madd: other tymes in a Laughing & singing Condic[i]on: other

tymes in a dispareing & disconsolat Condic[i]on and att other tymes in a very solitary & mute Condic[i]on.[106]

The illness entered a new phase when Dorothy Heron claims that she saw the two women in her room:

> And upon Saturday Last aboute three of ye Clock in the morneing: she tooke a most sadd & Lamentable fitt: Crying outt to this Informer who was Lyeing in bedd w[i]th her, that one Isabell Atcheson and Jane Simpson did afflict & Torment her body and were aboute ye bedd to carry her away: and this Informer had much to doe to hold & Keep her in bedd.[107]

This must have been a fantasy or dream, but the names of the two women had nevertheless been uttered, so they became suspects. According to Dorothy, they were beside her bed and tortured her body 'grievously'. Dorothy insisted that the women were in the room, and asked her husband whether he could see them:

> Looke where they both stand: And ye s[ai]d Dorothy: putting by the Curten: this Informer did visably and Clearly see ye s[ai]d Isabell Atcheson: standing att ye bedd side in her owne humane and bodyly shape Clothed w[i]th a Green wais[t]coate: in ye same habitt she dayly weares; and this Inform[er] calling upon ye Lord to be p[re]sent w[i]th him the s[ai]d Isabell: did vanish and disappeare.[108]

The name of the Lord seemed to be effective, making the women vanish from sight. Anthony Heron himself admitted that he had seen the figure of Isabel in the room, and he did not deny this in court. In this way, an inexplicable illness was turned into an act of witchcraft, and the two women—Jane Simpson and Isabel Atcheson—now faced a terrible situation. This incident, the vision of the two women in the bedroom, proved to be a pivotal point for the case.

Then, the situation changed again. The morning after Dorothy Heron had allegedly seen Isabel Atcheson and Jane Simpson in her room, she requested that they be sent for: 'And aboute 10: of ye Clock of ye same day according to ye desire of his Wife, hee sent for ye s[ai]d Isabell: and Jane to come upp to his howse: w[hi]ch they did Accordingly'.[109] Dorothy asked them to come to her home so they might help her recover from the illness: she had seen their presence in her room as a sign that they had been the ones to cast the affliction on her, and now she wanted them to remove it. The women came,

> and he asking the s[ai]d Isabell: what she did att his bedd side soe soone y[a]t Morneing shee replyed itt was not her butt ye Devill y[a]t was there: and ye s[ai]d Isabell: and Jane comeing into ye roome: where this Inform[er]s wife was Lyeing: she had a desire to have blood of them: telling them that they had wronged her, and she would be revenged of them.[110]

This is a strange statement, but the probable meaning is that she believed their blood would 'unwitch' her and therefore make her well again. Drawing blood from a person is known from traditional sorcery in other countries and is used in the same context.[111]

Both Jane Simpson and Isabel Atcheson agreed that Dorothy could scratch them to get some of their blood.[112] However, the word 'partly' in the quote below suggests that they might not have agreed immediately, and that there may have been some hesitation:

> they *p[ar]tly* Condescending thereunto she scratch[ed] there faces & Gott blood of them both and *w[i]thin a howre after* she Gott out of her bedd: caused her Clothes to be putt on and walked over ye floore called for meate: and ever since is very much amended and is every day better & better: and in a very recovering Condic[i]on: to ye admirac[i]on of all p[er]sons to see such a sudden alterac[i]on & Change: being soe infirme and weake in body before.[113] [My italics.]

The effect of getting some of the women's blood was apparently immediate, as after just one hour, Dorothy Heron was well again, out of bed, and dressed. It is emphasized in the above quote that the sudden recovery was permanent, to everybody's surprise. In addition, Dorothy asked for meat just after she was out of bed, which seemingly signalled that her health had miraculously improved, as she was strong enough to eat. This episode indicates that traditional beliefs about becoming 'unwitched' by drawing blood from those who performed the bewitchment was an understanding shared by all involved—and indeed the act of drawing blood worked as expected. This episode also illustrates that a belief rooted in ideas about malevolent witchcraft—likely existing before ideas about demonological witchcraft became widespread—remained prominent even at the end of the period of witchcraft persecution. Layers of witchcraft-related belief from different eras existed side by side in oral communities; a part of a common understanding among peasants that humans had to obey underlying forces that they believed in but could not see.[114]

Isabel Atcheson was examined before the town mayor in Newcastle on 20 July 1664. The records contain a rarity in witchcraft research, namely a complete rendering of the questions posed to her during this examination, as well as her answers. This is a treasure for courtroom discourse analysis, as the questions posed in most witchcraft trials were not fully recorded. We see the work of a professional scribe who had the objective to accurately enter the discourse into the records. The first question posed was whether Isabel knew 'one Dorothy hearon wife of Anthony hearon of this Towne Baker: & Brewer'.[115] The question is formulated in such a way that Isabel could simply answer 'Yes' or 'No'. However, this is not what Isabel did, instead answering that 'she hath seene ye s[ai]d Dorothy severall tymes'[116]—in other words, Isabel knew who Dorothy was, but she did not know her well.

The second question targeted the time just before the episode in which Dorothy Heron saw Isabel Atcheson and Jane Simpson in her bedroom. Isabel was asked 'where she was upon Saturday Morneing Last aboute 3 or 4 of ye Clock: and if she were not then in ye howse of anthony: hearons'.[117] This is a direct question; it is not open-ended. She was asked where she was on a certain night, and it is suggested directly afterwards that she was in the house of Anthony Heron. The way the last question is formulated made it possible to simply answer 'Yes' or 'No'; however, this is not what Isabel did. She answered,

> y[a]t she was in her owne howse and in bed untill six of ye Clock y[a]t Morneing: and came not att ye howse of ye s[ai]d Anthony: hearons untill she was sent for: p[er] Elezer Potts to come upp: att Tenn of ye Clock on Saturday Last.[118]

Of course she could not admit to having been in Dorothy's house in the middle of the night, as that would have meant admitting that she had cast the illness on Dorothy.

Isabel Atcheson was then asked a direct question as to whether she practised witchcraft—here, for the first time, in addition to the words 'witchcraft' and 'sorcery', the notion of the diabolical enters into the records: 'if ever she wronged ye s[ai]d Dorothy: or used or Exercised any *witchcraft sorcery: or any such diabolicall Art*: upon ye body of ye s[ai]d Dorothy hearons: to afflict Torment: waist or consume ye same'. [Italics in original.][119] It is interesting that terms from the witchcraft statutes, such as witchcraft and sorcery, were mentioned, while the diabolical part was a more recent addition.[120] For this question, too, the answer could have been a simple 'Yes' or 'No', but Isabel answered 'that she never wronged ye s[ai]d Dorothy in all her Life *neither by word or deed*: and as for *witchcraft: or such devellish Acts* she is altogether Ignorant of: and further sayes not'.[121] [My italics.] Isabel did not mention sorcery, but instead referred to 'witchcraft: or such devellish Acts', denying any knowledge of it. She changed the word 'diabolicall' to 'devellish', but still linked witchcraft to the devil. When Isabel stated that she did not wrong Dorothy, 'neither by word nor deed', this could have been a reference to specific sorcery-related practices, such as the use of charms or formulas, which would likely have been known among the peasants, villagers, and townsfolk. Because of the way the question is posed, answering in the affirmative would have been impossible for Isabel: if she had, she would have admitted guilt. The last sentence, stating that she had nothing more to say, may be the answer to a question about whether she wanted to add anything to her prior statements. No mentioning of pressure has been entered into the court records. The outcome of the case is unknown.

Jane Simpson was examined on 21 July, one day after Isabel. Jane had sold cherries to Dorothy Heron and had argued with her because Dorothy complained about the high price of Jane's cherries. When Jane was examined, she was asked three questions, just like Isabel Atcheson. The first was whether she had gone to Dorothy Heron's house five weeks before, with cherries to sell, and whether she had sold cherries to Dorothy Heron. Instead of answering 'Yes' or 'No', she gave a longer answer, saying 'y[a]t aboute the s[ai]d tyme she was att ye howse of Anthony hearons w[i]th Chirryes to sell: butt she sold none of them to Antho[ny] hearons wife'.[122] Here we have new information, because this is the first time it is stated that Jane did not, in fact, sell any cherries to Dorothy—Anthony Heron, by contrast, said in his testimony that Dorothy had purchased cherries from Jane, paying her one pound, and then complained that the cherries were too expensive.

The next question posed to Jane was whether she and Anthony Heron's wife 'were att any words: or ever fell outt'. To this, Jane answered 'y[a]t she never had any occation or cause to fall out w[i]th ye s[ai]d hearons: wife nor never abused or wronged her in her Life p[ro] word or deed'.[123] We see here that Jane denied that she had quarrelled with Dorothy, which was an important argument in Anthony Heron's testimony because it gave a reason as to why Jane had cast sickness on Dorothy. Again, Jane could have answered with one word, but instead she answered in the negative with a complete sentence.

The third question concerned the experience Dorothy Heron said she had had in the middle of the night,

> if she were not in ye howse of ye s[ai]d Anthony hearons upon: Saturday Morneing instant and did not then appeare to ye s[ai]d Anthony hearons [*sic*] in her owne bodyly shape: or afflicted or Torm[en]ted ye body of ye s[ai]d hearons wife: or Exercised & practised any *diabolicall Art of witchcraft sorcery* or: the Like upon her.[124] [My italics.]

This question resembles the second and third questions posed to Isabel, and again Jane could have answered 'Yes' or 'No'. However, Jane replied that

> she was not then in ye s[ai]d Anthony hearons howse: nor never appeared to her nor noe other p[er]son in any such manner: and as for *witchcraft sorcery or any such diabolicall Art* or practice she is altogether Ignorant of And further sayth not.[125] [My italics.]

The questioner mentions the words 'diabolicall Art', 'witchcraft', and 'sorcery'. However, unlike Isabel, Jane repeats all the words, saying 'diabolicall Art' instead of the phrase 'devellish Acts' that Isabel had used. It could be that Jane was more familiar with the learned terms than Isabel, or simply that Jane just repeated the words used in the question. The last sentence in the record is the same as Isabel's, and was probably an answer to a question asking if she had any more to say.

The Voice of Isabel Atcheson

The voice of Isabel Atcheson appears twice in the records: the first time only faintly, in the testimony of Anthony Heron, and the second time quite vividly, in her own answers when she is questioned.

In his testimony, Anthony Heron renders Isabel's answer in indirect speech. Encouraged by his sick wife to check if he, too, could see the two women in the bedroom in the middle of the night, Anthony had looked at a specific place in the bedroom and thought he had seen Isabel and Jane. When they were sent for the next morning, he had asked Isabel what she was doing in his bedroom so early in the morning, and she had replied that it was not she who had been there, but the devil. Isabel, as quoted by Anthony, thus brought the devil into the narrative. This possibly relates to oral speech, in that at that time, the devil could be mentioned in a way that was a bit rude (i.e., via swear words). If so, then Isabel answered Anthony Heron impolitely here, and definitely did not give him a response that answered his question. To mention the devil in this way would therefore have had nothing to do with diabolic witchcraft, but rather with an outspoken woman using rough language. This would mean that when Isabel came to the Herons' house that Saturday morning, she was not a timid person. However, it cannot be ruled out that Isabel really meant that the devil had appeared in the Herons' bedroom in her likeness.

The interrogation supports the impression that Isabel Atcheson was a strong-willed woman. The three questions posed to her are all formulated in such a way that it is unlikely they will get a positive answer. The first one, asking whether Isabel knew Dorothy Heron, is rather neutral, but the other two questions essentially invite the accused person to respond in the negative. It is almost like the examiner expects the accused to deny practising witchcraft. We do not know what state Isabel was in at this time, but she had likely been imprisoned for many days. As the selling of the cherries had occurred five weeks earlier, and the recorded documents are dated 20, 21, and 22 July, the case came up for examination fairly quickly. However, it seems quite clear from the answers Isabel gives that she still had the strength to resist. Her answers are rich in words, with a strong oral flavour. Reading the questions together with her answers gives a strong feeling of her resistance. This is not a woman who is giving in, nor is she nearing any kind of breakdown. She states quite definitely that she was in her own house when the Herons had seen the two women in their bedroom, and that she had never hurt Dorothy.

When the examiner introduces the term 'diabolical Art', she responds with 'devellish Acts', which is more colloquial. When the examiner uses 'witchcraft sorcery', Isabel Atcheson uses only the word 'witchcraft' in her response. 'Diabolical' is a word used here with reference to legal discourse and the laws, and adds a serious touch to the discourse. Thus, in the linguistic expression of the interrogation, we see two spheres of ideas meeting each other: the mayor's, with his connection to the ideas and language of the legal field, and Isabel's, with her connection to the ideas and language of the peasants. This difference can be traced stylistically, with the interrogator clearly echoing the Witchcraft Act, using solemn terms, while Isabel is speaking in the language of the common people, using words that reflect an oral sphere and additive linguistic structures. The voice of Isabel is not hesitant or afraid, but strong, independent, vigorous, and confident. Even if she has been imprisoned for the five weeks following her sale of the cherries to Dorothy Heron, she is not at a low point. By 1664, all inhabitants of England knew what it meant to be accused of witchcraft. This fear cannot be traced in her voice, however—perhaps she believes that she will be acquitted. She knows there is no evidence, that nothing can be proved, and that as long as she does not confess to anything, she has a strong case and cannot be convicted. It is also worth noting that in the 1660s, witchcraft persecution was on the decline across England, and accusations were treated with more leniency than previously. Trials were still possible as long as there was a witchcraft statute and officers were willing to enact it, but there were fewer witchcraft trials than before and conviction rates were low.[126]

The Voice of Jane Simpson

The voice of Jane Simpson is characterized by resistance and strength. She refuses every attempt to make her confess and answers in full and rich sentences. Additive noun constructions and additive verbal constructions surface in her confession, such as 'occasion or cause', 'abused or wronged', 'word and deed', which are oral features. She answers the last question briefly—she does not want to give any more information, and she wants the questioning to come to an end. Her voice is not weak. She protests, and there is no sign that she is on the verge of confessing to witchcraft.

Jane Simpson had been selling cherries, and was probably not very rich, as she was a widow. She would have been used to debating prices with customers, and perhaps she could be quarrelsome, although there is no evidence for this other than what Jane had allegedly told Anthony Heron's wife, according to his testimony. If we believe what Jane says, there was no argument between her and Dorothy Heron, so either Anthony Heron or Jane Simpson were wrong on this point.

Jane Simpson's voice provides a coherent narrative, which is precise with regard to the timeline, people's names, and other details. There is no contradiction between her narrative and Isabel Atcheson's narrative. Both women proclaim their innocence and there is no sign that they are surrendering. Jane's answers to the examiner's questions are clear and decisive.

Although she is in a dangerous situation, Jane Simpson, like Isabel Atcheson, does not show fear. Apparently both thought they were safe. We do not know what kind of pressure these two women had been exposed to during imprisonment in order to make them confess. They were examined on two different days, and we do not know whether they had the opportunity to talk to each other in the tolbooth.

Both Isabel Atcheson and Jane Simpson had the opportunity to reply with a short 'Yes' or 'No' to the questions posed, but neither did so. This supports an interpretation that the accused women in witchcraft trials were given the space to tell their stories, that they used these opportunities to speak, and also that the scribe recorded their words.[127]

The Voice of the Witness

There is only one witness in this case: Anthony Heron, the husband of the sick Dorothy. However, much of his testimony is a rendering of what his wife told him. His deposition consists of two parts: first, the story about the two women allegedly present in Dorothy's bedroom, seen in a vision; second, the summoning of Isabel Atcheson and Jane Simpson in order to have them unwitch Dorothy. The first part of his testimony does not support his wife's vision of both women being present in her bedroom, as Anthony says that he could see only Isabel. The second part of Anthony's testimony, dealing with Isabel and Jane being sent for in order to cure his wife's illness, provides information about the conversation taking place between him and Isabel. When questioned about what she did at his bed in the morning, she answered in a rather harsh way that it was not her, but the devil he had seen. The voice of Anthony is one blaming her; however, she paid him back in her own coin.

From Anthony Heron's voice, we learn that he and his wife, too, believed in witchcraft. They believed that spells could be the cause of illness. They believed that the person who cast a spell could also remove it. They believed that drawing blood from the person who cast a spell could reverse the process and take the illness away. Thus, the fear of malevolent witchcraft and the conviction that some people could cast and take away spells underlies Dorothy Heron's interpretation of her vision of the two women in the bedroom and her request for them to come back. Likewise, the same belief must have formed the basis of Anthony Heron's testimony, as he is willing to testify in court on his wife's behalf. However, the weakness of his testimony is that it is mostly a retelling of a ill woman's unrealistic vision.

The Voice of the Interrogator

There were two people in the courtroom who had the opportunity to influence the court records of the trials of Isabel Atcheson and Jane Simpson: the scribe and the interrogator. In general, the voice of the interrogator—here, the mayor—is more prominent in witchcraft trial records than the voice of the scribe. In these two trials, the voice of the interrogator is quoted directly and is vivid. As the interrogator was the one posing the questions, he was able to steer the examination by using leading questions. In these two cases, there were only a few questions, and each was phrased such that they could obtain one-syllable answers. The questions were standard and not very insistent; the kinds of questions that suggest that the interrogator was not convinced about Isabel's and Jane's guilt.

In both trials, the voice of the interrogator is interwoven with the accused persons' answers during a brief interrogation. The interrogator is efficient. In the course of a three-step inquiry in the questioning of Isabel Atcheson, he gets to know about the relationship between Isabel and Dorothy, where Isabel was at a crucial point in time, and whether she practised 'witchcraft sorcery: or any such diabolicall Art'. By equating witchcraft and sorcery with diabolical art, even labelling them as diabolical in the last question, he takes the interrogation in the direction of the demonic. The word 'diabolical' is not mentioned in the Witchcraft Act of 1604, which means that it is inserted by the interrogator and might point to the legal rhetoric that had developed over some decades. The interrogator does not ask direct follow-up questions, which might have been expected because of his third question about Isabel's witchcraft practice. We see the same procedure in the interrogation of Jane.

As both accused women answered the three questions negatively, there was not much the interrogation of the accused could have produced in terms of relevant information for the judiciary. The accusations against Isabel and Jane had to rely on Anthony Heron's testimony. In both trials, the interrogator probably gave the accused the chance to say something more at the end. The fact that the interrogator did not follow up the last question in particular might be a sign that he found the evidence very weak. Thus, the voice of the interrogator might be interpreted as one representative of a relatively late trial, held when the fear of evil witchcraft in the local courts was declining and likewise the interest in persecuting witches. Taking the content of the questions into consideration and the lack of interest to press for more information by posing more questions, it is not quite clear whether there was any interest to pursue these cases.

The Voice of the Law

The court's decision was made on 22 July 1664, two days after the case began, and it mentions both women:

> The Condic[i]on of this Recognizance is such that if the above bounden Anthony: hearon doe make his p[er]sonall appeareance att the next assizes or Generell gaole delivery w[hi]ch shall first happen to be holden for the Towne of Newcastle and ye Countyr of the same Towne Then and there doe frame & p[ro]ferr or cause to be framed & p[ro]ferred *a Bill of Indictm[en]t* ag[ains]t Isabell Atcheson wife of Raiph Atcheson y[e]om[an] and Jane Simpson widow: now prisoners in his Ma[jes]ties Gaol w[i]thin this Towne, ffor ye suspic[i]on of witchcraft in bewitching the body of dorothy: hearon wife of the s[ai]d Anthony hearon.[128] [My italics.]

Here, Anthony Heron is asked to present the indictments against the two women for suspicion of witchcraft before the assize at their next meeting, which means that he must present a written document based on his testimony and the questioning of the women. He also needs to provide additional witness testimonies, if possible.

The decision by the court concludes as follows: 'And further to doe what by the Court shall be Enjoyned him: and not dep[ar]t the Court w[i]thout Licence That then this recognizance to be voyd or else to stand in force'.[129] Thus, the continuation of the case rests upon Anthony Heron. If he is able to provide the indictment, the case will continue; otherwise, the women will be acquitted. Judging from the testimony and the examination of the women, Anthony's case is not very strong. His own testimony is based on a vision of one woman, and his wife's vision of two women, in his bedroom—the latter related to him by his wife when she was in a delirious state. There are no confessions from the accused, as they both denied any knowledge of witchcraft. The fact that Dorothy Heron had, by the time of the court proceedings, recovered from her illness also weakened Anthony's case. The alleged witchcraft resulted in neither death nor permanent illness, and it is not clear how much weight the court gives to Anthony's accusations. Unfortunately, the preserved sources do not provide any more information.

When studying the discourse in this case against Isabel Atcheson and Jane Simpson, it is interesting to ask how much content they contributed to the case themselves, and how much was contributed by Dorothy and Anthony Heron. As it happens, Isabel's and Jane's voices are only heard in direct rendered speech when they are answering questions before the mayor, and in these responses they deny that they had anything to do with witchcraft. They do not complement the testimony with any new elements but rather deny all accusations. The content thus comes from the voices of Dorothy and Anthony; in fact, most comes from the rendered voice of Dorothy, who told her husband about the incident. Dorothy had apparently resented the price of the cherries that Jane had sold her, and the whole story is rooted in that situation. The quarrel they had regarding the price of the cherries then connected the two women to Dorothy's illness, because she had allegedly seen them in her bedroom. The illness was grave and sudden, so it was necessary to generate an explanation for what had caused it—and then an explanation for her sudden recovery. Thus the entire testimony presented before the mayor was created by Dorothy and Anthony. The link between Dorothy's sickness and the two women's practice of witchcraft was never more than a fictive creation. Anthony's testimony is unrealistic, and based on very weak evidence.

The Voice of the Scribe

With regard to the voice of the scribe, the documents in Isabel Atcheson and Jane Simpson's case are unusual because the entire examination—questions as well as answers—is so closely rendered. The voice of the interrogator, the voice of the accused, and the voice of the witness can be reconstructed from the documents, as the scribe preserved many details and orality features, thus distinguishing the different voices. In this way, the documents provide a convincing impression of the scribe at work and of his aim to accurately render the discourse.

In this case, the voice of the scribe is very professional. His job was to write down what was said, and this he did. It is not possible to trace his own view, as he was simply recording what he heard. There is no sign that he was being selective, recording some statements while leaving out others. As such, the personal voice of the scribe does not come to the fore.

Conclusion

The analyses of the trials of Thomasine Read, Isabel Atcheson, and Jane Simpson have documented ideas about witchcraft in English witchcraft trials related to demonology as well as *maleficium*. The demonological ideas coming to the fore in the confession of Thomasine Read, who was accused during the witchcraft panic in the 1640s, show that the devil's pact was known in England. There was also a belief in a devil's mark, or a teat, and in the existence of familiars, demonic creatures owned by alleged witches. Further, the trial of Thomasine Read shows that ideas about *maleficium* and demonological ideas in witchcraft confessions were fused: the casting of evil spells on human beings and animals causing sickness and the transference of sickness from one person to another appear to have been merged with the appearance of the devil and other demonological features. The trials of Isabel Atcheson and Jane Simpson, both accused in trials in 1664, present several notions related to malevolent witchcraft in the accused persons' confessions as well as in the witness's testimony: casting spells resulting in illness, the power to unwitch, the taking away of a spell, and the belief that drawing blood from a person who had cast a spell could make the sick person recover.

The voices of women in courtroom discourse display a range of narrative strategies, documented in accused individuals' confessions as well as in witnesses' depositions. Many participants in these trials mastered the art of telling a story. We see this most clearly in the confession of Thomasine Read and the witnesses' depositions in her trial. The confession is formed according to clear narrative strategies, wherein coherence, speed, and timeline are central elements. The witnesses' testimonies also express habile language users who assigned great importance to cause and effect in order to make their accusations sound reliable. As for linguistic devices, a rich arsenal of orality features is documented in confessions as well as testimonies, bearing witness to the questioned people's lives in oral societies. The scribe's rendering of orality features emphasizes the individuality of the accused and the witnesses. The words and expressions they use are their own and give colour to the descriptions of the participants in the trial, be those accuser or accused.

The interrogation of the accused differs between the trial of Thomasine Read in 1647 and the trials of Isabel Atcheson and Jane Simpson in 1664. In the trial of Thomasine, which ended in a confession to witchcraft, it is possible to detect what she was asked about. The interrogator was interested in her knowledge about witchcraft ideas, details about her two familiars, and her power when it came to performing witchcraft and unwitching. In a way, he wanted to know how dangerous she was as a witch. Her confession came rather easily and fluently after the witnesses' testimonies. The demonological elements of familiars suckling and the contract with the devil initiated the confession, and this must have been regarded as the most important point. The follow-up questions from the interrogator had to do with his interest in knowing more about her demonic abilities. The elements related to *maleficium* were confessed to later on. It is interesting that the bewitchment of a person was confessed to as having been performed by the familiars, not by Thomasine herself, as this shows a fusion of demonological ideas and ideas about *maleficium*. It is also interesting that she showed her authority faced with the devil and refused to sacrifice her own child, which signals resistance even when she was delivering a serious confession.

The interrogations of Isabel Atcheson and Jane Simpson were not comprehensive or complete, with only three questions posed to each woman. Neither person confessed, and certainly the atmosphere in the courtroom must have been much calmer than in 1647. Direct demonological ideas were not mentioned, but the words 'diabolical' and 'devillish' were used, denoting the presence of the Evil One in the alleged performance of witchcraft. While demonological ideas in their pure form were absent in the trials from 1664, the devil crept into the judicial rhetoric, and this insertion most likely did not come from the witchcraft statutes but from language usage in the courts.

Thomasine Read, Isabel Atcheson, and Jane Simpson emerge as individuals in the court records because of their personalized language, not least in terms of orality features. The scribe rendered all of them as language users in their own right. Thomasine, who could not write herself, possessed a clear language, with details about the names of farms, personal names, and time inserted. She showed anger and knew how to formulate her anger in an elaborate threat when her own boy was fired from his job and another, stronger boy was taken in as a farmhand. She also knew exactly when her contract with the devil was signed. The words of Isabel Atcheson and Jane Simpson are rendered in the records in a way that shows that they were willing to talk. Instead of replying with one-syllable words to the interrogator's questions, they included names, times, and days of the week. These details show the richness of their language, and in addition show a scribe who was eager to record the words he heard being uttered in the courtroom, thus revealing shades of the accused individuals' way of speaking.

Certain types of pressure are documented in the English trials analysed above. The use of circumstantial evidence is seen in the trial of Thomasine Read, when she was pricked to find the devil's mark. Her confession was given well after the devil's mark was found. Even if we do not know the outcome of this trial, it is possible to point to the pricking as crucial for her confession. Also, the testimonies of three of the witnesses, retelling Thomasine Read's words as they remembered them, would have meant increasing pressure on Thomasine, particularly the testimony of Ellen Pope, the pricker. The fact that she personally knew Thomasine and that Thomasine had come to her house strengthened the reliability of Ellen Pope's testimony.

As for the trials of Isabel Atcheson and Jane Simpson, the testimony of the only witness, Anthony Heron, was weak, and the interrogator was rather lukewarm. No use of circumstantial evidence is recorded. Still, this is a situation involving power, starting in much the same way as many other witchcraft trials that had fatal outcomes. There is the power of the interrogator over the accused, rooted in learned knowledge about witchcraft; the power of the representatives of the law—in Isabel Atcheson's trial, the mayor—over ordinary people; the power of the assize; and the power of the wealthy over the poorer. All these factors indicate that all who were accused of witchcraft were vulnerable and likely to be victims of forces working against them on several levels. Once a witchcraft case was brought before the court, a merciless machinery started working, and during the most intense periods of witchcraft persecution, the odds of survival for those accused were low. Thus, an important feature of these trials was that they were judicial operations, conducted with the law in hand.

English witchcraft persecution is interesting because the ideas about witchcraft, the images of the devil, and the role that the devil played have been interpreted in various ways along historiographical lines. The analyses conducted in this chapter reinforce an understanding that the English witchcraft trials were, to a certain extent, influenced by demonological ideas. This goes for the devil's mark, the devil's pact, and the familiars seen in the trial of Thomasine Read. Further, the use of words like 'diabolic' and 'devillish' during interrogation in the 1664 trials points to the dominant role of the devil in the beliefs of lay and learned people alike, which existed in the last half of the 1600s. It is also clear from the trials analysed that there was no clear-cut division between demonological ideas about witch-craft and ideas related to *maleficium*. In the trial of Thomasine Read, malevolent witchcraft was performed by the familiars. In the trial of Isabel Atcheson and Jane Simpson, even the dreamlike vision of the women testified to by a sole witness was related to diabolical witchcraft. This seems to emphasize the impression of the devil as a strong player throughout witchcraft persecution in England.

7

NORWAY—CHARMS, BLÅKOLL, AND CHASING FISH

Norway, which was in a union with Denmark during the period of witchcraft persecution, was sparsely populated. Witchcraft persecution took place all over the country, most severely in the north. The three trials chosen for analysis in this chapter occurred in three different parts of Norway and represent different types of courts, clerical as well as secular. The first trial analysed is that of Anne Knutsdatter. It started in Stavanger in 1584 and continued in Bergen in 1594, with both towns situated on the south-western coast of Norway. This trial took place first before a church court: the Stavanger cathedral chapter, also known as the Stavanger *Domkapitel*, which was a forum where the bishop and the ministers of the cathedral discussed and decided on cases related to religious questions.[1] Ten years later, Anne Knutsdatter was tried in Bergen, before a city court. The second trial analysed is that of Sitru Pedersdatter in 1623. It was held before a local court in the village of Rygge in the Værne Monastery district, Eastern Norway. District accounts and attachments to the accounts are used as sources. The third trial analysed is that of Gundelle Olsdatter in 1663. It took place before a local court in the town of Vardø, in the district of Vardøhus in Finnmark, Northern Norway. Court records from the Archives of the Finnmark Magistrate document this trial. The three trials draw a chronological line from 1584 via 1623 until 1663, and display cases from the early, middle, and late period of witchcraft persecution.

Accusations and confessions in witchcraft trials encompass a range of elements, including various ideas of witchcraft, which will be highlighted in the analyses. The trials chosen for analysis complement each other and are suited to shedding light on mentalities of the time. The trial of Anne Knutsdatter deals with healing, the trial of Sitru Pedersdatter with *maleficium* and demonological ideas, and the trial of Gundelle Olsdatter with demonological ideas. The variety of ideas, particularly as they emerge during interrogation, provides insight into knowledge about

DOI: 10.4324/9781003255406-7

witchcraft that lay and learned people alike possessed. The chapter will discuss the interrogation, confession, verdict, and sentence of each trial.

In the sources which form the basis of this chapter, court records, the voices of women mainly surface in accused persons' confessions, in denunciations by other imprisoned women, and in the testimonies of female witnesses. In addition to court records, important information about the development of a trial is documented in district accounts. The sources are written in the Gothic hand, by magistrates.

The analyses will focus on courtroom discourse, especially the narration performed in the confessions. Narrative strategies from the oral field belonged to the inherent competence of the accused women. The analyses concentrate on individualizing linguistic features of the confessions in order to explore the differentiated speech that comes to the fore. The recorded discourse of the accused person, in either direct or indirect speech, will contribute to shedding light on the women's individual voices and on the scribe's work, particularly his accuracy.

The chapter will pay close attention to the interrogation. Questions posed by the interrogator can be traced, showing to which degree leading questions steered the confession in a certain direction. It is also fruitful to examine in which way, and with which content, these questions were answered. The interrogation may be looked upon as an arena in which elite culture and folk culture met.[2] The questions posed by the interrogator display a learned person's perspectives, beliefs, and knowledge. The answers given echo the ideas and knowledge that common people in an oral culture possessed, be that traditional beliefs or recently acquired ideas.

Court practice will be looked into as well, as this shows how witchcraft laws and decrees were interpreted and applied in various courts. Even though Norway was in a union with Denmark during the period of witchcraft persecution, it kept its own laws. Specific to Norway, as demonstrated in this chapter, is the very strict legislation with regard to healing a couple of decades before and after 1600. In addition, the sources analysed clarify the factual use of torture during witchcraft trials.

The analysis of each trial will start with a description, followed by an analysis of the voice of the accused woman. In addition, the voice of the law, the voice of the interrogator, and the voice of the scribe will be briefly discussed. In conclusion, the main findings of the chapters will be summarized.

Background

Persecution

The witchcraft trials in Norway took place in the period 1560–1695. During this period, around 750 women and men were accused of witchcraft, and about 310 of these were sentenced to death.[3] Norway had a population of 400,000 in 1600, increasing to 440,000 in 1665. When seen in a European context, the intensity of persecution in the entire country is average in proportion to the population.[4] On average, one-third of those accused of witchcraft in Norway were executed.

Like in most other European countries, two concepts of witchcraft appeared. On the one hand, there were trials held on an individual basis, dealing with traditional harmful witchcraft—*maleficium*, casting spells on people and animals—resulting in sickness or death. On the other hand, there was a collective performance of witchcraft: panics based on demonological ideas, particularly the devil's pact and witches' gatherings.[5] Both individual trials and witchcraft panics occurred, with the individual trials scattered over the total period of persecution, whereas the panics were concentrated in a shorter period of time, most often from some months to a couple of years. The panics primarily took place in the 1600s. The frequency of cases gradually decreased towards the end of the seventeenth century, and there are very few cases after 1700.[6] As for gender, 80% of those executed in Norway were women. This is in accordance with the average in Europe.[7]

The source material elucidating witchcraft trials consists mainly of the court records from local courts and the Court of Appeal. The position of a magistrate at the Norwegian local courts was established in 1591, and he was the one to record all trials taking place.[8] In addition to court records, district accounts provide valuable information, as they document expenses and income related to the burning of sentenced witches.[9] Source coverage varies geographically, as court records are inadequate for several Norwegian districts. The districts with the best continuity and completeness of witchcraft trials are Rogaland at the south-western coast of Norway and Finnmark in the north.[10]

Moreover, the intensity of witchcraft trials in Norway varied from district to district, as did the pattern of witchcraft persecution and the content of the trials. Witchcraft persecution in Norway was most intense from 1620 until 1665. Differences in the development of witchcraft trials are seen in the districts in which the three trials chosen for analysis took place, which will be clarified in the following.

The district of Rogaland in south-western Norway, around Stavanger, experienced witchcraft trials from 1611 until the 1740s. The oldest Norwegian court records from local courts come from Rogaland, with minutes written by the magistrate from 1613 onwards.[11] In this district, 112 people were accused of witchcraft, mainly in *maleficium* trials.[12] The majority of trials took place before 1660.[13] The execution rate was one in four, which points to the passing of sentences other than burning.[14]

The towns of Stavanger and Bergen had the highest concentration of witchcraft trials in south-western Norway.[15] In the Bergenhus district in Hordaland, witchcraft trials occurred from 1566 until the 1700s, with 119 cases, based on the court records, district accounts, and accounts of fines paid to the king, *sakefall*.[16] There were many more trials in Bergen town than in the countryside.[17] The town of Bergen had early witchcraft trials: already sixteen before 1600. Many of these were characterized by learned witchcraft beliefs such as the devil's pact, witches' gatherings, and shape-shifting. It should also be noted that in Bergen town, several persons with a high social and economic status were accused, which is different from the rest of Norway, where the majority of those accused had a low social and economic status.[18] For the Bergenhus district, smaller panics are found in the period 1580–1620, while larger witchcraft panics took place particularly in the 1650s and 1660s.[19]

Witchcraft trials in Eastern Norway, *Østlandet*, occurred from 1567 to 1730.[20] During this period, 192 witchcraft trials, around one-fourth of all Norwegian witchcraft trials, took place.[21] After a few trials at the end of the 1500s and the first two decades of the 1600s, a strong increase is seen from 1619 until 1625, and then a stable, but low number of trials until just after 1700.[22] Most of the death sentences were passed during the seven-year peak around 1620.[23] The execution rate for the district of in Eastern Norway is 36.5%.[24] While *maleficium* trials dominate, confessions to the devil's pact occur throughout most of the seventeenth century.[25] As for gender, around 85% of the accused were women in the 1500s, compared to 75% in the period of strong persecution, 1619–25. During the rest of the 1600s, only women were accused.[26] The influence of demonology due to the announcement of the 1617 Witchcraft Decree is seen as important for the pattern of witchcraft persecution in Eastern Norway.[27]

In the trial from Eastern Norway from 1623 analysed in this chapter, interesting ideas about witches' meetings surface. These ideas connect to trials in Sweden in 1594 and the 1660s and 1670s, Åland in Finland in 1666, and Rendalen in Norway 1670–74.[28] By 1620, demonological ideas were spread throughout Europe, also in the Nordic countries. The idea of witches' gatherings is fundamental for panics to occur, as during the interrogation of a suspected witch, the question about the identity of other participants at a named gathering was always posed. Witchcraft panics occurred mainly in the 1620s in Eastern Norway, during the most intense period of witchcraft persecution in the area.[29] In Denmark, too, the height of witchcraft persecution occurred during this decade, and this might have influenced the Rygge persecution.[30] Through the Witchcraft Decree of 1617, demonological ideas came into the letter of the law for the first time in Denmark and Norway. By 1623, this decree was probably well known by judicial officials, and court practice could have been influenced by the law's statement on who were 'true witches'.[31]

In the district of Finnmark, severe witchcraft trials took place in the period 1600–92. During this period, 135 women and men were accused of witchcraft, of whom 91 lost their lives: 77 women and 14 men.[32] During the first two decades of the 1600s, nine *maleficium* trials took place before the first panic was a reality, in 1620–21. For the first time, demonological ideas emerged in Finnmark. There is a link via the Scotsman John Cunningham to the appearance of the first demonological ideas in Finnmark.[33] Cunningham had been in the service of the Danish king since 1603 and was installed as district governor in Finnmark in 1619. Cunningham, born *c.* 1575, knew King James VI, knew Scottish witchcraft trials from his youth, knew the Danish language, and was active during interrogation during the first witchcraft panic in Finnmark in 1620–21.[34] I argue that he transmitted demonological ideas from Scotland to Finnmark, ideas that took root among the judiciary and in local communities and impacted further persecution in Norway's northernmost district.

Two additional panics took place in the district of Finnmark: one in 1652–53 and one in 1662–63, when Gundelle Olsdatter was accused.[35] As for gender, 82% of those accused in Finnmark were women.[36] The execution rate during the Finnmark witchcraft trials of 67% was high compared to that of other European countries. Seen in the context of the total Finnmark population of 3,000 *c.* 1600, the number of executions *per capita* was extremely high.[37] The epicentre of witchcraft persecution was the village of Vardø, where Vardøhus Fortress was situated.[38] Ethnic conditions in Finnmark were special, as two ethnic groups, the Norwegian and the Sami people, lived side by side. Members of both groups were accused during the witchcraft trials: the Samis constituted about 20% of the accused persons and the Norwegians about 80%. As for ethnicity, there was a marked gender difference: among the women accused of and executed for witchcraft in Finnmark, Norwegian women were absolutely the worst hit.[39] However, among the men accused and executed, Sami men were in the majority.[40]

Jurisdiction

The union between Denmark and Norway lasted for more than 400 years. In 1380, Olaf II of Denmark inherited the kingdom of Norway, titled as Olaf IV.[41] He died in 1387, and his mother, Margrete I, was from then on the ruler of Norway until her own death in 1412. From 1397 to 1523, Sweden, Denmark, and Norway were joined in a personal union[42] under a single monarch: the Kalmar Union.[43] Otherwise, their political and legal administrations were kept apart. Cristian III of Denmark (1503–59) formed close ties between the Lutheran Church and the crown.[44] After a two-year civil war (1534–36) between Protestant and Catholic forces—called the Count's Feud—Lutheranism was established in the king's realms as part of the Protestant Reformation.[45] The Reformation in Denmark took place in 1536, in Norway in 1537. Christian III was placed on Denmark's throne in 1536. All political power was vested in the king and his council, *Rigsraadet*, without Norwegian representation.[46] Like Jutland, Zealand, and Funen, Norway was now a province of the Danish kingdom.[47] In 1660, absolutism was introduced by Frederick III (1609–70).[48] The union between Denmark and Norway lasted until 1814, with mostly Danish representation on the king's council. The majority of district governors and bailiffs in Norway were Danish as well, with the latter mostly responsible for the administration of local affairs.[49] At this time, the two northernmost districts in Norway were Finnmark and Nordland. In Finnmark, most officials came from Denmark, while the deputy bailiffs and police officers often came from the local area.[50]

At the top of the hierarchy in Finnmark was the Royal Commander of Vardøhus Fortress. He was appointed district governor until 1660, after which he held the title of regional governor.[51] The Royal Commander—the king's man—was the most important person in seventeenth-century Finnmark. He resided at Vardøhus Fortress and was in charge of administrative duties and court meetings, but also of controlling Finnmark's borders with Iceland, Greenland, and the Faroe Islands.

In Finnmark's local courts, a jury of locally elected men decided on the verdict, after 1634 together with the magistrate.[52] Court of Appeal sessions were held every third year due to the judge having to travel north, which caused delay for cases brought to the Court of Appeal from the local courts.

The Nordic countries had codes of law written in the vernacular dating from the Middle Ages.[53] The thirteenth-century *Magnus Lagabøtes Landslov*, the national law of Magnus the Lawmender,[54] stated that *maleficium* was a capital offence. According to Hans Eyvind Næss, this statute seemed not to have been used much until after the Reformation: 'As far as we know some time went by until the death penalty in cases of witchcraft was generally accepted'.[55] The legal attitude towards witchcraft as *crimen exceptum* had already been stated in 1521–22, however. Within contemporary jurisdiction, if there was a rumour that someone had committed a serious crime, the rumour was considered equal to an accusation. Witchcraft was considered to be one such crime, on par with murder.

Witchcraft trials took place in Norway throughout the Middle Ages.[56] They seem to have been of a rather mild character. There is one well-known case from 1325, dealing with love magic and the use of charms.[57] The punishment was fasting and a seven-year-long pilgrimage to holy places outside Norway.

Throughout the period of a union with Denmark, Norwegian laws continued to be enforced. There were three levels in the court system: the local courts, the Court of Appeal, and central legal authorities in Copenhagen in addition to *Overhoffretten*, the highest court in Norway for the period 1667–1797. Local courts in Norway were allowed to pass a death sentence.[58] The Norwegian word for magistrate is *sorenskriver*, which originally means 'sworn scribe'. The magistrate, whose office was established in 1591, was initially a professional scribe who created the court records, but after legal reforms in 1634, he was granted the additional responsibility of judging alongside the jury. The vote of the magistrate was then equal to the vote of one jury member. When a new legislative act was passed in 1687, the magistrate replaced the jury altogether in minor cases. The magistrate was appointed by the district governor until 1660 and thereafter by the king. With respect to the functioning of the courts in Finnmark, the geographical distance between the courts' locations and central legal authorities in Copenhagen is relevant, especially regarding witchcraft trials, as it could have caused arbitrary judicial practice—such as local courts making rapid decisions on their own.

Sterner practices on the European Continent regarding procedures in witchcraft cases seem to have influenced Denmark and Norway, as the judiciary's approach to witchcraft became more intransigent just before the turn of the century. In 1584, the king in Copenhagen responded to a letter sent by the bishop in Stavanger. In this letter, the bishop described the consultation of wise men and women, common in Norway, as a deadly sin against God. As a result, healing, *signeri*, was made a capital offence in the diocese of Stavanger by royal decree. Through decrees in 1593 and 1594, this local law was extended to all over Norway, stating that all those who were seeking or using 'ungodly sorcery' should be sentenced to death without mercy.[59]

In 1604, the next code of laws was published—Christian IV's Norwegian Code of Laws—which retained witchcraft as a serious crime. This code was an edited version of the national law of Magnus the Lawmender. Then, the important Witchcraft Decree of 1617 was issued. Here, 'true' witches[60] were defined as those who had attached themselves to the devil or consorted with him. A clear demonological definition had thus found its way into the letters of the law. The 1617 decree had an obvious impact on witchcraft persecutions in Norway: a harsher attitude towards witchcraft is evident throughout the seventeenth century, with the demonological notions of the 1617 decree repeated in the Recess of 1643 and the Danish Law of 1683. In Norway, sentenced witches were burned alive. The 1617 decree changed the punishment for seeking acts of healing from death sentence to loss of property, and the punishment for healing from death sentence to exile.[61]

Anne Knutsdatter, 1584/1594

The Trial

Anne Knutsdatter, the wife of Christen Jyde,[62] was brought before the court twice: first at Stavanger Cathedral Chapter[63] on 17 June 1584, then in Bergen in 1594.[64] The first time, she was accused of healing, namely having read over a sick person.[65] This person was Tora, the wife of Court of Appeal Judge Kosmos Arildsen. She suffered from pain in her chest and was said to have been bewitched as well. The bishop of Stavanger, superintendent Jørgen Erikssøn, was in charge of the trial. Anne Knutsdatter confessed that a man called Cosmas[66] had fetched her to read over his sick wife.[67] The same day, Anne's daughter-in-law, Anne Torsdatter, and Ragnild from Meland were also brought to trial and interrogated, and they confessed the same: that they had been fetched to read over 'Tore Cosmassis'.[68] Another person was related to the healing of Tora Cosmassis as well: Jacob Jonson had been tried one week earlier.[69] The accusation was that he was reading over people to combat several diseases. He confessed that he had cut five bloody crosses in Tora's body. The accused women apparently offered healing and read charms or formulas, and the accused man in addition practiced the cutting of crosses in the body of the sick person. Jacob Jonson was sentenced to public penitence, and he promised under the threat of execution that he would never use such vanity again.[70] Anne Knutsdatter was banished from the Stavanger bishopric.

The belief in and use of healing in the family of the Court of Appeal Judge made the Stavanger bishop react.[71] He contacted Danish-Norwegian King Frederic II and requested a stricter punishment for healing. This was successful.[72] Royal decrees of 1584, 1593, and 1594 were issued. This was the first time after the Reformation that a specific law against witchcraft was issued in Norway.[73]

The 1584 decree stated that those who performed white magic, or healing, should be punished with a death sentence, just like those who sought their help. This meant that Kosmos Arildsen and his wife were accused, since they had sought the help of healers.[74] However, they were acquitted, and this case did not negatively affect the remaining career of Kosmos Arildsen. In 1591, he was appointed Court of Appeal Judge in Fredrikstad in Eastern Norway and left Stavanger.[75]

On 16 March 1594, Anne Knutsdatter was brought before the court in a secular trial in Bergen, having been accused of witchcraft.[76] In this town on the west coast of Norway, a famous witchcraft trial had taken place a few years earlier, namely the trial of Anne Pedersdatter in 1590. She was the widow of a high-ranking clerical person, Absalon Pedersson Beyer.[77] She was sentenced to death by fire at the stake. Anne Pedersdatter had earlier been accused of witchcraft in 1575, when she was aquitted. This case led to witchcraft accusations against two other women.[78] When the trial against Anne Pedersdatter became famous, one reason was that people of high social rank were involved. Understandably, the clergy in Bergen protested against the conviction of Anne Pedersdatter. However, it was not only social class affiliation that made her trial well known. The content of her confession differed from that of previous witchcraft trials. While *maleficium* witchcraft trials were well known in Bergen, new demonological ideas came up in her trial. Anne Pedersdatter confessed that she had taken part in night flights to a witches' gathering at the witch mountain Lyderhorn in Bergen. The two other accused women confessed to demonological ideas as well.

Four years after the trial of Anne Pedersdatter, Anne Knutsdatter was interrogated in Bergen's town hall. Among the judicial officials was Peder Thott, governor of Bergenhus Fortress,[79] in addition to the Judge of the Court of Appeal,[80] mayors, chief officers of the town's finance department,[81] and the jury. The Stavanger case is referred to, in which Anne Knutsdatter had obliged herself to give up her vain readings, healing, and drawing of the cross for magical purposes, and immediately flee and leave the bishopric of Stavanger.[82] If she thereafter would have anything to do with such art, she would bear the punishment that the authorities would lay down for her, according to documents from Stavanger, which give the reason why she had fled from there.[83]

Next, town bailiff Claus Meltzow[84] called forth a woman from Bergen named Magdalena, the wife of Henrik the Mason. She accused Anne Knutsdatter of having killed her (Magdalena's) first husband with witchcraft, and of having performed evil deeds against herself (Magdalena) afterwards, in different ways and at different times.[85] This was shown by her written confession, which Claus Meltzow, in the presence of honourable men,[86] had arranged to be recorded in detail. When Magdalena got a sudden illness, she became wild and out of her mind, the records say. Anne Knutsdatter came to her uninvited and asked Magdalena's maid Anna Hieronimusdatter why her mistress lay in such a state. And the girl had answered that God must know. Then Anne Knutsdatter confessed that she took a piece of ginger and put it in Magdalena's mouth, stroked her back, and read a charm for gout,[87] so that the next day, she was helped and could walk again as before.[88] The charm went like this: 'Fly away gout, you full shame, God free us from load and shame, In three names, God the Father, Son, and Holy Spirit. Amen'.[89]

In the same way, Anne Knutsdatter recited two other charms that she confessed she used in Bergen as well as in Stavanger previously. The first one was for the tying off of the umbilical cord when a child is born, and was a prayer for the first stools[90] of the child. The prayer goes like this: 'There were nine Marias, should pray and bind, the first prayed, the second bound three fingers below the navel. There you shall lie bound until doomsday, as long as the stone which lay there was from eternity'.[91] The third charm was for stomach pain.[92] It goes like this:

> Our Jesus rode over a bridge, there he met an evil woman. Where are you going? Christ said, I want to go to the homes of men. What are you going to do there? Christ said. I shall break limb from limb, back from back. No, said Christ, you shall hurt none and break none. You shall go in the blue mountain,[93] there you shall turn the rudder. In three names, God the Father, Son, and the Holy Spirit. Amen.[94]

Next, Anne Knutsdatter confessed that she also used a charm for bloodletting,[95] which she could not readily recite. In addition, she confessed that she had read geese feathers for stomach pain and sent them to Lame Mogens for good health in his sickness.[96]

Likewise, Magdalena's recorded testimony notes that Anne Knutsdatter allegedly said several times to Anna Hieronimusdatter, Magdalena's maid, that if Magdalena would be loyal to her and not tell anybody who had given her the information, then she would reveal who had done evil against Magdalena,[97] and she would show her that person, who would appear in front of her bed and ask for forgiveness. Anne Knutsdatter could not deny this testimony, but said that she had spoken those words during sickness and rage.

Moreover, Anne Knutsdatter confessed that she had asked Magdalena's maid to fetch church soil from the graveyard for Magdalena's cure.[98] And when Anne Knutsdatter had obtained the soil from St Morten's graveyard, and kept it until the third day, she had sent a message to Anna Hieronimusdatter with a blind woman named Mette, saying that Anna should come to her. And when she came, she was told to put one part of the soil under Magdalena's beer barrel, one part under the doorstep and one part under her bed.[99] This, Anne Knutsdatter, Anna Hieronimusdatter, and Mette confessed to as being true. And after this soil had lain next to Magdalena's bed for six weeks, Magdalena said that she had become crippled and lame, so that she did not know other than that she was dead. And when Anne Knutsdatter was asked why she fetched and used the soil from the graveyard,[100] she answered that a long time ago, she had received advice from a woman called Guron Fielder in Skjold's parish in Ryfylke[101] (whom she said was dead now), that if a dwarf or one of the hill people looked for anybody, then the church soil would help protect people from them. In the same way, Anne confessed to having taken and touched such a dwarf, and he had small, soft, and downy fingers. One time, he wanted to do something together with her and he wanted to get her out of bed.[102]

In the same way, the records continue, Anne Knutsdatter's husband, Christen Jyde, confessed that when his wife was sick, he delivered on request[103] some salt to Lisbett, the sister of Herr Wolfgang,[104] which she would bring to Magdalena for a cure. This salt, Magdalena and Lisbett said, had disappeared.[105] And when they wanted to burn the plate with pieces of cloth that this salt and also the church soil were placed on, rumbling was heard, as documented in Magdalena's and Lisbett's written testimonies, which they now confessed to before the court. Anne Knutsdatter answered that when somebody wants to throw a piece of cloth with salt into the fire, then the cloth cannot burn, and the salt becomes a lump.

Thereafter, a copy of a decree was brought forth, which learned men in Stavanger had sealed. The records state that Superintendent of the Stavanger bishopric, Jørgen Erikssøn, had received the decree from the Danish-Norwegian king when Anne Knutsdatter in Stavanger used her ungodly healing of Kosmos Arildsen's wife. However, the records continue, this court did not previously have a copy or knowledge of this decree, which originally was dated Copenhagen, 21 September 1584, and signed by His Royal Highness. Now, this decree was read out loud. It stated that all people who either use or perform disturbing healing by the sign of the cross, read over sick people, or used other ungodly or unchristian means,[106] then those who are found either to seek or use, or to perform such (deeds) should be punished with death without mercy, and with no such persons should this be taken lightly.[107] Otherwise, they would be brought before the Royal Court. In the same way, a royal letter dated 21 July 1593 was read out loud, with the same content as the letter from 1584.

After having examined the case of Anne Knutsdatter, the court found that many years after her first confession, she had engaged in her unchristian charms and witchcraft art again,[108] against His Royal Majesty's decrees and the promise she had made to the legal authority in Stavanger. Therefore, the court proclaimed that it was right that Anne should, following her own confession and the royal strict and serious command, be punished by losing her life.[109]

The Voice of Anne Knutsdatter

The voice of Anne Knutsdatter is characterized by the performance of healing acts for sick people who had allegedly been bewitched.[110] The first time she was interrogated, in Stavanger in 1584, she confessed that she had read a charm over a sick woman, and that she did this for payment. As the husband of the sick woman had fetched her to come visit his wife, it is clear that Anne Knutsdatter had a reputation in the local community for this type of healing. In this first interrogation, her voice is rendered in indirect speech, and very briefly so. It is not clear whether her confession is the result of pressure or torture, as it is only recorded that she was interrogated and that she confessed.[111]

Anne Knutsdatter's voice is heard in court records again in Bergen, ten years later. Her voice is recorded in direct as well as indirect speech, the latter using a reporting verb to initiate a reported clause. First, the court records from Stavanger are referred to. Next, the voice of Anne Knutsdatter is rendered in the written testimony of Magdalena, the wife of Henrik the Mason. She testifies that Anne came to her house and asked her maid, Anna Hieronimusdatter, 'Why is your mistress in such a state?'[112] This is the first time we hear the voice of Anne Knutsdatter rendered in direct speech. However, the utterance was passed on via several persons. It was first repeated by the maid, Anna, to her mistress. Then the mistress, in her testimony in court, used the same words that the maid claimed Anne Knutsdatter had used.

The court finds Anne's question interesting, because she apparently knew that Magdalena was miserable before she came to her house. An enigma is born, created by the question, and it is sufficient to cast suspicion on Anne. She had already been rumoured to practice witchcraft, and people would think that she had something to do with Magdalena's sickness. So in this case, the sickness is not said to have been the result of some evil words uttered by Anne Knutsdatter. Instead, the suspicion comes from a question, which might have been interpreted in several ways. Anne Knutsdatter must have interpreted Magdalena's testimony as convincing, because after this testimony was read, she confessed.

She related that she had put ginger in Magdalena's mouth, stroked her back, and read a charm over her, which resulted in Magdalena being well again the next day and being able to walk as before. These words uttered by Anne Knutsdatter are rendered in indirect speech, and there are no linguistic devices used to create a distance to what is told. Her voice is firm and signals that she believes in her art, and that the performance of witchcraft was efficient. The way Anne Knutsdatter's voice is rendered in the records—whether as a direct quotation of what she uttered in the courtroom or as a retelling in other witnesses' testimonies—shows steadiness when it comes to knowledge of an oral tradition concerning magic, coming to the surface both in direct speech and in the retelling of her utterances.

She displays her magical wisdom: her recitation of three charms shows a cunning voice. The charms she recites are prayers in the name of the Trinity and the nine Marias, signifying connections to Catholicism. She willingly recites the charms. In addition, Anne Knutsdatter confesses to having used a charm for healing, which she cannot recall. The knowledge of charms was essential to performing healing, and there certainly must have been pride connected to knowing many charms, one suitable for each occasion. She also confessed that she had read geese feathers 'for envy'[113] and had sent these to Lame Mogens to cure his illness. She shows that she knows about reading, charms, and remedies used for healing, and that she believes these methods are working.

Next, it emerges that Anne Knutsdatter dealt not only in healing, but in divination as well, as seen in Magdalena's testimony. Anne had told Magdalena that she was able to find the person who cast evil on Magdalena, and that she could press this person to appear in front of Magdalena's bed and ask for forgiveness. Anne Knutsdatter declares that she uttered these words 'in her sickness and rage'.[114] It seems that Anne regrets having confessed to this point, as she is making an excuse on her own behalf: she was not very strong, and was influenced by her afflictions when she said this. She is not comfortable with having given information about divination. She may have seen this knowledge as more dangerous than healing, as the intention was not benevolent. However, she does not deny that she offered to show Magdalena the identity of the person who was the cause of her suffering. Although she does not deny divination, she tries to excuse her performance. Divination seems to be part of the magical services she offered.

In addition, Anne Knutsdatter confesses that she asked Magdalena's maid to fetch soil from the churchyard. Such soil was believed to have strong magical powers and was used in folk medicine. Anne used this soil to heal Magdalena. When Anne is asked why she fetched the soil from the graveyard, she answers that a woman told her that it would help against dwarfs or hill folk who came to look for human beings. According to folk belief, such creatures might have bad intentions. She also confesses to having touched a dwarf and describes the sensation when she stroked his fingers. What the dwarf wanted to do with her is not said, but this is the closest we come to a description of a creature from another world in Anne Knutsdatter's confession.

The supernatural part of her confession touches on central elements of folk tradition, as it brings in both the churchyard and the hill folk. These tales belonged to oral tradition in the seventeenth century, since traditional Norwegian tales were written down only from the 1830s onwards.[115] Soil and bones from the churchyard were supposed to have strong magical powers, and fetching them is frequently confessed to in witchcraft trials. Also, witchcraft rituals could be performed at the churchyard. Closeness to the dead was considered intrusive.[116] The churchyard was a marginalized and dangerous area. When someone entered a churchyard at night to perform rituals or fetch soil, they entered a forbidden scene. Thus, when Anne Knutsdatter confesses that she used soil from the churchyard to perform healing, she has crossed a border to a field with some evil undertones. The power to heal is found where nobody should go. There is a great difference between using charms and using soil from the churchyard in the performance of healing. Still, the dark element is part of folk belief, and soil from the churchyard is an element found in folk medicine as well as in witchcraft in many countries.[117]

The other world, the world we cannot see, is central in folk belief all over the world. Various creatures inhabit these worlds, but they are usually hidden from humans. Some of these creatures live in the hills or underground.[118] They often appear on particular days of the year, when the border between our world and the world of the others can be permeated. For instance, there are tales in several countries about fairies or hill folk who come to fetch a human baby, particularly on Midsummer Eve, and leave their own baby, a changeling, in the cradle instead.[119] There are ways and means to protect oneself from hill folk. One means to protect babies is to place a cross in front of the cradle. Another is what Anne Knutsdatter mentions, soil from the churchyard.

The ideas that surface in Anne Knutsdatter's confession mainly deal with healing and white magic, not harmful witchcraft. She does not mention the devil or demonological ideas, like the devil's pact or witches' gatherings. She readily shares her wisdom related to healing without hesitation, but she has reservations about confessing to divination. Undoubtedly, she knows about protective rituals and the darker side of magical activities. There is no information about torture in the records. A potential turning point in her voice might have occurred before she started her confession.

Anne Knutsdatter's confession is a narrative. She is a good storyteller and structures her confession according to narratological strategies. The chronological order is established by a clear timeline, for instance when she states when she first came to Magdalena's maid and what took place afterwards. Duration, the effect of the story being told quickly or slowly, comes to the fore in passages that are descriptive, such as the story about the dwarf's hand. The delegation of voice from the narrator to the story's main characters is frequently used. Anne Knutsdatter expresses belief in the results of healing methods, also her own practice. Likewise, she thinks her performance of divination will work. The same seems to be the case with the other people involved in the trial: they are believers in the art.

Features of orality permeate Anne Knutsdatter's confession. When she received the soil from Magdalena, she kept it in her house for three days and then brought it to Magdalena's house, where she divided it into three parts. The soil remained next to Magdalena's bed for six weeks. This use of magic numbers is well known from oral tales. Closeness to the human world is demonstrated in details about geographical places, for instance the place where her mentor lives and the name of the graveyard. An abundance of details is seen in the records: among others in the description of the dwarf, the healing method used for Magdalena, the explanation of how churchyard soil was used, and the description of how the salt used for curing Magdalena was brought over to her. The charms contain set phrases and poetical devices like rhythm, rhyme, poetic images, and pregnant motifs.[120] Additive sentence structures are seen. Pointed remarks on the part of those interrogated are heard. All these features echo oral transfer, where interesting details play a role in spicing up a story and linguistic elements contribute to a rapid way of remembering and retelling.

The voice of Anne Knutsdatter emerges as the voice of a wise woman who possesses considerable knowledge. She has a reputation for healing and is asked to perform anti-magic to counteract the effects of bewitchment. However, the performance of magic to heal occasionally has the opposite effect, when the person one is trying to protect or help becomes worse. This was the case with Magdalena, and this was why Anne was accused of witchcraft. Anne's register also implies protective magic. Anne Knutsdatter's voice gives the impression that she is an experienced healer, and that people trust her and seek her advice. Her confession is considered reliable and strengthened by the testimonies of the maid Anna Hieronimusdatter and the blind woman, Mette.

The Voices of the Witnesses

Several witnesses are heard in this trial. In addition to the maid Anna, others testifying are the blind woman Mette, Lisbett, and Anne Knutsdatter's husband—Christen Jyde. Once, when Anne was ill, Christen brought some salt to Lisbett, who was the sister of a minister. Lisbett was to bring the salt to Magdalena as a cure for Magdalena's illness. However, Magdalena and Lisbett said that the salt had disappeared, and when they tried to get rid of the plate, the pieces of cloth that the salt was wrapped in, and the soil from the church, there was a lot of noise.

The voices of the witnesses—be they collaborators in the art of healing or messengers—signal a belief in the effect of the healing performed by Anne

Knutsdatter. They participate in the healing activities and follow the commands that Anne gives in order to carry out her act of healing. They all seem to be acquainted with the effect of church soil as well as salt when it comes to remedies being curative or potentially damaging. The performance of healing activities, as voiced by the witnesses, is consistent in its details. There is no contradiction in the way the healing remedies are presented, nor in the way these remedies were supposed to work. This seems to imply a common understanding among the local population that healing by using physical objects and charms was possible, and that some people, like Anne Knutsdatter, possessed this skill.

The Voice of the Interrogator

The voice of the interrogator comes to the fore in both trials through his interest in obtaining detailed explanations on methods of healing and divination. The questions posed to Anne Knutsdatter appear particularly in the 1594 trial, when her knowledge about charms is demonstrated to show her art. The interrogator is apparently not only interested in her performance of benevolent magic, but also in methods used for maleficent witchcraft and divination. With regard to her fetching soil from the graveyard, she is asked directly about why she did this. Thus, the interrogator's suspicion about the dark side of her art is demonstrated.

The interrogator is acquainted with the letter of the law. As the legislation on healing was severe during the years of Anne Knutsdatter's trials, the interrogator knew that a confession to healing and divination was sufficient for a death sentence. It was not necessary to enter into questions of a demonological character.

The Voice of the Law

The voice of the law in the trial of Anne Knutsdatter echoes the historically severest administering of justice in witchcraft trials in Norway, namely death sentences for those performing and those seeking healing. The strict decrees were not valid for Denmark.[121] When referred to in the indictment of Anne Knutsdatter's 1594 trial, the 1584 decree is recited for the first time in the court in Bergen,[122] as they had not had access to it before. The wording of the decree is quoted in detail as part of the indictment in the trial of Anne Knutsdatter, which indicates that close attention was paid to its contents. It also implies that it took several years before legal documents valid for both Stavanger and Bergen reached the judiciary in Bergen.

The voice of the law is formal and strong, and sticks very closely to the original wording of the royal decrees. The indictment emphasizes that many years after her previous confession in Stavanger, Anne Knutsdatter had continued with unchristian healing and witchcraft, going against what was stated in the royal decrees and the promises she had made to the authorities in Stavanger. As she herself confessed to this, there can be only one conclusion. The verdict and sentence state that Anne, according to her own confession and the royal command, should be punished by losing her life.[123]

The Voice of the Scribe

The voice of the scribe is neutral. The scribe does not offer his own opinion on or attitude towards the content of the records. He is reporting courtroom discourse and the development of the trial in a trustworthy manner. This goes for the factual information about the trial and its participants as well as for the content of Anne Knutsdatter's confession. The scribe aims to depict her confession in a way that preserves her individual language. Such a personalized way of recording provides access to Anne Knutsdatter's own language and her knowledge of healing methods as well as folk belief. The rendering of her discourse also shows her narrative strategies and her attitude towards what is told, be that her convictions about efficient healing methods or her regrets about having confessed to divination. The scribe had the option to delete and shorten the details about healing but chose to convey them. He also could have skipped her afterthoughts about regretting confessing to divination, but he did not. He strove to record what was actually said in the courtroom, not least the words uttered by Anne Knutsdatter.

Further, the scribe unveils the judicial climate in Norwegian witchcraft trials in the late 1500s. By bringing up the 1584 Stavanger trial of Anne Knutsdatter and the punishment she received then, the severity with which healing was viewed becomes clear. By accurately recording the verdict and sentence passed in 1584 and in 1594 and describing the factual content of the laws, the records clarify that the persecution of those performing healing has become much harsher in the course of these ten years. The new witchcraft legislation comprises not only witchcraft with the intention of doing harm but also magical acts with a benevolent purpose. For Anne Knutsdatter, this change becomes fatal.

The scribe is able to combine the complex elements of courtroom discourse into the recorded text. As a legal document, the records had to include all information about judicial context, judicial proceedings, and judicial decisions, not least in case the lawsuit would be passed on to a higher level of the court system for investigation. However, the scribe has also shaped the records into a personalized account, focusing on the discourse of the accused person and providing a glimpse of Anne Knutsdatter's knowledge. In this respect, the records' multiple levels reflect much more than this trial as an isolated legal case; they resonate with and echo the wider mentality of the time.

Sitru Pedersdatter, 1623

The Trial

Sitru Pedersdatter[124] was accused of witchcraft in a panic taking place in the village of Rygge in Eastern Norway in 1623. From spring until autumn 1623, six women were prosecuted and sentenced to death in witchcraft trials in Rygge village. The names of the accused were Anne Holter, Anne Vang, Maren Nabstad, Maren, the wife of Daniel, Sitru Pedersdatter, and Eline Grydstad. Maren, the wife of Daniel, was Danish and had lived in Denmark; the other women were Norwegian. One after another, women in the same neighbourhood were accused, interrogated, convicted, and executed. Complete court records from this panic have not survived; however, part of the records, including verdicts and sentences, are preserved.[125] In addition, accounts of expenses connected with the trials have been preserved, and these documents contain valuable information about the context of the trials as well as court practice.

Rygge was a village not far from the town of Moss, south of Oslo. In the Middle Ages, a monastery of the Order of St John was located in Rygge, which also ran a hospital for courtmen, *hirdmenn*.[126] The monastery was acquired by the crown in 1532 and kept in its ownership until 1675. After the Reformation in 1537, Værne Monastery became a district, or an administrative unit.[127] It also constituted the premises on which the district governor lived: a mansion with several buildings. In one of the buildings, the women accused in the witchcraft panic were imprisoned.

When Sitru Pedersdatter was brought before the court on 23 June 1623, the panic had been ongoing since April. She was called forth by bailiff Hans Pedersen, the official of district governor Sigvert Gabriel of Kringerup, who was not present.[128] The other judicial officials present were magistrate Christoffer Thamisen and police officer[129] Peder Backe. Also, the names of twelve men of the jury of Rygge parish are entered into the records, with the name of Hans Thøstad, a wealthy farm owner, first.[130] It was a local trial, and the location was Bakke.[131]

The trial of Anne Holter was the first one in this panic, and she was the first of the accused persons to be sentenced to death. In addition to witchcraft, she was accused of having killed her husband, which she confessed to.[132] She was burned about three months before Sitru Pedersdatter's trial. Anne Holter's confession contained a number of ideas about witchcraft, as it included several elements of *maleficium* as well as demonological witchcraft. Anne denounced three women for having learned and performed witchcraft, and Sitru Pedersdatter was one of these.[133] Anne Holter confirmed and stood by this denunciation at the hour of her death, and said that she did not reject anything but that she would die on her confession and that she had not lied about anyone.[134]

After being denounced, Sitru Pedersdatter fled from the parish, but was brought back. She was interrogated several times in the presence of honourable men, as the records state, and confessed to what was expressed in Anne Holter's accusation. Sitru was asked what she knew about this witchcraft's art and its contents.[135]

Then, she first confessed and stood by that she could do nothing else than milk cattle, and she confirmed that she could milk it (the cattle) until it was dry. The records go on to state that she said she had been to the farm of Fløgstad and milked the cattle of Nils Nabstad, that she could do no more witchcraft, and that Anne Holter had taught her. Furthermore, she confessed to having been to Blåkoll[136] together with Maren Nabstad, Anne Holter, and Anne Vang, and when they rode there, they gathered at Anne Holter's house and rode from there to Maren's and took the devil Maren Nabstad with them.[137] In the same way, Sitru Pedersdatter confessed that she rode to Blåkoll on a black calf, and that when they arrived at the gathering, they were merry and glad. Anne Holter provided wine to drink, and Maren Nabstad was sitting at the head of the table. Sitru Pedersdatter also confessed that her Apostle was named *Stub*, which means stump.[138]

When asked whether she could do more or knew more, she said that no, she could do only this and nothing more than milking, and that she would not come to confess anything more.[139] Still, she confessed that Nils Nabstad had come to her and asked her not to denounce his wife, Maren.[140] Then, the records state that on behalf of his Royal Majesty and his honoured master (Sigvert Gabriel), Hans Pedersen desired a final verdict and sentence.

The records continue to state that then, the indictment, response, and circumstances of the case were read, and these were clearly proved according to Sitru Pedersdatter's own confession, and also according to Anne Holter's accusation and confession. Likewise, the records continue, it is declared that the above-mentioned Sitru escaped and fled from the parish because she feared Anne Holter's accusation.[141] And it is declared that the aforementioned Sitru allegedly had learned the art of witchcraft. In addition, a rumour in this village was noted, stating that she had a reputation for the art of witchcraft.[142] So, the records continue, to us it seems that no further proof or testimony about this case is necessary, other than what was mentioned earlier.[143]

According to the circumstances of the case, the records carry on, we did not know better than that the aforementioned Sitru Pedersdatter should, according to the same confession and deprivation, be punished and burned by fire at the stake,[144] while her own confession in addition to Anne Holter's accusation will stand at their full power,[145] unless something other can be proved and experienced than what has happened now, or unless the authorities otherwise pardon her.

On 4 July, Sitru Pedersdatter was burned at Moss. At the place of execution, the verdict and sentence was read aloud to her in the presence of the common people from the local community. She confirmed that she stuck to the content of her sentence, and that she had not been lying to anyone but told the truth, and on this she would boldly go to her death. Moreover, she fully confessed that no person had influenced her or talked about other persons, and she had no one to blame for being an accomplice in performance and knowledge of witchcraft.[146]

The trial of Sitru Pedersdatter did not take a long time. In the accounts, it is stated that her food was paid for fourteen days. The executioner also had his food paid for fourteen days, and was paid for burning her.[147] This means that after her trial on 23 June, it took only eleven days before she was executed.

The Voice of Sitru Pedersdatter

The resistance of Sitru Pedersdatter is already broken before the trial starts. The denunciation by Anne Holter scared her and made her flee. This means that she knew the seriousness of being denounced for witchcraft and accused of having participated in a witches' gathering. It also means that demonological ideas were known in local society. In the voice of Sitru Pedersdatter, we hear echoes of Anne

Holter's as well as the other accused women's confessions. Sitru Pedersdatter's voice is rendered in indirect speech in the records: a reporting verb initiating a reported clause.[148] As Sitru's trial was part of a panic, her confession was influenced by demonological ideas that had been activated in Rygge in previous months and fuelled the trials.

From the beginning, Sitru Pedersdatter's voice is encircled in fear. It is clear that she has been questioned prior to the trial, in the presence of 'honourable men', probably the judicial officials. The kind of pressure she has been exposed to remains unknown, but being brought back to Rygge after her flight attempt to stand trial in a dangerous case constitutes strong pressure in itself. Whatever actually occurred, Sitru confesses to witchcraft before the trial starts, and she is afraid of the outcome of the trial. This is probably the reason that she repeatedly clings to her confession to traditional witchcraft, that is, milking cattle. This is the first point of her confession and the answer to the first question posed to her, which was on what she knew about witchcraft. Sitru Pedersdatter chooses to respond to this question by confessing to *maleficium*, and she might have hoped that this would suffice. Also, she offers the first name of a farmer whose cattle she milked. She underlines that this is the only witchcraft she knows. However, the interrogators do not spend much time on stealing milk; they want something else confessed to.

Then, the interrogation is directed towards demonology, and Sitru Pedersdatter confesses to having learned witchcraft from a mentor. She also confesses to night flight, riding on a calf, participation in a witches' gathering, and having a personal demon.[149] Sitru Pedersdatter's confession to these ideas is clearly directed by leading questions and is related to other confessions during this panic. The ideas of witches' flight and witches' meetings are mentioned by several of the accused women. A named demon is mentioned as well, carrying the colloquial name *Stub*, which connotes a short creature. In versions of the demonological narrative known from the Nordic countries, a demon is given to a witch when the latter enters into a pact with the devil. The confession of Sitru Pedersdatter, and likewise the other confessions from the 1623 Rygge panic, do not mention the devil in connection with witches' meetings. But the presence of demonic helpers implies a connection to the devil.

The voice of Sitru Pedersdatter retells a demonological narrative in a concise manner, and it should be expected that the interrogator wanted an expansion. However, he does not ask for more details. He knows that the point Sitru confessed to is sufficient as proof for a death sentence. She has admitted that she knows and has learned more than traditional witchcraft. And she has mentioned the place Blåkoll, a local hill the Rygge witches allegedly used to fly to.

The name Blåkoll emerges both in Sitru Pedersdatter's and in other accused persons' confessions in the same panic.[150] A trip to this hill encompassed phenomena such as riding through the air on calves, performing certain activities at the meeting, having personal demons, and shape-shifting into ravens.[151] Variations in details occur, as Sitru Pedersdatter confesses to having ridden on a black calf, not a blue one, as mentioned in local folklore.[152] Furthermore, she confesses that on the way to Blåkoll, the women first gathered at the farm of Anne Holter and then landed at the farm of the Nabstad family to fetch Maren Nabstad. The image of Blåkoll that Sitru Pedersdatter provides is one of a place of merriment and joy, in which participants are seated at a table, with one of them at the head, drinking wine. This story fits well within the frame of witches' gatherings known in Norway, where the witches' meetings are described as cosy and jolly, with food and drink. In Sitru Pedersdatter's voice, Blåkoll is not rendered as a frightening place, but more as a place at the edge of the home village, where one arrives by a secret night flight. The colour blue, which was part of the hill's name, signified the other world. Still, there is a danger connected to this place: to go there means to cross a border, not only between the visible and invisible but also between the legal and illegal. Thus, Sitru Pedersdatter's confession means that she violated an established order.

As for the name of Blåkoll, a variant of the name is known from a Swedish trial from Småland at the end of the 1500s, from Northern Sweden and Stockholm at the 1660s and 1670s, and from Åland trials in Finland in 1666: Blåkulla, a mythical place where famous witches' gatherings allegedly took place. However, in these mentioned trials it occurs in narratives devoid of any actual geographical ties.[153] Related to Eastern Norway, the name Blåkull is also known from local folk tradition: on certain days of the year, for instance Easter night, the witches used to fly to Blåkoll and home again, riding through the air on blue bucks.[154]

Sitru Pedersdatter is finally asked whether she can do more or whether she knows more. She responds as if this were a request to tell more about the witchcraft performed, but the question might also have been an invitation to denounce others. However, she had already mentioned Maren Nabstad three times in an otherwise short confession, thus she is thoroughly denounced. In addition, the fact that Nils Nabstad asked Sitru Pedersdatter not to denounce his wife shows that Maren Nabstad was in a vulnerable position. The interrogator does not pose any follow-up questions, perhaps because Sitru Pedersdatter was determined that she had confessed enough.

The voice of Sitru Pedersdatter is clearly marked by orality features. Additive structures surface, both in phrases where two words with identical meaning are joined[155] and in sentences combined with 'and'.[156] The last type contributes to establishing a timeline, as seen for instance when the witches started their flight at the Holter farm, rode from there to the Nabstad farm, and ended up in Blåkoll.[157] The constructed timeline makes it easy for the listener to follow the development of the story, creates an order in the occurrence of events, and adds to the speed of the narration. In addition, there are other orality features to be found, like scenes that are painted: Sitru Pedersdatter riding on a black calf to Blåkoll, Anne Holter providing the witches with wine to drink at Blåkoll, Maren Nabstad sitting at the head of the table. All together, these features point to the oral transfer of ideas about witchcraft.

Closeness to the human lifeworld permeates the confession of Sitru Pedersdatter. When narrating about the milking of cattle, she mentions a nearby farm where she is familiar with the farmer. She knows the consequences of milking cattle until they become dry.[158] It should be noted that milk is an important source of nourishment for the populace, thus to have the milk stolen would be a calamity. Also, the visit to well-known farms on the trip to Blåkoll and the mentioning of people's names demonstrate knowledge of the local community. The location of Blåkoll understood as an actual local hill is more realistic than witches going to a mythical hill in an unknown location. At the gathering in Blåkoll, they sit at a table and drink wine, much like a party at home. These features add credibility to the narrative and clearly show that ideas about witchcraft in oral transfer are connected to daily life in the village and to a geographical frame that is recognizable to the narrator as well as the listeners. Therefore, in Sitru Pedersdatter's confession, the magical flight has earthly stops, and the Blåkoll meal is a meal with real ingredients. The activity of witches is linked to down-to-earth activities and objects and mentioned *en passant* in the confession of Sitru Pedersdatter, which signifies that ideas about witchcraft formed part of the mentality of common people at the time.

The mood of Sitru Pedersdatter's confession, in terms of revealing her own attitude to the performance of witchcraft, is seen in her emphasis on *maleficium*. She repeats three times that she could do nothing more in terms of witchcraft than milking. Apparently, she believes that stealing milk from other people's cattle is possible by means of witchcraft, and that she can do it successfully. As for demonological ideas, these elements seem to be part of a witchcraft narrative that she has heard told in the village. This narrative is about Blåkoll as a tempting free space for female participants. In addition, she has a personal demon. In the demonological narrative, the personal demon helps with the performance of witchcraft.

The story about the trip to Blåkoll in Sitru Pedersdatter's version is related without any distancing devices. Thus, she subscribes to the content of the story and contributes her part to a united narrative valid for the women accused in this panic. Her confession does not imply that she sees her own witchcraft performance as related to the devil, but her Apostle might have played a demonic part.

One of the accused in the 1623 Rygge panic uses the expression 'in the name of a thousand devils' in cursing.[159] The same expression is used by a woman accused of witchcraft in Denmark in the late 1500s.[160] The image of the multitude of devils testifies to the oral field of transmission: with its emphasis on abundance, it becomes easy to remember and retell. In addition, bringing up the name of the devil is frightening and works well in a threat. Such a curse connotes an angry person and reveals negative emotions. However, Sitru Pedersdatter's confession does not bear the stamp of emotions, and she does not show anger.

From the beginning of her confession until the point of her execution, Sitru Pedersdatter has a cooperative voice. She willingly confesses to traditional harmful witchcraft. She willingly gives her demonological confession, stands by it, and confirms it at the place of execution. She tries to avoid denouncing many others, but has already given the name of Maren Nabstad. The appeal of Maren Nabstad's husband turns out to have been justified, as his wife is tried just as he feared. The denunciation of Maren Nabstad became deadly, even if this was probably not the intention. The confession of Sitru Pedersdatter reflects a wider climate of anxiety, which existed beyond this Eastern Norwegian village in 1623.

The last time Sitru Pedersdatter's voice is rendered in the records is in a comment in the margins, entered after her execution on 4 July 1623. She is a broken woman. She confirms her confession, says that she has not lied to anyone, and states that she has no one to accuse of performing and knowing witchcraft. It is recorded that she 'boldly'[161] goes to her death. Even if this is a postlude, her voice comes through as utterly sore in all her willingness to confirm. Her thread of life was cut. Maybe she could foretell this moment when she tried to flee from the trial just a few weeks previously?

The Voices of the Witnesses

Since this was a witchcraft panic, no formal witnesses were brought before the court. The evidence of crimes came from denunciations and confessions made by all accused women. Most likely, there had been a complaint from Nils Nabstad previously stating that his cattle was milked dry, as Sitru Pedersdatter mentions in her confession to maleficent witchcraft. Such a complaint, combined with a person being rumoured to engage in witchcraft, frequently led to accusations.

The Voice of the Interrogator

The voice of the interrogator is heard in questions rendered as indirect speech as well as in shadow questions. Sitru Pedersdatter was asked about several topics and then her answers were written down. The interrogation starts with an open question about what she knew about witchcraft. Then, the name of her mentor, the activities at the witches' gathering, and the flight to the witches' gathering come up. The interrogator takes her through an entire spectrum of dangerous ideas.

In Sitru Pedersdatter's interrogation, we see pressure to move towards demonological ideas. She starts by confessing to milking other people's cattle—and says that she could do nothing more with witchcraft, so it seems that she herself considers her confession to be finished.[162] However, the interrogator is not satisfied, and the trip to Blåkoll is next confessed to. It seems that the interrogator poses follow-up questions on this topic in order to enrich the demonological narrative; questions which are answered fluently, with details inserted. At the end, there is an open question about whether she knows more, to which she answers that she cannot confess to anything more.[163] She wants the interrogation to end. Thus, the records show that the interrogator was actively trying to obtain a demonological confession and continued his questioning after the woman said that she had nothing more to confess to. But the records also show that she answered in a way that confirmed her own knowledge of night flight on animals to witches' gatherings, of activities at witches' gatherings, and of named personal demons.

As a whole, the voice of the interrogator in the 1623 Rygge panic is active in steering interrogations from a focus on malevolent witchcraft to one on demonological ideas. The accused women themselves answer with what they know: performance of *maleficium* and a version of the demonological narrative about witches' gatherings and flights that they learned about through oral transmission in their local community.

The Voice of the Law

The trial records of Sitru Pedersdatter provide factual information about the trial: the names of judicial officials and men in the jury. It becomes clear that the court followed correct judicial procedure. For instance, members of the jury, who acted as judges, were not allowed to act as witnesses.[164] Further, the judiciary attaches importance to clarifying on what grounds the sentence is given: Sitru's own confession, Anne Holter's denunciation of her, and village rumours. This is repeated several times, signalling that the judiciary officials very much wanted to correctly carry out their appointment. Even in a local trial with few judicial officials, such as this one, the judiciary was knowledgeable about the letter of the law and referred to evidence that was needed for a sentence to be passed.

The voice of the law, as it emerges in the records, shows that proper court practice was followed. The main weight is placed on Sitru Pedersdatter's confession, wherein *maleficium* and demonological ideas are mixed. The other elements must be considered weaker as burden of proof in a legal context. However, the wording of the sentence signals that a strong fear of witchcraft was present among the judiciary, and that it believed witchcraft was possible, even flights to Blåkoll.

The Voice of the Scribe

The scribe does not give his own opinions on what is told but maintains a reporting accent throughout in terms of textual structure and expression. The sentences are mostly propositions, strengthening the accusatory party and building an impression of guilt on the side of the accused person.

There is one aspect that was not included in the records, namely the use of torture. Both torture and the water ordeal to press forth circumstantial evidence were used during this panic, but could not be entered into the records. However, torture is not documented in the trial of Sitru Pedersdatter, even if knowing that torture is a possibility is a clear means of pressure in itself.

An interesting feature in the records of Sitru Pedersdatter's trial is the word 'devil', which is used about Maren Nabstad. It is not clear whether this word is used by Sitru Pedersdatter or by the interrogator, or whether the scribe inserted it. It does not seem to fit in among the other words Sitru Pedersdatter used about the other women who went to Blåkoll. If the interrogator brought the word into court discourse, it shows an urge to describe Maren Nabstad in demonic terms. If the scribe inserted the word, then he leaves his neutral position and enters with a negative description of Maren. I think it is most likely that the word was used by the interrogator, as it contributes to painting a picture of Maren as being devilish, and also to mark that she would be the next one accused.

The voice of the scribe in the records of Sitru Pedersdatter's trial is a professional voice which strives for accuracy when it comes to the main elements of the interrogation, sentence, and verdict. At the same time, the scribe manages to include individual characteristics of the accused person's speech, among other orality features. The same goes for the recording of the trials of the other women in the panic. The wording of verdict and sentence is given textual space, so that the various voices heard in the courtroom appear in a balanced way.

Gundelle Olsdatter, 1663

The Trial

Gundelle Olsdatter was accused during the worst witchcraft panic in the district of Finnmark, which lasted from October 1662 until April 1663. Within a few winter months, more than thirty women from East Finnmark were accused of witchcraft, and twenty were sentenced to death by fire at the stake. The court records from these trials are preserved.[165] The records are written in the Gothic hand by the Finnmark magistrate in minute books, folio format. Of the women receiving death sentences, seventeen were questioned and tried at Vardøhus Fortress, two were tried in the neighbouring village of Vadsø, and one was tried in the neighbouring village of Kiberg.[166] By the time Gundelle Olsdatter was brought before the court, twelve women had already received their death sentences and were burned at the gallows at Steilneset. The first part of the name Steilneset, *steile*, refers to a method of execution,[167] while the second part means a headland. The witchcraft panic of 1662–63 was brutal. An extreme use of torture led to the death of two women on the rack before they were sentenced.[168] Because this was illegal, their trial records end abruptly. The accused simply disappear from the records without any explanation.

Gundelle Olsdatter was an ordinary woman who lived in Vardø. She was married to Christen Hansen and worked at Søren Christensen's house. She came to Finnmark from the island of Senja, a large island further south on the Northern Norwegian coast, and was thus one of many people who travelled north to Finnmark to find work. Most of those women worked as maids. Gundelle Olsdatter was denounced for witchcraft by Margrette Jonsdatter on 10 April 1663. Margrette Jonsdatter was first imprisoned and interrogated in October 1662, and brought before the court six times before she finally confessed and denounced others.[169] Margrette Jonsdatter said that Gundelle Olsdatter was just as skilled in witchcraft as she was. Gundelle allegedly participated in a witches' gathering with Satan on Domen Mountain[170] on Midsummer Night. The women had caroused and played board games with their gods, and Satan had played the fiddle. They had stayed there for an hour and a half. Gundelle Olsdatter and the other witches allegedly also drove the fish from the shore with stalks of seaweed the previous year and tried to cast a spell on Captain Jens Ottesen and his ship the previous autumn.[171]

On 10 March 1663, the same day as she was denounced, Gundelle Olsdatter was summoned to the court at Vardøhus Fortress. The regional governor himself, Christopher Orning, was present and took part in the interrogation. Also present in the courtroom were the bailiff, Nils Sørensen Fiil, the magistrate, and the sworn jurors.[172] In addition, people from the local community could attend the trial. Gundelle Olsdatter refused to confess and requested the water ordeal. She floated.[173]

Three other women were brought before the court on the same day as Gundelle Olsdatter.[174] One of these was Dorette Poulsdatter. She had been denounced by three women but denied knowing witchcraft[175] and was killed on the rack at Vardøhus Fortress in the night between 10 and 11 March 1663.[176] Then, on 11 March 1663, trials resumed, and the three surviving women were brought before the court again, one of them Gundelle Olsdatter. It was ascertained that she floated on the sea like a fishing bob when subjected to the water ordeal.[177] On this day, she must have known that a woman she knew well had been killed at Vardøhus the previous night, with all this implied. She now

> confessed the entire truth, which is that she was guilty of those very deeds that the aforementioned Margrette, Sigri and Ragnilde have denounced her for and ascribed to her before the court, namely those of witchcraft, and that she was just as adept as them at carrying out the aforementioned acts.[178]

She also confessed that the previous year, around Easter, she and the other witches were out at sea in the shape of seals, driving away fish from the shore with stalks of seaweed.[179] Furthermore, she confessed that last year, on the eve of St Hans's day, she and the three other aforementioned witches, Margrette, Sigri, and Ragnilde, were on Domen whither, she stated, she flew in the likeness of a crow. And there, the wicked Satan, Old Erich, joined them in the likeness of a crow.[180]

On one point, however, Gundelle Olsdatter's confession did not agree with that of the others. She firmly dismissed having seen or noticed a woman named Gjertrud Siversdatter, Søren Christensen's wife—whom the other accused, Margrette Jonsdatter, Sigri Jonsdatter, and Ragnilde, had named in connection with witchcraft—on Domen Mountain or at sea with the other witches.

To respond to and oppose the above-mentioned witches' accounts, Gjertrud Siversdatter appeared before the court to answer the accusations herself. Sigri Jonsdatter had diverged from parts of her previous confession about Gjertrud Siversdatter, claiming to have uttered untruths about her and that she (Gjertrud) was not present on Domen nor at the sea. Moreover, Sigri Jonsdatter maintained that when they gathered on a beach called Westersanden to drive the fish away from the shore, Margrette Jonsdatter had asked her to say that Søren Christensen's wife had gone with them.

After this confrontation, the final stage of the trial against the women was reached, and the verdict formulated:

> After such evil deeds, of which they give a full account and which they admit, unable to deny that they have learnt witchcraft and that they have

learnt and practised devilish crafts, His Royal Majesty's bailiff puts to the court that they should be punished by loss of life in fire at the stake for their evil misdeeds, and he requests judgement.[181]

The verdict and sentence followed the pattern of those of many other trials during this panic: 'Thus, after indictment and responses, and in accordance with the circumstances of the case',[182] it was found to be true that Margrette Jonsdatter, Styrk Olsen's wife, was one of the said witches, as she herself had confessed in detail on a most solemn oath before the court, also stating where she learned and subsequently practised her evil craft. Nor did she deviate from this, but said herself that she was a witch.

> In view of her committed misdeeds, she shall suffer and be punished corporally in this world and since she has also denounced, as she has, in addition to herself, the above Ragnilde Endresdatter,[183] item Siigrj Jonsdatter and Gundele Oelsdatter, also from this same place, maintaining that their craft is just as potent as hers, and they themselves have confessed truthfully in detail before the court that they have learnt witchcraft and consorted with her in various places, according to the lengthy confessions recorded here, we find, in view of the circumstances, that we cannot judge or decide otherwise than that they have forfeited their lives to fire at the stake.[184]

The convicted women were burned alive at the gallows. They suffered death at the stake, tied to a ladder toppled over into a burning pyre. The corpse of Dorette Poulsdatter was dragged out to the gallows and burned together with the living convicted women.[185] After these death sentences, the panic of 1662–63 led to four more women being sentenced to death and executed.[186] Then, during the remainder of the Finnmark witchcraft trials, fourteen people were brought before the court and accused of witchcraft, of whom three lost their lives.[187]

The Voice of Gundelle Olsdatter

The voice of Gundelle Olsdatter is one of many female voices heard during the 1662–63 panic. In the confessions, the names of others are frequently mentioned as participants in witchcraft activities, so that during the entire panic, the voices of the accused women are entangled. Therefore, a study of Gundelle Olsdatter's voice also requires looking at other accused people, as she was said to be part of a group in confessions related to the collective performance of witchcraft. The records provide important information about how an individual became a suspect of alleged witchcraft, what kind of ideas about witchcraft contributed to the continuation of a panic, and how the judiciary reacted to denunciations. In addition, the records show how witchcraft stories circulated among the women inside and outside the walls of Vardøhus Fortress and were told and retold, amended, and changed before they appeared in a confession. The three main accusations during this panic were casting a spell on Captain Jens Ottesen's ship, participation in a witches' meeting on the mountain Domen, and chasing fish from the shore. We find various versions of these in the confessions appearing in this panic as early as in November 1662. In addition, we find several other elements: a drinking party in Anders Pedersen's cellar on Christmas Eve in which the devil took part, a trip to Hell where the devil led the way, the destruction of the sledge of the regional governor, and the collective casting of a spell on the regional governor's arm by the use of pins.

Looking at the three main accusations in the denunciation of Gundelle Olsdatter, the spell against Jens Ottesen's ship first appears in this panic on 6 November 1662. Over the course of one day, Dorette Lauritsdatter, Maren Sigvaldsdatter, and Ragnild Clemidsdatter confess to having cast this spell. Then, three weeks later, the witches' gathering comes up. On 28 November, Maren Mogensdatter and Maritte Rasmusdatter confess to sailing on an overturned barrel to Domen Mountain, where they danced a folk dance[188] with the wicked Satan, who played for them on a sitar. Maren Henningsdatter is accused of the same. She denies witchcraft, but confesses to incest with two brothers twenty years earlier and receives a death sentence.

In the new year, more court meetings take place, and the accusations emerge again in confessions given on 26 January by Guri, Laurits's wife, and on 29 January by Solve Nilsdatter. The latter confession included chasing fish from the shore with stalks of seaweed.[189] So far, the name of Gundelle Olsdatter is not mentioned.

On 27 February, the panic continues with the examination of three young girls (the ages of eight and twelve years are mentioned) and the adult woman Ellen Gundersdatter. The same day, Karen Andersdatter is interrogated as well, and death sentences are passed for both Ellen and Karen. Still, the name of Gundelle Olsdatter has not yet been mentioned in the courtroom.

In total, six children were accused of witchcraft during this panic. The children interrogated this day are the sisters Ingeborg Iversdatter and Karen Iversdatter, and they confess to the devil's pact. In addition, Maren Olsdatter confesses to participating in a trip to Hell.[190] Also, the children confess to taking part in casting a spell on the regional governor (which did not succeed because he was very 'God-fearing')[191] and on the regional governor's woman, and to participating in witches' meetings on Domen and in Lærvigen, where they drank beer from a pitcher.[192] They denounce several adult women, who are subsequently tried and convicted. The denunciations made by the children are taken seriously. Their cases are sent on to the Court of Appeal, as the local court found it difficult to pass a sentence. The children were all acquitted by the Court of Appeal Judge.

On 9 March, Margrette Jonsdatter is called forth again, and denies witchcraft. She then requests to be tried by the water ordeal, and floats. The next day, she gives her confession. This is when Gundelle Olsdatter is mentioned for the first time. Gundelle is said to have been one of the participants in a witches' meeting on Domen, where there were six women altogether. Sigri Jonsdatter, Dorette Poulsdatter, Ragnilde Endresdatter, Gjertrud Siversdatter, and Gundelle [Gundle] Olsdatter are denounced by Margrette in connection with this meeting. Satan allegedly played the fiddle, and Gjertrud Siversdatter served them beer and wine in pewter cups.

Gundelle Olsdatter is said to also have taken part in chasing fish from the shore, as narrated by Margrette Jonsdatter in this beautiful way:

> She [Margrette] took part in beating the fish away from the shore with stalks of seaweed last Easter. And before the court, she also firmly denounces the following person, Søren Christensen's wife Giertrud from Krogen, saying that she was also there at the time, true enough in her own likeness, and she wore a black jacket, a red Bøffelbay[193] skirt, also a red cap with golden lace, and white linen around her neck. Besides, she sat on the water, holding and surrounded by seaweed. Margrette says that she herself was in the likeness of a gull, while Gundle [Gundelle] was in the likeness of a seal, Dorette, Waarøe Hans's wife, was in that of a porpoise, and Sigrj Jonsdatter was in that of a bluefin, and they were all holding stalks of seaweed, applying their craft to drive the fish from the shore, and this they did from land and from the islands.[194]

It is surprising to find such a poetic image in witchcraft court records. Here, seabirds and seals, golden lace and white linen are mentioned.

The next point in the confession of Margrette Jonsdatter is trying to cast a spell on the ship of Captain Jens Ottesen, creating a storm when he was sailing to Bergen the previous autumn. This operation was not successful because the crew 'evoked the Lord'.[195] The name of Gundelle Olsdatter is not mentioned on this occasion.[196] Still, when Gundelle is brought before the court, one accusation is that she attempted to cast a spell on Jens Ottesen's ship. It seems that the judiciary focused on a set series of accusations.

More women confess in the lead-up to the interrogation of Gundelle Olsdatter. Ragnilde Endresdatter and Sigri Jonsdatter confess that all that Margrette Jonsdatter had narrated was true, with Sigri saying that all those who were mentioned by Margrette Jonsdatter are truly witches. Thus, she confirms *en bloc* the names denounced by Margrette Jonsdatter, which include Gundelle Olsdatter. Dorette Poulsdatter is mentioned as having taken part in trying to cast the spell.

After the panic had been ongoing for four months, Gundelle Olsdatter, like the other women in Vardø, fearfully awaits who will be summoned to the court at Vardøhus Fortress next. With so many already burned during the winter months, no woman was safe. There was no warning and no indication of who would be next.

The Gundelle Olsdatter who enters the courtroom has been denounced for having been with the other accused women on the witch mountain Domen, for having driven fish from the shore with stalks of seaweed with the other witches the previous year, and for having tried to cast a spell on Captain Jens Ottesen and his ship with the other accused women the previous autumn. Gundelle Olsdatter does not confess or admit to any of these. Even though she has been accused in a panic that has already taken the lives of twelve women, she refuses to confess. To close her case and clear her name, she requests that she be tried by the water ordeal, a request that is granted. On 10 March, the day after she was denounced, we hear the voice of a strong woman who is unwilling to give in. It shows resistance, hope, and the strength to speak out. She possibly asks to be tested by the water ordeal because she still has a faint hope that she will not float, which did not happen. This becomes a turning point for her voice and in her trial.

The water ordeal clearly had an impact. Several of the women accused in this panic requested to be tried by it. They must have believed that this judgement from God could save them; it was a straw they could clutch at. As circumstantial evidence, it was not considered proof but only a sign, and even as such, it was much disputed within learned legal Europe.[197] It is recorded that Gundelle Olsdatter was tried by the same water ordeal and it was ascertained that she floated on the sea like a fishing bob, 'as could be seen'.[198] It is thus emphasized that the sign the ordeal constitutes is stronger and more convincing if many people witnessed the floating which they were also required to do by the authorities. The disappointment for the person tested must have been immense. The atmosphere at Vardøhus was surely heated the day of Gundelle Olsdatter's water ordeal. The judiciary desired a confession from the accused woman's own mouth. Gundelle Olsdatter knew that, after having floated, her odds were not good.

The next time we hear the voice of Gundelle Olsdatter in the court records is on 11 March 1663, the day after her water ordeal. Present in the courtroom are the regional governor, the bailiff, the magistrate, and the jurors. Gundelle Olsdatter's voice is subdued. She is the first woman interrogated before the court that day, and her confession must be interpreted in relation to what had just happened to Dorette Poulsdatter. Word of her death must have spread rapidly, and might explain Gundelle Olsdatter's willingness to confess.

In the records, it is entered that Gundelle Olsdatter confessed 'the entire truth' that day, which probably means that her confession included all the demonological ideas that the interrogators wanted to hear. She confesses that she was guilty of the deeds that Margrette Jonsdatter, Sigri Jonsdatter, and Ragnilde Endresdatter had ascribed to her before the court, and that she was just as adept as they were at carrying out acts of witchcraft.[199] Likewise, she mentions her mentor, who taught her witchcraft, and states that the powers came to her in beer that gave her a headache and made her deranged.[200] Satan had then come to her in the likeness of a crow and requested her services, to which she had agreed,[201] and he let himself be called her god by the name of Morten.[202] He promised her that she would know good fortune with regard to cattle and sheep and anything she might undertake.[203] Her mentor had given her some blue stuff,[204] which she tried out on a dog, after which the dog became demented and drowned itself.

This part of the confession shows that Gundelle Olsdatter knew about demonological ideas. She knew about learning witchcraft from another woman, a mentor; she knew about the devil's pact and the devil's promises; she knew that Satan could come in the likeness of a small demon—whom she called god—as a companion when performing evil deeds; and she knew about trying her art on an animal to see if it works. The mentor functions as a link to the devil, as Satan appeared just after she had received the drink from her. This role of the mentor constitutes a difference with *maleficium* and creates a bridge to demonology. The confession is in some respects similar to many others when it comes to elements of a story about the devil's pact and their narrative order. However, Gundelle Olsdatter's confession has a personal touch because of where she learned witchcraft and from whom, her reaction to drinking the beer, the name of her personal god, and the blue substance she received to try out her art.

Gundelle Olsdatter then confesses that around Easter in the previous year, she and the 'aforementioned witches' were out at sea in the form of seals, driving away fish with stalks of seaweed. This is not quite in accordance with Margrette Jonsdatter's confession, in which Gundelle Olsdatter was said to have taken the shape of a whale.[205] Gundelle also gives a reason for her participation: she was angry with her master, Søren Christensen, as he had asked a high price for his wares. We see similarities between the confessions, with economical motifs or personal grudges given as causes. For instance, Margrette Jonsdatter confesses that she took part in the chasing of fish because she was angry with her mistress; when Margrette asked for something from her, she did not get it. Margrette also narrates that Gjertrud Siversdatter, the wife of Søren Christensen who engaged in fish trade, took part in the witchcraft act because the fishermen she supplied were debt-free, so she felt that she did not have as much power over them as over other people, who were indebted.[206]

When Gundelle Olsdatter mentions why she chased the fish from the shore, she connects the unrealistic image of shape-shifting witches at sea to a realistic, factual situation: bad fisheries the previous spring and expensive wares she had to buy from her master. She thus points to harsh living conditions. Here, the promise of the devil when entering the pact, namely good fortune, also shows that many of Vardø's residents at the time were concerned with economic conditions and security of sustenance. This part of the confession clearly shows that the world view of an ordinary woman in Finnmark in 1663 was magical, as she seems to accept the possibility of fish-chasing in the form of a seal. However, her actual conditions were challenging. Thus, the unrealistic as well as the realistic features fused in her confession mirror the thoughts and living conditions of an ordinary woman.

Gundelle Olsdatter does not confess to casting a spell on Jens Ottesen's ship, but does confess to the witches' meeting. She narrates that the previous year, on St John's Eve, she and the three other women—Margrette Jonsdatter, Sigri Jonsdatter, and Ragnilde Endresdatter—were on the witch mountain Domen, to which she had flown as a crow. There, the 'wicked Satan, Old Erich', had joined them in the likeness of a crow. Gundelle Olsdatter knew about shape-shifting and witches' gatherings on particular days and in particular places. She strongly denies having seen or noticed Gjertrud Siversdatter—whom the other witches had named—on Domen or at sea with the other witches. Indeed, 'by the most solemn of oaths, and by whatever lot or share she might expect in the Kingdom of Heaven, she confirmed this'.[207] Gjertrud Siversdatter's case was passed on to the Court of Appeal, where she was acquitted in June 1663.[208] Perhaps Gjertrud got support from the other women because she had helped them at some point. She was more well-to-do than the rest, as she was the wife of a fish supplier,[209] a man trading in fish. Her position is also visible in the motif description of chasing the fish: Gjertrud Siversdatter is in the middle, in her own likeness, dressed in beautiful clothes. The apparent wish to protect Gjertrud shows that the accused women were aware of the serious consequences of denunciation. Still, Gundelle Olsdatter names other women who allegedly took part in these gatherings. This is most likely explained by the pressure put on her to denounce others and her fear of torture.

Gundelle Olsdatter confesses to two of the three points that she was accused of. One point is the chasing of fish. She explains why she took part, referring to social inequality. Her confession expresses the wish for revenge on those who had money and exploited ordinary people, for instance, her master charging too much for his goods. The other point is the witches' meeting on Domen, she mentions the day of St John's Eve (when witches were supposed to be out to perform evil deeds), the names of participants, that she flew in as a crow, and that the wicked Satan was also in the shape of a crow. She does not mention the pewter jug or cup or any drinking, like some of the other accused women, and does not mention the devil playing any instrument. As a whole, the confession of Gundelle Olsdatter includes the core elements of a basic demonological witchcraft narrative but is not very rich in details. After the water ordeal, Gundelle Olsdatter has given in. There is no longer any need to go into details; she wants to have it all finished. The courage she showed the previous day, when resistance and hope were reflected in her voice, is gone.

The voice of Gundelle Olsdatter, as it is rendered, is calm and not emotional. She does not show any fear for herself, but her refusal to confess and her request to be tried by the water ordeal are clear signals of a fear of the further development of the trial. Everyone in Vardø in 1663 knew the implication of being accused in a witchcraft trial. However, Gundelle shows a kind of compassion on behalf of Gjertrud Siversdatter, who is imprisoned and in the searchlight. Miraculously, her support might have had an effect.

Gundelle Olsdatter's confession is rather brief, and orality features are not prominent. However, the narratives about the Domen meeting and the chasing of fish came to her ears as stories passed from mouth to mouth in the village, and her confession in the courtroom is also an oral performance. Thus, both her learning of the story and her retelling of the demonological narrative in court were influenced by oral transfer. Colloquial expressions surface in her confession, like the name she uses for Satan, Old Erich, which is still in use in Norway today. This name also implies a certain humoristic tone. Gundelle Olsdatter's confession is close to the human lifeworld, which is a characteristic feature of oral tales. She refers to her own living conditions and obtained a promise from the devil about good fortune with her cattle. The occurrence of orality features in her confession shows that she has preserved her individuality as a user of language in a very threatening and challenging situation, and that narrating in fact is her last resort in a critical situation.

Thus, the voice of Gundelle Olsdatter provides a glimpse of the mentality of the time from the position of an ordinary woman, with a mix of learned and traditional aspects of witchcraft; a woman who shares the stories that circulate in local communities. However, she also shares the anxiety in the village. When Gundelle—who over the course of two days was brought before the local court, denied witchcraft, and was subjected to the water ordeal—willingly confessed to a very serious alliance with the devil, she must have felt compelled to do so. Knowledge of Dorette Poulsdatter's death on the night before she herself received her sentence must have been terrifying. Gundelle must have known that if she did not confess, the next step could be severe torture for her as well. It is difficult to view her confession as anything other than a confession under pressure, even if physical torture is not recorded in her case. Thus, an enforced narrative, containing all the elements the interrogators wanted to hear, is what she delivered.

The Voices of the Other Women

The Finnmark witchcraft panic of 1662–63 was not conducted following accusatory legal principles. There was no formal accusation, and no ordinary witnesses were brought before the court. The accused women were there because they were denounced by other interrogated women. For instance, the denunciation of Margrette Jonsdatter implicated four other women, all of whom were quickly tried. Instead of testimonies, a method of confrontation between the accused women in the courtroom was used. The confession of one woman could be countered by another woman, who did not agree with the content. Quite a few times, the laying-on of hands took place, where a confessing woman placed her hand on a denounced woman to reinforce the suspicion. This was done to confirm before the court that another woman was a witch. In the trial of Sigri Jonsdatter, who was first denounced by Margrette Jonsdatter, she (Sigri) initially refused to confess. Then Ragnilde Endresdatter, who had already confessed, was called forth to confirm that Margrette Jonsdatter had told the truth.[210] This shows an aspect of court practice in witchcraft panics in which women who confessed were used to put pressure on other women to confess as well.

It was dangerous to be a woman living in Vardø: the denunciations struck blindly, in all directions.[211] We do not know how the names mentioned in denunciations were chosen. In a small village like Vardø, it is likely that the women living there knew each other. Gundelle Olsdatter might have been just a familiar person for Margrette Jonsdatter, one she knew from daily life in Vardø, and therefore a name coming to her mind when she (Margrette) was under pressure. There is no indication that Margrette Jonsdatter carried hatred or envy against her. Gundelle Olsdatter was not rumoured to be a witch. Still, she suffered the same fate as many other women in Finnmark because of denunciation in a witchcraft panic, caught in a frenzy against women believed to be in league with the Evil One. The denunciation of Gundelle Olsdatter occurred after Margrette Jonsdatter had given in. Judicial officials had kept up the pressure on Margrette Jonsdatter for six months, led her before the court several times, tried to make her confess, but in vain. This shows her strength and perseverance. The result of the water ordeal changed it all.

After this ordeal, the judiciary got the confession they wanted, in which names never heard previously were included. The panic could continue.

The confessions of Gundelle Olsdatter and the other accused women are narratives. They are variations on a theme, a basic narrative, including all core elements of demonological witchcraft. This basic narrative as it is heard in the Finnmark courtrooms contains the following elements: where and from whom witchcraft was learned, the meeting with the devil, entering into the devil's pact, the promises of the devil, trying out the art, performing collective witchcraft, participating in a witches' meeting, activities at the witches' meeting, and denouncing others. The basic narrative appears in different versions in the various confessions, during the 1662–63 panic and during the other Finnmark witchcraft panics. Structurally, the main narrative has embedded narratives dealing with the performance of witchcraft, like witches' meetings and collective witchcraft operations. Each of the embedded narratives is fairly short and individually shaped, but activates several narratological categories: order, establishing a timeline, duration, the variation between fast- and slow-moving passages of the narrated story, voice, the delegation of voice from the narrator to the actors, and frequency—the repetition of textual segments—which results in extra attention for that particular point.

The variations in the different confessions are seen mainly when the stories about the witches' meeting and the chasing of fish are told. As for the witches' meeting, the detail about serving beer or wine differs: sometimes it is the devil who serves, sometimes it is one of the women. Sometimes the drink is poured from a pewter cup, sometimes from a pewter jug. The devil sometimes plays a fiddle, sometimes other instruments. The place of the witches' meeting is sometimes Domen, sometimes another mountain called Dovre. There is a detail about Margrette Jonsdatter losing one of her shoes dancing with Satan; this dance took place sometimes on Domen Mountain at St John's Eve, sometimes at Dovre Mountain on Christmas Night.[212]

As for the chasing of fish, the women sometimes shape-shift into birds, sometimes into whales, and sometimes into seals. In the confession of Gundelle Olsdatter, she tells about her own reaction when she obtained the power of witchcraft through drinking beer: she became delirious, and afterwards Satan came to her. This is one of the personal details in her confession. She also has an original detail when it comes to trying out the art of witchcraft, stating that she gave some blue stuff to a dog. Thus, she conveys her belief in the power of bewitched items. As always in a good story, the details are the spice, and the narrating women are aware of this: they note the details and vary them, while the main plot is kept unchanged.

The voices of the women contribute to a picture of learned and performed witchcraft. In different versions, the stories told deal with a pact with the devil, his promises, and the first try-outs of the art. Witches' gatherings are also described. Several women mention other acts, like chasing the fish from the shore, raising storms, and casting a spell on the regional governor. Each woman gives a slightly different account than those previously interrogated. The picture is extended for each new confession delivered. However, their confessions resemble each other when it comes to the devil's pact, witches' meetings, and the performance of collective witchcraft. As a whole, the voices of the women complement each other, such that we obtain a rich picture of the mentality of the women in Finnmark. Thus, the confessions cannot be described as simplistic.

In the women's stories, the common denominator is that witchcraft is possible, that shape-shifting is possible, that witchcraft is performed as a collective operation, and that the devil is their master. Other women are frequently named due to pressure and torture: it is repeatedly stated that women who are denounced are 'as good as' the woman who is being interrogated. Additionally, it appears that witchcraft will not work when the person to be bewitched strongly believes in God: 'For God was stronger than Satan'.[213]

The voices of the women that surface in the 1662–63 Finnmark panic show that magic is accepted in their narratives. Unrealistic elements found in their confessions include shape-shifting, flying to come to a witches' meeting, sitting at sea to chase fish with seaweed, and being tempted by the devil disguised as a dog. Also, there is a more pragmatic accent to be heard: a protest against powerful men, as the women explain why they performed acts of witchcraft. Frequently, they blame their employers or the regional governor for treating their minions too harshly. The voices as an entirety provide insight into the realm of ideas about witchcraft, daily village life with its challenges, fears of being denounced, hopes of clearing a suspicion of witchcraft through the water ordeal, willingness to denounce others when they know that their own fate is sealed, and a will to protect their children. The voices of the accused women show ordinary human reactions within a very dangerous and unusual setting.

The variations on a theme that come to the fore in the confessions of this panic might either imply that the basic demonological narrative about learning and performing witchcraft was known in the local community at this time or that the ideas were heard at Vardøhus Fortress during imprisonment. The last cannot be the only explanation, because several of the accused women were taken into Vardøhus right after denunciation, like Gundelle Olsdatter. This signals that the demonological witchcraft narrative must have been known in the local community which is a reasonable explanation, since demonological ideas were introduced in witchcraft trials in Vardø already in 1620 and were thereafter probably known among the villagers. The witchcraft confession that Gundelle Olsdatter gave must have been the result of a story told and retold in the local community, and then delivered in a trial. This may explain the personal touch of not only Gundelle Olsdatter's but also many other accused women's confessions. While several of the demonological ideas were preserved, like the pact, the devil's promises, the devil's mark, shape-shifting, and the witches' meeting, the confessions are attached to motifs known from folk belief.[214] In addition, the idea of shape-shifting has taken on a local valour, as the women confess to having been in the shape of sea-birds, seals, and whales, which all are shapes found in their own surroundings.[215] The atmosphere of the witches' meeting in Finnmark is coloured by sisterhood, dancing, and drinking—much milder in tone than the sabbaths further south in Europe. The accused woman brought a demonological story with her when she came to Vardøhus; however, it was a story in her own wrapping. The telling of such a story had a disastrous effect because it occurred in the frame of a witchcraft trial, in a forced setting.

The Voice of the Interrogator

Witchcraft studies have accentuated the extent to which leading questions influenced the confessions. Frequently one sees, also during this Finnmark panic, that leading questions were posed at the beginning of an interrogation—where and from whom one learned witchcraft. Judged from the textual ordering of the paragraphs in the court records, other questions posed during interrogation emphasize certain elements that the judiciary wants the accused to confess to. These questions must have been open. Often, the answer to a new question can be traced in the records by the opening of a new paragraph, for instance with the words 'Likewise', 'After this', 'Furthermore', 'Whereupon', 'Yet', '*Item*'. Demonological confessions are heard, interspersed with personal details. Demonological ideas, which originally must have been introduced by learned people, are apparent in Finnmark witchcraft trials since 1620. As ordinary people from the community and the members of the jury coming from the village could be present during the trials, these ideas were transmitted to the populace, retold orally, and finally returned to legal officials in personalized form in a witchcraft confession. The knowledge of demonology to a certain extent diverged from the full, learned European demonological doctrine— as seen in published demonological treaties—and resulted in local, regional, or national varieties.[216]

In Finnmark, several details found in learned demonology and in witchcraft trials in countries further south—such as sexual intercourse with the devil and the killing of babies—never occurred. Instead, we hear stories about collective witchcraft, particularly acts that accounted for tragedies which befell the local community. In the trial of Gundelle Olsdatter, the interrogator ensures that sufficient demonological ideas are confessed to in order for a death sentence to be passed. Therefore, he has to steer the course of the confessions through leading questions, inviting the accused person to talk. In return, he gets a narrative that circulates in the community. The content belongs to the accused woman, namely her understanding of the demonological narrative. In addition to posing questions aimed at obtaining a demonological confession, the interrogator is in a position where he can leave out elements or expand the questioning. In the trial of Gundelle Olsdatter, he does not follow up on one of the accusations: the spell against Jens Ottesen's ship. This might be because the witches' casting of the spell was unsuccessful.[217] Or it might be because the two points that Gundelle Olsdatter confessed to were considered sufficient. In either case, the interrogator knew that his main job was to obtain a confession, which was the best proof in a witchcraft trial. The interrogator had an important role to play in witchcraft trials, but in 1663, he was not solely responsible for the contents of the Finnmark confessions.

The Voice of the Law

The trial of Gundelle Olsdatter started with a denunciation and was conducted legally according to inquisitorial principles. She was summoned to court and accused by the bailiff. There were no witnesses testifying; the only references to statements confirming her guilt were references to those who denounced her. The voice of the law is heard most clearly at the end of the trial. As Gundelle Olsdatter's trial was part of a witchcraft panic that involved many accused individuals, it was common to have several people convicted at the same time. So also in this case. The verdict and sentence of Gundelle were pronounced together with the verdict and sentence of three other women.[218] All were sentenced to death by fire at the stake. It is emphasized that Margrette Jonsdatter's confession was decisive. The judges knew how important the confession was; hence the pressure to obtain one. In addition, the indictment was read out loud for the convicted woman, and she had to confirm it. The formal aspects of a trial were thus taken care of, as the court had laws to adhere to. For instance, in the trial of Margrette Jonsdatter, the oath of compurgation was mentioned: 'the law of twelve'. This gave her the opportunity to free herself if eleven women from the parish swore an oath together with her that she was innocent. Proper court practice had to be adhered to. If a trial was passed on to the next level of the judiciary, the Court of Appeal, it was important that the arguments for the sentence and the court procedure were clearly presented in the records, so that their validity could be evaluated.

In all Finnmark witchcraft panics, the voice of the law shows that legal officials believed that witches in alliance with the devil could perform evil acts. The attitude of the legal officials towards witchcraft, heard in indictments, verdicts, and sentences, was that witchcraft was possible and witches were dangerous. In the panic discussed here, there is no trace of doubt expressed on the part of the judiciary when it comes to the guilt of the adult women and their conviction. However, the sentencing of six young girls was found difficult. Moreover, Ragnilde Endresdatter and Gjertrud Siversdatter, who were sentenced together with Gundelle Olsdatter, were not executed but had their cases passed on to the Court of Appeal as well. The reason for this is not mentioned. However, each of them had a small child, and some of the denunciations of Gjertrud Siversdatter had been retracted.

The verdict and sentence of Gundelle Olsdatter is pronounced on 11 March 1663, just one month before the panic of 1662–63 ended and three months before the Court of Appeal Judge of Northern Norway, Mandrup Pedersen Schønnebøl,[219] would come to Finnmark. The Court of Appeal Judge came to Finnmark every third year and held court sessions along the Finnmark coast in the same places as the local court. Schønnebøl was a legal official who had held the position of Court of Appeal Judge since 1636, so he had practised for a long time.[220] When arriving in 1663, he brought recent ideas within the judiciary field about convictions in witchcraft trials with him, signalling a milder era in the prosecution of witches. This year, he acquitted the accused children and some adults.[221] The children were ordered to stay with their parents or foster parents, and the discussion of guilt was never brought up by Schønnebøl.[222] As a whole, managing to get a case passed to the Court of Appeal increased the chances of acquittal.[223]

Changing ideas about the seriousness and performance of witchcraft had not yet reached the local courts in Finnmark during the panic of 1662–63. In the wording of the verdict and sentence of Gundelle Olsdatter, there is no signal that a milder attitude towards convictions in witchcraft trials was coming. The rhetoric is an echo of previous decades, not a sign of a new way of thinking about witchcraft, in which the fear of 'true witches' gradually loosened its grip on the mindset of legal officials and the learned elite. The ideas about witchcraft that Schønnebøl, the Court of Appeal Judge, brought with him in the summer of 1663 were important in ending witchcraft persecution in Finnmark.[224]

The Voice of the Scribe

The court records of the 1662–63 Finnmark panic consist of fifty-five folio pages in minute books.[225] With many accused people brought before the court on the same day, the scribe faced the challenge of recording the voluminous court discourse and the content of the trials on paper. He has managed to report on around thirty people: factual information about time, place, judicial officials, names of jury members; biographical information about each of the accused women, the reasons they were brought before the court, and the accusations; factual information about circumstantial evidence, the interrogator's questions, and the accused person's confessions; and ending with information on the denunciation of newly suspected women and on the indictment, verdict, and sentence. Handling the names of so many women—not only those accused in a trial but also those who were related—requires orderliness. Recording the interrogation and confessions with so many details that even orality features and vernacular words are preserved requires good writing skills and the will to grasp as much as possible of the courtroom discourse. The task of the scribe was challenging, as he was trying hard to provide a broad picture of what happened in these winter months, mostly at Vardøhus Fortress.

The first day Gundelle Olsdatter was brought before the court, on 10 March 1663, she was the fourth woman to be questioned that day. After her, Dorette Poulsdatter was interrogated. Gundelle Olsdatter was presented, the accusations against her were listed, as was her request to be tried by the water ordeal. This is a short entry: eighteen handwritten lines in the records. The voice of the scribe is neutral but informative. The next day, when Gundelle Olsdatter was brought before the court, the killing of Dorette Poulsdatter had taken place. However, the voice of the scribe has not changed. It is expeditious, with all necessities written down. He notes the result of the water ordeal and takes down Gundelle Olsdatter's confession, which is rather brief. The brevity in, for instance, the narrative about chasing fish is perhaps a sign of an interrogation that was less intensive than previously during this panic, although Gundelle Olsdatter's reason for partaking in this act is included. However, in the narrative about the witches' meeting on Domen, details like St John's Eve and the vernacular name of Satan are inserted. In addition, Gjertrud Siversdatter's protest is given space in the records, and so is the information that Sigri Jonsdatter has retracted her denunciation of Gjertrud Siversdatter. The interrogator and the scribe know that the confession of Gundelle Olsdatter must be complete in order to end four trials. The interrogation, verdict, and sentence of four women are reported in the same way as in many earlier cases. Often, the reason that the confessing women have performed evil deeds is given, thus creating a link between the unrealistic narrative of the courtroom and their own lived experience and living conditions. This time, the scribe does not offer his own opinion or attitude to what he records.

The comprehensive scribe job is seen in the records from the entire 1662–63 panic. All factual information is reported. The scribe is trying to render utterances that were actually voiced in the courtroom. In addition, it is possible to get an impression of the interrogator's questioning and the points given priority during the interrogation. Furthermore, the content of the confessions is presented in a manner and with a degree of detail that makes it possible to obtain knowledge on ideas about witchcraft heard in the courtroom and the imagination of the questioned women. The voice of the scribe is not forthcoming with comments of his own; it is more like he is trying to keep a distance to the reported discourse and events. The scribe is characterized by a high degree of professionalism and an ambition to record the trial in such a way that the records are seen as reliable. The voice of the scribe is very closely connected to the *role* of the scribe: he sees his function as contributing with written documentation in a society that is barely mature enough, and has just started, to require records and build official archives.

Conclusion

In this chapter, the voices of three women from different parts of Norway have provided insight into ideas about healing, *maleficium*, and demonological witchcraft. In trials held in four courtrooms located far from each other, the voices of Anne Knutsdatter, tried in Stavanger and Bergen in 1584 and 1594; Sitru Pedersdatter, tried in Rygge in 1623; and Gundelle Olsdatter, tried in Vardø in Finnmark in 1663, display knowledge about not only harmful witchcraft but also healing and folkloric beliefs. The records present court practice, with a number of actors involved, in individual trials as well as panics. Courtroom discourse related to the judiciary, the witnesses, and the accused is rendered, with individualization and differentiation of the women's voices. When brought to trial, Anne Knutsdatter confessed at once to reading over a sick person, while Sitru Pedersdatter first confessed to stealing milk from cattle and later to a witches' gathering, and Gundelle Olsdatter first denied and then confessed to witchcraft after pressure. The three women were all executed by fire at the stake.

Ideas about healing as well as witchcraft come to the fore in the trials. Anne Knutsdatter's knowledge related to healing, both charms and objects, provides a glimpse of common people's belief in effective magical performance. There were charms believed to work against sickness, there was soil from the churchyard with magical powers, there was bloodletting, there were ways to reveal who was the thief. In her confession, Anne Knutsdatter willingly shared her knowledge of healing methods before the court. Divination, which was not a benevolent practice, was riskier to confess to, and afterwards she regretted having done it. People at the end of the 1500s knew that there was a division between magic used for good and for bad purposes, and they were aware of the severity that a confession to witchcraft implied.

Ideas about witchcraft encompassed *maleficium* as well as demonological ideas. Often, both concepts of witchcraft are documented in the same trial, as seen in the accusations against Sitru Pedersdatter. Ideas related to traditional harmful witchcraft—such as stealing milk—were not sufficient; therefore, demonological ideas about personal demons and flights to witches' meetings were activated. In a local community in Eastern Norway in the 1620s, orally transmitted demonological ideas played an important role. The place name of Blåkoll in this panic shows affinity with witchcraft trials occurring later in Norway and Finland, and both earlier and later in Sweden, in the versions Kullen and Blåkulla. The idea of a personal demon has a parallel in Danish trials. This signals the transnational transfer of ideas about witchcraft.

Moreover, in the trial of Gundelle Olsdatter, a spectrum of demonological ideas emerges, including the devil's pact, shape-shifting, collective witchcraft operations, and witches' meetings. In a frenzy of witchcraft persecution in Northern Norway in 1663, the voice of Gundelle Olsdatter shows that in the very north of Europe, learned ideas about witchcraft were well known by lay and learned people alike. These ideas found their way into the courtrooms, where a strongly pressured woman delivered her confession to devil service and devilish deeds.

Court practice was stern in the three trials, from the death sentence against Anne Knutsdatter in Bergen in 1594, via the death sentence against Sitru Pedersdatter in Rygge in 1623, to the death sentence of Gundelle Olsdatter in Vardø in 1663. The strictest laws in Norway, which applied in the area of Stavanger from 1583 until 1617, were practised in Anne Knutsdatter's trial, where healers and their accomplices were punished by death. Whether they were accused in a single trial or a panic did not matter. Once brought before the court, there seems to have been no way out for these women. The intensity of witchcraft persecution differed in different parts of Norway; however, the chapter has documented that the courts followed the laws on witchcraft to the letter.

Torture was used in Norwegian witchcraft trials all over the country in order to force confessions from the mouth of the accused person. In Norway, torture was allowed in witchcraft trials after the sentence was passed, in order to obtain the names of accomplices. This is when it could be entered into the records. Other uses of torture are not recorded. However, other sources clarify that deadly torture was applied illegally during the Finnmark panic of 1662–63, where the rack was in use. In Rygge, the district accounts state that torture was used during the panic in question.

The voices of the three women studied in this chapter provide a rich and fascinating range of ideas about witchcraft. Being good storytellers, the women knew by heart how to insert details and apply orality features, thus personalizing a narrative about demonic as well as malevolent witchcraft. Their voices changed from strong to weak. The turning point from denial to confession is most distinct in Gundelle Olsdatter's voice, for which the water ordeal and the terrifying news that her fellow accused had been killed on the rack silenced the attempt at resistance. Fear is voiced throughout in the three cases, from Anne Knutsdatter's regretting her confession to divination, to Sitru Pedersdatter's flight, to Gundelle Olsdatter's faint hope that she would not float when tried by the water ordeal.

In the sixteenth and seventeenth centuries, lay and learned people believed in witchcraft. Judicial officials, members of the jury, the accused, and witnesses all believed that witchcraft was possible. This was part of the mentality, of the way people looked upon the world, and of the oral stories passed on in local communities. However, witchcraft was impossible to prove. It was the laws that made this belief into a crime, and the courts that effectuated the punishment for this crime. In this respect, Norway joined the rest of the Northern European countries in treating witchcraft trials as governmental operations.

8

SWEDEN—KULLEN, BLÅKULLA, AND THE WATER MAN

In Sweden, the intensity of witchcraft persecution was average compared to that in other European countries.[1] The witchcraft trials were to a large extent characterized by *maleficium*, minor offences, and few death sentences. Most of the trials took place in the southern part of the country. However, there are some exceptions, most famously the Blåkulla[2] trials, in which demonological ideas were central. Sweden was divided into three regions: Götaland in the south, Svealand in the middle, and Norrland in the north. The Blåkulla trials began in Dalarne,[3] a province in the north of Svealand, and spread to Norrland, Uppland, and Stockholm from 1668 to 1676.[4] During these trials, a large number of child witnesses testified that they were abducted to a witches' sabbath at a hill called Blåkulla. The children denounced many adults.

I have chosen three Swedish witchcraft trials that exemplify chronology, different locations, and differences in content. The first is the trial of Ingegärd Andersdotter, which took place in 1594 in Kronoberg District,[5] in Småland in Götaland. The second is the trial of Karin Persdotter, which took place in 1653 in Uppvidinge municipality, also situated in Småland. The third is the trial of Karin, wife of Daniel Dantz, 1673–74. It took place before the local court in the town of Sundsvall in Norrland, close to the coast of the Gulf of Bothnia. The trial was part of the Blåkulla trials.

This timeline provides Swedish witchcraft trials occurring over a period of eighty years. It includes trials from Götaland and Norrland. As for content, the voices of women, in the accused persons' confessions as well as in witnesses' testimonies, display a range of ideas related to demonological witchcraft and maleficent witchcraft, in addition to beneficent magic (healing). The female voices heard in the trials provide glimpses of how new ideas about witchcraft connected to older ones in the mental realm of common people in seventeenth-century Sweden.

DOI: 10.4324/9781003255406-8

Both the confessions and the testimonies are narratives, and are formed according to narrative structures. Analysis of courtroom discourse will take into account the way these narratives were told and what kind of strategies the accused women and the witnesses used when communicating in the courtroom. The women lived in predominantly oral societies, and orality features colour the language. These also show an individualized language: each of the accused has put her own stamp on her formulations. The confessions also make it possible to trace leading questions posed during interrogation, thus echoing the interrogator's voice. In all confessions, new and learned ideas alongside with traditional ideas come to the fore.

The chapter aims at examining various accents of the female voices, particularly in the confessions. Through the close reading of confessions, a possible turning point of the trial will be looked for, as several trials start with the accused person denying witchcraft and then suddenly changing to confessing to it. This movement often reveals emotions, as a strong and protesting accent of the accused person's voice is replaced by a subdued and frightened accent.

The role of the scribe will be looked at, particularly whether his voice can be traced in the records. A professional attitude is present in a scribe's work, who records what is happening from the beginning to the end of a trial. However, he can also influence the court records. Whether he uses this possibility, abandoning a neutral position and surfacing as a subjective voice, reveals his attitude to what is being recorded.

For each of the trials, a description of the trial will be followed by an analysis of the accused woman's voice. This analysis comprises the main part of the chapter. In addition, comments on the voices of the witnesses, the voice of the interrogator, the voice of the law, and the voice of the scribe will be provided. In closing, the main findings of the chapter will be summarized.

Background

Persecution

The first documented Swedish witchcraft trial took place in 1471. The early trials (from 1471 to 1614) have been studied by Bengt Ankarloo, who found records from 171 cases: 4 from the late 1400s, 91 from the 1500s (of which 61 were from the period 1580–99), and the rest occurring in 1600–14.[6] The bulk of trials in this period took place between 1580 and 1614.

Sweden's later witchcraft trials from the southernmost area have been closely studied by Per Sörlin. The cases were brought before the Göta High Court, which was founded in 1634: 'In all, 515 cases of witchcraft and minor magic were submitted to the Göta High Court between 1634–1779, i.e. from the founding of the High Court to the abolishment of the death sentence for witchcraft by Gustav III'.[7] Between 1634 and 1754, 353 witchcraft cases were submitted, involving 880 persons.[8] Most of these were accused of 'innocent' forms of witchcraft, such as superstition[9] and 'white magic'. The majority of cases took place in the south of

Sweden.[10] Very few of these trials ended in a sentence of execution.[11] Punishment mostly ranged from fines to imprisonment. But those who practiced malevolent witchcraft often received harsher punishments, such as death by beheading or by fire at the stake. The prevailing accusation in witchcraft and magic cases submitted to the Göta High Court was superstition,[12] followed by *maleficium* and demono-logical witchcraft as the most frequent accusations.[13] In the latter half of the 1600s, witchcraft trials also occurred in areas that belonged to Sweden in the 1600s and to Finland today.[14] During the period of witchcraft persecution, the same legislation was valid for Sweden and Finland.

During the second half of the seventeenth century, the number of witchcraft trials increased. Demonological ideas influenced persecution. Interrogation tech-niques foreign to Swedish legal traditions began to be employed, such as torture and the water ordeal. This new type of demonic witchcraft was prosecuted along with *maleficium*. Sweden experienced outbreaks of large-scale witchcraft trials with the Blåkulla trials in the 1660s and the 1670s and the witchcraft trials of Bohuslän County (1669–72).

The first evidence of Blåkulla in Swedish folklore is found in church paintings in Uppland in the region Svealand in mid-Sweden from the latter half of the fif-teenth century.[15] Then, in 1555, Olaus Magnus mentions the image of a Nordic witches' meeting place in his well-known history book about the Nordic people. He writes about a place called Jungfrun,[16] a desolate and forbidding rock island in the southern Baltic.[17] This was the Northern Scandinavian equivalent to the Ger-man mountain Brocken.[18]

From the late 1500s onwards, the concept of Blåkulla, combined with demono-logical ideas, is found in witchcraft confessions in Sweden. Secular courts began to act against forms of witchcraft related to the witches' sabbath, journeys to Blåkulla, the devil's pact, and intercourse with the devil. At the same time, Continental legal practices can be distinguished. Interrogations were accompanied by water ordeals, shaving, and formal torture.[19] However, most of these trials were restricted to Götaland in the south. Bengt Ankarloo states that the first decades of the sev-enteenth century were crucial to the introduction of modern demonological and legal concepts of witchcraft in Sweden:

> The witches' sabbath was easily accepted in popular tradition, since it was perceived merely as an extension or elaboration of local beliefs, going back at least to the late Middle Ages, in night-flying women and a witches' gather-ing at Blåkulla.[20]

During the Blåkulla trials, the demonological notion of the witches' gathering was prominent. A great number of children's testimonies resulted in denuncia-tions and the subsequent imprisonment and execution of many individuals.[21] In addition, the Bohuslän trials were a mixture of *maleficium* trials and demonologi-cal trials. After these massive witch-hunts ended, the courts continued to pros-ecute magic-related crimes for at least a hundred years. In Southern Sweden's

Göta High Court (Göta Hovrätt), for example, three out of four cases took place after 1700.[22]

The execution rate in Swedish witchcraft trials varied with regard to time and location. Bengt Ankarloo argues that courts tended to be lenient in Swedish witchcraft trials, condemning only one in ten defendants while acquitting over 60%.[23] The number of executions during the Blåkulla trials is estimated to have been between 240 and 300.[24] As for witchcraft trials in the area of Bohuslän, the number of executions was 29.[25] Per Sörlin states that apart from the Blåkulla and Bohuslän witchcraft trials, no more than 100 persons were executed for witchcraft in Sweden from 1550 to 1750.[26] To sum up: in all of Sweden, which had a population of 800,000 in 1600, about 350–400 persons were sentenced to death in witchcraft trials, usually by beheading and then fire at the stake.[27]

Jurisdiction

In the Middle Ages, the provincial Swedish laws were concerned with harmful witchcraft. The oldest recorded laws were written down in the thirteenth century. For witchcraft that was physically injurious to human beings, *maleficium*,[28] the punishment was outlawing:

> the victim's kinsmen were free to take revenge and kill the witch. However, this very old form of penalty was soon replaced throughout the system by a formal death penalty. At the same time, the crime was extended so that the killing of cattle by magic was also deemed to be a capital offence.[29]

This tendency was most evident in Götaland, the southernmost of the three Swedish regions, and probably spurred on by the church. In the thirteenth century, statutes against superstitious practices of a less harmful nature were also adopted.[30] Such cases were to be brought before a bishop's court.[31]

To the north of Götaland, in the region of Svealand, provincial Swedish laws were different. Only fatal *maleficium* against human beings was included among capital offences. Other harmful but non-fatal forms were punished by fines. The bishop's court was not mentioned, so the church seemed to have less influence than in the southern provinces.[32]

The laws from Svealand were to be models for the witchcraft paragraphs in the national law code from the fourteenth century, the National Law of Magnus Eriksson,[33] and its fifteenth-century revision, the National Law of Kristoffer.[34] Both laws had statutes dealing with harmful witchcraft.[35] The National Law of Kristoffer legislated only against enrooted, harmful witchcraft, and prescribed death sentences only in cases of harmful witchcraft. These statutes were in force until the first half of the eighteenth century.[36] The laws provided no clear guidelines on how to deal with harmless magic, even if occasional supplements to the statutes were issued.[37]

A broader definition of witchcraft was applied in the sixteenth and first half of the seventeenth century.[38] Learned European ideas on demonology made their impact. Ideas about the devil's pact and witches' sabbaths entered the picture. Various forms of consorting with the devil were gradually placed on the same level as maleficent sorcery. In addition, biblical law was consulted when passing sentences for serious cases of witchcraft.[39] In 1609, biblical law[40] was accepted in Sweden, although some judges based their verdicts on the National Law of Kristoffer.

The court system in seventeenth-century Sweden was divided into three levels: the local courts, the High Courts, and the Supreme Court. The local courts were first instance courts, with a *häradshövding* in charge of the court district, the *tingslag*. There was a jury system, *en nämnd*, consisting of twelve trustworthy men from the community who decided on guilt. The first of the twelve was called *häradsdomare* and was to communicate the *nämnd*'s decision to the *häradshövding*. Local peasantry, often prominent persons, acted as co-judges while serving in the *nämnd*.[41] This was the same system as in Norway and Denmark. The High Courts were established in various parts of the Swedish kingdom during the first half of the seventeenth century. These courts were second instance courts, and functioned as courts for cases that had already been dealt with by local courts. The lower courts could pass cases over to the High Courts for a final decision. The Svea High Court in Stockholm was instituted in 1614 by Gustavus Adolphus. It was a second instance court. It was also possible to turn directly to the monarch for appeals, which were handled by the Justice Department of the Privy Council.[42] After 1614, the central authorities took firmer control of legal practice. All death sentences, except for murder, were to be brought to Stockholm for final approval. Sörlin states: 'Thus a system took shape whose main purpose was to strengthen state control over the local judiciary'.[43] Svea High Court cooperated with the church and upheld this procedure of final approval of witchcraft cases in Stockholm until the 1650s. This led to a low number of executions. After 1650, demonological ideas became more influential, which affected sentencing in witchcraft trials. During the Blåkulla trials, when evidence provided by children and accomplices was taken into account, the Svea High Court departed from its cautious line and confirmed many of the death penalties.[44]

Sweden's judicial system was based on accusatorial procedure: it required a plaintiff for each case. After 1600, royal officials in local courts assumed the role of public prosecutor in order to prosecute crimes that lacked a plaintiff. At the same time, secular courts gradually acquired the sole right to punish witchcraft of all sorts. Up to 1600, the church had gained support for the punishment of harmless magic.[45] Sweden's medieval laws were reformed in a way that had constraining as well as stimulating effects on witchcraft trials, not least seen in how torture was applied.

In witchcraft trials in general, a confession from the accused person's own mouth was imperative, because the crime was impossible to prove. Therefore, circumstantial evidence was used to increase the probability of guilt. In addition, torture to press forth a confession and obtain names of accomplices entered into the picture. Originally, torture was explicitly forbidden in Swedish legal proceedings. Still, coercive methods were openly and regularly employed in witchcraft cases. Exceptions with regard to the use of torture were made, for instance for special itinerant witchcraft courts or 'Troldoms commissioner'. A special law stated that these courts could do what they felt was reasonable.[46] The use of torture before a sentence was passed and threats of torture are documented also for the areas of today's Finland, for instance in the Åland witchcraft trials in 1666. These were used to force a confession and obtain names of accomplices.[47] A death sentence in Sweden required 'crystal-clear grounds and an unforced confession'.[48] The understanding of 'unforced confession' varied from country to country. In Norway, for instance, an 'unforced confession' was frequently interpreted as a confession given voluntarily in the courtroom shortly after torture had been applied.[49]

After the establishment of the High Courts, only they could grant a lower court permission to use forcible methods. However, the High Courts often played a passive role when it came to the use of torture. On the one hand, they did not sanction it; on the other, they did not disallow it. Even if they were prepared to reject applications for the use of torture, they accepted the method when confronted with its use.[50] Permission to use torture could also be given by direct royal decree. There are indications that both the High Courts and the king himself regarded torture as justifiable and suitable in witchcraft cases.[51] There was a connection with Continental doctrine.[52]

Also, accusations of gossip and slander were brought before the courts. A particular type of oath, *värjemålsed*, was important in Swedish litigation. It could be used in court to repudiate accusations, often when persons wanted to defend themselves. Those who swore this oath were called *edgärdsmän*. Through their oath, they had to convince the court that the accused person spoke the truth and was a man or woman of honour. Men swore to support men and women to support women.[53]

In 1665, the government issued a special regulation against white magic and superstition,[54] but it did not contain a clear recommendation for specific punishments. This regulation was renewed in 1687, this time with a relatively clear list of prescribed sentences.[55]

In the decades after 1687, scattered individual cases of witchcraft were still sent to the Court of Appeal. The experiences from the great witch-hunt were repeated in the 1720s, when tales of Blåkulla were told in Värmland in the western part of the country. All the verdicts from the lower courts, however, were in this case reversed in the Court of Appeal, and the most active persecutors were punished. In the New National Code of 1734, *maleficium* was still a capital offence. The statute was never used and finally taken off the book in 1779.[56]

Ingegärd Andersdotter, 1594

The Trial

On 4 June 1594, Ingegärd Andersdotter was brought before a court in a local trial held in Brännebo, Kronoberg County,[57] which was a part of the region Småland in Southern Sweden.[58] This was not Ingegärd's home town, as she lived in Vartofta[59]—in Habo Parish, Skaraborg County[60]—which is located a bit further to the north. She must therefore have been taken from her home town to be interrogated. There were a number of witchcraft trials in these regions in the late 1500s.[61] The court records of her trial, written in the Gothic hand, are kept in Vadstena Regional State Archives.[62]

During the trial, District Governor Lars Jonsson the older[63] of Visningsborg County[64] functioned as a 'law reader', *lagläsare*,[65] in the place of District Governor Hieronymus Augustinus von Udden[66] of Vartofta municipality in Skaraborg County. Lars Jonsson was an experienced legal official. He had held court in Habo Parish for a number of years, and on this occasion also in Brännebo.[67] In the records, he refers to himself in the first person, as 'I',[68] which probably means that he was also the scribe. The bailiff was Håkon Anderson,[69] and a jury composed of twelve local men, a *nämnd*, was to decide on the verdict and sentence. The executioner,[70] Håkon, lived in Jönköping, but he must have travelled to this examination location because his search for the devil's mark took place in the court building in Brännebo. The executioner was trained on the Continent so he could provide expertise on the subject in his home country.[71] Instruments of torture were available in Sweden at this time, as evidenced by the court records.

It is possible that Ingegärd Andersdotter was brought before the court in a county that was not her home county because she had been a witness in a trial in another district just before her trial.[72] She might also have been imprisoned in Vartofta and then sent to Brännebo for the trial. However, it is recorded that the bailiff, Håkon Anderson, and Håkon in Gulskog asked the public at the beginning of the court meeting on 4 June whether they, at any time, thought that they, the judicial officials, had hidden Ingegärd Andersdotter from the court when the court was held in Ebbarp. The response from the members of the public was that they 'never knew that anything like that had happened', and further, that Ingegärd Andersdotter 'herself confessed before the court that it never happened'.[73] This means that the court had had a session in Ebbarp outside Jönköping before they came to Brännebo, and thus that it was possible to bring an accused person before the court in various places outside their home town.

Ingegärd Andersdotter had a nickname—the German Beetle[74]—which might mean that she was originally German or had some kind of relation to Germany. She was accused in a trial that was linked to other witchcraft trials through denunciations. In her confession, she mentioned the name of the woman who had taught her witchcraft: Kirstin in Maden.[75] Several other names of suspects came up during the trial. Ingegärd Andersdotter was accused of having taught witchcraft to Karin Bengtsdotter. Several witnesses testified that they had seen another woman, Margrit in Knutshult, riding on a wolf, which might imply riding to a witches' sabbath, and that she performed witchcraft. After this, Margrit was immediately brought before the court.

Ingegärd Andersdotter gave a devil's pact confession, even though the trial began as a *maleficium* trial. She was first questioned about what kind of 'art' she used to perform the 'evil deed' she was suspected of: that she had taught Karin Bengtsdotter witchcraft—indeed, that she had taught Karin Bengtsdotter how to cast a harmful spell on her neighbours' cattle. As a result, Karin had allegedly carried witchcraft, in the form of some animal hair, to Nils in Hallbo's farm, and he had lost his best cow. Following this, two of his oxen were destroyed, such that their feet 'rotted off' and their ears 'fell from their heads'.[76]

After this line of questioning, however, the trial took a turn. The executioner, Håkon in Jönköping, examined and searched Ingegärd Andersdotter in the court building[77] in Jönköping. The Swedish verbs used in the records for his search are *ransakat* and *utletat*. These two words have almost the same meaning: *Ransaka* means to perform an examination, search for something; it may also mean to conduct a personal or bodily search. *Utleta* means to explore, investigate, also question.[78] This means that the executioner, with his Continental training and ideas, most probably searched her body for the devil's mark. In the late 1600s, many European countries used witch-pricking to provide circumstantial evidence in witchcraft trials.[79] In addition, he—or others—might have questioned her during the search, as Ingegärd Andersdotter confessed to witchcraft either during or just after the search. The same confession was given afterwards in the courtroom.[80] She was asked how she had learned 'the art of the devil' and answered that there was a little hill near a field close to Maden,[81] and that she and Kirstin in Maden went to this hill, Kullen. There, they had met a small companion,[82] who asked Ingegärd whether she would serve him. She responded: 'I will follow Kirstin in Maden—what she commands me to do, I will do'.[83] The small companion had then asked her to give him her hand. When she had done so, he had given her cheese and bread.[84] The next time Ingegärd Andersdotter went to Kullen, he had given her half a bushel of malt.

Ingegärd Andersdotter was sentenced to death;[85] the only death sentence in Habo in 1594. There were in fact five acquittals in 1594 in that county: one in Vista, two in Habo, one in Vartofta, and one in Hanekind.[86] With regard to Margrit in Knutshult, who was tried shortly after Ingegärd Andersdotter (in June 1594), two male witnesses testified that they had seen her ride a wolf in Knutshult. Other accusations against her were that she cast spells on a cow, causing its death, because she asked the owners for the cow but was not given it. Two other male witnesses testified that Margrit had cursed and threatened people, resulting in sickness and death. Even though the witnesses testifying in court were all men, they referred to women who had heard that Margrit had threatened others when she became angry. Many witnesses confirmed threats made by Margrit, which were allegedly related to envy, often led to misfortune on the part of those threatened.[87] The ruling of the local court, based on testimonies and proofs, was that 'I and the jury cannot acquit Margrit's life'.[88] Lars Jonsson, the *lagläsare*, emerged here as an 'I'. The case was sent to higher judicial authorities for further handling.[89]

The Voice of Ingegärd Andersdotter

The voice of Ingegärd Andersdotter is rendered in the court records in indirect and direct speech. It surfaces most clearly in her confession, which is a brief narrative. Her voice is rendered in third-person narration (indirect speech) as well as in first-person narration (direct speech) when the entering of the devil's pact is recounted. Indirect speech is also found in answers to questions posed to her by the interrogator and initiated by a reporting verb: 'then she answered'.[90] Inserted into this narrative is the direct speech of Karin Bengtsdotter in the first person: the answer she gives to the devil. She is quoting what she answered when the devil asked whether she would serve him. Also, the voice of Margrit in Knutshult is rendered in direct and indirect speech; direct speech is used particularly in her threats.

Ingegärd Andersdotter's voice may also be traced in the beginning of the trial, even if it is not rendered in the records. She is questioned about teaching witchcraft to Karin Bengtsdotter, and Ingegärd must have denied; otherwise, the executioner would not have been called in and it would not have been necessary to search her body.

The questions posed to Ingegärd Andersdotter initially come to the fore in the court records regarding her alleged teaching of witchcraft to Karin Bengtsdotter, resulting in Nils in Hallbo's loss of cattle. We hear an oral accent in the retelling of these incidents, with the exaggeration common in orally transmitted stories. Ingegärd Andersdotter is asked before the court what art she used so that Karin Bengtsdotter could perform this witchcraft, but she does not answer.

The first time we hear Ingegärd Andersdotter's own voice rendered during the trial is when members of the public present at court are approached and asked whether they heard that the judicial officials 'hid' Ingegärd from the court.[91] To this, the members of the public answer in the negative: they 'never knew such a thing to have happened'.[92] As Ingegärd Andersdotter herself denies this as well, we can surmise that she is asked to confirm that the judiciary did not previously help her escape.

The searching of her body leads to a concurrent change in the voice of Ingegärd Andersdotter. Torture is not mentioned. Permission to use torture in lower courts had to be requested from the High Court.[93] Very little torture was used in witchcraft trials within the jurisdiction of Göta High Court.[94] In this case, the executioner had an 'expert' reputation and certainly represented a threat. It is clear that Ingegärd first confessed to witchcraft during or just after the executioner's examination. Thus, the search is crucial to Ingegärd's resistance and to the turning point of her voice. It is also at this point that demonological ideas enter the trial. When Ingegärd Andersdotter is asked how she learned 'the devil's art', she answers with a demonological narrative that contains several core elements: the meeting with the devil at a hill, the devil's question about service, her acceptance of this by a gesture of giving the devil her hand, and the reception of gifts of food from the devil. The food was ostensibly offered to her by the devil as a token of the pact.

Narrative structures surface in her confession: it is a story with a timeline, an order of events during the ritual of entering the devil's pact, in which she meets the devil twice; there is variation between rapidly and slowly moving passages of text, as she inserts a quote in direct speech; there is a repetitive element in the devil's handing over of gifts, and the mood in Ingegärd Andersdotter's confession reveals no distance or scepticism on her behalf towards what is told. The way she appears as a narrator in her confession seems to confirm her own belief in the content of the devil's pact narrative. As a narrator, she uses her authority by assigning a voice to the devil in her narration about the pact. These narrative strategies point towards her being familiar with the major elements of a demonological narrative.

After her first denial of witchcraft, and after the search of her body, Ingegärd Andersdotter is cooperative in relating what she knows regarding the art of witchcraft. No hesitation is heard. The result of the executioner's search is not noted. Most likely, he found the devil's mark on her body, since the trial ended in a death sentence. In any case, the meeting with the executioner leads to her confession. If the devil's mark was found, she would have known the consequences.

The interrogator's question concerning how she learned the devil's art is clearly a question of a demonological nature, and her response is to relate her devil's pact narrative. The interrogation is steered in the direction of demonic witchcraft, inviting Ingegärd Andersdotter to respond with her knowledge. She willingly confesses, using a story that she obviously heard before: about Kullen, about the small companion and the pact, about the devil's promise and his command. Thus, we see that two mighty men became decisive in the development of her trial. The executioner was an important person when it came to pressing forth Ingegärd Andersdotter's confession. So was the interrogator in the courtroom, posing leading questions.

However, the coherent narrative about the devil's pact—as told in response to a question—must be Ingegärd Andersdotter's own. Her confession has details that only she could have known about. This points to an individualized confession: the name of her accomplice, Kirstin in Maden; the name of the meeting place, the hill named Kullen; the act of being initiated into the service of the devil; and, finally, her own words as she answered the devil on how she would serve him. It is very unlikely that all these details were placed in her mouth by the interrogators.

Orality features permeate Ingegärd Andersdotter's confession: for instance, the exaggeration in the image of the oxen's rotting feet and their ears falling off their heads. The exact description of the witchcraft brought to a man's farm—in the form of the hair of all animals on the farm—demonstrates orality features in its precision. The same holds true for other parts of Ingegärd Andersdotter's confession: she came twice to a meeting with the devil, and twice he gave her gifts. Even if the number three is not used, we see the increased tension in the text that is generated by repetition. An additive sentence structure is another marked linguistic feature in her confession: events are combined, using 'then', 'then', and 'then' in order to syntactically join elements at the sentence level. The liveliness of the short narrative of temptation and Ingegärd's entering the pact, with the variation in her voice between indirect speech and first-person narration, is typical for oral tales, as an important feature of an oral story is the variation in the speed of the narrative in order to retain the listeners' attention. The rendering of direct speech slows down the speed. Cause-and-effect logic is seen in the initial interrogation, when Ingegärd Andersdotter is asked which arts she used when she taught Karin Bengtsdotter how to cast spells. The connection is clear in that, first, witchcraft was carried to the farm of Nils in Hallbo, and immediately afterwards, the catastrophe happened. The notion here is that witches can plant objects in a specific place and cause misfortune and disaster. The order of events—what occurred first and what resulted (immediately) from this—is here used as important 'proof' to show that it was indeed witchcraft that had been performed. The cause-and-effect logic is also seen in the testimony against Margrit in Knutshult: once she promised evil, it occurred immediately.

The name of the place where Ingegärd Andersdotter allegedly met with the devil is Kullen, a hill located near Maden.[95] The first syllable of the name Kullen is orthographically and semantically identical to the second syllable of the name Blåkulla: *kull* or *kolle* means hill. The name Kullen or Blåkulla was used for a nearby hill or mountain where witches' gatherings took place.[96] It is likely that the notion of the hill entered Sweden from the south; however, it soon spread to Norway as well.[97] While Ingegärd Andersdotter's trial took place in Götaland in Southern Sweden, it was not until about seventy years later that a huge number of Blåkulla witchcraft trials took place in Northern Sweden.

The motif of Kullen must have been a new idea in 1594 Götaland. The trial of Ingegärd Andersdotter is an early documentation of this notion. In 1596, at a witchcraft trial in Stockholm, a woman confessed that she rode to Blåkulla, where she had intercourse with the devil.[98] In neighbouring Nordic countries, this motif is also found in witchcraft trials in the 1620s, when a meeting place for witches, called Blåkoll, is documented in the south-eastern part of Norway. It is also documented in the mid-eastern part of Norway, not far from the Swedish border, in the 1670s.[99]

The Kullen motif in Ingegärd Andersdotter's confession seems to stem from orally transmitted tales about the devil. Her way of narration, brief and effective, signals that she knew the main content before she was brought to trial. This means that ideas of witches' meetings and the devil's pact, related to Continental demonology, were known in a community in Småland by this time. Also, the executioner's search points to knowledge of demonological ideas in this region in the late 1500s.[100] When there is a turning point in a witchcraft trial from denial to confession, the question will always be, why did the accused person confess? If Ingegärd Andersdotter knew the basic story of the devil's pact, she also knew how dangerous it was to deliver such a confession—as such, it is likely that after having been searched by the executioner, she was exhausted and despairing.

Ingegärd Andersdotter's apparent initial refusal to confess was likely due to her fear of the trial's outcome. The turning point of the trial was the executioner's search. She must have been aware that further searching awaited her if she did not confess. As with most—if not all—others who confessed to demonological witchcraft, Ingegärd Andersdotter saw no way out of the situation, even if she knew that she was sealing her fate.

The trial of Ingegärd Andersdotter shows that a confession to the devil's pact and witches' meetings in Southern Sweden in 1594 resulted in a death sentence. Whether Ingegärd Andersdotter's nickname, German Beetle, signals that she had a connection to Germany and ideas on witchcraft there cannot be ascertained. What is clear is that demonological ideas in witchcraft trials in Sweden appeared about seventy years later in the north and had a particularly strong impact during the Blåkulla trials in the 1660s and 1670s. Shape-shifting is not mentioned in the trial of Ingegärd, but witnesses mention a woman allegedly riding on a wolf, a motif which is a mythological archetype and apparently was seen as a suspicious act. The trial emphasizes demonological witchcraft, based on leaving the pact with God and entering into the devil's pact. The ritual included getting a small companion, shaking hands with him, and receiving food, cheese, bread, and malt. However, the performance of *maleficium* also plays a role, providing a glimpse of traditional ideas about witchcraft.

Other Female Voices

In addition to the voice of Ingegärd Andersdotter, two other female voices can be heard in the court records. One is the voice of Margrit in Knutshult. Witnesses twice mention her threats: First, she was not content with a cow she bought, as she wanted to have another cow, and she said that the farmer would have little gain from the cow which he refused to sell to her.[101] Second, she wished the people on a farm a devilish journey.[102] In both cases, her threats came true. The cow died, the son of the farmer was bedridden with disease for eighteen weeks, before his thigh burst asunder and he became a cripple and finally died, and the wife and daughter of the farmer also lost their lives.[103] The way these incidents are told creates an unquestioned connection between her threat and the accidents that followed as a result. Margrit also had some negative comments about the cow that died. The testimonies against her portray a person to be feared: one who knows witchcraft and whose threatening words always come true. Her image is characterized by strong statements rooted in envy and anger and lay the groundwork for another trial.

The other female voice that can be listened out for in the records is the voice of a woman called Elinne, who visited Margrit in Knutshult and heard her curse the people of Jon in Lindholt by the table in Margrit's home.[104] Two male witnesses later visited Elinne and heard her retelling of Margrit's threatening words, which were in turn linked to tragic events. Thus, this testimony in court is a result of a retelling of Margrit's words in two rounds by different people. However, the judiciary still considered this valid proof.

The Voices of the Witnesses

Five witnesses are heard in this trial, all men. They testify against Ingegärd Andersdotter as well as Margrit in Knutshult. The arguments of the men are related to *maleficium*, except that one of them allegedly saw Margrit riding a wolf, which echoes the motif of a witch's night flight to sabbath. All witnesses point to maleficent witchcraft resulting in the sickness and death of human beings and cattle, and they argue that casting spells is effective and has disastrous results. By giving a detailed description of the charms used for witchcraft performance and by quoting the suspected women's direct and indirect speech, the testimonies stand as lively descriptions of malevolent witchcraft and the motives for casting evil spells. The tragic accidents of daily life in a sixteenth-century small Swedish village provide plenty of reasons to blame witches for what went wrong. There is a strict logic in the testimonies, and narrative strategies applied show that the male witnesses were good storytellers.

The Voice of the Interrogator

The voice of the interrogator is heard a few times during Ingegärd Andersdotter's trial. The first time has to do with the art she used to teach Karin Bengtsdotter witchcraft.[105] The maleficent witchcraft Ingegärd allegedly taught her is elaborated on, but the devil is not mentioned. The interrogator's voice emphasizes Ingegärd Andersdotter's role as mentor and underpins an accusation of *maleficium*, which was the main reason for legal action against persons suspected of witchcraft in Sweden at the end of the sixteenth century.[106] Ingegärd's own voice is not heard at this stage.

It is a bit unclear whether Ingegärd Andersdotter was interrogated in the course of the executioner's search or just afterwards. Either option is possible, because it is recorded that she confessed to the same before the court.[107] Who were present during the executioner's search is not noted. Usually, judicial officials as well as ministers were present during an executioner's examination of a suspect.[108] If the interrogator was present, he could have asked questions to press forth a confession. However, there is also the possibility that the executioner himself pressed for a confession and reported this to the judicial officials.

The next time we hear the interrogator is in the courtroom, after the search. The interrogator initiates her confession: he asks Ingegärd Andersdotter how she learned the devil's art.[109] This question displays the judiciary's conviction that her art was related to the devil. She answers with a narrative about the main elements of her entering the pact, agreeing to serve the devil, and sealing the pact with a ritual. The ritual retold in this confession is rather down-to-earth: She is asked whether she will serve him, she gives him her hand to seal the pact, and she agrees to follow the commands of one of the devil's allies. We do not hear about sexual intercourse with the devil as part of entering the pact. Indeed, the entire confession is short and without any ornamentation. There is no follow-up question, which means that no more details were considered necessary. The interrogator has obtained an answer that he is content with: a confession linked to demonology. It seems clear that the trial started as a *maleficium* case and was turned towards demonological content the moment the executioner was brought in. The voice of the interrogator shows that witchcraft as a devilish art was on the radar of the judiciary.

The Voice of the Law

The voice of the law is heard several times during the trial. It points to central legal principles, including the stipulation that according to the law, one who attributes evil to another person should not be believed.[110] Also, the practice of asking common people present at court for testimony about the correctness of the court's handling of a suspect shows that the court adhered to accepted rules. The witnesses swear their oaths on the criminal code book, which is a signal of the court's correct practice and its ambition to obtain reliable testimonies.

The voice of the law is also heard in the court records of the trial of Margrit in Knutshult. There is a formulation that strongly emphasizes the cause and effect of curses: many men testify that that many of those she quarrels with or envies certainly get what is evil.[111] It is stated that according to the testimonies and proof, the *lagläsare* and the jury cannot 'acquit Margrit's life' but are passing her case on to the High Court.[112] Lars Jonsson, *lagläsare*, comes to the fore as an 'I'.[113] This ruling shows that in capital cases a second instance court controlled legal practice.

Torture was not entered into the records. If the devil's mark was found, it could have served as circumstantial evidence. However, nothing more is said about the result of the search. No request to Göta High Court for the permission to use torture was sent.[114] Still, the local court's use of the executioner is an effective form of pressure. In this trial, what is called an 'unforced' confession might have been the one that Ingegärd Andersdotter delivered before the court after the executioner searched her. This is in accordance with Per Sörlin's argument that when it came to the use of force in lower courts, responsibility lay with a passive High Court: 'the moving forces behind the use of torture were the lower courts or regional officials, whose improvisational methods did not seem to have elicited much of a reaction from the High Court'.[115]

The Voice of the Scribe

The work of the scribe is diligent. All necessary information is recorded: date and location of the court session, the names of the judicial officials, the names of the jury members, the accusations, the names of the witnesses, the testimonies, the confession, the denunciation of others, the verdict, and the sentence. The court records are accurate as for the names of the participants in the trial, the places they live, and their words spoken in the courtroom. The events recorded are coherent and easy to follow from beginning to end. There is one point, however, that was possibly shortened: the work of the executioner. It remains unclear what kind of search he performed, and whether he himself questioned Ingegärd Andersdotter. If only a search for the devil's mark was performed, the rendering in the records covers the events. If torture was used, it was not recorded, possibly because torture was forbidden in Swedish legal proceedings.[116] Thus, the scribe is aware of what he should not include in the records.

Karin Persdotter, 1653

The Trial

On 30 September 1653, a trial was held before the local court[117] in Uppvidinge, at the Lenhovda court.[118] The court records are written in the Gothic hand and entered into a book of court proceedings, folio format. These minutes have been preserved in the Regional State Archives of Vadstena.

Lenhovda is a village in the Uppvidinge municipality in Småland's Kronoberg District, in the far south of Sweden. In this trial, Johan Johansen in Växjö[119]— accountant of Kronoberg District—functioned in the place of the district governor.[120] In addition, a *nämnd* was tasked with deciding the trial's outcome. In the margin of the court records is written: 'Karin Pedersdotter witch'.[121] The document was delivered from the local court to Göta High Court, the Court of Appeal, on 16 October 1653.

The records state that a very old[122] woman, Karin Persdotter from Ulvaskog, was led before the court because of complaints that she was dangerous and caused misfortune.[123] Accusations from several witnesses are recorded, and so are Karin Persdotter's own answers to the accusations. It is recorded that the previous winter, a woman living in a house on the same farm as Karin[124] had lost three calves that were half a year old. An unmarried woman,[125] Karin Persdotter, was believed to have caused this, as she always had been associated with sorcery.[126] Many people used to come to Karin to be taught things they wanted to learn from her.[127] For her trouble,[128] she charged them twelve *öre*;[129] money she would then hand over to 'him' in places with brooks or lakes, bridges over roaring water,[130] and related things.[131] The court records mention in brackets that by 'him' the Evil One was meant.[132] Most likely, this is a comment from the interrogator, but it might also be Karin Persdotter's answer to a question posed to her. She said that it was from 'him' that she obtained advice, lessons, and strength for her continued work. This, she said, was the same as what 'many trustworthy witnesses will testify under oath':[133] when she received the twelve *öre* from someone, she left every Tuesday or Thursday, at dinnertime or at sunrise or sunset, encouraged the Evil One to meet her, and had conversations with him about all that she might need.[134] This she expressed[135] of her own free will and in the presence of many people and, for this reason, she was often called the 'wise woman' in the neighbourhood.[136] It is recorded that for these reasons, everyone would prove her to be an old witch.[137] Thus an old man, Jon in Åmatorp, also spent twelve *öre* on her, so that she with her 'principals'[138] would help him with his severe illness, which did not happen; his illness only worsened.[139]

A woman, Kirstin in Håkonamåla, testified that eleven years ago, she had an ill mother's sister home on the bench,[140] and therefore she thought she would seek help from this cunning woman,[141] and gave her twelve *öre*, which she later demanded back because she did not get any help. The records further state that in Konga district,[142] Möre, and other places far away it is told that people sought out this woman[143] for the sake of her sorcery,[144] so that it is unheard of,[145] and that this creature lives and publicly assures people of help that will be provided. However, nobody was found who could speak of her work's good effects,[146] unless she promised anybody evil; they would say that it happens, as with the above-mentioned two [*sic*] calves.

The witness Per Gudmundson in Ulvaskog[147] testified that this Karin Persdotter said to his wife: 'Because you, Ramfred, hit me on the mouth (. . .) you shall have shame'.[148] Within two years, one cow would get loose, and the calves would die. The records go on to state that thereafter, the trustworthy man Per Gudmundson testified that eight weeks ago on this day, his wife fell sick with an illness which nobody understood, because she got worse day by day, and this sickness she herself thought was the result of the healer, who some days before his wife became sick had walked around by herself and muttered things (because she owned one-sixth of the farm and lived there).[149] What the trustworthy woman and her child had heard, was: '*Ja, Ja*, they should get shame'.[150] She repeated these words constantly[151] for several days.

At last, the wife told her husband about this daily threat: 'Husband, God bless us, what could happen to us now, as Karin still goes and mutters her threats'. Then her husband, the farmer, said to his wife: 'Do you know what she wants, when she walks around like this?'[152] She said: 'No, unless it is that she does not get from us everything that she wants'.[153] The night before the wife fell ill, the farmer's son, Jon Person, who was fourteen years old, lay in the same room as this Karin Persdotter, and then Karin said again and again: 'They should have shame. They should have shame'.[154] The boy asked her who should have shame. She answered: 'Your father and mother'. 'For what cause?' 'Yes', she said, 'because they do not pay me respect,[155] and do not believe that I can do neither good nor harm. They will well know me before they drop me'.[156] Thereafter, the wife immediately became ill, and since had had no peace, neither night nor day. It is recorded that several 'proper' people took Karin Persdotter and the boy for questioning, while the father listened, and the boy had with good reason convinced her (Karin) about what happened.[157]

Next, two widows came forward: Karin Persdotter's brother's daughter Maria Thoresdotter and Karin Persdotter's brother's wife, Ramfred Carlsdotter. And, the records state, of their own good will they told and testified that Karin had voluntarily expressed that she could cast a spell on a person with elves, so that this would bother the person day and night.

Therefore, the records continue, Karin Persdotter is mainly suspected of having, with God's permission, thrown this unspeakable[158] bothering upon his (Per Gudmundson's) wife, such sweat and pain on one side, so that she no longer is like a human being. Per Gudmundson also stated that he said to Karin Persdotter's brother, Thore Person in Karsahult: 'Thore, would you go together with me to the court and go bail for Karin, for I will no longer have anything to do with her'.[159] He (Thore) said immediately: 'This I will not do, and give God she will have a payment as deserved, because she has caused all the evil for me'.[160] Gudmundson also said: 'I fear she will strike me down as well before the court starts'.[161] Then the wife of her brother Thore answered: 'No, you must not fear her, for [even if] she has always said that she has made an effort in causing harm to you, she says you are a High Holy Day's child;[162] therefore she cannot do you any harm'. Per confirmed that he was a High Holy Day's child, and born at Christmas time, something she (Karin Persdotter) had not heard him say before. Then, it is inserted into the records that this without a doubt was revealed to her by her defender (the Water Man).[163] This insertion must be a comment from the scribe on the new information coming to the fore in the courtroom and Karin's reaction to it.

The records continue by stating that the previous spring, the tail and ears of one of his calves were cut off in the barn; first one died and then there were daily misadventures with the others,[164] and a cow died immediately thereafter. The accuser had these and several other complaints against this woman,[165] also that she assured soldiers that she was able to get him or them out of the burdensome military service without any problem, if only she first would get the twelve *öre* and, later on, what she otherwise desired. It seems that she used her competence to do business, and people knew this. Then, it is entered into the records that much could have been more fully recorded according to the testimonies given, but that this seemed not necessary because it was of the same type as noted previously.[166]

With this, the court took Karin Persdotter to a hidden interrogation,[167] meaning an interrogation away from the public court. She had not yet confessed, so some stronger measures were needed. She was protractedly admonished to confess the truth and, for the sake of her unrestful conscience, not conceal what she had been silent about.[168] Now, the records say, the time had come to think this over and restrain from devilry[169] so that she did not put herself in danger of condemnation. This is the first time the word 'devil' is used in the records. We do not know whether torture was applied during this interrogation. From other cases, we know that, first, a person may be tortured, and then the following day, the same person is recorded as having confessed 'of her own free will'.[170] Therefore, it is necessary to interpret the phrases 'good-willing' and 'without force' used in court records from witchcraft trials with great suspicion. It is, however, beyond doubt that when an accused person was taken to a 'hidden' interrogation during a witchcraft trial, this was because she refused to confess to whatever it is the interrogators wanted to hear. Pressure in some form or another was then used on this person, which usually resulted in the desired confession. In this trial, what the interrogators were after emerges later, namely a demonological confession that included sexual intercourse with the devil.[171]

After a long time to think it over and exposure to strong persuasion,[172] she gave the following 'voluntary' and 'unforced' confession,[173] which started with *maleficium*: that fourteen years prior, she suffered from a numb hand and was given the advice to go to a woman[174] who was renowned and who lived in the settlement of Taglarp.[175] This woman was called Ingeborg, and Karin Persdotter asked her for help and healing; the advice given was that she (Karin) should seek the Water Spirit, the Water Man, or the Stream Man[176] to find a cure, not only for the help she herself needed but also for the help of others.[177] This should without exception happen at certain times and days. At this point, the Evil One was brought into the picture. The name Lucifer, a classical name for the devil, was connected to the Water Man by some words inserted in brackets. Karin Persdotter said that she received money, which she then brought to 'running streams, bridges and other places to *him*'. [My italics.] Here is inserted, in parentheses: '(meaning by this the Evil One)'.[178] Karin introduced a figure with the pronoun 'him' in her narrative, without any explanation. It is likely that the words in parentheses were inserted by the judicial authorities—that is, that they provided a definition of who was meant by Karin Persdotter's 'him'. It might also have been an answer to a leading question or a suggestion from the interrogator. In any case, it is plausible that the connection between the Water Man and the Evil One was created by the interrogator. This shows how the link between folkloric ideas and demonological ideas may have been made. This establishes a connection between the Water Man and the Evil One, as being one and the same, a connection that continues throughout the rest of the trial.

The Water Man is described in the confession as a disembodied voice, talking from the water under the bridge, and money was always given to him. Karin Persdotter's confession was given immediately after her 'hidden' interrogation, which clearly was a turning point in the course of the trial. The development of the trial shifted when the interrogator identified the Water Man as also indicating the Evil One. This was a link that turned out to be dangerous for Karin. In this demonizing of the Water Man, we have an answer as to what could happen during an Early Modern witchcraft trial in order to secure links between old folk belief and new learned ideas of the demonological type.

Karen further confessed that she at once began to use her art, went to several lakes, streams, and under bridges. On some of her trips, she called forth the same pendant[179] of Lucifer, the Stream Man, in the Holy Trinity's name and sometimes in the other evil name. It is unclear whether the name Lucifer was introduced by a leading question during interrogation or whether it was a name that Karin Persdotter used. If she used to utter a charm, the Holy Trinity's name was frequently in use among people, particularly in charms employed for healing. Karin Persdotter continued her confession by saying that the same Water Man appeared by a bridge, not in person, but as it seemed to her swollen in the water. And he answered that her requests[180] would well be met, but only if twelve öre was delivered to him, and this she sacrificed as soon as she had received it.

Circumstantial evidence was produced via the testimonies of the witnesses, all pointing to the cause-and-effect connection between Karin's cursing and its results, and all the time dealing with malevolent witchcraft. When her appearance, the way she looked, could be used in the indictment as additional 'proof' of her immoral relation to the Evil One, one sees that the validity of the indictment—on which grounds she was sentenced—was very weak. She was asked whether she had had no other immoral relation[181] with him during this long period. To this she would not confess, and neither to the result of her assured healing, evil or good, even if innumerable persons sought her help.[182] Although the confession from the accused person's own mouth was lacking, the indictment is formulated as if a demonological confession took place: it clearly echoes the transition from *maleficium* to demonological witchcraft by using general legal formulations related to demonological witchcraft. Karin Persdotter herself denied all of this.

In the same way, she was asked whether she got help for her hand's numbness. She said not as much as she would have wanted to. Then, a comment is inserted into the records: when one looks at her hand, it seems as if it had previously been numb or to a certain extent out of function,[183] even if it was now somewhat vigorous.

Karin Persdotter would not name anyone who had been helped by her deeds,[184] or damaged, even if they allegedly were many, and the interrogator found it strange that she could deceive such large groups of people.[185] To this, she answered that she absolutely stuck to the assurance and mighty promises of the Water Man, and meant that she had little of this (deception) to blame herself for.[186]

The interrogators wanted an expanded confession. Their subsequent question was about whether Karin Persdotter had immoral relations[187] with 'him'. This, however, she denied. Karin stood her ground when it came to her own boundaries: she never confessed to having had a sexual relationship with the devil, and the interrogators could not move her from this stance. In this respect, the 'hidden' interrogation cannot be said to have been completely successful. But she was in a miserable state, which her behaviour shows.

One could not do anything more to get her to confess.[188] It is recorded that, unlike other people, she had not sought the Christian fellowship in church. She never came to the big celebration days of Christmas, Easter, or Pentecost. However, the court was concerned[189] that these accusations might have been raised towards her out of ill will or jealousy due to the one-sixth of farm she owned. Thus, it might be that distress and economic conditions[190] caused people who lived at the same farm as Karin Persdotter to complain about the heavy burden of evil[191] that befell them. The court listened to these accusations, which were dangerous for Karin, and entered them into the verdict and sentence.[192]

It was found that even if Karin Persdotter would not confess to having performed or encouraged anything evil, it was proved by the trustworthy witnesses that what she promised came upon them. Then, a 'Nota bene' is inserted into the records, containing the indictment in four points: (i) what she promised came upon people, including Per Gudmundson in Ulvaskog's wife, Ramfred; (ii) she refused to seek help from her Creator and went to the Stream Man; this she willingly confesses; (iii) she misused God's holy name and in that conjured[193] the Evil One; and (iv) all people desired to get rid of her. The records continue to state that she looked rather bad and that her eyes flickered. She was also unstable in behaviour and deeds, so that it was certainly clear that she had a bad relation with the Evil One.[194]

The first and second points, which pertain to Karin Persdotter promising evil and her leaving God and surrendering to the Water Man, echo indictments in many European countries, except that these usually are about renouncing the pact of baptism and entering into a new pact with the devil. The third point concerns Karin's misuse of God's holy name to evoke the Evil One. The fourth point about her appearance and behaviour is remarkable, as Karin Persdotter never confessed to any immoral relation with the Evil One.

On these grounds, the records continue, according to Karin Persdotter's confession, the jury could not do anything else but to sentence that she deserved to lose her life after God's commandment and law because she renounced her holy baptism pact. She was sentenced to be burned in fire at the stake after the laws Högmålsbalken 33:13 and 15 Capitel because she promised people evil, which later happened, and she had obviously practiced sorcery and healing for a long period.[195] This was the gracious 'resolution' by the High Court.[196] The proceedings of the court were signed by the law reader,[197] District Governor Gudmund Krok, and the jury.[198]

The Voice of Karin Persdotter

The voice of Karin Persdotter comes to the fore in many aspects of her confession. Her voice is complex. As for ideas about witchcraft, there is the accent of traditional cunning, of a woman who has learned witchcraft from another woman and who has, during her long life, performed healing and *maleficium*, receiving customers and taking payment for each act. This she admits to having done. In her confession, we hear the fusion of folk belief and demonological ideas in a narrative that is remarkable. On certain days and at certain times, Karin Persdotter walks to meet the Water Man under a bridge. She brings him the payment from her customers, and he gives her the answers she seeks. It is a kind of divination, or foreseeing.

Another accent of her voice is heard as an echo of leading questions. The court records describe the Water Man not only as a nature spirit but also as connected to the devil—to Lucifer, a connection that seems to have been made by the interrogator. The advice Karin Persdotter seeks from the Water Man turns into advice from the devil.

However, Karin Persdotter's voice also contains accents that pertain to her strength and her strategies as an accused person. There is the firm accent of denial: Karin Persdotter is a woman who has drawn a boundary around what she is willing to confess to—no matter the pressure or attempts at persuasion—as she refuses to confess to a loathsome relation with the Evil One. Karin Persdotter also refuses to denounce others. However, she is asked to denounce others as a healer and give names of those persons who came to her to be cured and were not skilled in magic themselves. The judicial officials did not act according to the demonological doctrine to get names of other witches belonging to a group, as Karin never confessed to a witches' meeting. Her performance was individual, but allegedly related to evil via the Water Man. She says that she trusted the assurance[199] of the Water Man. This means that the court pressed for a demonological confession from Karin, but when it came to denunciations, they asked for names of her clients. In my view, the court was after a demonological confession in order to secure a death sentence. In addition, they were after the names of those who sought healing. These persons might be future suspects, because this healer was connected to evil in order to obtain the advice that the clients desired. In this way, the clients were also related to evil. When it is clear that Karin Persdotter is not willing to answer any more, the interrogator can terminate the questioning, as he has been given enough. The rest of the court records render testimonies about neglect with regard to church attendance.

Karin Persdotter does not show remorse for having performed healing acts for people. On the contrary, she talks openly about the advice she received from the Water Man. She does not confess to performing evil deeds or casting spells. She does confess to meetings with the Water Man, but not to having immoral contact with him. When the interrogators want to extend the questions into more demonological territory, she refuses to cooperate. It is quite clear that Karin Persdotter herself believes that she has done nothing wrong. She learned about the Water Man when she sought a cure herself and has continued to use him as adviser. These are the pragmatic accents of her voice. However, many mythological threads are also woven into her narrative about the Water Man, through the water, the bridge, the swell of the water, the voice from the water, the sacrifice of coins—all elements known from old, religious worship in most cultures way back in history. Mikael Häll has studied folk belief about the male water creatures, particularly the Water Man, *näcken*, and points to the connection with death and sexuality.[200] Karin probably learned about these elements through orally transmitted tales.

In the 1650s, the incorporation of demonological terminology began surfacing in witchcraft trials in Sweden, which can be seen in Karin Persdotter's case. The verdict is based on the assumption that Karin was a dangerous person in an alliance with the devil, while her confession tells something else entirely. Through Karin Persdotter's voice, we see that she was multifaceted: she was an old woman, but not so easy to manipulate; she was firm and could not be pressed to toady to the interrogators; she was a knowledgeable person who knew tales with roots going back in time; she had a positive attitude towards life, believing that it was possible to get advice from the Water Man; she was also a businesswoman, requiring money from her clients, which she then gave to the Water Man. Karin Persdotter's self-image was based on the conviction that she possessed knowledge which others did not have. But she was not content with her living conditions, and felt she was entitled to more goods from the *huskvinna*[201] and her husband, who lived on the same farm. Therefore, she muttered 'shame on them'.

The word 'pact' is never mentioned in this trial. What Karin Persdotter does mention is having meetings with the Water Man. She has to interpret the Water Man through swelling water, because, as she states, he does not meet her in person. It could be that she has only seen the whirlpools of water and heard a voice coming from these. In any case, the link to the Evil One turns out to be fatal for her.

Karin Persdotter emerges as a complete person, with good and bad qualities. Her discontent, cursing, and wish for revenge can be detected in several negatively loaded situations. However, good qualities also appear in more positive situations: in her admiration for the Water Man, in her pride in people coming to her to seek help, in her cleverness as a businesswoman.

The Voices of the Witnesses

It was rumoured that Karin Persdotter was a healer—and a paid one at that. Many people reported and were willing to testify to having heard her say that she would go to the Water Man with money from clients; furthermore, that she would give him this money and would encourage him to meet her to answer her questions. Her rendered voice and the accusations against her are documented by the public, based on what they have heard her say. Their perceptions of her as a dangerous person are based on her words, her utterings and curses, which are well known in the community. The complaints had to do with *maleficium* and healing that went wrong.

The circle of witnesses is then personified from an impersonal 'many' to named individuals: neighbours and people from her close circle. Several persons testify that they went to Karin Persdotter to seek help for their own or others' illnesses and that they paid her the correct fee but had not been helped. Additionally, it is stated that people from nearby villages came to her to be healed, so there was never any doubt that she had a reputation for healing. However, according to the witnesses, nobody could confirm any positive effects from her acts.

Karin Persdotter's voice, as it exists in public rumours, is related to what the witnesses and people in general say about her. For example, she allegedly told others about her contact with the Water Man, the pieces of advice she received from him, and the rituals connected to these interactions.

Both Karin Persdotter's healing activities and the negative effects of her other activities are referenced. One witness, Per Gudmundson, delivered a testimony wherein the voice of Karin is heard rendered in direct speech. First, he gives an explanation regarding the main point of the accusation, which was that his wife, Ramfred, lost three of her calves. She beat Karin on the mouth, and Karin said: 'Because you, Ramfred, hit me on the mouth some weeks ago, shame on you! Within two years from this time, you shall have no cows'. This voice is a cursing and threatening voice. There was a reason for this threat, as the two women had apparently been arguing, but the serious element here is that Karin's curse, as rendered by Per, had an effect, namely the death of the calves. In a testimony like this, where Karin Persdotter's voice is rendered in direct speech by a witness, it is difficult to say whether her utterance was exactly as he remembered it. What we can say, however, is that Per Gudmundson is rendering a curse with many features of orality, and thus one that is easy to retell. The reason given for the anger is 'a blow' that required some form of revenge. The expression 'Shame on you!' is in common use as an angry exclamation. The timeline is important, as the result of Karin's alleged curse would occur within a defined time. The effect of the curse, too, is defined: Ramfred would lose all her cows. All these central points of Per Gudmundson's testimony can easily be stored in the oral collective memory and retold, and here they are depicted in their correct frame. Therefore, the words of Karin Persdotter, as rendered in the testimony of Per Gudmundson, could very well be exactly what she uttered.

Per Gudmundson has more to testify to, however: his wife has been ill for one week, and nobody knows what kind of illness she is suffering from. Her condition is gradually worsening. Ramfred believes that Karin Persdotter cursed her because Karin felt she did not receive what she wanted from her (Ramfred) and her husband. Per Gudmundson testifies that, before his wife fell ill, she heard Karin mumble: 'Yes, yes, shame upon them'.[202] Ramfred and Per's son, who slept in the same room as Karin Persdotter, also heard her mumble these words, which were explained to the boy by Karin as a lack of respect from Per Gudmundson and his wife. It was shortly after this, Per says, that his wife became ill.

Here, too, the voice of Karin Persdotter is rendered in ways that are easy to retell. The threat in Swedish—*Ja, Ja, de skola få skam*—contains the repetition of *Ja* and is a very rhythmic sentence. The same is true for the sentence overheard by the son. In these cases, the voice of Karin Persdotter is threatening and has clear oral features. Her utterance can be situated in a cause-and-effect argument, because the curse embedded within it is realized immediately. It also contains Karin's reason for the curse: a lack of respect and of desired essentials. This voice is one of revenge and discontent. The way this voice is rendered shows an attempt to be accurate but also echoes oral transmission in the variation between indirect speech and direct speech, a variation that enlivens a narrative. In addition, the pointed sayings, the repetitive features, and the rhythm preserved in the utterances as they were written down in the court records signal that the voice of Karin Persdotter rendered in the records is close to what she really said—in terms of both content and form.

We hear the voices of two female witnesses next, in the testimony of the widows Maria Thoresdotter and Karin Persdotter's brother's wife, Ramfred Carlsdotter. Both refer to what Karin herself has said she can do, namely to cast a spell on a person by the use of elves so that he or she will be 'bothered both night and day'.[203] Karin is therefore suspected of having severely bothered a woman, 'with God's allowance'.[204] The voice of Karin Persdotter rendered here is a boasting voice. They testify that Karin told many that she can cast 'deadly spells' on people, and that she detailed that the result of these would be illness, in which the person would be bothered 'just as the poor wife of Per Gudmundson'. Karin's voice here, as rendered in the voices of these women, is one to be feared, because she emphasizes that when she casts a spell, it will clearly come true.

The voices of the witnesses also bring in elements of protection. These elements might be based on a person's birthdate. For instance, the wife of her brother Thore says that Karin herself said that she tried to harm Per Gudmundson, but that it was not possible because he was a Holy Day child.[205] The voices of the witnesses carry the belief that those born on special days were immune against witchcraft.[206]

Both female and male witnesses are heard during the initial part of the trial, which focuses on *maleficium*. These probably came from Karin Persdotter's close circle. Looking at the voices of the female witnesses, their testimonies contain cause-and-effect arguments used as circumstantial evidence as well as information based on folk belief. Two female witnesses argue for the connection between Karin Persdotter's well-known and self-proclaimed ability to cast a certain spell—using elves as a means of harming people—and the sickness of the wife, who contracted the illness that the spell contained. The witnesses hold forth that the connection is proved by the symptoms of the illness. The evidence is based on common knowledge about Karin's cursing and the kind of illness the woman has contracted, which can be observed. The voices of these two female witnesses contribute not only common knowledge about what Karin Persdotter herself has said about her art of casting spells, but also show ordinary people's understanding of the connection between the two incidents: Karin's power and the wife's sickness. These female voices are most likely representative of the village people's opinions, and they are convincing as a type of proof that will bear weight and that the court will listen to.

The other female witness we hear, the wife of Thore Person, explains why Karin Persdotter's spells did not work on those who are High Holy Days children. This witness expresses a type of folk belief about Karin's unsuccessful spells and also provides comforting information to the man who is afraid that he will be hit by one of the spells Karin is uttering. She also expresses ideas on what protects against sorcery and witchcraft. Of the voices of the two female witnesses, the former is a testimony giving further evidence to the indictment of Karin as a witch and negatively influences the trial for the accused. The latter, more accidental information is about why not all of Karin's spells work, and does not influence the outcome of her trial. In general, the voices of female witnesses in this case can be said to echo common people's opinions and attitudes towards Karin Persdotter's practice and aspects of folk belief.

The witnesses show anger and fear: anger, because this woman is allowed to behave like she does; fear, because her curses seem to have an effect. The court records show a local community in which people strongly believe that witchcraft is possible, as is healing.

The Voice of the Interrogator

In this trial, the voice of the interrogator surfaces both in direct speech, via the reporting verb 'asked', and in shadow questions, in which the answers of the interrogated person make it possible to interpret what the person was asked about. The interrogator clearly influences the development of the interrogation from *maleficium* to demonological ideas, plays a major role in demonizing the Water Man, and has a decisive role in creating an indictment in which the factual confession of Karin Persdotter is set aside and a confession to immoral relations with the Evil One is inserted. How much the interrogator knew about demonological ideas is unknown, but fragments—like renouncing God and becoming an ally of the Evil One, using one of the devil's names as synonym, and having immoral contact with the devil—were known to him.[207] The interrogator's role during this trial was important to the outcome.

The Voice of the Law

The voice of the law is distinct in the references to the laws underlying verdict and sentence. Also, in the indictment, the voice of the law is heard through the formulations of the judiciary. The wording of the indictment displays accusations of malevolent witchcraft and the public's opinion regarding Karin Persdotter's 'bad' appearance. It shows that being gossiped about for malevolent witchcraft was frightening and could be dangerous. Its points are based on witnesses' testimonies. However, while the ideas related to *maleficium* came from the witnesses—neighbours who knew Karin—the demonological ideas were introduced by the judicial officials. It is the judiciary who creates the link between her appearance and her immorality. Details about what her relationship with the Evil One consisted of were added to the interrogation by persons who knew about demonological ideas to a certain extent. Even if a pact is not explicitly referred to, demonological ideas are mentioned. Here, we see a failed connection between what the voice of Karin literally confesses to and what has been made of her confessing voice in the indictment. The fact that Karin Persdotter never confessed to witchcraft is overshadowed by rather weak evidence. How this 'proof' against her could lead to a death sentence can only be explained by how the legal officials and the jury interpreted her confession.

The Voice of the Scribe

The scribe is accurate in describing ideas about witchcraft and healing, whether they originated from the accused person or from the witnesses. He is also accurate when it comes to accusations of *maleficium* and the presentation of witnesses. The rendering of courtroom discourse is to a certain extent complete, but has some weak points with regard to the interrogator's encroachment when he attempts to link the Water Man and the Evil One. Generally, the scribe seems to be more familiar with *maleficium* trials than with demonological trials, but he possesses the insight that demonological ideas were crucial to the severity of the trial and its outcome.

The question about Karin Persdotter's numb hand results in a comment from the scribe or from the interrogator, namely that when one looks at her hand, it seems like it has been numb or partly lacks function, even if it is now somewhat movable. This is a strange comment, as it must have been difficult to observe that a hand was numb before, but has now improved.

With the exception of the example above, the scribe does not reveal his attitude towards what is told. However, the way he includes insertions between brackets shows an interest on his part to include critical questions and comments in the court records, but the use of brackets signals that the comments are his own. The scribe has, as best he could, remained loyal to Karin Persdotter's description of the Water Man and her healing business. If this information was new to him, he must be said to have done a good job in terms of preserving details.

Karin Dantz, 1673–74

The Trial

This is a case that concerns the Blåkulla narrative—folkloric beliefs about the mysterious and hidden place called Blåkulla, where witchcraft gatherings took place. The Blåkulla trials are remarkable, particularly in their extensive use of child witnesses, who had allegedly been abducted to Blåkulla and could therefore denounce several adults they saw there.[208] Many Swedish witchcraft trials from the 1660s and 1670s relate to Blåkulla.[209] The Swedish Blåkulla trials became famous not only on a national level but internationally as well. One of the cities in which these trials took place was the town of Mora in Dalarne. In 1669, trials took place there that resulted in fifteen executions, of which one was of a man.[210] The condemned were first decapitated and then burned at the stake. These trials are described in George Sinclair's book *Satan's Invisible World Discovered*, published in Edinburgh as early as 1685.[211] The 'Relation' chapter about the Mora trials includes the Blåkulla narrative and is one of thirty-six relations, or chapters, of Sinclair's book.[212]

Karin Dantz, the wife[213] of Daniel Dantz, lived in the town of Sundsvall in Norrland, a town situated by the Gulf of Bothnia. She was brought before the local court three times, first on 22 December 1673. The original sources are court records from local trials in Sundsvall, written in the Gothic hand and preserved in the Regional State Archives in Vadstena. In addition, there are sentence minutes, *domböcker*, from Svea High Court preserved in the National Archives in Stockholm.[214] Present at the court meeting in 1673 were the mayor[215]—Johan Jöransson—and jury members Lars Hindersson, Siul Nielsson, Per Jönsson, and Per Michelsson. Karin Dantz was brought before the court again on 31 January 1674. Present were the mayor—this time, Johan Alander—and the members of the jury. The last time Karin was brought before the court was on 17 March 1674.[216] Present were the mayor—again Johan Alander—and the jury members. Karin Dantz confessed to having been to Blåkulla. Several other voices are heard in these court records, among them the voice of a seven-year-old boy.

At the first court meeting on 22 December 1673, the mayor, Johan Jöransson, first addressed the court with a lecture about witchcraft, warning of Satan and his eagerness to lead people astray. He stated that even children were hearing about witchcraft, and he admonished those in court to prevent children and others from overhearing talk about witchcraft. Those who 'ran around with such talk',[217] Jöransson said, would be fined forty *marker*.[218]

The trial started partly as a confession by Karin Dantz, partly as a speech of defamation on the part of Karin, in which Ingred, Olof Hansson's wife, was denounced. This case is special in that an adult woman confesses to the same as most children involved in the Blåkulla trials, namely that she was abducted to Blåkulla. Karin Dantz confessed on 22 December 1673 that she had been to Blåkulla one night, fourteen days prior. She had allegedly been brought to Blåkulla by Ingred, Olof Hansson's wife, and there she (Karin) had been 'sorely handled',[219] bruised in the eyes and blue around the neck, witnesses to which she pleaded were the wife of Lars Hansson Bruse[220] and the wife of Olof Båtsman, as she had shown them the bruises.[221] Karin, the wife of Daniel Dantz, was asked by the court whether she stood by her speech, and now she confessed formally that she imagined that she was taken to Blåkulla the same night by Olof Hansson's wife, Ingred, and went out of her house through the east corner,[222] but she did not know how she came there. She thought she went to the west above the old town, and she saw that it was a starlit sky, and even if it was cold, she felt she was in a warm wind, and as such she was carried to Blåkulla.

And she felt as if she had come to a kitchen, and inside it was a guest sauna, wherein candles were burning, and people 'danced and played in the same room'.[223] Karin Dantz confessed she had seen Ingred, the wife of Olof Hansson, who did not do anything in particular other than going back and forth.[224] And there, wife Dantz was ordered to weave and to wash the table. Whose command this was, she did not know.[225] The same person (who gave the command) had given Karin Dantz a large amount of silver coins, white money in a huge pile,[226] which were placed in three piles and wrapped in paper. Later, she confessed to having thrown steel over the money[227] with a knife she borrowed from Olof Hansson's maid, Marit Nilsdotter, who had also been there. But later on, when she looked closer at the coins, there was nothing but pine shavings and aspen leaves. And she stated that right after this, she had become speechless and called on God for help. With this, she wanted to take the money with her from there, and then someone had come and sort of cut her hand, and took out the money she thought she had in her fist, and afterwards she did not feel anything other than as if both the hand and the arm were cut off.[228]

Then, she narrated, it was like a voice took her up through the ceiling. She said that she was twice lifted up under the roof beam[229] and was received by a man in white clothes, who taught her and commanded her to sing the verse which teaches all people to 'perform recovery' in time.[230] The wife Dantz recalled the verse in court, even if she confessed that she previously had never known it. Then, she said that in Blåkulla, she was nearly thrown into a black house, where she thought they would burn her and her child, and where there seemed to be only fire and sulphur.[231] And the door was opened, where they wanted to have her inside, but the man in white clothes closed the door and defended her with the words: 'Let her be'.[232]

Thereafter, she thought she was standing in a black, soot-blackened barn, and after that, she confessed that she woke up in her own house and in her own bed, asking her husband Daniel to get up and light the fire,[233] and to observe how she had been handled during the night. The records continue to state that 'this wife Dantz' also confessed that she at the same time had seen her own one-year-old son in Blåkulla, and accused her neighbour, wife Ingred, of having transported her (Karin's) child there, whereupon wife Ingred, in response to such an accusation, had given Karin Dantz a box on the ear.[234]

The wife of Lars Hansson Bruse[235] states that she, together with her mother and the wife of Olof Båtsman,[236] on Saturday morning after the night she (Karin Dantz) stated she was taken away, had seen wife Dantz, that she was blue on her cheekbone, and that she had shown them the finger marks of a flat hand, which were all blue.[237] In the same way, there were two wounds on her nose, which she said she sustained when she went through the corner of the house, and in the same way, her right hand was swollen.

Olof Hansson's small boy, Nils Olofsson, who was seven years old, said that a wife[238] whom he did not know had pulled the blanket off his father at the time of night, smeared something onto half her and his father's fingers,[239] and left via the chimney to Blåkulla. Thereafter, he also followed, and the same wife who led the father also led the son. Later, when they came back, they again came down through the chimney. Later, this same woman had given his father her own water to drink. Nils testified that he went to Blåkulla five nights. Moreover, he said that his mother, wife Ingred, had moved herself up under the ceiling.[240] He also testifies that he saw Jon Nyborgare's daughter Brita in Blåkulla; likewise, he saw Per Larsson's daughter Sigrid and his (Nils's) brother Hampus and sister Sigrid playing together there. He also said that they had helped themselves to food in Blåkulla,[241] but a white man[242] had struck the food out of his hands, which (the food) was worms and toads.[243]

Nils moreover stated that in Blåkulla, a black dog had lain under the table, having horns on its head and knees; the dog even played on its ass,[244] whereafter his father had danced backwards with an unknown wife, and the whole crowd[245] likewise danced backwards. All of this, both Olof Hansson and his wife, Ingred, denied; wife Ingred solemnly swore herself to be free of this accusation, 'before God and their own conscience, even if evil people had brought such upon them'.[246] And wife Ingred was now seriously and solemnly admonished by the court on behalf of God to confess the truth, and if she knew that she was guilty, to confess in the name of Jesus, considering that it was better to suffer her punishment in this world than suffer everlasting and interminable pain together with all devils in hell, endlessly.[247]

On 31 January 1674, well over a month since the first interrogation, Karin, the wife of David Dantz, was again brought before the court in Sundsvall. This time, the mayor was Johan Alander, and the jury members were present.

She was first asked by the court whether she maintained the accusations against Ingred, the wife of Olof Hansson, that she presented on 22 December 1673,[248] that Ingred had transported herself (Karin) and her child to Blåkulla,[249] 'with more that the interrogation contains',[250] which were read out loud for her. Karin Dantz said that she maintained the same accusation, that she could say or know nothing else than that she was carried by wife Ingred, and saw her (Ingred) in Blåkulla.[251]

But she (Ingred) now as previously absolutely denied, swearing solemnly by her conscience to be free from this sin of witchcraft. And that God alone knew that she was free.[252] The court asked her which God she meant, the one she mentioned so often.[253] She answered that Jesus Christ, who suffered death for her and all people, knew her to be free.

The wife Ingred followed her children's story, namely that they heard Dantz's Karin say at the place of Kirstin, the wife of Bruse, that Brita, the wife of Lars Jonsson, gave her (Karin Dantz) money[254] in Blåkulla. The records continue stating that the wife Anna in Åkersvik, who died a few days previously, had cut off her (Karin's) finger,[255] Karin, the wife of Per Jönsson, had blown it together,[256] and the wife Ingred (who the wife Dantz had previously known) had given her (Karin Dantz) a box on the ear.[257]

After she took her oath, Kirstin Bruse was admonished to tell the truth and not conceal anything if she had heard such a thing being said by Karin, Dantz's wife. But she (Kirstin Bruse) said that she had never heard such things being said by her (Karin Dantz). Otherwise, however, Kirstin Bruse reports that the morning after Karin Dantz was allegedly taken away,[258] she (Karin) had come to her (Kirstin Bruse) and shown her how she had been handled during the night and how she was carried to Blåkulla, and that she (Karin Dantz) was taken out through the corner of the house by wife Ingred, whom wife Dantz now also confessed to have reported to Kirstin Bruse.[259] But she (Karin) said that she had not mentioned the other wives, whom wife Ingred copied according to what she had heard from her (Ingred's) children. But otherwise, wife Dantz confessed that she understood nothing other[260] than that the frequently mentioned wife Ingred brought her (Karin Dantz) to Blåkulla and had been there herself.

On 17 March 1674, a court session began in Sundsvall.[261] A few days later, on 23 March, in the presence of well-honoured mayor Johan Alander and the jury,[262] a young girl, Marit Nilsdotter, born in Torp Parish, was brought before the court because on 22 December, at the last held court session,[263] she was denounced by Karin, Dantz's wife, as having been to Blåkulla together with her (Marit Nilsdotter's) mistress, Ingred, wife of Olof Hansson. There (in Blåkulla), this girl (Marit) allegedly washed the table and lent Karin Dantz the knife to throw over the money she (Karin) was given there, according to Karin's story. This girl was previously examined by her vicar[264] in Torp, and absolutely denied having been to Blåkulla at any time, which she was accused of, as the letter by the honoured pastor of 12 March reported.[265]

According to the letter by Pastor[266] Olai, the court asked this girl—with serious admonition 'on God's road'[267] to confess the truth—whether she was guilty of the rumours that she had been to Blåkulla, washed the table, and lent a knife to Karin Dantz to throw over the money. This, Marit Nilsdotter absolutely and unequivocally denied[268] in high tones, avowing and pleading that God knew she was innocent,[269] and she knew nothing about it, unless she was brought there against her will, and in an unconscious state.[270] The records continue to state that Karin Dantz, who was also present in the courtroom, was asked whether it was correct that this girl thus was in Blåkulla and lent her the knife and so forth. To this, Karin Dantz answered: 'Yes', and said that she with good conscience could stand by this confession. And that it was all true what she previously had confessed about Ingred, Olof Hansson's wife, as well as about this girl, Marit Nilsdotter.

The court closely reflected upon the case and took it into consideration. Then, the records state, as one could get no further and clarify this obscured case,[271] even though the court as well as the vicar most seriously admonished all individuals concerned particularly and clearly to give true confessions,[272] both wife Ingred and the girl Marit Nilsdotter unanimously denied the accusation. They asserted that everything that wife Dantz had brought upon them was complete untruth.[273] And likewise, the records state, this wife Dantz was warned by the court with many admonitions not to bring anything more upon somebody than she knew she could stand by as truth. Still, she stood by her unchanged confession, as can be seen from the previous proceedings.

The records conclude that for that matter, there was no reason based on which this humble court could prove that the defamed persons were completely related to the accusations against them, nor was there any reason that Karin, the wife of Dantz, who brought them under suspicion, would have told untruth and given them a bad reputation,[274] while she so many times stated that she was abducted[275] by wife Ingred and treated badly,[276] and living witnesses also testified to having seen that wife Dantz was thus being sorely handled and treated, as the proceedings further show. However, the unanimous court could not bring this case to a definitive end, in this case (which was) concealed for human beings,[277] but had to, in all subservience, pass it on to the High Court,[278] with a deferential request for how this humble court could further proceed.[279] Upon this, the records state, the humble court subserviently awaited the High Court's very wise opinion and notification.[280] The verdict and sentence in the case of Karin Dantz are unknown, due to missing court records.[281]

The Voice of Karin Dantz

The voice of Karin, the wife of David Dantz, comes to the fore in direct and indirect speech, the latter as answers to questions posed to her. Her voice is most clearly heard during the trial in December 1673, when she narrates the Blåkulla story, while during the two subsequent trials, her voice is hardly audible. The story told by Karin Dantz differs from many other versions of the Blåkulla narrative, because an adult woman confesses that she was abducted to Blåkulla and in doing so denounces another adult woman, the one who abducted her. In most Blåkulla trials, a child testified about an abduction. As a narrator telling a tale influenced by children's perspectives and interpretation, Karin Dantz could utilize a story that was well known in the local community. Bengt Ankarloo states that the extensive and detailed cosmology of Blåkulla is dealt with in Dalarne, Norrland, Uppland, and Stockholm: 'The creative fantasy of the children and young women acting as witnesses gives minor individual variations on a given theme, apparently well known by all'.[282]

Karin Dantz's way of telling the Blåkulla story is familiar: she is economic with regard to the amount of words she uses, and the speed of the story is high throughout. She knows the storyline's sequence of events and manages to insert not only the main ideas but also details, moving steadily towards the end of the narrative. This is a story she has heard being told, be that by children or adults.

Karin Dantz's version of the Blåkulla story follows the well-known order of events from fairy tales: home—leave home—return home. The focus in traditional tales is on solving a difficult task or broadening the mind towards becoming a wiser person through the journey. In the Blåkulla narrative, the decision to embark on such a quest is less deliberate than in a traditional fairy tale, in which the desire to become a more mature person, making the right choices or winning the princess and half the kingdom, is the goal. In Karin Dantz's narrative, the person going to Blåkulla is taken there by another person, and the journey is not undertaken willingly. The journey starts inside the house and ends in bed in the same house. In the meantime, strange events take place in an even stranger place.

The Blåkulla story links to ideas about demonological witchcraft. In the version told by Karin Dantz, the main ideas of the narrative are recognizable as elements of confessions in witchcraft trials, particularly the ideas about witches' meetings. There is night flight and there is a meeting; a gathering at which many people assemble. In this place, there is a figure with high authority, described as a man in white clothes. Such a white man occurs in other Blåkulla narratives as well, along-side with angels, representing forces of good but evil as well. They are ambiguous, as certain aspects of their appearance were suspect. The white angel was also seen as the Evil One in disguise, as one of Satan's tricks allegedly was to appear as a white angel to seduce the ignorant.[283] In Karin Dantz's narrative, the man in white clothes acts as a helper, a rescuer from a scary place, and also a teacher.[284] In other Blåkulla narratives, the representatives of the forces of goodness are an ambiguous group.[285] However, in Karin's narrative, they are described positively, which denotes that the place Blåkulla was not understood solely as evil. Also, the man in white is the one who teaches Karin Dantz a verse that is used to make people better, most likely a charm for healing.[286]

Still, this gathering in Blåkulla is gloomy: the place is something else than pure merriness. On the one hand, there is dancing and playing at the gathering, as well as a table and food. On the other, there is the black burning, a terrible place to end, in fire and in pain. A crowd is present, people whom the narrator knows and people whom she does not know. All these features are common elements in demonological witchcraft confessions. However, versions of the Blåkulla story may contain many or few demonological ideas. In Karin Dantz's version, some impor-tant elements are missing. We do not hear about a devil's pact, even if the gift she received—the three piles of silver coins turning into aspen leaves—have clear con-notations of entering a devil's pact and receiving gifts in return, for instance money that changed into dirt. We do not hear about devil worship or rituals. However, we do hear about Karin being in peril outside a black house, a motif with a clear denotation of hell. We also hear about her recognizing other visitors to Blåkulla—a point of uttermost importance for the judiciary.

Karin Dantz's narrative contains both positive and negative descriptions of the trip. On the positive side, flying offered a spectacular view, and in Blåkulla, there had been a sauna and a kitchen, and there were burning lights. On the negative side, she sustained injuries and bruises during the trip, which she had shown to several people; she was close to being burned while in Blåkulla; and she felt like her hand was cut off when she wanted to grab the money she was given. Karin did not gain anything from this journey. She did not become rich, as the gift of money turned out to be a trick. The overall feeling we are left with is that she was exposed to something dangerous. Her trip home ended with her waking up in bed next to her husband. Hence, the whole journey may be seen as a dream; a vision she had about leaving the real world and entering another. In that respect, a retelling of the Blåkulla narrative has many features in common with the Norwegian visionary poem *Draumkvedet* from the late Middle Ages. In this poem, the protagonist, Olav Åsteson falls into a deep sleep on Christmas Eve; he wakes up on the thirteenth day of Christmas and tells about a journey to the underworld, positioning himself in the church door to tell everyone about what he experienced.[287] The difference is that Olav Åsteson was not contaminated with evil during his stay in the underworld, while Karin Dantz is alleged to have crossed a border where, in the eyes of the judiciary, she joined forces with evil, which inevitably became a part of her.

As for narrative structures, Karin Dantz masters the art of narrating. There are marked variations in tempo, which contribute to enlivening the story. The narrator's delegation of voices to various persons is handled well. Shifts between indirect and direct speech are elegant. Direct speech is scarce, and thus obtains prominence when it occurs. For instance, a short sentence from the man in white is inserted; a sentence that has a decisive impact on Karin Dantz's destiny. Indirect speech dominates the discourse, rendered as reported clauses introduced by a reporting verb: we hear the speech of the witnesses, the man dressed in white, Ingred, and Marit Nilsdotter. The language in these passages is clear, coherent, and concise, not staying too long with one single actor or one single occasion.

The speed of Karin Dantz's way of narrating is somewhat interrupted due to a number of detailed descriptions. The details pertain for instance to the incident of Karin leaving the house, how she was lifted up through the roof beam, where in the house this was, and also how the money she was given in Blåkulla was wrapped, how many piles of money there were, and how she had thrown a knife over the money—the use of steel being a well-known method to break witchcraft. Small images contribute to creating an atmosphere and provide—among other things— an unexpected frame to an illegal night-time flight. The narration displays a story-teller who knows that even in the dangerous and the frightening, small moments of peace are needed.

Also, orality features colour the Blåkulla narrative. These include additive sentence structures, contributing to an even pulse in the story, closeness to the human lifeworld through the kitchen and sauna in Blåkulla, and precision in people's names. These narrative strategies create a text which is spiced, thus making it Karin Dantz's own.

There is a marked timeline in Karin Dantz's story, distinguishing day and night, morning and evening. As a witches' flight in demonological terms strongly relies on secrecy, it is of importance that Karin's abduction took place when others were asleep. It is also significant that she came back before her husband woke up, and that she could show her bruises to other people in the morning after she had been to Blåkulla. The order of events on the timeline is important for the effect of the story and for the built-in credibility of the narrative. In Karin Dantz's narrative, this is marked by words denoting order: 'since', 'afterwards', 'subsequently', and 'previously'.

When some elements are given more weight than others in a narrative, this may have to do with repeated mentioning, or frequency. In Karin Dantz's story, an element mentioned several times is the movement of a person lifted through the ceiling to get out of a room or a house. It is a clearly unrealistic element. The emphasis on this act is probably related to a central question of this narrative, namely how a person could set off on the night flight to Blåkulla when they were in bed inside a house. It is more important to repeat that which is not understandable than that which is easily understandable.

The mood of the narrative comes to the fore in the narrator's attitude towards what is told. In this case, no linguistic devices are used to create a distance to the content of the story; the narrator seems to believe in what she tells. As the experience of Blåkulla was mixed, the unpleasant emerges in Karin Dantz's voice, particularly when she narrates about her bruises and the fright she experienced in the black barn. It seems important for Karin to demonstrate that she was exposed to a violent journey, since she contacted many people the morning after the trip. Thus, she signals that she was exposed to something dangerous and gives a warning to others.

There is a marked contrast between what we hear of Karin Dantz's voice in the first trial and what we hear in the next two trials, in January 1674 and March 1674. We do not know what happened to Karin in the meantime, but the storyteller has vanished; her play with language and her personal tone have gone. The interrogators have already got out of her what they wanted, and they are only interested in new names of persons who went to Blåkulla. Karin Dantz's voice is audible during the January and March trials only in a set frame, in which she responds to questions, confirming her previous denunciation. Looking at the questions posed, they circle around denunciation. In January 1674, Karin Dantz is brought before the court to confirm witnesses' testimonies and maintain her denunciation of Ingred. However, she still shows some resistance, as she denies that she mentioned the names of other women who went to Blåkulla, as Ingred's children state. This means that Karin protests that she was wrongly cited. In March 1674, when Marit Nilsdotter is interrogated, Karin is present in the courtroom and gives the short answer 'Yes' to confirm that she saw Marit Nilsdotter in Blåkulla, and in addition maintained her (Karin's) confession and the denunciation of Marit Nilsdotter and Ingred. Thus, Karin Dantz's voice changes from a willing voice with a narrative flow when it comes to the Blåkulla narrative during the first trial to a reduced voice during the second and third trial.

Karin Dantz must have known that it was dangerous to confess to a journey to Blåkulla. Still, in contrast to the other two women implicated in this trial, she gives the interrogators the story they want. She does not seem to regret the denunciations. Perhaps she gave in from the very beginning, thinking that denial was useless, that it would be a lost battle. There is no marked turning point in Karin Dantz's trial, but her voice clearly became silent between 22 December 1673 and 23 March 1674.

The Voices of Other Participants

The two other women mentioned—Ingred and Marit Nilsdotter—choose strategies opposite to Karin Dantz's. They deny that they went to Blåkulla at that time, swearing by God and Jesus Christ. Formulations from the Christian literature, especially the catechism, are included in their defensive speeches. Their strong denials seem to influence the court by introducing doubt about their guilt. Their voices, rendered in the court records, show that they were afraid of what would happen next, with good reason. Their strategy of denial made it necessary for Karin to confirm her denunciations twice. During the court meeting of 31 January 1674, Ingred in fact tried to denounce several other women, following her children, who said that Karin mentioned that these women went to Blåkulla. That Ingred took this step, which could have been disastrous for the women mentioned, might reveal anger or revenge, as she herself was in a pressed situation. However, Karin Dantz denied that she mentioned these women and thus managed to put a full stop to any further investigation.

In addition, the seven-year-old boy who testified knows a surprising number of demonological ideas.[288] He knows about how a Blåkulla journey is performed, leaving the house through the chimney, smearing half a finger, a black dog staying in Blåkulla with horns on its head and knees—a creature which played on its ass—people dancing backward, and the food in Blåkulla, which was transformed into snakes and toads. He is a child who fits well into the frame of a child witness testifying to having been abducted to Blåkulla and thus having first-hand knowledge of the women who frequented the place. To be aware of demonological ideas at such a young age means that he must have heard Blåkulla stories from very early on. The court seems to pay attention to his testimony, as there is no sign that they do not believe him. The abundance of children used as witnesses during the Blåkulla trials puts a special stamp on these trials, as children became serious actors responsible for the deaths of many adults.

The Voice of the Interrogator

The voice of the interrogator is heard in indirect speech, sometimes asking Karin Dantz for confirmation of the denunciations incorporated in her Blåkulla story, sometimes admonishing Ingred to confess her sins to avoid eternal agony with all devils in hell, and sometimes admonishing Marit Nilsdotter to confess that she went to Blåkulla. There is a tension between on the one side a witch-hunter's urge to obtain more names of Blåkulla visitors and on the other a religious warning, admonishing the suspects to confess in order to save their souls. This tension gives the voice of the interrogator a loaded character.

Following the trials mentioned above, it is clear that the voice of the interrogator moves towards pressure to obtain the names of new suspects and a confession to a Blåkulla journey. There is no mentioning of preliminary or hidden examinations in these trials. Karin Dantz's confession comes easily, but the two other women whom she denounces are not cooperative, and deny. Therefore, after the first court meeting in December 1673, Karin is important only in order to confirm her previous denunciations of Ingred and Marit Nilsdotter, which she does willingly. However, she refuses to name others. The interrogator's goal is therefore not to obtain details about Blåkulla or expand demonological ideas; he is after a statement that they were there. Thus, his goals are influenced by the demonological idea of a witches' gathering.

Another accent of the interrogator's voice, particularly coming to the fore during the two trials in 1674, is based on religion: confession to sins is decisive in saving one's soul. If the suspect knows that she is guilty of the sin of witchcraft, it is imperative that she confesses and suffers in this worldly life instead of experiencing hell's eternal agony. The interrogator appeals to the suspect's conscience and remorse. The fight between God and the devil is echoed in a question posed to Ingred, who uses the name of God and is asked which God she means, the one she often mentions.[289] On the whole, the interrogator's voice is coloured by religious terminology, reinforcing the understanding that a witch is an enemy of God.

The Voice of the Law

In the trial of Karin Dantz and the two other accused women, the voice of the law interestingly signals that new ideas have entered the minds of the judiciary. At this time, Europe is in the midst of a transitional period with regard to judicial authorities' views on witchcraft, and this is echoed in the court records. The first court meeting, on 22 December 1673, starts with a complaint: the court has been given cause to hold an investigation of some witchcraft, which was spread by some mad people and could not be proved.[290] The records continue to state that this is why Satan—the enemy of all people—likes to seek them out, in order to lead all people to their depravation.[291] Then follows a judicial lecture, warning about the power of Satan and the danger of choosing the wrong 'master'. Both adults and children are mentioned: the adults are warned within a religious frame, and a special warning is given to those who talk about witchcraft in a way that children can overhear.[292] These persons are to be punished with fines. This warning might be related to the large number of child witnesses who had been testifying during the great Northern Swedish Blåkulla persecution, which at the time of this trial was in its middle phase. When in 1673, the judiciary in Sundsvall warns against talking too much about witchcraft, this can be interpreted as an expression of doubt regarding the claims of children about having been taken to Blåkulla; specifically, an implication that they cannot be trusted as witnesses because they are easily influenced by stories they hear. Still, this address to the court is characterized by the understanding that witchcraft is possible if human beings choose the 'wrong side', and that witches are dangerous people who should be prosecuted by law.

During the last court meeting in this trial, in March 1674, the judiciary presents a thoughtful reflection on the nature of this case. This passage clearly shows that this case was considered to be difficult, and that doubt was expressed related to the question of guilt. Arguments pro and contra are brought forth, stating precisely what the accused actually confessed to and protested against. On the one hand, there is Karin Dantz's denunciation of Ingred and Marit Nilsdotter; on the other, there are their denials. Taken together, these questions are deemed too challenging for the court to handle; therefore, the case is passed on to higher legal authorities.

However, even in the face of a demonological confession, the judicial officials are very careful not to make inaccurate judgements in the cases of the three women. They find the cases difficult to judge; caution that would probably not have been seen fifty years earlier. The cases of Karin Dantz and the other two women signal—through the voice of the law—that new ideas entered the minds of the judiciary. Still, severe persecution was taking place in neighbouring districts. The pattern seen in Sundsvall could also represent a first phase, characterized by a scepticism which nevertheless develops into witchcraft panics. This insight into the judiciary's understanding of its own responsibility regarding serious cases of witchcraft accusation displays a new way of thinking; further, it points to the period after 1700 as critical for the changes seen throughout Europe in terms of the judgement of the crime of witchcraft.[293] The primary questions that arise here centre around whether the courts believed the confessions in witchcraft trials, which often contain completely unrealistic elements: could these events actually have happened? How seriously should such confessions be taken by the representatives of the law, and how severe should the final sentence be? The Sundsvall court's discussion in 1674 sheds light on these aspects, and shows that there was room for disbelief when it came to the content of witchcraft confessions. The view on witchcraft here is clearly in a transitional phase, the effect of which can be seen in each individual courtroom and the decisions made therein. This reflects a change in mentality that, a little later, would unfold into the Age of Enlightenment and a new era of understanding in the world.

The Voice of the Scribe

The scribe gives equal weight to the voices of the accused, the witnesses, the interrogator, and the law. Particular phrases denoting demonology, like 'Satan and his pendant', occur several times. The same goes for fear-provoking descriptions of hell and strong admonishments aimed at pressing forth a confession. The accused are most often rendered in indirect discourse, with the reporting verb intact, so that an individualized language emerges. The testimony of the child witness is rendered elaborately. The parts of the records which present the voice of the law has kept its legal style. It surfaces in passages containing shades of doubt about the possibility of performing witchcraft, but also containing the conviction that witches exist. The court records are balanced. The scribe does not present his own opinion, but strives to be loyal to the participants' expressions and thus to various accents of their voices. His professionalism shines through in the reliable recording of the courtroom's discourse.

Conclusion

The trials analysed in this chapter have displayed ideas of *maleficium* as well as demonological ideas. In a country in which mainly maleficent witchcraft trials took place, the trial of Ingegärd Andersdotter has shown that demonological ideas occurred in the late 1500s, and the trial of Karin Dantz has likewise demonstrated that demonological ideas were central during the Blåkulla trials about seventy years later. However, these trials, which were linked to other witchcraft trials, also contain ideas on *maleficium* and show how traditional ideas on maleficent witchcraft were intertwined with demonological notions throughout the period of persecution. Contrary to this, the trial of Karin Persdotter is an individual trial originally aimed at healing, which then became demonized during the trial. Taken together, the voices of these three women display a rich spectre of ideas about witchcraft within local Swedish communities throughout a century.

The three voices heard are voices of good narrators, which is displayed in their confessions. They have learned from oral transfer how to create narratives with an individual stamp, an element which is carefully preserved by the scribe: the records present all women as individual language users. The retelling of a demonological narrative in a courtroom signals that the women knew the Blåkulla story before entering the courtroom: core ideas had been told and retold in the local communities for a while. I argue that new and learned demonological ideas from further south in Europe were first introduced by a judicial official during a trial, as leading questions during interrogation, and later assimilated in the local community by oral transfer. In the trial of Ingegärd Andersdotter, the idea of the devil's pact was new. The personal factor must have been crucial to the introduction of demonological ideas: one single person within the judiciary had a strong influence on local witchcraft trials.[294] In the case of Ingegärd Andersdotter, there was also an executioner, trained at the Continent, who searched her for the devil's mark. Thus, several persons related to the trial would have known about the doctrine of demonology. In addition, since people from the village were also present at a local trial, and since the jury, the *nämnd*, consisted of local men, new ideas spread rapidly in the local community. The *nämnd* would also have knowledge of local folk beliefs about *maleficium*, and therefore be able to distinguish and pay close attention to demonological ideas when these occurred in witchcraft trials. Narratives about the devil's pact, the devil's mark, witches' meetings, and Blåkulla soon became knowledge shared by the village's inhabitants. Shape-shifting was not documented in the trials analysed above. What the confessions in witchcraft trials make clear, however, is that many versions of the demonological narrative thrived in different places. While the core demonological elements were always preserved, the frame and the details varied. This is demonstrated in this chapter in the confessions of Ingegärd Andersdotter and Karin Dantz, and in several other chapters in this book. Here, in two different regions of Sweden, stories with demonological content took different forms as they were told and retold over decades.

The trial of Karin Persdotter provides a close glimpse of the development of a witchcraft trial in which people of a local village turned against a quarrelsome old woman whom they considered burdensome and wanted to get rid of. As the witnesses and the judiciary worked towards the same aim and a hidden interrogation took place, the trial developed in an unfortunate direction: Karin Persdotter's words were twisted, and the case ended in a death sentence. The records provide an unusual peek into the imagination of Karin Persdotter, a poor seventeenth-century woman: the images she provides, her feelings, senses, strategies, and thoughts so deeply rooted in folk belief—a richness of layers. In the trial of Karin Persdotter, very weak testimonies were heeded by the judiciary, so she became an easy prey for anger and dissatisfaction. The village's judgement played a decisive role.

The trial of Karin Dantz represents the Blåkulla witchcraft trials, and differs from the other two with regard to the start of the trial and the content. It also differs from other Blåkulla trials, as Karin confessed to having been abducted to Blåkulla by an adult woman, not a child.

The Swedish cases show a century of witchcraft persecution in a Nordic country wherein the law had taken measures to secure the correct treatment of witchcraft trials. The demand that a local court pass on severe cases to High Courts certainly reduced the number of executions. However, even if torture during witchcraft trials was forbidden, exceptions were made in order to obtain the names of accomplices.[295] Traditional as well as new learned ideas about witchcraft made their impact during the period of witchcraft persecution in Sweden. Demonological and malevolent notions influenced the laws, the minds of the judiciary, and courtroom practice, bringing the number of executions in witchcraft trials in Sweden very close to what is found in the neighbouring Nordic countries.

9
FINLAND—MAGIC SALT, UNCOVERED HAIR, AND BLÅKULLA

The witchcraft trials in Finland differ in several respects from those in the other countries in this book. The trials started later, the rate of execution was low, a large proportion of the accused were acquitted, demonological elements were not prominent, and the gender proportion was about fifty–fifty, meaning that Finland had one of the largest percentages of men among those accused and sentenced in witchcraft trials in all of Europe.[1] In addition, national conditions were different some centuries ago. The 'Finland' referred to in this book should be understood as corresponding geographically to today's Finland. In the 1600s, this area was part of Sweden, as Finland did not become a state of its own until 1917.[2] At the time of the witchcraft trials, Sweden and Finland had the same judicial system.

The trials chosen for the analysis of women's voices in witchcraft trials in Finland are the cases of Gertrud Matsdotter from Eurajoki in Southern Finland, 1649; Maria Nilsdotter from Emkarby, 1666; and Brita Eriksdotter Pålsu from Kokkola, 1685. The three trials took place in the western and southern part of what today is Finland. The first was held in the municipality of Eurajoki, close to the Eura River. Eurajoki is situated at the south-western coast of Finland, in the region of Satakunta. The second was held in Emkarby in Åland. The Åland Islands group consists of 6,500 islands and is located in the Baltic Sea between Finland and Sweden. In the Early Modern period, from the 1300s onwards, Åland was connected to the church in the town of Turku, and from 1634, it was an administrative part of the district or province of Turku and Pori.[3] The third trial chosen for analysis was held in the municipality and town of Kokkola.[4] The town was part of the Swedish Empire and is among the oldest towns in Finland.[5] It is located in the Ostrobothnia Region on the coast of the Gulf of Bothnia, the northernmost part of the Baltic Sea. The courts belonged to the Turku Court of Appeal.

The language spoken in these three districts in the seventeenth century was Swedish in Åland and both Swedish and Finnish in Satakunta and Ostrobothnia,

DOI: 10.4324/9781003255406-9

with a Finnish-speaking majority in Satakunta and a Swedish-speaking majority in the coastal towns of Ostrobothnia. The court records are written in Swedish. Oral testimonies in Finnish were translated into Swedish for the court records. The Finnish lower court records have survived from the 1620s onwards, and provide very good sources for research due to their high level of detail and continuity over decades.[6] The records are written in the Gothic hand and preserved in regional and central archival institutions in Finland and Sweden.

The selected trials are from the middle and the last half of the 1600s. The choice for this period is related to the fact that most trials in Finland occurred between 1660 and 1700. By establishing a chronological line throughout four decades, it is possible to compare the intensity of persecution, the range of witchcraft ideas, court practice, courtroom discourse, and the nature of the accused women's confessions, including orality features. The selected records also provide insight into notions related to healing and traditional folkloric motifs. In order to carry out close readings of the court records, relatively detailed records were chosen.

In the trials selected for analysis, the voices of women mainly surface in accused persons' confessions and in the testimonies of female witnesses. Both the confessions and the testimonies are narratives and are structured as such. A narratological approach to analysis will highlight the way these narratives are told, with regard to both content and the linguistic features that tend to individualize the language user. Also, knowledge about witchcraft will come to the fore in the women's voices, mainly during interrogation and in the accused's confessions. Further, attention will be paid to a potential turning point in the trial.

The court records used for analysis were produced within a legal frame, which provides the context for analysis. The words expressed in the courtroom—by the accused person, the judiciary, and the witnesses—were uttered during a criminal trial. This affects the understanding and interpretation of courtroom discourse. The scribe made an effort to record this discourse in an accurate and reliable way. However, text-critical elements and an evaluation of the scribe's possibilities to influence the court records also form part of the analytical work that will be done.

Each trial is first given a description, followed by an analysis of the voice of the accused woman. Also, other voices heard during the trial, such as the voices of the witnesses, the voice of the law, the voice of the interrogator, and the voice of the scribe, are discussed. The factors dealt with in the analysis are comparable to those discussed for the other countries in this book. The chapter ends with a conclusion that summarizes the central findings of the analyses.

Background

Persecution

About 2,000 persons were accused of witchcraft in Finland; a large amount for a population of about 400,000.[7] Of these, 150 to 200 were given a death sentence.

The execution rate in the Finnish witchcraft trials was less than 10%, which is low compared to most other European countries. Half of all those accused were acquitted.[8] The remaining convictions resulted in fines and mild forms of corporal punishment.

The Finnish witchcraft trials took place between the mid-sixteenth and late eighteenth centuries. There were few trials between 1540 and 1620, and these were primarily concerned with benevolent magic, superstition, and *maleficium*.[9] The bulk of trials occurred after 1640, with most taking place during the last four decades of the 1600s. Ideas related to demonology, the devil's pact, and witches' gatherings appeared only in trials that took place between 1650 and 1689. There were a few witchcraft trials during the eighteenth century, mainly trials for super-stitious or fraudulent magic.[10]

The persons accused of witchcraft in Finland came from all levels of society, as stated by Raisa Maria Toivo, who discusses questions related to witches and power and challenges those who see the witches as victims only.[11] The gender distribu-tion in Finland was special.[12] Likewise, Iceland was exceptional within a European context, with only one woman accused out of a total of twenty-two individuals.[13]

The Lutheran religion was a state religion in seventeenth-century Sweden—after the Reformation, Lutheran dogma had been steadily imposed across North-ern Europe, and Sweden was no exception. However, this process was slow and took place over a long period, a fact that has been emphasized by several scholars.[14] Nevertheless, the impact of the Reformation on the Nordic witchcraft trials is clear—particularly in the wording of the records' verdict.

Jurisdiction

In the legal system in Early Modern Northern Europe, the accusatorial process gradually turned towards a more inquisitorial process, as judicial officials adopted the role of public prosecutors. The *talion* principle (persons who brought charges to court but failed to prove them risked the same punishment as their oppo-nents would have suffered, had the charges against them been proven) was losing its importance.[15] Most witchcraft trials in Northern Europe took place in local courts, and this was the case in Finland as well.[16] Like in the rest of Northern Europe, the judicial system in Finland was based on interaction between differ-ent governmental and jurisdictional levels. All records of the treatment of crimes possibly carrying the death penalty were reviewed in the Court of Appeal, the Turku High Court,[17] before the sentence was carried out.[18] This made it necessary for the lower court to strive to fulfil demands from higher judicial levels when it came to transparency, predictability, and verifiability.[19] There was only one High Court in the whole of Finland during the seventeenth century, and it was located in Turku.[20]

In Finland, District Courts and town magistrate courts were found at the lower level, and the accused were summoned to these courts in person. During the trials, the hearings were typically oral and were open to the public. As such, in addition to the accused, the defendants, and the witnesses, there would have been a crowd of local people in attendance who were allowed to voice their opinions.[21] Like the other Nordic countries, the judiciary in local courts consisted of judicial officials, and there was a jury of trustworthy men from the local community to decide on the verdict and sentence. In addition, the legal officials present would have included the judge and the scribe. The judge and the scribe were not local: they represented the central government and thus a higher level of learning. The jury, however, consisted of trustworthy individuals from the community who, in addition to their role in deciding on the verdict and sentence, were expected to act as local experts and provide information during the trial.[22]

Torture was not legal in lower courts.[23] However, exceptions were made.[24] Torture could be applied if special permission was granted by the Turku High Court, which also had to approve the sentences passed by the lower court. For two of the cases analysed below, torture was applied after a sentence was passed in order to obtain the names of the accused's alleged accomplices—such as others who had participated in witches' gatherings alongside the accused. Denmark and Norway followed the same court practice with regard to the application of torture at the time.

Gertrud Matsdotter, 1649

The Trial

The trial of Gertrud Matsdotter took place in Eurajoki Parish[25] in the south of Finland.[26] She was first brought before a local court on 9–10 November 1649. Local police official[27] Eskill Thomasson in Irjande[28] was in charge of the case. Gertrud Matsdotter was a married peasant woman living in the village of Hansby in Eurajoki. Her husband was Sigfred Thomasson. She had long been rumoured to practise witchcraft, and it was her neighbours who formally accused her. The first witness was one of her neighbours, Henrich Matsson, and he testified that eight years ago, there had been a conflict between him and Gertrud Matsdotter's husband. Gertrud then allegedly threatened Henrich with these words: 'Watch out, I will find you and give you a secret sign'.[29] The following day, Henrich Matsson became seriously ill. Henrich was then asked by the court how he could know that Gertrud had cast a spell[30] on him. He answered that she had done something to lift the spell, and that he had become better at once.

Next, the records mention the testimony of a chaplain, Herr[31] Mårthen, who reported that some time earlier, the aforementioned Henrich Matsson had been seriously ill and received the last rites. Herr Mårthen, too, believed that a spell had been cast on Henrich by Gertrud Matsdotter. Sigfred Thomasson, the husband of Gertrud, was adamant that he had not threatened Henrich, let alone that his wife had cast a spell on Henrich in such a way.

Henrich Matsson then testified,[32] the records continue, that seven years ago, he had regained a field from Sigfred Thomasson, which Sigfred had acquired illegally, as it belonged to Henrich. A few days later, Henrich was hit by a severe spell, an illness that lasted seven weeks, and he had nearly died of this spell, had it not been for the help in curing the illness with counter-magic he received from Dordei Matsdotter in Köyliöpolvi, Eurajoki Parish (who is now dead, the records clarify).[33] Henrich had lost some cows a few times, but did not think that Gertrud had cast a spell on them. However, because she had always hated and threatened him, and things happened as she said they would right afterwards, his suspicions were that she had caused the cows' death.[34] And Henrich swore an oath that Gertrud had threatened him in the presence of Lucas Jacobsen (who worked as a cleaner[35] in Sweden) who was now at Korsmäkeri. Afterwards, the records state, Henrich had asked Sigfred who had taught him the art. The latter answered right away, 'Yes, the art [of sending *tyror* after someone to hurt him] is perfectly learnt, but they are not yet thrown after you. But watch out, it will hereafter be too much infected', and he complained that he was afflicted with *tyror* many times.[36] Henrich said that he had been attacked by spells several times. However, he had no witnesses whom the other had threatened, and the witnesses had little complete knowledge on what illness he suffered from, other than that he had been very ill[37] (and even Henrich spread this word that he had a spell cast on him). This his neighbours confessed and testified to, the records state.

Henrich Matsson further reported that his animals or cattle[38] had become ill at his farm in Stopan some time before Michaelmas, and two cows and one kid were sent to Gertrud Matsdotter for healing. Gertrud confessed that the cattle were led to her, but said that she did not know how to cure them, let alone that she had received the *pertzelar*,[39] the aforementioned goods, but still the animals became better and were healed.

Also, the records continue, her other neighbour Michel Carlsen's son Mårthen Mikilson testified on several points. First, he testified that the aforementioned Gertrud Matsdotter had, without his knowledge, taken one sheep from his entire flock with the intention, he could not understand otherwise, to slaughter it. This sheep Gertrud had locked in her own barn, and when her sister Augnes heard the sound of the sheep, she had run to the door of Gertrud's barn mentioned before and let the sheep out, something her father heard. Then, Gertrud took a piece of wood and intended to strike Augnes, but the latter managed to escape. When Gertrud's evil deed could not be performed, she uttered the *formalia*[40] word *jacas*[41] (in the presence of another neighbour, the late Nils Jöranson). Two days later, she had cast a spell on him (Nils Jöranson), and with that he was bothered for a long time, until a woman in Raumo[42] allegedly healed it, and the spell was sent on to Mårthen. Gertrud was taken to court by the aforementioned Nils (Jöranson), but wanted to negotiate, and Mårthen found her forgiven because of her prayer, when the sheep was given back. Therefore, the records declare, the charges were dropped.

The records then state that Anders Nilsson, son of Nils, was called forth and confirmed what his father had said about the agreement, and he did not have anything more to say about the incident. As for the agreement about the sheep, Gertrud Matsdotter could not deny it, but as for casting a spell, she refused to confess.

Anders said that Sigfred Thomasson's pig had caused destruction on Mårthen Mikilson's seeds several times, and Mårthen had warned him that he should watch out,
but he (Sigfred Thomasson) did not care about this. Therefore, Mårthen once saw
himself obliged to hit him on the back, which he (Sigfred) some time afterwards
allegedly paid Mårthen back for when he was out at sea in Söbskäer,[43] because he
(Mårthen) was then very heavily attacked by a spell.

Second, the records continue, Mårthen Mikilson was asked how he knew that
it was a spell that had caused his illness, and he answered that at the same time,
Sigfred's wife Gertrud Matsdotter salvaged[44] hay from an inlet,[45] and she decided
that he should get what was mentioned above.[46] The same was stated by neighbour Henrich Matsson, who once transported him (Mårthen) from the beach with
oxen. He (Henrich) said that he was saved from this illness, and that he had been
cured from it by Dordei in Köyliöpolvi.[47] The aforementioned Gertrud confirmed
that Mårthen had been ill, but said that this was not a result of her witchcraft.[48]

Third, the records carry on, Mårthen Mikilson answered a question on how the
aforementioned Sigfred Thomasson took one of the horses belonging to his father-
in-law, Mats Bengstsen in Korpis, with the intention of ploughing his (Mårthen's)
field. But he could do nothing of the kind, since Mårthen's horse would not obey
at any time, but chased into a sandbank,[49] and Sigfred Thomasson was then to
blame for the mischief. And he was obliged to lead his father-in-law's horse home
again. One or two days after this incident, Mårthen's horse had been severely hit by
a spell, and had nearly died,[50] because he (Mårthen) had not used the appropriate
means[51] required. The same Henrich Matsson said that this was true, but he did not
know who was responsible for the harm performed through witchcraft.[52]

Fourth, the records continue, Mårthen Mikilson also declared that Sigfred
Thomasson's wife Gertrud Matsdotter had threatened his father's cattle shepherd,[53]
a young boy, just for the sake of some pieces of turnip,[54] which he (the boy) had
taken out of her turnip land, and said (however, nobody seems to have heard it, so
it could not be proved)[55] that he would pay for it dearly.[56] This then allegedly came
to pass,[57] so that the boy almost died if they had not found a remedy at Henrich
Larsen in Himilän, who confessed that he had obtained salt[58] from the late Bertil
Helli in Cumo Parish.[59]

Fifth, the above-mentioned Mårthen Mikilson, on his wife Ursula's behalf, testified
before the court how the aforementioned Gertrud Matsdotter had allegedly
scolded her (Ursula) several times with shameful words.[60] In particular, these words
were: 'Little have you been ill before, but hereafter this shall be improved, evil and
the like may happen'.[61] This also came to pass.[62] And even though the aforementioned Mårthen's wife had not herself sworn a full oath[63] as a witness, he hoped that
the deed would be remembered. And with this notification, he paused his case, as
there was no formal witness at this point.[64]

Gertrud Matsdotter's third neighbour, Erich Henderson, the records go on,
offered to swear an oath and said that he had heard perfectly well how Gertrud had
boasted and said that she could get as much butter as she herself wanted (namely
4 *Lispund*[65] from a cow and 1 *Lispund* from an animal).[66] Henrich Matsson said

that he had heard the same (her boasting), although he had not heard it specified. When asked whether her neighbours had suffered any harm in terms of butter, it was answered that Erich's mother had had no luck making butter for many years.[67] Then, after a while, Erich stated that some years ago, when he was to travel to Sassila farm[68] together with others and use the small boat[69] belonging to the farm, wife Gertrud threatened him with this formula:[70] 'Watch out, because before you come from there and back here, you will become worse; a flea shall bite you'.[71] This also happened, so that he got a big scar on his head.[72] Because of this, a witness was called forth, a member of the jury, namely Oleff Matsson in Lomplax. He explained that an old woman, Valborg Persdatter,[73] told him that she had heard Gertrud's boasting: 'What she promises with the mouth, she finishes off with the deed'.[74] The same was reportedly witnessed by Margretta, who lived in the same house, and who could not be brought before the court because of her old-age weakness.[75]

In addition, the records continue, Erich Henderson testified that he had gained, through inheritance, the farmstead that he now lived on, where Gertrud Matsdotter had lived before. During the time of the previous bailiff, Grels Matsson, Gertrud was placed at another farmstead,[76] where she did not have to pay taxes,[77] and Erich Henderson took over the farmstead where she lived. Gertrud had threatened Erich, saying that he should not be glad about this,[78] and after that he complained that he had had a lot of adversity. Among other things, his hand was injured.[79] He had obtained what he aimed for when he took over the farmstead. However, due to his injured hand, he could no longer cut trees at the farmstead,[80] and this became his downfall and ruin. Second, none of his cattle could thrive. Third, he suffered great damage through harmful fires several times and now, around last Michaelmas,[81] in a house where people lived,[82] a small child had burned to death (who belonged to a wife in the same house, Maisa Matsdotter).

This Maisa Matsdotter maintained that this fire happened because Gertrud Matsdotter had asked her to move from Erich's farmstead and come live with her in the house, and Maisa had not agreed. Gertrud had then let these words drop: 'You shall regret this before St Martin's Day[83] comes'. This came true when her child burned to death in a conflagration.[84] This, the records state, the oft-mentioned Maisa confirmed in her testimony; however, no witnesses were there who had heard Gertrud speak these words. Gertrud adamantly denied, and she said that she did not know how to practise the deed itself, just her own formula words:[85] *Cuka tietä Jos se tulle sitä mina Lausun*[86]—'It will happen that Our Lord punishes them who cause me pain'.

One of the jury members, Eskill Henderson in Päräby, declared that Gertrud's grandfather's father was born in Safwolax.[87] He had filled a bag with all types of witchery, and afterwards, he placed the above-mentioned things with the bag under the threshold of the barn of Eskill's father in Jngräffvit, and with that the aforementioned Eskill's father had had much adversity with cattle.[88] Then, at last, a beggar from Norrbotten[89] came, who foretold[90] that something must have been laid under the threshold of the barn. This was found as aforementioned, and once it was taken away, the cattle started to thrive again. And Eskill also said that he suspected Gertrud, that she knew something about such matters; as for her father, however, nothing other than honour and good was known to date.

Finally, the chaplain,[91] Herr Mårthen, on his daughter Margreta Mårthensdatter's behalf, testified that anno 1647, on Easter Sunday, during the time of the Easter service, Herr Mårthen's dog had made a very bad sound, and the daughter, the aforementioned Margreta herself, had felt unwell after the sound. And she saw a female person[92] walking in the field, but she could not recognize who it was (because it was at a distance). In addition, a young woman, Margreta Erichsdotter in Hansby, said in her testimony that on the same day and date, she witnessed Gertrud Matsdotter who had come running with bare feet, her hair uncovered and loose,[93] and this happened during the Easter dinner service. The aforementioned girl reportedly asked her what she looked like.[94] She answered that never in her life had she had an Easter day so terrible as she had suffered that day.[95] Gertrud adamantly denied this.

Concluding the trial, the records continue, the following sentence was passed: as much as Gertrud Matsdotter was thoroughly examined and admonished to confess the truth,[96] we could not bring her to do so. But nevertheless, it is recorded that such similarities are found in what is touched upon in the examination, that what she intended and threatened has partially occurred.[97]

Still, she was cleared of the charges (but not of loose speech) without any suspicion, which the jury placed confidence in. Therefore, the case was judged after Chapter 13 in Högmålsbalken.[98] The twelve men in the jury unanimously decided that she should free herself with an oath of compurgation,[99] given by eleven honest women, with herself as the twelfth,[100] after Chapter 19 in Tingsbalken.[101] The court required her, at the appointed time, to comply with[102] the punishment that could follow.

In Eurajoki, on 15–16 March 1650, Henrich Matsson and Erich Henderson in Hansby, both of them witnesses during the 1649 trial, appeared before the court and claimed a sentence[103] for their neighbour Sigfred Thomasson's wife, Gertrud Matsdotter, at the same place, who had been tried and sentenced at the last court session after Chapter 19 in Tingsbalken[104] and Chapter 13 in Högmålsbalken, stating that she should appear again at the next court session, following the rumour for witchcraft that she had become a subject of. Several points of the charges were made known to her husband, who had the obligation to bring her to court again. The records go on, saying that they further stated that, although she was accused of having been associated with[105] witchcraft and sorcery, which the attached testimonies show, she had been unable to procure the oaths of eleven honest women that she spoke the truth,[106] and so had fled to Ulfsby[107] Parish. The jury, in response, and in accordance with Chapter 19:34 *infinæ*[108] in Tingsbalken, sentenced Gertrud to be burned in fire at the stake, a punishment in accordance with Chapters 6 and 15 in Högmålsbalken—and herewith the sentence was most humbly[109] placed under the further resolution of the High Court.

The court records from the Court of Appeal have not been preserved, so we do not know whether they confirmed the sentence from the local court. Marko

Nenonen states that it is not known whether the sentence was executed. Therefore, the final outcome of the trial of Gertrud Matsdotter remains uncertain.[110]

The Voice of Gertrud Matsdotter

The voice of Gertrud Matsdotter can be heard in her responses to questions, in denials of accusations, and in the witnesses' testimonies, specifically in their recitation of her curses and threats.

Most of all, the voice of Gertrud Matsdotter is a voice of resistance. Several times, we hear Gertrud Matsdotter immediately denying accusations made by the witnesses. She denies all accusations against her. The judicial officials pay attention to her denials in court, and her voice of denial is respected. No confession to witchcraft is heard. A confession of guilt from her own mouth would have been decisive for the sentencing; however, it is clearly pronounced in the sentence that, although she was examined and admonished to confess the truth, she denied practising witchcraft. The suspicion against her could therefore not be confirmed, so she could not be convicted for witchcraft. She managed to uphold the strength of her resistance throughout the trial: no hesitation or weakness can be traced in the words that come from her mouth. Instead of supporting the suspicion against her, she strongly protests.

Gertrud Matsdotter's voice, as it is rendered in the witnesses' depositions, is threatening. She knew, and used, charms and cursing to cast spells on humans and animals. All cursing had to do with sickness and death. The neighbours claimed that her curses and spells came true, and that they were connected to accidents and tragedies which recently struck the local community.

Gertrud's use of formulaic expressions clearly comes to the fore in the witnesses' depositions. The closest she comes to a confession is admitting that she indeed uttered the words of a specific curse, but she repeatedly claims that the performance of witchcraft—the actual content of the curse itself—was never carried out. It seems, therefore, that in her understanding, there was a difference between pronouncing a curse and having that curse result in any evildoing. In the eyes of the law, however, by confessing to cursing, using charms and formulas, she had practised witchcraft. In addition, she admits to having offered her services for healing and counter-magic and having in fact received payment for this.

Gertrud Matsdotter herself is not thinking in terms of cause and effect, that is, that something harmful will happen as a consequence of her uttered words. The witnesses see it differently: a misfortune was promised and tragedy followed just after, in the form of the sickness or death of animals and humans. This is what the witnesses believed; it is a recurrent feature in all witnesses' depositions. Gertrud's words did not represent an empty threat. Gertrud's voice as it is rendered in the court records may be interpreted as the voice of an outspoken woman. Apparently, she had a conflict with her neighbours on several occasions, and her threats are claimed to have come true. Thus, she is portrayed as a dangerous person. In all the curses and threats, a particular stylistic tone is present, as there is always something uttered only halfway, while the rest of the meaning remains an enigma—an understatement which makes the uttering even more frightening. This is the semantic nature of a curse.

However, Gertrud Matsdotter's voice is not only threatening; it also has a boasting accent. The neighbours did not only react to her curses. They also reacted to her boasting about how much butter she could get from her cows. While some people got very little butter, including the mother of one of the witnesses, Gertrud says she can get a lot of butter. This was considered suspicious, as it could mean that she had supernatural powers which she could use to manipulate the amount of butter.

On one occasion, Gertrud Matsdotter's voice seems to have a humble accent. She must have been a versatile person. The witnesses testify about a sheep that Gertrud stole from a neighbour and placed in her barn. The neighbour accused her of stealing. In this case, an agreement was reached, and the sheep was given back to its owner. However, it is stated that Gertrud was forgiven due to her prayer, so she must have been begging for forgiveness.

In Gertrud Matsdotter's voice, we can discover some of her knowledge of ideas about witchcraft. While we hear no confessions of a demonological character, she apparently knew *maleficium*, even if she did not confess to it. In addition, she was used to providing counter-magic and healing, which means that she must have known charms and formulas, knowledge gained through oral transmission.

Features of orality are strong in Gertrud Matsdotter's voice: in her rendered expressions, her curses, and her threats. In particular, Gertrud's curses have preserved this oral accent: the sayings are short, pointed, and easy to remember, using rhythm, intonation, and contrast to capture attention. The court records occupy a specific place between oral and written text, as oral phrases and orally transmitted sayings uttered in the courtroom were taken down by the scribe. The oral accent of Gertrud's voice is strong in the witnesses' rendering of her threats. The type of threatening words that Gertrud is connected with is typical of threats in many cultures: the evil that is to come is undefined and can therefore imply many things. In the threat about the flea, we see first an exclamation ('watch out'), and then a timeline is established ('before you come from there and back here'). There is also a development from bad to worse in the sentence, which, together with the detail about the flea, makes the saying easy to remember. Orality features can also be seen when special days of the year—like St Martin's Day, Michaelmas, Easter Sunday, St Jacob's Day—are used to attach a certain event to a specific day of the year: one of the quarter days particularly days related to the supernatural.

Gertrud Matsdotter shows irritation and disappointment through cursing. She might have been an ill-tempered person who easily cursed people, but she also had her grounds for doing so. Several curses uttered by Gertrud were related to neighbours. She had to leave her farmstead when Erich Henderson moved in, so no wonder she felt anger and expressed it. She was angry with Maisa Matsdotter because she (Maisa) did not want to come live with her (Gertrud). She supported her husband in a conflict he had with Henrich Matsson. These incidents show a woman who reacted in an understandable manner when there were conflicts with neighbours or when her sustenance came under attack.

Gertrud also shows fear. When her case came up again in 1650, she fled to another town. She had not managed to get eleven women to swear for her. At this point in time, it was well known in local Finnish communities what a witchcraft trial might lead to. The trial records of Gertrud Matsdotter show that however strong and resistant her voice was, in the meeting with the law, she was helpless.

No torture or extreme pressure is mentioned as having been used to make Gertrud Matsdotter confess. The turning point during her trial did not occur until the sentence was passed: to free herself from rumours of witchcraft, the oath of compurgation had to be used. This requirement was very difficult to fulfil, and Gertrud did not manage to do so. With only denials and no confession from Gertrud's mouth, the jury had to base its verdict and sentence entirely on the depositions of the witnesses, as is clearly illustrated in the pronounced sentence.

We cannot hear Gertrud's voice in these final trial records because, by this time, she had fled to Ulfsby Parish. These records from Eurajoki, dated 15 and 16 March 1650—four months after Gertrud's first trial—indicate that the case was made known to her husband, so that she had to be brought before the court again. She was accused once again of having practised witchcraft and sorcery, by the same neighbours who testified against her in her first trial, Henrich Matsson and Erich Henderson. She was ultimately sentenced to be burned at the stake: a severe sentence, given that she never confessed to having practised witchcraft, nor did any demonological ideas appear in the case.

The Voices of the Witnesses

The voices of female witnesses are heard during the trial, but only faintly. We hear the testimonies of seven male witnesses, but only two female witnesses: Maisa Matsdotter, who lost her child in a fire, and Margreta Erichsdotter, who had seen Gertrud Matsdotter with her hair uncovered in the fields during an Easter dinner service. The impact of their voices was relatively weak, as there were no witnesses to support Maisa's accusation that Gertrud cursed her, nor could anyone confirm that Margreta had indeed seen Gertrud in the fields. In both instances, it was Gertrud's word against the word of the witness, and her denial was quite strong.

We also hear the voices of several other women, but only as rendered in court by male witnesses: the chaplain, Herr Mårthen, on behalf of his daughter Margreta Mårthensdatter, who said that she had seen a female person in the field during Easter service; Mårthen Mikilson, on behalf of Gertrud's sister Augnes; Mårthen, on behalf of his wife Ursula; and jury member Oleff Matsson, on behalf of the elderly woman Valborg Persdatter and Margretta, who lived in the same house as Valborg.

The weight and impact of the male witnesses' testimonies are much stronger than those of the female witnesses. Among the men, we have four of Gertrud Matsdotter's neighbours—Henrich Matsson, Mårthen Mikilson, Anders Nilsson, and Erich Henderson—along with two jury members, Oleff Matsson and Eskill Henderson, and the chaplain, Herr Mårthen. One after another, the men are brought before the court, each appearing to believe in Gertrud's power to curse others. Their depositions are narratives in which misfortune always followed Gertrud's threats. We see here the kind of cause-and-effect argumentation often used in accusations in witchcraft trials: if a threat comes true immediately after it is uttered, this supports a connection between the threat and the accident, as a threatening utterance leaves room for many interpretations.

The first witness, Henrich Matsson, believes that Gertrud Matsdotter cursed him, but also that she mastered healing and counter-magic. And he believes that a woman in another parish, Dordei Matsdotter, could break the spell. The second witness, Mårthen Mikilson, is the first to render one of Gertrud's curses before the court. Mårthen seems to believe in Gertrud's mastering of the art of witchcraft. The third witness, Anders Nilsson, only confirms what his father has said concerning an agreement on a sheep as payment for healing and also concerning an alleged curse. Gertrud does not deny having healed, but denies having cursed Anders's father. Here, we can hear Gertrud's own voice: she is present in court, so can react immediately to Anders's testimony. She has the same reaction to Anders's next accusation, which is that Gertrud cursed Mårthen. Again, we see the curse argument being used without any proof other than the witness's belief in Gertrud's intention. And again, Gertrud denies the accusation, saying that Mårthen's illness was not as a result of her *förgörning*, her alleged harming with witchcraft.

Next, we hear Mårthen Mikilson's testimony about a horse and a ram that were both attacked by spells. To cure the ram, he had to obtain a kind of magic salt.[111] Mårthen states that Gertrud Matsdotter cursed the horse and the ram, but did not render the words she used. Mårthen also testifies on his wife Ursula's behalf, stating that although Ursula had not filed an official complaint against Gertrud, Gertrud had on several occasions threatened Ursula. Mårthen wants the court to make a note of this in the hope that it would be remembered, even if he could not prove that the threats had occurred. Even if they did not find or name a witness during this short court session, he hoped that in the future he could provide witnesses. This is a legal note made by the scribe, in the third person; the scribe is recording what he thought Mårthen wanted.[112] Because the further legal procedure was uncertain, on the day of his testimony, Mårthen did not know whether a sentence would be passed that same day or if the case would be postponed until further witnesses could be heard. In Mårthen's opinion, the actual words of the curse were not important for the deed itself to be carried out, and the curse's effect could be observed even if the exact wording of the curse could not be proved.

Up to this point in the trial, Gertrud Matsdotter has been connected with threats and *maleficium*, through curses whose effects allegedly occurred shortly after the curses were uttered, and she has also been connected with healing. But with the testimonies of the neighbours Henrich Matsson and Erich Henderson, another type of witchcraft is introduced into the trial—namely the stealing of milk from other people's cows, producing large amounts of butter. Gertrud's boasting about being able to get butter was rendered as a recitation of a string of words. The suspicion cast on Gertrud is strengthened when Oleff Matsson, one of the jury members, recites remarks he had heard about Gertrud's deeds from two old women. Gertrud's boasting, as allegedly overheard and then retold by the old women, pertains to her power: people should know there is a reason to fear her—indeed, she wants people to fear her.

Erich Henderson's story about taking over Gertrud Matsdotter's homestead concludes with the rendering of her threat. This time, the accusation is that she caused a conflagration. However, she maintains that her words were never actually put into effect. Here, she admits to having uttered a curse, which is recited in Finnish, her mother tongue. The scribe chose to write down the curse in the language Gertrud was in fact speaking, as if her words became stronger when they were rendered *verbatim*.[113] She admits that she pronounced the curse, but she does not admit that there was any deed connected to the saying of the words.

Then, Gertrud Matsdotter's witchcraft heritage is brought up by a jury member, Eskill Henderson, who declares that her great-grandfather knew witchery and witchcraft. Gertrud's great-grandfather is brought into the picture in order to strengthen the idea that she knows witchcraft. This testimony shows that the jury was not neutral, but had certain attitudes that were likely to influence the sentencing. It also suggests that rumours about family witchcraft could cling to a person through generations and eventually play a part in the proceedings of a witchcraft trial. Thus, Gertrud's grandfather's witchcraft is brought to light in a way that might harm her—even though, with regard to her father, only honour and good were known.

Finally, we have the testimonies of the vicar, Herr Mårthen, speaking on his daughter's and another girl's behalf. These describe how Gertrud Matsdotter ran across the field with loose and uncovered hair during Easter service,[114] and how the minister's dog had made a bad sound. The implied meaning here is that Gertrud was up to no good on Easter Sunday, something Gertrud herself strongly denies.

The voices of the witnesses, male and female neighbours alike, signal that rumours about Gertrud Matsdotter's knowledge and practice of witchcraft were widespread. Mostly, the testimonies are weak in the sense that the majority are based on cause-and-effect argumentation The witnesses wanted to get rid of a person who they argued was not only quarrelsome, but also dangerous.

The Voice of the Interrogator

In the trial of Gertrud Matsdotter, the voice of the interrogator, the local police official in charge of the case, does not come to the fore often. However, the voice is echoed in Gertrud's denial and in her countering of witnesses' testimonies— occasions at which Gertrud was given the opportunity to respond. As the witnesses gave their testimonies in a fluent linguistic form, there was no need for leading questions. As for ideas about witchcraft, the interrogator does not force the trial into the direction of demonological notions. Neither does he ask follow-up questions related to healing, which was one of the elements of her practice mentioned in the testimonies. His main contribution was to conduct the trial in a formally correct manner.

The Voice of the Law

The voice of the law is clearly heard in the verdict and sentence of the 1649 trial and in the sentence of the 1650 trial. References to the laws were recorded. In the 1649 trial, the verdict notes that Gertrud Matsdotter has not confessed, in spite of examination and admonition. Still, she is not acquitted. The connection between her threats and the misfortune that followed her threats is given weight when it comes to the question of guilt.

As for the sentence, the jury has paid attention to doubt and does not find that the suspicion against her has been proved. She is given the chance to free herself by an oath of compurgation, having eleven trustworthy women from the parish to swear that she speaks the truth, with herself as the twelfth. Her husband has the obligation to bring her to court again during the next court session.

In the 1650 trial, two of the witnessing neighbours demand a sentence in the case, as Gertrud Matsdotter should appear again at the next court session. The requirement about the oath of compurgation was not fulfilled. Then, the death sentence of burning at the stake is passed, with reference to respective laws. No further reason is given. The fact that she did not confess has not changed. No additional witnesses were heard. So her conviction was implemented based on very weak testimonies from neighbours related to *maleficium*.

The Voice of the Scribe

The scribe's recording is professional. Most of the trial records in this case consist of witnesses' testimonies. The scribe used a structuring device to record each of the testimonies, as each new point in the testimony is marked with a number. No distancing linguistic devices can be traced on the part of the scribe, so it appears that he believed that sorcery and witchcraft could happen. However, the scribe also believed, as we can see in the example of Mårthen Mikilson's testimony on behalf of his wife Ursula, that cause and effect could be separated, such that the result of sorcery could be detected even if the spell was not heard. The scribe tried to accurately take down the courtroom's discourse in order to show what was said and thus provide a clear understanding of the trial in case it was sent to the Court of Appeal. Facts about the trial and the names and hometowns of jury members, witnesses, and accused person were recorded, as were the content of the testimonies, the verdict, and the sentence.

Still, there are some text-critical points to be noted. Original speech by the accused person in Finnish was translated into Swedish for the records, so that linguistic shades and details might have been amended. The brevity of the court records is sometimes a challenge when it comes to interpretation, as the recorded text was condensed. Nevertheless, the semantic meaning of the courtroom discourse and the rendering of oral features all point to an understanding that the court records are reliable and that the central elements of the trial proceedings were taken down as precisely as possible.

Maria Nilsdotter, 1666

The Trial

Maria Nilsdotter was accused of witchcraft during Finland's only European-style serious witch-hunt of 1666–70, presided over by the rural district judge Nils Psilander.[115] Maria Nilsdotter was denounced by a woman named Karin Persdotter,[116] who was executed for witchcraft on 8 August 1666. Karin Persdotter was first brought before the court in Finström Parish's court session at the home of Emkarby's police officer on 5 April 1666 and confessed the same day. Her confession contained demonological elements, such as the devil's pact and witches' gatherings inside a witch mountain called Blåkulla. Here, Blåkulla is described as a mountain; in other confessions it is described as a hill or a mysterious location.[117] During this interrogation, Karin denounced two women. The first was the mother of Staffan Nilsson in Emmenäs,[118] a wise woman who allegedly had convinced Karin to come along to Blåkulla the first time. The second was a woman from Finnö,[119] who had hanged herself in 1664. After this woman's death, there had been an investigation that had included a testimony stating that, when she was alive, she had been contaminated with witchcraft.

After her first confession, Karin Persdotter refused to confess to anything more, and the lower court could not coerce[120] her into any more confessions. The court was not allowed[121] to apply torture with handcuffs[122] but had threatened her with the torture chamber, which was called 'hell'.[123] Hence, the records continue, the rest had to be left to the confession that she most likely would give before her execution.[124] Karin said that her husband was completely innocent and had not known that she had gone to Blåkulla. On 5 April, Karin was sentenced to be executed by axe for witchcraft, and her body was to be burned at the stake.

Karin Persdotter's death sentence was sent to the Court of Appeal. The Court of Appeal refused to grant Karin clemency. Instead, it ordered that she should be carefully questioned about anyone else who had been party to witchcraft. This 'careful questioning' apparently included permission to use torture. Torture was forbidden in court procedure, and not directly referenced, but in the same way as in other countries, 'veiled and encoded expressions for it were used'.[125] In this case, application of torture was made after that local court and Court of Appeal settled on execution.[126] On 28 May 1666, this court confirmed her death sentence.[127] Her pact with the devil is cited as the explanation of her divination ability, as she could tell people when someone had something stolen and who had stolen it.[128] Three women who had visited Karin Persdotter to make use of her skills were fined; however, a boy who had stolen eight bundles of rye from Karin was acquitted.[129]

'The witch of Emkarby' could not be pardoned, and it is stated that many like her could be found.[130]

Several months would pass before Karin Persdotter was brought before the court in an extraordinary court session at Casteleholm on 6 August 1666.[131] During this interrogation, she gave a very long confession and denounced twelve women, among them Maria Nilsdotter in Marcusböle, whom Karin described as the daughter of the woman in Emmenäs who seduced Karin into witchcraft.[132] Due to this denunciation on 6 August, Maria Nilsdotter and another woman, Kirstin in Lemböte, were taken into custody by the caretaker at Casteleholm.[133] Both of them had been accused of witchcraft previously.[134] The other women denounced by Karin were released on bail until the next court session. Thus, Karin Persdotter was still alive when Maria was taken prisoner. Karin was executed two days later, on 8 August.[135] What happened to Karin between May and August 1666 is not known, but we know that she was tortured after the sentence of execution in the Court of Appeal. We also know that during these four months, she had lived under the pressure of a death sentence.

On 24 August 1666, eighteen days after Maria Nilsdotter had been taken into custody and sixteen days after Karin Persdotter's execution, a court session was held in Finström Parish, in Emkarby.[136] The court records were written in the Gothic hand and have been preserved in minute books,[137] folio format. Present were the governor,[138] Erland Törn, and the jury, twelve farmers from Finström.

The trial of Maria Nilsdotter, Axel Markusson's wife, was a fact.[139] Karin Persdotter had confessed that when she was about to enter Blåkulla mountain four or five years earlier, she met Maria Nilsdotter coming out of the mountain.[140] Karin Persdotter had also confessed, the records continue, that Maria milked the cattle from Finström's vicar's farm on the headland, after which the cattle unexpectedly died, like last winter with Herr Carl's cow—about which it was said that it had been perfectly on its feet and running around in the evening, and the next morning it was lying dead in the barn. Karin had claimed that Herr Carl and his old father found Maria in the barn once, but since Herr Carl was a pious and meek man, he had not wanted to create problems, so he had given her what she asked for: permission to milk the cow.[141] According to Karin, Maria had also caused trouble for many others, as she could destroy other people's cattle with one word only.[142] And finally, according to Karin, Maria could also heal, as several examples from the previous ten years had shown.[143]

The interrogation of Maria Nilsdotter is recorded in a style where both the questions posed to her and her answers, marked 'Responsum', are rendered. She was interrogated according to the points of the confession that Karin Persdotter had given: first, that Maria's late mother had taught both Karin and Maria witchcraft; second, that Karin had seen Maria leave Blåkulla;[144] and third, that Maria had used the same healing practices as her mother had taught Karin when Karin's brother was sick.[145] Further, it is recorded that it was also likely that the rest that Karin had confessed to about Maria was true:[146] that she had harmed with witchcraft, *förgjort*, other people's cattle and used other people's cows, especially with regard to the parish vicar in Finström's cow, which had suddenly died.

To all this, Maria Nilsdotter answered 'No' only, saying that Karin Persdotter had told lies about both her and her mother and that she had never known her mother as having anything to do with superstitious methods.[147] Maria had been accused of witchcraft previously but had been acquitted. She was now asked from whom she had learned the art that she had used before. She replied that the things that rumours said about her were absolutely not true, but were only whispered about because they could not be taken up in a church service or at a court session. To this, the interrogator objected that if every man had known as much about the habits of her home when she was gossiped about earlier as they did now, she would not have got away so easily.[148] The only thing she was required to answer now was where she had learned such an art. But she still denied, saying that the rumours had not been anything other than guesses.

It is then recorded that Maria Nilsdotter continued to hold up the court in this way for several hours. However, the scribe added that when one understood that it was not possible to win anything with the good, and when one saw that her old knowledge was similar to her late mother's, one threatened her [Maria] with the handcuffs.[149] And when she finally understood the seriousness of the situation, she said: 'Maybe I heard my mother say that one should throw silver in water when one gets sick from the sea, but I never asked my mother about such things'.[150] She was then asked how she had known that the illness of the child of the bailiff in Grelsby was caused by his urinating in the sauna at sea. She answered that she guessed that she found something to say. Then she was asked when she used to guess and when she knew what to say. It is recorded: 'Hereafter, *one could not get a categorical answer before one was obliged to set the handcuffs on (but screwed them only a little)*'.[151] [My italics.]

After this, the records go on, Maria Nilsdotter finally confessed to having used the following divination formula:[152] 'I ask you, Sigfredh Mårtinssån's son (from Grelsby's farm) where you have caught your sickness, either from the sea or from earth or when you threw your water into the sauna'.[153] And that when she had reached the last part of the formula, her body had shivered as if a cold had come upon her,[154] so she instructed the boy's mother to throw milk and silver into the sauna to cure him. She had used a similar formula for the son of Jöran in Finström: 'I ask you, Jacob Jöransson (who was swollen) where you have got your sickness, either you are crossed[155] or it has been blown upon you by members of the family'.[156] And then she had shivered. So therefore she taught Jacob's family to cast silver on the grave of his late mother, who had blown on Jacob. But she had not said by herself that Jacob's mother had blown on him in a shed by the gate; she was told that this was where Jacob had first become sick.[157]

She was further examined about when she first learned such knowledge and entered into a pact with Satan[158] since he would, through such shivering, reveal such secrets to her.[159] Then it is recorded that '*all work was in vain until the pure evening and until the court found it advisable to screw the handcuffs tighter even*'.[160] [My italics.] We see here that torture was used from the beginning of the interrogation, and that it was entered openly into the records before sentence was passed.[161] After this, Maria Nilsdotter confessed that once, in the summertime, when she had gone into the forest after some sheep, Satan had met her in boatman's clothes, 'looking black and shiny (that is leather)',[162] asking her whether she would serve him and promising her good luck with fish and knowledge to speak to people (that means knowledge to tell people about the causes and healing of illnesses), and for this he desired her soul.[163] In addition, she confessed that once, in the summertime (but not the week before Easter),[164] she had been taken to a mountain and saw how it was there. Following this statement, it is added in the court records: 'However, as she later confessed that she had here told untruth, it is not necessary to record more about this here'.[165]

The next day, Maria Nilsdotter was taken to be interrogated again, whereupon she confessed 'without any coercion' how, after her mother's death, she [her mother] had revealed herself to Maria and had taken her along to Blåkulla. However, as the court believed this to be a fable,[166] they pointed out to her what the conditions of the dead were, according to the knowledge 'revealed through the word of God',[167] and as she saw no other possibilities to get away, she finally confessed that her mother had tempted her to take part in two separate journeys to Blåkulla; however, this had happened after Maria was married to Marcusböle.[168] But after the journeys with her mother, Maria never went back, so it was not true that Karin Persdotter had seen her there recently. Maria confessed that the first time they went to Blåkulla, she was very much afraid of Satan, who had looked very shiny. Therefore, she had been thrown out because her errand was not successful, but her mother had spent some time there.[169] Maria did not know where she went, neither the way to nor from there, or where this mountain was, only that when she first recognized something, she found herself just west of Marcusböle village, on a small patch of field.[170]

But the year after, her mother persuaded her to enter Satan's service, and then her pact[171] with Satan was arranged such that Satan promised her good luck with seed from the field and fish from the sea, and also good luck with cattle, and in addition he promised her that she could tell people the cause of or remedies for illnesses. However, of seed, fish, and cattle she should not have an overabundance, but instead, when she had the necessary amount for her household, she should give back the rest.[172] And with that, he had beaten her on her back with his hand, saying: 'Here I take your blood to vindication, and then you shall also give me your red cow'.[173] She said that after this beating, she had been sore for a long time, and the red cow, which was her best, had languished[174] so that they had to raise her up for quite a time until she eventually died.

Maria Nilsdotter was then asked to take off her clothes; this also happened, whereupon it was found that she had a brown spot between the shoulders, so big that it could be covered with a glove. And it was there, the records continue, that Maria confessed she had been beaten. After the mark had been found, one of the interrogators maintained that nothing could be believed other than that she had to report to Satan each year, considering how they, on both sides, had lived after the pact.[175] Maria adamantly denied this, but said that besides, he had let himself be seen by her at home on the farm as a black man, as often as they (at home) had scolded each other (which the jury said happened too often, as she frequently engaged in a terrible commotion[176] with her young son's wife, while Satan had been standing grinning at them).[177] In addition, every other year, sometimes during summer and sometimes during winter, she was in the forest on Thursday evenings, when he (Satan) met her alone outside the farm, started to talk with her, dressed in black like a boatman,[178] and asked for his share. And then she answered that there was not much to be enjoyed,[179] and let him know, particularly in the later years, that she needed to buy seed (this the jury also confirmed was true).[180] He had replied: 'I take what is mine, you take what is yours where you want'.[181] And with this, their supply of fish had disappeared, and the best cattle died (which the jury also confirmed had happened).[182]

Maria Nilsdotter was next asked about the use Karin Persdotter said she had made of others' cattle, especially those of the parish vicar, and his biggest cow in particular. Maria would absolutely not confess to any of this, even though the parish vicar's brother, Herr Elias, assured her that this would not further be touched on by the vicar, the cow's owner.[183]

Later, the records continue, Maria Nilsdotter was admonished to denounce others (that she knew had been seduced by Satan in the same way),[184] but she said she did not know who they were, and even if there were other people than her mother in the mountain, she did not know who they were (but nevertheless, after she had received her sentence, she partly gave the expectation that she might confess to something more, when she had been able to think things over in a better way).[185]

Finally, Herr Elias pointed out to her that it was known[186] in the congregation that she did not go to church on the most important holidays or the most important days of prayer before this spring, when this rumour of witchcraft had come up (which even the jury and her neighbours testified to be true);[187] also, that the evenings before they awaited the Lord's holy rites, she had ruled in her house[188] as no Christian being.[189]

Everything was then sent over to the jury, the records state, who upon Maria Nilsdotter's detailed confession univocally testified that Maria had absolutely left her baptism-entered pact with God, her creator and redeemer, and there against entered into a pact with Satan receiving promises, and let this be reaffirmed with blood and a recognizable mark on her body, even if according to the same devilish pact Satan regretted his promises and took back his and his followers' subsistence on both water and land.[190] She had also used the same pact, using Satan's knowledge and cooperation, to confuse and irritate people by inventing hidden causes of sickness and afterwards healing them with witchcraft, and therefore she was truly a witch.[191]

The sentence, passed the same day and pronounced by the judge, stated that according to the jury's unanimous evidence,[192]

> I sentenced[193] that Maria Nilsdotter from Marcusböle, who thus partly with witchcraft and magical deeds was contaminated,[194] partly because she herself

admitted and confessed to it in court,[195] shall, according to God's holy law, described in Exodus 22:18, like a witch lose her life, and explicitly[196] according to the execution process in the native country for such a serious crime,[197] be executed with an axe, and her body afterwards should be burned in fire at the stake[198]—however, not without the High Court's gracious evaluation and confirmation.[199]

On 25 October 1666, Maria Nilsdotter's case was treated by the Court of Appeal.[200] It is stated that the witch[201] Maria Nilsdotter could not be pardoned, but should according to the wording of the local court lose her life: be executed by axe and then burned.[202] The accusation against her was that she practised healing and witchcraft, tried to find hidden causes of illness,[203] and let herself into a pact, community, and conversation with Satan.[204] As Maria Nilsdotter so far was the only woman denounced by Karin Persdotter who was tried, it was decided that before Maria would be executed, the district governor[205] Nils Psilander should let her be confronted with the other women denounced by Karin Persdotter, in order to provide more names of women to be tried by the law, and thus continue the trials.[206]

The Voice of Maria Nilsdotter

In Maria Nilsdotter's trial records, we have a long narrative recorded in her own voice. All questions and answers during the interrogation were written down, enabling us to know what she was asked about, the focus and direction of the interrogation, and her ways of responding to the questions. Maria's voice is rendered sometimes in first-person direct speech and sometimes in indirect speech, third-person narration.

The beginning of Maria Nilsdotter's interrogation is organized around points made in Karin Persdotter's denunciation. The points pertain to *maleficium*, demonological ideas related to the witches' gathering at Blåkulla, and healing. Maria denies everything and says that Karin's denunciation is not true, nor are the rumours that previously led to her being accused of witchcraft.

Maria Nilsdotter's strategy from the beginning is denial, and the interrogators are not sure what they can do to make her confess. It is the threat of using handcuffs which leads to a turning point of the trial, and little by little, Maria admits that she knows something about witchcraft: she heard her mother talk about throwing silver in water for healing—but she also says that she never asked her mother about such things.

The bulk of the confession, however, comes after the handcuffs are employed. It proves that torture is effective. She confesses that she knows the wording of a charm used to determine the cause of a person's illness. The charm contains several options, and she would start to shiver when the correct option was pronounced. This is the first confession given by Maria Nilsdotter. The interrogator then turns to demonological ideas and asks about the pact with Satan. Maria refuses to answer these questions. All effort on the part of the interrogator to obtain a confession related to demonology is in vain.

The next turning point does not come until the handcuffs are tightened, and this happens in the evening after a long day of interrogation. Now, Maria Nilsdotter confesses to meeting Satan, being promised luck and knowledge in exchange for her soul. And she confesses that once, she was taken into a mountain and saw things there. However, she withdraws this confession, saying that she had not told the truth, and therefore the scribe does not find it worthwhile to record it in detail. Maria must have understood that it was dangerous to confess about the mountain.

The next day, it is recorded that Maria Nilsdotter confesses without any coercion.[207] This is a phrase found in other countries in court records written the day after torture was applied.[208] The accused person had experienced what torture is like and knew that it would most likely be used again. On this day, Maria confesses that her mother initiated her into witchcraft and took her to Blåkulla, both when the mother was alive and even after her death. Maria had become a servant of Satan and received his mark. This confession is formed as a narrative, and is the longest part of Maria's confession. Maria has now confessed to having been to Blåkulla, entering into the devil's pact, and receiving the devil's mark, and has given the name of the person who taught her witchcraft.

The interrogator then insists that Maria Nilsdotter must have met with Satan each year to follow up on their pact. Initially, she strongly denied this, but the day after she was tortured, she confesses that she met him. She told him that there was not much to give him. But as he wanted his share, a large number of fish disappeared and also the best creatures. The way Maria vacillates, first denying follow-up meetings with Satan and then admitting to them, suggests that she has become exhausted and can no longer stand firm in her denial. Moreover, at this point, the content of her confessions is already sufficient for a sentence of execution to be passed.

Further questioning concerns spellcasting, particularly that directed at the vicar's largest cow. She does not respond. Then, the compulsory point of a demonological witchcraft trial is activated: She is urged to denounce others who were also deceived by Satan, but she replies that she knows of no others, and that, if anyone other than her mother had been at Blåkulla, she did not know who they were. The last point made by Herr Elias, the vicar's brother, was her lack of church attendance on holy days and the quarrelling in her house before she received the sacrament in church. She does not respond. During the last part of her interrogation, she is passive, and no names of accomplices are given. In the records, it is written in brackets that after Maria's sentence had been passed, she indicated that she might confess to more once she would be given time to think it over.

The voice of Maria Nilsdotter changes accents throughout the phases of the interrogation. Her resistance is gradually broken down. At first, she denies witchcraft, stating that she did not learn from her mother, did not go to Blåkulla, and did not enter into a pact with Satan. However, at the end, she confesses that she knows and practised witchcraft, went to Blåkulla twice with her mother, and entered into a pact with the devil. Then, although she said at first that she had not seen anyone else at Blåkulla, nor could she recognize anyone, after she receives her sentence of execution she says that she might remember some of the persons she saw there. The change is caused by the application of torture. She is being interrogated over long days, from morning to evening, and when the interrogators do not make any headway with her, they apply the handcuffs and tighten them gradually to cause pain. She is defeated again and again and tries to stay strong, but must give in at the end.

The use of torture was not allowed in Finnish lower-court trials unless the Court of Appeal gave permission. However, we clearly see torture being used in the trial of Maria Nilsdotter, aimed at coercing a confession. Handcuffs are used, first as a threat and then as an instrument of torture when night fell. After torture, she confesses to the most dangerous element.

We see during the interrogation that Maria Nilsdotter is driven away from her initial strategy of denial. She confesses to a combination of several features of folkloric belief from her traditional knowledge and also demonological features. The interrogators direct the questioning towards demonological features, about the devil's pact and the promises made by the devil, the devil's mark, and denunciation of others. The content of her confession can be interpreted as a mixture of *maleficium* and demonological witchcraft. Her images of the devil are those of a black man, a man dressed in the clothes of a boatswain, and an ordinary man, but there are no sexual connotations involved in the entering of the pact. Satan does not honour the promises he makes. The interrogators clearly have knowledge about demonological notions and so does Maria. She must have either known stories mentioning features of the devil's pact before her trial started or heard these stories while in custody. When she at last confesses, she claims to have been to Blåkulla herself, having been invited by her mother, who also taught her the *maleficium* spells and the practices she knows. At last, she opens up to maybe denouncing people she has seen in the Blåkulla mountain—in contradiction to all her previous refusals. I interpret this as her having given in: the attacks on her during interrogation have been successful, and the interrogators have made her as tractable as they want her to be.

The court records of Maria Nilsdotter clearly show how ideas connected to *maleficium* and ideas connected to demonology met in the courtroom, where demonological ideas were given weight during the interrogation and sentencing. Before the trial, Maria knew about Blåkulla, about the figure of the devil as a black man and his promises. These notions were not placed in her mouth by the interrogators at court—the confession in this trial is an example of a process of assimilation of demonological ideas that had taken place in the local community before the trial started. The questions posed to Maria were simple, while the answers she gave in return were detailed. She also knew much about *maleficium* ideas: traditional beliefs about witchcraft, the practice of healing magic, the use of charms and objects to perform witchcraft, and the casting of spells.

The voice of Maria, as it is heard in the court records, is strongly influenced by orality features. It is remarkable how prominent the oral accent is. In the rendering of Maria's direct speech and indirect speech, the oral accent can be heard in pointed utterances that are easy to remember, in language images and motifs, in the mentioning of special days of the year, in additive sentence constructions, and in the overall narrative structures.

Maria Nilsdotter shows fear at the beginning of the trial, trying to reduce the impact of the previous witchcraft accusation against her by saying it was based on guessing only. She shows hope that the interrogation would stop, underlining that she herself never asked her mother about knowledge on witchcraft or healing. She is trying to reduce her own knowledge of witchcraft even after the handcuffs were put to use and she had recited a charm, which means she still had some hope of a mild treatment then. She shows regret when she has confessed to the devil's pact, as she withdraws this confession. She shows despair when she understands that she cannot escape from the trial, and gives her long demonological confession. However, she has not completely given in, as she refuses to confess to harming the vicar's cows with witchcraft and she refuses to denounce others. Maria Nilsdotter understands that the trial is developing in a negative direction, and her hope of acquittal is gradually fading.

The Voice of the Interrogator

The voice of the interrogator is clearly audible in the court records, coming to the fore in the rendering of his questions. He leads the interrogation in a steadfast way, taking one step after another towards bringing about a demonological confession. He deliberately tries to secure a confession comprising malevolent witchcraft, demonological witchcraft, and healing. The interrogator is the person who brings in the question on whether she met the devil on a yearly basis to report how she followed the pact. He is the one who creates a connection between Maria Nilsdotter's way of getting to know secrets related to healing by the use of charms and the idea that it was the devil who revealed those secrets to her.

The interrogator seems to have thorough knowledge of ideas on *maleficium*, demonology, and healing, as he manages to pose questions that are very much to the point. He communicates with the jury during the interrogation, as they present comments on Maria Nilsdotter's confession, mostly confirming its content. The voice of the interrogator as well as the voices of the jury members show that in 1666, ideas on demonological content and the story of Blåkulla were well known in the local community, along with ideas of *maleficium* and folklore.

The Voice of the Law

The voice of the law is echoed in the court's decision to use torture. The interrogator had worked for an entire day to get Maria to confess. In the evening, the court decides to screw on the handcuffs. This is successful. The next day, it is recorded that she confessed without any force that her mother had taken her to Blåkulla. The use of handcuffs took place without permission from the High Court. In the court records, it is noted that when the interrogator did not manage to make her confess 'in the good',[209] the handcuffs were used, first as a threat, later physically. The importance of a demonological confession was the driving force. The judiciary clearly believed that Maria was guilty of performing demonological witchcraft,

312 Finland

and they sought to make her confess using any means necessary. To accomplish this goal, the use of torture and circumstantial evidence was accepted.

The voice of the law emerges most clearly in the wording of the sentence, which includes reference to the criminal code. Maria's sentence specifies that she has renounced her baptismal pact and therefore left God, her creator and redeemer, and entered into a pact with Satan, reaffirmed with blood and his marks on her body. This pact with the devil granted her the ability to use Satan's knowledge and cooperation to invent hidden causes of a sickness and later cure this sickness through witchcraft. All this, in the eyes of the court and the law, makes her a witch.

The Voice of the Scribe

In these trial records, the voice of the scribe comes to the fore in several ways. On the one hand, he was a professional person who carried out his job accurately and thus produced very rich court records. For instance, the oral features taken down so carefully by the scribe denote an ambition to record what was uttered in the courtroom. The features were so faithfully recorded that they can provide a glimpse of the mentality of ordinary people, their beliefs, and their ideas.

On the other hand, the scribe inserted several sentences which might be his own considerations, and in this way reveals his attitude towards what is told. These sentences show that at the beginning of the trial, he thought that it was unfortunate that the court was kept for several hours during the interrogation without coming closer to a confession. And when the court could not reach a result in a benevolent way, and saw that Maria's knowledge was the same as her mother's, it was acceptable that the handcuffs were used as a threat. Likewise, the handcuffs were put on because the court did not get any 'categorical' answer. However, in parentheses, it is written that they were tightened only a bit. Then, when more tightening of the screws was a reality, this was because the devil's pact was on the agenda. After a long day's work, where all had been in vain until the evening, the court found it 'advisable' to tighten the handcuffs. The way these sentences are formulated makes it clear that the scribe was of the same opinion as the court: when Maria would not cooperate, was obstinate, and delayed the court's work, it was necessary to use the handcuffs in order to make some progress. The scribe's sympathy lay with the interrogator and the jury: they were bothered by all this work with the stubborn woman. The voice of the scribe certainly supports the court's authority and the established order, and the alleged witch is seen as a disorderly element.

Brita Eriksdotter Pålsu, 1685

The Trial

The trial of Brita Eriksdotter Pålsu started in August 1685 and continued through 1686 and 1687 until her sentencing in December 1687. The trial was held before the Häradz Dommars Thingh—the local court.[210] The court records are written in the Gothic hand in minute books, folio format. The trial took place in Kokkola and Kälviä. The judicial official of the Crown was Oloff Sundell, and a jury of twelve trustworthy men decided on the question of guilt.

Brita Eriksdotter Pålsu was brought to court because it was rumoured that she could do bad things. The parish vicar[211] Isack Falander confirmed that bad and evil words had been said about her for a long time. The rumours about Brita Eriksdotter Pålsu included her late father and mother, who were alleged to have been 'witch people' and a 'bad lot', and to have cast a spell on a man named Germund Michelson because he stole a sheep from them. Brita's father in particular had been spoken badly about, as he had had a reputation of being a wicked sorcerer.[212]

Isack Falander testified that, on the third day of Christmas, Brita Eriksdotter Pålsu had come to Gabriel Olafson's home. Gabriel confirmed this, but stated that it was his daughter-in-law, not he himself, who had spoken with Brita and had given her a bowl of beer and two bundles of straw.[213] Brita confirmed that this had occurred, and told the following story:

> She had been at Johan Lasainen's place the entire night before the third day [of Christmas], but in the morning she had left and had been given a bowl of beer, and then she had come to Gabriel Olafson's house, where she had been given the other bowl of beer, and from there she had travelled to Johan Olafson's house, arriving around dinnertime, and there she had been given a big glass[214] of brandy[215] and two bundles of straw, and she had emptied the glass and become drunk, but Johan had not warned her. From there she had gone to the chapel, where she wanted to be on the fourth day [of Christmas] to attend the service. And when she came to the chapel, her horse got loose and ran around the chapel, so that she had dropped the straw bundles and fallen asleep in the snow. Because of this, she was suspected of performing *vidskepelse*,[216] which she denied, saying that she did not know about this at all.[217]

Hans Clemåla then testified that Brita Pålsu had harmed the eyes of his sister, Sisla Persdotter, with witchcraft[218] the summer before. Sisla had been sitting at the church with her friends, both girls and boys, waiting for the church to open.[219] They had been chatting and laughing together, and Brita had taken it the wrong way, thinking that they were laughing at her. Hans stated that his brother Erik told Brita, 'If you do not take your dog back,[220] you shall come onto the fire'.[221] After that, Hans said, Sisla's eyes immediately became better.

Gabriel and Johan Olafsöner were asked to swear an oath of compurgation for Brita Pålsu, together with two others, but refused to do this, so Brita could not be acquitted. The parish vicar, Magister Isack Falander, then asked the people present at court whether Brita had performed any additional bad and unjust deeds,[222] aside from what Hans Clemåla had told the court about his sister Sisla's eyes. It was answered that, had he been there, the farmer Erik Erikson Kainu would have testified about what Brita had done with his calf. Because Erik Kainu was not present, it was requested that the case be postponed to the winter court session, and the rest was left to the jury, who agreed that as the trial depended on additional information to be brought forth, it should be postponed to the next court session. The jury further decided that, at the next court session, because of the rumours associated with her and the fact that no one had been willing to swear an oath of compurgation for her, Brita would be required to swear an oath of compurgation together with eleven other persons, in accordance with Chapter 19 of the Mannhelge Balk, which was part of the law. It is stated that the local court most humbly relied on the 'Learned Royal High Beneficial's' further judgement and discretion.[223]

Brita Pålsu's trial continued in Kokkola on 6 October 1686.[224] The records state that dignified parish vicar Magister Isack Falander declared[225] that the court should further investigate the case against the tenant woman[226] Brita Pålsu, who was now brought before the court. However, they had to await a decision from the Court of Appeal. There was a legal requirement that if there was a trial where a death sentence was possible, the case had to be sent to the Court of Appeal for consideration.

The trial continued in Kokkola on 22 October 1687, where, the records state, an extraordinary court session was held in Old Carleby in the presence of the Crown's judicial official, the respected Oloff Sundell, and the jury, which consisted of eleven members. Erik Kainu and his wife, Karin Mårtensdotter, were called forth as witnesses first. Their testimonies concerned a calf that, some years previously, Brita Pålsu had harmed with witchcraft so that it died, as Erik had alleged. The court now asked Erik's wife, Karin, what she knew about this case, whereupon she testified that she had given Brita a meal when she came to fetch a calf which was hers. Karin intended to keep Brita away from the barn because she did not want to have her there. But Brita had gone to the barn anyway, without Karin noticing. Karin hurried after Brita, and when she went inside, Brita had been stroking one of Karin's calves on the back.[227] This was on a Tuesday. During the night, the calf became swollen like a bucket,[228] so much that it could not eat, and after a few days they were obliged to drag it to the dogs. Karin described further how, the Sunday following this incident, she had gone immediately to Johan Anderson Lasainen's place, because she knew Brita was there. She waited at the farm until Brita came out, and had then spoken to her, telling her that she left a bad dog and deed after herself, but that, if she would let everything be, Karin would be content and not go to court.[229] But if any more harm should come to Karin's cattle, then Brita would have to compensate her for all further damage. Brita had answered by saying that she would like to take Karin to court because she had scolded her for witchcraft.[230] All of this, Karin maintained under oath to be true and not the least invented, nor did she have any ill will or discontent towards Brita in her conscience,[231] but she could not think or believe otherwise than that the calf had become sick because of Brita. Brita, however, denied all of this, and told the court that she had not been in the barn, nor had she talked with Karin Mårtensdotter.

Karin Mårtensdotter then called forth Johan Lasainen's wife as a witness, as she had overheard them talking. Johan's wife, Margeta Eriksdotter, who, after having sworn an oath on the book, testified in response to questions that she did not know that Brita Pålsu had done anything other than sustain herself in the place where she now lived,[232] after she had been driven away from her farmstead like a poor tenant woman.[233] She further testified that Karin had spoken with Brita in Margeta's home on a holy day, when Brita had spent the night there. Then, Margeta's mother's sister, the aforementioned Karin Kainu, had come and spoken with Brita out at the farm. Margeta did not listen to their conversation, but went her own way, going about her business. She testified that Karin and Brita had separated from each other well and on friendly terms, and that not the least quarrel was heard. Margeta Eriksdotter further denied, on the bliss of her soul, that she did not have anything to tell about Brita Pålsu's wickedness and anger,[234] but would leave that to those who had knowledge of it and had started to spread the rumours about her.

The daughter of Erik Kainu, a young girl called Margeta as well, was then called forth. She did not swear an oath, but repeated everything that her mother, Karin, had said earlier, and declared that she could not, and neither in her conscience, believe and think otherwise than that their calf died as a result of Brita's deed.

Three persons who lived at the Clemåla farm were called upon next: the brothers Hans Person and Erik Person and their sister Margeta, the one who had first accused Brita Pålsu in the summer court in 1685.[235] They were asked whether they knew anything more about Brita than what they had told before, and whether they would stand by the testimony they had given in 1685, where they had accused Brita of having harmed the eyes of their sister Sisla by witchcraft.[236] Together with her likes, Sisla had allegedly laughed at Brita outside the church when she (Brita) came up to them. Hans, who had been the keenest accuser in the previous court session, answered that he had to excuse himself and could not in good conscience testify to this, because he had not actually been at home when the incident had occurred. He had been in Halsö in the fields, and only knew about the incident, as it had been described in the last court session, because he heard about it from his family. He finished his statement by saying that his brother Erik had better knowledge about what had happened.

Erik Person was therefore called forth and asked what he would like to tell and whether he would swear on his soul's bliss that the eye disease of his sister Sisla had happened through a deed of Brita Pålsu. Erik replied that 'he had not himself heard Pålsu's curse'.[237] The court then asked Hans Person about Sisla's eyes, and how long they had been sore, to which Hans replied that he did not know, because he had been five miles[238] away. Erik was asked the same question, and he testified that the sickness lasted four days and no longer. Margeta, their sister, was then called forth and asked where she had heard Brita's curse[239] on Sisla's eyes, and questioned about the illness that had stricken Sisla immediately after the incident at the chapel.[240] Margeta testified that she had been at Brita's home two weeks after St Jacob's Day,[241] when Brita had started talking about Sisla, who had laughed at her and winked at the other girls in order to make a fool of her. Brita had said: 'Our Lord finds ways to do something with the eyes of those who laugh and wink at poor people'.[242] Two weeks later, Sisla's right eye was sore and painful for three days. Sisla had told Margeta that when she was going to fall asleep, she called out the name Kuihu Porkå (Brita's nickname) in her sleep.[243]

It is then inserted in brackets in the court records: 'It comes to my mind that all this talk could not bring forth the most insignificant witness (to testify to it)'.[244] The jury found that the stories of the Clemåla people could not be anything other than invented envious talk, because the people eagerly persecuted this Brita Pålsu, and they also wanted to win back the farmstead[245] where she had lived before, which they finally did.

Isak Jönsson Lassiph was called forth as the next witness and asked to testify about Brita Pålsu's misdeeds.[246] After having sworn an oath on the book, requesting God's help,[247] he testified that he did not know anything about Brita. Johan Hendrichson Kainu then offered to convince Isak, and told him that Brita had come with cheese to Isak's wife and had demanded some tobacco. However, Isak's wife had not accepted the cheese. This, Isak absolutely denied, and he asked Johan Kainu not to place words in his mouth.[248]

The parish vicar, Magister Isack Falander, asked the court whether it was superstitious methods[249] that made Brita Pålsu ride around the chapel, as was recorded.[250] But all present testified that Brita knew nothing other than that she had been talked about too long and had a bad reputation.[251] The jury explained with regard to this case that they, in good conscience, could not say that any superstitious methods had been used, and even more, that this incident was due to Brita's age, her inebriated state, and the fact that she had her rather vertiginous horse before the sledge, which was about to foal.[252] They had not heard that anything evil had followed this incident. In particular one of the jury members,[253] a man named Oloff Lesjo, maintained that this riding around was nothing more than the horse's giddy behaviour, which Brita could not control.

Because nobody else who had anything further to testify against Brita Pålsu could be brought forth, and because all others said that they had nothing else to say about her other than that she had a bad reputation, the jury decided upon the sentence.

The court gave the Clemåla people some fines because they had come with an accusation that was impossible to prove, and, the records state, their talk could not be understood as anything other than envious and harsh stories, invented by Erik Kainu with his wife, and the same was true for the story about the sickness of an eye, and the same with a calf which died. Because Brita Pålsu was in general rumoured to have been practising witchcraft, but a full act of witchcraft could not be proved, the bad belief was what caused the bad talk. Therefore, Brita Pålsu was sentenced to swear an oath of compurgation[254] at the next court session that she could not cause malice, even less use such means,[255] and that her riding around the chapel did not show any conceivable superstitious methods, and thus she was free from all malevolent deeds and such like,[256] according to Chapter 9 in the Tingmål Balk.[257] This sentence was forwarded to the Royal High Court[258] for confirmation.

The court records from the Court of Appeal have not been preserved. Neither is it known whether Brita Eriksdotter Pålsu managed to free herself with an oath of compurgation. Thus, the final outcome of her trial remains uncertain. All matters which carried a potential death penalty were to be referred to the Court of Appeal. At this time, this court often changed death sentences into banishments and fines. Toivo states: 'During the latter half of the seventeenth century, Göta Court of Appeal, the material of which has been systematically studied, began to mitigate sentences except of the great witch-panics in Dalarna and Göta'.[259] With regard to death penalty, cases of infanticide, murder and suicide were the crimes for which extraordinary court sessions were organized between normal regular court sessions, but witchcraft rarely got that much attention.[260]

The Voice of Brita Eriksdotter Pålsu

Brita Pålsu's voice is rendered in direct and indirect speech in the court records, the latter with an introductory reporting verb. We hear her voice when she speaks about the event with her horse running around the chapel, in her denials, and in her speech rendered by the witnesses.

When Brita Pålsu's voice is audible for the first time, a storytelling accent emerges. She tells a story to contradict Hans Person Clemåla, who testified about an event that happened around Christmas 1684. Brita, who was a poor woman, says that during the first three Christmas Days, she had visited three neighbours, travelling by horse. She was offered drinks, beer and brandy, and subsequently became drunk. On the fourth day of Christmas, she went to the chapel in order to attend the upcoming service. Here, the horse started to run around the chapel, and she had then fallen asleep because of her inebriated state. Brita's voice has intact narrative structures and clear orality features. She hoped this story would explain to the court why she was found in a miserable state near the chapel and why her horse was running around. She hoped that the suspicion of performed witchcraft related to this event would be lessened.

However, her neighbours interpreted this incident as a very unusual happening and as connected to superstitious methods. To counter such an accusation, Brita Pålsu's voice is heard with an accent of protest and denial.

When Brita Pålsu's voice again is referred to, it is by Hans Clemåla, a brother of Sisla. He testifies that Brita understood the laughing of Sisla and her friends as ridicule, and she responded to this by harming with witchcraft. This sensitive accent of Brita's voice points to her vulnerable position in local society and shows that she is marginalized.

To the last accusation, namely that Brita Pålsu harmed a calf with witchcraft, she does not respond. However, she is told by the legal officials to clear herself through an oath of compurgation at the next court meeting. Even if she has not confessed, it becomes clear that rumours circulating about her can be dangerous, because it is difficult to find others willing to swear for her. This is the end of the first session of her trial, and her voice is still one of resistance.

The next time Brita's trial comes up before the court is in the winter court session in October 1686, and only a formal entry is made. Due to the absence of central persons, the case is postponed.

The third and final time Brita Pålsu's trial comes up before the court is in October 1687, more than two years after the initial court meeting. Again, harming the calf with witchcraft comes up, as testified to by Karin Mårtensdotter, whom Brita is said to have met at the farm when she performed the alleged witchcraft. Karin feared that Brita might harm the animals. However, Brita goes to the barn without Karin noticing it, and strokes one of the calves. Karin warned Brita that if she did more damage, Karin would formally accuse her of witchcraft. Karin Mårtensdotter further testifies that Brita Pålsu responded that she would have Karin brought before the court for accusing her of witchcraft. Brita is countering Karin's threat. She knows that an accusation of witchcraft might result in the accuser being punished. They are changing positions. Brita still has power to counter the warning.

As for the testimony about Sisla Persdotter's eye disease, the words uttered by Brita Pålsu and rendered by Margeta Eriksdotter were turned into a curse. This accent of Brita's voice is threatening. Even if Brita's uttering mentions Our Lord and not the devil, it is recited in court as if it was a curse. The witness finds that rendering Brita's voice in this way suits the purpose.

The Voices of the Witnesses

The witnesses' portrayal of Brita Eriksdotter Pålsu is characterized by her threatening voice and deeds. She had long been rumoured to be a witch in local society.[261] Her parents, too, had been rumoured to have practised witchcraft; therefore, the suspicion of harming with witchcraft is related to families, in Brita's case her mother and father. Her neighbours portray her as a suspicious person, an impression which is strengthened by the description of her intention to perform witchcraft when she hastened to the barn to stroke a calf. The voices of the witnesses signal a fear of witches throughout, which is heard for instance in the repeated threat of bringing somebody to the fire.

The voices of the female witnesses are not very different from the voices of the male witnesses. It seems they have equal authority, although the male witnesses give their testimonies first. The first female witness to testify is Karin Mårtensdotter, who states that Brita Pålsu harmed her calf with witchcraft, resulting in death. Karin calls upon another woman, Johan Lasainen's wife Margeta Eriksdotter, to strengthen her own testimony, but Margeta has nothing negative to say about Brita and says that Karin and Brita parted as friends. The third female witness—and the least credible—is another Margeta, the daughter of Karin and her husband. She simply confirms her mother's testimony. With regard to the accusation about the calf, the testimonies of the female witnesses from the Kainu family's side tend to be negative, and those from the other parties are positive.

Regarding the accusation about Sisla Persdotter's eye disease, Sisla's siblings testified: first two brothers and then one sister. The first brother had been absent when the incident occurred; the second brother says that he himself did not hear Brita utter the curse and only heard about it from his sister, Margeta. The latter introduces unexpected information, which weakens the accusation against Brita:

the timeline is changed and thus the cause-and-effect argument loses its convincing power. According to Margeta, the spell was not cast on the day outside the chapel, but two weeks later, and it was another two weeks until Sisla's eye became sore, and that lasted for three days only. Here, Margeta is rendering Brita's words as direct speech. As such, the spell and the eye disease are no longer connected to the chapel, nor to Brita's riding around the chapel. The jury found this talk to be rooted in nothing other than envy.

With regard to the witnesses, all effort at negative talk about Brita Pålsu fails. Brita herself is silent, also when the parish vicar, Isack Falander, once more brings up the episode related to the chapel. He seems from the beginning to have had an interest in having Brita found guilty of harming with witchcraft. The jury, however, supports her arguments that bring up old age, drunkenness, and the horse's wildness.

The Voice of the Interrogator

The voice of the interrogator is heard mainly in connection with questions posed to the witnesses. The intention is to throw more light on the main points of accusation. He seems eager to get to know the factual conditions related to the accusations, also in cases where the burden of proof is very weak, like in the accusation about Sisla's eye disease. His approach is balanced; he does not steer the interrogation in a predetermined direction.

The Voice of the Law

The voice of the law clearly comes to the fore in the wording of the sentence, in the reference to the Tingmål Balk, and in the formulations addressed to the Court of Appeal. The court is apparently of the opinion that the accusations against Brita Pålsu do not hold water. And, more important, she has not confessed to witchcraft. She has tried to convince the court that the riding around the chapel had explainable causes. She has denied harming the calf with witchcraft. It is only her being rumoured to practise superstitious methods that works against her, spurred on by some of her neighbours. To what extent her explanation and denial will be listened to is for the court to decide. But the little that is heard of her voice signals that this is not a woman who had broken down. She does not see herself as a witch.

The sentence stipulates that the Clemåla family should be fined because of an unprovable accusation, which is clearly supportive of Brita Pålsu. However, the demand that she was to free herself with an oath of compurgation would be hard to fulfil.[262] This might have been the turning point of Brita Pålsu's trial. In spite of her denials, the outcome of her trial is uncertain.

The Voice of the Scribe

In the case analysed above, it is clear what the accused persons as well as the witnesses were asked about and what they answered. The scribe is professional in rendering the voices of all people active during the trial. A picture thus emerges, showing the topics the judiciary wanted to expand on. The discourse allows the accused as well as the witnesses to react immediately with responses. The jury listens to the voices of female as well as male witnesses, and they pay attention not only to convincing points but also to the less credible points of the testimonies. A foundation is provided on the basis of which the jury could pass the verdict.

Conclusion

The voices of three women in the witchcraft trials from Finland analysed above show that ideas on *maleficium* as well as demonological ideas were part of common people's belief in the latter half of the seventeenth century. This study encounters the notion of Blåkulla in 1666, in a detailed narrative similar in content to the Blåkulla trials in the northern part of Sweden in the 1660s and 1670s. Thus, these demonological ideas were known in the Åland islands as early as in Norrland in Sweden.[263] The ideas on *maleficium* comprise casting spells on humans and animals, resulting in sickness of people and sickness and death of animals. In addition, ideas related to healing and counter-magic are documented in the voices of women as they come to the fore in this chapter.

Ideas on malevolent witchcraft appear in the trials of Gertrud Matsdotter and Brita Pålsu. They were accused by neighbours who feared their acts of harming with witchcraft. Due to conflicts in the local communities resulting in threatening words that immediately came true, the accusations were based on people suddenly becoming sick or animals falling ill or dying. There is no doubt that people in the villages believed that doing harm with witchcraft was possible, and that charms and formulas were effective, which clearly emerged in the trial of Gertrud Matsdotter. However, there was also a strong belief that spells cast on humans and animals could be removed, either by the same person who cast the spell in the first instance or by another skilful person. Magic salt is one of the remedies that was said to help heal sickness caused by harm with witchcraft. The idea that harm caused by witchcraft could be taken from one person and sent to another is seen in the trial of Gertrud Matsdotter. Also, the traditional method of milking other people's cattle, obtaining a large amount of butter, is documented in the trial of Gertrud. Reasons for suspicion were plenty. If a woman was seen outside with her hair uncovered, this could be a signal that she was out on a wrong errand.

In the trial of Brita Eriksdotter Pålsu, the ideas coming to the fore are related to *maleficium*. They deal with traditional witchcraft. Accusations by locals are based on weak evidence and deal with illness cast on animals and humans harmed with witchcraft due to conflicts. Neighbours wanted to get rid of a person who was quarrelsome and created displeasure in daily life, and the parish vicar supported the accusations by giving a testimony. In this late case from 1685, the threshold for accusing people of witchcraft seemed to be low, as the witnesses' argumentation was failing. Compared to Gertrud Matsdotter's trial of 1649, the fear of dangerous witches seems to have been waning, the accused person was not cooperative, and those accusing Brita Pålsu were punished themselves.

Very different accents are heard in the voice of Maria Nilsdotter, who was denounced in a panic and exposed to much harsher court proceedings. She started with denial, then came the threat of handcuffs, followed by her confession to throwing silver in the water for healing and the foretelling of the cause of a person's sickness. Next, the handcuffs were applied, and the interrogators obtained the confession to the devil's pact and to the Blåkulla gathering. In her trial, the confession of foretelling and healing came first, as she apparently saw this as something not very dangerous. Then, after pressure, the dangerous words came. This merging of malevolent and demonological ideas in a confession reveals the accused person's understanding of the severity of witchcraft performance and magic, but also the interrogators' urge to press for the confession they wanted to obtain: the one that would provide enough reason for a death sentence.

The court records are written in Swedish. A text-critical remark about the work of the scribe has to do with the bilingual aspects of the court records. The discourse of those accused women who had Finnish as their mother tongue was translated into Swedish. This could have led to misunderstandings. However, the courtroom discourse is rendered in a clear and understandable way, and the court proceedings are easy to follow. There is no doubt about the delegation of voices. The narrative structures of the testimonies in each of the three trials are marked, and so is the orality accent. This shows that the scribe has managed to individualize the voices of the accused women and let them come forth with the particular accents of their voices that belong to each one of them. The rendering of the different voices of the trial has been performed in a diligent and careful way.

10

COMPARISON AND CONCLUSION

A choir of female voices has come to the fore during the previous chapters: twenty-four voices from eight countries in Early Modern Northern Europe. In this concluding chapter, I would like to compare the eight countries in question, according to the set of ten factors described in the introduction: the accused person's confession, witnesses' testimonies, narrative structures, orality features, interrogation, torture and pressure, enforced narrative, the voice of the law, the voice of the scribe, and transnational transfer. Listening out for the voices of women in different phases of the trial will not only provide an understanding of how the development of a trial influences women's words, but also throw light on an important question: is there a turning point during the trial which leads to the confession?

In trial after trial, women's voices emerge in the courtrooms: in confessions, testimonies, and interrogation. The women show strengths and weaknesses: they flee, protest, argue, give in, and narrate—their words written down with a quill (feather pen) by a scribe in large books. The voices of women in witchcraft trials reveal important aspects of courtroom discourse. In addition, the voices of other participants in the trials are included in the analyses: the voices of the witnesses, interrogator, the law, and the scribe.

Based on the analyses performed in the preceding chapters, the comparisons aim at finding patterns valid for not only one country but for eight countries, including in terms of similarities and differences. The accused women's confessions have been the main focus of the analyses of the trials, as the voices of women come clearly to the fore in this part of the trial.

Two different concepts of witchcraft, demonological ideas and ideas about *maleficium*, surface in the women's confessions, the witnesses' testimonies, and the interrogation. These notions determine the severity of the trial. Persons in trials containing ideas about *maleficium* were punished more mildly than those in demonological trials.[1] An important question to try to answer is why the accused

DOI: 10.4324/9781003255406-10

women confessed to having performed the severe crime of witchcraft. In connection to this question, the use of pressure and torture during interrogation will be discussed.

Courtroom discourse will be paid attention to, as the way interrogation is performed influences the content of the confession. Also, particular linguistic features that come to the fore in the voices of women—narrative structures and orality features—will be assigned great importance, as they explain characteristic aspects of women's voices and contribute to explaining the transference of ideas about witchcraft. The transnational transference of ideas about witchcraft will be discussed. Finally, the conclusion of the analyses of all trial records in this study will be formulated.

The ten factors described in the introduction constitute a simplified analytical framework constructed around the main object, making it possible to compare the various countries with regard to parallel conditions. The analytical framework includes major factors characterizing the voices of women and provides insight into courtroom discourse and court practice, as well as the mentality of accused persons, witnesses, and the judiciary.

The voices of women in witchcraft trials have many accents. On the one hand, these voices serve to bring forward the individual accused person by rendering their personal language and ways of expression. On the other hand, the voices of women contribute to uncovering the development of witchcraft trials as a legal action. The various accents of the voices of women emphasize that court records are multilayered texts. While the women are the protagonists in this study, the voices of other participants in the trials serve to deepen the contextual understanding of women's voices.

Confession

The confession of the accused person is the first factor in the analytical framework. As the term witchcraft is broad, the confession echoes a range of ideas intended to cause harm. Randi Rønning Balsvik states:

> Witchcraft is close to the terms 'magic' and 'sorcery'. The concepts refer to the ability some people have of causing supernatural powers to interfere in the lives of fellow human beings to the detriment of their welfare. The forces are invisible and used to cause bad luck, sickness, and even death.[2]

A confession in a witchcraft trial was often given after initial denial and was a result of pressure. When an accused woman came to the stage of confession, the outcome of the trial could be guessed; in most cases, it was negative. Still, we do not hear only one, stereotypical linguistic expression voiced. An accused woman's confession displays a richness of language and a mastery of narration. In the following, I would like to start with a comparison of ideas about witchcraft coming to the fore in the confessions.

Demonological Ideas

I argue that demonological ideas had an impact on the European witch-hunt. In my view, demonological ideas were a vital force in Early Modern witchcraft persecution and should not be underestimated. These ideas play an important role in the voices of accused women, in the voices of the witnesses, in the voice of the law, in judging the severity of the accused's actions, and in the escalation of trials seen in witchcraft panics.

In all countries in this study, demonological ideas are heard in confessions. These ideas are heard consistently in confessions from Spanish Netherlands, Northern Germany, Denmark, Scotland, Norway, and Sweden from the end of the 1500s. Demonological ideas, even if to a lesser extent in this period, are also present in the confessions from Finland and England. This study has documented demonological ideas in England particularly in the 1640s and in Finland particularly in the 1660s.[3] However, the devil appeared in English witchcraft trials as early as in 1572.[4]

As knowledge of demonological ideas at the time of witchcraft trials varied among judicial officials and common people, several versions of a demonological narrative existed in Northern Europe. In some areas, these were detailed and close to elaborated demonological works. In other areas, only a few features of learned demonology were known, but these still constituted the backbone of the narrative heard in the confession. At an early stage of a witch-hunt, demonological ideas were less elaborate than at a later stage, seen for instance in the trial of the Swedish Ingegärd Andersdotter in 1594. These variants of demonological ideas that appear in the trials analysed point to the mentality sphere and to how the transfer of ideas occurs. While key demonological ideas about the devil's pact and witches' gathering are often preserved, other, less fundamental ideas might vary, such as ideas on shape-shifting, night flight, sex with the devil, and activities at witches' gatherings. Ideas about the devil's pact and the witches' gathering in particular had a great impact on witchcraft persecution. The latter was influential as it led to denunciation of other participants, which was an incredibly efficient method to get new names of suspected people, resulting in a witchcraft panic.

The first decade which stands out in this study when it comes to demonological ideas is the 1590s. Even if these ideas are found in several countries prior to 1590,[5] it seems that there was an increase in witchcraft persecution in this decade. Witchcraft panics occurred for the first time in some countries, for instance in Scotland during the North Berwick trials. The analyses document ideas about the pact ritual, the devil's mark, the witches' gathering, and personal demons called Apostles in the trial of Maren, the wife of Mogens in Denmark in 1590; the idea of a witches' gathering at a graveyard and in a church, the devil's pact, kissing the devil, the devil's mark, sex with the devil, and digging up corpses from the graveyard in the trial of Agnes Sampson in Scotland in 1590–91; the idea of witches' flight and witches' gathering in the trial of Anne Pedersdatter in Norway in 1590;[6] the idea of entering the devil's pact at a hill called Kullen in the trial of Ingegärd Andersdotter in Sweden in 1594; and the idea of an evil spirit in the trial of Lynken van Brugghe in Spanish Netherlands in 1596. The first trial from Northern Germany in this study is from the year 1607. However, demonological ideas had been known in Northern Germany from the 1540s onwards.[7] District laws issued in 1567, 1572, and 1591 stated that the death sentence should be used in trials concerning witchcraft performed after a pact with the devil had been made.[8] In Spanish Netherlands, demonological ideas are documented from an early stage as well, from the 1530s onwards.[9] In 1532, a woman submitted herself to the 'enemy from Hell' and denied God, and demonological ideas continued to occur in witchcraft trials throughout the century, characterizing several panics in the 1590s. In the 1596 trial in Spanish Netherlands analysed in this study, Lynken van Brugghe confessed to having an evil spirit (an evil enemy), thus signalling the devil's pact.

Therefore, central demonological ideas were known before the mid-1500s in both the Spanish Netherlands and Northern Germany. Rolf Schulte has documented persecution pressure from Southern to Northern Germany from the 1580s onwards.[10] These ideas seem to have appeared not much later in the Nordic countries and on the British Isles.[11] Around 1590, demonological ideas were known in Northern Europe, among judicial officials as well as lay people. These ideas must have been established within society's oral narratives as well as in written form, influencing judicial officials.

After the turn of the century, we find a great variety of demonological ideas activated during witchcraft confessions. In Northern Germany, the trial of Kistina Netelers in 1607 documents a pact including sex with the devil and promises of food and prospering cattle from the devil. In Denmark, in the trial of Mette Lauridsdatter Kongens in 1618, it was testified that a black-billed magpie always jumped after her, and she confessed that she herself participated in a witches' gathering, in which a man played a bagpipe and a scribe was recording. She denounced several of those who had been present at the witches' gathering. In the trial of Sitru Pedersdatter during the witchcraft panic in Norway in 1623, Sitru confessed to a witches' gathering at a hill called Blåkoll, whereto she rode on a black calf. She denounced other women who had allegedly attended the witches' gathering. She also had a personal demon named Apostle. In Spanish Netherlands, Mayken Karrebrouck in 1634 confessed to a number of demonological ideas: the name of her mentor, dances with the devil, sex with the devil, the likeness of the devil being a black man, receiving money from the devil, which later turned out to be faeces or dirt, night flight, and the performance of witchcraft. In Northern Germany, Anneke Rickers in 1641 confessed to leaving Jesus Christ, sexual intercourse with a red rider, a promise of money from the devil, having an idol called Beelzebub who took the shape of a black dog, and the use of witchcraft powder. In Scotland, in the trial of Helene Clerk in 1643–45, the accused was pricked for the devil's mark. In England, demonological ideas were activated in the trial of Thomasine Read in 1647: the devil's pact in the form of a contract, the devil's mark as a teat, and familiars in the shapes of a mouse and a cat.

The demonological ideas coming to the fore in the trials from 1618–53 show more detail than those of the trials from 1590–1607. A consolidation of such ideas has taken place, with rich descriptions of entering the devil's pact, the devil and his likenesses, sexual intercourse with the devil, the devil's promises and his disregard of the same, the demonic helpers given to those entering the pact, the witches' gatherings and the activities taking place there, shape-shifting, night flights, and the use of witchcraft powder. In all countries in question, the main elements of a demonological narrative seem to be known by this time; however, elements are weighed differently in the various countries. The demonic helper is known as an Apostle in Denmark, Norway, and Sweden, and as a familiar in England. Folkloric elements known from traditional fairy tales are related to the devil, for instance the red rider appearing in the confession of Anneke Rickers in Germany in 1641. Again, the devil's pact and the witches' gathering are the main demonological ideas confessed to.

The last period of trials in my study documenting demonological ideas in witch-craft confessions covers the time span 1652–78. In Spanish Netherlands, Clayse Sereyns in her trial from 1657 confessed to having met the devil—who was black and had black horse feet and, later, claws on his feet—having entered into the dev-il's pact and forsaken God and the Holy Mother, renouncing her baptism, having a physical relationship with the devil, receiving witchcraft powder from the devil, and receiving money from the devil for performed witchcraft deeds. In Northern Germany, in her trial from 1669, Anna Spielen confessed to having had personal contact with a name-given devil or spirit through the use of a stick, the devil's pact, sexual intercourse with the devil, a witches' gathering at Bloksberg, and rid-ing a male goat. In Denmark, Anna Bruds in 1652 confessed to having learned witchcraft from another woman, forsworn her Christendom, received a demonic servant boy, and participated in witches' gatherings. She denounced several other women for performing collective witchcraft. In Scotland, Isobell Eliot in a 1678 panic confessed to having met the devil, denounced her baptism, entered into a pact with the devil, had carnal copulation with the devil, and received a new name. In Norway, in a 1662–63 panic, Gundelle Olsdatter confessed to having learned witchcraft from another woman, entered the devil's pact, shape-shifting, attended a witches' gathering at a mountain together with Satan, and performed collective witchcraft. In Sweden, in the trial of Karin Persdotter from 1653, a demonologi-cal confession is pressed for. The judiciary equates the Water Man she described with the Evil One, Lucifer. Also in Sweden, Karin Dantz, in a panic, confessed in 1673–74 to having been abducted to a witches' gathering in Blåkulla, where they danced backwards and where she saw a black dog, which had horns on its head and knees and played on its ass. Further, she confessed to night flight and to hav-ing received money while staying in Blåkulla. In Finland in a panic in 1666, Maria Nilsdotter confessed to the devil's pact with Satan in a boatswain's clothes and receiving promises from him about having luck with fish and cattle and knowledge to speak to people. Further, she confessed that her mother had taken her to the mountain Blåkulla, where Satan was present, and the year after she, persuaded by her mother, went into his service. The devil beat her on the back, leaving a mark, and took her blood for vindication.

Names of the devil and evil spirits vary. In Spanish Netherlands, the name of the evil spirit of Lynken van Brugghe, *du warinne*, should probably be understood as a name pronounced when she was nearly out of her mind due to torture. In Northern Germany, Kistina Netelers's demonic lover was called Niβ, Anneke Rickers's idol was called Beelzebub, Anneke Ratke's idol was called Kreÿenfues, and Anna Spielen's lover was called Paul, so we see both biblical and colloquial names. In Scotland, Agnes Sampson's devil was called the Sprite, and when she called Eloa, the devil appeared. In Sweden, the name Lucifer was connected to Karin Persdotter's Water Man during interrogation. Naming the demon was a way of personalizing this creature. Using a colloquial name brought the demon closer to the local community and the personal sphere of the woman. Using a biblical name brought the demon closer to the religious sphere and the rhetoric used by the church. Also, when baptism was mentioned as part of the ritual when entering into the devil's pact, attention was drawn towards leaving Christianity and entering the darker side. Also, those entering into the devil's pact sometimes got new names. Scottish Isobell Eliot was named Jean by the devil when entering the pact, while Marion Veitch received a new name, Broad Back.

Demonic helpers, devils or Apostles, are found in confessions in the Nordic countries and in Northern Germany throughout the entire period of this study. Biblical and colloquial names of Apostles are seen, reflecting the spiritual as well as earthly side of these creatures. Often, there is a comic element included in the colloquial name; a mocking accent. The occurrence of Apostles seems to be frequent in Denmark and Norway. In Denmark, the Apostles in the 1590 trials also have biblical and colloquial names: Langinus, Pilhestskou, Smuck; the servant boy of Anna Bruds, the wife of Thomas, was Brud. In Norway, the Apostle was called Old Erich (*Gammel-Erik*). The English familiars give the Apostles company, appearing as the devil's prolonged arm. The personal demons appeared either at witches' meetings or during the individual performance of witchcraft. In Denmark, in 1590 and 1652, personal devils called Apostles or a servant boy in the shape of a red man appear as helpers when witchcraft is going to be performed. For instance, Anna Bruds cast sickness upon a boy, making him dumb and lame, by using her servant boy. The personal demons obeyed the command of the women who owned them and could be sent out to sea and to other places. In the confessions in which Apostles or familiars are described, they appear as important for the performance of the deed of witchcraft, always ready and willing to work. They were small and could easily be placed in small vessels. The inclusion of these creatures in a demonological narrative shows that local versions of how evil power was transmitted and activated thrived in several countries in Northern Europe. They represented a down-to-earth, sometimes factual link to the more abstract figure of the devil, and were in a way practical to handle.

A comparison of demonological ideas in the countries in this study shows that the two main notions—the devil's pact and the witches' gathering—emerged with differing intensity in the various countries. The demonic witch was a person who had made a pact with the devil, promised her soul to him, received evil power from him, worshipped him, and had become an evil person.[12] She had renounced her baptism and left her good master. These words are echoed in verdicts and sentences throughout the areas that suffered from witchcraft persecution in Europe. Therefore, the notion of the devil's pact is crucial to understanding and interpreting the voices of all persons accused of witchcraft, not least the voices of women.

The devil's pact was an important element in the demonological narrative, as this was the occasion where the devil showed his power and the woman entering the pact was given access to evil power. The choice of a wrong master was decisive for the power of the devilish witch and the danger and fear she connoted. It is also one of the major points on which demonological witchcraft differs from malevolent witchcraft. The devil's pact confessions in this study demonstrate to which extent the accused woman was aware of the devil's pact as a crucial entrance into the Evil One's realm. Whether the confession was given voluntarily or under pressure, it demonstrates that detailed and widespread knowledge of this notion existed among common people in Northern Europe from the late 1500s onwards. It also shows what the judicial interrogators were after: they insisted on women confessing to a pact with the devil, because women were able to manipulate the elements of nature by means of their alliance with evil forces. In the confessions analysed above, this is clearly expressed in the ability to raise storms and destroy the barley harvest. The capacity of humans to influence natural processes is emphasized by Julio Caro Baroja, who has stressed a perspective in which the dividing line between physical reality and the imagined mythical world was more obscure than it tends to be today. 'Between what physically exists and what man imagines, or has in the past imagined to exist, there lies a region in which the evidential real and the imaginary seem to overlap'.[13] In this obscure region, the witches' activities took place.[14] As the view of humankind's relationship with nature changed from a Greek to a Renaissance perspective in the seventeenth century, common people continued to hold on to the Greek perspective, which was based on an analogy between humankind and nature. In this view, nature is permeated by spirit, which is an integral part of it, not a separate entity. This outlook evoked the likelihood that humankind could manipulate nature by means of magic. It was possible that the spirit of humankind controlled the spirit of nature. In contrast, judicial authorities reflected views that coincided with a Renaissance perspective on nature, in which body and soul were seen as separate entities. This applied equally to humankind and to nature.[15] In this cosmological movement, laws of nature reflect an intelligence that is detached from nature, that of the Holy Creator and Lord. Since witches allied themselves with the devil and defied God, disasters would descend upon the world in order to punish humankind through God's will.[16] The transition from the Greek to the Renaissance perspective on nature was a condition for the new, learned concept of witchcraft to emerge. The tension between these two perspectives is particularly present in this study in the Swedish trial of Karin Persdotter, in the Copenhagen trials of 1590, in the North Berwick trials of 1590–91, and in the Finnmark panic of 1663.

The devil's pact is mentioned in all countries in this study, but the elements of the pact and rituals connected to this pact vary in terms of elaborateness. The first meeting with the devil is highlighted in Spanish Netherlands, Northern Germany, Scotland, Norway, Sweden, and Finland. Often, the woman meets the devil in a forest or on a field. The shape of the devil varies, from an evil spirit in Spanish Netherlands in 1596 to a black man in the same country in 1634 and a black man with black horse feet in 1657. In Northern Germany, the devil is a man, black and rough, in 1607; in 1641, he is a rider in red clothes. In Denmark in 1652, the devil has the likeness of a pig. In Scotland in 1590–91, the devil has many likenesses: a long, black thing, smoke, a black dog, and a man in a black gown and a black hat. In Finnmark in Norway in 1663, the devil appears in the likeness of a crow, as a personal god with a man's name, and also as a man. In Sweden in 1594, the devil is described as a small companion. In Finland in 1666, Satan is described as a man in boatswain's clothes and as a black man. In England, the familiars are helpers in performing witchcraft, but the devil himself is not described.

The different likenesses of the devil signal how the devil's pact is understood. When the devil is described as a man with masculine attributes, the sexual element of the pact is emphasized. The first meeting with the devil appears as very important, as this is the occasion during which he, as an erotic creature, tempts the woman he meets to enter into the pact. In some countries, sexual intercourse is seen as part of the alliance with the devil, exemplified among others in the trials analysed from Scotland in 1590–91, Northern Germany in 1607, and Spanish Netherlands in 1657. In Scotland, the element of embodiment in entering the devil's pact is underlined by an expression used, 'from the top of my head to the bottom of my sole', stating that both body and mind belonged to the devil from now on.[17] The sexual element is not present in the confessions of the Finnmark witchcraft trials in Norway, while the formal part of entering the pact and the joy and sisterhood at gatherings are strongly emphasized. However, in the minds of the elite in the Nordic countries of the time, the image of the lecherous witch as described in *Malleus Maleficarum* is strongly present.[18]

The sign of entering the pact could simply be a handshake, like in Sweden in 1594, or accepting the devil's offer by answering positively to his request for service and accepting his promises of cattle and food. The gifts related to the pact differed. In England in 1647, the devil wanted Thomasine Read's child, but she refused. The familiar, the spirit, allegedly sucked blood from Thomasine for seven years before a contract with the devil was made. In Spanish Netherlands in 1657, Clayse Sereyns said she received powder five or six times a year, in accordance with the pact. The powder was used to bewitch, and she was paid for each witchcraft deed. Also in Spanish Netherlands, a frog is mentioned, which was received from the devil. In Finland in 1666, the devil wanted the soul of the woman who entered into the pact, emphasizing the spiritual side of the pact. For the countries in which the women received a personal Apostle, the devil gave this personal demon to the woman who was entering into the pact, and the mission of these creatures was to help perform witchcraft.[19]

Notwithstanding differing details, in all trials analysed in this study, the pact is linked to promises from the devil and the power of performing witchcraft. The promise from the devil is more or less the same: good fortune with cattle and food, money, and—in Scotland—the all-encompassing 'You shall never want'. The promises from the devil show what the women wanted: sufficient food, good fortune with cattle, and enough money to sustain themselves. Thus, the promises made by the devil, as we hear them in accused persons' confessions, also point to harsh living conditions and a desire for a good life. When the promise given by the devil was not fulfilled, or the money given by him turned into dirt, the women became angry. Also, a certain authority over the devil is seen in the trial of Agnes Sampson in Scotland, where he appears as a dog and she sends him away howling.

Entering the pact meant crossing a border, leaving Christ, and, in Spanish Netherlands, leaving the Holy Mother. This point is clearly demonstrated in Northern Germany in 1641, when the woman entering the pact by physically walking over a nest repeated a charm saying that when she walked over the nest, she left the Lord Jesus Christ. Leaving God in Heaven is repeated as the first words in all sentences of execution in witchcraft trials, in which entering into the pact is portrayed as the sentenced person leaving the pact of baptism and giving herself to the Evil One. Often, the touch of the devil will constitute proof of the pact, as a 'waff', a waving movement of his hand, left a mark that could be detected. Such a mark turned out to be very important for spotting witches in Scotland and England, where witch-pricking was frequently applied. In Spanish Netherlands, Finland, Sweden, and Norway, however, the devil's mark was used as circumstantial evidence during witchcraft persecution. From the moment this type of 'proof' was used extensively in the countries in question, from the end of the 1500s, some key elements of demonological ideas had entered the minds of witch-hunters and left their stamp on witchcraft persecution in most of Northern Europe. Another type of circumstantial evidence was the water ordeal. In the material analysed in this study, only the Finnmark trial documented the use of this ordeal. However, secondary literature shows that the water ordeal was used in witchcraft trials all over Northern Europe.[20]

The other key notion among demonological ideas was that of the witches' gathering, which is also richly demonstrated in the accused persons' confessions in the analysed trials in this book. Like the devil's pact, it was very influential during the Early Modern persecution of witches, not least because it generated witchcraft panics in which many people were denounced and brought before the court. The notion of the witches' gathering is central in the analyses of trials from Spanish Netherlands, Northern Germany, Denmark, Scotland, Norway, Sweden, and Finland; the two last countries represented by the Blåkulla trials. The image of the witches' gathering is connected to the supernatural in the sense that the narrative contains marked unrealistic features: the gathering is a meeting place between visible and invisible elements.[21]

The witches' gathering in this study that presents the most elaborate description of activities is the North Berwick convention. With trials going on in Edinburgh from the end of 1590 lasting more than a year, the scene was set for an extraordinary performance, with the king of Scotland as one of the interrogators.[22]

As the trial records were published in a witchcraft pamphlet in 1591, details of this witches' gathering were widely spread and formed a sensation. The North Berwick convention was named after the coastal village North Berwick, on the Lothian side of Edinburgh. According to confessions, witches met at the graveyard outside the church, digging up bones from the graves to be used for making powder. They were dancing and having a merry time. A participant was playing a mouth harp. Next, they went into the North Berwick Kirk to listen to a speech given by the devil on the pulpit. He took a roll call of his audience, and asked them how much evil they had performed since the last meeting. They entered and left the church as part of a ritual, and they had to worship the devil by kissing his ass. The lively and exciting confession not surprisingly made an impact, and the North Berwick narrative shows a remarkable range of details. As this was the first time demonological ideas were heard in Scottish witchcraft trials, it is likely that the interrogators used leading questions to introduce the ideas. Not least, it should be emphasized that King James himself returned from Denmark in May 1590 with fresh knowledge about witches' gatherings.

As the voices of women provided so much energy and weight in narrating demonological ideas in the witchcraft confessions, these women demonstrated not only their knowledge of demonology but also their ability to tell stories. The witches' gathering was a happening to which many kinds of details could be attached, and the confessing women seized this opportunity. The main content consisted of the witches being subordinates to the devil, but the relationships between the participants were also rendered in a colourful way. That the North Berwick convention was held at the graveyard and in the church was a clear sign of mocking Christianity. The voices heard in the confessions do not only tell a remarkable story about a night in North Berwick, but also tell about the devil's power and what it was like to be an agent on the wrong side of the monarch's wishes. Judged from what was happening at this convention, it must have seemed absolutely interesting to participate in such an event.

In Denmark in 1618, the witches' meetings described were confessed to by Maren Alrøds and Mette Kongens. The gatherings took place on special days of the year: Michaelmas and St Valborg's Eve. Maren confessed that all women took the form of cats, so that they could not recognize each other. They danced and cast spells on human beings; spells which changed direction and came over the sheep. Mette Kongens and some others were said to have ploughed one evening to 'turn the rain'. In the shape of black horses, they went out to plough the field before the barley was sown in order to destroy it. Mette herself also confessed to the witches' gathering in which they tried to destroy barley, which was at Bjerrelide, a hill with a circle of oak trees at the top and a wide view of the fields around.[23] However, their evil deed did not succeed that time.

The witches' gathering in Spanish Netherlands in 1657 took place at secret locations and at crossroads, and is described as having involved dancing and playing, the devil playing on a drum, and an unknown person playing on a flute. The food was unsalted butter and unsalted sheep meat,[24] and the participants drank beer and water. They had their own devil, by whom they were caressed and who transported them to different places. In order to fly, participants were given black ointment, which they put on the broomstick, and they left the house through the chimney. This description of a witches' gathering seems to have all the standard ingredients, but is at the same time brief and concise. This signals that by the 1650s, this story had been told and retold many times in the community.

In Finnmark, the witches' gathering entered the confessions in witchcraft trials at the same time as when the first demonological ideas appeared, in the panic of 1620–21. All panics in Finnmark contained confessions to witches' gatherings, including the 1662–63 panic, from which the trial of Gundelle Olsdatter in this study is taken. The main activities at the witches' gatherings in Finnmark in Northern Norway in 1663 were dancing and drinking, a demonstration of sisterhood, with the devil as the polite host, who played his red violin and served beer from pewter cups. The activities could also be of a special kind, such as playing board games with the devil.[25] This type of witches' gathering was of an innocent character, and was described as a break from the harsh conditions of daily life.

In Northern Germany, the famous meeting place for witches' gatherings Bloksberg is mentioned in the trial of Anna Spielen in 1669. She confessed that she had been to Bloksberg twice and that she had ridden a male goat to get there. She had seen some well-known people there, but did not denounce anyone. A folkloric belief was that witches used to meet at Walpurgis Night to dance with the devil at Bloksberg, and the motif was depicted in art as early as 1650.[26] We see that quarter days were connected to witches' meetings with dancing and devil worship, and that transportation was a male goat, an animal frequently linked to the devil.

The Blåkulla trials in Sweden and Finland in the 1660s and 1670s became famous outside the Nordic countries, not least because some of the court records were translated into English right when the trials were in process.[27] The confessions from these trials highlight several demonological ideas, such as a night flight to reach the gathering, worshipping the devil at the sabbath through, among others, sexual intercourse, and receiving money and food at the gathering, which turn out to be faeces or dirt. The Blåkulla trials quickly increased in terms of number of people accused and also spread to new areas in Norrland. The notion is also found in witchcraft trials in Åland in Finland. An unusual factor in the Blåkulla trials was the large number of children who said they had been abducted to Blåkulla, and who were used as witnesses during the trials to provide information about whom they had seen there. The Blåkulla trials have been studied among others by Per-Anders Östling, Raisa Maria Toivo, Jari Eilola, and Per Sörlin. Their studies have contributed to knowledge about children's as well as adults' voices in witchcraft courtroom discourse.

The confessions to witches' gatherings in this study reveal a wide range of ideas. An unrealistic thread comes to the fore, alongside a down-to-earth and realistic attitude. The natural surroundings formed a backdrop that all people in a certain region knew. The meetings were held on fields or hills on the outskirts of nearby settlements, a common denominator, and representations of boundaries with the other world were 'located a few miles from the witches' home'.[28] In addition, the meetings could take place on well-known mountain tops, like Bloksberg in Germany, Domen in Finnmark, and Lyderhorn in Bergen. The influence of popular belief is seen in the mentioning of quarter days that have particular magical importance. Laura Paterson maintains that, as for the Scottish witches' sabbath, 'the witches were responding to the interrogator's questions based on their own knowledge and beliefs'.[29] This holds true for the descriptions given in this study. However, when comparing the confessions from the different countries, differences are found: sexual intercourse with the devil is not found in Finnmark. Digging up corpses from the graveyard in order to use the bones to make powder is found in Scotland only. Shape-shifting in connection with a witches' meeting is documented in Norway, Spanish Netherlands, and Denmark. Witches' flight on animals or broomsticks is mentioned in Norway, Sweden, Northern Germany, Spanish Netherlands, and England. Bodily flight, meaning 'the witch being physically carried by the devil or another demon',[30] is documented in Scotland, Finland, and Sweden. The use of ointment is mentioned in Spanish Netherlands, Scotland, and Sweden. Witchcraft territories organized in districts are mentioned in Denmark in 1618. Additional research increased the activities related to witches' gatherings, finding more differences. The element of cannibalism, eating babies, is found in Germany and also in Spain, but not in Northern Germany, in the Nordic countries, or on the British Isles.[31] The activities of witches' gatherings are portrayed in detail in Germany and France, both in court records and in visual art, particularly in a famous picture published in Paris in 1613.[32] Likewise, the witches' gathering held as a court session with a scribe is portrayed by artists.[33] Similarities in descriptions of witches' meetings within Northern Europe are remarkable. Ideas travelled.

The narrative constituting the witches' gathering has been discussed by witchcraft scholars, among others Willem de Blécourt.[34] With regard to historians' treatment of the topic, he states that from the start, the 'sabbath story was compartmentalized, broken up into its constitutive elements, such as devil worship, dancing, cannibalism, and flight'.[35] He argues that later historians continued this compartmentalizing process, thus decontextualizing the stories and losing the links between different elements, not paying sufficient attention to the interplay between the intellectual and 'popular' witchcraft discourse. The flexibility of sabbath imagery is underlined. I agree with De Blécourt that the sabbath story is flexible. However, the elements of devil worship, dancing, and flight are, with some amendments, useful for a description of the sabbath narrative. In fact, the terms 'transport/flight', 'location', and 'dancing/activities' cover the elements of the sabbath narrative. This is supported by Laura Paterson's research.[36] As for Northern Europe, 'cannibalism' does not occur often in confessions to witches' gatherings. Therefore, it should not be seen as a compulsory or frequent element.

The term 'transport' describes the opening and closure of the narrative. As exemplified in this study, the manner in which the participants came to the gathering is frequently mentioned. In Scotland in 1590, Agnes Sampson narrated that she rode a horse to the North Berwick convention. In Northern Germany in 1669,

Anna Spielen confessed that she rode a male goat to come to the witches' gathering. In Norway in 1623, Sitru Pedersdatter confessed that she rode to Blåkoll on a black calf.

As for 'flights', in Bruges in 1634, Mayken Karrebrouck flew to the meetings via the chimney, after having rubbed powder onto her body. Also in Scotland, flight is mentioned in witchcraft trials, either bodily flight—during which the witch was physically carried by the devil or another demon—or flight in spirit, which could mean that they actually flew either in spirit or in their 'imagination' or 'fantasy', as research by Julian Goodare shows.[37] In Sweden, confessions to riding to Blåkulla are known from 1596 onwards.[38] In the Swedish and Finnish Blåkulla trials in this study, Maria Nilsdotter in Finland in 1666 said that she was taken to Blåkulla and that the participants in the witches' gathering were transported through the air. Swedish Karin Dantz confessed that she was brought to Blåkulla by a neighbour, which is unusual. However, Karin said that she did not know how she had arrived there, but that she was carried to Blåkulla through the air and could feel the wind.[39] In Norway, Gundelle Olsdatter confessed to having attended a witches coven on Domen mountain on Midsummer Night in the guise of a crow.

The closing of the narrative is particularly marked in Sweden and Finland, when the women say that suddenly, they were standing outside their own house and did not know where they had been. Karin Dantz said that leaving Blåkulla was like a voice that took her up through the ceiling, and she was twice lifted up under the ceiling and was received by a man in white clothes, who decided that she should not be locked up in a black-sooted barn. The closing of the narrative is marked: she woke up in her own bed. As for Maria Nilsdotter's trip back from Blåkulla, she did not know where she went, only that she found herself west of Marcusböle village on a small patch of field, when she recognized something. From the secondary literature, it is known that witches travelled to Blåkulla on any item or animal available: brooms, rakes, cattle, goats, cocks, wolves, humans, wagons, and troughs. The witches did not use their own cattle as a means of transportation, but always took other people's cattle.[40] In Sweden, Norway, and Scotland, they transformed into birds.[41] In Northern Germany, flights were connected with travelling to witches' gatherings at Bloksberg.[42]

Location is also an important contextualizing element mentioned in the confessions to witches' gatherings. This element is frequently a clear indicator of the local context, as the confessions in Vardø in Finnmark mention the nearby field Ballvollen and the nearby mountain Domen; in Rygge the nearby place Kullen; in Bergen the nearby mountain Lyderhorn; in Viborg in Denmark the nearby hill Bjerrelide; in East Lothian in Scotland the village of North Berwick and the hill, the North Berwick Law; and in Bruges in Spanish Netherlands a nearby open field. These mentions account for local variants, in which the interplay between actual nearby fields and mountains and the hidden activities at witches' gatherings, part of common people's imaginations, meet in enforced narratives in a courtroom. Then, in addition, there are the mythical places, like some descriptions of Bloksberg and Blåkulla, which are apparently known in many countries.

The trials analysed in this book show contrasts when it comes to activities at witches gatherings. In the Scottish North Berwick trials, the activities described mention dancing, playing, and the digging up of bones from the graveyard. The devil is certainly the one in command of his allies. Some decades later, Scottish Isobell Eliot, one of the alleged Peaston witches, confessed to a witches' meeting in Crighton, in which activities included the use of 'flaming fire'. In Finnmark, the devil is the polite host who provides the participants with drinks and also music for their dance. The atmosphere is friendly, and the women are not commanded to do evil deeds; it is narrated more like a party. In Blåkulla, the activities documented in this study are eating, drinking, and dancing, with the devil present. In the Swedish version of the narrative, Karin Dantz is also weaving and washing the table, much like domestic activities. She received money and was lifted up under the ceiling, where she met a man in white clothes who taught her and made her sing a verse for healing. She was nearly thrown into a black house and thought they would burn her and her child. Other studies of the Blåkulla trials show that sexual intercourse with the devil took place in connection with the dance or afterwards.[43] Generally, the devil's sexual partner was a woman, and the connection between the devil and a woman was marked.[44] Finnish Maria Nilsdotter said that the first time she was in Blåkulla, she was very much afraid of Satan, and therefore she had been thrown out because her errand was not successful, probably as she did not perform evil deeds.

In Denmark, the 1590 Copenhagen trials show the use of objects and charms during witches' meetings. In the trial of Maren Alrøds in 1618, she said that they danced at a witches' gathering on Michaelmas in order to cast scabies and sickness on human beings. They also ploughed in order to destroy barley as a collective enterprise at the same meeting. Mette Kongens in 1618 also confessed to destroying barley, and she said there was a man playing bagpipe at the gathering and also a scribe. Anna Bruds in Ribe in 1652 confessed to a witches' meeting at a churchyard during which the women drank beer.

In Spanish Netherlands in 1634, Mayken Karrebrouck confessed that she had been to dances two or three times. At the meeting some danced, and they discussed what evil they would commit. Clayse Sereyns confessed in 1657 that she had attended meetings at secret locations. Her devil would be playing on a small drum, and an unknown creature played a flute. After dancing, they had eaten unsalted butter and sheep meat and drank beer and water.

Devil worship as an element is clearly described in the North Berwick records from 1590–91, in which the participants confessed that they paid homage to the devil by kissing his ass; a description common in many countries. It might be linked to the idea that the devil had a second face in that part of his body.[45] The whole meeting inside the North Berwick Kirk was devil worship, in which everything was turned upside down.[46] In Spanish Netherlands in 1634, Mayken Karrebrouck confessed that she did not show the devil any honours at the witches' gatherings and was often beaten because she did not want to cause much harm. In Finnmark, the devil is serving the witches, not the other way around. Devil worship took place at Blåkulla: witches greeted their lord who was in the seat of honour, they entered the dwelling of the devil with their backs first, after which they used to curtsey, shake hands, kiss him, and perform a greeting with the left hand. They also danced backwards in Blåkulla.[47] In Southern and Western Germany, gruesome rituals were common at alleged witches' gatherings as part of devil worship, but these are not often mentioned for witches' gatherings in Northern Germany.[48] Here, other types of rituals are described as a sign of renouncing the Christian faith.[49] Goodare emphasizes the symbolic inversion, which is related to many of the rituals at the sabbath: 'The horrific rites of the witches' sabbat were a symbolic inversion of positive human values: not just bad acts, but the imagined *opposite* of good acts'.[50]

Demonological ideas were not easily confessed to. The comparison shows that, with the exception of England, there is a pattern with regard to demonological ideas. The ideas are known in Northern Europe by lay and learned at the end of the 1500s, and demonological confessions were given after elaborate interrogation, torture, or severe pressure. Demonological narratives became more detailed as the decades went by.

The voices of women reveal how a string consisting of resistance, denial, protest, and defence was broken down during interrogation and pressure and turned into cooperation with the judiciary and resignation. Analyses of courtroom discourse display dramatic changes in the voices of the accused persons from the moment they are accused of witchcraft until the sentence is passed. Such changes could not have occurred unless judicial officials pressed for a demonological confession. Also, they required a court system in which instruments of coercion were available and were used willingly.

Central demonological ideas, like the devil's pact, sex with the devil, the devil's mark, the witches' gathering, personal demons, and familiars were heard in courtrooms in accused women's confessions throughout Northern Europe. These ideas, documented in the demonological confessions of this study, show a development over time: ideas and motifs circulate, and the main demonological narrative was enriched when it comes to elements and details, and expanded when it comes to the amount of words. In the process of telling and retelling the demonological narrative, colour from local society and existing traditional stories is added in terms of content and language. Thus, different versions of the demonological narrative, characterized by different aspects of the mentality of the societies, are heard in the accused persons' confessions. This study also shows the time span of the main occurrence of the notions of the devil's pact and the witches' gathering in Northern Europe, dealing with trials taking place from the late 1500s until the late 1600s. The analyses of demonological ideas in confessions demonstrate how these ideas influenced the judiciary's evaluation of the severity of the confessions and paved the way for an escalation of the trials. I assign considerable weight to these ideas, not least witches' gatherings, as do scholars from all countries included in this book, in which shades of the demonic are highlighted.[51]

Ideas About Maleficium *and Healing*

A wide range of ideas on *maleficium* comes to the fore in this study: traditional ideas about witchcraft, known all over Europe prior to the start of the witchcraft trials. Malevolent witchcraft deals mainly with casting spells that cause sickness in and death of people and cattle. To perform this type of witchcraft, charms, formulas, and objects were frequently used, even curses. Rituals and gestures were performed, and quarter days were often seen as suitable for practicing these deeds. Knowledge of *maleficium* was learned as an individual art. Often, a mentor—an elderly, cunning woman—was the one teaching the art, be that a mother, another relative, or a reputed person. The devil is not the one who provides evil power in the process of learning malevolent witchcraft. The performance was not collective, like demonological witchcraft. The accused persons were tried in single trials or small groups, not in panics.

For trials related to *maleficium*, the confessions contained a wide range of ideas related to traditional witchcraft and folklore, often including descriptions of how these ideas were practised and what kind of objects and charms were used. When the performance of healing is confessed to, ideas related to folk medicine appear, in addition to methods of counter-magic.

Looking at the ideas about *maleficium* and healing that surface in the voices of women as they are rendered in witchcraft court records in this study, it seems clear that the accused persons' view of magic and magical practice differed from the understanding of the elite. These contrasting views are discussed in Raisa Maria Toivo's close reading of the witchcraft trials of Agata Pekantytär,[52] in which the interpretation of common people's voices is highlighted. Charges against Agata included both benevolent magic and malevolent witchcraft: 'It is, then, a question of whose views and actions were the most plausible in court records: those of the local people or those of the authorities'.[53] The trials of Agata ended in acquittal, so that she could continue her life in the village. Hence, not all witchcraft trials ended in a death sentence; acquittal and, among others, a fine or banishment were also possible. Important research on the life trajectories of women accused of witchcraft who were subsequently acquitted has been performed in Finland and Sweden.[54]

The perspective of Toivo is supported by Bente Alver's research.[55] It also constitutes this study's approach, as a focus on the voices of women serves to display the beliefs and attitudes of common people. Folkloric motifs woven into the mentality of ordinary people and the belief that charms and spells worked, be that in a good or a bad way, were common throughout Northern Europe in the Early Modern period. Folkloric ideas did not fundamentally change over time, and here they differ from demonological ideas: maleficent ideas tended to be stable as centuries went by. In my view, the beliefs coming to the fore in accused women's utterances are convincing as an expression of the imagination of common people at the time.

It was believed that charms helped the spells be effective. They were orally transferred, learned by heart in the villages via rhyme, rhythm, alliteration, and motifs that were easily remembered. They could be words read out loud, like in the trial of Gertrud Matsdotter in Finland in 1649 and Helene Clerk in Scotland in 1643. Other remedies to support a spell could be a hand stretched out, as in the trial of Lynken van Brugghe in Spanish Netherlands in 1594, pots and jars with creamy arsenic that were found in Lynken van Brugghe's house, beggar books in the house of Mayken Karrebrouck in 1634, and other objects, like in Denmark in 1590, when clay pots were used to conjure a storm against the royal fleet, and in Scotland in 1590–91, when a piece of cloth belonging to a person or a picture of wax were confessed to have been used in the performance of witchcraft.

Spells allegedly could be lethal, as we see in the trial of Scottish Helene Clerk. To take revenge on a man because he did not engage her son as a servant, she said the man would not sail another year, whereupon he fell ill and died. Also, the death of a child, burned in a boiling kettle, is testified to have happened because Helene fell out with the mother of the child and uttered threatening words about her going home worse than she came. Helene allegedly obtained the power of witchcraft because she was washed with charmed water by a woman who was executed as a witch. The idea of Helene Clerk receiving the power to perform witchcraft from a woman who had a reputation for witchcraft is parallel to the way the art of healing is passed on personally by a reputed, often elderly woman to a younger woman. Not everybody could receive this art; a personal quality was required.

Diverse objects were confessed to as being used in spells. The idea of taking an object to church, or stealing what belonged to the church or the dead (like soil from graveyards or bones from a grave), is often connected to witchcraft.[56] The magical use of what belongs to God is seen in the trial of Anna Spielen in Northern Germany. Spielen confessed to having taken communion bread from her own mouth and given it to Satan in a handkerchief. The idea of digging up of bones from the graveyard is documented in the trial of Agnes Sampson. It was common belief that magic worked better when devices with religious connotations were used. Bente Alver maintains that the witches' efforts to get more of something through magical practice had to do with the distribution of fortune. In a society with food scarcity, the witches, through their contact with dark forces, seized good fortune that they were not allowed to claim.[57]

Divination, or the ability to foretell or see into the future, was a magical practice that was considered a crime. It could be used to tell something about the future, like in the prayer of Agnes Sampson's case in 1590–91, which could stop once or twice, thus providing information about the fate of the person who was prayed for. Or we can see it in the shivering of Maria Nilsdotter in Finland when she heard the name of the place where a person's sickness was contracted, or in the trials of Karin Persdotter in Sweden, who paid money to the Water Man to learn what was the cause of an illness. When standing before the court, the women knew that it was more dangerous to confess to divination than to healing, as we see in the trial of Anne Knutsdatter, Norway, who regretted that she had confessed to divination.

Love magic aimed at forcing another person to love the one who asked for their love. Rituals, prayers, and magical devices were used. It was regarded as harmful magic and punished as a crime. This practice is seen in Scotland in the trial of

Agnes Sampson, who had been given a ring by Barbara Napier to pray over, so that Barbara would obtain the favour of a desired woman. In Germany, love magic is seen in the trials of Kistina Netelers, who had two crosses out of rye straw with a red thread twined around them, objects to be placed under her husband's pillow to make him leave his mistress and love her again.

Ideas about *maleficium* and healing were interrelated. Healing was easily confessed to; the women regarded this as part of their competence, and they even seemed to be proud of their knowledge. It involved the healing or taking away of illness. Healing comprised the same methods as performing malevolent witchcraft: charms, formulas, prayers, objects taken to church for magical purposes, and graveyard soil. In the trial of Agnes Sampson, Scotland 1590–91, soil from the graveyard was confessed to having been put under the feet of a woman about to give birth.[58] In the trial of Anne Knutsdatter in Norway in 1594, soil from the graveyard was confessed to having been used as a cure for illness. The same trial documents the cutting of crosses in the body of a sick woman in order to heal her. Indeed, religious symbols were used. In Denmark in 1618, Mette Lauridsdatter Kongens confessed to having made the sign of the cross over a sick man, reciting a prayer, and giving his mother a drink that he was supposed to consume the following Sunday morning before the sun went up. Moreover, different types of food, herbs, and roots were used for healing. Agnes Sampson confessed that she used eggs as an ingredient in a remedy for a disease.

Common people were convinced that healing was possible if the right means were used. They knew whom to contact in case of illness, were aware of the reputation of this person, and knew where this person lived. In the trial of Agnes Sampson, we hear that her healing activity and her clients were spread in the East Lothian area, an amazing distance to most likely traverse by foot for the healer as well as for her clients.

In the courtroom, healing was judged by a judiciary that connected this performance to evil and a code of law that stated its criminality. In some countries, punishment for healing and those who contacted healers was very severe, such as in Norway from the 1580s until 1617, and somewhat milder in Denmark and Norway after 1617. Common people also knew about the 1617 decree of witchcraft issued in Copenhagen, and its content: Mette Lauridsdatter Kongens said in 1618 that she had performed no evil after the king's letter about witchcraft was issued.

The cunning persons who had a reputation of healing humans were also believed to have the power to heal animals. The sign of the cross was used to heal cattle in the name of the Holy Trinity, as confessed to by Mette Lauridsdatter Kongens in Denmark. In the trial of Kistina Netelers, Northern Germany, she confesses that a stocking tie was taken to church so that mass would be read over it, and was later used for healing a sick horse.

People in Early Modern Europe believed it was possible to manipulate forces when using the right devices. Religious expressions were frequently used in charms in Protestant countries, while the elements of Catholicism are found in Spanish Netherlands, where the Virgin Mary was included in the prayers. When it comes to ideas activated in this study, minor variations may be traced: the deed of destroying barley is found in trials in Germany and Denmark, elfshot and fairies are found in Scotland, throwing silver in water is mentioned in Sweden and in Finland in connection with divination, and sucking blood to recover from sickness is found in England and Scotland. In this way, variation between countries and within countries is seen, but the core elements of malefice and healing in the confessions are similar throughout Northern Europe. Comparison of the trials in this study shows that maleficent witchcraft and the unsuccessful practice of healing impact witchcraft trials due to consequences connected to evil and inexplicable tragedies.

The comparison between ideas of *maleficium* in the eight countries in this study displays a wide range of methods used to perform harmful magic. Similarities are marked between the countries when it comes to the content of curses, the way curses are formed, and the strong link between cause and effect, namely the word uttered and the harmful effect which followed. This linear occurrence of action influenced the sequentiality of the trial, as there would always be a sequence dominated by witnesses' testimonies before the sequence of the accused person's explanation and the passing of verdict and sentence. However, it is worth noting that the judiciary considered maleficent witchcraft to be less dangerous than demonological witchcraft, particularly during the last decades of the 1600, as seen in the Finnish case of Brita Pålsu. Several scholars have contributed with valuable studies on *maleficium*, not least from the Nordic countries.[59] Ideas about *maleficium* and healing continued to live in the communities after demonological witchcraft trials had ceased.

Ideas related to maleficent witchcraft and healing in the voices of Northern European women show the rich folk belief inherited via oral transfer through the centuries. This knowledge and competence was widespread and practised in the local communities, and the ideas certainly put their stamp on a number of witchcraft trials.

Merging of Ideas

Ideas about *maleficium* and demonological ideas could occur in the same trials. In addition, ideas about healing could be turned into demonological ideas during interrogation. One can even see that these ideas were fused. This study offers some interesting examples of how the merging of these ideas was made possible, most often due to the influence of the interrogator during the questioning of the accused person. On the part of the judiciary, there was a desire to press forth demonological confessions by changing the content of folkloric motifs into demonic content. In Sweden, the 1653 trial of Karin Persdotter is an example of demonizing folkloric beliefs. The demonizing became a fact when the Water Man was linked to the Evil One. While Karin confessed that she went to the Water Man to get advice, the indictment states that she left God and surrendered to the Water Man, who was called the Evil One and Beelzebub. Even if Karin never confessed to a loathsome relation with the Evil One, this point was twisted and turned in the sentence passed, as a connection was created between her unstable behaviour and her relationship with the Evil One. In her 1666 trial, Finnish Maria Nilsdotter was asked when she entered into a pact with Satan, so that he could reveal to her such shivering secrets as she confessed to. It is the interrogator who linked the shivering and Satan, thus connecting ideas about *maleficium* and divination to demonology. Again, the judiciary directed the confession according to its desire. In the trial of Agnes Sampson in Scotland in 1590–91, her comprehensive knowledge of healing is turned into demonological knowledge. From a starting point in which she willingly shared her knowledge of healing and even recited several of her prayers, the interrogation led her confession towards a demonic one. In the trial of Anna Spielen in Northern Germany, the points of the confession that are concerned with *maleficium* were fused with features of demonology. This is the case for the cow that died and for the communion bread taken from church. Her confession shows that she had knowledge of *maleficium* as well as of demonology.

The fusion of ideas that we see in several of the confessions reflects a difference in attitude to witchcraft between the judiciary and the accused persons. While the women who were brought before the court responded to questioning by using the knowledge they possessed, the interrogators had another agenda. Even if the accused women were acquainted with the content of the laws and the danger of a demonological confession, they still found themselves with the latter outcome. Thus, the voices of women show the broad knowledge of ideas about witchcraft that these women had, but they also echo the merciless judicial officials, who had a quite different mental baggage.

Witnesses' Testimonies

Most often, testimonies in witchcraft trials, heard in court records, came from neighbours in the local communities. So also in this study. Robin Briggs has emphasized the social context of witchcraft charges, 'the core of the belief lay in the notion that witches had peculiar powers to harm their neighbours and the community at large'.[60] The reason why neighbours gave these testimonies is a fear of witchcraft performed by a woman in the village, resulting in an accident or illness. The outset of such a testimony was often a threatening remark uttered in a quarrel or conflict situation. These words were followed shortly afterwards by an accident or illness, as seen in trial records from all countries in this study. Most often, rationalization after the fact took place, as people began to look for scapegoats when unexpected misfortune occurred. In most cases, the tragedy took place shortly after the threat was uttered. However, finding scapegoats for a shipwreck could take years, as we see in the first witchcraft panic in Finnmark in 1620–21.[61]

It was dangerous to utter threatening words in the seventeenth century. They were often linked to witchcraft: witnesses heard the accused person express threats in a quarrel, and the words came true. This cause-and-effect argumentation was an attempt to provide evidence in a case in which this was impossible. We see this exemplified in the *maleficium* trial of Anna Spielen: a spoken charm and the death of a cow; in the trial of Helene Clerk, as she had uttered that a man would never sail another year and he fell ill and died; as well as in the trials of Isabel Atcheson and Jane Simpson in 1664. In these two trials, we do not only get a testimony stating that threatening words were related to a strange illness, but we also see how the persons suspected of having cast a spell on a person were sent for to help the sick person recover. Thus, there was a belief that if a woman had the power to cast spells causing illness, that same woman also had the power to take the illness away.

A saying related to threats coming true was expressed in the Finnish trial of Gertrud Matsdotter in 1649: what she promised with the mouth, she finished off with the deed. Often, spells were interpreted to be related to human illness. Julian Goodare states that people in the villages were interested in 'whether an illness was "natural" or "unnatural"'.[62] Some diseases were feared in the period of witchcraft persecution, but were not blamed on witchcraft.[63] However, probably 'a witchcraft-induced disease had to have an unusual set of symptoms, one that had no "natural" explanation'.[64] As sudden illness was difficult to understand, common people explained it by spells having been cast on a person:

> The 'unnaturalness' of a disease ultimately lay, not in its symptoms, but in its aetiology—the way in which it was held to have been caused. This in turn was diagnosed, not from the symptoms themselves, but from the way in which the symptoms responded to treatment.[65]

Here is where the cunning person came in and could confirm, if the patient failed to recover after treatment, that the illness was caused by witchcraft.

The voices of women heard in the testimonies in the trials analysed demonstrate the power to 'unwitch', to use counter-magic to take away a spell. It seems that it was common to seek this type of help, as we see in the trial of Gertrud Matsdotter, in which a man who believed that a spell was cast on him readily contacted a cunning woman who was believed to be able to help. Sometimes the spell was sent on to another person, like in the same trial of Gertrud Matsdotter: the spell was transferred to another man. In the trial of Brita Pålsu, she was believed to have cast a spell on a woman causing eye sickness, and Brita was threatened by the sick woman's brother to take the sickness away; otherwise, he said, he would 'get her onto the fire'. After that, the woman's eyes immediately became better. A testimony of this kind given in court was a clear rationalization after the fact. The eye sickness might have improved after some days anyway. This accusation shows how easy it was to connect an illness to witchcraft, and how easy it was to claim that the illness had been taken away by witchcraft as well. Notably, in this late case of 1685, the jury did not believe in this charge, as it was impossible to prove.

The most frequent testimony revolved around the inexplicable illness and death of humans, although the illness and death of animals often occurred as well. This was a well-chosen accusation if neighbours wanted to get rid of a troublesome person, as we see in the German, Finnish, and Swedish trials. Methods were plenty: witchery might for instance be placed in the barn, under the doorstep. In the trial of Anneke Rickers, we get to know what kind of objects she used: a plait of hair, a brass ring, a leather shoelace, and the hoof of a pig. The result was the loss of five horses. Also, in the trial of Gertrud Matsdotter, Gertrud was said to have boasted that she could get as much butter as she wanted from an animal. This luck of hers was connected to a woman who had had no luck making butter for many years, and thereby an accusation was made. In the Finnish villages, this type of magic was looked upon as theft; 'milk thieves' were commonly spoken of.[66] Milking from a distance is exemplified in the trial of Kistina Netelers, through an axe struck in a block of wood, a motif which is also found in a woodcut from 1511.[67]

How seriously a witchcraft accusation was punished varied a great deal. Malevolent witchcraft, like the stealing of milk, which was widespread in traditional witchcraft,[68] received rather mild punishment. In the trial of Ingegärd Andersdotter, she confessed to having taught another woman how to cast a harmful spell on cattle: she had carried some animal hair to her neighbour's farm, with the result that he lost his best cow. Whether one animal or several animals were affected by witchcraft, whether the result was sickness or death, the fear of spells thrown upon animals shows the value of cattle and the catastrophe that losing animals represented to a farmer.

A comparison between the countries in this study with regard to witnesses' testimonies shows that the same content was evenly distributed throughout Northern Europe in the sixteenth and seventeenth centuries. Ideas about *maleficium* were central to the persecution of alleged witches in several countries, not least Finland. A pattern emerges, showing the uttering of a curse which is just afterwards connected to inexplicable tragedies and misfortunes. When comparing the countries of his study, it has been demonstrated that people believed that malevolent witchcraft was effective, as was healing.

Narrative Structures

From a narratological point of view, in which narratology is defined as the study of structures in narrative texts—an exploration of the narrator's function[69]—the entire court records of a trial can be interpreted as a narrative. Likewise, the confession given by an accused person is a narrative, as well as the testimony given by a witness. The narrator is seen as an absolutely necessary textual device, with the authority to delegate voices to the participants of the narrative. Court records bring several voices to the fore. The voices focused on in this study, the voices of women, appear in confessions given by accused persons and in testimonies of witnesses. The category of voice has great importance in a witchcraft narrative.

Throughout the analyses, we have seen a cohesion which kept the stories together, and this glue was based on a profound knowledge of narrative structures. These narrative structures are seen in demonological and malevolent confessions equally. However, the contents differ according to the two concepts of witchcraft discussed above.

The demonological narrative is based from the outset on a denunciation in a witchcraft panic. This narrative comprises some core elements: the devil's pact, the witches' gathering, and the performance of collective witchcraft. These core elements were developed into various versions, which became more detailed as the decades passed by. There was a 'set menu' in a demonological narrative that additional points were added to. Thus, it was a framed narrative in a way. The additions had to do with renouncing one's baptism, the power to perform witchcraft received from the devil, the ritual of the devil's pact, the devil's appearance, the devil's promises, shape-shifting, transport to the witches' gatherings, the activities at the witches' gathering, the type of collective witchcraft performed, and the denunciation of others.

The *maleficium* narrative is mainly formed according to narrative structures, like the confessions. The main structuring device is a cause-and-effect argument: first a threat was uttered, then an accident happened. The ability to master the art of *maleficium* is inherent, and this type of witchcraft was learned individually from a cunning person. This type of witchcraft was performed individually or in small groups. The main elements of the *maleficium* narrative are the casting of spells causing human or animal illness or death. This is facilitated by charms, formulas, and objects. It is an open narrative, in the sense that the elements to be included are not defined. The performance of malevolent witchcraft existed before and after the period of European witchcraft persecution.

For both these basic narratives, narrative structures were essential in the process of learning, transferring, and confessing to ideas about witchcraft. In the confessions to the devil's pact, witches' gatherings, and collective witchcraft, narrative structures are inherent. The narrative structures eased oral transference in communities. This study has applied the narratological categories of order, duration, frequency, voice, and mood in its analyses. Chronological order is established by a timeline, on which the actions are placed via linearity. Order is essential in the demonological narratives because it creates a connection between the actions, be that the elements constituting the ritual of the devil's pact, those constituting the activities at the witches' gathering, or those making up the performance of collective witchcraft. The linear construction adds a logical connection between realistic and unrealistic elements.

The category of order is strengthened by accuracy in the way transport was arranged, for instance in Maria Nilsdotter's flight to Blåkulla: the way she left her house, who carried her, and the views she noticed on her way. We see this in Agnes Sampson's confession, in which linearity is the structuring device which helps assemble all fragments of the preliminary interrogation into a coherent narrative, and in which the order of events—the dancing at the graveyard, the digging up of joints from the graves, the entry into the kirk, the calling of names by the devil in the kirk, and the exit from the kirk—contributes to increasing tension and to the excitement of the narrative. And we see it in the prayer of Agnes Sampson, which could stop once or twice: the order was a signal of life and death.

Order is seen in the establishing of a timeline. In a Blåkulla journey, it begins when the alleged witches leave the house by flight or other transport and ends with them going home. These points mark linearity. The mentioning of the location of the gathering gives the narratives a local touch and contributes to contextualiza-tion. Then there are the basic elements: the dance, the activities, and devil worship. These events are categories that are not strictly defined, and they allow for new fragments to be inserted without interfering with the basic elements. The order of the elements strengthens the coherence of the story. The narrative of the witches' gathering enables, through its flexibility, brief as well as detailed descriptions within the same frame.

The actions are points on a line, which in oral transfer helps with remembering. We see it in the trial of Helene Clerk in the story of the charmed water cast in the sea, after which a great storm arose and took the boats and houses of Newhaven. We see it in the confession of Anna Spielen, in which she first went to church, then did not swallow the communion bread, and then gave it to Satan in a handkerchief. We hear it in the confession of Gundelle Olsdatter in Finnmark, in which the order of the ritual of the devil's pact was strict: first she got beer, then she was deranged, then Satan appeared and wanted her service, then she pledged herself to Morten, her God, then he promised her good fortune with livestock and everything she undertook. By ordering the elements, the entering of the pact falls into a pattern that was learned and known all over Europe.

In a *maleficium* narrative, order is a requirement. We see it in the confession of Swedish Karin Persdotter, in which the visits to the Water Man could only hap-pen during certain times and days. We see it in the trial of Lynken van Brugghe, who visited a breastfeeding woman, stretched out her hand, and cast a spell on her, resulting in no production of milk the next day. We see it in the trial of Thomasine Read, in which a spell was cast on a boy: first, he came to her house, then he was given a root to eat, and a short time later, he had his first 'tormenting fitt'. For these devices to work intentionally in a *maleficium* narrative, there has to be order; in fact, success is dependent on order.

The narratological category of duration is understood as the effect of the narra-tive being told quickly or slowly: whether an event is told briefly, with few words, or with many words, and how rapidly the action moves according to a timeline. For instance, the rendering of direct discourse and descriptive passages tend to slow down the speed of the narrative. These slowed-down sections of the text are focused on and thus get most attention. In the trials of Isabel Atcheson and Jane Simpson, the description of a woman's dream, containing the two suspected witches inside her bedroom, receives considerable textual room within relatively brief records. In the trial of Clayse Sereyns, the powder she received from the devil as part of the initiation ritual is described by colour and ways of using it. In the trial of Lynken van Brugghe, retorts and dialogues are rendered in direct speech, in words uttered by Van Brugghe as well as by witnesses. In the trial of Anneke Rickers, the story about the red rider adds lustre to the records, and an accurate description of the witchery she placed in the barn does the same. In the trial of Anne Knutsdatter, the description of the small dwarf with the soft, downy fingers echoes fairy tales told and retold. In the trial of Helene Clerk, a considerable amount of words is used to describe how witch-pricking was performed. In the trial of Gertrud Matsdotter, weight is given to a description of her during the Easter dinner service, when she came running with bare feet and her hair uncovered in the field. In the trial of Karin Dantz, her arrival at Blåkulla stands out, when she was asked to weave and wash the table and another woman lent her a knife to throw over the money that Karin was given there. In the trial of Maren, the wife of Mogens, details are given about the Apostle placed in a beer barrel and commanded to go to the royal ships in the North Sea. In the trial of Mette Kongens, the testimony of one witness describes a black-billed magpie with holes through both wings jumping behind Mette, a motif which attracts the listener's attention because of visuality. The slowing down of the text gives room to details and 'spice', points of interest that made the narrative easier to learn and to tell. The way duration is handled in the witchcraft confessions displays a considerable competence in storytelling, and it reminds us that the narrators who brought these narratives to the courtrooms were living in predominantly oral societies.

The category of frequency, the repetition of story elements, is activated in all trials analysed. In the demonological confessions, repetition of textual elements is heard in the entering into the devil's pact, when the devil often appears several times in order to attain the woman's service, echoing the 'three-number-law' from fairy tales.[70] It is an element that builds tension in the text, at the same time as it provides a pattern and gives the expectation of success for the devil's effort. We see it in the Danish trial of Maren, the wife of Mogens, in which it is mentioned time and again that the witchcraft against the royal ships had to do with Princess Anne's *first-time* voyage to Scotland, as she also went to Scotland a second time. The repetition of *first time* links the performed witchcraft to a certain time, the autumn of 1589, while the witchcraft trials took place in the summer of 1590. It also underlines the failure of the first voyage, and the witches' power to conjure storms to hinder even the king's ships. The repetitive element is also at work in the dittay of Isobell Eliot, in which, through the help of judicial officials, the words 'divill' and 'carnall copulation' are mentioned frequently. In an indictment or dittay, repetition has a conjuring effect and displays the force of repetition as a strong linguistic device, also demonstrated in legal rhetoric.

In a *maleficium* narrative, repetition is often seen in the use of charms and formulas that are used to perform witchcraft. We hear it in the trial of Maria Nilsdotter, in the formula used when she asked for an answer about the cause of an illness, whether it came from the sea or the earth: her question started always in the same way. Repetition could be used in confessions to emphasize extenuating circumstances. We hear this in the trial of Brita Pålsu in the repetition of the holy days of Christmas in her confession: that she wanted to go to church to attend the service, which reinforced her presentation of herself as a Christian woman. We hear repetition used in an unusual way in the trial of Karin Persdotter, as she presented herself as a business woman: twelve öre is repeated, the money she gave to the Water Man, accentuating the point that people paid money to obtain her advice. As a *maleficium* narrative was most often constructed by witnesses, emphasizing the connection between a threat and the result of the threat, repetitive elements are also heard in different witnesses' testimonies, as they centre around a restricted number of performed evil actions in similar versions.

The category of voice express a multitude of accents, as the analyses above have shown. The rendered voices in demonological confessions display knowledge about a specific type of witchcraft. The voices of women emerge with authority, whether they confess to their first meetings with the Evil One in fields or forests, their flights to the Blåkulla, Domen, or Bloksberg Mountains, or their activities at witches' gatherings. Their knowledge is genuine, and is commonly shared and feared during the Early Modern period.

The voices of women come to the fore differently in a demonological narrative than in a *maleficium* narrative. First, the voices presenting the demonological narrative were heard during a relatively short period of witchcraft persecution, while the voices portraying the *maleficium* narrative were retelling an old story. Second, there is a difference related who constructs the narrative. The demonological narrative is a retelling of a story, told in a confession given by an accused woman. The narrative is unrealistic, containing shape-shifting and night flight. The *maleficium* narrative is constructed mainly by the witnesses: those who brought forward accusations, those who were wronged. The narrative was linked to a real event. Third, there is a difference related to delegation of voice. In a demonological narrative, the narrator most often delegated voice to the devil. His voice is heard in relation to entering the devil's pact, when he is asking the woman to serve him, when he wants to have a report of the evil deeds his servants have performed, and when he gives promises. His voice belonged to a recreated story, known in skeleton form throughout Europe. In a *maleficium* narrative, the narrator, frequently a witness, delegated voice to the woman uttering a threat, to the person or persons she had a conflict with, and to the people who had spells cast on them. The voice was always delegated to a human being. The witnesses were convinced that it was possible for human beings to manipulate powers, with illness and death as a result, and that those knowing and causing malefice lived in the neighbourhood. With the principle of cause-and-effect as the backbone of argumentation, the *maleficium* narrative was also presented with reliability, with the weight of centuries' beliefs behind it. There had to be a connection between a threat and a calamity, in the form of a cunning person, passing on an art which had survived in family memory for centuries.

In the discourse of a trial, the category of voice was central, because the words uttered by the participants were decisive in the interpretation of the charges. The content of the words uttered, who was uttering them, to whom they were spoken, in which way they were uttered, and the context of the words spoken are central questions for a scholar. However, the category of voice also becomes important because it has to do with the two different narratives' frame of reference. There is a distinction between voices rendered in a narrative in terms of whether they were related to real life, to living persons, or whether they belonged to actors in a story. This study has shown that there is a difference between the demonological narrative and the *maleficium* narrative when it comes to the delegation of voice. In a demonological narrative, voice is delegated to a non-human figure, most often the devil. His voice is part of a story detached from real life. In a *maleficium* narrative, voice is delegated to human beings. Their voices are part of events that actually took place. Thus, the backdrop is different in these two types of narrative. The demonological narrative relates to a fictional universe. The *maleficium* narrative relates to a realistic universe. What is new and significant in the Early Modern courtrooms is that a fictional narrative was regarded as valid evidence in witchcraft trials.

The narrative category of mood is audible in the court records as an expression of the narrator's point of view: her or his attitude towards what is told, be that in a confession or a testimony. This includes the question of whether those who told the narratives believed in witchcraft. It also includes the question of how to interpret a narrative that clearly belonged to fiction. There is no doubt that people in Early Modern Europe believed that witchcraft could be performed, and that it worked. However, the attitude to a confession was not a confirmation of the belief that witchcraft was possible, but rather an acceptance of magical elements as part of a demonological narrative.

In the demonological narrative, unrealistic elements could occur without problem. In the *maleficium* narrative, it is believed that the events described could take place and had taken place in real life. The content in a demonological narrative also differed from the *maleficium* narrative in that it was connected to the demonic sphere, with the devil in a central role as participant in the narrative. This is an important difference, as it points to a dividing line when it comes to the narrator's attitude towards what was told. When a woman accused of witchcraft gave a demonological confession, she retold a story she had heard. The magic happened within the story. Gundelle Olsdatter confessed that she had been to Domen Mountain, Maria Nilsdotter and Karin Dantz that they went to Blåkulla, Agnes Sampson that she went to 'foreign coasts', and Anna Spielen that she went to Bloksberg. The flight they confessed to was part of a magical event. They heard such stories, and this is what they reproduced.

When a witness gave a testimony about performed malevolent witchcraft, he or she narrated about an event they believed had really taken place. This is seen for instance in the description of concrete objects connected to malevolent witchcraft; physical objects that could be touched. When narratives were heard in the courtrooms, the one most feared was the demonological one, perhaps because it dealt with the powerful evil figure and because it was far from the daily lifeworld, and thus fascinating. Malevolent witchcraft, on the contrary, was easy to explain and to hold on to because the magical performance and the surroundings of the magical performance were recognizable elements in the local village. In spite of this closeness to the recognizable world that we hear in the testimonies, a comparison between the countries in this study shows that what the interrogators wanted to hear was the demonological narrative.

The comparison of narrative structures shows a pattern. Compared with a *maleficium* narrative, a demonological narrative was treated differently by the courts with regard to interrogation, the use of pressure, and sentence. The concept of *maleficium* and the concept of demonology led to different types of trials. Narrative structures are seen in confessions and testimonies in all countries in this study, as these structures form the base of confessions and testimonies told in the courtroom. The two types of narratives may contribute to an explanation of the difference in intensity of persecution in witchcraft trials in various countries. Words uttered in the courtroom were judged according to the danger they were assumed to represent, and a narrative based on the demonological doctrine, for a few centuries, was taken as red-hot speech.

Orality Features

The comparison of orality features in women's voices in eight countries show a mastery of storytelling that is deeply rooted. This knowledge enabled demonological narratives to thrive and prosper in Northern European villages, as they spread from mouth to mouth. What seems clear from the analyses of trials in this study is that around 1580–1600, the demonological narrative obtained a foothold among common people in Northern European countries. What emerges from the confessions and testimonies in courtrooms is the retelling of narratives that are composed according to certain patterns and orally transferred. The words presented by the women in their confessions and testimonies are the foundation for our understanding of common people's mentality and narrative competence.

The particular position of court records, between oral and written text, is pointed out by Elizabeth S. Cohen:[71] These documents enable an interpretation in which orality is taken into account.[72] Cohen suggests to approach court records as documents based on oral utterances given in a courtroom. The confessions of the accused persons as well as the witnesses' testimonies are in third-person narration, past tense. Inserted in these narratives, we find quotations of utterances and charms in first person, present tense. This way of telling is lively and easy to follow in an oral setting. Kathleen Doty and Daniel Collins argue, based on studies of the Salem witchcraft documents and Russian sources, respectively, that the use of indirect speech in court records fits orality.[73] Collins even suggests that the shift to indirect speech may signal a suppression of orality. He concludes that this shift can be traced in the law's needs and structures. I think the same might hold true for most trial documents analysed in this book.[74]

Orality features are frequently present in the confessions and in the witnesses' testimonies, made visible in the records' markers of orality as additive sentence structures, redundancy, cause-and-effect relations, folkloric elements, closeness to the human lifeworld, and an agonistic tone.[75] All these features are documented in the confessions and testimonies of the women in the trials analysed in this book, giving the impression that the documents occupy a particular textual space between oral and written discourse.

Orality features show the accused women as individual language users, with accents of their personal language emphasized. The rendering of charms, prayers, formulas, and spells known in traditional folk beliefs as part of the confession underlines oral transference. Spells are most often related to witchcraft, while charms and prayers are often related to healing. Such a charm is heard in Germany in Kistina Netelers's confession, in which the fusing of colloquial and religious language is reflected in the invocation of Christ and St John in combination with the colloquial name Jens, thus getting close to local culture. In addition, the prayer is characterized by rhythmic elements, which facilitate oral transference. Also, the charm rendered in Anna Spielen's confession is formed according to conventions within the oral sphere, while the content—that she is leaving God and joining the devil—represents a fundamental demonological idea. In this case, we see how demonological ideas were merged with traditional beliefs and were apparently used to perform malefice. In Spanish Netherlands, charms were used to take away evil spells, as we hear in the confessions of Lynken van Brugghe and Mayken Karrebrouck; however, Van Brugghe is reluctant to recite the charm for the interrogators. Also, in Denmark, the recital of charms as well as the use of objects is frequent when *maleficium* is performed, as we hear in the confessions of Maren, the wife of Mogens, and Mette Kongens. In Scotland, prayer and charms are used in connection with divination and healing, in particular brought to the fore in the confession of Agnes Sampson, in which the reading of a prayer for life and death was said to foretell the future. Also, the charmed water heard about in the trial of Helene Clerk shows strong belief in the charm: that it was powerful and lasting. In Norway, we hear about charms and prayers in the confession of Anne Knutsdatter: she read them over sick people and over the first stools of a child, one in the name of the nine Marys. In Sweden, charms surface in the confessions of Ingegärd Andersdotter and Karin Persdotter in connection with malefice and healing. The names of the Trinity are used for healing, while spells are used for the performance of malevolent witchcraft. In Finland, Gertrud Matsdotter's voice, as it is rendered in the witnesses' depositions, uses charms and cursing to cast spells on humans and animals.

The way in which charms, prayers, spells, and formulas are rendered in the confessions, and also in witnesses' testimonies, shows that the accused persons as well as the witnesses believed in the power of these words. They paid attention to signs given by the prayers. Furthermore, it is apparent that charms and spells were often seen as a necessary part of a ritual, whether related to demonology, *maleficium*, or healing. The charms, prayers, spells, and formulas were passed from mouth to mouth. Per Sörlin emphasizes that stories were told and retold in local communities, and I share this emphasis. Words had power: they could be deadly, but they could also be a blessing. The confessions from the eight countries above strengthen the impression that among common people, the belief in magical words was strong.

The comparison shows that another prominent orality feature is the use of additive structures. Additive structures are observed in the court records on a sentence, paragraph, and word level. With regard to the sentence level, we see the conjunction 'and' used frequently, for instance in the confession of Gundelle Olsdatter from Finnmark, in which she confessed about the women shaped as birds, chasing fish from the shore.[76] With regard to the paragraph level, in the Nordic countries a new paragraph is frequently started with *Item*, which gives a feeling of addition. On a word level, we have heard in the confession of Kistina Netelers the description of the devil as *schwart und rugh, kort und dick und kalt*.[77]

Then there is the device of redundancy, wherein several words with the same semantic content are used to describe a person, an object, or a happening. Often, two words are combined, like in Jane Simpson's trial: 'occasion or cause', 'abused or wronged'. The frequency of additive structures in witchcraft confessions shows in particular the focus on rhythm in oral storytelling.

A characteristic oral element that we find in many of the confessions and witnesses' testimonies is the mentioning of quarter days. There are some particular days of the year, like All Hallows and St John's Eve, when according to folk tradition, witches were out. It was widely believed that on these days, the boundary between the world we see and the world we do not see could be crossed. This resulted in tales, passed on orally, which are echoed in witchcraft trials. Then, there were quarter days which served as a calendar, like Michaelmas, used in the Danish and Scottish witchcraft confessions. Christmas Eve was often used in the same manner. Altogether, the mentioning of particular days of the year in witchcraft trials tends to connect a happening or a deed to a specific time of the year.

Closeness to the human lifeworld is an aspect attributed to the oral field. In Kistina Netelers's confession, the devil came to her when her husband was away; the devil ate cabbage, the husband was out drinking, she wished to get the love of her husband back, the devil made the promise of enough food—formulations connected to subsistence needs and basic experiences and emotions. These orality features contribute substantially to an understanding of the living conditions of common people.

Agonistic accents of the voices of women are first and foremost heard in witnesses' testimonies, related to ideas of *maleficium*. The female witnesses render events and words which strengthen the suspicion against a person. Most often, such testimonies contained short narratives about a situation in which the accused person scolded or threatened another person. A short time thereafter, the threat came true, leading to sickness or death in humans or animals.

The comparison of orality features in women's voices in Northern European witchcraft trials shows that throughout, oral expressions were taken down in the court records. This gives the language of each speaker a unique nuance. Each confession contains individualized expressions, making it a confession that only this woman could have given. Gunvor Simonsen says in her book about the West Indian courts that 'historians talk about voices as a means of reconstructing the historical subjectivity of enslaved people'.[78] This can also be said about the voices of the women we have encountered in the analyses, as they come to the fore with oral accents. The personal touch present in every witchcraft confession is clear. Features of orality emphasize the personal influence on as well as the personal expression of the confession.

Interrogation

The interrogation was an extremely important part of witchcraft trials, often resulting in the turning point of the trial and determining the content of the confession and the outcome of the trial. Therefore the comparison between the eight countries in this study with regard to interrogation is of strong interest. In all trials analysed in this book, interrogation is rendered in the records. It is also possible to find the questions the interrogator posed to the accused woman. This can be done either by finding a recorded verb denoting a question, like 'being asked', or by using the technique of 'shadow questions', in which the questions can be reconstructed based on the answers given. In some countries, a questionnaire could be used during interrogation in witchcraft trials, to make sure that items vital to the verdict and sentence were answered. Questionnaires resulted in numbered, itemized recorded confessions. These confessions show that certain items like the devil's pact, the witches' gathering, and the denunciation of other witchcraft suspects were required by the legal authorities to be part of a witchcraft confession. For the countries included in this book, such a questionnaire was used in Northern Germany and in Spanish Netherlands. The content of the articles activated in Kistina Netelers's confession shows that when a questionnaire was used during interrogation in a witchcraft trial in the Northern Germany in the early 1600s, central demonological elements as well as the denunciation of other suspects were included. In the countries wherein a questionnaire was not in use, the same elements were required to be part of the confession; however, the questioning was performed in a more open, fluent way.

In an accusatory witchcraft trial, focused on malevolent witchcraft, the first part of the interrogation often dealt with ideas about *maleficium*: spells that had been cast causing sickness in and death of people and animals, the stealing of milk, and divination. In a demonological witchcraft trial, the interrogation might from the beginning focus on the demonic: the devil's pact, the witches' gathering, and the performance of collective witchcraft. In some trials, ideas about *maleficium* as well as demonological ideas appear during interrogation. Often, such interrogations see a shift from *maleficium* towards demonological ideas, with denunciation as the last item focused on. In Spanish Netherlands, this pattern can partly be seen in the trial of Lynken van Brugghe, 1596, in which the ten items of the court records show such a change in the questions posed. Also, in the case of Mayken Karrebrouck, the trial started with a concrete accusation of malefice and turned into a clear demonological trial, with denunciation of others and pressure for additional denunciation.

The change towards the demonic is also seen in the trial of Karin Persdotter in Sweden and in the trial of Agnes Sampson in Scotland. In the latter case, there was an interest in her healing activity and divination, her prayers and charms, but the interrogators also had, from the very beginning, a keen interest in collective witchcraft operations, witches' gatherings, and other demonological ideas. Already from the very first interrogation of Agnes Sampson, many names came up that were related to either the North Berwick convention or other witches' meetings or collective witchcraft operations. Thus, the trials developed rapidly, from two persons accused to many more people accused—an escalation symptomatic of demonological trials starting with denunciation.

In all eight countries in this study, leading questions were used during interrogation. The trial of Anneke Rickers started with interrogation related to malefice, sickness of cattle, but was directed towards demonology. She finally—and after pressure—confessed to the demonological ideas that the interrogators wanted to hear.[79] We see the same in the trial of Mayken Karrebrouck: a trial that started with a concrete accusation turned into a clearly demonological trial, with denunciation of others and pressure for additional denunciation. In Scotland, the interrogation of Agnes Sampson developed in the direction of confession to demonological notions, like the devil's pact and sexual intercourse with the devil, after healing had been shown serious interest. In Sweden, we also see in the trial of Karin Persdotter that the judiciary took an interest in her knowledge of a folkloric character, before pressure to move towards the demonic was performed by strongly leading questions. In Denmark, the interrogation of Maren, the wife of Mogens, clearly aimed at a confession to collective witchcraft, and likewise with Mette Kongens, a professional healer, who was associated with a witches' gathering. Also, Anna Bruds was exposed to an interrogation that was directed towards demonology and the collective performance of witchcraft. In Norway, Anne Knutsdatter was an experienced healer, but was also, with the help of witnesses' testimonies, related to the more serious practice of divination, which the interrogator focused on. Sitru Pedersdatter changed her confession from the rather innocent stealing of milk to dangerous demonology and witches' gathering due to intense interrogation. Gundelle Olsdatter confessed to witches' gatherings, shape-shifting, and flights after severe pressure. In Finland, Gertrud Matsdotter was accused of *maleficium* but failed to prove her innocence by an oath of compurgation, Maria Nilsdotter was led, via a spell of divination she confessed to, to a Blåkulla confession, while Brita Pålsu's constant denial of maleficent witchcraft left more hope for an unknown outcome of the trial. In England, Thomasine Read confessed after several witnesses' depositions, ending with a combined malefice and demonological confession. However, also in England, the trials of Isabel and Jane show that it was possible to resist leading questions, since the women well knew that without a confession, no sentence could be passed.

In a few trials included in this book, the interrogator argued on religious grounds about the afterlife. Karin Persdotter was admonished to confess the truth and, for the sake of her unrestful conscience, reveal what had been concealed. The religious dimension is also included in the trial of Swedish Ingred, who was seriously admonished by the court on behalf of God to confess the truth for the sake of salvation. However, such considerations are rarely expressed in the trials of this study; the interrogations do not linger much on the afterlife.

In all trials analysed, the interrogator is the one steering the questioning. Also, we see that he directs the interrogation towards the worst possible outcome, be that confessions to demonic witchcraft, *maleficium*, or divination, all considered crimes which were given a strict punishment. Further, in trials in which a mild sentence was passed in a local court, like the trial of Brita Pålsu, the demand for an oath of compurgation to be sworn in order for Brita to free herself made the situation very uncertain for her, as this was a difficult task to achieve.

The interrogator questioned according to his competence. This brings up the question of what a witch-hunter in local courts knew about demonology, a question discussed by Raisa Maria Toivo and other witchcraft scholars.[80] In some places, they might have known a lot, in other places less so. The majority of judicial officials in first instance courts probably had knowledge of what Julian Goodare calls 'middle-range demonology' and James Sharpe calls 'practical demonology', which could be used in the daily work of judiciary officials.[81] This meant that during interrogation, they activated demonological ideas only on a superficial level. We see this in, among others, the Blåkulla trials in Sweden and Finland, in which the accused person apparently knew a more detailed narrative than the interrogator.

Also related to the interrogator is the question of the extent to which the interrogator knew about the beliefs of the populace. In the Nordic countries, the judges and scribes in local courts came from other circles of society and were probably not acquainted with popular belief. However, the jury members might have been active in giving information on local folklore during the trial, and thus helped transfer ideas. We see from the analyses above that the judiciary was interested in knowing more about popular beliefs about *maleficium*, healing, and folklore. In the interrogations of Agnes Sampson, Maria Nilsdotter, and Anne Knutsdatter, the judiciary was eager to have prayers and formulas recited in the courtroom.

There is also the language question to consider. In Finland, for instance, the court records were written in Swedish, and the interrogation of an accused woman speaking Finnish had to be translated. Here, the *lensmann* of members of the *nämnd* might have been needed as translator for a Swedish-speaking interrogator. This is certainly a point where the jury members might have transferred their knowledge of the local community and their mentality to the judiciary. Thus, there is the possibility that the interrogator, if he was sitting in his position for some time and if he was interested, might have gotten acquainted with some local beliefs. In Finnmark in Norway, the language situation was similar if a Sami person was accused, as the Sami *lensmann* would have had to translate the Sami language into Norwegian during interrogation. We see this for instance in the case of Anders Poulsen in 1692.[82]

Next is the knowledge of the accused persons. How much did the suspected person who was brought before the court in a witchcraft panic know beforehand about demonological ideas, and to what extent was she influenced during the trial by leading questions from the interrogator? To what extent can we say that demonizing happened during interrogation? These are not easy questions to answer, but the analyses in this book can provide some information.

First, the interrogators clearly aimed at a demonological confession. If the suspected woman first confessed to *malefice* or healing, but refused to confess to demonological ideas, the interrogator was not satisfied. He went for a new round of interrogation to get the kind of confession he wanted. We see this in

Spanish Netherlands in the trial of Mayken Karrebrouck, in Finland in the trial of Maria Nilsdotter, and in Scotland in the trials of Agnes Sampson and Helene Clerk. What the interrogators wanted was a confession containing demonological ideas.

Second, in some trials there is an indication that demonizing occurred by the devil or the evil spirit being introduced by the interrogator. It might be the case that, like in the trial of Lynken van Brugghe in Spanish Netherlands, a woman was forced into a devil's pact confession by confirming the interrogator's statement, and the confession consisted of just one word. However, answering with a simple 'Yes' or 'No' to questions related to demonological notions was not the rule. Another example of demonizing is seen in the trial of Agnes Sampson in Scotland, in which her healing activities are turned into the devil's pact, pressed forth in her confession. However, in Agnes Sampson's trial, her answer is not a brief 'Yes' but a narrative about entering the devil's pact and the North Berwick convention. Thus, it seems that she was aware of a version of the demonological narrative before she was interrogated. It is not possible that a narrative as fleshed out as the one she gave was placed in her mouth by the interrogator. It seems that the accused woman heard a story about the devil and his work either before she was imprisoned or while in prison.

Third, there are some trials, for instance the trial of Gundelle Olsdatter from Finnmark, in which the accused person clearly knew a demonological narrative before the interrogation started. Gundelle was denounced by Margrette Jonsdatter on 10 March 1663, brought before the court the same day, and sentenced to death the next day.[83] As this is a late trial, demonological ideas were certainly widespread in the local communities of Finnmark at the time, since demonological witchcraft trials had been going on since 1620. In all likelihood, Gundelle acquired this knowledge from Vardø, the town where she lived.

Fourth, we do not find stereotypical confessions, which are similar from one woman to another. This indicates that each confessing woman created her own version of a narrative of which the core elements were known. In particular, the personalized language of the accused woman is substantiated by individual variations compared with other women's confessions in the same panic and the occurrence of orality features in the wording of the confession.

This leads to my understanding that from the end of the sixteenth century and throughout the seventeenth century, demonological ideas were known among townsfolk and villagers to a certain extent. This means that a woman, when interrogated in the courtroom, was able to answer with a narrative showing that she knew many of the elements. More elaborate versions of this narrative, with new details added, appeared as decades went by. However, the analyses of the trials also show that this confession was not given voluntarily. The woman had the knowledge of demonological ideas beforehand, but they had to be activated by the interrogator during the trial through the use of leading questions, and the confession in the form of a narrative was often brought forth by coercive methods.

Torture and Pressure

Comparing twenty-four trials from Northern Europe in this study has made it more than clear that torture and pressure during interrogation had an impact in all eight countries. Torture to force confessions in witchcraft trials was frequently used and created a turning point in the trial; a pattern common to all countries that used it. We see this in the trials from Spanish Netherlands in 1596 and 1634, the trial from Finland from 1666, the trial from Denmark from 1652, the trial from Northern Germany from 1669, and the trial from Sweden from 1673. The severity of torture varied. In Spanish Netherlands and Northern Germany, where the *Carolina* law code was in use, severe torture was applied almost immediately after the trial started. It should also be noted that torture resulting in deaths on the rack took place in Finnmark, Northern Norway, an area that saw witchcraft persecution as harsh as on the Continent. Rita Voltmer points to the influence of Roman law on the legal system and criminal court practice in Continental Europe: 'Procedural law all over continental Europe defined torture as a legal instrument necessary for extracting the confessions needed to secure a clear verdict'.[84] The form and duration of torture during a criminal procedure remained unregulated in the *Carolina* code and was left to the arbitrary judgement of the courts. It should be noted that torture was in use for other capital crimes as well.[85] In Denmark-Norway, torture was not allowed until a sentence had been passed. Still, it is documented that torture was used in both countries before this.[86] In Sweden and Finland, the trials analysed in this study document mild torture during interrogation, with the use of handcuffs. In Scotland, several types of torture were used to press forth confessions.[87] The only country in Northern Europe where torture was not allowed and not used in witchcraft trials was England.[88]

The most serious cases of torture seen in this study occurred in the trial of Lynken van Brugghe in Spanish Netherlands, who was first tortured by flogging and sleep deprivation and later killed during torture in an attempt to extract the name of her evil spirit—a clear demonological notion. The trial of Mayken Karrebrouck started with an accusation but changed character when she refused to confirm witnesses' testimonies, in which she was suspected of performing witchcraft causing illness and the deaths of children. After having been tortured on the rack and with the collar several times, she confessed to entering the devil's pact, sexual intercourse with the devil, receiving gifts from the devil, and participating in witches' gatherings. She also denounced several others.

In Northern Germany, we find that torture was used in the three trials analysed. In 1607, Kistina Netelers, was tortured from the start of the trial, which was allowed judicially, and confessed to demonological ideas, *maleficium*, and healing. In 1641, Anneke Rickers was exposed to torture after she denied performing witchcraft. The use of torture was based on the accusation and testimony of only one witness. Interrogation took place before and after torture, and the use of torture was recorded. Anneke Rickers confessed to having renounced her Christian faith and entering into the devil's pact but also to ideas related to *maleficium*. In 1669,

Anna Spielen was interrogated first 'in the good' and afterwards under torture. She confessed to the devil's pact, to participation in a witches' assembly, and to having stolen sacred communion wafers from the church and given them to the devil.

In Denmark, torture was used in 1590 in the trial of Ane Kolding to make her confess to witchcraft against the ships of the Danish king. The rack might have been in use during the trials of the summer of 1590. Mette Kongens was accused of witchcraft in 1618. She gave eight confessions related to a witches' gathering, and torture was most likely used. In 1652, Anna Bruds confessed after torture to having a personal demon. She denounced a number of people.

In Scotland, torture was used in the trial of Agnes Sampson in 1590–91. She denied witchcraft from the beginning of the trial, but confessed to demonological ideas after torture, thrawing, had been used. A torture method which was often used in Scotland was sleep deprivation, with a guard engaged to keep the suspected person awake. It has been documented that after a few days of being awake, the suspect was clearly out of her mind.[89]

In Norway, torture during witchcraft trials was used frequently in Finnmark, also during the panic of 1662–63, in which Gundelle Olsdatter was tried. Even if torture is not mentioned specifically in her trial, severe legal torture was used at Vardøhus Fortress, where she was imprisoned: a woman was killed on the rack the night between the two days of Gundelle's trial.

In Sweden, Ingegärd Andersdotter was searched for the devil's mark and possibly tortured during her trial in 1594. She confessed to the devil's pact. In 1653, Karin Persdotter was taken to an interrogation away from the public court; a 'hidden interrogation'. Afterwards, it is recorded that she confessed by her own good will, and with no use of force.

In Finland, during the trial of Maria Nilsdotter in 1666, handcuffs were screwed tighter and tighter to force a confession. She initially denied witchcraft, but after torture confessed to *maleficium* as well as demonological ideas.

These examples show that, in response to torture, women reacted in the same way everywhere. From an initial strategy of denial, a rather quick turning point was reached when torture began. Resistance was broken down within a short time. The interrogators were pressing for a confession and wanted to hear that the devil was the one who had given the woman the power to perform witchcraft. After torture, the women delivered demonological narratives, including the devil's pact and the witches' gathering, and ended with denouncing other people. This movement from denial to confession shows not only the power of torture but also how efficient torture was in extracting specific content, in the sense that the accused person confessed to what the interrogators wanted to hear within a short time.

The way the use of torture is documented in witchcraft court records in Northern European countries varies strongly. In Northern Germany and the Spanish Netherlands, the use of torture was openly recorded. There is information about when torture started and when it stopped. The use of torture is recorded both when it led to a confession and when it did not, as seen in the trials from Spanish

Netherlands. In Scotland, torture was used in witchcraft trials, and in a number of trials it is written down in the records. Sometimes, warrants from the Privy Council allowing the use of torture in witchcraft trials were given.[90] In some countries, however, the use of torture in witchcraft trials could not openly be written into the records until sentence was passed, for instance in Norway and Denmark. Still, in some trials, torture before the passing of a sentence is recorded in legal documents from these countries.

Several torture instruments are documented in the trial records analysed in this book. The types of instruments varied from country to country. Some torture instruments had a stronger effect than others. The rack, used in Finnmark, Denmark, and Spanish Netherlands, was terrifying. So was thrawing, which was performed with a rope around the head that was twisted with sudden and strong movements. This was used in the trial of Agnes Sampson in Scotland. Sleep deprivation was also common in Scotland. The collar, used in the trials of Lynken van Brugghe, proved to be effective after a few hours. The use of torture with handcuffs is documented in trials from Finland. In addition to actual torture, the threat of torture had an impact on confessions. In the trial of Gundelle Olsdatter in Finnmark in 1663, an overhanging fear of the rack must have influenced her confession, as a woman had been killed on the rack at Vardøhus the night before Gundelle confessed.

Methods to obtain circumstantial evidence—like the water ordeal, the pricking of witches, and the devil's mark—were also in use during witchcraft trials. Often, threatening to use these methods was enough to press forth a confession.[91] Of the regions in this study, the water ordeal was frequently used in Finnmark, where one-third of those sentenced to execution had been through this test.[92] Witch-pricking was used extensively in England and Scotland, where witch-prickers were engaged by the state to travel around and perform their job.[93] The devil's mark has been documented in this study in trials from England, Scotland, Northern Germany, Spanish Netherlands, Sweden, and Norway. Sleep deprivation was common in Scottish witchcraft trials.[94] The use—and fear—of circumstantial evidence must have created an atmosphere of anxiety in local communities. This is echoed in the voices of the accused women.

There is a clear connection between the use of torture and pressure and a confession to demonological ideas. Rita Voltmer has emphasized that 'interrogation and torture were not actions with an open end', but a struggle in which 'the accused person had few or no chances to cling to their own narratives and emotional habits'.[95] I agree that the use of torture during interrogation in witchcraft trials was influential. As seen in several of the analyses above, there was a turning point in many of the trials. This turning point was torture, the threat of torture, or use of or threat of circumstantial evidence. A common denominator in the trials analysed in this book is that torture led to deadly confessions. However, in spite of what should be expected, the enforced narratives were told with an individual stamp. There was a personal touch to each confession: it was a personal expression. Therefore, I maintain that the accused persons in witchcraft trials did in fact cling to their own narratives, even in the most severe situations, and this is what is rendered in the court records.

Enforced Narratives

Parallel to the unambiguous result of torture and pressure, the comparison of the trials shows distinctly that the confessions given were enforced. The women presented demonological ideas with difficulty. They did not want to tell these narratives because they knew it was dangerous. In the twenty-four trials analysed in this study, fifteen women denied witchcraft at first. The amount of pressure put on accused persons in order to obtain a confession varied from country to country, and varied according to legal principles applied in the trial. In a trial following inquisitorial principles, pressure during interrogation was strong. In an accusatorial trial, pressure was often milder. Pressure could take various forms. In Sweden, Ingegärd Andersdotter was searched for the devil's mark by the executioner, who was trained on the Continent and knew demonological ideas from abroad. This search led to a demonological confession. She told a narrative about the devil's pact and about receiving food from the devil. The same is the case for Anna Bruds, Gundelle Olsdatter, Kistina Netelers, Anneke Rickers, and others.

The analyses have shown that women fled from their homesteads because they were afraid of the outcome, and rightly so. They wanted to survive. They resisted the trial. They rejected denunciation. They tried to use the strategy of denial. They confessed to *maleficium*, for instance stealing milk, because they knew it was more dangerous to give a demonological confession. In this way, they showed that they hoped that the confessed element of malefice was sufficient. After torture and pressure, however, they confessed to what the interrogators required. The narratives were enforced, but the individual woman, standing in the courtroom and deprived of many things, still owned her language. She had the power to tell a narrative, even while knowing that these words would seal her death sentence. She was telling a story, thus maintaining the dignity to use her language skills to the very end of her life. When the accused woman's words manage to penetrate legal rhetoric and the judiciary's discourse, we can get a glimpse of a woman's way of speaking. Thus, 'enforced' did not mean that her ability to narrate had been cut off. She was still a storyteller, clinging to her art.

As I see it, the telling of enforced narratives reveals emotions. Elizabeth Cohen's thesis on the double modes of reading when analysing court records reminds us that due to their multilayered character, these documents can reveal some of the accused person's feelings.[96] Other witchcraft scholars think differently. Rita Voltmer states:

> Whatever kind of anger, fear, shame, despair, resignation, or depression lingered in the minds and the hearts of the persons involved, be it the accusers or the accused, these fluid feelings are lost. In the texts we find labels, stereotypes, norms, narratives of emotion fixed in black and white to be

communicated to readers and audiences. Standardized emotions were written down because they were meant to stabilize a legal, and thus political and
religious, truth.[97]

This statement can be disputed. It is correct that court records were written to
communicate within a legal field, not least to document why a particular verdict
and sentence were passed if the case was transferred to a Court of Appeal. It is also
correct that verdict and sentence were passed on religious grounds. It is likewise
true that it is impossible to enter the hearts of seventeenth-century people; we
have only the words they uttered and their recorded actions to relate to. However,
my research shows that we are not talking about 'standardized emotions' but about
individual women's feelings and reactions. And that signifies a profound difference
in interpretation.

The narratives confessed to during witchcraft trials were part of the mentality of
the time. The local community is where demonological and popular culture met,
and where fully fledged stories surfaced in the oral field. As decades went by, from
the end of the 1500s and onwards, demonological ideas became known among the
populace in Northern Europe. Per Sörlin has shown that in Sweden, by the time
of the great witchcraft persecution in the later 1600s, the idea of the witches' sabbath was firmly implanted in the popular imagination.[98] Knowledge about learned
witchcraft could enter a society in multiple ways. It is likely that a judicial official
introduced demonological ideas during interrogation in witchcraft trials in an area,
and thus enabled oral transference because local people and local members of the
jury were present in the courtroom. Still, there were alternative ways in which
demonological ideas could enter the popular imagination of a society and influence
the enforced narratives confessed to in witchcraft trials.

Written literature as well as oral transference might have influenced the spreading of ideas. In the written field, numerous demonological treaties, pamphlets and
tracts were published in Europe from the late 1400s until around 1600. Also, novels
and plays mattered. In addition, religious literature and sermon books were published, influencing church preaching, which admonished the people to choose the
right master and avoid the snares of the powerful devil. These influences following
written paths prepared the ground for confessions to a devil's pact and the witches'
gathering. In the oral field, demonological pamphlets and tracts were read out loud
in places where many people gathered, transferring ideas. Travellers also brought
ideas with them to be retold in a new place.[99]

The mental baggage of an individual mattered in the transfer of ideas, as we have
seen in the North Berwick trials, the Finnmark trials, and the Åland trials. In this
process, the mind of a person was echoed. For transfer based on written material,
this person could be an author of a book, an author, known or unknown, of a
pamphlet, a creator of a broadsheet, or a sender of a diplomatic letter. For the oral
transfer of narratives, there had to be a narrator. This was a necessary device for a
narrative to come into being. The personal factor was always at hand, whether in
the form of a statesman, a judicial official, a preaching vicar, a sailor, a fisherman,

a tradesman, a travelling person seeking work in a new place, or a traveller visiting family and friends. Travelling persons brought stories with them and retold stories. These stories came to influence the enforced narratives we hear in witchcraft trials.

The Voice of the Law

In the trials analysed in this study, the voice of the law comes to the fore in varying degrees of distinctness and varying types of punishment. In Europe, witchcraft was criminalized during the late Middle Ages. Brian P. Levack says:

> The identification of witchcraft as a crime that could be prosecuted in the church courts came about as a result of its gradual assimilation with the crime of heresy, on the basis of the belief that the witch made a pact with the devil. There was no clear statement of the crime of witchcraft in canon law.[100]

This assimilation was brought about by a variety of means, from a papal decree of 1258 to the publishing of *Malleus Maleficarum* in 1486, which defined the offence of witchcraft as involving both maleficent magic and the devil's pact.[101] Malevolent witchcraft was practised all over Europe.[102]

The Early Modern Period brought about a change in the legal system. Jørn Øyrehagen Sunde and Poul J. Jørgensen document that a harsher attitude towards witchcraft can be seen in legislation in several European countries throughout the sixteenth and seventeenth centuries.[103] Even if the legal order aimed at attractive and peaceful ways of solving conflicts as an alternative to violence, the state still had to handle crime, in the Nordic countries in the name of the king. The legal order established in the Middle Ages turned out not to be up to this task.[104] Sunde states that the goal in Norway was to establish a legal system consisting of three instances: local, intermediate, and central courts. What connected the three instances was the possibility of sending an appeal from an inferior to a superior court.[105] During this transition, magic became legally relevant. This was a pre-condition for sixteenth- and seventeenth-century witchcraft persecution.[106] A similar development within the legal system took place in several Northern European countries. The practice of passing cases carrying a death penalty from a first instance court to the Court of Appeal is seen in this study in trials in Sweden, Finland, and Denmark.

Witchcraft scholars have discussed whether witchcraft trials started 'from below', with accusations coming from neighbours, rooted in the mentality of common people and first instance courts having strong authority, or 'from above', due to the role of the state. In my opinion, witchcraft trials were governmental operations. This has been argued by several witchcraft scholars, among others Julian Goodare and Hans Eivind Næss, who have pointed to the criminological context.[107] Witchcraft trials were criminal trials, taking place in courtrooms, with judicial officials holding the trial and laws deciding the sentence. Such persecution could not have been carried out without a decisive role for the state. This enabled sentences of execution in witchcraft trials.

In the voice of the law as it comes to the fore in this study, I would like to look at the religious element, reference to the laws, and legal principles employed. The religious element is present in the verdict in all countries in this study: the witch has renounced her baptism and entered into a pact with the devil. We see this in Spanish Netherlands, in the trials of Lynken van Brugghe and Mayken Karrebrouck, the mention of forsaking God and Mother Mary, and a pact with the enemy from hell. We see it in Northern Germany, where the Holsten Court stated that Anneke Rickers had renounced her Christian faith and become an apostate from God. We see it in Denmark, where Anna Bruds is said to have forsworn baptism and Christendom. Moreover, we see it in the trial of Mette Kongens, who confessed to having made the sign of the cross over Brunk Pedersen and having cured cattle in the name of the Holy Trinity. We see it in Sweden in the trial of Karin Persdotter, who was said to have left God and surrendered to the Water Man, as well as misused God's holy name to evoke the Evil One. Further, we see it in the trial of Karin Dantz, where we are presented with a judicial lecture underlining the power of Satan and the danger of choosing the wrong 'master'. We hear it in Norway in the trial of Gundelle Olsdatter, one of the 'true witches' according to the 1617 decree, who consorted with the devil and forfeited her life. In Scotland, Isobell Eliot renounced her baptism and blasphemed God. Thus, we see the understanding of the witch as an enemy of God formulated within the legal field throughout Northern Europe. The voice of the law is unanimous: the crime of witchcraft is rooted in the fact that the witch has left God and chosen the wrong master.

Looking at reference to laws in the course of the trials, we see that this was done in most countries. It was important for the judiciary to clarify on what grounds the sentence was given. In Norway, in the trial of Anne Knutsdatter, the king's decree about healing is referred to. In Finland and Sweden, references to the laws were recorded. Also, the accused person knew about the laws, for instance Mette Kongens, who said that she had performed no evil after the king's letter about witchcraft was issued, which included healing as a deed to be punished. In the trial of Helene Clerk, the wording of the Witchcraft Act is echoed in courtroom discourse.

The courts adhered to accepted rules. In the trial of Anne Knutsdatter, who was twice brought before the court, we see that in the second trial, the proceedings of the first trial were referred to. In the trial of Sitru Pedersdatter, proper court practice was followed, and judicial officials were acquainted with the laws. For instance, members of the jury could not act as witnesses, since they were judging. In Sweden, witnesses swore their oaths on the Law Book, which is a sign of the court's correct practice and its ambition to obtain reliable testimonies. In the trial of Gundelle Olsdatter, the written confession was read out loud for the convicted woman, and she had to confirm it; thus, the formal aspects of a trial were taken care of. The same is the case in Northern Germany. In Denmark, we see in the trial of Anna Bruds that the sentence correctly passed in local court was sent to be confirmed by *Landstinget*. In Finland and Sweden, which shared the same legal system at the time, all cases from local courts where a death sentence was expected were passed on to the Court of Appeal.

These elements point to a court system that strove to keep up with laws and proper court practice. At the same time, however, it was convinced about dangerous witchcraft and feared it. This also comes to the fore in the rhetoric used, like in the sentence of Anneke Rickers, in which it is stated that she should pay not with money or property, but with flesh and blood; a strong linguistic expression. The same is seen in the indictment of Helene Clerk: the rhetoric is characterized by an emphasis on a malicious and deplorable art and evil deeds. In the evaluation of Helene Clerk's dittay, judicial arguments are evaluated, and some articles are repelled. In the late case of Karin Dantz in Sweden, one can note some sceptical thoughts about witchcraft, and a thoughtful reflection on the nature of the case is presented by the judiciary. The same scepticism is seen in the trial of Brita Pålsu, in which those who accused her were actually punished. However, in the late trials in Finland, when an acquittal was likely, the accused woman was still required to free herself by an oath of compurgation; a requirement which was difficult to meet.

There is a clear difference in court proceedings when it comes to legal principles followed. In accusatory trials, there was an accuser and a clear accusation and witnesses were brought before the court. These were most often *maleficium* and single trials. In the trials of English Isabel Atcheson and Jane Simpson, we see that the responsibility to continue the case rested with Anthony Heron, who had to provide a written document based on his testimony and the questioning of the women, and also additional witnesses. The latest witchcraft trials all over Northern Europe fall in the accusatory category.

In inquisitorial trials, the accused person was denounced by the first confessing woman in a witchcraft panic, no witnesses were brought before the court, and the trials were linked. The content of these trials was demonological. A witchcraft panic developed quickly due to the idea of the witches' gathering, and names of participants were forcibly obtained. The voice of the law in demonological trials is exemplified in this study in the trial of Lynken van Brugghe, wherein the fanatic coercion to make her confess to the devil's pact attained tragic dimensions, and in which self-criticism on the part of judicial officials seemed non-existent. In several of the other trials with demonological content, the pressure to obtain a confession was strong and torture was used. It should be noted that in Schleswig-Holstein, for instance, trials that started as accusatory trials often turned into inquisitional trials.[108]

It is interesting to note the role of the jury, consisting of elected trustworthy men from the local communities, and its authority to decide on guilt or innocence on the part of the accused.[109] These men knew maleficent witchcraft and local folk belief. To a certain extent, they also had knowledge of demonological ideas, although this varied. Nevertheless, they were able to recognize demonological ideas in accused persons' confessions and followed the evaluation of the judicial officials presiding over the trials when it came to the severity of the confessions and the question of guilt. In my work with witchcraft sources, I have seen only one instance where the jury did not follow the indictment pleas by the judiciary, and that was during the last panic in Finnmark, when six young girls were accused of witchcraft and had given demonological confessions. The jury disagreed with the indictment and said that this case was so difficult that they could not judge it. The cases were passed on to the Court of Appeal, and all children were acquitted.

The voice of the law as it comes to the fore in this study shows that legal officials in office during most of the seventeenth century were convinced that witchcraft was possible, and that unrealistic elements such as shape-shifting and flight could happen. It is not until the late in the century that sceptical thoughts about the reality of witchcraft made themselves felt, like in the trials of Brita Pålsu, Isabel Atcheson, and Jane Simpson. Trials centred on demonological ideas faded away in the later decades of 1600s, while trials with *maleficium* content still took place. However, from the perspective of the judiciary, it was no longer as urgent to prosecute witches. The reasons for this change within the history of criminal justice may be manifold: in a Norwegian context, Sølvi Sogner points to changes of mental attitudes in governments generally, and Hans Eyvind Næss points to the measures taken by the *lagmenn*, the Court of Appeal Judges.[110] The reduction in witchcraft persecution was a tendency all over Europe, with relatively few witchcraft trials taking place after 1700.

The Voice of the Scribe

The comparison of trials in this study indicates that the scribe was a very professional person. His profession was to be a scribe of formal, official documents. He wanted to provide a reliable image of courtroom discourse. The words of accused witches were important, vital evidence and needed accurate recording and careful consideration. The scribe worked as correctly as he could; this is seen not least in the strong impact of orality on the accused persons' confessions. This feature originates from their own utterances and could not have been imposed by the scribe. In the voice of the scribe, his own attitude towards what was told is heard only a few times; otherwise, his voice is silent and does not comment on what the participants in the trial narrated. While taking ordinary text-critical considerations into account, in my view the records are reliable. The interpretation of court records rests upon the assumption that the recorded text carries meaning about factual courtroom discourse as well as historical conditions. This is supported by the findings of this study.

The role of the scribe in producing witchcraft court records has been discussed among witchcraft scholars. One point of view is that the voices of judges impacted the content of elaborated demonology in confessions and depositions, and that it was their voices which were recorded by the scribe. Rita Voltmer refers to Virginia Krause: 'Virginia Krause has noted that, with the help of learned judges, elaborated demonology crept into the court room, torture chambers, and interrogatories, and it infested, reframed, and standardized the witches' confessions'.[111] Further, it is argued that what we hear in the confessions is not the voices of those confessing but the lore of judges and scribes.[112] This is an argument advocating not only that the voices of the judges influenced the confessions and depositions, but also that these voices are the only ones which can be discerned in the records. In addition, the confessions are said to be standardized. This argumentation is not supported by my research.

First, it is possible to approach court records as reliable documents, wherein the scribe has done his uttermost to take down on paper what was said in the courtroom during the trial. This is a view supported by many Northern European witchcraft scholars, and formulated among others by Malcolm Gaskill, Raisa Maria Toivo, Alison Rowlands, and me.[113] Gaskill emphasizes the recording of words that were factually uttered, and states that it was not possible for the scribe to distort something which was not said in the first place.[114] I agree with this.

Second, the content of the confessions when it came to demonological ideas might have come from the interrogator, but also came from the confessing witch. It is likely that demonological ideas were introduced into witchcraft trials by a learned person, but the same ideas were quickly assimilated into the mentality of the populace due to oral transference. During the trial, members of the local community might have been present, and all jury members were local men who had their families and acquaintances in the locality. This must have contributed to a rapid transmittance. As for folkloric ideas, it is an open question whether judicial officials knew the peasant mentality, as these officials most often belonged to upper classes of society.

In my view, therefore, it is not likely that we hear only the lore of judges and scribes in confessions and depositions. What we hear are individual versions of the demonological narrative or individual testimonies on malefice. In many cases, the narratives must have been known by the accused from the local mental realm before they entered the courtroom. The voices of women heard in the courtroom are voices with individual expressions, and some of the content was rooted in a mentality they knew. In addition, learned demonological ideas interacted with ideas of folk belief, as we can hear in the voices of women in this study. In my view, both the personal factor of the interrogator and common people's ideas within the local community were decisive for the ideas that appear in witchcraft courtroom discourse and that are rendered by the scribe.

Transnational Transfer

The comparison of the voices of women in witchcraft trials shows that ideas about witchcraft displayed in accused persons' confessions can change character within one and the same country as decades pass, and they can also travel across national borders.

If we regard separate countries, a motif is often enriched over the years, as oral narratives in general are told and retold and are thus likely to be expanded by the insertion of new details. So also with the demonological narratives that can be found in the witchcraft records. Within Spanish Netherlands, there is a great difference between Lynken van Brugghe's confession in 1596 and Clayse Sereyns's confession in 1657, the latter having a rich register of demonological elements. In Northern Germany, the brief demonological element about Kistina Netelers's demonic lover in her confession of 1607 is greatly enriched in the confession of Anneke Rickers in 1641 in the narrative about the red rider, and further expanded in the confession of Anna Spielen in the narrative about her spirit Paul and her trip to Bloksberg, riding a male goat. As decades go by, folkloric elements may be inserted in the demonological narrative, and details added about witches' gathering places, the flight to these places, and activities at witches' gatherings. In Norway, a simple devil's pact narrative confessed to in Rygge in 1623 had been embellished with numerous details during a trial in Finnmark in 1663. Often, elements added to a previous version echo local or regional conditions. The Finnmark version not only adheres to the main demonological elements but is spiced with local notions, like women flying to places for witches' gatherings not only in the likeness of birds but also in the specific likenesses of a variety of sea birds.

Geographical distance and connection between areas matter when it comes to the oral transference of ideas. The voices of women in this study document that there was a circulation of names to denote places for witches' gatherings. With a basis in the German name Bloksberg, known as a place for witches' gatherings, the mountain or hill where witches' gatherings were allegedly held in the Nordic countries is slightly altered. It is called Kullen in Sweden in 1594, Blåkoll in Norway in 1623, Blåkulla in Åland in Finland in 1666, Blåkulla in Rendalen in Norway in 1670–74, and Blåkulla in Sweden in 1678. The brief description of the devil's pact in Kullen from Southern Sweden in 1594 has swelled to a comprehensive narrative on Blåkulla in the 1670s. Simultaneous with the expansion of the story, the number of trials increases. The core element of the name of the location, Kullen/Koll/Kulla, meaning a hill or peak or rounded mountain top, is kept. The names of the gathering place have the same semantic meaning, and the main orthographic form is the same, while the final spelling belongs to a region or country. The name Kullen in Sweden and the name Blåkoll in Norway occur not far from each other in geographical distance, and are found in the southern parts of the countries. The Blåkulla trials further north in Norway and further north in Sweden occur a few decades later and signal that stories travel. The Blåkulla trials revolved around women leaving the house during the night, flying to the gathering, experiencing strange things, and returning home without knowing the route and without other family members knowing they had been away. While the idea of witches flying to witches' sabbaths on mountains and hills was standard in many Northern European countries by 1590, for instance in Bergen in Norway, the Blåkulla trials in the 1660s and 1670s represent a rather late flare-up of demonological trials in the Nordic region. The use of child witnesses to denounce adult Blåkulla participants puts a special stamp on the Swedish and Finnish Blåkulla trials. The Blåkulla confessions in Finland from 1666 and Sweden from 1674 are rendered with severity and fluency, which signals that the accused person was well acquainted with the story.

The travelling of ideas across borders is seen not only in names used, but also in the use of motifs, for instance in the flight to a witches' meeting. In Northern Germany in 1607, Kristina Netelers mentions Bloksberg in her confession, which was reached by flight. The idea of witches flying at night is retold in confessions in Bergen and Rygge in Norway, in Swedish and Finnish Blåkulla stories, and in Scottish confessions to witches' flight.[115] A study of transmission from Northern Germany to Denmark bears witness to how the motif of beating a glass drum was transferred.[116] Likewise, the idea of a child being sacrificed to the devil by its mother or a mother teaching her oldest daughter witchcraft is heard in the Finnmark witchcraft panic of 1662–63, most likely transmitted by a learned couple from the capital of Norway to Finnmark.[117]

The spread of demonological ideas most likely happened on several levels, through written and oral transference. Witchcraft scholars have used the term 'acculturation' to refer to this transmittance of ideas, which is seen as a pre-condition for the spread of witchcraft persecution: an understanding that 'some élite ideas penetrated into the lower strata';[118] a perspective 'from above'. I myself think that assimilation is a better term to explain the transference of demonological ideas in local communities. It is likely that demonological ideas about witchcraft were spread in many ways, to be embedded in frequently retold stories in local communities. Both the 'from above' perspective and the 'from below' perspective might contribute to understanding the spread of ideas about witchcraft.

Looking at all of Europe during the period of this study, I argue that due to an intense wave of witchcraft persecution in the Trier and St Maximin area of Germany, demonological ideas were transmitted via Schleswig-Holstein to Denmark and further on to Scotland in the 1580s and 1590s. The transmittance was influenced by written transfer and personal factors. There was persecution pressure in Europe related to the strong witch-hunt in South-Western Germany from the 1580s onwards, as stated by Rolf Schulte.[119] Around thirty years later, demonological ideas were transmitted from Scotland to Finnmark through personal transfer. These ideas strongly impacted witchcraft trials in Schleswig-Holstein, Denmark, Scotland, and Finnmark, and the findings of this study emphasize the importance of transnational history.

Hence, the analyses performed show that in the course of the late sixteenth century and the seventeenth century, demonological ideas became common knowledge in Northern Europe. Both written and oral transference of demonological ideas about witchcraft reached lay and learned people during the time span of this study, emphasizing witchcraft as a powerful crime and impacting witchcraft persecution. Related to the trials analysed in this study, Niels Hemmingsen's treatise about witchcraft of 1575 is of importance in the written field, as King James VI met Hemmingsen in Denmark in 1590, and Danish witchcraft ideas (most likely about witches' gatherings) carried by the Scottish monarch himself influenced the Scottish North Berwick trials. Knowledge about the North Berwick trials spread quickly through a London-published pamphlet,[120] and a number of witchcraft pamphlets and tracts were circulated in England.[121] The Blåkulla trials in Sweden were known to an English-reading audience in 1685. Demonological ideas in Sweden might have come from Germany or from Denmark, as they were known in both countries around 1590 and these ideas might have influenced the trial of Ingegärd Andersdotter in 1594.[122] The transfer of ideas about witchcraft can thus be traced in printed material. Next, and in my opinion of uttermost importance, transference might have happened through the influence of persons of authority who had such ideas in their mental baggage. When these had the power to start and continue witchcraft trials, often a witchcraft panic occurred. We see this with regard to the introduction of demonological ideas in witchcraft trials in Scotland in 1590. We see it in Finnmark in 1620; ideas that came to influence Finnmark's witchcraft persecution until 1663, including the trial of Gundelle Olsdatter. We see it also in the Åland trials in Finland.

Conclusion

This study of the voices of women in witchcraft trials in eight countries in Northern Europe from the late 1500s until the late 1600s has shown both similarities and differences between the countries, but mostly similarities. These recurring features emerging in all trials display a pattern in the way women's voices come to the fore.

First, the voices of women reflect a period in legal history during which witchcraft was defined as a crime that should be severely punished. Women accused of demonological witchcraft, maleficent witchcraft, and—to a certain extent—healing were brought before the court in criminal trials. As witchcraft was a *crimen exceptum*, circumstantial evidence was used to make the performance of the crime more probable. The best proof in order to pass a sentence, however, was a confession from the accused woman's own mouth. This is echoed in the voices of women as they are rendered in court records.

Second, the voices of women clearly surface in accused women's confessions and in female witnesses' testimonies. In the confessions, a wide range of ideas related to demonology, *maleficium*, and healing are expressed. Demonological ideas appear in confessions in witchcraft panics. These were linked trials with denunciation of participation at a witches' gathering as a starting point, which were conducted according to inquisitorial legal principles. Ideas on *maleficium* appear in confessions in single trials or small groups with an accusation of maleficent witchcraft as a start, which were conducted according to accusatory legal principles. Some trials began with an accusation of *maleficium* and developed into a demonological trial due to leading questions during interrogation. Ideas related to healing were confessed to by practising healers, and trials were sometimes related to unsuccessful healing, when original benevolent witchcraft was turned into maleficent witchcraft. The testimonies of female witnesses appeared in maleficent witchcraft trials. They voice the fear of malefice in a local community, expressing a cause-and-effect logic connected to the uttering of a curse which came true shortly afterwards. The study exemplifies a width of ideas about witchcraft, known by common people and part of the mentality of the time.

Third, the voices of women in demonological confessions appear in enforced narratives, delivered after severe pressure or torture. The pressure for a demonological confession was a dominant feature of the trials in all eight countries. There was a clear turning point in the trials when the confession was a fact. Through close readings of the interrogation records, the study has documented the impact of the interrogator on the transformation from a malevolent to a demonological witchcraft trial. The confession narratives were not given voluntarily. Still, in spite of the pressure and coercion used to extract a confession, these narratives are characterized by the mastering of the art of storytelling. The demonological ideas emerging in these narratives may partly have been a result of leading questions during interrogation and partly a result of assimilation processes in the local communities. The enforced narratives display a richness of orality features and show how oral discourse is echoed in the confessions. Orality features documented in the confessions emphasize the individual language touch of each woman and the diversity of the modes of storytelling. Furthermore, the accused women's steadfastness in clinging to her art of storytelling until the end of her life bears witness to how language can display strength.

Fourth, the voices of women document the travelling of ideas about witchcraft from Southern Europe to Denmark, Scotland, Norway, Sweden, and Finland. These ideas, for instance the names of locations of witches' gatherings, can be heard in demonological confessions and emphasize the impact of transnational transmittance within the history of mentalities. Narrative devices surface in the confessions and signal why the ideas were easily transmitted. The study has documented, through close readings of confessions, how pregnant motifs and expressions were carried across borders in an astonishing way and how women's voices made arduous efforts to keep and retell the linguistic images in their proper context. The skill of narration promoted accurate ideas within cultural exchange. The study has also pointed to the personal factor of travelling judicial officials as significant in the spreading of ideas, probably explaining why some local areas had much more intense witchcraft persecution than others.

Fifth, the voices of women in witchcraft trials bring us all the way to the sentencing. Then, the voice of the law takes over. The religious element is emphasized: the danger of being ensnared by the devil. Leaving the pact with God in baptism and entering into a new pact with the Evil One is how the wording of every sentence passed begins. A witch has received evil powers from the devil, enabling her to practice witchcraft. Her evil deeds are weighted. Following her own confession and the government's laws, a witch should be punished by losing her life. The scribe is the one to take these words down on paper. He appears as a professional person who carried out his job of producing formal documents. This study has been performed according to the view that court records are reliable historical documents, which render courtroom discourse as well as historical context in a trustworthy manner.

After the similarities we can see in the voices of women in all countries, a few differences between countries can be mentioned. The clearest differences are found in the legal arena and have to do with the use of torture and the first instance court's authority to pass a death sentence. England differs from the other countries, because torture was not allowed in trials, which may explain the low conviction rate. However, with regard to conviction in capital cases, a confession was not required in England; a jury could convict a suspect on indirect evidence. In the other countries in this study, torture was allowed in witchcraft trials before a sentence was passed in Spanish Netherland and Northern Germany, which used the *Carolina* law code, contrary to the other countries' national law codes. In the other countries, torture was allowed only after a sentence was passed, and then to obtain names of accomplices only. Another point related to torture was its recording. In this study, Spanish Netherlands and Northern Germany differ from the other countries in that the application of torture before sentencing was openly recorded in the court records in these two countries, while in the other jurisdictions, torture was recorded only after sentencing. Spanish Netherlands and Northern Germany were also the only ones to use questionnaires during interrogation. When it came to the authority to pass and carry out death sentences, Norway differs from the other Nordic countries in that the first instance court, the local court, had the authority to pass and carry out a death sentence: it did not have to pass the case to the Court of Appeal to get the death sentence confirmed. These differences, which were all related to the legal system, obviously tended to either reduce or increase the execution rate in witchcraft trials in the respective countries. There is no doubt that the use of torture in particular influenced the voices of women tried for witchcraft.

This study has shown, through careful research, that voices can carry meaning. My interest in retrieving women from history as well as the interpretation of language has motivated this book. The same can be said about my trust in what language can convey. The accused woman in a witchcraft trial was fighting for her right to use her language and amplify her voice until the very end of the trial. She was fighting with words against being helpless and crushed. The firmness we hear in her voice is remarkable. Still, her voice was silenced.

NOTES

1 Introduction

1 Orig. *Escucho con mis ojos a los muertos.* The line is from his book *Historia de la vida del Buscón.* Francisco Gomez de Quevedo y Villegas (1580–1645) was a Spanish poet.

2 Roger Chartier, *The Author's Hand and the Printer's Mind: Transformations of the Written Word in Early Modern Europe* (Cambridge, 2014), 3.

3 Chartier, *Author's Hand,* vi.

4 Julian Goodare, *The European Witch-Hunt* (Abingdon, 2016), 27.

5 For witchcraft trials in the Spanish Netherlands, I received transcriptions of primary sources which, with the help of translators, were translated into English and Norwegian. I would like to thank Professor Dr Dries Vanysacker (KU Leuven Belgium) for letting me use the transcriptions that Professor Jos Monballyu (KU Leuven Belgium) made of the original court records; see www.kuleuven-kulak.be/facult/rechten/Monballyu/Rechtlagelanden/Heksenvlaanderen/heksenindex.htm.

6 Brian P. Levack, 'Witchcraft and the Law', in Brian P. Levack (ed.), *The Oxford Handbook of Witchcraft in Early Modern Europe and Colonial America* (Oxford, 2013), 471–72.

7 Brian P. Levack, 'Introduction', in Levack, *Oxford Handbook of Witchcraft,* 4; Goodare, *European Witch-Hunt,* 10–11, 97–99, 112.

8 Levack, 'Witchcraft and the Law', 472–74.

9 Liv H. Willumsen, *Witches of the North: Scotland and Finnmark* (Leiden, 2013), 7–8.

10 Orig. *Es zeichnet sich wohl ab: Wir müssen mit beträchtlichen Eigenheiten der schleswig-holsteinischen Hexenverfolgung rechnen (. . .) Es ist nicht zu übersehen, daß der akkusatorische Prozeß nach seiner Einleitung in die Regel wie ein inquisitorischer verlief.* Dagmar Unverhau, 'Akkusationsprozess—Inquisitionsprozess. Indikatoren für Intensität der Hexenverfolgung in Schleswig-Holstein' [Accusatorial Trial—Inquisitional Trial. Indicators of the Intensity of the Witch-Hunt in Schleswig-Holstein], in Christian Degn, Hartmut Lehmann, and Dagmar Unverhau (eds.), *Hexenprozesse. Deutsche und skandinavische Beiträge* [Witch Trials. German and Scandinavian Contributions] (Neumünster, 1983), 116.

11 Goodare, *European Witch-Hunt,* 7, 80–81, 85, 124.

12 Gerhild S. Williams, 'Demonologies', in Levack, *Oxford Handbook of Witchcraft,* 69–83.

13 Liv H. Willumsen, 'Board Games, Dancing, and Lost Shoes: Ideas About Witches' Gatherings in the Finnmark Witchcraft Trials', in Julian Goodare, Rita Voltmer, and Liv

H. Willumsen (eds.), *Demonology and Witch-Hunting in Early Modern Europe* (Abingdon, 2020), 261–81.

14 To free from or as if from a magic spell, also (obsolete): unbewitch. *Merriam-Webster*, s.v. 'unwitch', www.merriam-webster.com/dictionary/unwitch (accessed 20 December 2020).

15 Bente G. Alver, *Mellem mennesker og magter: Magi i hekseforfølgelsernes tid* [Between Humans and Powers: Magic in the Time of Witchcraft Persecution] (Oslo, 2008), 288.

16 Alver, *Mellem mennesker og magter*, 289.

17 Alver, *Mellem mennesker og magter*, 289.

18 Willumsen, 'Narratologi', 69.

19 Stuart Clark, *Thinking with Demons: The Idea of Witchcraft in Early Modern Europe* (Oxford, 1997), 3.

20 Stuart Clark, 'Introduction', in Stuart Clark (ed.), *Languages of Witchcraft: Narrative, Ideology and Meaning in Early Modern Culture* (Basingstoke, 2001), 8.

21 Clark, *Thinking with Demons; Languages of Witchcraft*.

22 Quentin Skinner, 'Review of Stuart Clark, *Thinking with Demons*', *Common Knowledge*, 25, nos. 1–3 (April 2019), 412.

23 Clark, 'Introduction', 7.

24 Jan Machielsen (ed.), *The Science of Demons: Early Modern Authors Facing Witchcraft and the Devil* (Abingdon, 2020).

25 Marion Gibson, *Reading Witchcraft: Stories of Early English Witches* (London, 1996).

26 Liv H. Willumsen, *Seventeenth-Century Witchcraft Trials in Scotland and Northern Norway* (Ph.D. thesis, University of Edinburgh, 2008), 29–33; *Witches of the North*, 29–37; Julian Goodare, 'Witchcraft in Scotland', in Levack, *Oxford Handbook of Witchcraft*, 307.

27 Marion Gibson, *Witchcraft: The Basics* (Abingdon, 2018).

28 Sierra Dye, *'Devilische Wordis': Speech as Evidence in Scotland's Witch Trials, 1563–1736* (Ph.D. thesis, University of Guelph, 2016).

29 This is Genette's main work, a study developing a narratological methodology through the analysis of a fictional work (Marcel Proust's *À la recherche du temps perdu*, seven volumes published during the years 1913–27). It was published in English with the title *Narrative Discourse. An Essay in Method* (Ithaca, 1980).

30 The English editions are titled *Narrative Discourse: An Essay in Method* (Ithaca, 1980), *Narrative Discourse Revisited* (Ithaca, 1988), and *Fiction and Diction* (Ithaca, 1993).

31 Cf. Genette, *Narrative Discourse Revisited*, 101.

32 Genette, *Fiction and Diction*, 55–56.

33 In English, the term for non-fictional prose is not as distinct as in Norwegian, which uses the word *sakprosa*, a term used almost exclusively in Nordic countries. Johan Tønnesson has discussed different terms in English for this type of prose. He maintains that a negative definition like 'non-fiction', which literally means 'everything other than fiction', is too superficial. Tønnesson discusses whether the terms 'factual prose' and 'subject-oriented prose' could be used to denote this type of prose, and maintains that the latter of the two is the best, but that neither of these terms catches the history of meaning related to the Norwegian word *sakprosa*. Johan L. Tønnesson, *Hva er sakprosa* [What Is Factual Prose] (Oslo, 2008), 24.

34 Lubomír Doležel, 'Fictional and Historical Narrative: Meeting the Postmodernist Challenge', in David Herman (ed.), *Narratologies. New Perspectives on Narrative Analyses* (Columbus, 1999), 247.

35 Liv H. Willumsen, 'Narratologi som tekstanalytisk metode' [Narratology as Text-Analytical Method], in Mary Brekke (ed.), *Å begripe teksten* [To Understand the Text] (Kristiansand, 2006), 39–72.

36 Genette, *Narrative Discourse*, 35, 87–88, 113, 186; Genette, *Narrative Discourse Revisited*, 161–62.

37 Gérard Genette, 'Voice', in Susana Onega and José Á. Landa (eds.), *Narratology: An Introduction* (London, 1996), 172–73.

38 Willumsen, 'Narratologi som tekstanalytisk redskap', 43.

39 On the category of 'Voice', see Genette, *Narrative Discourse*, 212–62.

40 Raymond Grew, 'The Case for Comparing Histories', *American Historical Review*, 85, no. 4 (1980), 765; Willumsen, *Witches of the North*, 24.

41 Elizabeth S. Cohen, 'Back Talk: Two Prostitutes' Voices from Rome *c.* 1600', *Early Modern Women*, 2 (2007), 95.

42 Elizabeth S. Cohen, 'Between Oral and Written Culture: The Social Meaning of an Illustrated Love Letter', in Barbara Diefendorf and Carla Hesse (eds.), *Culture and Identity in Early Modern Europe (1500–1800): Essays in Honour of Natalie Zemon Davis* (Ann Arbor, 1993), 181–201.

43 Gunvor Simonsen, *Slave Stories: Law, Representation and Gender in the Danish West Indies* (Aarhus, 2017), 13.

44 Poul J. Jørgensen, *Dansk Strafferet fra Reformationen til Danske lov* [Danish Criminal Law from the Reformation to the Danish Law] (Copenhagen, 2001), 34–103; Willumsen, *Witches of the North*, 234–35; John H. Langbein, *Torture and the Law of Proof: Europe and England in the Ancien Régime* (Chicago, 2006); *The Origins of Adversary Criminal Trial* (Oxford, 2003); Björn Åstrand, *Tortyr och pinligt förhör—väld och tvång i äldre svensk rätt* [Torture and Interrogation Under Pressure—Violence and Force in Older Swedish Courts] (Ph.D. thesis, Umeå University, 2000).

45 Liv H. Willumsen, 'A Witchcraft Triangle. Transmitting Witchcraft Ideas Across Early Modern Europe', in Marina Montesano (ed.), *Folklore, Magic, and Witchcraft: Cultural Exchanges from the Twelfth to Eighteenth Century* (Abingdon, 2021), 247–49.

46 The Finnish Declaration of Independence was adopted by the Parliament of Finland on 6 December 1917.

47 LHAK, 211, No. 2223, fos. 1–51; trials of Barbara Kremer zu Longuich 1587, Grethen Sundtgen zu Fell 1588; Maria von Kirsch/Maria Wolf, Meiers zu Fell 1588; Trein Beckers zu Fell 1590; Logen Faßbender zu Fell 1595; Martenß Christ zu Fell 1595. Stadtarchive Trier, No. 1533/170, fos. 243–61; Depositum Kesselstadt, Abt. 54K, no. 3643; Abt. 54K, no. 3644; Abt. 54K, 657, fos. 67–208, 225–50.

48 Rita Voltmer and Karl Weisenstein (eds.), *Das Hexenregister des Claudius Musiel* [The Witch Register of Claudius Musiel] (Trier, 1996).

49 Rolf Schulte, 'Ein Kinderhexenprozess aus St. Margarethen' [A Child Witch Trial from St. Margarethen], in *'Wider Hexerey und Teufelswerk. . .'. Von Hexen und ihrer Verfolgung* ['Against Witchcraft and the Work of the Devil. . .'. About Witches and Their Persecution], exhibition catalogue (Itzehoe, 2000), 48–55.

50 Peter Morton (ed.), *The Trial of Tempel Anneke: Records of a Witchcraft Trial in Brunswick*, trans. Barbara Dähms (Peterborough, 2006).

51 C. L'Estrange Ewen, *Witch Hunting and Witch Trials: The Indictments for Witchcraft from the Records of 1373 Assizes Held for the Home Circuit AD 1559–1736* (London, 1929); *Witchcraft and Demonianism: A Concise Account Derived from Sworn Depositions and Confessions Obtained in the Courts of England and Wales* (London, 1933); Malcolm Gaskill, 'Witches and Witnesses in Old and New England', in Clark, *Languages of Witchcraft*, 55–80.

52 Lawrence Normand and Gareth Roberts, *Witchcraft in Early Modern Scotland. James VI's Demonology and the North Berwick Witches* (Exeter, 2000).

53 Liv H. Willumsen, *The Witchcraft Trials in Finnmark, Northern Norway* (Bergen, 2010).

54 Ole P. Grell (ed.), *The Scandinavian Reformation* (Cambridge, 1995), 114–43.

55 See Niels Hemmingsen, *Admonitia de superstionibus magical vitandis* (Copenhagen, 1575); Jesper Brochmand, *Systema universæ theologia, vol. 1–2* (Hafniæ/Copenhagen, 1633); Hans P. Resen, *De sancta fide* (Copenhagen, 1614); Danish translation of the Bible (1604–07). The three were bishops of Zealand and professors at the University of Copenhagen. Liv H. Willumsen, *Trollkvinne i nord i historiske kilder og skjønnlitteratur* [Witch in the North in Historical Sources and Literature] (M.A. thesis, University of Tromsø, 1984; published in 1994), 60–61.

56 Jeffrey B. Russell, *Witchcraft in the Middle Ages* (London, 1972), 79.

Notes

57 Rita Voltmer, 'Wissen, Media und die Wahrheit', in Heinz Sieburg, Rita Voltmer, and Britta Weimann (eds.), *Hexenwissen: Zum Transfer von Magie- und Zauberei-Imaginationen in interdisziplinärer Perspektive* (Trier, 2017), 17.
58 Willumsen, 'Witchcraft Triangle', 252.
59 Hans de Waardt, 'Netherlands, Northern', in Richard M. Golden (ed.), *Encyclopedia of Witchcraft: The Western Tradition*, vol. 3 (Santa Barbara, CA, 2006), 810.
60 Willumsen, 'Witchcraft Triangle', 248, 250, 252.
61 Johannes Dillinger, *'Böse Leute': Hexenverfolgungen in Schwäbisch-Österreich und Kurtrier in Vergleich* (Trier, 1999), 359.
62 Rita Voltmer, 'Debating the Devil's Clergy. Demonology and the Media in Dialogue with Trials (14th to 17th Century)', *Religions*, 10, no. 12 (2019), 648; Wolfgang Behringer, *Hexen und Hexenprozesse in Deutschland* (first published 1988; München, 2010), 180–84.
63 Willumsen, 'Witchcraft Triangle', 253.
64 Willumsen, 'Witchcraft Triangle', 253.
65 Willumsen, 'Witchcraft Triangle', 253.
66 Orig. *Europaweite Verfolgungsdruck.* Rolf Schulte, *Hexenverfolgung in Schleswig-Holstein 16.–18. Jahrhundert* [The Witch-Hunt in Schleswig-Holstein 16th–18th Century] (Heide, 2001), 68.
67 Brian P. Levack, *Witch-Hunting in Scotland: Law, Politics and Religion* (New York, 2008).
68 Diane Baptie and Liv H. Willumsen, 'From Fife to Finnmark. John Cunningham's Way to Finnmark', *The Genealogist*, 28, no. 2 (Fall 2014), 191.
69 Arne Kruse and Liv H. Willumsen, 'Magic Language: The Transmission of an Idea Over Geographical Distance and Linguistic Barriers', *Magic, Ritual, and Witchcraft*, 15, no. 1 (Spring 2020), 13.
70 Barbara Kryk-Kastovsky, 'Historical Courtroom Discourse: An Introduction', *Journal of Historical Pragmatics*, 7, no. 2 (2006), 213–45; Kathleen L. Doty, 'Telling Tales. The Role of Scribes in Constructing the Discourse of the Salem Witchcraft Trials', *Journal of Historical Pragmatics*, 8, no. 1 (2007), 25–41.
71 Jürgen Macha et al. (eds.), *Deutsche Kanzleisprache in Hexenverhörprotokollen der Frühen Neuzeit* [German Chancery Language in Witchcraft Trial Interrogation Minutes of the Early Modern Period] (Berlin, 2005).
72 Elvira Topalovic, '"Ick kike in die Stern vnd versake Gott den Herrn". Versprachligung des Teufelpaktes in westfälischen Verhörprotokollen des 16./17. Jahrhunderts' ['Ick kike in die Stern vnd versake Gott den Herrn'. Representation of the Devil's Pact in Westphalian Interrogation Minutes of the 16th/17th Century], *Augustin Wibbelt-Gesellschaft. Jahrbuch* 20, 69–86.
73 Jürgen Macha and Wolfgang Herborn, *Kölner Hexenverhöre aus dem 17. Jahrhundert* [Cologne Witches' Interrogation from the 17th Century] (Berlin, 1992). See also Jürgen Macha, 'Redewiedergabe in Verhörprotokollen und der Hintergrund gesprochener Sprache' [Speech Reproduction in Interrogation Minutes and the Background of Spoken Language], in Sabine Krämer-Neubert and Norbert R. Wolf (eds.), *Bayerische Dialektologie. Akten der Internationalen Dialektologischen Konferenz 26.–28. Februar 2002* [Bavarian Dialectology. Proceedings of the International Dialectological Conference, 26–28 February 2002] (Heidelberg, 2005), 171–78; Macha et al., *Deutsche Kanzleisprache*; Topalovic, 'Ick kike in die Stern'.
74 Rita Voltmer, 'Demonology and the Relevance of the Witches' Confessions', in Goodare, Voltmer, and Willumsen, *Demonology and Witch-Hunting*, 26; 'Witch in the Courtroom: Torture and the Representations of Emotion', in Laura Kounine and Michael Ostling (eds.), *Emotions in the History of Witchcraft* (Basingstoke, 2017), 97–116; 'The Judges' Lore? The Politico-Religious Concept of Metamorphosis in the Peripheries of Western Europe', in Willem de Blécourt (ed.), *Werewolf Histories* (Basingstoke, 2015), 163–67.

75 Peter Rushton, 'Texts of Authority: Witchcraft Accusations and the Demonstration of Truth in Early Modern England', in Clark, *Languages of Witchcraft*, 31, 35.
76 Alison Rowlands, *Witchcraft Narratives in Germany: Rothenburg, 1561–1652* (Manchester, 2003), 2.
77 Kryk-Kastovsky, 'Historical Courtroom Discourse', 167–68; 'Representations of Orality in Early Modern English Trial Records', *Journal of Historical Pragmatics*, 1, no. 2 (2000), 201–30; 'How Bad Is "Bad Data"? In Search for the Features of Orality in Early Modern English Legal Texts', *Current Issues in Unity and Diversity of Languages. Collection of Papers Selected from the CIL 18, Held at Korea University in Seoul on July 21–26, 2008* (Seoul, 2009); Doty, 'Telling Tales', 27.
78 Gaskill, 'Witches and Witnesses', 56–58.
79 Malcolm Gaskill, 'Reporting Murder: Fiction in the Archives in Early Modern England', *Social History*, 23, no. 1 (1998), 2.
80 Clark, 'Introduction', 12.
81 Silvia Federici, *Witches, Witch-Hunting and Women* (Oakland, 2018), 11–14.
82 Laura Gowing, *Domestic Dangers: Women, Words and Sex in Early Modern London* (Oxford, 1996), 232–76; 'Language, Power and the Law: Women's Slander Litigation in Early Modern London', in Jenny Kermode and Garthine Walker (eds.), *Women, Crime and the Courts in Early Modern England* (London, 1994), 26–47.
83 Garthine Walker, *Crime, Gender and Social Order in Early Modern Cheshire* (Ph.D. thesis, University of Liverpool, 1994), 46–74; 'Women, Theft and the World of Stolen Goods', in Kermode and Walker, *Women, Crime and the Courts*, 95–97.
84 Kryk-Kastovsky, 'Historical Courtroom Discourse'; 'Representations of Orality'; 'How Bad Is "Bad Data"?'; Doty, 'Telling Tales'; Kathleen L. Doty and Risto Hiltunen, 'I Will Tell, I Will Tell', *Journal of Historical Pragmatics*, 3, no. 2 (2002), 299–335.
85 Cohen, 'Back Talk'; 'Between Oral and Written Culture'.
86 Simonsen, *Slave Stories*.
87 Miles Ogborn, *The Freedom of Speech: Talk and Slavery in the Anglo-Caribbean World* (Chicago, 2019), 3.
88 Emma Wilby, *The Visions of Isobel Gowdie: Magic, Witchcraft and Dark Shamanism in Seventeenth-Century Scotland* (Eastbourne, 2010).
89 Rowlands, *Witchcraft Narratives in Germany*; Natalie Z. Davis, *Fiction in the Archives: Pardon Tales and Their Tellers in Sixteenth-Century France* (Cambridge, 1987).
90 Davis, *Fiction in the Archives*, 4.
91 Davis, *Fiction in the Archives*, 4.
92 Petter Aaslestad, *Pasienten som tekst* [The Patient as Text] (Oslo, 1997).
93 Liv H. Willumsen, 'Children Accused of Witchcraft in 17th-Century Finnmark', *Scandinavian Journal of History*, 38, no. 1 (2013), 18–41; 'A Narratological Approach to Witchcraft Trials: A Scottish Case', *Journal of Early Modern History*, 15 (2011), 531–60.
94 Allison Coudert, 'Female Witches', in Golden, *Encyclopedia of Witchcraft*, 357–59; William Monter, 'Male Witches', in Golden, *Encyclopedia of Witchcraft*, 712–13; Alison Rowlands, 'Witchcraft and Gender in Early Modern Europe', in Levack, *Oxford Handbook of Witchcraft*, 449–67.
95 Raisa M. Toivo, *Witchcraft and Gender in Early Modern Society. Finland and the Wider European Experience* (Aldershot, 2008).
96 Raisa M. Toivo, 'Gender, Sex and Cultures of Trouble in Witchcraft Studies: European Historiography with Special Reference to Finland', in Marko Nenonen and Raisa M. Toivo (eds.), *Writing Witch-Hunt Histories* (Leiden, 2013), 87–108; 'Discerning Voices and Values in the Finnish Witch Trials Records', *Studia Neophilologica*, 84, no. 1 (2012), 143–55.
97 Jari Eilola, 'Witchcraft, Women and the Borders of Household', *ARV: Nordic Yearbook of Folklore*, 62 (2006), 33–50.
98 Marie Lennersand and Linda Oja, *Livet går vidare: Älvdalen och Rättvik efter de stora häxprocesserna 1668–71* [Life Goes on: Älvdalen and Rättvik After the Great Witchcraft

Trials of 1668–71] (Hedemora, 2006); 'Vitnande visionärer: Guds och Djävulens red-skap i Dalarnas häxprocesser' [Witnessing Visionaries: God's and the Devil's Tool in the Witchcraft Trials of Dalarne], in Hanne Sanders (ed.), *Mellem Gud og Djævelen: Religiøse og magiske verdensbilleder i Norden 1500–1800* [Between God and the Devil: Religious and Magical World Images in the Nordic Countries 1500–1800] (Copenhagen, 2001), 177–84.

99 Jacqueline van Gent, *Magic, Body and the Self in Eighteenth-Century Sweden* (Leiden, 2009).

100 Åsa Bergenheim, *Den liderliga häxan: Häxhammaren och de svenska häxprossesserna* [The Lewd Witch: The Witches' Hammer and the Swedish Witchcraft Trials] (Stockholm, 2020).

101 Merete Birkelund, *Troldkvinden og hendes anklagere: Danske hekseprocesser i det 16. og 17. århundrede* [The Witch and Her Accusers: Danish Witch Trials in the 16th and 17th Centuries] (Århus, 1983).

102 Louise N. Kallestrup, *I Pagt med Djævelen. Trolddomsforestillinger og trolddomsfor-følgelser i Italien og Danmark efter Reformationen* [In Pact with the Devil: Witchcraft Imaginations and Witchcraft Persecution in Italy and Denmark After the Reformation] (Frederiksberg, 2009).

103 Ellen Alm, *Trondheims siste heksebrenning* [The Last Witch Burning in Trondheim] (Trondheim, 2014).

104 Willumsen, *Trollkvinne i nord.*

105 Willumsen, *Witches of the North*, 70–77, 88, 93–94, 262; *Dømt til ild og bål* [Sentenced to Death in Fire at the Stake] (Stamsund, 2013), 48, 407.

106 Ulla Manns and Fia Sundevall (eds.), *Methods, Interventions, and Reflections: Report from the 10th Nordic Women and Gender History Conference* (Bergen, 2012).

107 Dagmar Unverhau, 'Frauenbewegung und historische Hexenverfolgung' [Women's Movement and Historical Witch-Hunts], in Andreas Blauert (ed.), *Ketzer, Zauberer, Hexen. Die Anfänge der europäischen Hexenverfolgungen* [Heretics, Sorcerers, Witches. The Beginnings of the European Witch-Hunts] (Frankfurt am Main, 1990), 241–83.

108 Lyndal Roper, *Witch Craze: Terror and Fantasy in Baroque Germany* (New Haven, 2004).

109 Laura Kounine, *Imagining the Witch: Emotions, Gender and Selfhood in Early Modern Germany* (Oxford, 2018).

110 Marion Gibson, *Early Modern Witches: Witchcraft Cases in Contemporary Writing* (Florence, 2000).

111 Marion Gibson, *Witchcraft Myths in American Culture* (New York, 2007).

112 Diane Purkiss, *The Witch in History: Early Modern and Twentieth-Century Representations* (Abingdon, 1996), 74.

113 See Christine Middleton, *The Witch & Her Soul: A Novel* (Lancaster, 2012); Blake Morrison's, *Pendle Witches* (London, 1996). With etchings by Paula Rego.

114 Malcolm Gaskill, 'Witchcraft and Power in Early Modern England: The Case of Margaret Moore', in Kermode and Walker, *Women, Crime and the Courts*, 125–45.

115 Jim Sharpe, 'Women, Witchcraft and the Legal Process', in Kermode and Walker, *Women, Crime and the Courts*, 106–24.

116 Christina Larner, 'Was Witch-Hunting Woman-Hunting?' *New Society* (October 8, 1981), 11–13.

117 Julian Goodare, 'Women and the Witch-Hunt in Scotland', *Social History*, xxiii (1998), 288–307; 'Men and the Witch-Hunt in Scotland', in Alison Rowlands (ed.), *Witchcraft and Masculinities in Early Modern Europe* (Basingstoke, 2009), 149–70.

118 Lauren Martin, 'The Devil and the Domestic: Witchcraft, Quarrels and Women's Work', in Julian Goodare (ed.), *The Scottish Witch-Hunt in Context* (Manchester, 2002), 73–89.

119 Lara Apps and Andrew Colin Gow, *Male Witches in Early Modern Europe* (Manchester, 2003), 45.

120 Kirsten Hastrup, 'Iceland: Sorcerers and Paganism', in Bengt Ankarloo and Gustav Henningsen (eds.), *Early Modern European Witchcraft: Centres and Peripheries* (Oxford, 1990), 386; Rune B. Hagen, 'Witchcraft Criminality and Witchcraft Research in the Nordic Countries', in Levack, *Oxford Handbook of Witchcraft*, 382.

121 Apps and Gow, *Male Witches*.

122 Rowlands, *Witchcraft and Masculinities*.

123 Rolf Schulte, *Hexenmeister: Die Verfolgung von Männern im Rahmen der Hexenverfolgung von 1530–1730 im Alten Reich* [Sorcerers: The Persecution of Men as Part of the Witch-Hunt of 1530–1730 in the Old Kingdom] (Frankfurt am Main, 2001); *Man as Witch: Male Witches in Central Europe* (Basingstoke, 2009).

124 Rune B. Hagen, 'Images, Representations and the Self-Perception of Magic among the Sami Shamans of Arctic Norway', in Louise N. Kallestrup and Raisa M. Toivo (eds.), *Contesting Orthodoxy in Medieval and Early Modern Europe: Heresy, Magic, and Witchcraft* (Cham, 2017), 279–300; 'Sami Shamanism: The Arctic Dimension', *Magic, Rituals and Witches*, 1, no. 2 (2006), 227–33; *The Sorcery Trial of Anders Poulsen in 1692* (Karasjok, 2012).

125 David J. Collins (ed.), *The Cambridge History of Magic and Witchcraft in the West: From Antiquity to the Present* (Cambridge, 2015).

126 Julian Goodare, 'Women, Men, and Witchcraft', in Goodare, *European Witch-Hunt*, 267–316.

127 Brian P. Levack, *The Witch-Hunt in Early Modern Europe* (Essex, 1995; first published in London, 1987).

128 Wolfgang Behringer, *Witches and Witch-Hunts. A Global History* (Cambridge, 2004); Wolfgang Behringer, 'Weather, Hunger and Fear: Origins of the European Witch-Hunts in Climate, Society and Mentality', *German History*, vol. 13, no 1, pp. 1-27.

129 Laura Stoke, *Demons of Urban Reform: Early European Witch Trials and Criminal Justice, 1430–1530* (Basingstoke, 2011).

130 Eva Österberg and Sølvi Sogner (eds.), *People Meet the Law. Control and Conflict-Handling in the Courts* (Oslo, 2000).

131 Gregory Durston, *Witchcraft and Witch Trials: A History of English Witchcraft and Its Legal Perspectives, 1542 to 1736* (Chichester, 2000).

132 Langbein, *Torture and the Law*.

133 Langbein, *Origins of Adversary*.

134 Åstrand, *Tortyr och pinligforhör*.

135 Jørgen C. Jacobsen, *Danske Domme i Trolddomssager i øverste Instans* [Danish Sentences in Witchcraft Trials at the Highest Court Level] (Copenhagen, 1966).

136 Jørgensen, *Dansk Strafferet*. This edition has an introduction by Ditlev Tamm and Helle Vogt.

137 Jørn Ø. Sunde, *Speculum legale—rettsspegelen* [Speculum Legale—The Mirror of the Law] (Bergen, 2005).

138 Bente Alver, *Heksetro og trolddom* [Witchcraft Beliefs and Sorcery] (Oslo, 1971).

139 The use of Norwegian charms and spells related to witchcraft is well documented in Alver, *Mellem mennesker og magter*.

140 Julian Goodare and Martha McGill (eds.), *The Supernatural in Early Modern Scotland* (Manchester, 2020).

141 Euan Cameron, *Enchanted Europe: Superstition, Reason and Religion 1250–1750* (Oxford, 2010).

142 Sydney Anglo (ed.), *The Damned Art: Essays in the Literature of Witchcraft* (London, 1977).

143 Ankarloo and Henningsen, *Early Modern European Witchcraft*.

144 Jens C. Johansen, 'Tavshed er guld. En historiografisk oversigt over amerikansk og europæisk hekseforskning 1966–1981' ['Silence Is Gold. A Historiographical Survey of American and European Witchcraft Research, 1966–1981'], *Historisk tidsskrift*, 81 (1982), 401–23.

145 Darren Oldridge (ed.), *The Witchcraft Reader* (Philadelphia, 2002).

146 Alan C. Kors and Edward Peters, *Witchcraft in Europe, 400–1700. A Documentary History* (Philadelphia, 1972).

147 Jonathan Barry, Marianne Hester, and Gareth Roberts (eds.), *Witchcraft in Early Modern Europe: Studies in Culture and Belief* (Cambridge, 1996).

148 Owen Davies and Willem de Blécourt (eds.), *Beyond the Witch Trials. Witchcraft and Magic in Enlightenment Europe* (Manchester, 2004).

149 Jonathan Barry, Owen Davies, and Cornelie Usborne (eds.), *Cultures of Witchcraft from the Middle Ages to the Present: Essays in Honour of Willem de Blécourt* (Cham, 2018).

150 Marijke Gijswijt-Hofstra, Brian P. Levack, and Roy Porter (eds.), *Witchcraft and Magic in Europe: The Eighteenth and Nineteenth Centuries* (London, 1999).

151 Kors and Peters, *Witchcraft in Europe, 400–1700*.

152 Brian P. Levack, *The Witchcraft Sourcebook* (New York, 2004).

153 Marion Gibson, *Witchcraft and Society in England and America, 1550–1750* (New York, 2003).

154 J. S. Cockburn, *Calendar of Assize Records, Home Circuit Indictments. Elizabeth I and James I.* 10 vols. (London, 1975–85).

155 Ewen, *Witch Hunting and Witch Trials; Witchcraft and Demonianism*.

156 Morton, *Trial of Tempel Anneke*.

157 Macha and Herborn, *Kölner Hexenverhöre*.

158 *Wider Hexerey und Teufelswerk*.

159 Normand and Roberts, *Witchcraft in Early Modern Scotland*.

160 John Hungerford Pollen (ed.), *Letter from Mary Queen of Scots to the Duke of Guise, Scottish History Society*, series 1, vol. 43 (Edinburgh, 1904); C. H. Firth (ed.), *Miscellany of the Scottish History Society (Second Volume)*, Scottish History Society, series 1, vol. 44 (Edinburgh, 1904); *The Bannatyne Miscellaney Containing Original Papers and Tracts Chiefly Relating to the History and Literature of Scotland*, vol. 3, *The Bannatyne Club* (Edinburgh, 1855).

161 David Grønlund, *Historisk Efterretning om de i Ribe Bye forfulgte og brændte Mennesker* [Historical Account of Those People Persecuted and Burned in Ribe Town], 2nd ed. (1973; first published in Viborg, 1780).

162 Leif Ljungberg and Einar Bager, *Malmø tingbøger 1577–83 og 1588–90* [Malmø Court Records 1577–83 and 1588–90] (Copenhagen, 1968).

163 Lilienskiold was in office in Finnmark from 1684 to 1701. Rune B. Hagen and Per E. Sparboe (eds.), *Lilienskiold, Hans H.: Trolldom og ugudelighet i 1600-tallets Finnmark* [Lilienskiold, Hans H.: Witchcraft and Ungodliness in Seventeenth-Century Finnmark] (Tromsø, 1998).

164 Willumsen, *Witchcraft Trials in Finnmark*. These original sources have also been published in *verbatim* transcription in Danish and in modernized Norwegian. Liv H. Willumsen, *Trolldomsprosessene i Finnmark. Et kildeskrift* [The Finnmark Witchcraft Trials. A Source Book] (Bergen, 2010); Liv H. Willumsen, *Kilder til trolldomsprosessene ei Finnmark. Modernisert språklig utgave* [Sources to the Finnmark Witchcraft Trials. Edition in Modernized Language] (Leikanger, 2017).

165 Andrew C. Gow, Robert B. Desjardins, and François V. Pageau (eds., trans.), *The Arras Witch Treatises* (Pennsylvania, 2016).

166 Called the Republic of the United Provinces or Low Countries in the late Middle Ages and the Early Modern period.

167 Marijke Gijswijt-Hofstra and Willem Frijhoff (eds.), *Witchcraft in the Netherlands: From the Fourteenth to the Twentieth Century* (Rotterdam, 1991); de Waardt, 'Netherlands, Northern'; 'Witchcraft and Wealth: The Case in the Netherlands', in Levack, *Oxford Handbook of Witchcraft*, 237–38; Marijke Gijswijt-Hofstra, 'From the Low Countries to France', in Bengt Ankarloo and Stuart Clark (eds.), *Witchcraft and Magic in Europe, vol. 4: The Period of the Witch Trials* (London, 2002), 95–188; Willem de Blécourt, 'Contested Knowledge: A Historical Anthropologist's Approach to European Witchcraft', in Barry, Davies, and Usborne, *Cultures of Witchcraft*, 1–22.

168 Dries Vanysacker, 'Netherlands, Southern', in Golden, *Encyclopedia of Witchcraft*, 814; *Hekserij in Brugge. De magische leefwereld van een stadsbevolking, 16de-17de eeuw* [Witchcraft in Bruges. The Magical World of an Urban Population, 16th–17th Century] (Bruges, 1988).

169 Dagmar Unverhau, 'Kieler Hexen und Zauberer zur Zeit der großen Verfolgung (1530–1676)' [Kiel Witches and Sorcerers at the Time of the Great Persecution (1530–1676)], in Jürgen Jensen (ed.), *Mitteilungen der Gesellschaft für Kieler Stadtgeschichte* [Communications of the Society for Kiel City History], Band 68 (Gesellschaft für Kieler Stadtgeschichte, 1981–83), 41–96; Schulte, *Hexenverfolgung in Schleswig-Holstein*; 'Ein Kinderhexenprozess'; Karen Lambrecht, *Hexenverfolgung und Zaubereiprozesse in den schlesischen Territorien* [Witch-Hunts and Sorcery Trials in the Silesian Territories] (Köln, 1995); Eva Labouvie, *Zauberei und Hexenwerk. Ländlicher Hexenglaube in der frühen Neuzeit* [Sorcery and Witchcraft. Rural Belief in Witches in the Early Modern Period] (Frankfurt am Main, 1991).

170 Gisela Wilbertz, Gerd Schwerhoff, and Jürgen Scheffler (eds.), *Hexenverfolgung und Regionalgeschichte. Der Grafschaft Lippe im Vergleich* [Witch-Hunt and Regional History. The County of Lippe in Comparison], Studien zur Regionalgeschichte, b. 4 (Bielefeld, 1994).

171 Degn, Lehmann, and Unverhau, *Hexenprozesse*.

172 Unverhau, 'Akkusationsprozess—Inquisitionsprozess'.

173 Dagmar Unverhau, *Von Toverschen und Kunstfruhwen in Schleswig, 1548–1557, Quellen und Interpretationen zur Geschichte der Zauber- und Hexenwesens* [Of 'Toverschen' and 'Kunstfruhwen' in Schleswig, 1548–1557, Sources and Interpretations on the History of Magic and Witchcraft] (Schleswig, 1980).

174 Schulte, *Hexenverfolgung in Schleswig-Holstein*.

175 Schulte, *Man as Witch*.

176 Schulte, *Hexenmeister*.

177 Behringer, *Hexen und Hexenprozesse*; Sönke Lorenz and Jürgen Schmidt, *Wider alle Hexerei und Teufelswerk: Die Europäische Hexenverfolgung* (Ostfildern, 2004).

178 Wolfgang Behringer, *The Shaman of Oberstdorf: Chonrad Stoeckhlin and the Phantoms of the Night* (Charlottesville, 1998); *Witchcraft Persecutions in Bavaria: Popular Magic, Religious Zealots and Reason of State in Early Modern Europe* (Cambridge, 1997).

179 Henrik C. Liisberg, *Vesten for Sø og østen for Hav: Trolddom i København og i Edinburgh 1590: et Bidrag til Hekseprocessernes Historie* [West of the Sea and East of the Ocean: A Contribution to the History of Witchcraft Trials] (Copenhagen, 1909).

180 Liv H. Willumsen, 'Witchcraft Against the Royal Danish Ships in 1589 and the Transnational Transfer of Ideas', *International Review of Scottish Studies*, 45 (2020), 54–99; 'Trolldom mot kongens skip 1589 og transnasjonal overføring av idéer' [Witchcraft Against the King's Ship 1589 and Transnational Transfer of Ideas], *Historisk Tidsskrift*, 2 (2019), 309–44.

181 Gustav Henningsen, *The Witches' Advocate. Basque Witchcraft and the Spanish Inquisition* (Reno, 1980).

182 Birkelund, *Troldkvinden*; Jens C. Johansen, *Da Djævelen var ude . . . Trolddom i det 17. århundredes Danmark* [When the Devil Was Out . . . Witchcraft in Seventeenth-Century Denmark] (Viborg, 1991); 'Denmark', in Golden, *Encyclopedia of Witchcraft*, 265; 'To Beat a Glass Drum: The Transmission of Popular Notions of Demonology in Denmark and Germany', in Goodare, Voltmer, and Willumsen, *Demonology and Witch-Hunting*, 233–42.

183 Louise N. Kallestrup, *Trolddomsforfølgelser og trolddomstro: En komparasjon af det posttridentine Italien og det luthersk protestantiske Danmark i det 16. og 17. århundrede* [Witchcraft Persecution and Witchcraft Belief: A Comparison of Post-Tridentine Italy and Lutheran Protestant Denmark in the Sixteenth and Seventeenth Centuries] (Ph.D. thesis, Aalborg University, 2007); *I Pagt med Djævelen*; *Heksejagt* (Aarhus, 2020).

184 Louise N. Kallestrup, 'Maleficium ò "abuso di sacramento"?' *Dansk Historisk Tidsskrift*, 102, no. 2 (2002), 282–305; '"When Hell Became Too Small": Constructing Witchcraft in Post-Reformation Denmark', in Tyge Krogh, Louise N.

Kallestrup, and Claus B. Christensen (eds.), *Cultural Histories of Crime in Denmark, 1500–2000* (London, 2017), 38–57; ' "He Promised Her So Many Things": Witches, Sabbats, and Devils in Early Modern Denmark', in Goodare, Voltmer, and Willumsen, *Demonology and Witch-Hunting*, 243–60; Kallestrup and Toivo (eds.), *Contesting Orthodoxy*.

185 Thyge Krogh, *Oplysningstiden og det magiske: henrettelser og korporlige straffe i 1700-tallets første halvdel* [The Age of Enlightenment and the Magical: Executions and Corporal Punishments in the First Half of the Seventeenth Century] (Copenhagen, 2000).

186 Karsten S. Jensen, *Trolddom i Danmark 1500–1588* [Witchcraft in Denmark 1500–1588] (Copenhagen, 1988).

187 Christina Larner (née Ross), *Scottish Demonology in the Sixteenth and Seventeenth Centuries and Its Theological Background* (Ph.D. thesis, University of Edinburgh, 1962).

188 Christina Larner, *Enemies of God: The Witch-Hunt in Scotland* (London, 1981).

189 Larner, 'Was Witch-Hunting Woman-Hunting?' 11–13.

190 Goodare, *Scottish Witch-Hunt in Context*; Julian Goodare, Lauren Martin, and Joyce Miller (eds.), *Witchcraft and Belief in Early Modern Scotland* (Basingstoke, 2008); Julian Goodare (ed.), *Scottish Witches and Witch-Hunters* (Basingstoke, 2013). The last contains a useful bibliography of Scottish witchcraft.

191 See www.arts.ed.ac.uk/witches (archived January 2003, accessed February 2007).

192 Julian Goodare, 'The Finnmark Witches in European Context', in Reidun L. Andreassen and Liv H. Willumsen (eds.), *Steilneset Memorial. Art, Architecture, History* (Stamsund, 2013), 57–63; 'The Framework for Scottish Witch-Hunting in the 1590s', *Scottish Historical Review*, 81 (2002), 240–50; 'The Scottish Witchcraft Act', *Church History*, 74, no. 1 (2005), 39–67; 'John Knox on Demonology and Witchcraft', *Archiv für Reformationsgeschichte*, 96 (2005), 221–45; 'The Scottish Witchcraft Panic of 1597', in Goodare, *Scottish Witch-Hunt in Context*, 51–72; 'Women and the Witch-Hunt'; 'Men and the Witch-Hunt'; 'Scottish Witchcraft in Its European Context', in Goodare, Martin, and Miller, *Witchcraft and Belief*, 26–50; 'Flying Witches in Scotland', in Goodare, *Scottish Witches*, 159–76; 'Witches' Flight in Scottish Demonology', in Goodare, Voltmer, and Willumsen, *Demonology and Witch-Hunting*, 147–67; 'Emotional Relationships with Spirit-Guides in Early Modern Scotland', in Goodare and McGill, *Supernatural in Early Modern Scotland*, 39–54.

193 Lauren Martin, 'Scottish Witchcraft Panics Re-Examined', in Goodare, Martin, and Miller, *Witchcraft and Belief*, 119–43; *The Devil and the Domestic: Witchcraft, Women's Work and Marriage in Early Modern Scotland* (Ph.D. thesis, New School for Social Research, 2003); Lauren Martin and Joyce Miller, 'Some Findings from the Survey of Scottish Witchcraft', in Goodare, Martin, and Miller, *Witchcraft and Belief*, 51–70; Joyce Miller, 'Men in Black: Appearances of the Devil in Early Modern Scottish Witchcraft Discourse', in Goodare, Martin, and Miller, *Witchcraft and Belief*, 144–55; *Cantrips and Carlins: Magic, Medicine and Sorcery in the Presbyteries of Haddington and Stirling, 1600–1688* (Ph.D. thesis, University of Stirling, 1999); Louise Yeoman, 'Away with the Fairies', in Lizanne Henderson (ed.), *Fantastical Imaginations* (East Linton, 2009), 29–46; 'Hunting the Rich Witch in Scotland: High-Status Witchcraft Suspects and Their Persecutors, 1590–1650', in Goodare, *Scottish Witch-Hunt in Context*, 106–21; Dye, *'Devilische Wordis'*; Michelle D. Brock, *Satan and the Scots: The Devil in Post-Reformation Scotland c. 1560–1700* (London, 2016).

194 Peter G. Maxwell-Stuart, *Satan's Conspiracy: Magic and Witchcraft in Sixteenth-Century Scotland* (East Linton, 2001); *An Abundance of Witches. The Great Scottish Witch-Hunt* (Gloucestershire, 2005); Stuart Macdonald, *The Witches of Fife. Witch-Hunting in a Scottish Shire, 1560–1710* (East Linton, 2002); Jenny Wormald, 'The Witches, the Devil and the King', in Terry Brotherstone and David Ditchburn (eds.), *Freedom and Authority: Scotland c. 1050–c. 1650* (East Linton, 2000), 165–80.

195 Anna Cordey, *Witch-Hunting in the Presbytery of Dalkeith, 1649 to 1662* (M.Sc. thesis, University of Edinburgh, 2003); 'Reputation and Witch-Hunting in Seventeenth-Century

Dalkeith', in Goodare, *Scottish Witches*, 103–20; Laura Paterson, *The Witches' Sabbath in Scotland* (M.Sc. thesis, University of Edinburgh, 2011); 'Executing Scottish Witches', in Goodare, *Scottish Witches*, 196–214; 'The Witches' Sabbath in Scotland', *Proceedings of the Society of Antiquaries of Scotland*, 142 (2012), 371–412.

196 Levack, *Witch-Hunting in Scotland*.

197 Willumsen, *Seventeenth-Century Witchcraft Trials*.

198 Willumsen, *Witches of the North*.

199 Willumsen, 'Narratological Approach'; 'Witches in Scotland and Northern Norway: Two Case Studies', in Peter Graves and Arne Kruse (eds.), *Images and Imaginations: Perspectives on Britain and Scandinavia* (Edinburgh, 2007), 35–67; 'The Ninety-Nine Dancers of Moaness: Orkney Women Between the Visible and Invisible', in Goodare and McGill, *Supernatural in Early Modern Scotland*, 72–85; 'Exporting the Devil Across the North Sea: John Cunningham and the Finnmark Witch-Hunt', in Goodare, *Scottish Witches*, 49–66; Baptie and Willumsen, 'From Fife to Finnmark'; Kruse and Willumsen, 'Magic Language'.

200 Alan Macfarlane, *Witchcraft in Tudor and Stuart England: A Regional and Comparative Study* (London, 1971); Keith Thomas, *Religion and the Decline of Magic: Studies in Popular Beliefs in Sixteenth and Seventeenth-Century England* (London, 1971).

201 James Sharpe, *Instruments of Darkness* (Philadelphia, 1996).

202 James Sharpe, *Witchcraft in Early Modern England* (London, 2001).

203 James Sharpe, 'English Witchcraft Pamphlets and the Popular Demonic', in Goodare, Voltmer, and Willumsen, *Demonology and Witch-Hunting*, 127–46.

204 Marion Gibson, 'French Demonology in an English Village: The St Osyth Experiment of 1582', in Goodare, Voltmer, and Willumsen, *Demonology and Witch-Hunting*, 107–26; Marion Gibson (ed.), *Early English Trial Pamphlets* (London, 2003).

205 Malcolm Gaskill, *Crime and Mentalities in Early Modern England* (Cambridge, 2000).

206 Malcolm Gaskill, 'Witchcraft Trials in England', in Levack, *Oxford Handbook of Witchcraft*, 283–99; 'Witches and Witnesses'.

207 Malcolm Gaskill, *The Witchfinders: A Seventeenth-Century English Tragedy* (London, 2006).

208 Jonathan Barry, *Witchcraft and Demonology in South-West England 1640–1789* (Basingstoke, 2012); Jonathan Barry and Owen Davies, *Palgrave Advances in Witchcraft Historiography* (Basingstoke, 2007).

209 Ronald Hutton, 'Anthropological and Historical Approaches to Witchcraft: Potential for a New Collaboration?' *Historical Journal*, 47, no. 2 (2004), 413–34; 'Witch-Hunting in Celtic Societies', *Past and Present*, 212 (2011), 43–71.

210 Charlotte-Rose Millar, *Witchcraft, the Devil, and Emotions in Early Modern England* (London, 2017).

211 Hans E. Næss, *Trolldomsprosessene i Norge på 1500–1600-tallet: En retts- og sosialhistorisk undersøkelse* [Witchcraft Trials in Norway During the Sixteenth and Seventeenth Centuries. A Legal and Socio-Economic Study] (Oslo, 1982).

212 Hans E. Næss, *Med bål og brann* [In Fire at the Stake] (Oslo, 1984); *Fiat justitia! Lagmennene i Norge 1607–1797* [Fiat Justitia! Court of Appeal Judges in Norway 1607–1797] (Oslo, 2014); 'Norway: The Criminological Context', in Ankarloo and Henningsen, *Early Modern European Witchcraft*, 367–82; *Source Editions Court Records for Rogaland* (Stavanger, 1979, 1982, 1984); 'Presters og prestefruers roller I norske trolldomsprosesser' [The Roles of Ministers and Ministers' Wives in Norwegian Witchcraft Trials], in Nils O. Østrem (ed.), *Nedstrand kyrkje 150 år: I tru, håp og kjærleik* [Nedstrand Church 150 Years: In Faith, Hope, and Love] (Nedstrand, 2019), 113–22.

213 Gunnar W. Knutsen, *Trolldomsprosessene på Østlandet* [Witchcraft Trials at Østlandet] (Oslo, 1998); *Servants of Satan and Masters of Demons. The Spanish Inquisition Trials for Superstition, Valencia and Barcelona, 1478–1700* (Turnhout, 2009).

214 Gunnar W. Knutsen, 'Norwegian Witchcraft Trials: A Reassessment', in *Continuity and Change*, 28, no. 2 (2003), 185–200; 'The End of the Witch Hunts in Scandinavia', *ARV: Nordic Yearbook of Folklore*, 57 (2006), 143–64; 'Topics of Persecution: Witchcraft

Historiography in the Iberian World', in Nenonen and Toivo, *Writing Witch-Hunt Histories*, 167–90.

215 Willumsen, *Trollkvinne i nord; Seventeenth-Century Witchcraft Trials; Witches of the North; Dømt til ild og bål.*

216 Liv H. Willumsen, *Witchcraft Trials in Finnmark; Steilneset: Memorial to the Victims of the Finnmark Witchcraft Trials* (Oslo, 2011).

217 Willumsen, 'Board Games'; 'Anders Poulsen—Sami Shaman Accused of Witchcraft, 1692', *Folklore*, 131, no. 2 (2020), 135–58; 'Oral Transference of Ideas About Witchcraft in Seventeenth-Century Norway', in Thomas V. Cohen and Lesley K. Twomey (eds.), *Spoken Word and Social Practice: Orality in Europe (1400–1700)* (Leiden, 2015), 46–83; Arne Kruse and Liv H. Willumsen, 'Ordet Ballvollen knytt til transnasjonal overføring av idéar' [The Word Ballvollen Connected to Transnational Transfer of Ideas], *Historisk tidsskrift*, no. 2 (2014), 407–23.

218 Rune B. Hagen, 'Sami Shamanism'; *Sorcery Trial of Anders Poulsen*; 'Witchcraft and Ethnicity: A Critical Perspective on Sami Shamanism in the Seventeenth-Century', in Nenonen and Toivo, *Writing Witch-Hunt Histories*, 141–66; 'Images, Representations', 279–300; *Ved porten til helvete* [At the Gate to Hell] (Oslo, 2015); Willumsen, *Witches of the North*, 246.

219 Rune B. Hagen, *Hekser: Fra forfølgelse til fortryllelse* [Witches: From Persecution to Enchantment] (Oslo, 2003); *Dei europeiske hekseprosessane* [The European Witchcraft Trials] (Oslo, 2007); 'At the Edge of Civilisation: John Cunningham Lensmann of Finnmark 1619–51', in Andrew Mackillop and Steve Murdoch (eds.), *Military Governors and Imperial Frontiers c. 1600–1800: A Study of Scotland and Empires* (Leiden, 2003), 29–52.

220 Rune B. Hagen and Per E. Sparboe, *Kongens reise til det ytterste nord: Dagbøker fra Christian IV's tokt til Finnmark og Kola 1599* [The King's Voyage to the High North: Diaries from Christian IV's Trip to Finnmark and Kola 1599] (Tromsø, 2004).

221 Nils Gilje, *Heksen og humanisten: Anne Pedersdatter og Absalon Pederssøn Beyer: en historie om magi og trolldom i Bergen på 1500—tallet* [The Witch and the Humanist: Anne Pedersdatter and Absalon Pedersson Beyer: A Story About Magic and Witchcraft in Sixteenth-Century Bergen] (Bergen, 2003); ' "Djevelen står alltid bak": Demonisering av folkelig magi på slutten av 1500—tallet' [The Devil Is Always Behind: Demonizing of Traditional Magic at the End of the Sixteenth Century], in Bjarte Askeland and Jan F. Bernt (eds.), *Erkjennelse og engasjement: Minneseminar for David Roland Doublet (1954–2000)* [Recognition and Engagement: Seminar in Memory of David Roland Doublet (1954–2000)] (Bergen, 2001), 93–107.

222 Ellen Alm, *Statens rolle i trolldomsprosessene i Danmark og Norge på 1500-og 1600-tallet: En komparativ studie* [The Role of the State During the Witchcraft Trials in Denmark and Norway in the Sixteenth and Seventeenth Centuries: A Comparative Study] (M.A. thesis, University of Tromsø, 2000); *Trondheims siste heksebrenning.*

223 Emanuel Linderholm, *De stora häxprocesserna i Sverige* [The Great Witchcraft Trials in Sweden] (Uppsala, 1918).

224 Bengt Ankarloo, *Trolldomsprocesserna i Sverige. Skrifter utgivna av institutet för rättshistorik forskning, Serien I: Rättshistoriskt bibliotek* [Witchcraft Trials in Sweden. Books Published the Department of Legal Historical Research], vol. 17 (Ph.D. thesis, University of Lund, 1971; 2nd ed. 1984, with postscript).

225 Ankarloo and Henningsen, *Early Modern European Witchcraft.*

226 Per-Anders Östling, *Blåkulla, magi och trolldomsprocesser: En folkloristisk studie av folkliga trosföreställningar och av trolldomsprocesserna inom Svea Hovrätts jurisdiktion 1597–1720* [Blåkulla, Magic and Witchcraft Trials: A Folkloristic Study of People's Witchcraft Beliefs and of Witchcraft Trials in Svea Court's Jurisdiction 1597–1720] (Ph.D. thesis, University of Uppsala, 2002).

227 Per Sörlin, *Trolldoms- och vidskepelseprocesserna i Göta Hovrätt 1635–1754* [Witchcraft and Sorcery Trials in Göta Court 1635–1754] (Ph.D. thesis, Umeå University, 1993).

228 Per Sörlin, 'Wicked Arts', in *Witchcraft and Magic Trials in Southern Sweden, 1635–1754* (Leiden, 1999).

229 Per Sörlin, *Sakören, soning och soldater* [Fines, Atonement and Soldiers] (Oslo, 2004); 'Om saköreslängderna som historisk källa' [On Fines Records as Historical Source], in Olof Holm, Georg Hansson, and Christer Kalin, *Böter och Fredsköp: Jämtlands och Härjedalens saköreslängder 1601–1645* [Fines and Purchase of Peace. The Fines Documents from Jämtland and Härjedalen 1601–1645] (Östersund, 2016), 9–37.

230 Linda Oja (ed.), *Vägen till Blåkulla: Nya perspektiv på de stora svenska häxprocesserna* [The Road to Blåkulla: New Perspectives on the Great Swedish Witchcraft Trials] (Uppsala, 1997).

231 Linda Oja, *Varken Gud eller natur: synen på magi i 1600- och 1700-talets Sverige* [Neither God Nor Nature: Views on Magic in Sixteenth- and Seventeenth-Century Sweden] (Ph.D. thesis, Uppsala University, 1999).

232 Karin Granquist, 'Thou Shalt Have No Other Gods Before Me (Exodus 20:3). Witchcraft and Superstition Trials in the 17th and 18th Century Swedish Lapland', in Peter Sköld and Kristina Kram (eds.), *Kulturkonfrontation i Lappmarken: Sex essäer om mötet mellan samer och svenskar* [Cultural Confrontations: Six Essays on the Meeting Between Sami and Swedes] (Umeå, 1998), 13–21.

233 Maria Lennersand, *Rättvisans och allmogens beskyddare: Den absoluta staten, kommissionerna och tjänstemännen, ca 1680–1730* [The Protection of Justice and the Common People: The Absolute State, Commissioners and Public Officials, c. 1680–1730] (Ph.D. thesis, Uppsala University, 1999).

234 Lennersand and Oja, 'Vitnande visionärer', 356.

235 Lennersand and Oja, *Livet går vidare.*

236 Per Sörlin, 'Witchcraft and Causal Links: Accounts of Maleficent Witchcraft in the Göta High Court in the Fifteenth and Sixteenth Centuries', *ARV: Nordic Yearbook of Folklore*, 62 (2006), 51–80; Per-Anders Östling, 'Blåkulla Journeys in Swedish Folklore', *ARV: Nordic Yearbook of Folklore*, 62 (2006), 81–122.

237 Soili-Maria Olli, *Visioner av världen: hädelse och djävulspakt i justitierevisionen 1680–1789* [Visions of the World: Blasphemy and Devil's Pact in Records of the Justiciary 1680–1789] (Ph.D. thesis, Umeå University, 2007).

238 Mikael Häll, *Skogsråets famn och Djävulens hamn: föreställningar om erotiska väsen i 1600- och 1700-talens Sverige* [The Roe's Bosom and the Devil's Guise: Imaginations of Erotic Beings in 17th- and 18th-Century Sweden] (Ph.D. thesis, Lund University, 2013).

239 Van Gent, *Magic, Body and the Self*; Bergenheim, *Den liderliga häxan.*

240 Toivo, *Witchcraft and Gender*; Nenonen and Toivo, *Writing Witch-Hunt Histories*; Marko Nenonen, 'Witch-Hunts in Europe: A New Geography', *ARV: Nordic Yearbook of Nordic Folklore*, 62 (2006), 165–86; Toivo, 'Discerning Voices and Values'.

241 Raisa M. Toivo, *Faith and Magic in Early Modern Finland* (Basingstoke, 2016).

242 Toivo, 'Gender, Sex and Cultures of Trouble'.

243 Raisa M. Toivo, 'What Did a Witch-Hunter in Finland Know About Demonology?' in Goodare, Voltmer, and Willumsen, *Demonology and Witch-Hunting*, 282–301.

244 Kallestrup and Toivo, *Contesting Orthodoxy.*

245 Nenonen, 'Witch-Hunts in Europe'; Nenonen and Toivo, *Writing Witch-Hunt Histories*, 1–16.

246 Jari Eilola, 'Lapsitodistajien kertomukset Ruotsin noitatapauksissa 1668–1676' [Child Witnesses' Stories in Witchcraft Trials in Sweden 1668–1676], E-journal *Kasvatus and Aika*, no. 3 (2009); 'Interpreting Children's Blåkulla Stories in Sweden (1675), in Goodare, Voltmer, and Willumsen, *Demonology and Witch-Hunting*, 327–44.

247 Marko Lamberg, *Häxmodern. Berättelsen om Malin Matsdotter* [The Witch's Mother. The Story about Malin Matsdotter] (Helsinki, 2021).

2 Spanish Netherlands—Holy Water, Witchcraft Powder, and the Collar

1 Gijswijt-Hofstra, 'From the Low Countries', 103.

2 The dialect of Dutch spoken in Flanders is also referred to as 'Flemish', but is not a language as such.

3 Vanysacker, 'Netherlands, Southern', 814.

4 I would like to thank Professor Dr Dries Vanysacker (KU Leuven, Belgium) for letting me use the transcriptions Professor Jos Monballyu (KU Leuven, Belgium) made of the original court records (see www.kuleuven-kulak.be/facult/rechten/Monballyu/Recht-lagelanden/Heksenvlaanderen/heksenindex.htm). I am also very grateful to Dr Alinda Damsma who provided me with the first, important assistance in translating Dutch court records into English. I would also like to thank Dr Marieke Krijnen for translating the Dutch court records into English and Professor Emerita Synnøve des Bouvrie for translating the Dutch court records into Norwegian.

5 Contrary to the court records from the other countries that are analysed in this book, in which case I knew the languages and could read the original court records myself, my knowledge of the Dutch language is restricted. I have received good help with the translation of the original court records; cf. note 4.

6 Spain had already conquered it, then left, and then came back to conquer it again in 1556.

7 Also called the Dutch Republic. De Waardt, 'Netherlands, Northern', 810.

8 De Waardt, 'Witchcraft and Wealth', 234.

9 De Waardt, 'Witchcraft and Wealth', 234.

10 There were two types of local officers in the Netherlands: a *baljuw* representing the prince in a county district, and a *schout*, an officer in a town.

11 De Waardt, 'Witchcraft and Wealth', 241.

12 Groningen had fifty executions, Gelderland forty-six, and Holland thirty-nine. De Waardt, 'Witchcraft and Wealth', 241.

13 Hans de Waardt underlines that the figure of 164 executed people is a minimum, and that 200 executions in witchcraft trials within the boundaries of the Republic of the United Provinces is a likely number. De Waardt, 'Witchcraft and Wealth', 241.

14 De Waardt, Witchcraft and Wealth', 241.

15 Vanysacker, 'Netherlands, Southern', 813, 814.

16 In the French-speaking counties of Artois, Cambrésis, Lille-Orchies, and Tournai, forty-seven people were executed; in the county of Hainault, thirty-one; in the Duchy of Brabant, thirty-one; in the county of Namur, 144; and in the Duchy of Luxembourg, between two and three thousand people were executed. Vanysacker, 'Netherlands, Southern', 815, Table 1.

17 Vanysacker, 'Netherlands, Southern', 816.

18 Vanysacker, 'Netherlands, Southern', 817.

19 One case in Bruges in 1459–60, and five cases in Bruges and Diksmuide in 1468.

20 Vanysacker, *Hekserij in Brugge*, 151; 'Netherlands, Southern', 815.

21 Vanysacker, 'Netherlands, Southern', 816.

22 Vanysacker, 'Netherlands, Southern', 816.

23 Orig. *viant*, meaning both 'enemy' and 'devil'. See Vanysacker, *Hekserij in Brugge*, 151.

24 Bruges, City Archives (SABrugge), OSA, 192, Verluydboeck 1490–1537, fo. 231v.

25 SABrugge, OSA, 192, Verluydboeck 1490–1537, fo. 12v.

26 SABrugge, OSA, 192, Verluydboeck 1490–1537, fo. 12v.

27 SABrugge, OSA, 192, Verluydboeck 1490–1537, fo. 12v.

28 SABrugge, OSA, 192, Verluydboeck 1490–1537, fo. 12v.

29 De Waardt, 'Witchcraft and Wealth', 236.

30 Practice of Criminal Matters.

31 Justinian Code.

32 De Waardt, 'Netherlands, Northern', 810.

33 De Waardt, 'Witchcraft and Wealth', 236.

34 Goodare, *European Witch-Hunt*, 246, with reference to Robert Muchembled, *Sorcières, justice et société aux 16ᵉ et 17ᵉ siècles* [Sorcerers, Justice and Society in the 16th and 17th Centuries] (Paris, 1987), 96–97.

35 Levack, *Witch-Hunt in Early Modern Europe*, 29–49.
36 A cumulative concept of witchcraft emerged from the late 1400s onwards. Willumsen, *Witches of the North*, 5; Levack, *Witch-Hunt in Early Modern Europe*, 32–51.
37 Vanysacker, 'Netherlands, Southern', 817.
38 It is still like this in Flanders today.
39 The Dutch word *schepen* has its origins in the Old Saxon word *scepino*, meaning judge. It is related to the German word *Schöffe*, a lay magistrate.
40 In Dutch *oordeelvinders*.
41 In English 'thing'.
42 In Dutch *dingplicht*.
43 *Schepenen* are often assigned portfolios such as culture, education, or city planning. They have several executive responsibilities relating to their portfolios, and thus assist the mayor in governing the town or city.
44 *The Witches' Hammer* (Speyer, 1486).
45 Martin del Rio, *Disquisitiones Magicae Libri Sex* (Leuven, 1599/1600). See Vanysacker, 'Netherlands, Southern', 817.
46 Jean Bodin, *De la demonomanie des sorciers* (Antwerp, 1586).
47 Willumsen, 'A Witchcraft Triangle', 252.
48 Warhem is a commune in today's Nord department in Northern France, on the border with Belgium. The distance from Warhem to Hondschoote is 8.3 kilometres.
49 Hondschoote, Archives communales, FF 7, fos. 16v–18v.
50 Orig. *Mahieu ghy en hadt my zulcx niet belooft.*
51 Orig. *Meester.*
52 Dunkirk is today a commune in Northern France, 10 kilometres from the Belgian border. The distance from Hondschoote to Dunkirk is 15.79 kilometres.
53 Ieper is the official name of this municipality in West Flanders; Ypres is the French name, which is commonly used. The distance from Hondschoote to Ieper is 28.1 kilometres.
54 Orig. *hebbende over de haeghe aldaer gheworpen een pacxken met een paer slaeplaeckens, een hemde, een lyveken ende voorts ghemeent te abondonneren ten zelven huuze een bedde, oorpal, slaeplaekens ende anders.*
55 Orig. *tardele.*
56 Orig. *Wat gaetet u an als ghy betaelt zyt?*
57 Orig. *Ende laet ons niet vallen in tentatie etc excluz.*
58 Orig. *dat myne heeren van der wet in heur examen tzelve hadden voorghezeit ende heur gheleert.*
59 Orig. *Waerop ende meer andere diversche indicien ende presumptien tvoornoompde Lynken gheen suffisante satisfactie hebbende connen gheven ende by dien metter torture van gheesselynghe gheexamineert gheweest hebbende.*
60 Orig. *voorts daernaer bloot ghemaect metten scheerze van alle heur haar ende ghezet omme bewaert te worden zonder slaepen.*
61 Orig. *Wat grote boezems zyn dat, ghy hebt de dobbel crone, tzyn boezems om een cuenyncken te zoghen.*
62 Orig. *Wiste ick dat eenich mensch tzelve ghedaen hadde, ick zoude hem zyn herte in zyn handt gheven.*
63 Orig. *Compere zyt gherust, tzal wel beteren.*
64 Orig. *Beyt ick zalt gaen zegghen.*
65 Orig. *den boosen gheest.*
66 Orig. *Jae.*
67 Orig. *Ende want op heur gheropen wiert dat zou Sathanas zoude afgaen ende heur betrouwen op God stellen, en heeft niet willen ofte connen spreken.*
68 Orig. *O Jhesus, Davids zone, ontfermt u mynder.*
69 Orig. *ghelyc oft pyne dede tzelve inne te nemen.*
70 The meaning of the second word is unclear. The first word, *du*, might mean 'you'.
71 Orig. *den boozen gheest.*
72 Orig. *den boozen vyandt haer gheholpen heeft an heure zoo haestighe ende subite doot.*

73 Probably incidents of *maleficium*.
74 Bruce Lincoln, 'Festivals and Massacres: Reflections on St. Bartholomew's Day', in Bruce Lincoln (ed.), *Discourse and the Construction of Society: Comparative Studies of Myth, Ritual, and Classification* (New York, 1989), 89–102.
75 Lincoln, 'Festivals and Massacres', 97.
76 Lincoln, 'Festivals and Massacres', 100.
77 Lincoln, 'Festivals and Massacres', 100.
78 Willumsen, 'Oral Transference of Ideas', 47.
79 Orig. *bezetene.*
80 Orig. *Ende want op heur gheropen wiert dat zou Sathanas zoude afgaen ende heur betrouwen op God stellen.*
81 De Waardt, 'Witchcraft and Wealth', 239.
82 De Waardt, 'Witchcraft and Wealth', 237–38.
83 Dries Vanysacker, *Hekserij in Brugge*, part IV, 159*ff*.; Rijksarchief Brugge (RAB), Stad Brugge, 624, fos. 9v–42r en 666 fos. 107r–185r (passim); Stadsarchief Brugge (SABrugge), Oud stadsarchief Brugge, 192, Verluydboeck 1611–1676, fo. 144r; Germain Vandepitte, 'Van heksen . . . en de boze vijand' [Of Witches . . . and the Evil Enemy], *Rond de Poldertorens*, 26, no. 1 (1985), 23–40. The *Verluidboeck* is a 'serial court source that recorded the sentences in serious criminal cases for the period 1490 to 1795, with a gap between 1555 and 1611', Lowagie Hannes, *Par desperacion. Zelfmoord in het graafschap Vlaanderen tijdens de Bourgondische periode* (1385–1500). Een sociologische aanpak [Par Deperacion. Suicide in the County of Flanders During the Burgundian Period 1385–1500. A Sociological Approach] (Ph.D. thesis, Ghent University, 2007), 23.
84 Capuchin, literally 'cloak', refers to 'a member of the Order of Friars Minor Capuchin forming since 1529 an austere branch of the first order of St Francis of Assisi engaged in missionary work and preaching'. *Merriam-Webster*, s.v. 'capuchin (*n.*)', www.merriam-webster.com/dictionary/capuchin (accessed 13 March 2020).
85 In Dutch *griffier.*
86 In Dutch *griffier van de Brugse vierschaar.*
87 In Dutch *keek.*
88 In Dutch *kanunnik.*
89 In Dutch *pastoor.*
90 Orig. *pypen ofte schreemen.*
91 In Dutch *de burgemeester van het 'corps'.*
92 Orig. *geusche boucken.* The word *geuzen* means beggars. This was a name assumed by the confederacy of Calvinist Dutch nobles, who from 1566 opposed Spanish rule in the Netherlands. In the Eighty Years' War, the Capture of Brielle by the Watergeuzen in 1572 provided the first foothold on land for the rebels, who would conquer the Northern Netherlands and establish an independent Dutch Republic. The name *geuzen* became a party title. The patriot party adopted the emblems of beggary, the wallet, and the bowl. As part of a propaganda campaign, prints and pamphlets were spread. The *geusche* books referred to during the trial of Mayken Karrebrouck were books related to the patriot party. See Maurits Sabbe, 'Brabantsche spotdichten op de nederlaag van Christian IV van Denemarken te Lutter 1626' [Brabant Satirical Poems About the Defeat of Christian IV of Denmark at Lutter 1626], *Verslagen en Mededelingen van Koninklijke Vlaamse Academie voor Taal- en Letterkunde* (1931), 747–57.
93 In Dutch *doekje voor vrouwen*, presumably sanitary towel for women.
94 Orig. *Ick zal het besterven, ick zal hier niet licht van af komen.*
95 Orig. *wonende in de Lane.*
96 In Dutch *het 'franchijne'-briefje met kruisjes.*
97 Orig. *geschrifte.*
98 Orig. *tegenschlagen.*
99 Orig. *ter torture metten bank.*

100 In Dutch *rokende pijnkeldertje*.
101 Orig. *daer is alreede (reeds) een jonghen duyvel*.
102 Orig. *schudde en beefde*.
103 Orig. *ghenoueh clouekeliek*.
104 Orig. *alleene op haer beenen*.
105 In Dutch *schepenbank*.
106 Orig. *maar Mayken bleef volhouden dat ze niets misdaan had*.
107 Orig. *tooveresse*.
108 Orig. *Ick behoire Godt Almachtich toe ende dat men haer pynichde ten onghelycke*.
109 Orig. *de bosen*.
110 In Dutch *hadden beiden elkaar uitgescholden voor tovenares*.
111 In Dutch *schepenbank*.
112 Orig. *tooveresse*.
113 In Dutch *baljuw van de gevangenis*.
114 Orig. *Mayken, sijt ghij daer, ick en weet van u niet te segghen*.
115 Orig. *noch ick van u*.
116 A neck collar, which was a tool of torture. A metal collar with a lock was placed around the necks of the imprisoned people in witchcraft trials during interrogation under torture. Such collars were thick and heavy; they often had protruding spikes.
117 In Dutch *bezweek ze volledig*.
118 Orig. *dat van al die zij betoovert heeft, haer leet es ende daervan rekenynghe zal gheven voor God*.
119 Presumably the devil, as she confessed earlier that she called him 'her friend'.
120 Orig. *de conste*.
121 In Dutch *Haar duivel was een zwarte man die zich nooit als een hond, geit of bok vertoonde*.
122 In Dutch *ingesmeerd met poeder*.
123 In Dutch *door de schouw naartoe gevlogen in gezelschap van haar lief*.
124 In Dutch *welk kwaad ze zouden aanrichten*.
125 Orig. *vleselijke conversatie*.
126 In Dutch *De conversatie verliep zoals met een gewone man, maar zijn zaad voelde ijskoud aan*.
127 In Dutch *Ze had hem geen eerbetuigingen bewezen, en ze had vaak een pak slaag gekregen, aangezien ze niet veel kwaad wou aanrichten*.
128 In Dutch *daarop werd ze van de halsband bevrijd*.
129 SABrugge, Verluydboeck 1611–1676, fo. 144r.
130 Morbecque is today a commune in the Nord department in Northern France. It is an inland commune, 57 kilometres southeast of Dunkirk.
131 The court for judicial matters related to the district, the *leen*.
132 Gent, Universiteitsbibliotheek, Hs. 654, fos. 126v–127v.
133 Orig. *ghenaemt soo gy beleden hebt Abraham Hoghelaer*.
134 Orig. *dat gy den raedt van den duyfel [volghende]*.
135 Orig. *u begheven hebt tot het abominabel crimen van tooverye*.
136 Orig. *ghemaeckt hebt een accoordt en compact afgaende ende loochenende Godt almachtigh met syne heylighe moeder*.
137 Orig. *met den selven alsdan nemende vleeschelycke conversatie, als wanneer gy van hem ontfanghen hebt een teecken ofte stigma op uwen rugghe, afgaende alsdan oock uw doopsel*.
138 In the court records of witchcraft trials, 'examination' is often used in the same meaning as 'interrogation'.
139 Orig. *hebbende u altoos gheaccompangniert naer texamen ende van daer wederom naer de vanghenisse, u troostende dat hy u nimmer meer soude verlaeten*.
140 Orig. *met uwen aesem, ende het selve raeckende met uw handt, soo tselve lagh in de wiegh*.
141 Orig. *eenen stuyver* (five-cent piece).
142 Orig. *eenen Luyckschen vyfgrootnaer*.
143 Orig. *daervan sy corts daernaer gheswolten is*.
144 Orig. *vyf stuyvers*.
145 Orig. *Jae, gy altoos continuerende in uw boos leven*.

146 Orig. *eenen dobbelen stuyver.*
147 Orig. *eenen scheut van der mauwe.*
148 Orig. *stuyver*, a five-cent piece, five pennies.
149 Orig. *oortkens*, a specific Flemish coin.
150 Orig. *met blaesen van uwen aesem in haeren necke.*
151 Orig. *heusel*: a small animal living in a meadow or pasture.
152 Orig. *over welcke persoonen gy nochtans geen macht en hebt ghehadt, so ghy seght.*
153 Orig. *Is maer ghecommen te quelen, so sy noch doet.*
154 Orig. *thien oortkens.*
155 Orig. *cruysstraete.*
156 Orig. *dycken.*
157 Orig. *van de welcke sy seer ghecaresseert wierden.*
158 Orig. *Tot welcke plaetsen gy vertransporteert wiert door toedoen van den selven uwen duyvel.*
159 Orig. *vlooght daermede ter vierstede uyt.*
160 Orig. *verscheyde stonden met u commen slaepen, u vleesschelyk bekennende, wesende van ander posture als eenen man, als ghevoelt hebbende dat hy klauwen hadde aen syn voeten.*
161 Orig. *Soo al tselve behoorlyck ende volcommentlyck tuwen laste is ghebleken, by uwe eyghen confessie ende andersints.*
162 Orig. *waerom ende [om] alle dese abominabele feyten ende tooveryen, mannen van desen hove wysen ende condemneren u gheiusticeert te worden metten viere soo datter de doot naer volght ende het lichaem alsoo verbrant, ghestelt te worden ter plaetse patibulaire, dienende ander voor exempel.*
163 Orig. *verclaerende voorts alle uwe goederen, al waer de selve ghestaen ofte ghelegen mochten wesen, gheconfisqueert ten profyte van de geene daerop recht hebbende.*
164 Orig. *de costen ende impensen van iustitie alvooren ghededuceert.*
165 See for instance the case of Karen Jonsdatter, Vardø 1654, who tried to cast a spell on Laurits Olufsen's boat, but did not succeed because his crew was God-fearing. Statsarkivet i Tromsø (SATØ) [Regional State Archives of Tromsø], Sorenskriveren i Finnmarks arkiv (SF) [Archives of the Finnmark District Magistrate], no. 8, fo. 132v.
166 Orig. *Ende alsoo wesende int voornomde verbondt, hebt van uwen duyvel vyf of ses keeren tiaers onfaen poeder van het coleur van grofnaghele.*
167 See the chapters on Denmark and Norway in this book.
168 Orig. *sonder nochtans ghesien te hebben wie met tfluytken speelde.*
169 Cohen, 'Back Talk'.

3 Northern Germany—Bloksberg, Red Rider, and Torture 'in a Humane Way'

1 As Denmark was in a union with Norway until 1814, the duchy of Schleswig fell under Norway for a period as well. From 1376 to 1386, the district was occupied by the duchy of Holstein-Rendsburg; from 1386 to 1390, the district was Holstein-Rendsburg's fief, *len*, under Denmark, which changed its name to Schleswig; in 1424, Danish supremacy over Schleswig was acknowledged.
2 The town of Bordesholm developed around 1330, when the abbey of Neumünster, founded in 1127, was moved to an island in Lake Bordesholm. A village grew around the shore of the lake, likely providing services for the abbey. Because of the abbey, Bordesholm became the cultural and economic centre of the region between Kiel and Neumünster. The abbey was closed in 1566, during the Reformation. Duke Hans the Elder of Schleswig-Holstein-Haderslev converted Bordesholm Abbey into an educational institution the same year. Duke Hans died in 1580. It then became a Latin school, which was dissolved in 1665. This was the beginning of the University of Kiel. Today, the district is called Rendsberg-Eckenförde. Caspar Danckwerth, *Neue Landesbeschreibung der zwey Herzogthümer Schleswich und Holstein* [New Description of the Two Duchies Schleswig and Holstein] (1652), 191.

3 In German *Freie Reichsstadt*.
4 In German *Reichsunmittelbarkeit*. In Danish *rigsumiddelbarhed*. The city was founded in 1143. Friedrich II elevated the town of Lübeck, in German *Hansestadt Lübeck*, to the status of an imperial free city in 1226. It was the leading city of the Hanseatic League.
5 *Domkapitel* refers to the jurisdiction of a Catholic cathedral. Næss, 'Presters og prestefruers roller, 113.
6 Schulte, *Hexenverfolgung in Schleswig-Holstein*, 107.
7 Thomas Robisheaux, 'The German Witch Trials', in Brian P. Levack (ed.), *The Oxford Handbook of Witchcraft in Early Modern Europe and Colonial America* (Oxford, 2013), 179–98, at 179.
8 Goodare, *European Witch-Hunt*, 29.
9 Volmer and Wisenstein, *Das Hexenregister*, 31; Rita Voltmer, *Hexen: Wissen was stimmt* [Witches: Knowing What Is True] (Freiburg im Breisgau, 2008), 23; Rita Voltmer, 'Hexenverfolgungen im Maas-Rhein-Mosel-Raum' [Witch-Hunts in the Meuse-Rhine-Moselle Region], in Franz Irsigler (ed.), *Beziehungen, Begegnungen und Konflikte in einem europäischen Kernraum von der Spätantike bis zum 19. Jahrhundert* [Relations, Encounters and Conflicts in a European Core Area from Late Antiquity to the 19th Century] (Trier, 2006), 153–87; Behringer, *Witchcraft Persecutions in Bavaria*, 122, 232; Goodare, *European Witch Hunt*, 239, 245; Robisheaux, 'German Witch Trials', 186; H. C. Erik Midelfort, *Witch Hunting in Southwestern Germany 1562–1684* (Stanford, 1972), 85–163; Behringer, *Hexen und Hexenprozesse*, 53, 183, 196–97, 361–64; Gerhard Schormann, *Hexenprozesse in Nordwestdeutschland* (Hildesheim, 1977), 1–30; *Hexenprozesse in Deutschland* (Göttingen, 1981), 13, 84; Willumsen, 'Witchcraft Triangle', 247–52.
10 Goodare, *European Witch-Hunt*, 27–29.
11 The duchy of Schleswig covered an area of about 60 kilometres north and 70 kilometres south of the current border between Germany and Denmark.
12 Frederik III (1415–93) ruled from 1452 until his death. He was crowned king of Germany as Frederick IV in 1440.
13 Adolf was duke of Schleswig-Holstein-Gottorp (1527–86) and resided in Gottorp Castle, which is situated close to the town Schleswig; he died in Schleswig; John the Elder [Hans den Ældre] (1521–80), was duke of Schleswig-Holstein-Haderslev, resided in Hansborg Castle, Haderslev, and died in Haderslev.
14 The House of Gottorp was a branch of the House of Oldenburg. The duchy of Holstein was a Danish rigslen until 1864. Holstein was part of the German-Roman Empire until the disintegration in 1806.
15 The Treaty of Roskilde in 1658 and the Treaty of Copenhagen in 1660.
16 Schulte, *Hexenverfolgung*, 115–43.
17 Unverhau, *Von Toverschen und Kunsthfruwen*.
18 Schulte, *Hexenverfolgung*, 67; Goodare, *European Witch-Hunt*, 28; Behringer, *Hexen und Hexenprozesse*, 194.
19 Schulte, *Hexenverfolgung*, 69.
20 Schulte, *Hexenverfolgung*, 68–69.
21 Christian V ruled from 1670 until 1699.
22 In Danish, *Danske Lov av 1683*.
23 Schulte, *Hexenverfolgung*, 70.
24 Schulte, *Hexenverfolgung*, 70–71.
25 Schulte, *Hexenverfolgung*, 72.
26 Schulte, *Hexenverfolgung*, 72.
27 Schulte *Hexenverfolgung*, 72.
28 Of the total accused, 714 were women and 75 were men. Schulte, *Hexenverfolgung*, 97.
29 Schulte, *Hexenverfolgung*, 98.
30 Robisheaux, 'German Witch Trials', 180.
31 Robisheaux, 'German Witch Trials', 180.
32 The Copenhagen articles of 1547 and Article 8 in the Kalundborg Recess of 1576.

33 Orig. 'Peinliche Gerichtsordnung Kaiser Karls V'. Schulte, *Hexenverfolgung*, 35; Johann Diefenbach, *Der Hexenwahn in Deutschland* [The Witch Mania in Germany]. Verlag von Franz Kirchheim (Mainz, 1886; repr., Fotomechanischer Neudruck, Leipzig, 1978), 156.

34 Schulte, *Hexenverfolgung*, 38.

35 Schulte, *Hexenverfolgung*, 35.

36 Schulte, *Hexenverfolgung*, 37.

37 In German *kaiserlicher Anteil*. During the period dealt with in this chapter, 1607–69, the German-Roman Emperors, the House of Habsburg, were: Rudolf II (1575–1612), Matthias (1612–19), Ferdinand II (1619–37), Ferdinand III (1636–57), Ferdinand IV associate king (1653–54), and Leopold I (1658–1705).

38 In German *die Rechtsprechung sogenannten Volksgerichten. Sie setzen sich aus der Gruppe bäuerlicher Hufner, d. h. Bauern im Besitz vollständiger (Boden-)Hufen, zusammen, die unter Vorsitz eines landesherrlichen Beamten urteilen.* Schulte, *Hexenverfolgung*, 41.

39 Schulte, *Hexenverfolgung*, 41–42.

40 Schulte, *Hexenverfolgung*, 82.

41 Goodare, *European Witch-Hunt*, 194.

42 Schulte, *Hexenverfolgung*, 82.

43 Jens C. Johansen, 'Denmark: The Sociology of Accusation', in Ankarloo and Henningsen, *Early Modern European Witchcraft*, 339–65, at 340; Schulte, *Hexenverfolgung*, 82–83.

44 In a European context, this was the first example of automatic appeal in witchcraft cases heard at secular courts. Johansen, 'Denmark: Sociology of Accusation', 341.

45 Goodare, *European Witch-Hunt*, 195.

46 Article 48 of the *Carolina* formulates five *Indizien zu einer Anzeige wegen Zauberei für ausreichend halt.* Schormann, *Hexenprozesse in Nordwestdeutschland*, 1.

47 *Hexenprozesse sind Strafverfahren ohne Straftat.* Schormann, *Hexenprozesse in Nordwestdeutschland*, 1.

48 Orig. *Die Folter war im Rahmen des neuen Beweisrechts da Mittel zur Wahrheitsfindung. Geständnis und Folter bildeten eine 'unheilige Allianz.* Unverhau, 'Kieler Hexen und Zauberer', 82.

49 Goodare, *European Witch-Hunt*, 195.

50 Orig. *Es zeichnet sich wohl ab: Wir müssen mit beträchtlichen Eigenheiten der schleswig-holsteinischen Hexenverfolgung rechnen (. . .) Es ist nicht zu übersehen, daß der akkusatorische Prozeß nach seiner Einleitung in die Regel wie ein inquisitorischer verlief.* Unverhau, 'Akkusationsprozess—Inquisitionsprozess', 116.

51 Robisheaux, 'German Witch Trials', 193.

52 *Das dreimalige Durchstehen der Tortur.* Schormann, *Hexenprozesse in Nordwestdeutschland*, 39.

53 Diefenbach, *Hexenwahn in Deutschland*, 157.

54 *Carolina*, Article 48, *eins guten Vernunfftigen Richter.* Schormann, *Hexenprozesse in Nordwestdeutschland*, 39.

55 Schulte, *Hexenverfolgung*, 36.

56 Diefenbach, *Hexenwahn in Deutschland*, 156.

57 Robisheaux, 'German Witch Trials', 193.

58 Titled *Das Licht der Seele.* Schulte, *Hexenverfolgung*, 16.

59 Schulte, *Hexenverfolgung*, 17–19.

60 Unverhau, *Von Töverschen und Kunsthfruwen*, 30–32.

61 Schulte, *Hexenverfolgung*, 38.

62 Rolf Schulte, *Man as Witch* (Basingstoke, 2009), 196.

63 Professor Niels Hemmingsen's book had a great impact on Denmark and Schleswig, not least because it was used by students of theology for many years. It was titled *Admonitio de superstitionibus magicis vitandis* [Admonition to Avoid Witchcraft]. Nortorf minister Samuel Meiger's book was titled *Von List bzv. der Verschlagenheit der Hexen.* Schulte, *Hexenverfolgung*, 22–26.

64 The term is found in court records from the Preetz Priory. Schulte, *Hexenverfolgung*, 16.

65 Schulte, *Hexenverfolgung*, 38.
66 In Danish *Trolddomsforordning av 1617*.
67 Orig. *rette troldfolck*.
68 Schulte, *Hexenverfolgung*, 83.
69 *Ankläger und Zeugen sind Männer, aber auch Frauen; Verfolger und Gerichtsorgane sind bereitwillige Obrigkeiten in Gestalt eines Gutsherrn, eines protestantischen Domkapitels, eines Bauerngerichtes in einem Amt oder des Rates einer Stadt; der Tathergang ist eine absurd erscheinende Beschuldigung, aufgrund derer mehrere Menschen in einer sadistischen Quälerei schließlich umgebracht oder ihnen die Lebensgrundlagen entzogen werden.* Schulte, *Hexenverfolgung*, 13.
70 A. Wolff, *Flensburger Hexenprozesse, Aus Flensburgs Vorzeit, Beiträge und Geschichte der Stadt Flensburg* (Flensburg, 1887), 17–37.
71 Schulte, *Hexenverfolgung*, 10–11.
72 These are loanwords that entered into the German language.
73 Dagmar Unverhau, 'Flensburger Hexenprozesse (1504, 1607/08) erneut betrachtet. Die "Hexe" als "Ärztin"?' [Flensburg Witch Trials (1504, 1607/08) Revisited. The 'Witch' as 'Doctor'?], *Grenzfriedenshefte*, no. 3/4 (1984–85), 171–87, at 175.
74 Orig. *Das Visier des Rates zu Flensburg*.
75 Orig. *Toverei*.
76 Orig. *Königlichen Stadtfogedes*.
77 Orig. *Achtbarn*, meaning honest, revered, of high esteem.
78 Orig. *Kämmerer*.
79 Unverhau, 'Flensburger Hexenprozesse', 179.
80 Unverhau, 'Flensburger Hexenprozesse', 176.
81 Orig. *wegen allehandt anzeigen und vordachts pinlich examiniert unde aufgehört worden*.
82 Orig. *Demnach ist sie durch einhellige Votis beider Bürgermeister und Ratsverwandten zum Feuer condemniert und verurteilt*.
83 Orig. *der habe auch sonsten, wenn ihr Mann nicht zu Hause gewesen, bei ihr gelegen*.
84 Orig. *unheimliche*.
85 Orig. *druddehalf*.
86 Orig. *schwart und rugh*. Today, *rugh* is spelled *ruug*.
87 Orig. *se hebbe ehme grueth und koll tho etende gegeven up dem Boens und he ethe vele*. Today, *Boens* in Low German is *Böhn*, referring to the German word for stage, *Bühne*.
88 Orig. *bewunden*.
89 For an illustration, see *Die Emeis von Dr. Johannes Geiler von Keiserperg*, 1517.
90 Orig. *dass se vor 3 oder 4 Jahren wehre von der Welt gewesen*.
91 Orig. *Wedefruive*.
92 Orig. *hasenbandt*.
93 Orig. *Abwehrzauber*.
94 Orig. *Eggestall, eiserne Eggenzähne*.
95 Orig. *Norder Porten*.
96 Schulte, *Hexenverfolgung*, 10.
97 Orig. *Demnach ist sie durch einhellige Votis beider Bürgermeister und Ratsverwandten zum Feuer condemniert und verurteilt*.
98 Orig. *Da könnte jede Zauberin lernen, was sie vielleicht selbst einmal hersagen mußte*. Schormann, *Hexenprozesse in Nordwestdeutschland*, 133.
99 Unverhau, 'Flensburger Hexenprozesse', 185; Schulte, *Hexenverfolgung*, 10–11.
100 *Hexenmuster* is the word used by Unverhau. Unverhau, 'Flensburger Hexenprozesse', 178.
101 This personal demon differs from the personal demons mentioned in the chapters of Denmark and Norway when it comes to sexual intercourse with the woman entering into the devil's pact.
102 Walter J. Ong, *Orality and Literacy. The Technologizing of the Word* (London, 1982), 36–75.
103 Dagmar Unverhau states that such ideas are found in court records from Schleswig in the 1540s and 1550s. Unverhau, *Von Toverschen und Kunsthfruwen*, 30–32.
104 Orig. *Amt Bordesholm*. Today, this area belongs to the district of Rendsberg-Eckenförde.

105 Frederick III was son of Princess Augusta of Denmark, daughter of King Frederick II of Denmark and Duke Johann Adolf of Schleswig-Holstein. One of the daughters of Frederick III, Hedwig Eleonore (1636–1715) was married to King Charles X of Sweden in 1654. Lis Granlund, 'Queen Hedwig Eleonora of Sweden: Dowager, Builder, and Collector', in Clarissa Campbell Orr (ed.), *Queenship in Europe 1660–1815: The Role of the Consort* (Cambridge, 2004), 56–76.

106 Anton II von Wietersheim (1587–1647), jurist and chancellor of Duke Friedrich III of Schleswig-Holstein-Gottorf. Theodor Stenzel, 'Zur Genealogie der Familie von Wietersheim', *Vierteljahrsschrift für Wappen-, Siegel- und Familienkunde*, 8 (1880), 135–63.

107 Orig. *Amtsscreiber.*

108 Schulte, *Hexenverfolgung*, 135.

109 Schulte, *Hexenverfolgung*, 135.

110 Landesarchiv Schleswig-Holstein (LSH), Abt. 7, No. 1758[I], Anneke Rickers, fo. 6rv.

111 The pages belonging to the dossier are kept together in a folder. In the dossier, the pages are mixed when it comes to chronology. Fos. 6rv, 7rv are dated 14 May 1641. Fo. 5rv concerns the permission to use torture and is dated 22 May 1641, in ink. At the bottom of fo. 5r, 26/5 1641 is written in pencil. Fo. 8v contains an inscription addressed to Anton von Wieterszheimb, Geheimerath und Candtzler, dated 26 May 1641. Fo. 9r begins with *Friedrich* and is dated 16 May 1641, addressed to Johann Pundt, and received 26 May. Fo. 9v is blank. Fo. 10r is dated 5/6 1641. On fo. 12v, 5 June 1641 is written on the page. Fo. 13r begins with 'Friederich' and is dated with ink 5 June 1641. In the page's margin 5/6, 1641 is also written in ink. Fo. 13v is blank. Fo. 14r is blank. Fo. 14v is addressed to Johann Pundt, dated 5 June 1641. Fo. 1r is dated 10 June 1641. Fo. 1v is blank. Fos. 2r–4v are dated 10 June 1641. Fo. 15a begins with *Friederich* and is dated, in ink, 13 June 1641. The same date in pencil is written in the page's margin. Fo. 15v is blank. The next page is blank. On the back of this page, *den 13 Junij ao 41* [The 13 June Anno 1641] is written. The next two pages are blank. The next is paginated fo. 16r, a blank page. Fo. 16v has the inscription *Friedrichen*, dated *Gottorff, den 11 Junij 1641.*

112 Von Buchwald was a noble family in Schleswig-Holstein, with wide outrunners. In older times, the family name was written as Bockwolde, which has its origin in the old Wagrien in the outskirts of the city Lübeck.

113 Orig. *Candtzler.*

114 Orig. *Lottding.*

115 Orig. *Zauberey.*

116 Orig. *eine Flechte Haer, einen mißinges ringk einen ledern sonnkell und ein Kluwen Zwirn.*

117 It remains unclear whether Hans Embke ran a farm owned by Jurgen Nefen, or whether Embke owned the farm himself.

118 Orig. *Kaeks.*

119 Orig. *Beclagtinne Verleüchnet es abermalß, und will nirgent worum wißen.*

120 The group of peasants who decided on the verdict.

121 Orig. *Landrecht.*

122 Orig. *Lottding.*

123 LSH, Abt. 7, No. 1758[I], Anneke Rickers, fo. 8v. Fo. 8v is the back page of a large sheet of paper starting with fo. 5r and contains an inscription addressed to 'Anton von Wieterszheimb, Geheimerath und Candtzler', dated in ink 26 May 1641. A note in the margin on page 5r reads'16/5 1641'.

124 Orig. *unser gnedigen befehlig.*

125 Orig. *vermittelst corporlichen Eydes verificiren werden, du darauff der Holsten erkandtnus volnstrecken, Jedoch menschlicher Weise nach mit dem scharffen examine verfahren laßest* (. . .) *vermittelst corporlichen Eydes verificiren werden, du darauff der Holsten erkandtnus volnstrecken*. LSH, Abt. 7, No. 1758[I], Anneke Rickers, fo. 9r, headline Friedrich, dated 26 May 1641.

126 Fo. 10r–11r. On fo. 10r, line 3, it is written that she was tortured on 2 June. On fo. 10r, 5/6 1641 is written in pencil. On fo. 12v is written: *Vhrgicht detz zum Bordesholm*

eingezogenen Weibes Anneke Rickers. On fo. 12v, at the bottom of the page, it says: 'P. Gottorff d. 5 June 1641'. The document *Vhrgicht* consists of a total of five written folio pages and is the longest continuous text in the dossier.

127 Orig. *ausserhalb der Tortur.*

128 Orig. abbreviated Thlr., Thaler, a currency used. In the Nordic countries, this currency was called *Daler.*

129 Orig. *hat Abgeschlagen.*

130 Orig. *sie thäte es woll begehren.*

131 Orig. *in der scheune.*

132 Orig. *Ich trede hir auer dat Nest, und vorlathe unsern Hern Jesum Christ.*

133 *Anneken, wiltu mir freÿen, so will ich dir woll haben, unnd dir einen Himbten geldt geben, doch mustu Zuforderst mit mir wrangen.* The verb *wrangen*, according to Otto Mensing in his *Schleswig-Holsteinischer Wörterbuch* [Schleswig-Holsteinian Dictionary], vol. 5 (Neumünster, 1935), has four meanings: (i) to work hard (against any kind of resistence); (ii) to push, urge, press; (iii) to wrestle, scuffle, beat; or (iv) sitting on a chair/lying on a bed, but moving all the time. The word *wrangen* might also be interpreted as 'first we must work together in performing evil deeds'. However, looking at the rest of the confession, it is likely that here, *wrangen* means having sexual intercourse.

134 Orig. *er hette Sie bedacht, Sie muste ihm etwas wieder geben.*

135 Orig. *welches Sie ihm dan gegeben.*

136 Orig. *abfurdern'.*

137 Orig. *herfurgelanget.*

138 Orig. *dar sich dan befunden das es kein geldt, sondern Pferdedreck gewesen.* LSH, Abt. 7, No. 1758[I], Anneke Rickers zu Buchwald, Amt Bordesholm, wegen Zauberei, unpaginated document dated 10 June 1641, point 9.

139 Orig. *Übell angeführet.*

140 Orig. *Eiderbrocks Holtz.*

141 Orig. *Du dienest io mich waß wiltu nach der Kirchen thun, Des Sontages habe ich mit dir Zuwircken, darauff Sie wieder Zurugke gang.*

142 Orig. *wirken.*

143 Orig. *in eines schwartzen hundes gestaldt ihr erschienen.*

144 Orig. *du bist nun mein, unnd solt auch mein bleiben.*

145 Orig. *des Hirdten Frau to Bockwald.*

146 Orig. *Hirauff ist Ihr Zugemüthe geführet das Sie velleichte dieses alles der Ratkschen mit unwahrheit nachredete.*

147 Orig. *wan sie auch in stucken Zurißen wurde.*

148 Orig. 'To J. Pundt' is written in the margin. The document begins with 'Frederich'.

149 Orig. *Nothding.*

150 The word 'not' could be omitted without changing the meaning. It makes the question resemble a 'tag question', which consists of operator plus pronoun, with or without a negative particle; the choice and tense of the operator are determined by the verb phrase in the superordinate clause. If the superordinate clause is positive, the tag is negative, and vice versa.

151 Orig. *Zurerst ob nicht wahr daß (. . .).*

152 Orig. *unnd Sie in der güte gefraget worden.* This is an expression often found in court records to denote that confirmation is given of the accused person's own free will, willingly, not as a result of torture on that occasion.

153 Orig. *Dieser Reüter wehre sie in der scheüne erschienen, sagde sie furm gerichte.*

154 Orig. *freüen.*

155 Orig. *daß Sie in sein begehren gewilliget.*

156 Orig. *Ob nicht wahr, dass Sie sich darauff gegen der Ratschen beclaget dass dieselbe sie übell angeführet welche ihr da Zufrieden gesprochen und einer thaler vorehret.* LSH, Abt. 7, No. 1758[I], Anneke Rickers zu Buchwald, Amt Bordesholm, wegen Zauberei, unpaginated document dated 10 June 1641, point 10.

157 Orig. *Stuten.*

158 Orig. *Ob nicht wahr daß daßelbe Pulver schwartz anzusehen unnd lebendig gewesen.*
159 Orig. *Sie wolte ihm woll rath Zue seinen Pferden schaffen.*
160 Orig. *unnd solte sich anstellen, alß ob Sie es herauß genommen hette.*
161 Orig. *daß konte ihr gleich viel thun.*
162 Orig. *sie solte aber Jurgen Neven Frawen sagen daß solches Clauß Embken unnd Eggert Resen Frawens Veruhrsachten.*
163 Orig. *Diese Puncte sein der Rickerschen im Gerichte offentlich vorgehalten, und hat Sie diesselbe mit Ja bekrefftiget, daß Sie darauff leben und sterben wolle.*
164 Orig. *denselben ganck auch gehen mugte, welchen sie vielleicht gehen müsste.*
165 Orig. *Hirauff ist von Holsten erkandt.*
166 Orig. *In Peinlichen Sachen Anneke Rickers welche ihren Christlichen glauben verleuchnet und von Gott abgefallen, auch dem Ancleger Jurgen Nefen an seinem Viehe schaden zugefügt.*
167 Orig. *Eure Fÿrstliche Gnaden.*
168 The letter is addressed to 'Fÿrsten' and 'Herrn Fredrichen', to be opened by the 'Candtzler' at the 'Candtzlery', dated 11 June 1641, 'Prad: Gottorff'. LSH, Abt. 7, No. 1758[l], Anneke Rickers zu Buchwald, Amt Bordesholm, wegen Zauberei, fo. 16v.
169 See the chapters on Denmark, Scotland, and Norway in this book.
170 The Romantic Movement in Europe started towards the end of the 1700s and reached its peak in most areas in the period from approximately 1800 to 1850. The best-known works from Germany are the collections of folk tales by the brothers Grimm, published from 1812 onwards.
171 Willumsen, *Witches of the North*, 255.
172 Orig. *Buler.*
173 Orig. *Unnd wehre d. Pulver Schwartz wie Büchßenpulver anzusehen: unnd lebendig gewesen.*
174 Orig. *solches solte weiß machen.*
175 Schulte, *Hexenverfolgung*, 77–79.
176 Schulte, *Hexenverfolgung*, 79.
177 Konrad v. Anten was executive officer in legal questions at Lübeck Chapter. His tractate was published in Lübeck one year before he died in 1591. Schulte, *Hexenverfolgung*, 28–29.
178 Ericus Mauritius (1631–91) was Professor of Law at the University of Tübingen, later at Kiel. From 1671, he held a position at the highest German court, *Reichskammergericht*, in Speyer. Schulte, *Hexenverfolgung*, 29–30.
179 Henricus Michaelis (1627–78) was executive officer in legal questions, *Syndikus*, at Stralsund and in 1665–68 docent at the University of Kiel, then executive officer in legal questions in Lübeck. Schulte, *Hexenverfolgung*, 30–31.
180 Friedrich Spee von Langenfeld (1591–1635) was a Jesuit, ordained as Catholic priest in Mainz in 1622. He became professor at the University of Paderborn 1622 and taught later at the universities of Speyer, Wesel, Trier, and Cologne. In 1631, he anonymously published in 1631 *Cautio Criminalis*, a book which became very influential in learned, judicial discussions. Schulte, *Hexenverfolgung*, 29–31.
181 Orig. *Anno 1669.5. 'Octobr: Dienstags ist auss geheiss und im nahmen Rev: Capituli Lubecens: Zu Hemmelstörff vorm gehöffte peinlich Recht über hernachgenannte und daselbst för offenem Gerichte geführte person gehegt und gehalten'.* LSH, Abt. 268 No. 673. The court records contain three unpaginated folio pages. On the last page is written '*Vhrgichte Vnd Bekentniße auch Vrteil Vm dem Execution Anna Speieln im Jahre benefi iij*'. Hemmelsdorf is a small village close to Lake Hemmelsdorf. Gramsdorf is close to Hemmelmark, a manorial estate. The *Domkapitel* in Lübeck was the authority for that area. It owned villages and estates, *Lübsche Dörfer*. 'Die Freie und Hansestadt Lübeck hatte wie andere große Städte größere Arelae außerhalb der Stadtmauern zum Schutz ihrer Handelsmöglichkeiten (. . .) der juristische Raum übertraf die geographische Stadt beträchtlich.* Schulte, *Hexenverfolgung*, 154, note 270.
182 Schulte, *Hexenverfolgung*, 140.
183 Anna Spielen confessed that she had *von der jüngst verbranten Trine Hildebrandes gelehrt.* LSH, Abt. 268 No. 673.

184 LSH, Abt. 268 No. 675, Expences Hemmelsdorfer trials. During her imprisonment, Catrine Hildebrand cut open her windpipe, so that air could not pass through her mouth, and she had to be treated and bandaged for this. The cost was entered into the documented expenses. Hemmelsdorf was a town at the beach of Hemmelsdorfer See, to the north of Lübeck, close to the Baltic Sea.

185 *Gebiet Domkapitel Lübeck.* Orig. *So hat Ein hochwollwürdiges Dohmcapitul dess hohen Stiffts Lübeck dero von Gott den Allmächtigen auf dieser welt anbefohlenes Ampt verrichten.* LSH, Abt. 268 No. 673.

186 Orig. *und diese Anna Spielen, alss eine wegen vorbesagter ubeltaht berüchtigte person in Ihre des Dohmcapitulss Verwahrsam und gefängniss, eine solche berüchtigung zu erforschen, und den zu schüldiger fortsetzung der Heiligen Justitz diess orts einweisen und bewahren lassen.* LSH, Abt. 268 No. 673.

187 Orig. *beÿ Verschiedenen in Gramstörff wohnhafften Ihren benachbahrten Zauberey halber in argwohn genommen anrüchtig und* deferiret *worden.* LSH, Abt. 268 No. 673.

188 Orig. *Und demnach anfangs* Venerabilis Capituli *Herren Deputirte dieselbe in der güthe, auch nachgehend durch die scharffe frage examiniren laßen.* LSH, Abt. 268 No. 673.

189 Orig. *so hat sich endlich aussgesagt und gestanden.* LSH, Abt. 268 No. 673.

190 Orig. *Daß sie Zaubern könte, und solches vor etzlichen jahren von der jüngst verbranten Trine Hildebrandes gelehrt: die Ihr einen weissen Stock gegeben, welchen sie angegriffen, und gesagt, Ick griep an dissen Stock, verlate Gott, und wilt mit dißen Düfel holden.*

191 Orig. *Bekennet, daß sie dadurch Ihren Geist oder Teüfel verstanden, so Paul geheißen.* LSH, Abt. 268 No. 673.

192 Orig. *Bekennet, daß Sie mit dem Teüfel etzlich mahl gebuhlet.* LSH, Abt. 268 No. 673.

193 Orig. *Bekennet daß sie etzliche mahl auf den Bloxberg gewesen, und auf einem Zigenbock dahin geritten.* LSH, Abt. 268 No. 673.

194 Orig. *Bekennet, daß sie daselbst einige nahmhaffte personen gesehen.* LSH, Abt. 268 No. 673.

195 Orig. *Bekennet, daß sie eine Blaue Kuh umgebracht, so der Kühirtin zu Willmstörff (: itzo zu Gramstörff wohnhafft.) umgebracht.* LSH, Abt. 268 No. 673.

196 Orig. *Bekennet, daß Sie beÿ empfang des H. Abendmahls den oblaten auß dem Munde genommen und denselben in einem Schnupftuch den Satan hingegeben.* LSH, Abt. 268 No. 673.

197 Orig. *Alss nun solchene bekenntniss und aussage der gegenwertigen Anna Spielen zu unterschiedenen mahlen und noch itzo für diesem öffentlichen gerichte wiederhohlet und gestanden.* LSH, Abt. 268 No. 673.

198 Orig. *In peinlichen sachen Anna Spielen in puncto* Veneficij *erkennen und sprechen Wir Dechand, senior und gantzes Capitul deß hohen Stiffts Lübeck nach angestalter fleißiger inquisition und getahner gütlicher und peinlicher bekentniße Vorbesagter Annen Spielen für recht: Weil dieselbe beÿ sothaner Ihrer gütlicher und peinlicher bekentniße für diesem gehegtem öffentlichen peinlichem Halßgerichte freÿwillig und bestendig verbleibet, daß demnach Sie mit dem Feüer vom Leben zum tode abzustraffen und hinzurichten seÿ, wozu Sie der hirmit condemniret und verurteilet wird. Von Rechts-wegen.*

199 Orig. *Ick gripe an diesen Stock, verlate Gott, und wilt mit dißen Düfel holden.* LSH, Abt. 268, No. 673, unpaginated document dated 5 October 1669.

200 *Deutsches Sprichwörter Lexicon,* s.v. 'Teufel, Düfel', http://proverbs_de.deacademic.com/21767/Teufel(accessed 23 December 2021).

201 Walpurgis Night, an abbreviation of St Walpurgis Night, is the eve of the holiday of St Walpurga. It is celebrated on the night of 30 April and the day of 1 May. The holiday commemorates the canonization of St Walpurga and the movement of her relics to Einstätt, both of which took place on 1 May 870. St Walpurga was hailed by the Christians in Germany for battling the plague, rabies, and whooping cough, as well as witchcraft. In parts of Christendom, people light bonfires on St Walpurga's Eve in order to ward off evil spirits and witches.

202 There are several mountains or hills called Bloksberg in Germany—the most famous, however, is the mountain of Brochen, which has the highest elevation in the Harz

Mountains in Lower Saxony. Another German witches' mountain is Dorste, now part of Osterode, in the Harz.

203 Orig. *menschlicher Weise*. LSH, Abt. 7, No. 1758¹, Anneke Rickers, fo. 9r, headline Friedrich, dated 26 May 1641.

4 Denmark—Weather Magic, Witches' Dance, and Personal Demons

1 Louise N. Kallestrup discusses popular notions of witchcraft in *Agents of Witchcraft in Early Modern Italy and Denmark* (Basingstoke, 2015), 116–29.
2 Willumsen, 'Witchcraft Against'.
3 Jacobsen, *Danske Domme*, 137.
4 In Danish *jernbyrd*.
5 Jacobsen, *Danske Domme*, 138.
6 Orig. *Landskabslove*. See Jutland Law III-69 on witchcraft. Jacobsen, *Danske Domme*, 138.
7 In Danish *Nævn i Kirkesogn*. See note 144 for more information on this oath. Grønlund, *Historisk Efterretning*, 165.
8 Recess of 6 December 1547. Jacobsen, *Danske Domme*, 141.
9 Recess of 13 December 1558. Jacobsen, *Danske Domme*, 141.
10 Jacobsen, *Danske Domme*, 141–42.
11 Orig. *udædiske Mennesker*, whereof *Troldkarle eller Troldkvinder*. Jacobsen, *Danske Domme*, 168.
12 Goodare *European Witch-Hunt*, 324; Kallestrup, *Agents of Witchcraft*, 2.
13 Article 8 in the Copenhagen Recess of 6 December 1547 and article 18 in the Kolding Recess of 13 December 1558.
14 Article 17 in the Copenhagen Recess of 6 December 1547 and article 19 in the Kolding Recess of 13 December 1558. Article 8 in the Kalundborg Recess of 21 November 1576.
15 Decree of 12 October 1617, 'Om troldfolck oc deris medvidere' [About Witches and Their Accomplices], which was common for the union of Denmark-Norway; Hjördis A. Kasch, *Trollmenn og trollkvinner: En undersøkelse av kjønn i Norges trolldomsforfølgelser i tidlig moderne tid* [Male and Female Witches: A Study of Gender in Witchcraft Persecution in Norway in Early Modern Period] (M.A. thesis, University of Bergen, 2015), 79; Næss, *Trolldomsprosessene*, 82–84.
16 Orig. *rette troldfolck*.
17 Jacobsen, *Danske Domme*, 13–14.
18 On witchcraft, see 6th Book, 1 Chapter, Articles 9–13; Jacobsen, *Danske Domme*, 201.
19 A work institution for criminals.
20 Orig. *Spindehuset*; Jacobsen, *Danske Domme*, 202.
21 Orig. *da skulde de have forbrut deris Boeslod, og Rømme Kongens Riger og Lande*. Jacobsen, *Danske Domme*, 202; Birkelund *Troldkvinden*, 31.
22 Orig. *aabenbare Skrifte*. Jacobsen, *Danske Domme*, 202.
23 Article 13. Jacobsen, *Danske Domme*, 202.
24 Højesteret. Jacobsen, *Danske Domme*, 203.
25 Harald III (Harald the Whetstone, Danish: Harald Hen); c. 1040–April 17, 1080.
26 Johansen, 'Denmark'.
27 Charles Zika, 'Images of Witchcraft in Early Modern Europe', in Levack, *Oxford Handbook of Witchcraft*, 141–56.
28 Willumsen, 'Trolldom mot kongens skip', 314–16.
29 Charles V reigned in 1519–56.
30 Willumsen, 'Trolldom mot kongens skip', 315; 'Witchcraft Against', 70.
31 Voltmer, 'Debating the Devil's Clergy', 15.
32 Printed in Copenhagen in 1591. Willumsen, 'A Witchcraft Triangle', 253.
33 Willumsen, 'Trolldom mot kongens skip', 337.
34 Willumsen, 'Trolldom mot kongens skip', 337–43.

35 *Malmø tingbøger 1577–83; 1588–90* [Malmø Court Records 1577–83; 1588–90]. Edited by Leif Ljungberg and Einar Bager in cooperation with Erik Kroman from Selskabet for udgivelse af kilder til dansk historie (Copenhagen, 1968); Louise N. Kallestrup, '"Kind in Words and Deeds, but False in Their Hearts": Fear of Evil Conspiracy in Late-Sixteenth-Century Denmark', in Barry, Davies, and Usborne, *Cultures of Witchcraft*, 137–53, at 142.
36 Johansen, 'Denmark', 266.
37 This nobleman was Jørgen Arenfeldt, who held many trials at his manor.
38 Jørgen C. Jacobsen, *Den sidste Hexebrænding i Danmark 1693* [The Last Burning of a Witch in Denmark] (Copenhagen, 1971).
39 Hagen, 'Witchcraft Criminality, 376.
40 Goodare, *European Witch-Hunt*, 28.
41 Goodare, *European Witch-Hunt*, 86; Willumsen, 'Trolldom mot kongens skip', 314–18, 327–34; Birkelund, *Troldkvinden*, 80–85.
42 Johansen, 'Denmark', 267.
43 Goodare, *European Witch-Hunt*, 131; Willumsen, 'Trolldom mot kongens skip', 317.
44 Willumsen, 'Trolldom mot kongens skip', 317.
45 Johansen, 'Denmark', 267.
46 Kallestrup, *I Pagt med Djævelen*, 72–73.
47 Krogh, *Oplysningstiden og det magiske*.
48 Johansen, 'Denmark', 268.
49 Means 'through the agency'. Used to indicate that a person is signing a document on behalf of another person; in this case, that King James had a stand-in in Denmark during this marriage arrangement.
50 Mary, Queen of Scots (reign 1542–67) was beheaded in London 1587 after being held in custody by Elizabeth I of England for eighteen years.
51 A. Francis Steuart (ed.), *Memoirs of Sir James Melville of Halhill 1535–1617* (London, 1929), 328. With an introduction by A. Francis Steuart.
52 Liisberg, *Vesten for Sø*, 30.
53 William Ashby til Burghley. *Calendar of the State Papers Relating to Scotland and Mary, Queen of Scots*, vol. 10 (Edinburgh, 1936), no. 236, October 10, 1589.
54 This means three times twenty, which equals sixty. Liisberg, *Vesten for Sø*, 30.
55 Thomas Fowler in a letter dated 20 October. *Calendar of the State Papers Relating to Scotland and Mary, Queen of Scots*, vol. 1. Thomas Fowler (1540–90) was an English lawyer, diplomat, adviser to King James VI, and Scottish ambassador to London.
56 William Ashby to Burghley. *Calendar of the State Papers relating to Scotland and Mary, Queen of Scots*, vol. 1, no. 236, October 10, 1589.
57 William Ashby to [Michael] Throckmorton. *Calendar of the State Papers Relating to Scotland and Mary, Queen of Scots*, vol. 1, no. 299, November 28, 1589. Michael Throckmorton was the son of George Throckmorton and his second wife, Mary Brydges. 'Throckmorton Family', *Welcome to My Tudor Court*, www.tudorplace.com.ar/THROCKMOR-TON1.htm (accessed 24 May 2018).
58 The trial of Maren Mogens, Rigsarkivet [National Archives], Copenhagen (RAD), A232, Danske Kancelli (DK) 1572–1660, Sjællandske Tegnelser (SJT) 1588–90, folder marked 'No. 117 Færeöe Præst og Jndbÿggere som er beskÿlt for Signerie og Troldoms Konster derom Landstings dom'; The trial of Agnes Sampson, Normand and Roberts, *Witchcraft in Early Modern Scotland*, 233, 239.
59 National Library of Scotland (NLS), Special Collections, Adv. Ms. 35.5.3. In 1527, Hector Boece published *Historia Gentis Scotorum* [History of the Scottish People].
60 Dated 8 October 1589. Ashby to Lord Burghley. *Calendar of the State Papers Relating to Scotland and Mary, Queen of Scots*, vol. 10.
61 Steuart, *Memoirs of Sir James Melville*, 328.
62 Thomas Tennecker was the English ambassador to Denmark in 1589. *List and Analysis of State Papers, Foreign Series Elizabeth I: August 1589–June 1590*. Edited by Richard Bruce Wernham (London, Her Majesty's Stationery Office, 1964), 458.

63 National Archives London (NAL), State Papers Denmark (SPD) 75, II, D7.

64 Dated 20 October—'Discourse of James VI on taking his Voyage'.

65 William Ashby to Burghley. *Calendar of the State Papers relating to Scotland and Mary, Queen of Scots*, vol. 10, no. 262, October 30, 1589.

66 The British Library, London (BL), Egerton Manuscript 2, 598, fo. 190.

67 Old Bishop's Palace was founded at the beginning of the 1200s by Bishop Nikolas Arnesson, and it was a place of great national importance. David Stevenson, *Scotland's Last Royal Wedding* (Edinburgh, 1997), 34–39.

68 Tycho Brahe (1546–1601) was a Danish nobleman, astronomist, and author. He is known for his accurate and comprehensive astronomic observations. Tycho Brahe was on friendly terms with King Frederik II and was given means to build a research centre. However, due to a disagreement with King Christian IV in 1597, he went to Prague and died in exile there. During the last part of his research work, he was assisted by Johannes Kepler.

69 Niels Hemmingsen was dismissed from his professorship in theology at the University of Copenhagen because his view of the Lord's Supper diverged from the Lutheran understanding. Hemmingsen was known for his book *Admonitio de superstionibus Magicis vitandis* (Copenhagen, 1575), which became influential.

70 Stevenson, *Scotland's Last*, 49.

71 Published in Edinburgh.

72 J. T. Gibson Craig, *Papers Relative to the Marriage of King James the Sixth of Scotland, with the Princess Anna of Denmark; A.D. MDLXXXIX*, Bannatyne Club (Edinburgh, 1936), 47–55.

73 Gibson Craig, *Papers Relative to the Marriage*, 39.

74 RAD, A232, DK 1572–1660, SJT 1588–90.

75 Liisberg, *Vesten for Sø*.

76 Ljungberg and Bager, *Malmø tingbøger 1577–83 og 1588–90*; Niels M. Pedersen, 'Dokumenter til en Troldomssag under Christian III' [Documents Related to a Witchcraft Trial Under Christian III], *Danske Magazin*, 3 (1843), 52–67; Thomas Riis, *Should Auld Acquaintance Be Forgot. . .: Scottish-Danish Relations c. 1450–1707*, vol. I (Odense, 1988), 267; Kallestrup, 'When Hell Became Too Small', 25; '"Kind in Words and Deeds"', 139–40.

77 One expects the records to be archived under Copenhagen City Court Proceedings. Instead, they were archived under SJT. The records were archived together with local court records from Fæøe island. On the outside of the folder of the SJT documents was written: "Fæøes Præst og Indbyggere som er beskÿlt for Signerie og Troldoms Konster derom Landstinget dom" [Fæøe island's minister and inhabitants who are accused of sorcery and witchcraft, the sentence of Landstinget], exactly the same wording as used in Liisberg's book. However, these words have now been crossed out by archivists. The 1590 trial records were archived under SJT together with an early witchcraft trial from Fæøe.

78 I at once informed my Danish colleague Louise Nyholm Kallestrup about the references to these documents, as she had been searching for these documents but could not find them.

79 All quotations from the original court records are my transcriptions. The trial documents are not paginated. Therefore, references are given using date of trial and name of accused person.

80 RAD, A232, DK 1572–1660, SJT 1588–90. Folder marked: 'Sag imod: Margrethe Jacob Skrivers for Trolddom 2 Stk. Dokumenter 1590 13 Juli. Oktbr' [Trial Against Margrethe Jacob the Scribe's Wife for Witchcraft].

81 RAD, A232, DK 1572–1660, SJT 1588–90.

82 The idea of an alleged witch having a personal demon, an 'Apostle', is also known from witchcraft trials in Finnmark in Norway. In England, a familiar—a domestic animal, most often a cat—was alleged to be the personal demon of a witch.

83 The Danish word *Frøkenen* is used in the original source, meaning an unmarried woman.

84 Orig. *første gang*.

85 In Danish *byting*.

86 Information about the date varies, either 15 or 17. In a letter sent from Denmark to the English court, the date is 17 June.

87 Gibson Craig, *Papers Relative to the Marriage*, 47–55.
88 London Archives Kew: S.P. Denmark, Dr Parkins to Burghley, dated Rødby, 25 June.
89 Robert Bowes, Queen Elizabeth's new ambassador to Scotland (after Ashby), to Burghley.
90 Literally, the surname Söndags means 'Sunday's'.
91 The name Langinus is sometimes written as Longinus in these sources. Longinus refers to the soldier that stuck his lance, which is called 'the holy lance', into the side of Christ on the cross to expedite his death. Gospel of John, 19: 31–37. His name is not mentioned in the Bible, but in sources outside the Bible this man is called Longinus or Logginus.
92 Orig. *Frøkenen.*
93 'The first time' refers to the voyage in the autumn of 1589. This was the first time Princess Anne tried to get over to Scotland.
94 Orig. *med sott och Siugdom.*
95 Orig. *udj Raad och gierning.*
96 Orig. *paa siell och Sallighedt.*
97 Kolding Recess, 1588, stated in Article 19 that nobody should be tortured before sentence was passed. However, after sentence was passed, the use of torture to get hold of accomplices was allowed. Willumsen, *Trollkvinne i nord*, 56.
98 In Danish, the word *Noch* is used here.
99 Orig. *förste gang adt skottlanndt.*
100 Liisberg, *Vesten for Sø*, 32.
101 Orig. *war medt Att forgiöre Kongenns skibbe.*
102 Orig. *war Lige saa god wdj troldoms konster som hunn och the Andre.*
103 Orig. *ware forsambled thill Karenn weffuers.*
104 Orig. *och ther will hunn gaa til döde.*
105 Orig. *Bekiende Marenn Att Anne Kollings haff(ue)r Bekienndt for hinnde Att Jacob shriffuer haffde Beditt hinnde ther om, Attj skulle forgiöre Kongenns skibbe.*
106 A single article or unit in a collection, enumeration, or series; a clause of a document, such as a bill or charter.
107 Liisberg is of the opinion that the rack was in use during these trials. Liisberg, *Vesten for Sø*, 59.
108 Orig. *om Sonstj mickelßdags thidt.*
109 Orig. *Maren Mogenßis Bekiende och soer saa sanndt hunn Agth(ed) Att bliffue ett gudz barn.*
110 *Pilhestesko* means literally 'Horse Arrow Shoe'.
111 The Danish word *Smuck* means 'handsome'.
112 Orig. *och ßee huorledis thed war fatt medt thennom, effter Jacob shriffuers Begiering.*
113 Orig. *och war same tid hoß skibbene.*
114 L. Laursen (ed.), *Kancelliets Brevbøger vedrørende Danmarks indre forhold* (Copenhagen, 1908), 404–405.
115 The diary of Peder Christensen. Liisberg, *Vesten for Sø*, 65–66.
116 In Finnmark, Northern Norway, personal demons are called *Apostler*. In England, these demons, most often cats or other animals, were called *familiars*, as mentioned above.
117 *Borgmester* was the title of the leader of the Town Council.
118 Means 'with pestilence and sickness'.
119 V. A. Secher, *Forordninger, Recesser og andre Kongelige Breve 1558–1660* [Decrees, Recesses, and Royal Letters, 1558–1660], vol. 2 (Copenhagen, 1887), 33.
120 Orig. *Och ther fore wdj thennd meninng, Att ieg Fattige manndt paa Margrette Jacob schrif-fuers wegnne, Jcke kunde forstaa, om the 16 mennd Soere Rett eller wrett.* RAD, A 232, DK 1572–1660, SJT 1588–90 Folder: Sag imod: Margrette Jacob Skrivers for Trolddom 2 Stk. Dokumenter 1590 13. Juli–Oktbr.
121 National Archives of Britain, London (NAB), SP, vol. 75, II, Danish Domestic Affairs, HH4. Paul Knibbe [Knibbius] to Dr Daniel Rogers, letter dated Kolding 3 September. Original in Latin.
122 RAD, A232, DK 1572–1660, SJT 1588–90 Folder: Sag imod: Margrette Jacob Skrivers for Trolddom 2 Stk. Dokumenter 1590 13. Juli–Oktbr.

123 RAD, A232, DK 1572–1660, SJT 1588–90. Folder: Sag imod: Margrette Jacob Skrivers for Trolddom 2 Stk. Dokumenter 1590 13. Juli–Oktbr.; Liisberg, *Vesten for Sø*, 68–79.

124 Liisberg, *Vesten for Sø*, 89.

125 Steuart, *Memoirs of Sir James Melville*, 328.

126 Means literally 'master of interest', treasurer. The *Rentemester* was chief of the *Rentekammeret*, one of the three organs of the state, and the organ that had to do with finance. The other two were *Danske Kancelli* and *Tyske Kancelli*. The leadership of the *Rentekammeret* was a powerful position, as the centre of power was found in the cooperation between the king, the leaders of the three *Kancellis*, and other councillors appointed by the king.

127 Christoffer Valkendorf (1525–1601) served as treasurer and Stadtholder. He was Steward of the Realm in 1596–1601.

128 Orig. Lat. *Obruendo*. The word has a double meaning: normally to overwhelm or to bury; in this context it probably means to drown.

129 NAL, SP, vol. 75, II, Danish Domestic Affairs, HH4. Paul Knibbe [Knibbius] to Dr Daniel Rogers. Letter dated Kolding 3 September. Original in Latin.

130 Paul Knibbe to Dr Daniel Rogers, letter from Kolding.

131 Orig. *Frijbÿtter*. The Danish word *fribytter* means scoundrel or criminal.

132 Orig. *Att Margrette skulle haffe spurdt thennom adt, huilcken shib ther heed Gedionn, som Fröknen war paa.*

133 Orig. *For thed spörsmaal Siunis mig Jcke, Att margrette kunde Sigis thill döde, Effterdj Att ther Jngenn skade eller forderffuelße.*

134 Orig. *hellig giest hus.* The holy guest house was a house used by the church to accommodate visitors.

135 Probably meaning plague.

136 Orig. *ett Christelige Och Erligdt skudzmaal och winndißbÿrdt.*

137 Orig. *Lÿder om ett maall Att margrette skall haffue maallett med sine föder, wdj Hanns Bagers.* Measuring, in Danish *maalen*, was a kind of white magic; magical healing performed by means of measuring, usually measuring a body. In this case, measuring was allegedly used to perform harmful witchcraft, and the measuring was performed inside a house.

138 Orig. *Och ther efftir skall werre kommen nogenn thudßer wdj hanns Siudekiell Och Att hannem er Faldenn stor wlöcke thill.*

139 Orig. *Effterdj Knud Bager his wife, Jcke wed om margrette haffde ther nogenn skÿlt wdj, Och hanns höstru siger Att the icke wide, huem the skulle skÿlle, for skade och wlöcke, wdenn gudt.*

140 Orig. *omsonstj Mikkelsmess.*

141 The suffix -*datter* means 'daughter of', in the case, daughter of Laurids.

142 Orig. *Hans Hiorde.*

143 Three districts from Eastern Jylland (Eastern Jutland) were under the jurisdiction of Viborg Landsting: Åkjær, Skanderborg, and Århusgård.

144 Birkelund, *Troldkvinden*, 138.

145 Orig. *lensmand.*

146 There might also have been witchcraft trials in 1600 and 1614, but documentation is scarce. Birkelund, *Troldkvinden*, 141.

147 Orig. *forvisne som dug for solen.* Birkelund, *Troldkvinden*, 141.

148 A legal instrument dating back to ecclesiastic law from the early Middle Ages: if the court was unable to prove guilt and the person charged found six peers, including him- or herself, who were willing to swear in support of his or her uprightness, the charge would be dropped. It was also called six-man sentence. This type of oath could also be made by twelve peers. For a minor offence, fewer people were required.

149 In Danish *kirkenævningenes ed og tov.*

150 Orig. *rode.*

151 Literally *Kongens* means 'the king's'.

152 St Valborg's day is 30 April, and St Valborg's night is the night to 1 May. It is celebrated to commemorate St Valborg. According to folk belief, witches' gatherings took place this night, and bonfires would protect against evil powers. The celebration is related to the growth of the soil.

153 Orig. *haver hun også givet sig fanden i vold.*

154 Nørre Jylland (Northern Jutland).

155 Orig. *Lauridzs Ebbeβen till tulstrup, befalingsmand Paa Skander borig hans Wiβe boedt Erlig och Fornommstige Jacob Jensen Ridefogett der ib(i)d(em).* Landsarkivet for Nørrejylland (LAN), Viborg Landsting (VL), Dombog B, 1618, B 24–535, fo. 177v.

156 Orig. *for troldoms gierninger och bedrefft hun schall haffue giort och begangitt.* LAN, VL, Dombog B, 1618, B 24–535, fo. 177v.

157 Orig. *att hun haffde Indtit Ontt giort siden Kong: Maystz: breffue komb.* The letter referred to is the royal witchcraft decree of 1617, 'About witches and their accomplices'. Orig. *Om troldfolck oc deris medvidere.*

158 Orig. *oversværged.*

159 In Danish *Nævningeeden.*

160 Birkelund *Troldkvinden,* 144.

161 Birkelund, *Troldkvinden,* 144.

162 Orig. *da hand Icke Sielff for hans Siugdom och schröbeligheds schyld kunde komme till tingett.* LAN, VL, Dombog B, 1618, B 24–535, fo. 177v.

163 Orig. *badskær.*

164 Orig. *kopsætte,* to bleed.

165 Orig. *och denom Kand thamis beschier icke Rade eder buode for.* LAN, VL, Dombog B, 1618, B 24–535, fo. 179r.

166 Orig. *och saa gick hand till hinder thj hand war da saa föer att hand Kunde gange till hinder.* LAN, VL, Dombog B, 1618, B 24–535, fo. 178r.

167 Orig. *Miste hand sine bienn och siden gick hand Aldrigh.* LAN, VL, Dombog B, 1618, B 24–535, fo. 179r.

168 Orig. *med spögelβe, Kaars Och segnellβe.* LAN, VL, Dombog B, 1618, B 24–535, fo. 179r.

169 Orig. *de sige at min Kone haffuer Werret i med marenn Alleröds.* LAN, VL, Dombog B, 1618, B 24–535, fo. 179r.

170 Orig. *ieg haff(ue)r en kou den vil ieg gierne giffue // Kongen och en sou den Will ieg giffue dig.* In this quotation, '//' denotes page shift. LAN, VL, Dombog B, 1618, B 24–535, fo. 179r.

171 *Landstinget* was the second instance court, whereto all witchcraft trials from local courts were sent.

172 Orig. *dett gaar icke Anderledis end hun komme till En Ild.* LAN, VL, Dombog B, 1618, B 24–535, fo. 179v.

173 Orig. *gud giffue ieg war Wde i dett blaae wandt som dett er dybest, thj ieg befrychter mig ieg schall bliffue saatt i denne Afften.* LAN, VL, Dombog B, 1618, B 24–535, fo. 179v.

174 Orig. *sagde sigh wdi troldombs konst Vscheldig.* LAN, VL, Dombog B, 1618, B 24–535, fo. 180v.

175 Orig. *Da giorde ieg Kaars offuer dett och dett finge bedre.* LAN, VL, Dombog B, 1618, B 24–535, fo. 178v.

176 Orig. *Bekiend och wedgaaed att hun signedt och giorde Kaars Offuer brunck Pierβenn och finge hans moder en dryck till honom som war ickon Edicke.* LAN, VL, Dombog B, 1618, B 24–535, fo. 178v.

177 Orig. *da will ieg giöre Kaars offuer Eder Igienn schall i med guds hielp faae boedr.* LAN, VL, Dombog B, 1618, B 24–535, fo. 178r.

178 Orig. *och da löste hun dise ord offuer brunck pierβen att de her styng de schulle bliffue stönglös som Jomfru Maria föde en sönn mandlös i Jesus Naffnn Amenn.* LAN, VL, Dombog B, 1618, B 24–535, fo. 179r.

179 Orig. *bekiend och wedgaaet, for^{ne} mete Kongens ydermiere att haffue sagt att hun haffde Jndtid Ontt giort siden Kong: Maystz: breffue komb.* LAN, VL, Dombog B, 1618, B 24–535, fo. 178v.

180 Orig. *Saa och loffued for^{ne} mete Kongens Att der som hun skulde lide nogett her paa hinhis lagoms Wegne da schulle brunk piers(en)siell bliffue i pinne till Evig tid dett schule hun loffue hanom.* LAN, VL, Dombog B, 1618, B 24–535, fo. 179r.

181 Orig. *da sagde for^{ne} mete Kongsdater till hinder att wille hun Komme Off(ue)r till hinder en Afften da schal der schie itt sielsomt mirackell.* LAN, VL, Dombog B, 1618, B 24–535, fo. 180r.

182 Orig. *och forstörredt dennomb i deres besteling saa de Jngen fremgangh der med fick.* LAN, VL, Dombog B, 1618, B 24–535, fo. 180r.

183 Orig. *och sagde ieg haffde faaet eders moder Enn drÿck.* LAN, VL, Dombog B, 1618, B 24–535, fo. 178r.

184 Orig. *hvilkenn Karll hun Wide haffue.* LAN, VL, Dombog B, 1618, B 24–535, fo. 179v.

185 Orig. *roder.* LAN, VL, Dombog B, 1618, B 24–535, fo. 179v.

186 Orig. *Der sammeledis da Kunde de schabbe denom i Katte Ligenelser och Andett diefuelsschab, som de giorde Ved S: Michelsdags tide sist forledenn.* LAN, VL, Dombog B, 1618, B 24–535, fo. 180r.

187 Birkelund, *Troldkvinden*, 144.

188 Birkelund, *Troldkvinden*, 145.

189 Birkelund, *Troldkvinden*, 144.

190 Grønlund, *Historisk Efterretning*.

191 Grønlund, *Historisk Efterretning*, 102–36.

192 Orig. *Korsbrødre Gaard. Korsbrødre* means 'Brothers of the Cross', a monastery of the Order of Malta, 'Johanitterkloster', first mentioned in Danish sources in 1311.

193 Orig. *en Troldqvinde.* Grønlund, *Historisk Efterretning*, 138.

194 Mogens Sehested, or Mogens Clausen von Sehested, belonged to the nobility. He was born 1598 at Højris Slot (Højris Castle). He studied in Padova, got a position at the court as *Hofjunker*, and accompanied several Danish kings abroad. Sehested was appointed district governor, *lensherre*, of Copenhagen Castle in 1629–32, and in the same period held the position of *lensmand*, police officer, in Copenhagen, and was the accuser in a witchcraft trial against the alleged male witch Lamme Heide. This trial was related to royal circles. He was the owner of his ancestors' mansions Holmgaard and Nørre Holmgaard, where he died in 1657, http://roskildehistorie.dk/stamtavler/adel/Sehested/Sehested.htm; www.geni.com/people/Mogens-Sehested-Broholmlinjen/6000000006266691685 (accessed 23 December 2021).

195 A castle scribe was the secretary and accountant of a *lensherre*, a district governor. The castle scribe Povel Jensen was employed by Mogens Sehested. In the trial of Anna Bruds, Povel Jensen was the interrogator. It is not likely that Jensen was the scribe, because in the records he is spoken about in the third person. Since this was a local trial, it is likely that the local court had its own scribe.

196 Orig. *Dreng.* This is a personal demon with the same function as an Apostle, like we hear about in the Copenhagen trials of 1590.

197 Orig. *Bruhuus. Bryg-hus, Bryggers,* building for brewing of beer. Grønlund, *Historisk Efterretning*, 163.

198 Orig. *Liv og Levnet.* Grønlund, *Historisk Efterretning*, 137.

199 Orig. *Volborg Nielsdatters Fuldmægtig.* A *procurator* who gave legal advice. Grønlund, *Historisk Efterretning*, 137, 171.

200 This is probably the same person who is previously named Volborg Nielsdatter, as the defender, Carsten Sørensen, speaks first on behalf of Volborg Nielsdatter, then changes to speak on behalf of Volborg Michelsdatter.

201 Orig. *Troldkarl.*

202 Orig. *Maren Jelle Skræders.*

203 Orig. *Maren Christen Bundtmagers.*

204 Orig. *Bruhuus.* Grønlund, *Historisk Efterretning*, 163.

205 Orig. *Vee og Smerte.*

206 Orig. *Ribe Raadhus.*

207 Orig. *viide vi ikke imod de 15 Mænds Eed og Tyding at sige, mens ved Magt at være*. Grønlund, *Historisk Efterretning*, 141.

208 According to the law, it was correct to use torture after the *Raadstueretten* confirmed the oath of trustworthy men who had sworn that the accused was a witch. Grønlund, *Historisk Efterretning*, 173–74.

209 Means literally 'The Dog's Street'.

210 Orig. *Herpaa blev Sagen d. 7 April 1652 af Byefogden med Borgemestere og Raad endelig paadømt, at hun skulle lide som en vitterlig Troldqvinde*. Grønlund, *Historisk Efterretning*, 142, 174.

211 Orig. *og siden hun haver forsvoret Daab og Christendom*. Grønlund, *Historisk Efterretning*, 142.

212 Orig. *Hun torde ikke være den bekjent i Volborg Michelsdatters Nærværelse*. Grønlund, *Historisk Efterretning*, 141.

213 According to Jutland Law, there should be six weeks between the start of a trial and the passing of a sentence; usually, three or four court meetings were held. Grønlund, *Historisk Efterretning*, 171.

214 Grønlund, *Historisk Efterretning*, 137, 163.

5 Scotland—Devil's Pact, Gatherings, and Sleep Deprivation

1 I am grateful to Diane Baptie for transcription of the Scottish unpublished court records.

2 This database, created by a group of scholars led by Julian Goodare at the University of Edinburgh, contains registration of all Scottish witchcraft trials. The database was finished in 2003. For the spelling of accused people's names, I follow the orthography used in the Survey of Scottish Witchcraft.

3 Goodare, 'Witchcraft in Scotland', 302.

4 Willumsen, *Seventeenth-Century Witchcraft Trials*, 39.

5 Willumsen, *Seventeenth-Century Witchcraft Trials*, 38; Goodare, *Scottish Witches*, 302, note 2.

6 Willumsen, *Seventeenth-Century Witchcraft Trials*, 41.

7 Goodare, *European Witch-Hunt*, 27–29; *Scottish Witches*, 302. Willumsen, *Seventeenth-Century Witchcraft Trials*, 57–69.

8 Willumsen, *Seventeenth-Century Witchcraft Trials*, 38.

9 Goodare, *European Witch-Hunt*, 160–61; Willumsen, 'Trolldom mot kongens skip', 334.

10 Larner, *Enemies of God*, 200.

11 Brock, *Satan and the Scots*, 171.

12 Goodare, *Scottish Witches*, 309; Willumsen, *Seventeenth-Century Witchcraft Trials*, 39.

13 Willumsen, *Seventeenth-Century Witchcraft Trials*, 43, 69–78.

14 Willumsen, *Seventeenth-Century Witchcraft Trials*, 51–53.

15 Goodare, *Scottish Witches*, 302.

16 Goodare, *Scottish Witch-Hunt in Context*, 5.

17 Goodare, *Scottish Witch-Hunt in Context*, 5.

18 Larner, *Enemies of God*, 5.

19 Julian Goodare, 'Witch-Hunting and the Scottish State', in Goodare, *Scottish Witch-Hunt in Context*, 124.

20 David M. Robertson, *Goodnight My Servants All. The Sourcebook of East Lothian Witchcraft* (Glasgow, 2008), 29.

21 Goodare, *Scottish Witches*, 303.

22 In this chapter, the word 'church' is used as a general body, while the Scottish word 'kirk' is used in official titles.

23 Introduction to the Survey of Scottish Witchcraft (SSW).

24 Willumsen, *Seventeenth-Century Witchcraft Trials*, 44–45.

25 Goodare, *European Witch-Hunt*, 302.

26 Goodare, 'Witch-Hunting and the Scottish State'.

27 Willumsen, *Seventeenth-Century Witchcraft Trials*, 45.

28 Levack, *Witch-Hunting in Scotland*, 21.

29 Willumsen, *Seventeenth-Century Witchcraft Trials*, 45.

30 Goodare, *Scottish Witches*, 303.

31 Goodare, *Scottish Witches*, 303.

32 Christina Larner: 'if the picture given here of the way in which the persecution developed in Scotland is anywhere near accurate, it shows the witch panic developing from the beliefs and attitudes of the elite, rather than as a spontaneous expression from below'. *Witchcraft and Religion,* 21.

33 Brian P. Levack, 'State-Building and Witch Hunting in Early Modern Europe', in Barry, Hester, and Roberts, *Witchcraft in Early Modern Europe*, 96–115.

34 Goodare, *Scottish Witches*, 306; 'Witch-Hunting and the Scottish State'.

35 Brian P. Levack, 'Absolutism, State-Building and Witchcraft', in Levack, *Witch-Hunting in Scotland*, 98–114; Goodare, 'Witchcraft in Scotland', 306.

36 Goodare, 'Witchcraft in Scotland', 306.

37 Willumsen, *Seventeenth-Century Witchcraft Trials*, 83.

38 Willumsen, *Seventeenth-Century Witchcraft Trials*, 84.

39 R. D. Melville, 'The Use and Forms of Judicial Torture in England and Scotland', *Scottish Historical Review*, 2 (1905), 225–48; Christina Larner, *Witchcraft and Religion: The Politics of Popular Belief* (Oxford, 1984), 107–9; Levack, *Witch-Hunting in Scotland*, 22–23; Stuart Macdonald, 'Torture and the Scottish Witch-Hunt: A Re-examination', *Scottish Tradition*, 28 (2002), 95–114; Maxwell-Stuart, *Satan's Conspiracy*, 74–75, Goodare, *Scottish Witches*, 307; Willumsen, *Seventeenth-Century Witchcraft Trials*, 78–84.

40 Willumsen, *Seventeenth-Century Witchcraft Trials*, 80.

41 Levack, *Witch-Hunting in Scotland*, 21–22.

42 Goodare, *Scottish Witches*, 306–7; Goodare, *European Witch-Hunt*, 195–96; Brian P. Levack, 'Judicial Torture in Scotland During the Age of Mackenzie', *Stair Society Miscellany*, 4 (2002), 185–98; 'Witchcraft and the Law in Early Modern Scotland', in Levack, *Witch-Hunting in Scotland*, 21–24; Macdonald, 'Torture and the Scottish Witch-Hunt'.

43 This is 1736 by modern dating; it was January 1735–36, because the new calendar year was then taken to begin on 25 March.

44 Larner, *Enemies of God*, 78.

45 Edward J. Cowan and Lizanne Henderson, 'The Last of the Witches? The Survival of Scottish Witch Belief', in Goodare, *Scottish Witch-Hunt in Context*, 198–217, at 200–1.

46 Normand and Roberts, *Witchcraft in Early Modern Scotland*.

47 Goodare, 'Witchcraft in Scotland', 303–5, for references see notes 4–14; Willumsen, 'Witchcraft Against', 91.

48 Larner, *Scottish Demonology*, 90.

49 Wormald, 'Witches, the Devil and the King', 171–72; Peter G. Maxwell-Stuart, 'James VI and the Witches', in William Naphy and Penny Roberts (eds.), *Fear in Early Modern Society* (Manchester, 1997), 209–25, at 211–14.

50 Paterson, 'Witches' Sabbath in Scotland', 375.

51 Riis, *Should Auld Acquaintance*, i, 266–69.

52 Goodare, 'John Knox on Demonology', 221–45.

53 Goodare, 'Framework for Scottish Witch-Hunting'; 'Witchcraft in Scotland', 304–5.

54 Goodare, 'Scottish Witchcraft Panic', 60–66; 'Witchcraft in Scotland', 305.

55 Goodare, 'Witchcraft in Scotland', 305.

56 Willumsen, 'Witchcraft Against', 69–76.

57 Normand and Robert, *Witchcraft in Early Modern Scotland*, 137, 144; Willumsen, 'Witchcraft Against', 69.

58 Normand and Robert, *Witchcraft in Early Modern Scotland*, 136; Willumsen, 'Witchcraft Against', 77.

59 Berit V. Busch, 'They Shipped All in at North Berwick in a Boat like a Chimney'. Fores-
tillinger om samlinger knyttet til de hekseanklagede i North Berwick-prosessene [Ideas About
Witches' Gatherings Related to Accused Persons During the North Berwick Trials]
(M.A. thesis, University of Tromsø, 2018), 41.

60 Normand and Roberts, Witchcraft in Early Modern Scotland, 135–49, 154–57, 231–46.
I quote Normand and Roberts with regard to the documents dated pre-December and
December 1590, and the original court records with regard to the formal trial of Agnes
Sampson in January 1591.

61 JC2/2, National Records of Scotland (NRS). The pre-trial documents are loose items
of varying size, the earliest documents from the interrogation that are extant. The indictment, dittay, is recorded in the official series of Books of Adjournal, folio size. The dittay
is a compilation of pre-trial interrogation.

62 The four individuals are John Fian, alias Cunningham, Agnes Sampson, Barbara Napier,
and Euphame MacCalzean. Normand and Roberts, Witchcraft in Early Modern Scotland,
203. All primary trial documents are written in secretary hand. The indictment is written by one scribe.

63 Robertson, Goodnight My Servants All.

64 Robertson, Goodnight My Servants All, 13.

65 Robertson, Goodnight My Servants All, 29.

66 Robertson, Goodnight My Servants All, 29.

67 Robertson, Goodnight My Servants All, 29.

68 Maxwell-Stuart, 'James VI and the Witches', 215, with reference to note 17, 224;
George P. MacNeill (ed.), The Exchequer Rolls of Scotland (Edinburgh, 1903), 22:
160.

69 Robertson, Goodnight My Servants All, 7.

70 The first examinations of Agnes Sampson took place on two separate days, both before
December 1590, date unknown. Normand and Roberts, Witchcraft in Early Modern Scotland, 135; Maxwell-Stuart, 'James VI and the Witches', 215.

71 Willumsen, 'Trolldom mot kongens skip', 335.

72 In the court records, it is stated as 1590, because the new calendar year was then taken
to begin on 25 March.

73 The pre-trial examination of Agnes Sampson is referred to as Document 1, Document 2,
and Document 4 in Normand and Roberts, Witchcraft in Early Modern Scotland, 135–57.

74 NRS, JC2/2, fo. 207r.

75 SSW, sub Agnes Sampsoun. Also another accused person, John Fian, was strangled and
burnt at the end of January 1591.

76 Normand and Roberts, Witchcraft in Early Modern Scotland, 136.

77 RAD, A232, DK 1572–1660, SJT 1588–1590. Unpaginated court records.

78 Willumsen, 'Witchcraft Against', 69–70.

79 William Asheby, English Ambassador in Edinburgh, letter to Lord Burghley, Queen
Elizabeth I's chief minister, dated 10 October 1589. NAL, SP Denmark, SP 75, II, D7;
Paterson, 'Witches' Sabbath in Scotland', 375; Willumsen, 'Witchcraft Against', 77.

80 Normand and Roberts, Witchcraft in Early Modern Scotland, 137.

81 Brock, Satan and the Scots, 157.

82 Normand and Roberts, Witchcraft in Early Modern Scotland, 137.

83 Normand and Roberts, Witchcraft in Early Modern Scotland, 138.

84 Normand and Roberts, Witchcraft in Early Modern Scotland, 138.

85 Normand and Roberts, Witchcraft in Early Modern Scotland, 137.

86 Especially that is one more or less round or conical in shape; often applied to isolated
hills of this sort. Dictionary of the Older Scottish Tongue (DOST), now included in Dictionary of the Scots Language, s.v. 'law'.

87 Normand and Roberts, Witchcraft in Early Modern Scotland, 138.

88 Normand and Roberts, Witchcraft in Early Modern Scotland, 137.

89 It appears during a later interrogation that this letter was written by John Fian and delivered to Geillis Duncan to be brought to Leith to Janet Fairlie. Normand and Roberts, *Witchcraft in Early Modern Scotland*, 148.

90 Normand and Roberts, *Witchcraft in Early Modern Scotland*, 138.

91 See Yeoman, 'Hunting the Rich Witch', 107, 114–15.

92 Normand and Roberts, *Witchcraft in Early Modern Scotland*, 139.

93 Normand and Roberts, *Witchcraft in Early Modern Scotland*, 140.

94 Normand and Roberts, *Witchcraft in Early Modern Scotland*, 139.

95 Normand and Roberts, *Witchcraft in Early Modern Scotland*, 139.

96 Normand and Roberts, *Witchcraft in Early Modern Scotland*, 139.

97 Some of the items are numbered, from 5 until 14.

98 Normand and Roberts, *Witchcraft in Early Modern Scotland*, 143.

99 Kruse and Willumsen, 'Magic Language', 7.

100 Normand and Roberts, *Witchcraft in Early Modern Scotland*, 144.

101 Oslo.

102 *Newes from Scotland*, in Normand and Roberts, *Witchcraft in Early Modern Scotland*, 309–24, at 316.

103 Normand and Roberts, *Witchcraft in Early Modern Scotland*, 145.

104 Normans and Roberts, *Witchcraft in Early Modern Scotland*, 146.

105 See Normand and Roberts, *Witchcraft in Early Modern Scotland*, 142.

106 In Fife.

107 Normand and Roberts, *Witchcraft in Early Modern Scotland*, 144.

108 On 8 October 1589, William Asheby to Walsingham, no. 233; William Asheby to Lord Burghley, no. 234. *Calendar of the State Papers relating to Scotland and Mary, Queen of Scots*, vol. 10 (Edinburgh, 1936), 165–66.

109 Willumsen, 'Trolldom mot kongens skip', 319, 322, 'Witchcraft Against', 62–66.

110 Normand and Roberts, *Witchcraft in Early Modern Scotland*, 145.

111 Normand and Roberts, *Witchcraft in Early Modern Scotland*, 146. See DOST, law.

112 Normand and Roberts, *Witchcraft in Early Modern Scotland*, 145.

113 Normand and Roberts, *Witchcraft in Early Modern Scotland*, 145.

114 For storm-raising in 1618, see Larner, *Enemies of God*, 32, with reference to: Trial, Confession, and Execution of Isobel Inch, John Stewart, Margaret Barclay, and Isobel Crawford for Witchcraft at Irvine, Anno 1618; reprinted 1855; see also the trial of Helene Clerk below; for other connections between witchcraft and disasters at sea, see Larner, *Enemies of God*, 82.

115 Brock, *Satan and the Scots*, 159; Busch, *They Shipped All In*, 41.

116 Unusual descriptions of the devil, among others the devil as smoke, are known from scripts of demonic possession in the Middle Ages. See Sari Katajala-Peltomaa, *Demonic Possession and Lived Religion in Later Medieval Europe* (Oxford, 2020).

117 Normand and Roberts, *Witchcraft in Early Modern Scotland*, 147.

118 Normand and Roberts, *Witchcraft in Early Modern Scotland*, 148.

119 Normand and Roberts, *Witchcraft in Early Modern Scotland*, 148.

120 Busch, *They Shipped All In*, 36.

121 Maxwell-Stuart also mentions William Schaw, the Master of the King's Works, as one of the interrogators. Maxwell-Stuart, 'James VI and the Witches', 215, with reference to NRS, JC 26/2/3.

122 Agnes was accused of participating, together with nine other alleged witches, in a convention in Foulstruther where they plotted the destruction of a man named David Seton.

123 Agnes Sampson's head was thrawn, wound, and twisted with a rope for an hour. *Newes from Scotland*, Normand and Roberts, *Witchcraft in Early Modern Scotland*, 314, 99, 149, 302–3.

124 Normand and Roberts, *Witchcraft in Early Modern Scotland*, 211–12.

125 Normand and Roberts, *Witchcraft in Early Modern* Scotland, 156. This is Jean Lyon, countess of Angus. See Victoria Carr, 'The Countess of Angus's Escape from the North Berwick Witch-Hunt', in Goodare, *Scottish Witches*, 34–48.

126 Normand and Roberts, *Witchcraft in Early Modern Scotland*, 156.
127 The word 'fylit' is the imperfect tense of the verb 'fyle', which means 'to find guilty, to convict'.
128 Normand and Roberts, *Witchcraft in Early Modern Scotland*, 233–35.
129 The form 'maiesteis' is written in the original court records. NRS, JC2/2, fo. 206r.
130 NRS, JC2/2, fos. 206v–207r.
131 Busch, *They Shipped All In*, 40.
132 Articles 1 and 9, NRS, JC2/2, fo. 201v.
133 NRS, JC2/2, fo. 201v.
134 'Elfshot' is part of fairy belief, a 'shot' sent out by the fairies to hurt humans. Willumsen, *Witches of the North*, 137; Lizanne Henderson and Edward J. Cowan, *Scottish Fairy Belief: A History* (East Linton, 2004), 18, 32, 77–9; article 2, NRS JC2/2, fo. 201v.
135 A cripple. NRS, JC2/2, fo. 201v, article 3.
136 See for instance German trials: the trial of Susanna Grethen Sundtgen from Fell, Landeshauptarchiv Koblenz (LHAK), Bestand 211, no. 2222, Kriminalischer proceß Grethen Sundtgen zu Fell, fos. 1–18.
137 Normand and Roberts, *Witchcraft in Early Modern Scotland*, 144. *Bairns* means 'children'.
138 *Quhilk* in the Older Scottish tongue means 'which'.
139 *Quha* in the Older Scottish tongue means 'who'.
140 NRS, JC2/2, fo. 203r.
141 Normand and Roberts, *Witchcraft in Early Modern Scotland*, 155.
142 In this quotation, '//' denotes page shift. NRS, JC2/2, fos. 205v–206r.
143 Normand and Roberts, *Witchcraft in Early Modern* Scotland, 145.
144 Willumsen, *Witches of the North*, 34; Willumsen, *Dømt til ild og bål*, 45.
145 NRS, JC2/2, fo. 201v.
146 Paterson, 'Witches' Sabbath in Scotland', 387; Brock, *Satan and the Scots*, 119, 122, 164–67; Dye, *Devillische Wordis*, 61–140.
147 Christina Larner, 'James VI and I and Witchcraft', in Larner, *Witchcraft and Religion*, 8.
148 George F. Warner, 'The Library of James VI', *Miscellany of The Scottish History Society* 1 (1893), xlviii; Normand and Roberts, *Witchcraft in Early Modern Scotland*, 330.
149 Normand and Roberts, *Witchcraft in Early Modern Scotland*, 327–28.
150 Reginald Scot, Johann Weyer, Jean Bodin, Andreas Gerardus Hyperius, Niels Hemmingsen, and Cornelius Agrippa are mentioned. Normand and Roberts, *Witchcraft in Early Modern Scotland*, 353–56.
151 Normand and Roberts, *Witchcraft in Early Modern Scotland*, 137.
152 Normand and Roberts, *Witchcraft in Early Modern Scotland*, 136.
153 The alleged witches' means of transport to the convention, however, might have been unrealistic. One participant at the North Berwick convention, Jean Fian, is said to have been brought through the air from his home in Tranent to North Berwick.
154 Normand and Roberts, *Witchcraft in Early Modern Scotland*, 139, 148.
155 NRS, JC26/13 (separate document).
156 NRS, JC26/13 (separate document).
157 NRS, JC26/13, Bundle 1, 'Examination by the Minister, Andrew Fairfull'.
158 Additions to the formal document.
159 NRS, JC26/13, separate document, six articles, and two eiks.
160 NRS, JC26/13, Bundle 1, list of witnesses.
161 In the presence of Mr Alexander Colville of Blair, His Majesty's Justice deputy. NRS, JC26/13, Bundle 1.
162 The primary documents used for this analysis consist of court records from the central court in Edinburgh, 1643, in addition to a number of loose documents related to the same case: additions to Helene Clerk's dittay; examination by the minister, Andrew Fairfull 1643; list of witnesses, 10 March 1645; Helene Clerk's petition; and the list of accusations against her and whether they were repelled or deemed relevant.
163 NRS, JC26/13, Examination before Mr Fairfull.

164 Goodare, 'Scottish Witchcraft Act'. The Witchcraft Act was passed in 1563, during the reign of Mary Stuart, Queen of Scots. This was three years after the establishment of Protestantism, coincidentally the same year it was passed in England.
165 Conjuration of the spirits of the dead for purposes of magically revealing the future or influencing the course of events.
166 Orig. *sheitis*.
167 Orig. *toomed*.
168 Orig. *repair*.
169 NRS, JC26/13, Bundle 1, 'Examination by the Minister, Andrew Fairfull'.
170 NRS, JC26/13, Bundle 1, 'Examination by the Minister, Andrew Fairfull'.
171 Testify, give evidence upon oath.
172 Orig. *acquirit how the pairtie accused wes hir reply wes scho will be weill for they neidit not to send for hir seing thair wes nothing that wes done bot the pairtie accused could doe the samyn hirselff*. NRS, JC26/13, Bundle 1, Examination by the Minister, Andrew Fairfull.
173 NRS, JC26/13, Bundle 1, 'Examination by the Minister, Andrew Fairfull'.
174 NRS, JC26/13, Bundle 1, 'Examination by the Minister, Andrew Fairfull'.
175 Orig. *indweller*.
176 Orig. *fasterence evin*.
177 Orig. *Margaret Boyll indweller in leith sworne depones that thair being ane veriance betuixt the deponer and the pairtie accuset anent sum oysteris the pairtie accuset affirmit yit the deponer sould now it, at that tyme And th[air]efter the deponer tuik seiknes and lay auchtene oulkis seik dwyneing And the pairtie accused haveing sent in ane mccrell about fasterence evin w[i]th helene sword now deid scho then recoverit heir health and became weill, and when the said helene brocht in the mcrell scho gave the deponer ane strait comand that scho sould under the paine of hir lyff eit of it yit micht bot to eit it the morne neirest hir hairt*. NRS, JC26/13, Bundle 1, 'Examination by the Minister, Andrew Fairfull'.
178 Orig. *Barbara purves indweller in leith being solemnelie sworne befoir us & in our presence depones that about ten yeir syne or th[air]by the pairtie accuset hir husband being addettit to the deponer Sevin pundis and the deponer haveing cumet to hir and inquyreing hir money the pairtie accused sayd go home go home, tho sould go worse home nor scho cam afield Quhairupon scho haveing cumet home the deponer hir bairne wes taikin out of ane seithing kettill*. NRS, JC26/13, Bundle 1, 'Examination by the Minister, Andrew Fairfull'.
179 Orig. *Helene thomsone spous to williame craig in newheavin being solemnelie sworne befoir us & in our presence that Johne Smith haveing cumet in to hir hous and affirmeing the pairtie accused wald be his deathe seing that he had not maried the pairtie accused hir dochter contractit seiknes and suspecting the said helene clark pairtie accused to be the occasioner thairof went to the pairtie accuset at the dwelling house of the deponer so craved his healthe and send about ane pynt of aill to the quhilk pairtie accused gave him tua eggis quhilk he eitit and quhan he wes telling the pairtie accused that he wald go to ane doctor to mend his bak scho sayd that he could not doe it and ane schort tyme th[air]efter he died*. NRS, JC26/13, Bundle 1, 'Examination by the Minister, Andrew Fairfull'.
180 Orig. *deponed*.
181 Orig. *Williame Scobie in musselburt haveing sichtit the pairtie accused and scho haveing cassing af hir clois*. NRS, JC26/13, Bundle 1, 'Examination by the Minister, Andrew Fairfull'.
182 NRS, JC26/13, Bundle 1, 'Examination by the Minister, Andrew Fairfull'.
183 Parishioners.
184 NRS, JC26/13. Separate sheet.
185 In Orkney, demonological ideas were known in 1615. Also in the trial of Katherene Grieve alias Miller in 1633, such ideas appeared. Register of the Privy Council (RPC), 2nd series, vol. 5, 544–48, 556–59.
186 NRS, JC26/13, Bundle 1, 'Examination by the Minister, Andrew Fairfull'.
187 NRS, JC26/13. Separate sheet.
188 NRS, JC26/13, Bundle 1, 'Evaluation of articles'.
189 NRS, JC26/13, Bundle 1, 'Evaluation of articles'.

190 NRS, JC26/13, Bundle 1, 'Evaluation of articles'.
191 NRS, JC26/13, Bundle 1, 'Evaluation of articles'.
192 NRS, JC26/13, Bundle 1, 'Addition to helene clerk hir dittay'.
193 The metal lead. Dictionary of the Older Scottish Tongue (DOST), s.v. 'lede/leid'.
194 A hoop for a tub. DOST, 'girth/girth'.
195 *Quhilk sho hes affirmit to be of veritie in p[rese]nce of the Laird of benholme, James Halybur-*
    toun, Ro[ber]t Robertson, John Luikup & Mr Alexr Wairdrope. NRS, JC26/13, Bundle 1,
    'Addition to helene clerk hir dittay'.
196 NRS, JC26/13, Bundle 1, 'Addition to helene clerk hir dittay'.
197 Orig. *According to the q[uhi]lk thraitini[n]g he nevir mad ony th[air]eftir Bot w[i]thin aucht*
    dayis th[air]eftir be yo[u]r sorcerie & witchcraft ye laid ane heavie diseas & seiknes upone the said
    W[illia]m Oswale Quha dwynet & pynet away dyv[eris] dayis and nytis w[i]th grit dolloris &
    payne th[air]intill And means be yo[u]r sorcerie & witchcraft deceissit th[air]of. NRS, JC26/13,
    Bundle 1, 'Addition to helene clerk hir dittay'.
198 NRS, JC26/13, Bundle 1, 'Addition to helene clerk hir dittay'.
199 NRS, JC26/13, Bundle 1, 'Addition to helene clerk hir dittay'.
200 Orig. *About ane 15 days befoir his daith, being in the deponers hous sit doun at the fyre*
    syd w[i]th his goodsister in cu[m]panie w[i]th him And being wonderfullie pynet spak thir wordis
    to the deponet schoe haveing regratit his waiknes & p[rese]nt estait In good faith Jonet thair is
    none ye wyt of my waiknes bot helene clerk and schoe will be my daith for I am trublit with hir
    in the nycht & uth[e]r thrie women w[i]th hir. NRS, JC26/13, Bundle 1, 'Jonet Mcinlay
    deposition concernes the witch of Newheavin tane up the xij of mairch 1645'.
201 Orig. *Item in the moneth of [blank] the year of god jajvjct [blank] yeiris Ye the said helene*
    haveing sauld to margaret runsieman than servant to Lucres alias Luse Cokburne indweller in
    [blank] ane laid gallone full of oisteris And cu[m]ing at that tyme to the said Lucres hous th[air]
    w[i]th, ye set doun the laid gallone and bad the said servand namitt margaret runsieman to toome
    the leid gallone Quhilk servand ansring yow in ruche and hard woirdes I haif nothing to toome it
    ye marking that hir misbehavior & angrie countenance ye come & toomed the lead gallone yo[u]r
    selffe Quhairupone the said servand woman tuik up the said lead gallone and slang it frome hir
    and th[air]w[i]th brak ane of the girthes th[air]of Quhilk being sa done be hir in yo[u]r pres-
    ence & in sic dispyte, ye than said to the said servand woman, hes thow done this I sall gar the
    rew and repent the same Accordingly to the q[uhi]lk malicious thraitini[n]g sua utterit be yow
    the said m[ar]garet runsieman the same verie nycht be yo[u]r sorcerie & witchcraft laid be yow
    upoun hir hir leg was brunt. Quhilk sho hes affirmit to be of veritie in p[rese]nce of the Laird
    of benholme, James Halyburtoun, Ro[ber]t Robertson, John Luikup & Mr Alexr Wairdrope.
    NRS, JC26/13, Bundle 1. 'Addition to Helen Clerk's dittay'.
202 Orig. *ffor.*
203 NRS, JC26/13, Bundle 1, 'Addition to helene clerk hir dittay'.
204 Orig. *Q[uhai]rupone it followit that w[i]thin fyftene dayis th[ai]reftir the s[ai]d James bisset tuik*
    bed & lay pyneing w[i]th seiknes the space of 29 weikes eftir and wald have swat su[m]tymes
    thrie sarkis in a day and soe dwynet & deit'. NRS, JC26/13, Bundle 1, 'Jonet Mcinlay
    deposition concernes the witch of Newheavin tane up the xij of mairch 1645'.
205 Probably means 'Give it was undone, what is done'.
206 NRS, JC26/13, Bundle 1, 'Jonet Mcinlay deposition concernes the witch of
    Newheavin tane up the xij of mairch 1645'.
207 This contradicts the beginning of the court records, where it is said that Elspeth
    washed her.
208 NRS, JC26/13 (separate document).
209 NRS, JC26/13 (separate document).
210 NRS, JC26/13, Bundle 1, 'Mr Fairfull's examination'.
211 NRS, JC26/13, Bundle 1, 'Mr Fairfull's examination'.
212 NRS, JC26/13 (separate document).
213 Whereupon.
214 NRS, JC26/13, Bundle 1, 'Mr Fairfull's examination'.

215 *Albueris* might be a misspelling for *labueris, labouraris*: labourers, one who performs manual work, a land worker, a peasant.

216 Heritors: a landowner, a landed proprietor.

217 NRS, JC26/13 (separate document).

218 Orig. *The said helene and the deponer haveing ane long tyme befoir that space not speking togidder in respecte of the former contraversie betuixt the deponers husband and the pairtie accused.*

219 NRS, JC26/13, Bundle 1, 'Mr Fairfull's examination'.

220 Orig. *q[uhai]rof lykas the said helen a litle befoir his daith viz at the pace monday im[m]ediatlie preceiding came to Jonet anisone spous to the said James bisset quha had not spokin w[i]th hir ane lang tyme of befoir.*

221 NRS, JC26/13 (separate document).

222 NRS, JC26/13, Bundle 1, 'Mr Fairfull's examination'.

223 NRS, JC26/13 (separate document).

224 NRS, JC26/13, Bundle 1, 'Mr Fairfull's examination'.

225 The others were the Laird of Benholme, James Halyburtoun, Ro[ber]t Robertson, and John Luikup.

226 NRS, JC26/13, Bundle 1. 'Addition to Helen Clerk's dittay'.

227 Weeks. DOST, wouk, wo(u)lk, weke, wik(e).

228 NRS, JC 26/13 (separate document).

229 NRS, JC 26/13 (separate document).

230 When Helene brought in the mackerel, she gave the deponer a direct command that under the pain of her life she was to eat it in the morning close to her heart. NRS, JC26/13, Bundle 1, 'Mr Fairfull's examination'.

231 Orig. *deponer*, one who made a formal or sworn statement.

232 NRS, JC26/13, Bundle 1, 'Mr Fairfull's examination'.

233 NRS, JC26/13 (separate document).

234 Goodare, 'Scottish Witchcraft Act'.

235 A professional law agent or advocate. Ref. DOST, procurato(u)r.

236 NRS, JC26/13, Bundle 1, 'Helene Clerk's petition'.

237 Informers, accusers. Ref. DOST, dilator.

238 NRS, JC26/13, Bundle 1, 'Helene Clerk's petition'.

239 NRS, JC26/13, Bundle 1, 'Helene Clerk's petition'.

240 NRS, JC26/13, Bundle 1, 'Helene Clerk's petition'.

241 RPC, 3rd series, vol. 6 (1678–80), 627–29.

242 Investigators were Minister James Calderwood, Minister James Cockburn, court messenger David Chalmer, schoolmaster William Cockburn, Richard Dalgleish, miller John Fowler, Malcolm Greive, Sir of Keith, Robert Hepburn, John Pringle of Woodhead, William Sheil, indweller in Keith, James Youle, indweller in Keith.

243 RPC, 3rd series, vol. 6, 628.

244 Sir Robert Hepburn of Keith. He bought the estate of Peaston from the Cockburn of Ormiston family in 1657 (*Register of the Great Seal of Scotland*, x, no. 610). He was one of two lairds commissioned to arrange the witches' execution (RPC, 3rd series, vol. 6, 627).

245 RPC, 3rd series, vol. 6, 628.

246 The same amount (three dollars) had been given to George Rae, servitor to Mr Thomas Hay, for writing out four commissions several times.

247 RPC, 3rd series, vol. 6, 628. Money was written in Roman numerals: l, li, or lib was short for the Latin 'libra' = a pound; Sh or s = shilling; d = pennies; c or ct stands for centum = 100. There were 20 shillings in a pound and 12 pennies in a shilling; a merk was worth two-thirds of a Scots pound; from 1600 one pound Scots was worth one-twelfth of one pound Sterling. See www.scotsarchivesearch.co.uk.

248 A partly ceremonial junior court official.

249 The clerk of the criminal court affirmed that the King's Advocate's dues for the indictment of each witch was *ij merks, inde for 13 indytments is 93 lb. 6 s. 8 d.,* so the Laird

himself gave to the Kings Advocat, first in gold 45 lib., and last 14 dollors; is 40 lb. 12 s.; inde, given to the Kings Advocat in all 85:12.0. RPC, 3rd series, vol. 6, 628.

250 RPC, 3rd series, vol. 6, 629.
251 Orig. *Jacobum ffoulis.*
252 Orig. *Robertum.*
253 Orig. *Joannem.*
254 Orig. *Davidem Balfour de fforret.* Initial double 'ff' is F.
255 NRS, JC2/15.
256 A waving movement.
257 A sprinkling of dew or water.
258 NRS, JC2/15.
259 *Hauch, halch, haw, haughie, hauchie.* A piece of level ground on the banks of a river, river-meadow land. DOST, s.v. 'haugh'.
260 NRS, JC2/15.
261 NRS, JC2/15.
262 Larner, *Enemies of God,* 130.
263 NRS, JC2/15.
264 NRS, JC2/15.
265 NRS, JC2/15.
266 NRS, JC2/15.
267 A craftsman using a hammer for metal work.
268 A tin-plate smith.
269 A baker.
270 The names of the members of the assize were Robert Pringle in Templehall, Robert Fouler [orig. ffouler], in Overkeith, John Hempseed in Morris, James Symspon mer[chan]t in Ed[inbu]r[gh], Thomas Gray mer[chan]t in Ed[inbu]r[gh], John Fouler [orig. ffouler], in Humbie-milne, William Henryson in Ormiestoun, James Paterson skinner, Thomas Fisher [orig. ffisher], elder taylor, John Adam mer[chan]t, James Warrock mer[chan]t, Alexr Wilson hammerman, Henry Barclay baxter, Alexr Laying whitironman, Thomas Kincaid skinner.
271 NRS, JC2/15.
272 The ritual to return a woman to church after childbirth.
273 Crichton, Midlothian.
274 NRS, JC2/15.
275 William Thomson is apparently the same person as William Hair, whose name is mentioned in the dittay.
276 Presumably, *cleuchs* means claws, although the spelling is unusual. See Goodare, 'Flying Witches', 164.
277 Orig. *Leswade Loanhead* without any connecting word in between. These are two places, Lasswade and Loanhead. Lasswade is a village and parish in Midlothian, on the River North Esk, nine miles south of Edinburgh City centre, between Dalkeith and Loanhead. Melville Castle lies to the north and east.
278 Goodare, 'Flying Witches', 164; Willumsen, *Witches of the North,* 124.
279 JC2/15.
280 JC2/15.
281 Also mentioned by Brock, *Satan and the Scots,* 157.
282 See the trial of Susanna Grethen Sundtgen from Fell, Landeshauptarchiv Koblenz (LHAK), Bestand 211, no. 2222, Kriminalischer proceβ Grethen Sundtgen zu Fell. See also Pierre de Lancre, *Tableau de l'inconstance des mauvais anges et démons* [Tableau of the Inconstancy of Evil Angels and Demons] (Paris, 1613). For other Scottish examples, see Goodare, 'Men and the Witch-Hunt'. See also the chapter on Denmark this volume, in specific the trial of Mette Kongens.
283 JC2/15. In the margin of the document is written 'The proba[tio]n'.
284 Orig. *ffind.*

285 Orig. *fforrester*.
286 JC2/15. In the margin of the document is written 'The verdict of the assyse'.
287 The Gallowlee of Edinburgh was at Pilrig, between Edinburgh and Leith. The women mentioned are probably among the ones who were declared fugitives. RPC, 3rd series, vol. 6, 629.
288 Orig. *ffryday*.
289 JC2/15. In the margin of the document is written 'The doom'.
290 RPC, 3rd series, vol. 6, 627.
291 RPC, 3rd series, vol. 6, 627.
292 The women had probably been given plaids, blankets, to keep them warm while imprisoned.
293 Orig. *damster*. A minor ceremonial court official who declared the sentence formally, but played no role in deciding the verdict or sentence.
294 Carpenter.
295 RPC, 3rd series, vol. 6, 627.

6 England—Familiars, Teats, and Witchfinders

1 I would like to thank Malcolm Gaskill for kindly lending me his transcriptions of the court records of these trials.
2 Cambridge University Library (CUL), Ely District Records (EDR) E12 1647/11.
3 NAL, earlier Public Record Office (PRO), Home Circuit Assize Records (ASSI) 45/7/1/7.
4 Ewen, *Witch Hunting and Witch Trials*; *Witchcraft and Demonianism*; Gaskill, 'Witchcraft Trials in England'.
5 Goodare, *European Witch-Hunt*, 7.
6 J. S. Cockburn, *A History of English Assizes 1558–1714*, edited by D. E. C. Yale (Cambridge, 1972).
7 The archives of the ecclesiastical courts of Essex have survived, as well as records of the Northern and Oxford circuits of the assizes and goal books from the Western circuit. Sharpe, *Instruments of Darkness*, 119–21; Ewen, *Witch Hunting and Witch Trials*; Gaskill, 'Witchcraft Trials in England', 283–98.
8 Sharpe, *Instruments of Darkness*, 125.
9 Gibson, *Reading Witchcraft*; 'French Demonology'; Millar, *Witchcraft, the Devil and Emotions*; Sharpe, 'English Witchcraft Pamphlets'.
10 Macfarlane, *Witchcraft in Tudor and Stuart England*; Thomas, *Religion and the Decline of Magic*; Goodare, *European Witch-Hunt*, 250–52, 370–71.
11 Sharpe, *Instruments of Darkness*, 125.
12 Sharpe, *Instruments of Darkness*, 114.
13 Gaskill, *Witchfinders*; Sharpe, *Instruments of Darkness*, 128–47; Gaskill, 'Witchcraft Trials in England', 295.
14 Millar, *Witchcraft, the Devil, and Emotions*.
15 Goodare, *European Witch-Hunt*, 28–29, 410–11.
16 Sharpe, *Instruments of Darkness*, 125; Gaskill, 'Witchcraft Trials in England', 289.
17 Goodare, *European Witch-Hunt*, 410; Sharpe, *Instruments of Darkness*, 125; Millar, *Witchcraft, the Devil, and Emotions*, 3–7; Sharpe, *Witchcraft in Early Modern England*.
18 Levack, *Witch-Hunt in Early Modern Europe*, 22.
19 The first indictment printed in Ewen's book is from 1560. Ewen, *Witch Hunting and Witch Trials*, 117; Gaskill, 'Witchcraft Trials in England', 291.
20 Macfarlane, *Witchcraft in Tudor and Stuart England*, 147–207.
21 Gaskill, 'Witchcraft Trials in England', 293.
22 Gaskill, 'Witchcraft Trials in England', 294; Sharpe, *Instruments of Darkness*, 77, 99, 101, 127; Gibson, *Reading Witchcraft*, 134–39; Robert Poole (ed.), *The Lancashire Witches. Histories and Stories* (Manchester, 2002), with chapters on the trials by, among others, James

Sharpe, Stephen Pumfrey, Marion Gibson, and Jonathan Lumby; Peter G. Maxwell-Stuart, *The British Witch: The Biography* (Stroud, 2014), 210–12. These trials have also resulted in fictional works, among them Robert Neill, *Mist over Pendle* (London, 2011); Rachel A. C. Hasted, *The Pendle Witch-Trial 1612* (Preston, 1987); Walter Bennett, *The Pendle Witches* (Preston, 1957).

23 The pamphlet has resulted in several publications, among them Bennett, *Pendle Witches*; Hasted, *Pendle Witch-Trial*.

24 Gaskill, 'Witchcraft Trials in England', 293.

25 Ewen, *Witchcraft and Demonianism*, 244–51.

26 Goodare, *European Witch-Hunt*, 172, 240.

27 Gaskill, 'Witchcraft Trials in England', 295; *Witchfinders*, 259, 271; Gibson, *Early English Trial Pamphlets*; Sharpe, *Witchcraft in Early Modern England*.

28 Gaskill, 'Witchcraft Trials in England', 295; *Witchfinders*; Sharpe, *Instruments of Darkness*, 128–47; Maxwell-Stuart, *British Witch*, 241–43; Millar, *Witchcraft, the Devil and Emotions*, 4, 7, 12, 120–30; Levack, *Witch-Hunting in Scotland*, 75–76.

29 Gaskill, 'Witchcraft Trials in England', 295.

30 Barry, *Witchcraft and Demonology*, 9.

31 Barry, *Witchcraft and Demonology*, 9.

32 Gaskill, 'Witchcraft Trials in England', 298.

33 Brian P. Levack, 'The Decline and End of Persecutions', in Ankarloo and Clark, *Witchcraft and Magic in Europe*, 77.

34 W. B. Carnochan, see Millar, *Witchcraft, the Devil, and Emotions*, 22, note 22.

35 The case of George Lukins. Barry, *Witchcraft and Demonology*, 206–55.

36 Jonathan Barry, 'Public Infidelity and Private Belief? The Discourse of Spirits in Enlightenment Bristol', in Owen Davies and Willem de Blécourt (eds.), *Beyond the Witch Trials: Witchcraft and Magic in Enlightenment Europe* (Manchester, 2004), 117–43; Brian Hoggard, 'The Archeology of Counter-Witchcraft and Popular Magic', in Davies and de Blécourt, *Beyond the Witch Trials*, 167–86.

37 Ewen, *Witchcraft and Demonianism*.

38 For instance Gaskill, 'Witchcraft Trials in England', 286–96.

39 Goodare, *European Witch-Hunt*, 370.

40 Macfarlane, *Witchcraft in Tudor and Stuart England*; Thomas, *Religion and the Decline of Magic*.

41 Goodare, *European Witch-Hunt*, 370.

42 Sharpe, *Instruments of Darkness*, 105–27; *Witchcraft in Early Modern England*.

43 Sharpe, *Witchcraft in Early Modern England*, 12.

44 Sharpe, *Witchcraft in Early Modern England*, 12–13; *Instruments of Darkness*, 11–12.

45 Larner, *Enemies of God*; Levack, *Witch-Hunting in Scotland*, 92; Goodare, 'Witch-Hunting and the Scottish State', 122–45.

46 Goodare, *European Witch-Hunt*, 95.

47 Goodare, *European Witch-Hunt*, 252. Other countries who experienced this development are France and Italy.

48 Levack, *Witch-Hunting in Scotland*, 27.

49 Levack, *Witch-Hunting in Scotland*, 27; Langbein, *Origins of Adversary*, 24.

50 Scotland in fact had a system of administering criminal justice in the districts that resembled the English assizes, but this made itself felt primarily when the number of witchcraft trials were on the decline. Willumsen, *Seventeenth-Century Witchcraft Trials*, 47–50; Cockburn, *History of English Assizes*, 127–28.

51 Sharpe, *Witchcraft in Early Modern England*; Gaskill, 'Witchcraft Trials in England'; Levack, *Witch-Hunting in Scotland*, 2–14.

52 Gibson, *Witchcraft and Society*, 4; Millar, *Witchcraft, the Devil and Emotions*, 21, note 10.

53 Millar, *Witchcraft, the Devil and Emotions*, 3.

54 Millar, *Witchcraft, the Devil and Emotions*, 3–4.

55 Gibson, *Witchcraft and Society*, 5.

56 Gibson, *Witchcraft and Society*, 3–7.

57 Gibson, *Witchcraft and Society*, 5–6.

58 C. L'Estrange Ewen, *Witch Hunting and Witch Trials*, 65, with reference to David Jardine, *A Reading on the Use of Torture in the Criminal Law of England Previously to the Commonwealth* (London, 1837). On the use of torture in England, see also Goodare, *European Witch-Hunt*, 195.

59 Goodare, *European Witch-Hunt*, 195.

60 Levack, *Witch-Hunting in Scotland*, 3.

61 Goodare, *European Witch-Hunt*, 86.

62 Clive Holmes, 'Women: Witnesses and Witches', *Past and Present*, 140 (1993), 49–50.

63 Levack, *Witch-Hunting in Scotland*, 45.

64 Levack, *Witch-Hunting in Scotland*, 54.

65 Goodare, *European Witch-Hunt*, 199.

66 Goodare, *European Witch-Hunt*, 200.

67 Gaskill, *Witchfinders*.

68 Gaskill, *Witchfinders*, 252.

69 Gaskill, *Witchfinders*, 252.

70 Gaskill, *Witchfinders*, 252.

71 Gaskill, *Witchfinders*, 252.

72 Gaskill, *Witchfinders*, xiii, 3, 38, 41, 43, 51, 69, 187–88, 269–70.

73 In the 1640s, the conviction rate was between 42% and 46%, compared to between 23% and 28% previously. Gaskill, *Witchfinders*, 293, 295.

74 CUL, EDR E12 1647/11.

75 CUL, EDR E12 1647/11.

76 CUL, EDR E12 1647/11.

77 CUL, EDR E12 1647/11.

78 CUL, EDR E12 1647/11.

79 CUL, EDR E12 1647/11.

80 CUL, EDR E12 1647/11.

81 CUL, EDR E12 1647/11.

82 CUL, EDR E12 1647/11.

83 Gaskill, 'Witchcraft Trials in England', 295.

84 Gaskill, *Witchfinders*, 48.

85 Gaskill, *Witchfinders*, 4, 14, 149, 196; Levack, *Witch-Hunt in Early Modern Europe*, 149.

86 CUL, EDR E12 1647/11.

87 In a Finnmark case from 1663, Sigri Olsdatter emphasized after her confession that her child was not present during a witches' gathering. Willumsen, *Witchcraft Trials in Finnmark*, 205.

88 Willumsen, *Kilder til trolldomsprosessene*, 123, 125; *Witchcraft Trials in Finnmark*, 210, 215.

89 Liv H. Willumsen, 'Historical Approaches to Child Witches', *Oxford Bibliographies in Childhood Studies*, 2015. DOI:10.1093/OBO/9780199791231-0156, www.oxfordbibliographies.com/viao/document/obo-9780199791231/obo-9780199791231-0156.xml.

90 Willumsen, *Witches of the North*, 132–33, 207.

91 Normand and Roberts, *Witchcraft in Early Modern Scotland*, 235.

92 CUL, EDR E12 1647/11.

93 CUL, EDR E12 1647/11.

94 CUL, EDR E12 1647/11.

95 In the 1662 trial of Jonet Morrison in Bute, the fairies' whirlwind is also called 'blasting'. Willumsen, *Seventeenth-Century Witchcraft Trials*, 142.

96 See for instance the trial against Susanna Grethen Sundtgen from Fell. Landeshauptarchiv Koblenz, LHAK Bestand 211, no. 2222, Kriminalischer proceß Grethen Sundtgen zu Fell, fos. 1–18. See also the chapter on Denmark in this book.

97 The witches' sabbath was known in England, but rarely mentioned in trials due to legal restrictions. Goodare, *European Witch-Hunt*, 86.

98 CUL, EDR E12 1647/11.

99 CUL, EDR E12 1647/11.

100 Gibson, *Witchcraft and Society*, 3–7; Sharpe, *Instruments of Darkness*, 91; Gaskill, *Witchfinders*, 27–30.
101 Gaskill, *Witchfinders*, 30.
102 Millar, *Witchcraft, the Devil, and Emotions*, 48.
103 Millar, *Witchcraft, the Devil, and Emotions*, 4–5.
104 NAL, PRO, ASSI 45/7/1/7r. In 2003, the Public Record Office, London, became the National Archives, London.
105 Orig. 'flitts'.
106 NAL, PRO, ASSI 45/7/1/7r.
107 PRO, ASSI 45/7/1/7r.
108 PRO, ASSI 45/7/1/7v.
109 PRO, ASSI 45/7/1/7v.
110 PRO, ASSI 45/7/1/7v.
111 See Shetland trial, Marion Pardoun alias Peblis, 1644. Willumsen, *Witches of the North*, 207.
112 In the case of Marion Pardoun alias Peblis, Shetland, 1644, blood is obtained through biting. Willumsen, *Witches of the North*, 207.
113 PRO, ASSI 45/7/1/7r–45/7/1/7v.
114 Alver, *Mellem mennesker og magter*.
115 PRO, ASSI 45/7/1/8.
116 PRO, ASSI 45/7/1/8.
117 PRO, ASSI 45/7/1/8.
118 PRO, ASSI 45/7/1/8.
119 PRO, ASSI 45/7/1/8.
120 After Elizabeth's accession in 1558, a bill was read in Parliament in 1559, and the Witchcraft Act was enforced by 1560, even if it was not fully ratified until 1563. Norman Jones, 'Defining Superstitions: Treasonous Catholics and the Act against Witchcraft of 1563', in Charles Carlton, Robert L. Woods, Mary L. Robertson, and Joseph S. Block (eds.), *States, Sovereigns and Society in Early Modern England: Essays in Honour of A.J. Slavin* (Stroud, 1998), 187–203; Sharpe, *Instruments of Darkness*, 88–94; Ewen, *Witch Hunting and Witch Trials*, 15–18.
121 PRO, ASSI 45/7/1/8.
122 PRO, ASSI 45/7/1/6r.
123 PRO, ASSI 45/7/1/6r.
124 PRO, ASSI 45/7/1/6r.
125 PRO, ASSI 45/7/1/6v.
126 Gaskill, 'Witchcraft Trials in England', 296.
127 See Simonsen, *Slave Stories*, 46.
128 PRO, ASSI 45/7/1/9.
129 PRO, ASSI 45/7/1/9.

7 Norway—Charms, Blåkoll, and Chasing Fish

1 Næss, 'Presters og prestefruers roller', 113.
2 Sörlin, *Trolldoms- och vidskepelseprocessarna*, 12*ff.*
3 Hagen, 'Witchcraft Criminality', 385.
4 Hagen, 'Witchcraft Criminality', 376, 385; Goodare, 'Finnmark Witches in European Context', 59.
5 Willumsen, *Witches of the North*, 241.
6 Hagen, 'Witchcraft Criminality', 385; Næss, *Trolldomsprosessene*, 24.
7 Goodare, *European Witch-Hunt*, 267.
8 Næss, *Trolldomsprosessene*, 19; Hans E. Næss (ed.), *For rett og rettferdighet i 400 år: Sorenskrivere i Norge 1591–1991* [For Right and Justice During 400 Years: The Magistrates of Norway 1591–1991] (Oslo, 1991), 23.

9 District accounts for the whole of Norway are preserved in the National Archives, Oslo, Rentekammeret.

10 Næss, *Trolldomsprosessene*, 20.

11 There is one series of court records from Jæren and Dalane, starting in 1613, and one from Ryfylke, starting in 1616. Næss, *Trolldomsprosessene*, 19.

12 Næss, *Trolldomsprosessene*, 29.

13 This is shown by a comparison of the periods 1621–60 and 1661–1700. For Rogaland, 68 trials took place in the first period, and 40 in the last. Næss, *Trolldomsprosessene*, 30.

14 Næss, *Trolldomsprosessene*, 34.

15 Næss, *Trolldomsprosessene*, 33 The Witchcraft Decree of 1617 was standing law until 1842; however it did not have any real power during the last 150 years.

16 Ragnhild Botheim, *Trolldomsprosessane i Bergenhus len 1566–1700* [The Witchcraft Trials in Bergenhus District, 1566–1700] (M.A. thesis, University of Bergen, 1999), xviii.

17 Botheim, *Trolldomsprosessane i Bergenhus*, lx.

18 Botheim, *Trolldomsprosessane i Bergenhus*, xix.

19 Botheim, *Trolldomsprosessane i Bergenhus*, lvii.

20 Knutsen, *Trolldomsprosessene på Østlandet*, 24.

21 Knutsen, *Trolldomsprosessene på Østlandet*, 21.

22 Knutsen, *Trolldomsprosessene på Østlandet*, 29–30.

23 Indeed, 47 out of 70 death sentences were passed in 1619–25. Knutsen, *Trolldomsprosessene på Østlandet*, 29.

24 Knutsen, *Trolldomsprosessene på Østlandet*, 22.

25 Knutsen, *Trolldomsprosessene på Østlandet*, 80, 91–94, 141.

26 Knutsen, *Trolldomsprosessene på Østlandet*, 201–2.

27 Knutsen, *Trolldomsprosessene på Østlandet*, 196–97; 'End of the Witch Hunts'; 'Norwegian Witchcraft Trials.

28 For Swedish and Åland trials, see the chapters on Sweden and Finland in this book. For Rendalen trials, see Anne-Sofie Schjøtner Skaar, 'Da djevelen var løs i Rendalen—en av de siste trolldomsprosessene i Norge' [When the Devil Was Loose in Rendalen—One of the Last Witchcraft Trials in Norway], *Heimen*, no. 2 (2021), 115–35.

29 Knutsen, *Trolldomsprosessene på Østlandet*, 27.

30 Hagen, 'Witchcraft Criminality', 382.

31 'Trolldomsforordningen av 1617, Om troldfolck oc deris medvidere' [The 1617 Decree: About Witches and Their Accomplices]. Trolddomsforordningen, 12. oktober 1617, available at https://danmarkshistorien.dk/leksikon-og-kilder/vis/materiale/forordning-om-troldfolk-og-deres-medvidere-12-oktober-1617/ (accessed 23 December 2021).

32 Willumsen, *Steilneset*, 5.

33 Kruse and Willumsen, 'Magic Language', 6, 23–24, 26–32.

34 Willumsen, *Seventeenth-Century Witchcraft Trials*, 261–63; Kruse and Willumsen, *Magic Language*, 13.

35 Willumsen, *Dømt til ild og bål*, 267, 268.

36 Willumsen, *Witches of the North*, 246.

37 In Finnmark, 60 times the European average. Willumsen, *Seventeenth-Century Witchcraft Trials*, 307; Goodare, *European Witch-Hunt*, 83; Goodare, 'Finnmark Witches in European Context', 59.

38 Together with Hammerfest, Vardø was the first place in the district of Finnmark to get status as town in 1789. Randi R. Balsvik, 'Vardø i verden' [Vardø in the World], in Randi R. Balsvik and Jens P. Nielsen (eds.), *Forpost mot øst* [Outpost Towards the East] (Stamsund, 2008), 15–25.

39 Of the accused women, around 90% were Norwegian, the rest Sami. For those executed, the percentage is about the same. Willumsen, *Steilneset*, 6.

40 Willumsen, *Steilneset*, 6.

41 Olaf IV inherited the Kingdom of Norway after the death of his father, Haakon VI of Norway (1340–80).

42 A personal union is a league between two or more countries where one has the ruler of the state in common. Each of the states is independent of each other, but the grade of independence varies strongly in relation to how much power the leader of the state has. Lokalhistoriewiki, s.v. 'Personalunion', last modified 20 May 2014, 13:48, https://lokalhistoriewiki.no/wiki/Personalunion.

43 Steinar Imsen, 'The Union of Calmar: Northern Great Power or Northern German Outpost?' in Christopher Ocker (ed.), *Politics and Reformations: Communities, Polities, Nations, and Empires* (Leiden, 2007), 471–90.

44 Christian III was king of Denmark from 1534 and king of Norway from 1537.

45 In 1534, Christian III was proclaimed king in Rye, in Jutland. However, the royal council refused to accept this and turned to Count Christopher of Oldenburg, who was proclaimed regent at Ringsted and Scania. This resulted in the Count's Feud, a two-year civil war between Protestant and Catholic forces. Christian III sought help from the Swedish king Gustav Vasa. Count Christopher's forces surrendered in 1536. Øystein Rian, 'Christian 3', in *Norsk biografisk leksikon* [Norwegian Biographical Lexicon] (Oslo, 2000), 180–82; Arnved Nedkvitne, *The German Hansa and Bergen 1100–1600* (Cologne, 2014); Justyna Wubs-Mrozewicz and Stuart Jenks (eds.), *The Hanse in Medieval and Early Modern Europe* (Leiden, 2013).

46 After the Dano-Swedish War, the Treaty of Copenhagen was signed in May 1660.

47 Paul D. Lockhart, *Denmark, 1513–1660. The Rise and Decline of a Renaissance Monarchy* (Oxford, 2007); Øystein Rian, *Danmark-Norge 1380–1814* [Denmark-Norway 1380–1814] (Oslo, 1997).

48 Sebastian Olden-Jørgensen, 'Den ældre danske enevælde 1660–1730: Et historiografisk essay' [The Older Danish Absolute Power, 1660–1730: A Historiographic Essay], *Historie/Jyske Samlinger*, 2 (1998), 291–319.

49 Næss, *For rett og rettferdighet*, 34.

50 Willumsen, *Seventeenth-Century Witchcraft Trials*, 11–16.

51 In Norwegian, respectively *lensherre* and *amtmann*. In the original sources, Vardøhus Fortress was sometimes called *Vardøhus Slot*, which means Vardøhus Castle.

52 Willumsen, *Witches of the North*, 232.

53 Stephen A. Mitchell, *Witchcraft and Magic in the Nordic Middle Ages* (Philadelphia, 2011), 146–74.

54 In 1274, Magnus Lagabøte [Magnus the Lawmender], Magnus VI of Norway, issued Magnus Lagabøtes Landslov, a unified code of laws to apply to the whole country. In 1276, he issued a code for the towns, Magnus Lagabøtes bylov. Knut Helle, *Norge blir en stat, 1130–1319* [Norway Becomes a State, 1130–1319] (Oslo, 1974), 134–46.

55 Næss, *Trolldomsprosessene*, 40.

56 Mitchell, *Witchcraft and Magic*, 6–12, 149–53, 204–5.

57 The trial of Ragnhild Tregagås from Fusa, south of Bergen.

58 Botheim, *Trolldomsprosessane i Bergenhus*, 165.

59 Næss, *Trolldomsprosessene*, 78; Siegwarth Petersen and Otto Gr. Lundh (eds.), *Norske Rigs-Registranter*, b. 2 (Christiania, 1863), 571–72; Otto Gr. Lundh and Johan Ernst Sars (eds.), *Norske Rigs-Registranter*, b. 3 (Christiania, 1865), 302.

60 Orig. *rette troldfolck*.

61 Botheim, *Trolldomsprosessane i Bergenhus*, 35.

62 The surname Jyde is the name of a Germanic people who lived on the Jylland Peninsula in Denmark, and is the name of those who live there today.

63 Norwegian *domkapitel*, an assembly of priests at a cathedral, *domkirke*.

64 Stavanger domkapitels protokoll [The Minute Book of Stavanger Cathedral Chapter] no. 1, 1571–1630, 1901 edn., 31.

65 Orig. *Att læse offuer hende for skerffue*, meaning pain in the chest, *cardialgi*. Norsk Ordbok 2014, skjerve, vol. 9, column 1571. Stavanger domkapitels protokoll nr. 1, 1571–1630, 1901 edn., 31. In Ingjald Reichborn-Kjennerud, *Vår gamle trolldomsmedisin* [Our Old Sorcery Medicine], vol. 1 (Oslo, 1928), 150, there is description of cutting of a cross into the skin in order to cure *skjerva*.

66 Kosmos Arildsen was Court of Appeal Judge in Stavanger from 1575 until 1585 and Court of Appeal Judge in Fredrikstad in 1591–99. He belonged to an old noble family. Næss, *Fiat Justitia!*

67 Orig. *Cosmas haffde ladet hende hente till sin høstru.*

68 Orig. *oc lesde lige saananne fabell som de andre.* Stavanger domkapitels protokoll, 31.

69 Orig. *Anno 84, 10 junij, bleff den forfengelig drømmer Jacob Jonson paa Løchen vdi Tymens sogen paa capitelet forhørt.*

70 Orig. *oc loffuit vnder liffs straff aldrig att bruge saadan forfengelighed mere.*

71 Næss, *Trolldomsprosessene,* 258.

72 In fact, in his work of revising the laws in the 1520s, Christian II had already suggested the death penalty for both *maleficium* and healing, but this did not enter into the final laws. However, the laws of Christian II were changed by his successor, Frederic I.

73 Næss, *Trolldomsprosessene,* 78.

74 Næss, *Trolldomsprosessene,* 548.

75 Næss, *Trolldomsprosessene,* 258.

76 Bergen Rådhusprotokoll 1592–1594, *Norske Samlinger* [Norwegian Collections], 1 (1852), 253–57.

77 Anne Pedersdatter was twice accused of witchcraft. The first time was in 1575, when she was acquitted. The second time was in March 1590, and this time she was sentenced to death by being burned at the stake in April 1590.

78 The first was Marit Andersdatter, the wife of Jens Jyde, 1578. Jens Jyde was a bailiff. The second was Johanne Jensdatter Flamske, 1580, 1594. She was a weaver and taught young girls how to weave. The third was Anne Pedersdatter, 1575, 1590. She was the widow of Absalon Pedersson Beyer (1528–1575), teacher at Bergen Cathedral School, *notarius publicus* at Bergen Cathedral Chapter and Castle minister, a theologian who had studied in Copenhagen and Wittenberg. Ragnhild Botheim emphasizes that the elite from the church and from the legal apparatus were involved in these trials. Botheim, *Trolldomsprosessane i Bergenhus,* 104.

79 Orig. *Peder taatt Slotzherren paa Bergenhuus.*

80 Orig. *Laugmannd.*

81 Orig. *Raadtmennd.*

82 Orig. *Och strax römme oc Vnduige aff Staffuangers stichtt.*

83 Orig. *som oc Wijdere Vdi hendis missgierningh wdj gode menndz Missiuez breffuer aff Staffuangerr er antegnitt, for huilcke sager hunn war der aff Staffuangers stichtt römptt.*

84 Claus Meltzow had close family relations with the wife of Absalon Absalonson Beyer (1559–1639), son of Absalon Pederson Beyer and Anne Pedersdatter. Absalon Absalonson Beyer was minister in Gloppen Parish from 1603 onwards.

85 Orig. *oc sidenn giordt hender sielff megett ondt wdi asschillige maader oc paa adschillige tijder.*

86 Orig. *Dannemend,* singular is *dan(n)emand:* reputable, reliable, honorable men.

87 Orig. *Ichtt,* Norwegian *gikt* (pronounced *jikt*), meaning gout or rheumatism. In parts of Norway, there is a tendency in dialects for the 'j' before an 'i' to weaken or disappear, so in fact we should expect *jichtt* with a standing initial 'j' in the original phonetic form.

88 Orig. *saa att hun om anndenn dagen bleff derepther hiolpenn oc kunnde gaa igien som thilforne.*

89 Orig. *Flye bort icht du fulle skam, gud frij os fra laster oc skam, i tre naffn gud faders, sönns og helligaandtz. Amen.*

90 Orig. *Begh,* Norwegian *bek.* A baby's first stools is called *barnebek* in Norwegian.

91 The use of the name Mary is clearly a remnant from the Catholic period. Orig. *Der war Nie Marier schulle bede binnde, den ene bad, den anden bandt 3 fingre nedenfor naufflenn, Der schaltt du bunndenn ligge indthill Domsdegi saalenge den Stein laug der war fra Doms effue.* See Doms effue, doms æve, ex. 5 of I dom, Norsk Ordbok 2014, vol. 2, column 8. Often, there are set phrases in the charms, frequently occurring, like Domsdegi and Doms effue.

92 Orig. *Vreed,* meaning pain, for instance in the stomach. Otto Kalkar, *Ordbog til det ældre danske sprog (1300–1700)* [Dictionary of the Older Danish Language (1300–1700)

(Copenhagen, 1881–1907), sub vrid, ex. 3 of vrid; *Norsk Ordbok* [Norwegian Dictionary] 2014, sub vrid, ex. 5a av vrid, vol. 12, column 1267.

93 Orig. *Bergen blaa*, Norwegian *berget blå*, an expression often found in traditional Norwegian fairy tales. It is connected to Norwegian *blåne* (noun), a place situated so far away that is seems to be blue; or *blåne* (verb), become blue, get a tint of blue.

94 Orig. *Wor herre Jesus reed offuer ein bro der mötte hannom ein Ond quinde, huorth schalttu sagde Christus, Jeg will mig i Mannde hiem, huad schaltu der sagde Christus, Jeg schall brytte lem fra lem, ryg fra Ryg, neij sagde Christus, Du schaltt ingenn lytha oc inngen brytha, Du schaltt dig i Bergen blaa, der schaltu steffne paa i tre naffn gud faders sönns oc hellingaandtz Amen.* 'Steffne paa' means turn the stern (of a boat) in a certain direction.

95 Orig. *Læd*, Norwegian *lade*, Norwegian dialect *lata seg*, Old Danish *lade en arm*, *lade blod af en arm*, English let blood, a method in which cups or suckers are placed on the skin to create a suction, which may facilitate healing with blood.

96 Orig. *att haffue lest wdi gaasefiedt for Vred oc sentt Halte Mogens for Helseboed for hans Kranckdomb.*

97 Orig. *att dersom Magdalena wille were hender tro, oc icke sige fra, Da wiste hun huem dett onde haffde giordt for^{ne}: Magdalena.*

98 Orig. *Oc derhois bekiender for^{ne}: Anna Knudzdaater at haffue bedett for^{ne}: Magdalenes pige hente hennder Kiekeiord aff Kierkegaardenn, thil for^{ne}: Magdalenis helseboedt.*

99 Orig. *Och der hun kom antuordit hun hende samme Kierkeiordt med saadan befalning att hun ein partt deraff schulle legge Vnder Magdalenes Öltönne, oc nogett Vnder dörstockenn, oc nogett Vnder henndis seng.*

100 Orig. *for huad Orsage hun loed hempte oc bruge denn Kirkeiordt.*

101 Ryfylke is a district in the county of Rogaland on the south-western coast of Norway.

102 Orig. *Och hand eingang wille haft med hender att giöre, oc wilde haft hennder aff sengenn.*

103 Orig. *antuordett hand.*

104 In sixteenth- and seventeenth-century Norway, the title 'Herr' indicated a minister.

105 Orig. *Huilchet Saltt for^{ne}: Magdalena oc Lisbett saugde att haffue forsuundet fra dennom.*

106 Orig. *at huor nogenn saadann folck finndes som enten bruge eller giöre forargelig wchristelig middell enten med kaarssignelse lesing oc anndenn saadann wgudelig oc wchristelig hanndell.*

107 Orig. *Da at schulle lade Dennom som befindes enten at söge eller bruge, eller att giöre saadant straffis paa liffuett wdenn all naade, oc med Ingenn saadanne see igiennom fingre.*

108 Orig. *haffde omgaett med henndis wchristelig signelser oc Troldomskaanster.*

109 Orig. *bör at straffes paa Liffuit.*

110 Orig. *forgiort.*

111 Orig. *forhørt oc bestod.*

112 Orig. *Huj ligger din Matmoder i saadann schick.*

113 Orig. *lest wdi gaassefiedt for Vred.*

114 Orig. *Vdi henndis Krarckdom oc Raserij.*

115 Peter Christen Asbjørnsen and Jørgen Moe were the first to publish Norwegian traditional tales from the middle of the 1830s. They published *Norske folkeeventyr* [Norwegian Folk Tales] in pamphlets during the period 1841–44, with a main edition in 1852.

116 See the chapter on Scotland in this book.

117 Willumsen, *Witches of the North*, 173–74, 217.

118 There is a Norwegian fauna of various hill folks: *underjordiske*, literally creatures living under the ground; dwarfs, *dverger*, trolls, *troll*, usually living in the forest; fairies, *alver*; and, not to forget, *hulder*, a beautiful female temptress, unfortunately with a tail. Knut Liestøl, 'Innleiing' [Introduction], in *Norsk folkedikting* [Norwegian Folk Tales] vol. I (Oslo, 1960), 11–60; Olav Bø, *Norsk folkedikting I: Eventyr* [Norwegian Folk Tales I: Fairy Tales] (Oslo, 1977).

119 In Norwegian, this kind of changeling is called *en bytting*. In Scotland, there is a painting by Sir Joseph Noel Paton (1821–1901) displaying such a fairies' ride. See Willumsen, *Dømt til ild og bål*, 199.

120 The use of Norwegian charms and spells related to witchcraft is well documented in Alver, *Mellem mennesker og magter*, 208–65.

121 Johansen, *Da Djævelen var ude*, 37, 88.

122 Orig. *Bergen Rådstue.*
123 Orig. *Oc effteratt wij haffde Rannsagett for^{ne}: Anna Knudtzdaaters saig, Da befinndes wdj san-nhedt att hun wdj mange aar epther denne forschreffne henndis eigen bekienndelse haffde omgaett med henndis wchristelig signelser oc Troldomskaanster emod hågbe^{te}: Konnge Maytts breffuer, oc den forplicht som hunn for Öffrighedenn i Stffuanger giordt haffuer, Thi saugde wij for rette at forne Anna Knudtzdaatter epther saadann henndis eigen bekienndelsse oc Kongelig strenge oc alffuorlig befalning bör att straffes paa Liffuit.* Bergen Rådhusprotokoll 1592–1594, *Norske Samlinger*, bd. 1, 1852, s. 256–57.
124 Orig. *Sittru Peders daatter.*
125 RA, Rentekammeret, Lensregnskaper for Akershus len [National Archives of Norway, District Accounts for Akershus, the Exchequer], Verne Kloster len, 1613–26, 96, Process no. 5, www.trolldomsarkivet.uio.no/perl/ikos/prosesslist.cgi.
126 Around 1180, King Sverre Sigurdsson transferred a royal building at Værne in Rygge to The Order of St John, also called The Malteser Order. This Order was a clerical knight order erected in 1113 based on Kypros. The name of the Order today is The Most Venerable Order to the Hospital of St John of Jerusalem. The order established Værne Monastery in Rygge, where a hospital was built.
127 Sven G. Eliassen, *Østfolds historie* [The History of Østfold], vol. 2 (Sarpsborg, 2005), 269.
128 Jens Paulsøn was bailiff at Værne Monastery in 1621–35. In 1629, he became the king's publican at Værne Monastery. During his period in office, he is the one who signs the district account.
129 Orig. *lendzmanden.*
130 The first jury member mentioned usually acted as deputy bailiff. Hans Clemmetsøn Tøstad was a wealthy farm owner and also sold timber, once together with Peder Backe, the present police officer. He was the police officer, *lensmann*, in Rygge in 1593, and he was a sexton in the church. He is mentioned as a tax payer in the taxation register from 1593 to 1634, https://pettersen-dahl.no/Personer/PersH/Hans%20 Clemmetsen%20Toestad.html (accessed 23 December 2021).
131 Orig. *Backe.*
132 Riksarkivet, Rentekammeret, Lensregnskaper for Akershus len, Verne Kloster len, 1613–26, 96, Process no. 1, www.trolldomsarkivet.uio.no/perl/ikos/prosesslist.cgi.
133 Orig. *och forschr^{ne}: Anne Holter, daa haffuer beschyltt och bekiend for^{ne}: Sittru medt andre flerre medt sig att were belehrt och begaett [sic] medt throlddoms konstir.*
134 Orig. *huilchen hindis beschyldning hun i sin dödz stund stadfestid och ved stoed och aldellis jntted i fra gich mens sagde sig der paa att ville döe och att hun jngen haffde löiett paa.*
135 Orig. *haffuer wij der fore nu her for rettin i mange flere dannemendz affhör och offueruerilße hörtt for^{ne}: Sittru Peders daatters bekiendelße effter forschr^{ne}: Anne Holters beschylding och till spurt hinder, huis hinder var beuist medt samme throlddombs konst och lerdom.*
136 Orig. *Blakholl.* Between Jarle and Storedal in the municipality of Skjeberg is a hill named Blåkoll. According to folk tradition, it was here that the witches had a stopover on their flight to the witches' gathering.
137 Orig. *och daa de reed did forsamlledis de i Holter och red der i fra och till Nabstad och toeg den dieffuill med.*
138 Orig. *Jtem bekiende for^{ne} Sittru dett hun red did till Blakholl paa en sortt kalffue, Jtem beki-ende och saa daa di kom did, var de løstig och glade, och Ane Holtter schaffett dennom vin att driche, Jtem att Marin Nabstad sat der öffuerst thill bordz, Jtem bekiende och dett hindis apos-til hed Stub.* Riksarkivet, Oslo, Værne klosters lensregnskap 2.3.1623–24 med beviser [National Archives of Norway, Oslo, The Accounts of Værne Monastery 2.3.1623–24 with Proofs]. Eliassen, *Østfolds historie* ('Trolldom' chapter); *Hekseprosesser i Østfold* [Witch Trials in Østfold] (Sarpsborg, 1983).
139 Orig. *sagde hun iche kunde komme till att bekiende mere.*
140 Orig. *jtem bekiende dett Niels Nabstad var hos hinder och bad hun iche schulle schylle paa hans quinde Marin.*
141 Orig. *jtem och saa ehrfaris och till kiende giffuis, i dett for^{ne}: Sittru ehr vnduigt och römitt her fra sognitt och sig befrögttid for samme Anne Holters beschyldning.*

142 Orig. *sampt ehrfaris i dette bögde rögtte dett hun haffuer veritt i rob for slike throlddoms konstir.*

143 Orig. *saa osβ siunis jngen vider prouff eller vindisbyrd, her om dene sag fornöden giöris vider en som förre er rörtt.*

144 Orig. *Effter forberörtt leyglighed viste wij iche rettere end att forne Sittru Pedersdatter bör io effter samme bekiendelse och beröffuilβe for samme throlddom att straffes och brendis paa boell och brand.*

145 Orig. *emedens forschr^{ne}: hindis egin bekiendilβe samt Ane Holttters beschylding staa ved deris fulde magtt.*

146 Orig. *saa vell som bekiende fuldkomeligen, ingen menisches person att haffue hendir till stundit eller omreditt noggin menisches person, att paaschylle medt sig att were begoett och belert medt troldoms konstir.*

147 The amount for her food was 1.5 daler; the payment for the executioner's food was 2 daler, and the payment to the executioner for burning her amounted to 6 daler. Riksarkivet, Rentekammeret, Lensregnskaper for Akershus len, Verne Kloster len, 1613–26, 96, Process no. 5, www.trolldomsarkivet.uio.no/perl/ikos/prosesslist.cgi.

148 Orig. *bekiende, sagde,* and *bestoed.*

149 The idea of personal devils called Apostles is known from both Denmark and Finnmark in Norway.

150 Also mentioned by Anne Holter and Anne Vang.

151 See the confessions of Anne Holter and Anne Vang, plus ravens in the confession of Maren, the wife of Daniels. Eliassen, *Hekseprosesser,* 7.

152 Eliassen, *Hekseprosesser,* 6.

153 On different names of this hill in various countries, see Bengt Ankarloo, 'Sweden: The Mass Burnings (1668–1676)', in Ankarloo and Henningsen, *Early Modern European Witchcraft,* 288–92. For more on the Blåkulla trials, see the chapter on Sweden in this book.

154 On Easter Eve one had to draw tar crosses over the doors in the cowshed and stable, so that the Easter witches could not harm the cattle. On Easter night, the Easter witches rode through the air on blue bucks. They used to ride to Blåkullen and home again. Eliassen, *Hekseprosesser,* 6.

155 Orig. *löstig og glade.*

156 Orig. *och bestod dett; och bestoed hun; och att haffue weritt; och saa bekiende; och daa de reed.*

157 Orig. *och daa de reed did forsamlledis de i Holter och red der i fra och till Nabstad.*

158 It is a well-known notion that witches could milk buckets of milk, until blood came out, and then the cow died.

159 Anne Vang uses this expression.

160 The Devil's mother, Ane Koldings, see the chapter on Denmark.

161 Orig. *frimodeligen.*

162 Orig. *Daa for det förste haffuer hun bekientt och bestod dett hun iche kunde anditt en att malche fe (. . .) och sagde hun jnttet andett kunde medt throldomb.* Riksarkivet, Rentekammeret, Lensregnskaper for Akershus len, Verne Kloster, 1613–26, 96. Process no. 3.

163 Orig. *Bleff hinder till spurtt om hun kunde mere eller viste mere, sagde hun ney hun ekon kunde dett och jntted mere en att malche, sagde hun iche kunde komme till at bekiende mere.* Riksarkivet, Rentekammeret, Lensregnskaper for Akershus len, Verne Kloster, 1613–26, 96. Process no. 3.

164 In the panic of 1623, Peder Hasle was in the jury in one trial, acting as judge, and was a witness in another trial, testifying against one of the women. During the 1623 Rygge panic, between the court sessions of 28 May, 23 June, and 7 July, several men in the jury were replaced. For a court session on 6 August, all jury members were replaced. Knutsen, *Trolldomsprosessene på Østlandet,* 163–64.

165 SATØ, SF, no. 10, Records of court proceedings 1654–1663, fos. 210v–277v.

166 Willumsen, *Steilneset,* 11–101; *Witches of the North,* 273.

167 The first part of the word, 'steil' refers to a method of execution called 'steile og hjul', stake and wheel, where the sentenced person was beheaded, the body placed on a stake and the head placed on a wheel.

168 The two women killed during torture on the rack were Ingeborg, Peder Krog's wife, brought before the court at Vardøhus Fortress on 26 January 1663, and Dorette Poulsdatter, brought before the court at Vardøhus Fortress on 10 March 1663. Willumsen, *Witches of the North*, 257; *Trollkvinne i nord*, 39.

169 SATØ, SF, no. 10, Records of court proceedings 1654–1663, fos. 259v, 263v; Willumsen, *Steilneset*, 91.

170 An alleged witch mountain outside Vardø.

171 Jens Ottesen was captain of a ship from Bergen which was shipwrecked.

172 SATØ, SF, no. 10, Records of court proceedings 1654–1663, fo. 258v.

173 Orig. *Huor for^ne: Gundele om deß Beschaffenhed indtit i nogen maader wille Bekiende; heller wedgaae; Mens til hendis Sags opliußning och befrielße waar hun Begierendis at maatte Lade sig a probere paa Siøen; huilchet och bleff Hende tilsteed.* SATØ, SF, no. 10, Records of court proceedings 1654–1663, fo. 263v.

174 Margrette Jonsdatter, Sigri Jonsdatter, Dorette Poulsdatter. Willumsen, *Steilneset*, 91–94.

175 Dorette Poulsdatter was denounced by Margrette Jonsdatter, Ragnilde Endresdatter, and Sigri Jonsdatter. Willumsen, *Steilneset*, 94.

176 Willumsen, *Steilneset*, 94; *Witchcraft Trials in Finnmark*, 253.

177 SATØ, SF, no. 10, Records of court proceedings 1654–1663, fo. 264r.

178 Willumsen, *Witchcraft Trials in Finnmark*, 253–54.

179 Orig. *Thaare Legger.*

180 SATØ, SF, no. 10, Records of court proceedings 1654–1663, fo. 265r.

181 SATØ, SF, no. 10, Records of court proceedings 1654–1663, fos. 265v–266r.

182 SATØ, SF, no. 10, Records of court proceedings 1654–1663, fo. 266r.

183 The case of Ragnilde Endresdatter was subsequently heard by the Court of Appeal. On 23 June 1663, she was acquitted by the presiding judge of the Court of Appeal. Regional State Archives of Trondheim (SAT), LF 1647–1668, fo. 157.

184 SATØ, SF, no. 10, Records of court proceedings 1654–1663, fo. 266r.

185 SAT, LF 1647–1668, fo. 166. The same was the case with Ingeborg, Peder Krog's wife, who was killed on the rack, dragged out to Steilneset, and burned together with living convicted women. Willumsen, *Steilneset*, 86.

186 These were Barbra Olsdatter, Bodel Clausdatter, Brigitte Olufsdatter, and Karen Olsdatter. Willumsen, *Steilneset: Memorial*, 95–98.

187 Those who lost their lives were Sami Elli, 1670; Synøve Johannesdatter, 1678; and Anders Poulsen, 1692. Willumsen, *Steilneset*, 99–101; *Witchcraft Trials in Finnmark*, 415.

188 Orig. *Krytzdands.*

189 Willumsen, *Steilneset*, 79–88.

190 Willumsen, 'Children Accused of Witchcraft', 25–26.

191 SATØ, SF, no. 10, Records of court proceedings 1654–1663, fo. 252v.

192 SATØ, SF, no. 10, Records of court proceedings 1654–1663, fo. 252v.

193 A soft, thick material of carded wool, loosely spun, woolly on one side, smooth on the other, also used to make coats. Åsa Elstad, *Moteløver og heimføingar: Tekstiler og samfunnsendringer i Øksnes og Astafjord 1750–1900* [Moths and Homesteaders: Textiles and Community Change in Øksnes and Altafjord, 1750–1900] (Stamsund, 1997), 153.

194 SATØ, SF, no. 10, Records of court proceedings 1654–1663, fo. 260r–260v.

195 SATØ, SF, no. 10, Records of court proceedings 1654–1663, fo. 261r.

196 SATØ, SF, no. 10, Records of court proceedings 1654–1663, fo. 261r.

197 Goodare, *European Witch-Hunt*, 199; Willumsen, *Seventeenth-Century Witchcraft Trials*, 202–4.

198 SATØ, SF, no. 10, Records of court proceedings 1654–1663, fo. 264r.

199 Orig. *hun waar Liggesaa som de Goed wdi forbemeltte gierninger.*

200 Orig. *forwillit.*

201 Orig. *Huilchett hun och hannom tilsagde.*

202 In this case, Satan himself acts as a personal demon in one of his shapes.

203 Orig. *alt Andit huis hun paa Slog.*

204 Probably powder.
205 SATØ, SF, no. 10, Records of court proceedings 1654–1663, fos. 260 rv.
206 SATØ, SF, no. 10, Records of court proceedings 1654–1663, fo. 260v.
207 Orig. *och ded wed dend høysete Eed och dend Lod och part hun haffuer at formoede sig wdi Guds Rige.*
208 SAT, LF 1647–1668, fos. 159, 162.
209 In Norwegian *utreder.*
210 SATØ, SF, no. 10, Records of court proceedings 1654–1663, fo. 262v.
211 See the sketch of a web of denunciations during the Finnmark panic 1662–63. Willumsen, *Witches of the North*, 276.
212 SATØ, SF, no. 10, Records of court proceedings 1654–1663, fo. 250r.
213 SATØ, SF, no. 10, Records of court proceedings 1654–1663, fo. 268r.
214 For instance the Cinderella motif of losing one shoe. Willumsen, 'Board Games', 269.
215 We see the same in Shetland witchcraft trials, where shape-shifting into a seal is mentioned. Willumsen, *Witches of the North*, 210.
216 Gibson, 'French Demonology', 109.
217 SATØ, SF, no. 10, Records of court proceedings 1654–1663, fo. 261r.
218 The others are Margrette Jonsdatter, Ragnilde Endresdatter, and Sigri Jonsdatter. SATØ, SF, no. 10, Records of court proceedings 1654–1663, fo. 266a.
219 Mandrup Schønnebøl (1603–82) was Court of Appeal Judge for Vardøhus and Nordland during this period. He was living in Steigen in Nordland and came travelling north to Finnmark every third year to hold court sessions along the coast of Finnmark, from east to west.
220 This year, Schønnebøl obtained 'expectancy' to his position as Court of Appeal Judge: a royal letter, *ekspektanse*, with promise that he would get this position. He remained in his position till he died in 1682.
221 The case of Ragnilde Endresdatter was subsequently heard by the Court of Appeal. On 23 June 1663 she was acquitted by the presiding judge of the Court of Appeal. SAT, LF 1647–1668, fo. 157. The case of Gjertrud Siversdatter and her child was heard the same day, and they were acquitted. SAT, LF 1647–1668, fos. 159, 162.
222 Willumsen, 'Children Accused of Witchcraft', 31.
223 Willumsen, *Seventeenth-Century Witchcraft Trials*, 101.
224 Rune B. Hagen, 'Mandrup Pedersen Schønnebøl', in *Store norske leksikon*, January 28, 2019, https://snl.no/Mandrup_Pedersen_Schønnebøl.
225 SATØ, SF, no. 10, Records of court proceedings 1654–1663, fos. 226r–277v.

8 Sweden—Kullen, Blåkulla, and the Water Man

1 Goodare, *European Witch-Hunt*, 28.
2 Means blue hill.
3 Means the valleys.
4 Sörlin, 'Wicked Arts', 49; Ankarloo, 'Sweden', 285.
5 In Swedish *Kronoberg län.*
6 Ankarloo, *Trolldomsprocesserna i Sverige*, 23, 340–43.
7 Sörlin, 'Wicked Arts', 16.
8 Sörlin, 'Witchcraft and Causal Links', 53; 'Wicked Arts', 16.
9 In Swedish *förgjörning*, vexation.
10 In Götaland.
11 Sörlin, 'Witchcraft and Causal Links', 53.
12 In Swedish *vidskepelse.*
13 Sörlin, 'Wicked Arts', 40. In Swedish, *vidskepelse* is the word for superstition.
14 Witchcraft trials took place in the islands of Åland and the province of Österbotten on the east side of the Baltic Sea. Both *maleficium* and demonological ideas were activated,

the devil's pact and the devil's mark were focused on in particular. In Åland, seven women were sentenced to death from 1666 till 1670, in a witchcraft panic led by district judge Nils Psilander. In Österbotten province in 1665–85, 152 persons were accused of witchcraft, and the execution rate was 13%. Toivo, 'What Did a Witch-Hunter', 282; Antero Heikkinen and Timo Kervinen, 'Finland: The Male Domination', in Ankarloo and Henningsen, *Early Modern European Witchcraft*, 321, 333–35.

15 Östling, 'Blåkulla Journeys', 82.
16 Means the virgin.
17 Olaus Magnus, *The History of the Nordic People*, book II, chapter 23 (1982; first published in Rome in 1555), 113.
18 Ankarloo, 'Sweden'.
19 Ankarloo, 'Sweden', 290.
20 Ankarloo, 'Sweden', 290.
21 Sörlin, 'Wicked Arts', 1.
22 Sörlin, 'Wicked Arts', 3.
23 Ankarloo, *Trolldomsprocesserna i Sverige*, 340–42.
24 Sörlin, 'Wicked Arts'. Note 1 on page 1 refers to Linderholm, *De stora häxprocesserna i Sverige*, 55, who stipulates the number of executions between 275 and 300, and Ankarloo, *Trolldomsprocesserna i Sverige*, 228; Per Sörlin, 'Sweden', in Golden, *Encyclopedia of Witchcraft*, 1092–93.
25 Sörlin, 'Wicked Arts'. Note 1 on page 1 refers to Lars M. Svenungsson, *Rannsakningarna om trolldomen i Bohuslän 1669–1672* [The Persecution of Witchcraft in Bohuslän, 1669–1672] (Uddevalla, 1970), 327.
26 Sörlin, 'Sweden', 1093.
27 Hagen, 'Witchcraft Criminality', 376; Sörlin, 'Sweden', 1093; Bergenheim, *Den liderliga häxan*, 60.
28 In Swedish *förgörning*; this word included both maleficent witchcraft and vexation, all forms of injury not resulting from overt acts of violence. Sörlin, 'Wicked Arts', 42, 53, 239.
29 Ankarloo, 'Sweden', 286.
30 Ankarloo, 'Sweden', 286.
31 Ankarloo, *Trolldomsprocesserna i Sverige*, 29–34.
32 Ankarloo, 'Sweden', 286–87.
33 Orig. Magnus Erikssons Landslag.
34 Orig. Kristoffers Landslag.
35 Ankarloo, 'Sweden', 285.
36 Ankarloo, *Trolldomsprocesserna i Sverige*, 35–37.
37 Sörlin, 'Sweden', 1093.
38 Sörlin, 'Sweden', 1093.
39 Sörlin, 'Sweden', 1093.
40 The Pentateuch, the first five books of the Bible.
41 The twelve men were called *nämndemän*; a *nämnd* was the same as *häradsrätt*. Bergenheim, *Den liderliga häxan*, 49.
42 In Swedish *Justitierevisionen*. From this institution, during the 1700s, emerged what would be the highest court in Sweden.
43 Sörlin, 'Wicked Arts', 15.
44 Ankarloo, 'Sweden', 294–95.
45 Sörlin, 'Sweden', 1093.
46 Marie Lennersand, 'Responses to Witchcraft in Late Seventeenth- and Eighteenth-Century Sweden', in Davies and de Blécourt, *Beyond the Witch Trials*, 63–65.
47 Toivo, 'What Did a Witch Hunter', 283–84. See the chapter on Finland in this book, specifically the trials of Karin Persdotter and Maria Nilsdotter.
48 Sörlin, 'Wicked Arts', 54, 64.
49 Willumsen, *Trollkvinne i nord*, 29; *Witches of the North*, 270.
50 Sörlin, 'Sweden', 1093.

51 Ankarloo, 'Sweden', 290.

52 Ankarloo, 'Sweden', 290.

53 It was an oath of compurgation, in which twelve character witnesses, the accused person being the twelfth. This oath was considered supplementary to other evidence. Sörlin, 'Wicked Arts', 19, 48, 51–52; Bergenheim, *Den liderliga häxan*, 54–55.

54 Sörlin defines *förgörning* as maleficent witchcraft and *vidskepelse* as superstition, minor magic. Sörlin, 'Wicked Arts', 18, note 3.

55 Per-Anders Östling, 'Witchcraft Trials in 17th-Century Sweden and the Great Northern Swedish Witch Craze of 1668–1678', *Studia Neophilologica*, 84 (2012), 100.

56 Ankarloo, 'Sweden', 300.

57 Kronoberg is a county (*län*) in Southern Sweden. Its main town is Växjö. Skaraborg County existed between 1634 and 1997, was situated between Vättern and Vänern lakes, and was part of the region Västergötland.

58 There were a number of witchcraft trials in the regions Småland and Västergötland in the late 1500s. Ankarloo, *Trolldomsprocesserna i Sverige*, 340–43, documents many trials in Småland and Västergötland; Sörlin, 'Wicked Arts', 26.

59 Vartofta is the name of a village as well as a district. One hundred years later, Vartofta Hundred, or Vartofta *härad*, was divided between Småland and Västergötland in Sweden.

60 Until 1997, Skaraborg was a district (*län*) of its own, situated on the western side of Lake Vättern.

61 Ankarloo, *Trolldomsprocesserna i Sverige*, 340–43, documents many trials in Småland and Västergötland; Sörlin, 'Wicked Arts', 26.

62 Vadstena Landsarkiv (VLA), Göta Hovrätt (GH), Advokatfiskalens arkiv, Renoverade dom böcker t.o.m. 1700, Skaraborgs län 1590–1610, E VII AAAA:1, Habo Sokn af Vartofta häred för 1594–1603, fos. 2r–3r.

63 Lars Jonsson the older (1515–94) to Herrtorp in Bjärklunda parish, Skaraborgs län. He belonged to the noble family Lagerberg. See www.adelsvapen.com/genealogi/Lagerberg_nr_1112 (accessed 24 December 2021).

64 Visningsborg was situated on Visningsö, which is Lake Vättern's largest island.

65 There was a system of 'law readers', in Swedish *lagläsare*, who replaced the noble holders of *häradshövdingeräntan*, the Häredz Höfding position.

66 Orig. *Häredz Höfding*. On 31 May 1594, at the Vista County Court, von Udden is called the honoured and well-learned man, *ärlige och vällärde man*, and on 10 October 1594, at the court in Nykyrka, the noble man of good descent, *den ädle och välbördige Junker*.

67 In 1593, Lars Jonsson requested a testimony for his work (*häradsbevis*), and got words of praise from the court and the congregation for justice, knowledge, and wisdom in judging.

68 Orig. *Jagh*.

69 Orig. *M. N. H. fougte, wälachtigh Håkon Anderßon*. The abbreviation M. N. H. means 'My Gracious Lord's' (*Min Nådige Herres*).

70 Orig. *Mestermannen*.

71 Annika Sandén, *Bödlar* [Executioners] (Stockholm, 2016), 182.

72 This might be related to the fact that areas in various *län*, districts, belonged to Visningsborg county (*Visningsborgs grevskap*).

73 Orig. *På samma tid Hade Håkon Anderßon och Håkon i Gulskogh sigh tilfrågat mz [med] mehnigi man, om thi Hade nogon (tidh) // Tidh förstått at the skulle hafua förstuckit förne: Jngierdh Tyske billan ifrå rätten, den tid tingit war i Ebbarp: ther till suarede menige man, at the sådant aldrig wiste skedt wahr, thet Hon och sielf in för rätten bekende, at the theth aldrigh giorde.* In this quotaion, '//' denotes page shift. VLA, GH, Advokatfiskalens arkiv, Renoverade dom böcker t.o.m. 1700, Skaraborgs län 1590–1610, E VII AAAA:1, Habo Sokn af Vartofta häred för 1594–1603, fos. 2r, 2v.

74 Orig. *Tyska billan*.

75 Orig. *Mathen* or *Maden*, means a swampy or wet field. In Swedish *träskmark*. *Maden* might have been a place or a field with stagnant water or a field close to the beach.

76 Orig. *så att fötterni rottnade of them och öhrena föllo ifrå Hofuodet på them*.

77 Orig. *på tinghgården*.

78 *Utletat* may be a pleonasm for *ransakat* (searched). See www.saob.se/artikel/?seek= utleta&pz=2#U_U1083_25422.
79 Julian Goodare, 'Pricking of Suspected Witches', in Golden, *Encyclopedia*, 931–32.
80 Orig. *thet samma Hon och för rätten bekiende.*
81 Orig. *der war en liten Kolle wid Maden.*
82 Orig. *en liten Kåmpan*, a companion. The word *Kumpan* comes from Latin, *companio*, to share bread. *Compan* is used with the same connotation in the case of Gundell Olsdatter (1624), during the Finnmark witchcraft trials in Norway. Willumsen, *Witchcraft Trials in Finnmark*, 43, 407.
83 Orig. *Jagh will efther följgia Kirsthin J Maden Huad hon befaler migh giöra, thet will Jagh giöra.*
84 Orig. *thå bödh han henne räckia sigh hånden, thet hon och giördi, thå gaf han henne ost och brödh.* Handing over of food in connection with entering the devil's pact is also found in the Blåkulla trials and in the Bohuslän witchcraft trials. Per Sörlin, 'The Blåkulla Story: Absurdity and Rationality', *ARV: Nordic Yearbook of Folklore*, 53 (1997), 131–52 at 135 and also note 12.
85 Ankarloo, *Trolldomsprocesserna i Sverige*, 341, no. 56.
86 Ankarloo, *Trolldomsprocesserna i Sverige*, 341, nos. 57–61.
87 Orig. *Witnade och betÿgade monger man, at så många som Ho trätter meth eller får afuundh till, them fåt wißerliga thet som ondt är.* 'The testimonies about Margrit in Knutshult riding on a wolf correspond to a Jungian archetype. Ref. Clarissa Pinkola Estés, *Women Who Run With The Wolves: Myths and Stories of The Wild Woman Archetype* (London, 1992)'
88 Orig. *ickie frij förn(n)ede [frifinna] Margrites lif i Knutzholt.*
89 Orig. *och efther sådana witne och bewijs, Kan Jagh och Nemden ickie frij förn(n)ede [frifinna] Margrites lif i Knutzholt, wthen ställa thenna saken till Höge öfuer Hetenes betenkiende, Huru ther om widare Handlas skall.*
90 Orig. *Tå hafuer hon suaret.*
91 Orig. *at the skulle hafua förstuckit för^{ne}: Jngierdh Tÿske billan ifrå rätten.*
92 Orig. *ther till suarede menige man, at the sådant aldrig wiste skedt wahr.*
93 Sörlin, 'Wicked Arts', 60.
94 Sörlin, 'Wicked Arts', 58.
95 Orig. *en liten Kolle wid Maden.* See note 75.
96 Ankarloo, 'Sweden', 289.
97 See the case of Sitru Pedersdatter, Rygge 1623, in the chapter on Norway in this book, and in Rendalen 1670–74, ref. Skaar, 'Da djevelen var løs', 115–35.
98 Ankarloo, 'Sweden', 289; Goodare, *European Witch-Hunt*, 210.
99 See the trial of Sitru Pedersdatter, 1623, and the reference to the trials in Rendalen 1670–74 in the chapter on Norway in this book.
100 Ankarloo means that the idea of searching for the devil's mark was new in Sweden at the end of the 1500s. Ankarloo, 'Sweden', 289.
101 Orig. *tu mott latha migh hafua then Ko Jagh will hafua, om tu ickie wilt, thå skallt tu litit gagn hafua af tin Koo.*
102 Orig. *hon lofuade at Jons folch i lindholt skulle fara ena fahnens färdh.*
103 Orig. *Nogra dager ther efther siuknade en af Jons söner, och lågh på sotta sängh i 18 weckor, och brasth sönder låhrit på honom, och är nu en krÿplingh, och på endelÿchten mosthe sättia lifuit till, sampt Jons Hustro och Hans dotter.*
104 Orig. *the hade warit i Bosaryd och hört Elinnes ordh huadh hon tilförne af Haralz hustro i Knutzholt hört hade Hema wid Hennes bordh i Knutzholt.*
105 Orig. *och blef för Hörd Huadt Konsther Hon brukade till then Mißgierningh Hon wittis föri.*
106 Ankarloo, *Trolldomsprocesserna i Sverige*, 46–47.
107 Orig. *thet samma Hon och för rätten bekiende.*
108 Goodare, *European Witch-Hunt*, 204; Willumsen, *Witches of the North*, 87; *Dømt til ild og bål*, 378.
109 Orig. *Huruledes hon den diefuulz Konst lährt hade.*

110 Orig. *Så efther lagen Holler, att then som enom ont Jäter, er illa troendes. Jäta, gäta* means *omtala, nämna, berätta:* talk about, mention, tell about.
111 Orig. *Witnade och betÿgade mongir man, at så många som Ho trätter mx [meth] eller får afuundh till, them fåt wißerliga thet som ondt är.*
112 Orig. *wthen ställa thenna saken till Höge öfuer Hetenes betenkiende, Huru ther om widare Handlas skall.*
113 Orig. *och efther sådana witne och bewijs, Kan Jagh och Nemden ickie frij förn(n)ede [frifinna] Margrites lif i Knutzholt.*
114 Sörlin, 'Wicked Arts', 58.
115 Sörlin, 'Wicked Arts', 61.
116 Ankarloo, 'Sweden', 290.
117 Orig. 'laga tingh'.
118 Landsarkivet i Vadstena (LAV), Göta hovrätts arkiv (GH), EVAA, Criminalia 1635–1688, Uppvidinge härad den 30 september 1653, Kronobergs län, Göta hovrätts dom 7 and 9 november 1653.
119 The administrative, cultural, and industrial centre of Kronoberg County. It had an episcopal see since the twelfth century. The city got its charter in 1342, issued by Magnus Eriksson.
120 Orig. *Landzhöffdingen.*
121 Orig. *Karin Peders dotter trålKona'.*
122 Orig. *Vthgammall.*
123 The trial of Karin Persdotter is mentioned in Sörlin, 'Wicked Arts', 73–74.
124 Orig. *gårdsqvinna.*
125 Orig. *Pige,* which means 'girl', but is also used to refer to a woman who is not married.
126 Orig. *effther som then altidh pläger Vmgåeß medh Kupplerie.*
127 Orig. *och taga VnderVijßningh på dhet, dhe aff henne begjära at Veta.*
128 Orig. *omak.*
129 Orig. *12 ör:* a Swedish coin.
130 Orig. *gjälar, broer.* Due to the two words following each other, there is a possibility that this is a reference to Gjallarbrui. However, in the original source it is written with a comma in between the two words, which means that it is two separate words. Gjallarbrui in Norse mythology is a bridge which leads over the river *Gjǫll,* 'the roaring' which lies on the road leading to the death empire, Hel, the road which leads north and down and creates the border between the world of the living and the dead. Gjallarbrui, which had sharp spikes and dangerous creatures acting as guardians, is the narrow bridge to Paradise. The image of the bridge leading to the other world is universal. The word *Gjallar* is also found in *Gjallarhorn,* the horn of the god Heimdall in Norse mythology. This horn was used in case of danger and in case anyone tried to get across the bridge between Åsgard and Midgard, which Heimdall guards. The horn would also mark the start of Ragnarok. Gro Steinsland, *Norrøn religion: myter, riter, samfunn* [Norse Religion: Myths, Rites, Society] (Oslo, 2005).
131 Orig. *Vedh rinnande Strömmer, Siöer, gjälar, broer och annat.*
132 Orig. *menandes dhen Ondhe dherm[edh].*
133 Orig. *seger och sielff som monga trovärdige Eedeligen Vitna Vilia.*
134 Orig. *Vthi alt hvadt henne tilträngja Kan.*
135 Orig. *Vtsagt.*
136 Orig. *dhen Kloka Quinnan.*
137 Orig. *trullbacha.*
138 Orig. *principalß.*
139 Orig. *Vthan siukdomen Jfrade sigh Mehra sedan änn förr.*
140 A wooden bench, used as a bed, was often found inside the houses, as part of the furniture.
141 Orig. *Och dher före tänkte dhenne Signerskan sökia om hielp.*
142 Orig. *Konga härad.*
143 Orig. *Kona,* which in this context probably is a diminutive expression.

144 Orig. *Kupplorie.*
145 Orig. *ohörligitt.*
146 Orig. *och offenteligen försäkrar folk om hielp Ehvru [tross alt] dhet fullbordeß, ty ingen ännu bespaneß som nogon godh* Effect *om henne thala kan.*
147 Orig. *Ölfuaskog,* in Lessebo, Kronobergs *län,* which implies that Karin Persdotter also came from Ulvaskog.
148 Orig. *emädan du Ramfredh slogh migh på Munnen (. . .) skall tu få skam.*
149 Orig. *effther hon ther i garden äger 1/6 och boer dher.* These words are inserted in brackets in the records.
150 Orig. *Ja, Ja, dhe skola få skam.*
151 Orig. *Jdkeligen,* in modern Swedish *ideligen.*
152 Orig. *Veeta J hvadh henne Voller, Mädan hon gåer så.*
153 Orig. *Neij sade hon, Vthan dhet Mote Vara dherfore, at hon iche fåer alt dhet hon begjärer och aff oß hafua Vill.*
154 Orig. *dhe skola få Skam, dhe Skola få Skam.*
155 Orig. *för dhet dhe acta eller Vÿrda migh intet.*
156 Orig. *tro eij heller iagh kan giöra huarken ont eller gott, dhe skola Vell Kenna migh Innan dhe slippa migh.*
157 Orig. *Athshillige Monge reedeliga Folk j Faderenß åhöra hafue hafft henne och Poiken till förhör, tå han medg goda Skiäll henne dhetta öfuertÿgat hafuer.*
158 Orig. *osegeligh.*
159 Orig. *Vilt tu gåå m(edh) till Tinget och borga för Karin, ty iagh Vill intet länger Vette aff henne.*
160 Orig. *ty hon haf(ue)ʳ alt ont giort Migh.*
161 Orig. *iegh früchter hon legger migh och Neder förr änn tinget blifuer.*
162 Orig. *högtidtz barn.*
163 Orig. *Vthan tviffuell henne dhet Vppenbahret aff sin försvararer.*
164 Orig. *Mißgångna,* misfortune or misadventure.
165 Orig. *Kona.*
166 Orig. *Mÿchit Vore fuller effter berettelser her till Jnnföra Men iche sÿnes Nödigt ty dhet är alt åff Ver som dhete ofuentechnadhe.*
167 Orig. *skÿlt förhör.*
168 Orig. *först förmanteß longhsamlingen bekenne sanningen och iche för oroligitt samVett skull dhen förtiga besinnandeß att.*
169 Orig. *och sin diefuulskaper afstå.*
170 Willumsen, *Seventeenth-Century Witchcraft Trials,* 226.
171 Bergenheim, *Den liderliga häxan,* 69.
172 Orig. *Jnnthalanden,* persuasion.
173 Orig. *godvillige och otvungne.*
174 Orig. *Jnnhyßquinna,* probably a woman who lodged in a house.
175 There is a settlement named Taglarp in Vaggeryd. Vi parish is mentioned in the original source. This might be a name of a parish that has now disappeared.
176 Orig. *Nächen, VaterMannen eller StrömKarlen.* The Stream Man may be compared to an elf.
177 Orig. *iche allenast till dhen hielp hon behöfde Vthen och bota andre Medh.*
178 Orig. *Menandes dhen Ondhe dherm(edh).*
179 Orig. *Annheng.*
180 Orig. *anhollan.*
181 Orig. *otjdigt Vmgenge.*
182 Orig. *dhet Vill hon intet bekenna eij heller föge ont eller gott aff hennes försäkredhe läkedom, ehuruväl oräkneligt folk henne om hielp besöcht hafuer.*
183 Orig. *Eendeleß borttagen.*
184 Orig. *Annslagh.* Could also mean effort.
185 Orig. *Och dher före är Vnderligit huorföre hon så store partier aff folk bedraga Kunde.*
186 Orig. *her till svarar hon, dhet hon aldeleß hölt sigh Vedh StrömKarlenß försäkran och Mechtige tillsegelser och Meente sådant föga hafue på sigh.*
187 Orig. *otjdigt Vmgenge.*

188 Orig. *Mehr kan Man hoes henne Jntet Vtrette eller till bekennelse Vppbringa.*
189 Orig. *Befahredeß.*
190 Orig. *nød.*
191 Orig. *Myckne Onda.*
192 Orig. *betenchende och domb.*
193 Orig. *VppMaant.*
194 Orig. *Är och ostadigh j åthäfuor och gerningar så att Vißerligen är klart henne hafua eet faeßligitt Vmgange medh dhen Onde.* This means she behaved as if she was guilty. It was not unusual that the records noted how a person accused of witchcraft looked and talked. It might indicate bad conscience or guilty feelings. Sörlin, 'Wicked Arts', 56.
195 Orig. *Vidhskipelser och Signerier.*
196 Orig. *Dhette alt till dhen Höghlogl. Kongl. Hoffstedtz Nådige* resolution.
197 In this case, the district governor was the law reader and signed the records.
198 Gudmund Krok, Härads Höfding in Allbo, Kron, died in 1663 or 1664 and belonged to the Krok family. He was the brother of Andreas Krok, who was ennobled Gyllenkrook in 1674. Gudmund Krok was a son of Nils Krok, who was bishop in Växjö. See https://sok.riksarkivet.se/Sbl/Presentation.aspx?id=11786 (accessed 23 December 2021).
199 Orig. *Tillsegelser.*
200 Mikael Häll says that people often told stories about such supernatural creatures around life crises, trauma, and death. Häll primarily examines court records from the 1600s and the first part of the 1700s, to explore how Early Modern imaginations about the Water Man—in Swedish *näcken*—could be related to states of transition, death and sexuality, or theology and folk belief. This understanding of the Water Man as a phenomenon connected to the vague border areas of the imagination might well be descriptive of Karin Persdotter's experience of a diffuse creature, more by hearing him through the water than by sight. Mikael Häll, 'Näckens dödloga dop: manliga vattenväsen, död och förbjuden sexualitet i det tidligmoderna Sverige [Näckens Deadly Drug: Male Water Creatures, Death and Forbidden Sexuality in Early Modern Sweden], *Historisk tidskrift*, 131, no. 3 (2011), 590.
201 A woman married to a *husmann*, a tenant who did not own any land on his own.
202 Orig. *Ja, Ja, dhe skola få skam.*
203 Orig. *plåga een Natt och dagh.*
204 Orig. *effter gudz tillstädielse.*
205 Orig. *högtidz barn.*
206 Sörlin, 'Wicked Arts', 109.
207 Toivo, 'What Did a Witch-Hunter', 283–85.
208 Sörlin, 'Wicked Arts', 49–40; Östling, *Blåkulla, magi och trolldomsprocesser,* 'Witchcraft Trials'; 'Blåkulla Journeys; Eilola, 'Lapsitodistajen kertomukset'.
209 See the 1594 Swedish trial in this chapter, wherein Kullen is mentioned. See also the chapters on Norway and Finland about the Blåkulla notion, documented in Norway in the 1620s and 1670s and in Finland in the 1660s.
210 Later, some suspended executions took place. There is a famous German illustration of the Mora witch trial, dated 1670.
211 Mr George Sinclair, *Satan's Invisible World Discovered. A Choice Collection of Modern Relations, Proving Evidently Against the Saducees and Atheists of This Present Age, That There Are Devils, Spirits, Witches, and Apparitions, from Authentic Records, Attestations of Famous Witnesses and Undoubted Verity* (Edinburgh, 1685). Printed by John Reid.
212 Relation XXVII. 'A Relation of the Strange Witch-craft discovered in the Village Mohra in Swedeland. First, of their Journey to Blo-kula. The Contents of their Confession', In Sinclair, *Satan's Invisible World*, 112–24.
213 Orig. *hustru.*
214 RAS, Serie EXIe: 3155/3156.SH. Renov. Domböcker. Häradsrätten Gävleborgs län 1672–1674, nr. 21. Rådstuvorätt in Sundsvall 22 december 1673, fos. 395r–397r; Riksarkivet, Stockholm, Serie EXIe: 3155/3156. Svea hovrätt. Renov. Domböcker.

Häradsrätten Gävleborgs län 1672–1674, nr. 22. Rådstuvorätt in Sundsvall 31 januari 1674, fo. 148; 7 mars 1674, fo. 161. Quotations are from Emanuel Linderholm's copy of local court proceedings in Sundsvall, early 1900s, Rannsakning inför Rådstuvorätten in Sundsvall 22 december 1673, fos. 395r–397r; 31 januari 1674, fo. 148; 17 mars 1674, fo. 161.

215 Orig. *Borgmästare.*
216 The headline of these court records is dated 17 March 1674, but the court records are dated 23 March 1674.
217 Orig. *dhen som medh sådant tahl funnes löpa kring.*
218 This currency—singular *mark*, plural *marker*—was common at the time.
219 Orig. *illa handterat.*
220 Orig. *Bekenner och denne hust[ru] Karin samma gång der sedt sin son om 1 åhr gammal. beskyllandes hon sin grannhustru hust[ru] Ingredh att hon och sitt barn hafwer dijt fördt.*
221 Orig. *sönder rifvin i ögorne och blå om halsen, som hon beropade sigh til vittne på Lars Hansson Bruusse och Oluff Båttzmans hustru sigh hafva syhnt.*
222 Orig. *östre knuten.*
223 Orig. *dantzatz och speelatz på samma rum.*
224 Orig. *bekenner hon hafwa sedt Oloff Hans hustru Ingredh hwarest hon bekenner ingett ting hafft för sigh, uthan eliest gådt aff och ann.*
225 Orig. *ähr och der hustru Karin föresatt att göra tvist, tvetta bordet, hvilkens befallning han icke viste hvars den var.* göra tvist, use a special technique of weaving.
226 Orig. *hwiite penninger till en stoor hop.*
227 Orig. *hafva kastat stååk öfver samma penningar.* I interpret *stååk* as a misspelling of *ståål.* In folkloric belief, there is a notion that you can keep witchcraft away by throwing steel over the bewitched objects or use steel as a protection against witchcraft.
228 Orig. *och hon sedan intet annat kändt än att båden armen och handen skulle wara afskuren.*
229 Orig. *Kroppåsen,* roof beam.
230 Orig. *hvilken lärde och befalte henne siunga den verssen; lärer menniskior alla göra bettring i tijd etc.* The sentence is ambiguous. It may mean that the healer who is singing this verse has learned how to perform recovery, successful healing. It may also mean that the clients seeking the healer to get help will become better as time goes by. Particulary 'i tijd', in time, is difficult to interpret. If it had been 'i tijde', it would have meant 'in time, early enough', meaning that people might learn how to perform improvement (on clients) before it is too late.
231 Orig. *blef sedan häfvan uthj swart huuss, som henne tycktes, der dhe willie upbrenna henne och hennes barn, hwarest syntes ijdell eeldh och swafwell.*
232 Orig. *låth blifva henne.*
233 Orig. *göra op elden.*
234 Orig. *en öhrfijht.*
235 Orig. *Lars Hansson Bruusse.* However, from the context and the pronouns it is clear that it is his wife who witnesses.
236 Orig. *Oloff Båttzmans hustru*; surname means boatswain.
237 Orig. *om lördagzmorgon affter samma natten hon bekenner sigh warit förder, hafha syhndt wife Karin, att hon war blå på kindbeenet och syhntes fingersporen effter flaata handen hwilket alt war blådt.*
238 Orig. *hustru.*
239 In order to leave for a witches' flight, only half of the finger should be smeared, not the whole finger. In the records, it is not noted what she smeared onto their fingers.
240 Orig. *fördt sigh up onder thaaket.*
241 Orig. *the hafva gifvit sigh math j Blåkulla.*
242 Orig. *hvijt man.*
243 Other child witnesses tell about white angels at Blåkulla, acting as protectors from the devil, and encouraging children to reveal witches so that they could be punished. The white man at Blåkulla also possessed this protective quality. Östling, 'Blåkulla Journeys', 117–18; Sörlin, 'Blåkulla Story', 137.

244 Orig. *iembväl speelat på rumpan.*
245 Orig. *heele hopen.*
246 Orig. *ehuruväl onda menniskior hafva them sådant påfördt.*
247 Orig. *betrachtandes fast bettra vara lijda sitt straff här i verlden, än vmgälla den evige och oändelige pijnan medh alla dieflar uthj helfvetit för uthan, ända.*
248 Orig. *Förehades hustru Karin Daniel Dantz hustru, och rätten henne tillfrågade, om hun ännu tilstår samma beskyllning hon sidstleden den 22 december tillwitte Oloff Hanssons hustru Ingredh.*
249 Orig. *hafwa fördt sigh och sitt barn till Blåkulla.*
250 Orig. *medh mehra som ransakningen innehåller.*
251 Orig. *Hustru Karin säger sigh ännu stå widh samma bekennelse, att hon intet annat kan säija och weth, än hon ähr blefwen dijth fördh aff hustru Ingredh, och henne sedt i Blåkulla.*
252 Orig. *men hon nu som tillförände entständigt neckar, sigh högeligen beswärjandes på sitt samwetta wara frij för denne trulldoms syndh. Och Gud allena wetta att hon ähr frij.*
253 Orig. *rätten tillfrågar henne, hwadh hon mehnar för en Gudh, den hon så offta nämpner?*
254 Orig. *penningar.*
255 Orig. *skurit af henne fingret.*
256 Orig. *blåst i hoop dhet.* Probably they blew onto the finger to heal it.
257 Orig. *gifuit sigh öhrfijten.*
258 Orig. *uthan elliest referererar Kierstin att morgon effter sedan denna Karin skulle warit förder.*
259 Orig. *hwilket och nu hustru Karin tillstår sigh således hafwa Kierstin refererad.*
260 Orig. *men elliest tillstår hustru Karin sigh icke annat förstådt.*
261 Orig. *Ransakning inför Rådhusrätten i Sundsvall den 17 Mars 1674.* The date is written at the first page of the court records, the date when the court meeting started.
262 Orig. *Anno 1674 den 23 martij hölltz allmenna rådhstugu närwarandes borgmestaren well^t Johan Alander med rådhmennerne.*
263 Orig. *å håldne rådhstufwu sidstledne d. 22 december 1673.*
264 Orig. *körkieherde.*
265 Orig. *som wyrd. pastoris breff Torp aff den 12 martij sidstledne förmähler.*
266 Orig. *pastor.*
267 Orig. *medh alfwarlig förmahning på Gudz wäg.*
268 Orig. *hwar till Marith alldeles och ensidigt neckar.*
269 Orig. *sigh högeligen bedyrandes och beroopandes sigh till wittne att Gudh wetta sigh wara frij.*
270 Orig. *emot sin willia och owettandes.*
271 Orig. *och såssom man intet wijdare kunde komma till oplysning i denne förborgade saaken.*
272 Orig. *ehuruväl rätten som kyrkieherden alfwarligast hafwa alle vederböranderne så serskillt som uppenbarligen till sann bekennelse förmahnat.*
273 Orig. *påståendes wara ijdell osanning alt dhet hustru Karin dehm påfördt hafwer.*
274 Orig. *att hustru Dantes som dhem berychtat hafwer skall alldeles medh osanning fahrit, och them rychbare giordt.*
275 Orig. *bortfördh.*
276 Orig. *medhfarin.*
277 Orig. *i denne menniskiom förborgade saaken.*
278 Orig. *uthan denne saaken i all vnderdänigheet den höglofl. kongl. hoffrätten heemställer.*
279 Orig. *medh vnderdånig förfrågan huru ringa rätten må här vthinnan wijdare procedera.*
280 Orig. *der uppå och denne ringa rätten vnderdånigst afwachtar höglofl. kongl. hoffrättens högwijsse sentiment och vthslagh.*
281 The original court records from High Court, documenting verdict and sentence, were lost in a fire.
282 Ankarloo, 'Sweden', 295.
283 Sörlin, 'Blåkulla Story', 137.
284 Ankarloo, 'Sweden', 315; Östling, 'Blåkulla Journeys', 117–18.
285 Sörlin, 'Blåkulla Story' 137.
286 Orig. *men aff en hwijt klädder man emottagen, hwilken lärde och befalte henne siunga den werssen, lärer menniskior alla göra bettring i tijd etc.*

287 Steinsland, *Norrøn religion*, 82–96.
288 The same is documented in the Finnmark witchcraft trials, in which six young girls were accused of witchcraft and interrogated. The confessions of the children are paid attention to, even denunciations of adult women. Willumsen, 'Children Accused of Witchcraft', 29.
289 Orig. *rätten tillfrågar henne, hwadthon mehnar för en Gudh, den hon så offta nämpner.*
290 Orig. *emedhan man wedh denne tijden har warit förorsakat, hålla ransakning öfwer något trollwessende, som af någre wahnactige menniskior ähr kringfördt och iche bewijstligit finnes.*
291 Orig. *emedan man wedh denne tijden har warit förorsakat hålla ransakning öfwer något trollwessende, som af någre wahnartige menniskior ähr kringfördt, och icke bewijsligit finnes, hwarföre så som sathan alla menniskiors fiende gerna kringsöker, att föhra alla menniskior till sitt förderff.*
292 In the trials of the young girls during the Finnmark witchcraft trials, the judiciary argued for death sentences against the children, so that they would not lead other children astray. Willumsen, 'Children Accused of Witchcraft', 31.
293 Knutsen, 'End of the Witch Hunts', 143.
294 Toivo, 'What Did a Witch-Hunter', 282, 285–87; Willumsen, 'Exporting the Devil', 49–52.
295 Lennersand, 'Responses to Witchcraft', 63–65.

9   Finland—Magic Salt, Uncovered Hair, and Blåkulla

1 Goodare, *European Witch-Hunt*, 268.
2 Toivo, *Faith and Magic*, 3.
3 Åbo and Björneborg's district.
4 Karleby.
5 The Finnish name *Kokkola* means 'place of bonfire' or 'place of eagle', because the Finnish root word *kokko* means both bonfire and white-tailed eagle (the suffix -la denotes location).
6 Toivo, *Witchcraft and Gender*, 13.
7 Toivo, *Witchcraft and Gender*, 112.
8 Toivo, *Witchcraft and Gender*, 9.
9 Toivo, *Faith and Magic*, 3, 13.
10 Emmi Lahti, *Tietäjiä, taikojia, hautausmaita. Taikuus Suomessa 1700-luvun jälkipuoliskolla* [Cunning Folk, Practitioners of Magic and Cemeteries: Magic in Late 18th-Century Finland] (Ph.D. thesis, University of Jyväskylä, 2016).
11 Toivo, *Witchcraft and Gender*, 77–81.
12 Toivo, 'Gender, Sex and Cultures of Trouble', 91.
13 Hagen, 'Witchcraft Criminality', 382.
14 Toivo, *Faith and Magic*, 6; Goodare, *European Witch-Hunt*, 8, 22; Christopher Ocker, *Luther, Conflict and Christendom: Reformation Europe and Christianity in the West* (Cambridge, 2018), 212–29, 281–99.
15 Toivo, *Witchcraft and Gender*, 13.
16 Toivo, 'Discerning Voices and Values'.
17 Turku Hovrätt.
18 Toivo, *Witchcraft and Gender*, 112.
19 Toivo, *Witchcraft and Gender*, 14.
20 Toivo, 'Discerning Voices and Values', 145.
21 Toivo, 'Discerning Voices and Values', 145.
22 Toivo, 'Discerning Voices and Values', 145.
23 Toivo, *Witchcraft and Gender*, 14.
24 For example, special itinerant witchcraft courts, or 'Troldoms commissioner' in Sweden, passed a special law saying that these courts could do what they felt was reasonable. Lennersand, 'Responses to Witchcraft', 63–65.
25 In modern Finnish Eura Parish.

26 Ala-Satakunnan renovoidut tuomiokirjat I:KO a 6: Eurajoki 9–10 Nov. 1649, 623v–626v and 15–16 March 1650, 34v.

27 Orig. *Ländzman.*

28 In modern Finnish Irjanne, a village in Eurajoki.

29 Orig. *Paβ icke opå, iagh will digh wäll finnas, och göra digh et Lönligit teckn.* Ala-Satakunnan renovoidut tuomiokirjat I:KO a 6: Eurajoki 9–10 Nov. 1649, fo. 624r.

30 Orig. *tÿrer,* also written *tÿror* in the original. These were a kind of magical, semi-sentient weapons. There was an idea that *tÿror* could be thrown on humans and animals. They resemble *gand,* known in Norway, a spell that could be thrown on humans and animals, causing sickness and death. An interesting parallel to *tÿrer* practiced among the Navahos is exemplified in Clyde Kluckhohn's, *Navaho Witchcraft* (Harvard, 1944), which uses the expression 'supernatural techniques for injuring their fellow tribesmen', sometimes referred to by English-speaking Navahos as 'the bad side'. Kluckhohn, *Navaho Witchcraft*, 6.

31 In the Nordic countries during the Early Modern period, the title 'Herr' was used for chaplains, ministers, pastors, and vicars.

32 Orig. *förkunndhe.*

33 In Modern Finnish *Köyliöpolvi,* Eura Parish.

34 Orig. *Men medhan hon haffuer altijdh haatadt och Vndsagdt, och strax der effter skeer, derföre sadhe sigh bäre Miβtanker opå henne were wållande till deras dödh.*

35 Orig. *den i Swerige åhr stedder. Stedder,* modern Swedish *städare/städdare,* means a cleaner. Ala-Satakunnan renovoidut tuomiokirjat I:KO a 6: Eurajoki 9–10 Nov. 1649, fo. 624r.

36 Orig. *Suarret ginest, Ja, Konsten åhr full komligen Lärdt, men digh skud her icke åhn nu, Paβ Man icke opå, det skall här effter bliffue för betent och altså besuärat sigh många gånger medt tÿror warit bekajat. Skud* means *skjut,* literally meaning a tool for shooting during hunting, in transferred or symbolic sense, shooting speed. Ala-Satakunnan renovoidut tuomiokirjat I:KO a 6: Eurajoki 9–10 Nov. 1649, fo. 624r.

37 Orig. *doch ingen witne Henrich der opå hadhe, att den andra honom ondt Jäfftat haffuer, mÿcket minder någon fullkomligen wista seija hwadh siukdom hadhe dragas medh, annat åhn hon siuker warit.*

38 Orig. *refererade för en tijdh sedan Michaelistijd fåår hadde ondt skäät i Stopan; fåår* is mentioned here; however, since cows and kid are mentioned later, it most likely means cattle.

39 *Pertzelar,* goods or produce often used instead of money in trade and transaction.

40 Orig. *formalia,* could here mean 'the wording of charm', but it can also mean 'a formal confession'.

41 *Jacas,* a version of *jaka,* means yes.

42 Modern Finnish *Rauma.*

43 Orig. *uthi Siön på Söbskäer.* It might be Säbbskär, an island in the Baltic Sea. An island with a light-house in Luvia, Satakunta, fi. Säppi. Institutet för de inhemska språken: Svenska ortnamn i Finland. https://kaino.kotus.fi/svenskaortnamn/?a=find&qfind=S%C3%A4bbsk%C3%A4r (accessed 21 December 2021).

44 Orig. *inbergadh.*

45 *Holma.* It might be a pasture belonging to the farm at this inlet, as pastures often go by names like Holm and Sund. It seems that Holm might belong to Säbbskär; it could be the same place that is referred to.

46 Orig. *och hon sinnat honom haffua det som förb:te åhr.*

47 Orig. *huor uthaff hon detta βiukdoom unkom, förebär sigh haffue bliffuit i mehre tijdh aff inneberöede Dordei i Köyliöpolvi befrijat.*

48 Orig. *öfverb:te Ghertrudh Väll tillstedh Märthen Varit siuk, doch icke eftter hennes förgäringh skall haffue bliffuitt; forgöring,* to harm with witchcraft. It does not necessarily involve any words, or even actions: it can be a result of a pure, strong will.

49 Orig. *dyyn,* sandhill.

50 Orig. *och så när hadhe stört.* In modern Swedish *styrtet.*

51 Orig. *medhell.* In modern Swedish *middel.*

52 Orig. *doch icke uiste hwem till satte elden förgiorde.*
53 Orig. *bagge.*
54 Orig. *Rooffuor*, means *rova*, a type of food for the animals, turnip.
55 This piece of information in brackets is inserted by the scribe, as a comment.
56 Orig. *at han den dÿrt nock betala sall.*
57 Orig. *effter kommit.*
58 Orig. *salt*, must be *auffuinds salt*, a remedy used when performing sorcery and witchcraft.
59 Orig. *doch ingen finer haffua å hördt:) at han den dÿrt nock betala sall, det således skulle haffua bliffuit medh tÿror effter kommit, at Poijken hadhe så när i genom döden aff gången, det dhe icke skulle haffua funnit medhell hoos Henrich Larßen i Himilän, huilken bekende sigh haffua fååt salt aff framledne Bertill Helli i Cumo Sochn.* Today, Cumo parish is called Kokemäki parish.
60 Orig. *Thill det fempte effterb:ᵗᵉ Mårthen opå sin hustrus Wrsula wegna Rätten förkunnadhe huruledes öffrb:te Ghertrudh skulla haffue henne åthskillige gånger honom öffwer luppit medh ohöffwitzs smedhelige ordh.*
61 Orig. *Lithet haffuer du werit siuk tillforenne, Men här effter skall sådhant förbätres, Ont och såledhes kan skee.*
62 Orig. *bliffuit effter kommit.*
63 Orig. *full fälgh.*
64 Orig. *När han detta förnämer, stilladhe han sit företagande opsåådt, opå denne* Puncton *finnas inga vitne.* Ala-Satakunnan renovoidut tuomiokirjat I:KO a 6: Eurajoki 9–10 Nov. 1649, fo. 625v.
65 *Lispund* is a measure of weight.
66 Orig. *tiur*, cattle, animal.
67 Orig. *Thillfrågades om hennes granner hadhe Lijdhit någen skadhe opå Smör, Suarendes Erich Henderßons Modher hadhe inga Lÿcke ell:r fortgång i många åhr.*
68 Orig. *Saßila gårdh.*
69 Orig. *Lådhia*, modern Swedish *lodja*, a type of rowing vessel used on shallow waters.
70 Orig. *formalica*, here meaning 'the wording of charm', but it can also mean 'a formal confession'.
71 Orig. *Paß men icke opå, för ähn du kommer der ifrån tillbacke, skulle du bliffue Verße, at een Låppa skall digh bijda.*
72 Orig. *det och såledhes effter kommit, så at hon fick een stoor sk(r)åma på huffuidhet.*
73 Orig. *Päärß datter.*
74 Orig. *huadh hon Låffwer medh Munnen, det fullborder hon med gärningen.*
75 Orig. *det samma skulle Margretta inhÿses der sammestedhes vitna och bekomma, hwilcken ey kunde för hennes ålderdoms suagheetz skull fram hämptas.*
76 Orig. *ödhes godz*; *öde* literally means deserted. Here it means that she only lived on the farmstead, and a new farmer was assigned, which was what the bailiff, the *fogd*, had done.
77 The Crown's right to assign a new farmer, in this case Erich Henderson, in the hope of getting tax returns had been used.
78 Orig. *det han skulle icke der öffuer glädhias.*
79 Orig. *för derffuadh.*
80 Orig. *sigh Hafföa een sack Affter sin villia fååt, medhen han eij fåår hugga Trädher.* Ala-Satakunnan renovoidut tuomiokirjat I:KO a 6: Eurajoki 9–10 Nov. 1649, fos. 625v–626r.
81 Orig. *Michaelitidh*, 29 September.
82 Orig. *Pörte*, from Finnish *pirtti*: a house where people live.
83 Orig. *Martini dagh*, which is 19 June.
84 Orig. *Våndhe eldh.*
85 Orig. *formalia ordh.*
86 A Finnish expression. In English, 'Who knows if it comes from what I say'.
87 Savonia.
88 Orig. *och der medh hans förb:ᵗᵉ Eskills fadher mÿkit Mootgångh opå booskap hafft.*

89 Orig. *Norbothn.*
90 Orig. *spådde.*
91 Orig. *Capplan,* someone who works under the direction of the *KyrkoHerre,* often on a smaller sub-part of a parish that has its own chapel, but not a proper church.
92 Orig. *een Qvins Perßon.*
93 Orig. *på fää tää medh öpen Huffuidh och uthbristat Håår.*
94 Orig. *Hvordan hon skulle komme.*
95 Orig. *Aldrigh uthi hennes Liffs tijdh haffuer hafft på Påska dagh, sådant* defect, *som hon samma dagh hadhe Lijdhit.*
96 Orig. *forment till at bekenna sanningen.*
97 Orig. *Men Lijkwäll befinnes effter dhe skääll sådhan Lijknelße som i Ransaakningen omröres, at hvadh hon haffver hootet och vndsagdt, det endeles till gångit.*
98 Högmålsbalken: refers to the laws regarding grave or treasonous matters.
99 The oath of compurgation was abandoned in 1695 by a separate royal order.
100 Orig. *Ährlige danne Quinners Eedh.* The same phrase and the same practice is used in Denmark-Norway.
101 The law book referred to is the *Konung Kristoffers landslag* (the rural law of King Christoffer the Bavarian) from 1442, renewed as the rural law of Sweden in 1608 by Charles IX. In 1608, the Mosaic Law was added to the rural law and printed as an appendix, but this court case refers to the Bible. Tingsbalken refers specifically to the law's chapter on court proceedings.
102 Orig. *effter komme.*
103 They claimed that the trial of Gertrud Matsdotter should be finalized.
104 The law book referred to is *Konung Kristoffers landslag* (Rural Law of King Christoffer the Bavarian) from 1442, renewed as the rural law of Sweden in 1608 by Charles IX. In 1608, the Mosaic Law was added to the rural law and printed as an appendix, but this court case refer to the Bible. Tingsbalken means the law's Chapter on Court proceedings.
105 Orig. *omgås haffde.*
106 Bergenheim, *Den liderliga häxan,* 54.
107 Orig. Vlffsby, or modern-day Ulvila.
108 Unlimited.
109 Orig. *ödhmiuckeligste,* means in the humblest of ways.
110 Marko Nenonen, *Noituus, taikuus ja noitavainot Ala-Satakunnan, Pohjois-Pohjanmaan ja Viipurin Karjalan maaseudulla 1620–1700* [Witchcraft, Magic and Witch-Hunts in Rural Lower Satakunta, Northern Ostrobothnia and Vyborg Karelia, ca. 1620–1700] (Helsinki: Finnish Historical Society, 1992), 47–48.
111 Orig. *salt,* which must refer to *auffuinds salt,* a remedy used when performing sorcery and witchcraft.
112 Orig. *opå denne* Puncton *finnas inga vitne.*
113 There are similar examples in Scotland and in Finnmark, in Northern Norway, where persons accused of witchcraft who spoke in a language other than the official language of the courts had their spells and utterings recorded in that language. We see the same in the case of Janet Morrison, in Bute, Scotland. Willumsen, *Seventeenth-Century Witchcraft Trials,* 134. The same is seen in the case of Anders Poulsen, in Finnmark. Willumsen, *Seventeenth-Century Witchcraft Trials,* 241.
114 Loose and flying hair was considered a sign of a witch's appearance. Ankarloo, 'Sweden', 287.
115 Toivo, 'What Did a Witch-Hunter', 282.
116 Reinhold Hausen, *Rannsakningar och domar rörande trolldomsväsendet på Åland* [Persecution and Sentences Related to Witchcraft in Åland] (Helsingfors, 1894–98), 274.
117 Toivo, 'What Did a Witch-Hunter', 281–85; Eilola, 'Interpreting Children's Blåkulla Stories', 327–28, 335–41.
118 Hausen, *Rannsakningar och domar rörande,* 260, 261.

119 Orig. *Finnöö.*

120 Hausen, *Rannsakningar och domar rörande,* 262.

121 Orig. *tilstädes.* It means that the bailiff (the provost) was not present to use the handcuffs. However, this may have been due to the fact that coercion was not yet allowed.

122 Orig. *prophos.*

123 Orig. *uthan recta till pijnorummet, som elliest kallas helfwetet.* Hausen, *Rannsakningar och domar rörande,* 260.

124 Hausen, *Rannsakningar och domar rörande,* 262–63.

125 Toivo, 'What Did a Witch-Hunter', 283.

126 Toivo, 'What Did a Witch-Hunter', 284.

127 Riksarkivet Sverige, Stockholm (RAS). Åbo hovrätt skrivelse till Kungl. Majt. 1666 (vol. 4). Rotulus oppå dhe Criminal Saker, som uthi den Konungh: HofRätt J Stoor-furstendömmet Finlandh resolveredeähro pro Anno 1666, 28 May.

128 Orig. *Een Hussmanns i Emkarbÿ Sigfredh Erichsens Hustru, Karin ben:ᵈʰ, Hvilchen fördett Hoon Hafwer Hafft gemenskap och förbundh medh Satan, och således Kunnat genom hans ingifvande uppenbara och seija när någrom något ifrån stulit ähr, Hvem det samma stulet hafver. Dömbder är efter Gudz lagh att mista lifvet och i Båhlet brännas.*

129 Orig. *sampt dhe trenne Hustruer i Engeby, Maria og Brijta som denne Trullkona uthi widh-skieppeligh mening sökt hafva, till sine 40. shs Hvardera saat: fölte, iämbwähl att undergaa KÿrKioplicht, men gåsen Johan Hanßson, Hvilchen är af Trullkonan uthnämbder att Hafva dhe bort-Kompne åtta Rågbanden stulet är derföre frijkiendh.*

130 Orig. *Trullkonan i Emkarbÿ Karin, Kan inthet benådas, uthan skall after Häradzdomens lÿdelse, mista lifvet, rättas med ÿxe, och i båhle brennas, Så som och vijdh uthförandet, Hennes sidsta bekiennelse granneligen annoteras, enkannerligen om och Huru många medh henne Herutfinnas.*

131 Probably at Casteleholm Castle, which had previously been the administrative and military centre for the region. The castle was destroyed by the forces of Charles IX in 1599, but repaired in 1631. It lost its administrative status in 1634 due to a change in the county system, as Åbo was joined with the County of Åbo and Bjørneborg. However, the trial of Karin Persdotter was an extraordinary court session, thus the location might have been Casteleholm Castle.

132 Orig. *Maria Nilsdotter benemnd, som är dhen hustruns j Emmenääs dotter af hwilcken Karin sielf til trulldom blef förfördt.* Hausen, *Rannsakningar och domar rörande,* 266.

133 Hausen, *Rannsakningar och domar rörande,* 273.

134 Hausen, *Rannsakningar och domar rörande,* 268, 273.

135 A detailed survey of the costs of Karin Persdotter's execution, with reference to the accounts, is given in Hausen, *Rannsakningar och domar rörande,* 265.

136 Orig. *Emkarby länssmansgård,* the house where the local constable lived.

137 Åland domBøker.

138 Orig. *befallningsmann.*

139 Åland Domsaga (ÅD) 1664–1673 [Åland Court Records, 1664–1673], 331–59; Hausen, *Rannsakningar och domar rörande,* 274–80.

140 Orig. *och j synnerheet at hon sågh Marja j Markussböle komma uthur berget, då hon sielf gick dehr inn.* Hausen, *Rannsakningar och domar rörande,* 274.

141 Orig. *är ock en gång af herr Carls framledne fadher, salig herr Per, funnen opå hans fähuusbotn, men så som han war en fromm och sachtmodighh man, örkiade han dhet inthet, uthan gaf henne dhet til, mädan hon så myckit dherom badh honom.* Hausen, *Rannsakningar och domar rörande,* 267.

142 Orig. *Om dhenne Maria berättade också Karin, at hon jämwäl hafwer warit mången annan förnähr, efter hon är så arg, at hon alleenest med ett ord en annans creatur förderfwa kan.* Hausen, *Rannsakningar och domar rörande,* 267.

143 Hausen, *Rannsakningar och domar rörande,* 267.

144 Blåkulla was a well-known place for witches' gatherings in Sweden.

145 Orig. *at witterligit wore huru Maria hadhe tilförene brukat efwen sådane medel til at boota, som hennes moder lärde Karin, då hennes broder war siuk.* Hausen, *Rannsakningar och domar rörande,* 275.
146 Orig. *Och wore alltså troligit at jämväl dhet öfriga wore sant, som Karin om Maria hadhe bekändt.* Hausen, *Rannsakningar och domar rörande,* 275.
147 Orig. *widskepelse,* superstitious methods; they often meant witchcraft.
148 Orig. *Dherpå man inwände at hwar man wid dhen tijdhen hadhe haft om hennes heemseder så godh kundskap som nu, hadhe hon då inthet sluppit så lätt som hon giorde.* Hausen, *Rannsakningar och domar rörande,* 275.
149 Orig. *Omsijder när man förnam sigh inthet winna medh godho, och man lijkwäl görligen sågh at hennes gamble kundskap kom alldeeles öfwereens medh hennes framledne moders, hotade man henne med handklofwarne.* Hausen, *Rannsakningar och domar rörande,* 275.
150 Orig. *Kanske jagh hörde moor säija at man skal kasta silfwer j watn när man blifwer siuk af siöön; men aldrigh frågade jagh mijn moor om sådant.* Hausen, *Rannsakningar och domar rörande,* 276.
151 Orig. *Härpå fick man inthet categoriskt swar förr än man nödgades sättia handklofwarne på (:doch skrufwades dhe föga åth:).* The parenthesis were inserted by the scribe. Hausen, *Rannsakningar och domar rörande,* 276.
152 Orig. *sådane formalier.* Hausen, *Rannsakningar och domar rörande,* 276.
153 Hausen, *Rannsakningar och domar rörande,* 276.
154 Orig. *Och när hon frågade dhetta sidsta ryste hon j kroppen som en köldh hadhe kommit henne opå.* Hausen, *Rannsakningar och domar rörande,* 276.
155 Meaning that the sign of the cross had been used.
156 Orig. *anten är du krossad eller opbläst af släckten.* Hausen, *Rannsakningar och domar rörande,* 276.
157 Orig. *Men inthet hadhe hon af sig sielf sagt, at moderen blåste på Jacob j portlideret, uthan dhe sadhe henne sielfwe, at han war dher först blefwen krank.* Hausen, *Rannsakningar och domar rörande,* 276.
158 Orig. *förbundh.*
159 Orig. *at han skulle förmedelst sådant rysande uppenbara henne slijka hemligheeter.* Hausen, *Rannsakningar och domar rörande,* 276.
160 Hausen, *Rannsakningar och domar rörande,* 276.
161 Toivo, 'What Did a Witch-Hunter', 284.
162 Orig. *seendes swart och blister (:thet är leeder) uth.*
163 Orig. *anmodandes henne om tienst // och lofwandes henne lycka til fisk sampt wetenskap til at tala åth folk (:dhet är weeta säija folk orsaker och boot til siukdomar:), och dheremot begärade han hennes siäl.* In this quotation, '//' denotes page shift. Hausen, *Rannsakningar och domar rörande,* 276–77.
164 Orig. *dymbelweckan.* The scribe inserted the parentheses.
165 Orig. *Men alldenstund hon sedan bekände sig hafwa j dhet fallet berättat osanning, dy är ock onödigt dherom meera införa.* Hausen, *Rannsakningar och domar rörande,* 277.
166 Orig. *fabel.*
167 Orig. *Men såsom Rätten upptogh sammaleedhes dhet för een fabel och förehölt henne uthj hwadh tilstånd dhe dödhe äre, efter dhen kundskap oss uthj Guds ord uppenbarat är.* Hausen, *Rannsakningar och domar rörande,* 277.
168 Orig. *Marckussböle,* Marcus farm.
169 Orig. *och dherföre wardt hon med oförrättat ährende dhen gången uthkastad; men moderen dröijdes dher efter henne.* Hausen, *Rannsakningar och domar rörande,* 277.
170 Orig. *wreet.* Hausen, *Rannsakningar och domar rörande,* 277.
171 Orig. *förbund.*
172 Orig. *lycka med sädh uthaf åkeren sampt fisk uthaf siön, så som och lycka til boskap, och dherbredewid kunna tåla åth folk, doch så at hon af sädh, fisk eller boskap inthet skulle hafwa til öfwerflödh, uthan när hon hadhe sin nödtorfft til hushållet, skulle hon få taga igjen dhet öfrige.* Hausen, *Rannsakningar och domar rörande,* 277.

173 Orig. *Här tager jagh ditt blodh til stadhfästelsse, så skall du också gifwa migh dijn röda koo.* Hausen, *Rannsakningar och domar rörande*, 277.

174 Orig. *trånade sedan bort.*

175 Orig. *urgerade sedan huru dhet kunde inthet annars wara troligit än at hon åhrligen hafwer sedan most sigh hoos Sathan inställa til at öfwerläggia huru the förbundet å bägge sijdor hadhe efterlefwat.* Hausen, *Rannsakningar och domar rörande*, 278.

176 Orig. *grufweligit lefwerne*, terrible quarrel, could also mean bad habits, bad customs, bad ways of living.

177 Orig. *då han hafwer stått och glijst åth dhem.* Scribe-inserted parentheses. Hausen, *Rannsakningar och domar rörande*, 278.

178 Orig. *uthi en swart båtzmans habit.*

179 Orig. *dher är fuller inthet stoort til bästa.*

180 Orig. *dhet ock nembden witnade wara sant.* Scribe-inserted brackets. Hausen, *Rannsakningar och domar rörande*, 278.

181 Orig. *Mitt tager jagh, tagh du ditt hwar du will.* Hausen, *Rannsakningar och domar rörande*, 278.

182 Orig. *hwilket nembden också wittnade wara skedt.* Scribe-inserted parentheses. Hausen, *Rannsakningar och domar rörande*, 278.

183 Orig. *at sådant inthet widare skulle blifwa yrkiat uthaf kyrkioheerden.*

184 Orig. *som hon wiste wara j så måtto af Sathan förförde.* Scribe-inserted parentheses. Hausen, *Rannsakningar och domar rörande*, 279.

185 Orig. *men lijkwäl efter undfängen dom gaf hon eendeles förhopning at weela bekänna något meera framdeles, när hon finge sigh bättre betänkja.* Scribe-inserted parentheses. Hausen, *Rannsakningar och domar rörande*, 279.

186 Orig. *wäl witterligit.*

187 Orig. *hwilket jämwäl nembden och grannehustrurna bekände wara sant.* Scribe-inserted parentheses. Hausen, *Rannsakningar och domar rörande*, 279.

188 Orig. *hon hafwer regerat uthi sitt huus.*

189 Orig. *som ingen Christen menniskia om aftnarna forrän dhe ärnade sigh til H. nattward.* Hausen, *Rannsakningar och domar rörande*, 279.

190 Orig. *opå dhenna Marias omständeligen giorde bekännelse enhälleligen witnade, at Maria fullkomligen hadhe ifrån sitt medh Gudh, sinom skapare och återlösare, ingångne döpelses förbund afträdt och dheremot gifwit sigh j förbund med Sathan, låtandes dhet stadfästa med blodh och warteckn på sin kropp; jämwäl ock efter samme diefwulske förbund hemställt och förtrodt Sathan sitt sampt sin anhöriges uppehälle bådhe af wathn och landh.* Hausen, *Rannsakningar och domar rörande*, 279.

191 Orig. *trullkona.*

192 Orig. *jntygande.*

193 Orig. *dømbde jagh.* First person singular of personal pronoun is used here.

194 Orig. *som således med truldom och widskepelige åtgärningar deels är beträdd.*

195 Orig. *deels dhet ock å tinget sielf wedergångit hafwer och bekänt.*

196 Orig. *enkannerligen.*

197 Orig. *urboota måhl*, what could not be atoned for by a fine.

198 Orig. *såsom en trullkona mista lif och enkannerligen efter den executions process j fäderneslandet wid slika urboota måhl öfweligit är, blifwa afrättad med yxa, och hennes kropp sedan å bååle opbrännas; ubotamål* is a crime that is *obotlig*: for which it is not possible to pay a fine.

199 Hausen, *Rannsakningar och domar rörande*, 279–80.

200 RAS, Åbo hovrätt till Kongl Maijt vol 4. Rotulus Opå de Criminalie saker 1666, 25 October, item 43.

201 Orig. *Trullkonan.*

202 Orig. *kan inthet benådaß, uthan skall effter Häredzdomens lydelse mista lijfwet, rättaß med yxe och brinnaß.* SRA, Åbo hovrätt till Kongl Maijt vol 4. Rotulus Opå de Criminalie saker 1666, 25 October, item 43.

203 Orig. *brukat Signeri och Truldom till att upfinna Siukdomars förborgade orsaker.* SRA, Åbo hovrätt till Kongl Maijt vol 4. Rotulus Opå de Criminalie saker 1666, 25 October, item 43.

204 Orig. *lätat sigh i förbundh, gemenskap och samtal med Sathan*. SRA, Åbo hovrätt till Kongl Maijt vol 4. Rotulus Opå de Criminalie saker 1666, 25 October, item 43.

205 Orig. *Heredzhöfdingen Nillβ Peerson Psilander*. The witchcraft trials in Åland are taken to be the result of Psilander's personal interest or character. Toivo, 'What Did a Witch-Hunter', 282.

206 Orig. *henneβ tahl och sidsta bekennelse, medh deraβ där å gifna swar, granneligen* annotera *och med de beskyltes lagförande sedan fortfahra*. SRA, Åbo hovrätt till Kongl Maijt vol 4. Rotulus Opå de Criminalie saker 1666, 25 October, item 43.

207 Orig. *uthan något twång*.

208 Willumsen, *Seventeenth-Century Witchcraft Trials*, 226.

209 Orig. *man förnam sigh inthet winna medh godho*. Hausen, *Rannsakningar och domar rörande*, 275.

210 Pohjois Pohjanmaan renovoidut tuomiokirjat (PPRT)/ Northern Ostrobothnia domböker [Court Records from Northern Ostrobothnia], Kokkola (KO) A 5, Kokkola og Kälviä (Gamla Carleby & Kälviä), 27–29.8.1685, 253–55.

211 Orig. *KÿrcKioheerden*.

212 Orig. *Argh Tråll Karl*.

213 Orig. *Kärfwor halm*.

214 Orig. *βtoop*, a big glass, could also be *stein* or a *tankard*.

215 Orig. *brändewijn*, brandy or a strong distilled liquid, like vodka, which would be cheaper and locally made.

216 Orig. *viddskepelse*, superstitious methods, often they did mean witchcraft.

217 PPRT /Norra Österbotten Domböker, KO A 5, Kokkola og Kälviä (Gamla Carleby & Kälviä), 27–29.8.1685, 254.

218 Orig. *förgjort*, past participle of *förgöra*, to harm with witchcraft. It does not necessarily involve any words, or even actions; it can be a result of a pure, strong will. Originally it also carried the meaning of poisoning and using poison.

219 Orig. *Siβla wedh KÿrKian medh andre sine Lijkar, Flickor och Pygor suttit // och bÿdh at till theβ KÿreKian skulle öppnas*. In this quotation, '//' denotes page shift. PPRT / Northern Ostrobothnia domböker Domböker, KO A 5, Kokkola og Kälviä (Gamla Carleby & Kälviä), 27–29.8.1685, 255–56.

220 The dog probably means the evil she had done, but there is also the possibility that they are quarrelling about a dog.

221 Orig. *Tager du ej din Hundt tilbaka, skall du Komma på elden*. PPRT / Northern Ostrobothnia domböker, KO A 5, Kokkola og Kälviä (Gamla Carleby & Kälviä), 27–29.8.1685, 255.

222 Orig. *hwadt argt og vförett hon entteligen mera bedrefvit*.

223 Orig. *Heriste Ret ödmiåckeligest Heemstältes i Högl: Kongl. Rättz Höggunstigaste wijdare omdöme och gåttfinnande*.

224 PPRT /Norra Österbotten Domböker, KO A 6, Kokkola og Kälviä (Gamla Carleby & Kälviä), 6.10.1686, 524

225 Orig. *proponerade*.

226 Orig. *huusQuinnan*.

227 Orig. *Strukit inn af Karins Kalfwen öfwer Rÿggen*. PPRT / Northern Ostrobothnia domböker, KO A 7, Kokkola og Kälviä (Gamla Carleby & Kälviä), 22.10.1687, 561.

228 Orig. *Embare*; Norwegian *ambar*, amber, means bucket, from Greek *amphora*.

229 Orig. *deth hon lemnat een elak hundh och gerningh effter sigh, och om hon nu skolle lita beroo der wedh, will hon Karin gifva sigh tilfredz, ocj ej gåå till Ting*.

230 Orig. *Trolldom*.

231 Orig. *alt detta sitt tahl erhölth Karin Mårtensdr: medh sinå lifliga Edh å book wara sant, och icke deth ringaste opdichtat, eller at Någon ont allwillia och afundt på Britha berettat, ehrhållandes i sitt samwette*.

232 Orig. *huuβ Råta*, meaning *Huus Tota*, the place where she lived, which was a system of charity wherein those unable to work for a living were placed into groups of a certain

number of houses (depending on the number of houses available) to be cared for in each of the houses in their turn.

233 Orig. *som een fattigh huus quinna*. *Huskvinna*, a woman married to a *husmann*, a tenant who did not own any land.

234 Orig. *onsko och argheet*.

235 Orig. *hwilke denne Pålsu 1685 wedh Såmmar tinge först angafwå*. PPRT / Northern Ostrobothnia domböker, KO A 7, Kokkola og Kälviä (Gamla Carleby & Kälviä), 22.10.1687, 562.

236 Orig. *förgiort*.

237 Orig. *och på sin Siehl βaligheet tage, effter sin Syster Margetas tahl fast han ej sielf hört Pålβus Vndsejelse*. PPRT / Northern Ostrobothnia domböker, KO A 7, Kokkola og Kälviä (Gamla Carleby & Kälviä), 22.10.1687, 563.

238 Orig. *fem mihl*.

239 Orig. *Undseielse*.

240 PPRT / Norra Österbotten Domböker, KO A 7, Kokkola og Kälviä (Gamla Carleby & Kälviä), 22.10.1687, 564.

241 The day when the cursing was initially meant to have occurred.

242 Orig. *wåhr Herre finner fuller dem och deβ ögon, som leer och blinckar åth fattigt fålck*. PPRT / Northern Ostrobothnia domböker, KO A 7, Kokkola og Kälviä (Gamla Carleby & Kälviä), 22.10.1687, 564

243 Orig. *och twå wekor der effter är merbndtt: Siβlas Högre öga blifwit såår, och werkt i tree dagar, och Siβa [sic] enär hon skolla insåmna, ropat i drömma Kuihu Pirkå*. PPRT / Northern Ostrobothnia domböker, KO A 7, Kokkola og Kälviä (Gamla Carleby & Kälviä), 22.10.1687, 562.

244 Orig. *Kåmmer på mig till alt detta tahl Kunde ej ringaste wittne framtes*. PPRT /Norra Österbotten Domböker, KO A 7, Kokkola og Kälviä (Gamla Carleby & Kälviä), 22.10.1687, 564.

245 Orig. *tårpstelle*.

246 Orig. *att han och skolle witna åm denne Brijtas odygdh*.

247 Orig. *effter aflagdan Edh å boock tagandez sigh gudh til Hielph*. PPRT / Northern Ostrobothnia domböker, KO A 7, Kokkola og Kälviä (Gamla Carleby & Kälviä), 22.10.1687, 564.

248 Orig. *och badh Kainu eij göra Ordh j Hans Munn*. PPRT / Norra Österbotten Domböker, KO A 7, Kokkola og Kälviä (Gamla Carleby & Kälviä), 22.10.1687, 564.

249 Orig. *widskepelse*.

250 Orig. *stor widskepelse*, great superstitious methods, often in the meaning witchcraft. PPRT / Northern Ostrobothnia domböker, KO A 7, Kokkola og Kälviä (Gamla Carleby & Kälviä), 22.10.1687, 565.

251 Orig. *uthan alle nerwarande tilstod å sigh om Pålsu ej annat weta än det att hon är utjattat och elakt Rychte*.

252 Orig. *Nembden förklarade sig häruthinnan ej Kunna finna i sith samwete, deth sketh till Någon widskepelse, utan fast mere igennom hennes äldrige Menförheet medan hon då och warit drucken och hafft een temlig yhr föllβiugh för slädan*. PPRT / Northern Ostrobothnia domböker, KO A 7, Kokkola og Kälviä (Gamla Carleby & Kälviä), 22.10.1687, 565.

253 Orig. *Tålfinan*, meaning the twelfth man on the jury. There was an arrangement that there was always a deputy person on the jury in case somebody else got sick.

254 Meaning that she could free herself as the twelfth person to swear the oath.

255 Orig. *att hon eij Kan Kåmma ondt åstedh mÿckit mindre sådant Bruukat*.

256 Orig. *Lÿkmätigt*.

257 Orig. *T:B:L:L:.*

258 Orig. *Högl: Kongl: Höf Retten*, very learned Royal High Court, Court of Appeal.

259 Toivo, *Witchcraft and Gender*, 38.

260 Toivo, *Faith and Magic*, 17.

261 Orig. *Trullquinna*.

262 Toivo, *Witchcraft and Gender*, 40.

263 Also, these ideas in various versions were known in Småland in Sweden in 1594, in South-Eastern Norway in 1623, and in mid-eastern Norway in 1670–74.

10 Comparison and Conclusion

1 Russia is also a country in which malevolent witchcraft was central. Nenonen and Toivo, *Writing Witch-Hunt Histories*, 3–9; Willumsen, *Seventeenth-Century Witchcraft Trials*, 78, 103.
2 Randi R. Balsvik, 'Religious Beliefs and Witches in Contemporary Africa', in Andreassen and Willumsen, *Steilneset Memorial*, 90.
3 Toivo, 'What Did a Witch-Hunter', 282.
4 Gaskill, 'Witchcraft Trials in England', 291.
5 For instance, Anne Pedersdatter in Bergen in Norway 1575/1590; Susanna Grethen from Fell 1588. See the chapters on Norway and Northern Germany in this book.
6 A witches' meeting on the mountain Lyderhorn in Bergen is confessed to.
7 Unverhau, *Von Toverschen und Kunstfruhwen*, 30–32.
8 Schulte, *Hexenverfolgung in Schleswig-Holstein*, 38.
9 Vanysacker, 'Netherlands, Southern', 813, 814.
10 Schulte, *Hexenverfolgung in Schleswig-Holstein*, 68.
11 Willumsen, 'A Witchcraft Triangle', 247–58.
12 Goodare, *European Witch-Hunt*, 10.
13 Julio C. Baroja, *The World of the Witches*, trans. Nigel Glendinning (London, 1964), 13.
14 Willumsen, 'Ninety-Nine Dancers', 78.
15 Robin G. Collingwood, *The Idea of Nature* (Oxford, 1965).
16 Alver, *Mellem mennesker og magter*, 265–73; Willumsen, *Trollkvinne i nord*, 68–69.
17 Van Gent, *Magic, Body and the Self*, 28.
18 Bergenheim, *Den liderliga häxan*, 79.
19 Sharpe, *Instruments of Darkness*, 71–74.
20 Goodare, *European Witch-Hunt*, 199; Sörlin, 'Wicked Arts', 57.
21 Willumsen, 'Ninety-Nine Dancers', 72.
22 Normand and Roberts, *Witchcraft in Early Modern Scotland*, 145.
23 Birkelund, *Troldkvinden*, 83, has photos of Bjerrelide.
24 A lack of salt is known from Norwegian folklore, in which the people living underground, *de underjordiske*, only eat food without salt. Reichborn-Kjennerud, *Vår gamle trolldomsmedisin*, vol. 2, 236.
25 Willumsen, 'Board Games', 261.
26 For activities at witches' sabbaths, see 'Sabbath at Blocksberg' by Michael Herr, 1650, printed in Bergenheim, *Den liderliga häxan*, 144.
27 Sinclair, *Satan's Invisible World*.
28 Paterson, 'Witches' Sabbath in Scotland', 391.
29 Paterson, 'Witches' Sabbath in Scotland', 387.
30 Goodare, 'Witches' Flight', 148.
31 Baroja, *World of the Witches*, 39–40; Willumsen, *Trollkvinne i nord*, 73; Schulte, *Hexenverfolgung in Schleswig-Holstein*, 91–93.
32 Pierre de Lancre, *Tableau de l'inconstance*.
33 Abbildung deβ abschüligen Hexenwercks und unerhörten Teufflishen verführung im Königreich Schweden [Depiction of the Abominable Witchcraft and Unherd-of Devilish Seduction in the Kingdom of Sweden], German copper-plate graving, 1670. Printed in Goodare, Voltmer, and Willumsen, *Demonology and Witch-Hunting*, 329.
34 Willem de Blécourt, 'Sabbath Stories: Towards a New History of Witches' Assemblies', in Levack, *Oxford Handbook of Witchcraft*, 88.
35 Blécourt, 'Sabbath Stories', 90.
36 See the chapter on Scotland in this book.
37 Goodare, 'Witches' Flight', 148; 'Flying Witches', 149.

38 Also Bloksberg is mentioned in a Skåne trial in 1670. Sörlin, 'Wicked Arts', 28–31.
39 This is the same with John Fian in the North Berwick trials, who was moved from his house in Tranent to the convention in North Berwick.
40 Östling, 'Blåkulla Journeys', 93, 94.
41 Östling, 'Blåkulla Journeys', 96; Willumsen, *Steilneset*, 11–101.
42 Schulte, *Hexenverfolgung in Schleswig-Holstein*, 191.
43 Bergenheim, *Den liderliga häxan*, 11.
44 Goodare, *European Witch-Hunt*, 301.
45 Goodare, *European Witch-Hunt*, 203 and note 98 at 315.
46 Normand and Roberts, *Witchcraft in Early Modern Scotland*, 147.
47 Östling, 'Blåkulla Journeys', 100; see also the trial of Maria Nilsdotter in the chapter on Finland in this book.
48 Schulte, *Hexenverfolgung in Schleswig-Holstein*, 94.
49 Schulte, *Hexenverfolgung in Schleswig-Holstein*, 90, 95.
50 Goodare, *European Witch-Hunt*, 12.
51 Studies by Christina Larner, Åsa Bergenheim, Laura Paterson, Anna Cordey, Michelle Brock, Sierra Dye, Brian P. Levack, Julian Goodare, James Sharpe, Charlotte-Rose Millar, Rolf Schulte, Alison Rowlands, Jens Chr. V. Johansen, and Louise Kallestrup also emphasize the importance of demonological ideas.
52 Agata was brought before the court several times: in 1675, 1676, 1678, 1686, 1687, and 1688.
53 Toivo, *Gender and Witchcraft*, 42.
54 Toivo, *Gender and Witchcraft*; Lennersand and Oja, *Livet går vidare*.
55 Alver, *Mellem mennesker og magter*, 37–61.
56 Alver, *Mellem mennesker og magter*, 53.
57 Alver, *Mellem mennesker og magter*, 55.
58 Normand and Roberts, *Witchcraft in Early Modern Scotland*, 156.
59 Among others, Raisa Maria Toivo, Per Sörlin, Michael Ostling, Robin Briggs, and Hans Eyvind Næss in his studies of witchcraft trials related to social history.
60 Robin Briggs, *Witches and Neighbours: The Social and Cultural Context of European Witchcraft*, 2nd ed. (Oxford, 2002; first published in 1996), 2.
61 Willumsen, *Steilneset*, 20–30.
62 Goodare, *European Witch-Hunt*, 97.
63 For instance the Bubonic plague. Goodare, *European Witch-Hunt*, 97, 146.
64 Goodare, *European Witch-Hunt*, 97.
65 Goodare, *European Witch-Hunt*, 97.
66 Toivo, *Gender and Witchcraft*, 41.
67 Illustration of a witch milking from a distance, see Schulte, *Hexenverfolgung in Schleswig-Holstein*, 113.
68 See the chapter on Norway in this book: Old Norse laws on witchcraft existed from the 1200 onwards.
69 Genette, *Narrative Discourse Revisited*, 101.
70 In folklore, the numbers 3 and 7 are often used as a recognizable element. Reichborn-Kjennerud, *Vår gamle trolldomsmedisin*, vol. 2, 112.
71 Cohen, 'Between Oral and Written Culture'.
72 Cohen, 'Back Talk', 95.
73 Collins, *Reanimated Voices*, 46, 47, 56, 253–59, 274–80, 283, 286–302; Doty, 'Telling Tales', 26.
74 Willumsen, 'Oral Transference of Ideas', 61.
75 Willumsen, 'Oral Transference of Ideas', 47, 57; Ong, *Orality and Literacy*, 37–45.
76 Described in the analyses of Gundelle Olsdatter's trial in this book.
77 See the chapter on Northern Germany in this book: the trials of Kistina Netelers.
78 Simonsen, *Slave Stories*, 17; Carolyn Steedman, 'Enforced Narratives: Stories of Another Self', in Tess Cosslett, Celia Lury, and Penny Summerfield (eds.), *Feminism and Autobiography. Texts, Theories, Methods* (London, 2000), 25–39.

79 Blécourt, 'Sabbath Stories', 99.
80 Toivo, 'What Did a Witch-Hunter', 282.
81 Goodare, 'Witches' Flight', 163; Voltmer, 'Demonology and the Relevance', 36.
82 SATØ, SF, no. 25, Records of court proceedings 1692–1695, fo. 1r.
83 SATØ, SF, no. 10, Records of court proceedings 1654–1663, fos. 244v, 263v, 266r.
84 Voltmer, 'Witch in the Courtroom', 99.
85 Voltmer, 'Witch in the Courtroom', 99.
86 Willumsen, Steilneset, 86, 94.
87 Willumsen, Seventeenth-Century Witchcraft Trials, 83; Goodare, 'Witchcraft in Scotland', 307.
88 Ewen, Witch Hunting and Witch Trials, 65, with reference to David Jardine, Reading on the Use of Torture.
89 See the case of Marion Pardoun, Shetland. Willumsen, Witches of the North, 211.
90 Willumsen, Witches of the North, 87; Goodare, 'Witchcraft in Scotland', 306–7.
91 Witch-pricking in Scotland, England; water ordeal in Norway.
92 Willumsen, Steilneset, 6.
93 Levack, Witch-Hunting in Scotland, 23.
94 Willumsen, Witches of the North, 85–86.
95 Voltmer, 'Witch in the Courtroom', 100.
96 Cohen, 'Back Talk', 95.
97 Voltmer, 'Witch in the Courtroom', 98.
98 Sörlin, 'Wicked Arts', 29.
99 A famous play dealing with the devil's pact was Christopher Marlowe's The Tragic History of Doctor Faustus. First public performance 1594–1597. The play was based on the German Faustbuch. Willumsen, 'A Witchcraft Triangle', 260 ; E. J. Kent, 'Tyrannic Beasts: Male Witchcraft in Early Modern English Culture', in Kounine, Emotions, 79.
100 Levack, 'Witchcraft and the Law', 479.
101 A decree by the pope in 1258, a handbook for inquisitors in 1376, a document from the theological faculty in Paris in 1376, and Formicarius in 1437 and Malleus Maleficarum in 1486. Levack, 'Witchcraft and the Law', 470.
102 Briggs, Witches and Neighbours, 8–9; Goodare, European Witch-Hunt, 98–101, 150–52.
103 Recesses of 1547 and 1558, statutes of 1593 and 1594, the law of 1604, the decree of 1617, recess of 1643, the Danish Law of 1683. Sunde, Speculum legale, 183–96; Jørgensen, Dansk strafferet, 390–411.
104 Sunde, Speculum legale, 183.
105 Sunde, Speculum legale, 197.
106 Sunde, Speculum legale, 183–84.
107 Næss, 'Norway: The Criminological Context', 367–70; Goodare, 'Witchcraft in Scotland', 305–7.
108 Unverhau, 'Akkusationsprozess—Inquisitionsprozess', 116.
109 For instance in Sweden and Finland, the nämnd, and in Norway the lagrettemenn.
110 Næss, 'Norway: The Criminological Context', 381.
111 Voltmer, 'Demonology and the Relevance', 26.
112 Voltmer, 'Demonology and the Relevance', 26.
113 Willumsen, Witches of the North, 33–37.
114 Gaskill, 'Reporting Murder', 2.
115 Östling, 'Blåkulla Journeys'; Sörlin, 'Wicked Arts', 55; Goodare, 'Flying Witches', 159–76.
116 Johansen, 'To Beat a Glass Drum'.
117 Willumsen, Seventeenth-Century Witchcraft Trials, 212–15.
118 Ankarloo, Trolldomsprocesserna i Sverige. Skrifter utgivna, 14.
119 Schulte, Hexenverfolgung in Schleswig-Holstein, 68.
120 Normand and Roberts, Witchcraft in Early Modern Scotland, 290–95; Willumsen, Dømt til ild og bål, 358.
121 Millar, Witchcraft, the Devil, and Emotions, 37
122 Willumsen, 'Trolldom mot kongens skip', 315.

BIBLIOGRAPHY

Primary Manuscript Sources

Denmark

Landsarkivet for Nørrejylland (LAN) [Regional State Archives of Northern Jutland], Viborg Landsting (VL) [Viborg District Court], Dombog B, 1618, B 24–535.

Rigsarkivet Danmark, Copenhagen (RAD) [National Archives of Denmark, Copenhagen], A232, Danske Kancelli (DK) [Danish Chancellery] 1572–1660, Sjællandske Tegnelser (SJT) [Records from Zealand] 1588–90.

England

British Library, London (BL), Egerton Manuscript 2, 598.
Cambridge University Library (CUL), Ely District Records (EDR) E12 164 7/11.
NAL, ASSI 45/7/1/7.
NAL, ASSI 45/7/1/8.
NAL, ASSI 45/7/1/9.
NAL, Home Circuit Assize Records (ASSI) 45/7/1/6.
NAL, SPD, vol. 75, II, Danish Domestic Affairs, HH4.
National Archives of Britain, London (NAL), State Papers Denmark (SPD) 75, II, D7.

Finland

KAH, Ålands Domsaga (ÅD) [Åland Court Records], Kokkola og Kälviä (Gamla Carleby & Kälviä), 27–29.8.1685.
KAH, Pohjois Pohjanmaan renovoidut tuomiokirjat (PPRT)/Northern Ostrobothnia domböker [District Court records (Sent to the Court of Appeal) from Northern Ostrobothnia], Kokkola (KO) A 5, Kokkola og Kälviä (Gamla Carleby & Kälviä), 27–29.8.1685; KO A6, Kokkola og Kälviä (Gamla Carleby & Kälviä), 6.10.1686; KO A7, Kokkola og Kälviä (Gamla Carleby & Kälviä), 22.10.1687.

Kansallisarkisto, Helsinki (KAH) [National Archives of Finland, Helsinki (NAFH)], Ala-Satakunnan renovoidut tuomiokirjat [The Court Records of Lower Satakunta], I:KO a 6: Eurajoki 9–10 Nov. 1649, 623v–626v and 15–16 March 1650, 34v.

Kansallisarkisto, Turku (KAT) [National Archives of Finland, Turku (NAFT)], ÅD, 1664–1673, 331–59.

Germany

Landesarchiv Schleswig-Holstein (LSH) [State Archives of Schleswig-Holstein], Abteilung 7, no. 1758[I].

Landeshauptarchiv Koblenz (LHAK) [State Archives of Koblenz], Bestand 211, no. 2222, Kriminalischer proceβ Grethen Sundtgen zu Fell, fos. 1–18.

LHAK, Bestand 211, no. 2223, fos. 1–51.

LSH, Abteilung 268, no. 673.

LSH, Abteilung 268, no. 675.

Stadtarchiv Trier (ST) [City Archives of Trier], no. 1533/170; Depositum Kesselstadt, Abteilung 54K, no. 3643; Abteilung 54 K, no. 3644; Abteilung 54K, no. 657.

Norway

RA, Rentekammeret, Lensregnskaper for Akershus len [District accounts for Akershus, the Exchequer], Verne Kloster len, 1613–26, 96, Process no. 5. www.trolldomsarkivet.uio.no/perl/ikos/prosesslist.cgi.

RA, Værne klosters lensregnskap 2.3.1623–24 med beviser [Accounts of Værne Monastery 2.3.1623–24 with proofs].

Riksarkivet Norge, Oslo (RA) [National Archives of Norway, Oslo], Rentekammeret, Lensregnskaper for Akershus len [District accounts for Akershus, the Exchequer], Verne Kloster len, 1613–26, 96, Process no. 3.

SATØ, SF, no. 10, Records of court proceedings 1654–63.

Statsarkivet i Tromsø (SATØ) [Regional State Archives of Tromsø], Sorenskriveren i Finnmarks arkiv (SF) [The Archives of Finnmark District Magistrate], no. 8, Records of court proceedings 1648–54.

Statsarkivet i Trondheim (SAT) [Regional State Archives of Trondheim], Lagtingsprotokoll for Nordland og Finnmark 1647–1668 (LF) [Court records of the Court of Appeal for Nordland and Finnmark 1647–1668].

Scotland

National Library of Scotland, Edinburgh (NLS), Special Collections, Adv. Ms. 35.5.3.

National Records of Scotland, Edinburgh (NRS), Books of Adjournal, JC2/2.

NRS, Books of Adjournal, JC2/15.

NRS, JC26/2/3.

NRS, JC26/13, Bundle 1.

NRS, JC26/13 (separate document).

Spanish Netherlands

Hondschoote, Archives communales [Municipal archives], FF 7.

Rijksarchief Brugge (RAB) [State Archives of Bruges], Stad Brugge [City of Bruges], 624.

SABrugge, OSA, 192, Verluydboeck 1611–1676.

Stadsarchief Brugge (SABrugge), Oud Stadsarchief (OSA) [Old City Archives], 192, Verluydboeck 1490–1537.

Universiteitsbibliotheek Gent (UG) [University Library Ghent], Hs. 654.

Sweden

RAS, Åbo hovrätt skrivelse till Kongl. Maijt. [Åbo Court of Appeal Rolls Sent to His Royal Majesty, 1666] (vol. 4). Rotulus Opå de Criminalie saker 1666, 25 October, item 43.

RAS, Serie EXIe: 3155/3156.SH. Renov. Domböcker. Häradsrätten Gävleborgs län 1672–1674 [Copies of Court Records, Regional Court Gävleborg's District 1672–1674], nr. 21. Rådstuvorätt in Sundsvall 22 December 1673.

RAS, Serie EXIe: 3155/3156. Svea hovrätt. Renov. Domböcker. Häradsrätten Gävleborgs län 1672–1674 [Copies of Court Records, Regional Court Gävleborg's District 1672–1674], nr. 22. Rådstuvorätt in Sundsvall 31 January 1674.

Riksarkivet Sverige, Stockholm (RAS) [National Archives of Sweden, Stockholm]. Åbo hovrätt skrivelse till Kungl. Majt. 1666 [Åbo Court of Appeal Rolls Sent to His Royal Majesty, 1666] (vol. 4). Rotulus oppå dhe Criminal Saker, som uthi den Konungh: Hof-Rätt J Stoorfurstendömmet Finlandh resolverede ähro pro Anno 1666, 28 May.

Uppsala universitetsbibliotek (UU) [University Library Uppsala], Emanuel Linderholms samling, kaps. 85, nr. C 83, Handlingar till häxprocesserna i Sverige. Medelpad. Avskrifter [Uppsala University Library, Copies of Emanuel Linderholm's Collection, capsule 85, no. C 83, Records of witchcraft trials in Sweden, Medelpad]. II:4, Ransakning inför rådsturätten i Sundsvall d. 22 dec. 1673. (Orig. RAS, GRDD 21 (1673), fol. 395).

Vadstena Landsarkiv (VLA) [Swedish National Archives Vadstena], Göta Hovrätt (GH) [Göta High Court], Advokatfiskalens arkiv, Renoverade domböcker t.o.m. 1700, Skaraborgs län 1590–1610, E VII AAAA:1, Habo Sokn af Vartofta häred för 1594–1603.

VLA, GH, EVAA, Criminalia 1635–1688, Uppvidinge härad den 30 september 1653, Kronobergs län, Göta hovrätts dom 7 and 9 November 1653.

Primary Printed Sources

Bodin, Jean, De la demonomanie des sorciers (Antwerp, 1586).

Boyd, William K., and Henry W. Meikle (eds.), Calendar of the State Papers Relating to Scotland and Mary, Queen of Scots, vol. 10 (Edinburgh, 1936).

Brandrud, Andreas (ed.), Stavanger domkapitels protokoll 1571–1630 [The Minute Book of Stavanger Cathedral Chapter 1571–1630], no. 1 (Christiania, 1901).

Brown, Peter H. (ed.), The Register of the Privy Council of Scotland (RPC), 2nd series, vol. 5 (1633–35), H. M. Register House (Edinburgh, 1904).

Brown, Peter H. (ed.), The Register of the Privy Council of Scotland (RPC), 3rd series, vol. 6 (1678–80), H. M. Register House (Edinburgh, 1908).

Cockburn, J. S. (ed.), Calendar of Assize Records, Home Circuit Indictments. Elizabeth I and James I, 10 vols. (London, 1975–85).

Ewen, C. L'Estrange, Witch Hunting and Witch Trials: The Indictments for Witchcraft from the Records of 1373 Assizes Held for the Home Circuit AD 1559–1736 (London, 1929).

Ewen, C. L'Estrange, Witchcraft and Demonianism: A Concise Account Derived from Sworn Depositions and Confessions Obtained in the Courts of England and Wales (London, 1933).

Firth, C. H. (ed.), The Bannatyne Miscellaney Containing Original Papers and Tracts Chiefly Relating to the History and Literature of Scotland, vol. 3, The Bannatyne Club (Edinburgh, 1855).

Firth, C. H. (ed.), *Miscellany of the Scottish History Society (Second Volume)*, Scottish History Society, series 1, vol. 44 (Edinburgh, 1904).

Gibson Craig, J. T. (ed.), *Papers Relative to the Marriage of King James the Sixth of Scotland, with the Princess Anna of Denmark; A.D. MDLXXXIX*, Bannatyne Club (Edinburgh, 1936).

Grønlund, David, *Historisk Efterretning om de i Ribe Bye forfulgte og brændte Mennesker* [Historical Account of those People Persecuted and Burned in Ribe Town], 2nd ed. (1973; first published in Viborg, 1780).

Hagen, Rune B., and Per E. Sparboe (eds.), *Lilienskiold, Hans H.: Trolldom og ugudelighet i 1600-tallets Finnmark* [Lilienskiold, Hans H.: Witchcraft and Ungodliness in Seventeenth-Century Finnmark] (Tromsø, 1998).

Hausen, Reinhold, 'Ransakningar och domar rörande trolldomsväsendet på Åland 1666–1678' [Proceedings and Sentences Related to Witchcraft in Åland], in Reinhold Hausen (ed.), *Bidrag till Finlands historia . . . II*, Finlands Statsarkiv (Helsingfors, 1894–1898), 253–367.

Jacobsen, Jørgen C., *Danske Domme i Trolddomssager i øverste Instans* [Danish Sentences in Witchcraft Trials at the Highest Court Level] (Copenhagen, 1966).

Laursen, L. (ed.), *Kancelliets Brevbøger vedrørende Danmarks indre forhold* [insert translation] (Copenhagen, 1908).

Ljungberg, Leif, and Einar Bager, *Malmø tingbøger 1577–83 og 1588–90* [Malmø Court Records 1577–83 and 1588–90] (Copenhagen, 1968).

Lundh, Otto Gr., and I. E. Sars (eds.), *Norske Rigs-Registranter*, b. 3 [Norwegian State Papers] (Christiania, 1865).

Macha, Jürgen, and Wolfgang Herborn, *Kölner Hexenverhöre aus dem 17. Jahrhundert* [Cologne Witches' Interrogation from the 17th Century] (Berlin, 1992).

Monballyu, Jos, 'Witches in Flanders', www.kuleuven-kulak.be/facult/rechten/Monballyu/Rechtlagelanden/Heksenvlaanderen/heksenindex.htm.

Morton, Peter (ed.), *The Trial of Tempel Anneke: Records of a Witchcraft Trial in Brunswick*, trans. Barbara Dähms (Peterborough, 2006).

Nicolaysen, N. (ed.), 'Uddrag af Bergens Raadhus-Protokol 1592–1594', in *Norske samlinger* [Norwegian Collections], vol. 1 (Christiania, 1850), 221–82.

Normand, Lawrence, and Gareth Roberts, *Witchcraft in Early Modern Scotland. James VI's Demonology and the North Berwick Witches* (Exeter, 2000).

Pedersen, Niels M., 'Dokumenter til en Troldomssag under Christian III' [Documents Related to a Witchcraft Trial Under Christian III], *Danske Magazin*, 3 (1843), 52–67.

Petersen, Siegwarth, and Otto Gr. Lundh (eds.), *Norske Rigs-Registranter*, b. 2 [insert translation] (Christiania, 1863).

Pollen, John H. (ed.), *Letter from Mary Queen of Scots to the Duke of Guise*, Scottish History Society, series 1, vol. 43 (Edinburgh, 1904).

Register of the Privy Council (RPC), 2nd series, vol. 5.

Secher, V. A., *Forordninger, Recesser og andre Kongelige Breve, Danmarks Lovgivning Vedkommende 1558–1660* [Decrees, Recesses, and Royal Letters, 1558–1660], vol. 2 (Copenhagen, 1887).

Steuart, A. Francis (ed.), *Memoirs of Sir James Melville of Halhill 1535–1617* (London, 1929).

Stevenson, John H., and William K. Dickson (eds.), *The Register of the Great Seal of Scotland, A. D. 1303–1668*, vol. 10, H. M. Register House (Edinburgh, 1904).

Survey of Scottish Witchcraft (SSW). www.arts.ed.ac.uk/witches.

Voltmer, Rita, and Karl Weisenstein (eds.), *Das Hexenregister des Claudius Musiel* [The Witch Register of Claudius Musiel] (Trier, 1996).

Wernham, Richard B. (ed.), *List and Analysis of State Papers, Foreign Series Elizabeth I: August 1589–June 1590* (London, 1964).

Willumsen, Liv H., *Kilder til trolldomsprosessene i Finnmark. Modernisert språklig utgave* [Sources to the Finnmark Witchcraft Trials. Edition in Modernized Language] (Leikanger, 2017).

Willumsen, Liv H., *Trolldomsprosessene i Finnmark. Et kildeskrift* [The Finnmark Witchcraft Trials. A Source Book] (Bergen, 2010).

Willumsen, Liv H., *The Witchcraft Trials in Finnmark, Northern Norway* (Bergen, 2010).

Wolff, A., *Flensburger Hexenprozesse, Aus Flensburgs Vorzeit, Beiträge und Geschichte der Stadt Flensburg* [Flensburg Witch Trials, from Flensburg's Past, Contributions and Histories of the City of Flensburg] (Flensburg, 1887).

Secondary Sources

Aaslestad, Petter, *Pasienten som tekst* [The Patient as Text] (Oslo, 1997).

Alm, Ellen, *Statens rolle i trolldomsprosessene i Danmark og Norge på 1500-og 1600-tallet. En komparativ studie* [The Role of the State During the Witchcraft Trials in Denmark and Norway in the Sixteenth and Seventeenth Centuries. A Comparative Study] (M.A. thesis, University of Tromsø, 2000).

Alm, Ellen, *Trondheims siste heksebrenning* [The Last Witch Burning in Trondheim] (Trondheim, 2014).

Alver, Bente G., *Heksetro og trolldom* [Witchcraft Beliefs and Sorcery] (Oslo, 1971).

Alver, Bente G., *Mellem mennesker og magter: Magi i hekseforfølgelsernes tid* [Between Humans and Powers: Magic in the Time of Witchcraft Persecution] (Oslo, 2008).

Andreassen, Reidun L., and Liv H. Willumsen, *Steilneset Memorial. Art, Architecture, History* (Stamsund, 2013).

Anglo, Sydney (ed.), *The Damned Art: Essays in the Literature of Witchcraft* (London, 1977).

Ankarloo, Bengt, 'Sweden: The Mass Burnings (1668–1676)', in Bengt Ankarloo and Gustav Henningsen (eds.), *Early Modern European Witchcraft: Centres and Peripheries* (Oxford, 1990), 288–92.

Ankarloo, Bengt, *Trolldomsprocesserna i Sverige. Skrifter utgivna av institutet för rättshistorisk forskning, Serien I: Rättshistoriskt bibliotek* [The Witchcraft Trials in Sweden. Books Published at the Department of Legal Historical Research], vol. 17 (Ph.D. thesis, University of Lund, 1971; 2nd ed. 1984, with postscript).

Ankarloo, Bengt, and Stuart Clark (eds.), *Witchcraft and Magic in Europe, Vol. 4: The Period of the Witch Trials* (London, 2002).

Ankarloo, Bengt, and Gustav Henningsen (eds.), *Early Modern European Witchcraft: Centres and Peripheries* (Oxford, 1990).

Apps, Lara, and Andrew C. Gow, *Male Witches in Early Modern Europe* (Manchester, 2003).

Åstrand, Björn, *Tortyr och pinligt förhör—väld och tvång i äldre svensk rätt* [Torture and Interrogation Under Pressure—Violence and Force in Older Swedish Courts] (Ph.D. thesis, Umeå University, 2000).

Balsvik, Randi R., 'Religious Beliefs and Witches in Contemporary Africa', in Reidun L. Andreassen and Liv H. Willumsen (eds.), *Steilneset Memorial. Art, Architecture, History* (Stamsund, 2013), 89–99.

Balsvik, Randi R., 'Vardø i verden' [Vardø in the World], in Randi R. Balsvik and Jens P. Nielsen (eds.), *Forpost mot øst* [Outpost towards the East] (Stamsund, 2008).

Baptie, Diane, and Liv H. Willumsen, 'From Fife to Finnmark: John Cunningham's Way to the North', *Genealogist*, 28, no. 2 (Fall 2014), 180–201.

Baroja, Julio C., *The World of the Witches*, trans. Nigel Glendinning (London, 1964).

Barry, Jonathan, 'Public Infidelity and Private Belief? The Discourse of Spirits in Enlightenment Bristol', in Owen Davies and Willem de Blécourt (eds.), *Beyond the Witch Trials: Witchcraft and Magic in Enlightenment Europe* (Manchester, 2004), 117–43.

Barry, Jonathan, *Witchcraft and Demonology in South-West England 1640–1789* (Basingstoke, 2012).

Barry, Jonathan, and Owen Davies, *Palgrave Advances in Witchcraft Historiography* (Basingstoke, 2007).

Barry, Jonathan, Owen Davies, and Cornelie Usborne (eds.), *Cultures of Witchcraft in Europe from the Middle Ages to the Present: Essays in Honour of Willem de Blécourt* (Cham, 2018).

Barry, Jonathan, Marianne Hester, and Gareth Roberts (eds.), *Witchcraft in Early Modern Europe: Studies in Culture and Belief* (Cambridge, 1996).

Behringer, Wolfgang, *Hexen und Hexenprozesse in Deutschland* [Witchcraft and Witch Trials in Germany] (first published 1988; Munich, 2000).

Behringer, Wolfgang, *The Shaman of Oberstdorf: Chonrad Stoeckhlin and the Phantoms of the Night* (Charlottesville, 1998).

Behringer, Wolfgang, 'Weather, Hunger and Fear: Origins of the European Witch-Hunts in Climate, Society and Mentality', *German History*, 13, no 1, pp. 1-27.

Behringer, Wolfgang, *Witchcraft Persecutions in Bavaria: Popular Magic, Religious Zealots and Reason of State in Early Modern Europe* (Cambridge, 1997).

Behringer, Wolfgang, *Witches and Witch-Hunts. A Global History* (Cambridge, 2004).

Bennett, Walter, *The Pendle Witches* (Preston, 1957).

Bergenheim, Åsa, *Den liderliga häxan: Häxhammaren och de svenska häxprossesserna* [The Lewd Witch: The Witches' Hammer and the Swedish Witchcraft Trials] (Stockholm, 2020).

Birkelund, Merete, *Troldkvinden og hendes anklager. Danske hekseprocesser i det 16. og 17. århundrede* [The Witch and Her Accusers. Danish Witch Trials of the 16th and 17th Centuries] (Århus, 1983).

Blécourt, Willem de, 'Contested Knowledge: A Historical Anthropologist's Approach to European Witchcraft', in Jonathan Barry, Owen Davies, and Cornelie Usborne (eds.), *Cultures of Witchcraft in Europe from the Middle Ages to the Present: Essays in Honour of Willem de Blécourt* (Cham, 2018), 1–22.

Blécourt, Willem de, 'Sabbath Stories: Towards a New History of Witches' Assemblies', in Brian P. Levack (ed.), *The Oxford Handbook of Witchcraft in Early Modern Europe and Colonial America* (Oxford, 2013), 84–100.

Blécourt, Willem de (ed.), *Werewolf Histories* (Basingstoke, 2015).

Bø, Olav, *Norsk folkedikting I: Eventyr* [Norwegian Folk Tales I: Fairy Tales] (Oslo, 1977).

Botheim, Ragnhild, *Trolldomsprosessane i Bergenhus len 1566–1700* [The Witchcraft Trials in Bergenhus District, 1566–1700] (M.A. thesis, University of Bergen, 1999).

Briggs, Robin, *Witches and Neighbours: The Social and Cultural Context of European Witchcraft*, 2nd ed. (Oxford, 2002; first published in 1996).

Brochmand, Jesper, *Systema universæ theologia*, vol. 1–2 (Hafniæ/Copenhagen, 1633).

Brock, Michelle D., *Satan and the Scots: The Devil in Post-Reformation Scotland, c. 1560–1700* (London, 2016).

Busch, Berit V., *'They Shipped All in at North Berwick in a Boat like a Chimney'. Forestillinger om samlinger knyttet til de hekseanklagede i North Berwick-prosessene* [Ideas About Witches' Gatherings Related to Accused Persons During the North Berwick Trials] (M.A. thesis, University of Tromsø, 2018).

Cameron, Euan, *Enchanted Europe: Superstition, Reason and Religion 1250–1750* (Oxford, 2010).

Carlton, Charles, Robert L. Woods, Mary L. Robertson, and Joseph S. Block (eds.), *States, Sovereigns and Society in Early Modern England: Essays in Honour of A.J. Slavin* (Stroud, 1998).

Carr, Victoria, 'The Countess of Angus's Escape from the North Berwick Witch-Hunt', in Julian Goodare (ed.), *Scottish Witches and Witch-Hunters* (Basingstoke, 2013), 34–48.

Chartier, Roger, *The Author's Hand and the Printer's Mind: Transformations of the Written Word in Early Modern Europe* (Cambridge, 2014).

Clark, Stuart, 'Introduction', in Stuart Clark (ed.), *Languages of Witchcraft. Narrative, Ideology and Meaning in Early Modern Culture* (New York, 2001), 1–18.

Clark, Stuart (ed.), *Languages of Witchcraft. Narrative, Ideology and Meaning in Early Modern Culture* (London, 2001).

Clark, Stuart, *Thinking with Demons: The Idea of Witchcraft in Early Modern Europe* (Oxford, 1997).

Cockburn, J. S., *A History of English Assizes 1558–1714*, ed. D. E. C. Yale (Cambridge, 1972).

Cohen, Elizabeth S., 'Back Talk: Two Prostitutes' Voices from Rome *c.* 1600', *Early Modern Women*, 2 (2007), 95–126.

Cohen, Elizabeth S., 'Between Oral and Written Culture: The Social Meaning of an Illustrated Love Letter', in Barbara Diefendorf and Carla Hesse (eds.), *Culture and Identity in Early Modern Europe (1500–1800): Essays in Honour of Natalie Zemon Davis* (Ann Arbor, 1993), 181–201.

Collingwood, Robin G., *The Idea of Nature* (Oxford, 1965).

Collins, Daniel, *Reanimated Voices. Speech Reporting in a Historical-Pragmatic Perspective* (Amsterdam, 2001).

Collins, David J. (ed.), *The Cambridge History of Magic and Witchcraft in the West: From Antiquity to the Present* (Cambridge, 2015).

Cordey, Anna, 'Reputation and Witch-Hunting in Seventeenth-Century Dalkeith', in Julian Goodare (ed.), *Scottish Witches and Witch-Hunters* (Basingstoke, 2013), 103–20.

Cordey, Anna, *Witch-Hunting in the Presbytery of Dalkeith, 1649 to 1662* (M.Sc. thesis, University of Edinburgh, 2003).

Coudert, Allison, 'Female Witches', in Richard M. Golden (ed.), *Encyclopedia of Witchcraft: The Western Tradition* (Santa Barbara, 2006), 357–59.

Cowan, Edward J., and Lizanne Henderson, 'The Last of the Witches? The Survival of Scottish Witch Belief', in Julian Goodare (ed.), *The Scottish Witch-Hunt in Context* (Manchester, 2002), 198–217.

Danckwerth, Caspar, *Neue Landesbeschreibung der zwey Herzogthümer Schleswich und Holstein* [New Description of the Two Duchies Schleswig and Holstein] (1652).

Davies, Owen, and Willem de Blécourt (eds.), *Beyond the Witch Trials: Witchcraft and Magic in Enlightenment Europe* (Manchester, 2004).

Davis, Natalie Z., *Fiction in the Archives: Pardon Tales and Their Tellers in Sixteenth-Century France* (Cambridge, 1987).

Degn, Christian, Hartmut Lehmann, and Dagmar Unverhau (eds.), *Hexenprozesse, Deutsche und skandinavische Beiträge* [Witch trials. German and Scandinavian Contributions] (Neumünster, 1983).

Del Rio, Martin, *Disquisitiones Magicae Libri Sex* (Leuven, 1599/1600).

Diefenbach, Johann, *Der Hexenwahn in Deutschland* [The Witch Mania in Germany] (Mainz, 1886; repr., Fotomechanischer Neudruck, Leipzig, 1978).

Dillinger, Johannes, '*Böse Leute': Hexenverfolgungen in Schwäbisch-Österreich und Kurtrier in Vergleich* (Trier, 1999).

Doležel, Lubomír, 'Fictional and Historical Narrative: Meeting the Postmodernist Challenge', in David Herman (ed.), *Narratologies. New Perspectives on Narrative Analyses* (Columbus, 1999), 247–73.

Doty, Kathleen L., 'Telling Tales. The Role of Scribes in Constructing the Discourse of the Salem Witchcraft Trials', *Journal of Historical Pragmatics*, 8, no. 1 (2007), 25–41.

Doty, Kathleen L., and Risto Hiltunen, 'I Will Tell, I Will Tell': Confessional Patterns in the Salem Witchcraft Trials, 1692, *Journal of Historical Pragmatics*, 3, no. 2 (2002), 299–335.

Durston, Gregory, *Witchcraft and Witch Trials: A History of English Witchcraft and Its Legal Perspectives, 1542 to 1736* (Chichester, 2000).

Dye, Sierra, 'Devilische Wordis': Speech as Evidence in Scotland's Witch Trials, 1563–1736 (Ph.D. thesis, University of Guelph, 2016).

Eilola, Jari, 'Interpreting Children's Blåkulla Stories in Sweden (1675)', in Julian Goodare, Rita Voltmer, and Liv H. Willumsen (eds.), Demonology and Witch-Hunting in Early Modern Europe (Abingdon, 2020), 327–44.

Eilola, Jari, 'Lapsitodistajien kertomukset Ruotsin noitatapaukissa 1668–1676' [Child Witnesses' Stories in Witchcraft Trials in Sweden 1668–1676], E-Journal Kasvatus and Aika, no. 3 (2009).

Eilola, Jari, 'Witchcraft, Women and the Borders of Household', ARV: Nordic Yearbook of Folklore, 62 (2006), 33–50.

Eliassen, Sven G., Hekseprosesser i Østfold [Witch Trials in Østfold] (Sarpsborg, 1983).

Eliassen, Sven G., Østfolds historie [The History of Østfold], vol. 2 (Sarpsborg, 2005).

Elstad, Åsa, Moteløver og heimføingar: Tekstiler og samfunnsendringer i Øksnes og Astafjord 1750– 1900 [Moths and Homesteaders: Textiles and Community Change in Øksnes and Altafjord, 1750–1900] (Stamsund, 1997).

Estés, Clarissa P., Women Who Run With The Wolves: Myths and Stories of The Wild Woman Archetype (London, 1992).

Federici, Silvia, Witches, Witch-Hunting and Women (Oakland, 2018).

Gaskill, Malcolm, Crime and Mentalities in Early Modern England (Cambridge, 2000).

Gaskill, Malcolm, 'Reporting Murder: Fiction in the Archives in Early Modern England', Social History, 23, no. 1 (1998), 1–30.

Gaskill, Malcolm, 'Witchcraft and Power in Early Modern England: The Case of Margaret Moore', in Jenny Kermode and Garthine Walker (eds.), Women, Crime and the Courts in Early Modern England (London, 1994), 125–45.

Gaskill, Malcolm, 'Witchcraft Trials in England', in Brian P. Levack (ed.), The Oxford Handbook of Witchcraft in Early Modern Europe and Colonial America (Oxford, 2013), 283–99.

Gaskill, Malcolm, 'Witches and Witnesses in Old and New England', in Stuart Clark (ed.), Languages of Witchcraft. Narrative, Ideology and Meaning in Early Modern Culture (Basingstoke, 2001), 55–80.

Gaskill, Malcolm, The Witchfinders: A Seventeenth-Century English Tragedy (London, 2006).

Genette, Gérard, Fiction and Diction (Ithaca, 1993).

Genette, Gérard, Narrative Discourse. An Essay in Method (Ithaca, 1980).

Genette, Gérard, Narrative Discourse Revisited (Ithaca, 1988).

Genette, Gérard, 'Voice', in Susana Onega and José Á. Landa (eds.), Narratology: An Introduction (London, 1996), 172–73.

Gent, Jacqueline van, Magic, Body and the Self in Eighteenth-Century Sweden (Leiden, 2009).

Gibson, Marion (ed.), Early English Trial Pamphlets (London, 2003), vol. 2 in the series Richard M. Golden and James Sharpe (eds.), English Witchcraft 1560–1736.

Gibson, Marion, Early Modern Witches: Witchcraft Cases in Contemporary Writing (Florence, 2000).

Gibson, Marion, 'French Demonology in an English Village: The St Osyth Experiment of 1582', in Julian Goodare, Rita Voltmer, and Liv H. Willumsen (eds.), Demonology and Witch-Hunting in Early Modern Europe (Abingdon, 2020), 107–26.

Gibson, Marion, Reading Witchcraft: Stories of Early English Witches (London, 1996).

Gibson, Marion, Witchcraft: The Basics (Abingdon, 2018).

Gibson, Marion, Witchcraft Myths in American Culture (New York, 2007).

Gibson, Marion, Witchcraft and Society in England and America, 1550–1750 (New York, 2003).

Gijswijt-Hofstra, Marijke, 'From the Low Countries to France', in Bengt Ankarloo and Stuart Clark (eds.), Witchcraft and Magic in Europe, vol. 4: The Period of the Witch Trials (London, 2002), 95–188.

Gijswijt-Hofstra, Marijke, and Willem Frijhoff (eds.), *Witchcraft in the Netherlands: From the Fourteenth to the Twentieth Century* (Rotterdam, 1991).

Gijswijt-Hofstra, Marijke, Brian P. Levack, and Roy Porter (eds.), *Witchcraft and Magic in Europe, Vol. 5: The Eighteenth and Nineteenth Centuries* (London, 1999).

Gilje, Nils, ' "Djevelen står alltid bak": Demonisering av folkelig magi på slutten av 1500—tallet' [The Devil Is Always Behind: Demonizing of Traditional Magic at the End of the Sixteenth Century], in Bjarte Askeland and Jan F. Bernt (eds.), *Erkjennelse og engasjement: Minneseminar for David Roland Doublet (1954–2000)* [Recognition and Engagement: Seminar in Memory of David Roland Doublet (1954–2000)] (Bergen, 2001), 93–107.

Gilje, Nils, *Heksen og humanisten: Anne Pedersdatter og Absalon Pederssøn Beyer: en historie om magi og trolldom i Bergen på 1500—tallet* [The Witch and the Humanist: Anne Pedersdatter and Absalon Pedersson Beyer: A Story About Magic and Witchcraft in Sixteenth-Century Bergen] (Bergen, 2003).

Golden, Richard M. (ed.), *Encyclopedia of Witchcraft: The Western Tradition* (Santa Barbara, 2006).

Golden, Richard M., and James Sharpe (eds.), *English Witchcraft 1560–1736* (London, 2003).

Goodare, Julian, 'Emotional Relationships with Spirit-Guides in Early Modern Scotland', in Julian Goodare and Martha McGill (eds.), *The Supernatural in Early Modern Scotland* (Manchester, 2020), 39–54.

Goodare, Julian, *The European Witch-Hunt* (Abingdon, 2016).

Goodare, Julian, 'The Finnmark Witches in European Context', in Reidun L. Andreassen and Liv H. Willumsen (eds.), *Steilneset Memorial. Art, Architecture, History* (Stamsund, 2013), 57–63.

Goodare, Julian, 'Flying Witches in Scotland', in Julian Goodare (ed.), *Scottish Witches and Witch-Hunters* (Basingstoke, 2013), 159–76.

Goodare, Julian, 'The Framework for Scottish Witch-Hunting in the 1590s', *Scottish Historical Review*, 81 (2002), 240–50.

Goodare, Julian, 'John Knox on Demonology and Witchcraft', *Archiv für Reformationsgeschichte*, 96 (2005), 221–45.

Goodare, Julian, 'Men and the Witch-Hunt in Scotland', in Alison Rowlands (ed.), *Witchcraft and Masculinities in Early Modern Europe* (Houndmills, 2009), 149–70.

Goodare, Julian, 'Pricking of Suspected Witches', in Richard M. Golden (ed.), *Encyclopedia of Witchcraft: The Western Tradition* (Santa Barbara, 2006), 931–32.

Goodare, Julian (ed.), *The Scottish Witch-Hunt in Context* (Manchester, 2002).

Goodare, Julian, 'The Scottish Witchcraft Act', *Church History*, 74, no. 1 (2005), 39–67.

Goodare, Julian, 'Scottish Witchcraft in Its European Context', in Julian Goodare, Lauren Martin, and Joyce Miller (eds.), *Witchcraft and Belief in Early Modern Scotland* (Basingstoke, 2008), 26–50.

Goodare, Julian, 'The Scottish Witchcraft Panic of 1597', in Julian Goodare (ed.), *The Scottish Witch-Hunt in Context* (Manchester, 2002), 51–72.

Goodare, Julian (ed.), *Scottish Witches and Witch-Hunters* (Basingstoke, 2013).

Goodare, Julian, 'Witch-Hunting and the Scottish State', in Julian Goodare (ed.), *The Scottish Witch-Hunt in Context* (Manchester, 2002), 122–45.

Goodare, Julian, 'Witchcraft in Scotland', in Brian P. Levack (ed.), *Oxford Handbook of Witchcraft in Early Modern Europe and Colonial America* (Oxford, 2013), 300–17.

Goodare, Julian, 'Witches' Flight in Scottish Demonology', in Julian Goodare, Rita Voltmer, and Liv H. Willumsen (eds.), *Demonology and Witch-Hunting in Early Modern Europe* (Abingdon, 2020), 147–67.

Goodare, Julian, 'Women and the Witch-Hunt in Scotland', *Social History*, xxiii (1998), 288–307.

Goodare, Julian, 'Women, Men, and Witchcraft', in Julian Goodare (ed.), *The European Witch-Hunt* (Abingdon, 2016), 267–316.

Goodare, Julian, Lauren Martin, and Joyce Miller (eds.), *Witchcraft and Belief in Early Modern Scotland* (Basingstoke, 2008).

Goodare, Julian, and Martha McGill (eds.), *The Supernatural in Early Modern Scotland* (Manchester, 2020).

Goodare, Julian, Rita Voltmer, and Liv H. Willumsen (eds.), *Demonology and Witch-Hunting in Early Modern Europe* (Abingdon, 2020).

Gow, Andrew C., Robert B. Desjardins, and François V. Pageau (eds., trans.), *The Arras Witch Treatises* (Pennsylvania, 2016).

Gowing, Laura, *Domestic Dangers: Women, Words and Sex in Early Modern London* (Oxford, 1996).

Gowing, Laura, 'Language, Power and the Law: Women's Slander Litigation in Early Modern London', in Jenny Kermode and Garthine Walker (eds.), *Women, Crime and the Courts in Early Modern England* (London, 1994), 26–47.

Granlund, Lis, 'Queen Hedwig Eleonora of Sweden: Dowager, Builder, and Collector', in Clarissa Campbell Orr (ed.), *Queenship in Europe 1660–1815: The Role of the Consort* (Cambridge, 2004), 56–76.

Granquist, Karin, 'Thou Shalt Have No Other Gods Before Me (Exodus 20:3). Witchcraft and Superstition Trials in the 17th and 18th Century Swedish Lapland', in Peter Sköld and Kristina Kram (eds.), *Kulturkonfrontation i Lappmarken: sex essäer om mötet mellan samer och svenskar* [Cultural Confrontations: Six Essays on the Meeting Between Sami and Swedes] (Umeå, 1998), 13–21.

Graves, Peter, and Arne Kruse (eds.), *Images and Imaginations: Perspectives on Britain and Scandinavia* (Edinburgh, 2007).

Grell, Ole P. (ed.), *The Scandinavian Reformation* (Cambridge, 1995), 114–43.

Grew, Raymond, 'The Case for Comparing Histories', *American Historical Review*, 85, no. 4 (1980), 763–78.

Hagen, Rune B., 'At the Edge of Civilisation: John Cunningham Lensmann of Finnmark 1619–51', in Andrew Mackillop and Steve Murdoch (eds.), *Military Governors and Imperial Frontiers c. 1600–1800: A Study of Scotland and Empires* (Leiden, 2003), 29–52.

Hagen, Rune B., *Dei europeiske hekseprosessane* [The European Witchcraft Trials] (Oslo, 2007).

Hagen, Rune B., 'Harmløs dissenter eller djevelsk trollmann?' [Harmless Dissenter or Devilish Sorcerer?], *Historisk Tidskrift*, 81, no. 2–3 (2002), 319–46.

Hagen, Rune B., *Hekser: Fra forfølgelse til fortryllelse* [Witches: From Persecution to Enchantment] (Oslo, 2003).

Hagen, Rune B., 'Images, Representations and the Self-Perception of Magic Among the Sami Shamans of Arctic Norway', in Louise Kallestrup and Raisa M. Toivo (eds.), *Contesting Orthodoxy in Medieval and Early Modern Europe: Heresy, Magic, and Witchcraft* (Cham, 2017), 279–300.

Hagen, Rune B., 'Mandrup Pedersen Schønnebøl', *Store norske leksikon* (January 28, 2019), https://snl.no/Mandrup_Pedersen_Sch%C3%B8nneb%C3%B8l.

Hagen, Rune B., 'Sami Shamanism: The Arctic Dimension', *Magic, Rituals and Witches*, 1, no. 2 (2006), 227–33.

Hagen, Rune B., *The Sami—Sorcerers in Norwegian History* (Karasjok, 2012).

Hagen, Rune B., *The Sorcery Trial of Anders Poulsen in 1692* (Karasjok, 2012).

Hagen, Rune B., *Ved porten til helvete* [At the Gate to Hell] (Oslo, 2015).

Hagen, Rune B., 'The Witch-Hunt in Early Modern Finnmark', *Acta Borealia*, 16, no. 1 (1999), 43–62.

Hagen, Rune B., 'Witchcraft Criminality and Witchcraft Research in the Nordic Countries', in Brian P. Levack (ed.), *The Oxford Handbook of Witchcraft in Early Modern Europe
and Colonial America* (Oxford, 2013), 375–92.

Hagen, Rune B., 'Witchcraft and Ethnicity: A Critical Perspective on Sami Shamanism
in the Seventeenth-Century', in Marko Nenonen and Raisa M. Toivo (eds.), *Writing
Witch-Hunt Histories* (Leiden, 2014), 141–66.

Hagen, Rune B., and Per E. Sparboe, *Kongens reise til det ytterste nord: Dagbøker fra Christian
IV's tokt til Finnmark og Kola 1599* [The King's Voyage to the High North: Diaries from
Christian IV's Trip to Finnmark and Kola 1599] (Tromsø, 2004).

Häll, Mikael. 'Näckens dödloga dop: manliga vattenväsen, död och förbjuden sexualitet i
det tidligmoderna Sverige' [Näckens Deadly Drug: Male Water Creatures, Death and
Forbidden Sexuality in Early Modern Sweden], *Historisk tidskrift*, 131, no. 3 (2011),
590–620.

Häll, Mikael, *Skogsråets famn och Djävulens hamn: föreställningar om erotiska väsen i 1600- och
1700-talens Sverige* [The Roe's Bosom and the Devil's Guise: Imaginations of Erotic
Beings in 17th- and 18th-Century Sweden] (Ph.D. thesis, Lund University, 2013).

Hannes, Lowagie. *Par desperacion. Zelfmoord in het graafschap Vlaanderen tijdens de Bourgondische
periode (1385–1500). Een sociologische aanpak* [Par Deperacion. Suicide in the County of
Flanders during the Burgundian Period 1385–1500. A Sociological Approach] (Ph.D.
thesis, Ghent University, 2007).

Hasted, Rachel A. *The Pendle Witch-Trial 1612* (Preston, 1987).

Hastrup, Kirsten, 'Iceland: Sorcerers and Paganism', in Bengt Ankarloo and Gustav Henningsen (eds.), *Early Modern European Witchcraft: Centres and Peripheries* (Oxford, 1990),
383–401.

Hausen, Reinhold, *Rannsakningar och domar rörande trolldomsväsendet på Åland* [Persecution
and Sentences Related to Witchcraft in Åland] (Helsingfors, 1894–1898).

Heikkinen, Antero, and Timo Kervinen, 'Finland: The Male Domination', in Bengt Ankarloo and Gustav Henningsen (eds.), *Early Modern European Witchcraft: Centres and Peripheries* (Oxford, 1990), 319–38.

Helle, Knut, *Norge blir en stat, 1130–1319* [Norway Becomes a State] (Oslo, 1974).

Hemmingsen, Niels, *Admonitia de superstionibus magical vitandis* (Copenhagen, 1575).

Henderson, Lizanne (ed.), *Fantastical Imaginations* (East Linton, 2009).

Henderson, Lizanne, and Edward J. Cowan, *Scottish Fairy Belief: A History* (East Linton, 2004).

Henningsen, Gustav, *The Witches' Advocate. Basque Witchcraft and the Spanish Inquisition*
(Reno, 1980).

Hoggard, Brian, 'The Archeology of Counter-Witchcraft and Popular Magic', in Owen
Davies and Willem de Blécourt (eds.), *Beyond the Witch Trials: Witchcraft and Magic in
Enlightenment Europe* (Manchester, 2004), 167–86.

Holmes, Clive, 'Women: Witnesses and Witches', *Past and Present*, 140 (1993), 45–78.

Hutton, Ronald, 'Anthropological and Historical Approaches to Witchcraft: Potential for a
New Collaboration?' *Historical Journal*, 47, no. 2 (2004), 413–34.

Hutton, Ronald, 'Witch-Hunting in Celtic Societies', *Past and Present*, 212 (2011), 43–71.

Imsen, Steinar, 'The Union of Calmar: Northern Great Power or Northern German Outpost?' in Christopher Ocker (ed.), *Politics and Reformations: Communities, Polities, Nations,
and Empires* (Leiden, 2007), 471–90.

Jacobsen, Jørgen C., *Den sidste Hexebrænding i Danmark 1693* [The Last Burning of a Witch
in Denmark] (Copenhagen, 1971).

Jacques-Chaquin, Nicole, and Maxime Préaud (eds.), *Les sorciers du carroi de Marlou: Un procès
de Sorcielle en Berry (1582–1583)* [The Sorcerers of Crossroads of Marlou: A Witchcraft
Trial in Berry (1582–1583)] (Grenoble, 1996).

Jardine, David, *A Reading on the Use of Torture in the Criminal Law of England Previously to the Commonwealth* (London, 1837).

Jensen, Karsten S., *Trolddom i Danmark 1500–1588* [Witchcraft in Denmark 1500–1588] (Copenhagen, 1988).

Johansen, Jens C., *Da Djævelen var ude . . . Trolddom i det 17. århundredes Danmark* [When the Devil Was Out . . . Witchcraft in Seventeenth-Century Denmark] (Viborg, 1991).

Johansen, Jens C., 'Denmark', in Richard M. Golden (ed.), *Encyclopedia of Witchcraft: The Western Tradition* (Santa Barbara, 2006), 265.

Johansen, Jens C., 'Denmark: The Sociology of Accusation', in Bengt Ankarloo and Gustav Henningsen (eds.), *Early Modern European Witchcraft: Centres and Peripheries* (Oxford, 1990), 339–65.

Johansen, Jens C., 'Tavshed er guld. En historiografisk oversigt over amerikansk og europæisk hekseforskning 1966–1981' ['Silence Is Gold. A Historiographical Survey of American and European Witchcraft Research, 1966–1981'], *Historisk tidsskrift*, 81 (1982), 401–23.

Johansen, Jens C., 'To Beat a Glass Drum: The Transmission of Popular Notions of Demonology in Denmark and Germany', in Julian Goodare, Rita Voltmer, and Liv H. Willumsen (eds.), *Demonology and Witch-Hunting in Early Modern Europe* (Abingdon, 2020), 233–42.

Jones, Norman, 'Defining Superstitions: Treasonous Catholics and the Act Against Witchcraft of 1563', in Charles Carlton, Robert L. Woods, Mary L. Robertson, and Joseph S. Block (eds.), *States, Sovereigns and Society in Early Modern England: Essays in Honour of A.J. Slavin* (Stroud, 1998), 187–203.

Jørgensen, Poul J., *Dansk Strafferet fra Reformationen til Danske lov* [Danish Criminal Law from the Reformation to the Danish Law] (Copenhagen, 2001).

Kalkar, Otto, *Ordbog til det ældre danske sprog (1300–1700)* (Copenhagen, 1881–1907).

Kallestrup, Louise N., *Agents of Witchcraft in Early Modern Italy and Denmark* (Basingstoke, 2015).

Kallestrup, Louise N., '"He Promised Her So Many Things": Witches, Sabbats, and Devils in Early Modern Denmark', in Julian Goodare, Rita Voltmer, and Liv H. Willumsen (eds.), *Demonology and Witch-Hunting in Early Modern Europe* (Abingdon, 2020), 243–60.

Kallestrup, Louise N., *Heksejagt* (Aarhus, 2020).

Kallestrup, Louise N., *I Pagt med Djævelen. Trolddomsforestillinger og trolddomsforfølgelser i Italien og Danmark efter Reformationen* [In Pact with the Devil: Witchcraft Imaginations and Witchcraft Persecution in Italy and Denmark After the Reformation] (Frederiksberg, 2009).

Kallestrup, Louise N., '"Kind in Words and Deeds, but False in Their Hearts": Fear of Evil Conspiracy in Late-Sixteenth-Century Denmark', in Jonathan Barry, Owen Davies, and Cornelie Usborne (eds.), *Cultures of Witchcraft in Europe from the Middle Ages to the Present: Essays in Honour of Willem de Blécourt* (Cham, 2018), 137–53.

Kallestrup, Louise N., 'Maleficium ò "abuso di sacramento"?' *Dansk Historisk Tidsskrift*, 102, no. 2 (2002), 282–305.

Kallestrup, Louise N., *Trolddomsforfølgelser og trolddomstro: En komparasjon af det posttridentine Italien og det luthersk protestantiske Danmark i det 16. og 17. århundrede* [Witchcraft Persecution and Witchcraft Belief: A Comparison of Post-Tridentine Italy and Lutheran Protestant Denmark in the Sixteenth and Seventeenth Centuries] (Ph.D. thesis, Aalborg University, 2007).

Kallestrup, Louise N., '"When Hell Became Too Small": Constructing Witchcraft in Post-Reformation Denmark', in Tyge Krogh, Louise Kallestrup, and Claus B. Christensen (eds.), *Cultural Histories of Crime in Denmark, 1500–2000* (London, 2017), 38–57.

Kallestrup, Louise N., and Raisa M. Toivo (eds.), *Contesting Orthodoxy in Medieval and Early Modern Europe: Heresy, Magic, and Witchcraft* (Cham, 2017).

Kasch, Hjördis A., *Trollmenn og trollkvinner: En undersøkelse av kjønn i Norges trolldomsforfølgelser i tidlig moderne tid* [Male and Female Witches: A Study of Gender in Witchcraft Persecution in Norway in Early Modern Period] (M.A. thesis, University of Bergen, 2015).

Katajala-Peltomaa, Sari, *Demonic Possession and Lived Religion in Later Medieval Europe* (Oxford, 2020).

Kent, E. J., 'Tyrannic Beasts: Male Witchcraft in Early Modern English Culture', in Kounine, Laura, and Michael Ostling (eds.), *Emotions in the History of Witchcraft* (Basingstoke, 2017), 77–94.

Kermode, Jenny, and Garthine Walker (eds.), *Women, Crime and the Courts in Early Modern England* (London, 1994).

Kluckhohn, Clyde, *Navaho Witchcraft* (Harvard, 1944).

Knutsen, Gunnar W., 'The End of the Witch Hunts in Scandinavia', *ARV: Nordic Yearbook of Folklore*, 57 (2006), 143–64.

Knutsen, Gunnar W., 'Norwegian Witchcraft Trials: A Reassessment', *Continuity and Change*, 28, no. 2 (2003), 185–200.

Knutsen, Gunnar W., *Servants of Satan and Masters of Demons. The Spanish Inquisition Trials for Superstition, Valencia and Barcelona, 1478–1700* (Turnhout, 2009).

Knutsen, Gunnar W., 'Topics of Persecution: Witchcraft Historiography in the Iberian World', in Marko Nenonen and Raisa M. Toivo (eds.), *Writing Witch-Hunt Histories* (Leiden, 2014), 167–90.

Knutsen, Gunnar W., *Trolldomsprosessene på Østlandet* [Witchcraft Trials at Østlandet] (Oslo, 1998).

Kors, Alan C., and Edvard Peters, *Witchcraft in Europe 400–1700: A Documentary History* (Philadelphia, 1972).

Kounine, Laura, *Imagining the Witch: Emotions, Gender and Selfhood in Early Modern Germany* (Oxford, 2018).

Kounine, Laura, and Michael Ostling (eds.), *Emotions in the History of Witchcraft* (Basingstoke, 2017).

Krogh, Thyge, *Oplysningstiden og det magiske: henrettelser og korporlige straffe i 1700-tallets første halvdel* [The Age of Enlightenment and the Magical: Executions and Corporal Punishments in the First Half of the Seventeenth Century] (Copenhagen, 2000).

Krogh, Tyge, Louise Kallestrup, and Claus B. Christensen (eds.), *Cultural Histories of Crime in Denmark, 1500–2000* (London, 2017).

Kruse, Arne, and Liv H. Willumsen, 'Magic Language: The Transmission of an Idea Over Geographic Distance and Linguistic Barriers', *Magic, Ritual and Witchcraft*, 15, no. 1 (Spring 2020), 1–32.

Kruse, Arne, and Liv H. Willumsen, 'Ordet Ballvollen knytt til transnasjonal overføring av idéar' [The Word Ballvollen Connected to Transnational Transfer of Ideas], *Historisk tidsskrift*, no. 2 (2014), 407–23.

Kryk-Kastovsky, Barbara, 'Historical Courtroom Discourse: An Introduction', *Journal of Historical Pragmatics*, 7, no. 2 (2006), 213–45.

Kryk-Kastovsky, Barbara, 'How Bad Is "Bad Data"? In Search of the Features of Orality in Early Modern English Legal Texts', in *Current Issues in Unity and Diversity of Languages. Collection of Papers Selected from the CIL 18, Held at Korea University in Seoul on July 21–26, 2008* (Seoul, 2009).

Kryk-Kastovsky, Barbara, 'Representations of Orality in Early Modern English Trial Records', *Journal of Historical Pragmatics*, 1, no. 2 (2000), 201–30.

Labouvie, Eva, *Zauberei und Hexenwerk. Ländlicher Hexenglaube in der frühen Neuzeit* [Sorcery and Witchcraft. Rural Belief in Witches in the Early Modern Period] (Frankfurt am Main, 1991).

Lahti, Emmi, *Tietäjiä, taikojia, hautausmaita. Taikuus Suomessa 1700-luvun jälkipuoliskolla* [Cunning Folk, Practitioners of Magic and Cemeteries: Magic in Late 18th-Century Finland] (Ph.D. thesis, University of Jyväskylä, 2016).

Lamberg, Marko, *Häxmodern. Berättelsen om Malin Matsdotter* (Helsinki, 2021).

Lambrecht, Karen, *Hexenverfolgung und Zaubereiprozesse in den schlesischen Territorien* [Witch-Hunts and Sorcery Trials in the Silesian Territories] (Köln, 1995).

Lancre, Pierre de, *Tableau de l'inconstance des mauvais anges et démons* [Tableau of the Inconstancy of Evil Angels and Demons] (Paris, 1613).

Langbein, John H., *The Origins of Adversary Criminal Trial* (Oxford, 2003).

Langbein, John H., *Torture and the Law of Proof: Europe and England in the Ancien Régime* (Chicago, 2006).

Larner, Christina, *Enemies of God: The Witch-Hunt in Scotland* (Oxford, 1983; first published in London, 1981).

Larner, Christina, 'James VI and I and Witchcraft', in Christina Larner (ed.), *Witchcraft and Religion: The Politics of Popular Belief* (Oxford, 1984), 3–22.

Larner, Christina (née Ross), *Scottish Demonology in the Sixteenth and Seventeenth Centuries and Its Theological Background* (Ph.D. thesis, University of Edinburgh, 1962).

Larner, Christina, 'Was Witch-Hunting Woman-Hunting?' *New Society* (October 8, 1981), 11–13.

Larner, Christina, *Witchcraft and Religion: The Politics of Popular Belief* (Oxford, 1984).

Lennersand, Marie, *Rättvisans och allmogens beskyddare: Den absoluta staten, kommissionerna och tjänstemännen, ca 1680–1730* [The Protection of Justice and the Common People: The Absolute State, Commissioners and Public Officials, c. 1680–1730] (Ph.D. thesis, Uppsala University, 1999).

Lennersand, Marie, 'Responses to Witchcraft in Late Seventeenth- and Eighteenth-Century Sweden', in Owen Davies and Willem de Blécourt (eds.), *Beyond the Witch Trials: Witchcraft and Magic in Enlightenment Europe* (Manchester, 2004), 61–80.

Lennersand, Marie, and Linda Oja, *Livet går vidare: Älvdalen och Rättvik efter de stora häxprocesserna 1668–71* [Life Goes on: Älvdalen and Rättvik after the Great Witchcraft Trials of 1668–71] (Hedemora, 2006).

Lennersand, Marie, and Linda Oja, 'Vitnande visionärer. Guds och Djävulens redskap i Dalarnas häxprocesser' [Witnessing Visionaries: God's and the Devil's Tool in the Witchcraft Trials of Dalarne], in Hanne Sanders (ed.), *Mellem Gud og Djævelen. Religiøse og magiske verdensbilleder i Norden 1500–1800* [Between God and the Devil. Religious and Magical Images of the World in the Nordic Countries 1500–1800] (Copenhagen, 2001), 177–84.

Levack, Brian P., 'Absolutism, State-Building and Witchcraft', in Brian P. Levack (ed.), *Witch-Hunting in Scotland: Law, Politics and Religion* (New York, 2008), 98–114.

Levack, Brian P., 'The Decline and End of Witchcraft Prosecutions', in Bengt Ankarloo and Stuart Clark (eds.), *Witchcraft and Magic in Europe, vol. 4: The Period of the Witch Trials* (London, 2002), 1–93.

Levack, Brian P., 'Judicial Torture in Scotland During the Age of Mackenzie', *Stair Society Miscellany*, 4 (2002), 185–98.

Levack, Brian P., *The Oxford Handbook of Witchcraft in Early Modern Europe and Colonial America* (Oxford, 2013).

Levack, Brian P., 'State-Building and Witch Hunting in Early Modern Europe', in Jonathan Barry, Marianne Hester, and Gareth Roberts (eds.), *Witchcraft in Early Modern Europe: Studies in Culture and Belief* (Cambridge, 1996), 96–115.

Levack, Brian P., *The Witch-Hunt in Early Modern Europe* (Essex, 1995; first published in London, 1987).

Levack, Brian P., *Witch-Hunting in Scotland: Law, Politics and Religion* (New York, 2008).

Levack, Brian P., 'Witchcraft and the Law', in Brian P. Levack (ed.), *The Oxford Handbook of Witchcraft in Early Modern Europe and Colonial America* (Oxford, 2013), 468–84.

Levack, Brian P., 'Witchcraft and the Law in Early Modern Scotland', in Brian P. Levack (ed.), *Witch-Hunting in Scotland: Law, Politics and Religion* (New York, 2008), 21–24.

Levack, Brian P., *The Witchcraft Sourcebook* (New York, 2004).

Liestøl, Knut, 'Innleiing' [Introduction], in *Norsk folkedikting* [Norwegian Folk Tales], vol. I (Oslo, 1960), 11–60.

Liisberg, Henrik C., *Vesten for Sø og østen for Hav: Trolddom i København og i Edinburgh 1590: et Bidrag til Hekseprocessernes Historie* [West of the Sea and East of the Ocean: A Contribution to the History of Witchcraft Trials] (Copenhagen, 1909).

Lincoln, Bruce, 'Festivals and Massacres: Reflections on St. Bartholomew's Day', in Bruce Lincoln (ed.), *Discourse and the Construction of Society: Comparative Studies of Myth, Ritual, and Classification* (New York, 1989), 89–102.

Linderholm, Emanuel, *De stora häxprocesserna i Sverige, I: Inledning. Bohuslän* [The Large Witchcraft Trials in Sweden, I: Introduction. Bohuslän] (Uppsala, 1918).

Lockhart, Paul D., *Denmark, 1513–1660. The Rise and Decline of a Renaissance Monarchy* (Oxford, 2007).

Lorenz, Sönke, and Jürgen Schmidt, *Wider alle Hexerei und Teufelswerk: Die Europäische Hexenverfolgung* (Ostfildern, 2004).

Macdonald, Stuart, 'Torture and the Scottish Witch-Hunt: A Re-Examination', *Scottish Tradition*, 28 (2002), 95–114.

Macdonald, Stuart, *The Witches of Fife. Witch-Hunting in a Scottish Shire, 1560–1710* (East Linton, 2002).

Macfarlane, Alan, *Witchcraft in Tudor and Stuart England: A Regional and Comparative Study* (London, 1971).

Macha, Jürgen, 'Redewiedergabe in Verhörprotokollen und der Hintergrund gesprochener Sprache' [Speech Reproduction in Interrogation Minutes and the Background of Spoken Language], in Sabine Krämer-Neubert and Norbert R. Wolf (eds.), *Bayerische Dialektologie. Akten der Internationalen Dialektologischen Konferenz 26.–28. Februar 2002* [Bavarian Dialectology. Proceedings of the International Dialectological Conference, February 26–28, 2002] (Heidelberg, 2005), 171–78.

Macha, Jürgen, Elvira Topalovic, Iris Hille, Uta Nolting, and Anja Wilke (eds.), *Deutsche Kanzleisprache in Hexenverhörprotokollen der Frühen Neuzeit* [German Chancery Language in Witch Interrogation Minutes of the Early Modern Period] (Berlin, 2005).

Machielsen, Jan (ed.), *The Science of Demons: Early Modern Authors Facing Witchcraft and the Devil* (Abingdon, 2020).

MacNeill, George P. (ed.), *The Exchequer Rolls of Scotland* (Edinburgh, 1903).

Magnus, Olaus, *The History of the Nordic People* (1982; first published in Rome in 1555).

Manns, Ulla, and Fia Sundevall (eds.), *Methods, Interventions, and Reflections: Report from the 10th Nordic Women and Gender History Conference* (Bergen, 2012).

Martin, Lauren, 'The Devil and the Domestic: Witchcraft, Quarrels and Women's Work', in Julian Goodare (ed.), *The Scottish Witch-Hunt in Context* (Manchester, 2002), 73–89.

Martin, Lauren, *The Devil and the Domestic: Witchcraft, Women's Work and Marriage in Early Modern Scotland* (Ph.D. thesis, New School for Social Research, 2003).

Martin, Lauren, 'Scottish Witchcraft Panics Re-Examined', in Julian Goodare, Lauren Martin, and Joyce Miller (eds.), *Witchcraft and Belief in Early Modern Scotland* (Basingstoke, 2008), 119–43.

Martin, Lauren, and Joyce Miller, 'Some Findings from the Survey of Scottish Witchcraft', in Julian Goodare, Lauren Martin, and Joyce Miller (eds.), *Witchcraft and Belief in Early Modern Scotland* (Basingstoke, 2008), 51–70.

Maxwell-Stuart, Peter G., *An Abundance of Witches. The Great Scottish Witch-Hunt* (Gloucestershire, 2005).

Maxwell-Stuart, Peter G., *The British Witch: The Biography* (Stroud, 2014).

Maxwell-Stuart, Peter G., 'James VI and the Witches', in William Naphy and Penny Roberts (eds.), *Fear in Early Modern Society* (Manchester, 1997), 209–25.

Maxwell-Stuart, Peter G., *Satan's Conspiracy: Magic and Witchcraft in Sixteenth-Century Scotland* (East Linton, 2001).

Melville, R. D., 'The Use and Forms of Judicial Torture in England and Scotland', *Scottish Historical Review*, 2 (1905), 225–48.

Mensing, Otto, *Schleswig-Holsteinischer Wörterbuch* [Schleswig-Holsteinian Dictionary], vol. 5 (Neumünster, 1935).

Middleton, Christine, *The Witch & Her Soul: A Novel* (Lancaster, 2012).

Midelfort, H. C. Erik, *Witch Hunting in Southwestern Germany 1562–1684* (Stanford, 1972).

Millar, Charlotte-Rose, *Witchcraft, the Devil, and Emotions in Early Modern England* (London, 2017).

Miller, Joyce, *Cantrips and Carlins: Magic, Medicine and Sorcery in the Presbyteries of Haddington and Stirling, 1600–1688* (Ph.D. thesis, University of Stirling, 1999).

Miller, Joyce, 'Men in Black: Appearances of the Devil in Early Modern Scottish Witchcraft Discourse', in Julian Goodare, Lauren Martin, and Joyce Miller (eds.), *Witchcraft and Belief in Early Modern Scotland* (Basingstoke, 2008), 144–55.

Mitchell, Stephen A., *Witchcraft and Magic in the Nordic Middle Ages* (Philadelphia, 2011).

Monter, William, 'Male Witches', in Richard M. Golden (ed.), *Encyclopedia of Witchcraft: The Western Tradition* (Santa Barbara, 2006), 712–13.

Morrison, Blake, *Pendle Witches, with Etchings by Paula Rego* (London, 1996).

Muchembled, Robert, *Sorcières, justice et société aux 16e et 17e siècles* [Sorcerers, Justice and Society in the 16th and 17th Centuries] (Paris, 1987).

Næss, Hans E., *Fiat justitia! Lagmennene i Norge 1607–1797* [Fiat Justitia! Court of Appeal Judges in Norway 1607–1797] (Oslo, 2014).

Næss, Hans E. (ed.), *For rett og rettferdighet i 400 år: Sorenskrivere i Norge 1591–1991* [For Right and Justice During 400 Years: The Magistrates of Norway 1591–1991] (Oslo, 1991).

Næss, Hans E., *Med bål og brann* [In Fire at the Stake] (Oslo, 1984).

Næss, Hans E., 'Norway: The Criminological Context', in Bengt Ankarloo and Gustav Henningsen (eds.), *Early Modern Witchcraft: Centres and Peripheries* (Oxford, 1990), 367–82.

Næss, Hans E., 'Presters og prestefruers roller I norske trolldomsprosesser' [The Roles of Ministers and Ministers' Wives in Norwegian Witchcraft Trials], in *Nedstrand kyrkje 150 år* [Nedstrand Church 150 Years: In Faith, Hope, and Love] (Nedstrand, 2019), 113–22.

Næss, Hans E., *Source Editions Court Records for Rogaland* (Stavanger, 1979, 1982, 1984).

Næss, Hans E., *Trolldomsprosessene i Norge på 1500–1600-tallet: En retts- og sosialhistorisk undersøkelse* [Witchcraft Trials in Norway During the Sixteenth and Seventeenth Centuries. A Legal and Socioeconomic Study] (Oslo, 1982).

Nedkvitne, Arnved, *The German Hansa and Bergen 1100–1600* (Cologne, 2014).

Neill, Robert, *Mist over Pendle* (London, 2011).

Nenonen, Marko, *Noituus, taikuus ja noitavainot Ala-Satakunnan, Pohjois-Pohjanmaan ja Viipurin Karjalan maaseudulla 1620–1700* [Witchcraft, Magic and Witch-Hunts in Rural Lower Satakunta, Northern Ostrobothnia and Vyborg Karelia, ca. 1620–1700] (Helsinki, 1992).

Nenonen, Marko, 'Witch-Hunts in Europe: A New Geography', *ARV: Nordic Yearbook of Folklore*, 62 (2006), 165–86.

Nenonen, Marko, and Raisa M. Toivo (eds.), *Writing Witch-Hunt Histories* (Leiden, 2013).

Niemi, Einar, 'Hans Hansen Lilienskiold—embetsmann, vitenskapsmann og opprører [Hans Hansen Lilienskiold—Official, Scholar and Rebel], in *Portretter fra norsk historie* [Portraits from Norwegian History] (Oslo, 1993), 43–72.

Ocker, Christopher, *Luther, Conflict and Christendom: Reformation Europe and Christianity in the West* (Cambridge, 2018).

Ogborn, Miles, *The Freedom of Speech. Talk and Slavery in the Anglo-Caribbean World* (Chicago, 2019).

Oja, Linda (ed.), *Vägen till Blåkulla: Nya perspektiv på de stora svenska häxprocesserna* [The Road to Blåkulla: New Perspectives on the Great Swedish Witchcraft Trials] (Uppsala, 1997).

Oja, Linda, *Varken Gud eller natur: synen på magi i 1600- och 1700-talets Sverige* [Neither God nor Nature: Views on Magic in Sixteenth- and Seventeenth-Century Sweden] (Ph.D. thesis, Uppsala University, 1999).

Olden-Jørgensen, Sebastian, 'Den ældre danske enevælde 1660–1730: Et historiografisk essay' [The Older Danish Absolute Power, 1660–1730: A Historiographic Essay], *Historie/Jyske Samlinger*, 2 (1998), 291–319.

Oldridge, Darren (ed.), *The Witchcraft Reader* (Philadelphia, 2002).

Olli, Soili-Maria, *Visioner av världen: hädelse och djävulspakt i justitierevisionen 1680–1789* [Visions of the World: Blasphemy and Devil's Pact in Records of the Justiciary 1680–1789] (Ph.D. thesis, Umeå University, 2007).

Ong, Walter J., *Orality and Literacy. The Technologizing of the Word* (London, 1982).

Österberg, Eva, and Sølvi Sogner (eds.), *People Meet the Law. Control and Conflict-Handling in the Courts* (Oslo, 2000).

Östling, Per-Anders, 'Blåkulla Journeys in Swedish Folklore', *ARV: Nordic Yearbook of Folklore*, 62 (2006), 81–122.

Östling, Per-Anders, *Blåkulla, magi och trolldomsprocesser: En folkloristisk studie av folkliga trosföreställningar och av trolldomsprocesserna inom Svea Hovrätts jurisdiktion 1597–1720* [Blåkulla, Magic and Witchcraft Trials: A Folkloristic Study of People's Witchcraft Beliefs and of Witchcraft Trials in Svea Court's Jurisdiction 1597–1720] (Ph.D. thesis, Uppsala University, 2002).

Östling, Per-Anders, 'Witchcraft Trials in 17th-Century Sweden and the Great Northern Swedish Witch Craze of 1668–1678', *Studia Neophilologica*, 84 (2012), 97–105.

Paterson, Laura, 'Executing Scottish Witches', in Julian Goodare (ed.), *Scottish Witches and Witch-Hunters* (Basingstoke, 2013), 196–214.

Paterson, Laura, *The Witches' Sabbath in Scotland* (M.Sc. thesis, University of Edinburgh, 2011).

Paterson, Laura, 'The Witches' Sabbath in Scotland', *Proceedings of the Society of Antiquaries of Scotland*, 142 (2012), 371–412.

Poole, Robert (ed.), *The Lancashire Witches. Histories and Stories* (Manchester, 2002).

Purkiss, Diane, *The Witch in History: Early Modern and Twentieth-Century Representations* (Abingdon, 1996).

Reichborn-Kjennerud, Ingjald, *Vår gamle trolldomsmedisin* [Our Old Sorcery Medicine], vol. 1 (Oslo, 1928).

Resen, Hans P., *De sancta fide* (Copenhagen, 1614).

Rian, Øystein, 'Christian 3', in *Norsk biografisk leksikon* [Norwegian Biographical Lexicon] (Oslo, 2000), 180–82.

Rian, Øystein, *Danmark-Norge 1380–1814* [Denmark-Norway 1380–1814] (Oslo, 1997).

Riis, Thomas, *Should Auld Acquaintance Be Forgot . . . Scottish-Danish Relations c. 1450–1707*, vol. I (Odense, 1988).

Robertson, David M., *Goodnight My Servants All. The Sourcebook of East Lothian Witchcraft* (Glasgow, 2008).

Robisheaux, Thomas, 'The German Witch Trials', in Brian P. Levack (ed.), *The Oxford Handbook of Witchcraft in Early Modern Europe and Colonial America* (Oxford, 2013), 179–98.

Roper, Lyndal, *Witch Craze: Terror and Fantasy in Baroque Germany* (New Haven, 2004).

Rowlands, Alison, 'Witchcraft and Gender in Early Modern Europe', in Brian P. Levack (ed.), *The Oxford Handbook of Witchcraft in Early Modern Europe and Colonial America* (Oxford, 2013), 449–67.

Rowlands, Alison, *Witchcraft Narratives in Germany: Rothenburg, 1561–1652* (Manchester, 2003).

Rowlands, Alison (ed.), *Witchcraft and Masculinities in Early Modern Europe* (Houndmills, 2009).

Rushton, Peter, 'Texts of Authority: Witchcraft Accusations and the Demonstration of Truth in Early Modern England', in Stuart Clark (ed.), *Languages of Witchcraft. Narrative, Ideology and Meaning in Early Modern Culture* (New York, 2001), 21–39.

Sabbe, Maurits, 'Brabantsche spotdichten op de nederlaag van Christian IV van Denemarken te Lutter 1626' [Brabant Satirical Poems About the Defeat of Christian IV of Denmark at Lutter 1626], *Verslagen en Mededelingen van Koninklijke Vlaamse Academie voor Taal- en Letterkunde* (1931), 747–57.

Sandén, Annika, *Bödlar* [Executioners] (Stockholm, 2016).

Sanders, Hanne (ed.), *Mellem Gud og Djævelen. Religiøse og magiske verdensbilleder i Norden 1500–1800* [Between God and the Devil: Religious and Magical World Images in the Nordic Countries 1500–1800] (Copenhagen, 2001).

Schormann, Gerhard, *Hexenprozesse in Deutschland* (Göttingen, 1981).

Schormann, Gerhard, *Hexenprozesse in Nordwestdeutschland* (Hildesheim, 1977).

Schulte, Rolf, 'Ein Kinderhexenprozess aus St. Margarethen' [A child Witch Trial from St. Margarethen], in *'Wider Hexerey und Teufelswerk . . . '*, Von Hexen und ihrer Verfolgung, Exhibition Catalogue (Itzehoe, 2001), 48–55.

Schulte, Rolf, *Hexenmeister. Die Verfolgung von Männern im Rahmen der Hexenverfolgungen von 1530 bis 1730 im Alten Reich* [Sorcerers: The Persecution of Men as Part of the Witch-Hunt of 1530–1730 in the Old Kingdom] (Frankfurt am Main, 2001).

Schulte, Rolf, *Hexenverfolgung in Schleswig-Holstein 16.–18. Jahrhundert* [The Witch-Hunt in Schleswig-Holstein 16th–18th Century] (Heide, 2001).

Schulte, Rolf, *Man as Witch: Male Witches in Central Europe* (Basingstoke, 2009).

Sharpe, James, 'English Witchcraft Pamphlets and the Popular Demonic', in Julian Goodare, Rita Voltmer, and Liv H. Willumsen (eds.), *Demonology and Witch-Hunting in Early Modern Europe* (Abingdon, 2020), 127–46.

Sharpe, James, *Instruments of Darkness* (Philadelphia, 1996).

Sharpe, James, *Witchcraft in Early Modern England* (London, 2001).

Sharpe, Jim, 'Women, Witchcraft and the Legal Process', in Jenny Kermode and Garthine Walker (eds.), *Women, Crime and the Courts in Early Modern England* (London, 1994), 106–24.

Simonsen, Gunvor, *Slave Stories: Law, Representation and Gender in the Danish West Indies* (Aarhus, 2017).

Sinclair, George, *Satan's Invisible World Discovered. A Choice Collection of Modern Relations, Proving Evidently Against the Saducees and Atheists of This Present Age, That There Are Devils, Spirits, Witches, and Apparitions, from Authentic Records, Attestations of Famous Witnesses and Undoubted Verity* (Edinburgh, 1685).

Skaar, Anne-Sofie Schjøtner, 'Da djevelen var løs i Rendalen—en av de siste trolldomsprosessene i Norge' [When the Devil Was Loose in Rendalen—One of the Last Witchcraft Trials in Norway], *Heimen*, no. 2 (2021), 115–35.

Skinner, Quentin, 'Review of Stuart Clark, Thinking with Demons', *Common Knowledge*, 25, no. 1–3 (April 2019), 411–12.

Sörlin, Per, 'The Blåkulla Story: Absurdity and Rationality', *ARV: Nordic Yearbook of Folklore*, 53 (1997), 131–52.

Sörlin, Per, 'Om saköreslängderna som historisk källa' [On Fines Records as Historical Source], in Olof Holm, Georg Hansson, and Christer Kalin (eds.), *Böter och Fredsköp: Jämtlands och Härjedalens saköreslängder 1601–1645* [Fines and Purchase of Peace. The Fines Documents from Jämtland and Härjedalen 1601–1645] (Östersund, 2016), 9–37.

Sörlin, Per, *Trolldoms- och vidskepelseprocesserna i Göta Hovrätt 1635–1754* [Witchcraft and Sorcery Trials in Göta Court 1635–1754] (Ph.D. thesis, Umeå University, 1993).

Sörlin, Per, *Sakören, soning och soldater* [Fines, Atonement and Soldiers] (Oslo, 2004).

Sörlin, Per, 'Sweden', in Richard M. Golden (ed.), *Encyclopedia of Witchcraft: The Western Tradition* (Santa Barbara, 2006), 1092–93.

Sörlin, Per, 'Wicked Arts', *Witchcraft and Magic Trials in Southern Sweden, 1635–1754* (Leiden, 1999).

Sörlin, Per, 'Witchcraft and Causal Links: Accounts of Maleficent Witchcraft in the Göta High Court in the Fifteenth and Sixteenth Centuries', *ARV: Nordic Yearbook of Folklore*, 62 (2006), 51–80.

Steedman, Carolyn, 'Enforced Narratives: Stories of Another Self', in Tess Cosslett, Celia Lury, and Penny Summerfield (eds.), *Feminism and Autobiography. Texts, Theories, Methods* (London, 2000), 25–39.

Steinsland, Gro, *Norrøn religion: myter, riter, samfunn* [Norse Religion: Myths, Rites, Society] (Oslo, 2005).

Stenzel, Theodor, 'Zur Genealogie der Familie von Wietersheim', *Vierteljahrsschrift für Wappen-, Siegel- und Familienkunde*, 8 (1880), 135–63.

Stevenson, David, *Scotland's Last Royal Wedding* (Edinburgh, 1997).

Stoke, Laura, *Demons of Urban Reform: Early European Witch Trials and Criminal Justice, 1430–1530* (Basingstoke, 2011).

Sunde, Jørn Ø., *Speculum legale—rettsspegelen* [Speculum Legale—The Mirror of the Law] (Bergen, 2005).

Svenungsson, Lars M., *Rannsakningarna om trolldomen i Bohuslän 1669–1672* [The Persecution of Witchcraft in Bohuslän, 1669–1672] (Uddevalla, 1970).

Thomas, Keith, *Religion and the Decline of Magic: Studies in Popular Beliefs in Sixteenth and Seventeenth-Century England* (London, 1971).

Toivo, Raisa M., 'Discerning Voices and Values in the Finnish Witch Trials Records', *Studia Neophilologica*, 84, no. 1 (2012), 143–55.

Toivo, Raisa M., *Faith and Magic in Early Modern Finland* (Basingstoke, 2016).

Toivo, Raisa M., 'Gender, Sex and Cultures of Trouble in Witchcraft Studies: European Historiography with Special Reference to Finland', in Marko Nenonen and Raisa M. Toivo (eds.), *Writing Witch-Hunt Histories* (Leiden, 2013), 87–108.

Toivo, Raisa M., 'What Did a Witch-Hunter in Finland Know about Demonology?' in Julian Goodare, Rita Voltmer, and Liv H. Willumsen (eds.), *Demonology and Witch-Hunting in Early Modern Europe* (Abingdon, 2020), 282–301.

Toivo, Raisa M., *Witchcraft and Gender in Early Modern Society. Finland and the Wider European Experience* (Aldershot, 2008).

Tønnesson, Johan L., *Hva er sakprosa* [What Is Factual Prose] (Oslo, 2008).

Topalovic, Elvira, '"Ick kike in die Stern vnd versake Gott den Herrn". Versprachligung des Teufelpaktes in westfälischen Verhörprotokollen des 16./17. Jahrhundert' ['Ick kike in die Stern vnd versake Gott den Herrn'. Representation of the Devil's Pact in Westphalian Interrogation Minutes of the 16th/17th Century], *Augustin Wibbelt-Gesellschaft Jahrbuch*, 20, 6–86.

Unverhau, Dagmar, 'Akkusationsprozess—Inquisitionsprozess. Indikatoren für Intensität der Hexenverfolgung in Schleswig-Holstein' [Accusatorial Trial—Inquisitional Trial. Indicators of the Intensity of the Witch-Hunt in Schleswig-Holstein], in Christian Degn, Hartmut Lehmann, and Dagmar Unverhau (eds.), *Hexenprozesse. Deutsche und skandinavische Beiträge* [Witch Trials. German and Scandinavian Contributions] (Neumünster, 1983), 59–142.

Unverhau, Dagmar, 'Flensburger Hexenprozesse (1504, 1607/08) erneut betrachtet. Die "Hexe" als "Ärztin"?' [Flensburg Witch Trials (1504, 1607/08) Revisited. The 'Witch' as 'Doctor'?], *Grenzfriedenshefte*, no. 3/4 (1984–85), 171–87.

Unverhau, Dagmar, 'Frauenbewegung und historische Hexenverfolgung' [Women's Movement and Historical Witch-Hunts], in Andreas Blauert (ed.), *Ketzer, Zauberer, Hexen. Die Anfänge der europäischen Hexenverfolgungen* [Heretics, Sorcerers, Witches. The Beginnings of the European Witch-Hunts] (Frankfurt am Main, 1990), 241–83.

Unverhau, Dagmar, 'Kieler Hexen und Zauberer zur Zeit der großen Verfolgung (1530–1676)' [Kiel Witches and Sorcerers at the Time of the Great Persecution (1530–1676)], in Jürgen Jensen (ed.), *Mitteilungen der Gesellschaft für Kieler Stadtgeschichte* [Communications of the Society for Kiel City History], Band 68. (Gesellschaft für Kieler Stadtgeschichte, 1981–1983), 41–96.

Unverhau, Dagmar, *Von Toverschen und Kunstfruhwen in Schleswig, 1548–1557, Quellen und Interpretationen zur Geschichte der Zauber- und Hexenwesens* [Of 'Toverschen' and 'Kunstfruhwen' in Schleswig, 1548–1557, Sources and Interpretations on the History of Magic and Witchcraft] (Schleswig, 1980).

Vandepitte, Germain, 'Van heksen . . . en de boze vijand' [Of Witches . . . and the Evil Enemy], *Rond de Poldertorens*, 26, no. 1 (1985), 23–40.

Vanysacker, Dries, *Hekserij in Brugge. De magische leefwereld van een stadsbevolking, 16de-17de eeuw* [Witchcraft in Bruges. The Magical World of an Urban Population, 16th–17th Century] (Bruges, 1988).

Vanysacker, Dries, 'Netherlands, Southern', in Richard M. Golden (ed.), *Encyclopedia of Witchcraft: The Western Tradition* (Santa Barbara, 2006), 814.

Voltmer, Rita, 'Debating the Devil's Clergy. Demonology and the Media in Dialogue with Trials (14th to 17th Century)', *Religions*, 10, no. 12 (2019), 648.

Voltmer, Rita, 'Demonology and the Relevance of the Witches' Confessions', in Julian Goodare, Rita Voltmer, and Liv H. Willumsen (eds.), *Demonology and Witch-Hunting in Early Modern Europe* (Abingdon, 2020), 19–48.

Voltmer, Rita, 'The Judges' Lore? The Politico-Religious Concept of Metamorphosis in the Peripheries of Western Europe', in Willem de Blécourt (ed.), *Werewolf Histories* (Basingstoke, 2015), 163–67.

Voltmer, Rita, *Hexen: Wissen was stimmt* [Witches: Knowing What Is Correct] (Freiburg im Breisgau, 2008).

Voltmer, Rita, 'Hexenverfolgungen im Maas-Rhein-Mosel-Raum' [Witch-Hunts in the Meuse-Rhine-Moselle Region], in Franz Irsigler (ed.), *Beziehungen, Begegnungen und Konflikte in einem europäischen Kernraum von der Spätantike bis zum 19. Jahrhundert* [Relations, Encounters and Conflicts in a European Core Area from Late Antiquity to the 19th Century] (Trier, 2006), 153–87.

Voltmer, Rita, 'Wissen, Media und die Wahrheit', in Heinz Sieburg, Rita Voltmer, and Britta Weimann (eds.), *Hexenwissen: Zum Transfer von Magie- und Zauberei-Imaginationen in interdisziplinärer Perspektive* (Trier, 2017).

Voltmer, Rita, 'Witch in the Courtroom: Torture and the Representations of Emotion', in Laura Kounine and Michael Ostling (eds.), *Emotions in the History of Witchcraft* (Basingstoke, 2017), 97–116.

Waardt, Hans de, 'Netherlands, Northern', in Richard M. Golden (ed.), *Encyclopedia of Witchcraft: The Western Tradition*, vol. 3 (Santa Barbara, 2006), 810.

Waardt, Hans de, 'Witchcraft and Wealth: The Case in the Netherlands', in Brian P. Levack (ed.), *The Oxford Handbook of Witchcraft in Early Modern Europe and Colonial America* (Oxford, 2013), 237–38.

Walker, Garthine, *Crime, Gender and Social Order in Early Modern Cheshire* (Ph.D. thesis, University of Liverpool, 1994).

Walker, Garthine, 'Women, Theft and the World of Stolen Goods', in Jenny Kermode and Garthine Walker (eds.), *Women, Crime and the Courts in Early Modern England* (London, 1994), 95–97.

Warner, George F., 'The Library of James VI', *Miscellany of The Scottish History Society*, 1 (1893), XLVIII.

'*Wider Hexerey und Teufelswerk* . . . ', *Von Hexen und ihrer Verfolgung*, Exhibition Catalogue (Itzehoe, 2001).

Wilbertz, Gisela, Gerd Schwerhoff, and Jürgen Scheffler (eds.), *Hexenverfolgung und Regionalgeschichte. Der Grafschaft Lippe im Vergleich* [Witch-Hunt and Regional History. The County of Lippe in Comparison], Studien zur Regionalgeschichte, b. 4 (Bielefeld, 1994).

Wilby, Emma, *The Visions of Isobel Gowdie: Magic, Witchcraft and Dark Shamanism in Seventeenth-Century Scotland* (Eastbourne, 2010).

Williams, Gerhild S., 'Demonologies', in Brian P. Levack (ed.), *The Oxford Handbook of Witchcraft in Early Modern Europe and Colonial America* (Oxford, 2013), 69–83.

Willumsen, Liv H., 'Anders Poulsen—Sami Shaman Accused of Witchcraft, 1692', *Folklore*, 131, no. 2 (2020), 135–58.

Willumsen, Liv H., 'Board Games, Dancing, and Lost Shoes: Ideas About Witches' Gatherings in the Finnmark Witchcraft Trials', in Julian Goodare, Rita Voltmer, and Liv H. Willumsen (eds.), *Demonology and Witch-Hunting in Early Modern Europe* (Abingdon, 2020), 261–81.

Willumsen, Liv H., 'Children Accused of Witchcraft in 17th-Century Finnmark', *Scandinavian Journal of History*, 38, no. 1 (2013), 18–41.

Willumsen, Liv H., *Dømt til ild og bål* [Sentenced to Death in Fire at the Stake] (Stamsund, 2013).

Willumsen, Liv H., 'Exporting the Devil Across the North Sea: John Cunningham and the Finnmark Witch-Hunt', in Julian Goodare (ed.), *Scottish Witches and Witch-Hunters* (Basingstoke, 2013), 49–66.

Willumsen, Liv H., 'Historical Approaches to Child Witches', *Oxford Bibliographies in Childhood Studies* (2015). DOI:10.1093/OBO/9780199791231-0156.

Willumsen, Liv H., 'Narratologi som tekstanalytisk metode' [Narratology as Text-Analytical Method], in Mary Brekke (ed.), *Å begripe teksten* [To Understand the Text] (Kristiansand, 2006), 39–72.

Willumsen, Liv H., 'Oral Transference of Ideas About Witchcraft in Seventeenth-Century Norway', in Thomas V. Cohen and Lesley K. Twomey (eds.), *Spoken Word and Social Practice: Orality in Europe (1400–1700)* (Leiden, 2015), 46–83.

Willumsen, Liv H., 'A Narratological Approach to Witchcraft Trials: A Scottish Case', *Journal of Early Modern History*, 15 (2011), 531–60.

Willumsen, Liv H., 'The Ninety-Nine Dancers of Moaness: Orkney Women Between the Visible and Invisible', in Julian Goodare and Martha McGill (eds.), *The Supernatural in Early Modern Scotland* (Manchester, 2020), 72–85.

Willumsen, Liv H., *Seventeenth-Century Witchcraft Trials in Scotland and Northern Norway* (Ph.D. thesis, University of Edinburgh, 2008).

Willumsen, Liv H., *Steilneset: Memorial to the Victims of the Finnmark Witchcraft Trials* (Oslo, 2011).

Willumsen, Liv H., 'Trolldom mot kongens skip 1589 og transnasjonal overføring av idéer', *Historisk Tidsskrift*, 2 (2019), 309–44.

Willumsen, Liv H., *Trollkvinne i nord i historiske kilder og skjønnlitteratur* [Witch in the North in Historical Sources and Literature] (M.A. thesis, University of Tromsø, 1984; published in 1994).

Willumsen, Liv H., *Witches of the North: Scotland and Finnmark* (Leiden, 2013).

Willumsen, Liv H., 'Witches in Scotland and Northern Norway: Two Case Studies', in Peter Graves and Arne Kruse (eds.), *Images and Imaginations: Perspectives on Britain and Scandinavia* (Edinburgh, 2007), 35–67.

Willumsen, Liv H, 'Witchcraft Against the Royal Danish Ships in 1589 and the Transnational Transfer of Ideas', *International Review of Scottish Studies*, 45 (2020), 54–99.

Willumsen, Liv H., 'A Witchcraft Triangle: Transmitting Witchcraft Ideas Across Early Modern Europe', in Marina Montesano (ed.), *Folklore, Magic, and Witchcraft: Cultural Exchanges from the Twelfth to Eighteenth Century* (Abingdon, 2021), 247–64.

Wormald, Jenny, 'The Witches, the Devil and the King', in Terry Brotherstone and David Ditchburn (eds.), *Freedom and Authority: Scotland c. 1050–c. 1650* (East Linton, 2000), 165–80.

Wubs-Mrozewicz, Justyna, and Stuart Jenks (eds.), *The Hanse in Medieval and Early Modern Europe* (Leiden, 2013).

Yeoman, Louise, 'Away with the Fairies', in Lizanne Henderson (ed.), *Fantastical Imaginations* (East Linton, 2009), 29–46.

Yeoman, Louise, 'Hunting the Rich Witch in Scotland: High-Status Witchcraft Suspects and Their Persecutors, 1590–1650', in Julian Goodare (ed.), *Scottish Witches and Witch-Hunters* (Basingstoke, 2013), 106–21.

Zika, Charles, 'Images of Witchcraft in Early Modern Europe', in Brian P. Levack (ed.), *The Oxford Handbook of Witchcraft in Early Modern Europe and Colonial America* (Oxford, 2013), 141–56.

INDEX

The main headings of case study individuals are in **bold**. Index references to chapter endnotes are denoted by the format, 'pgnen'. For example, '421n169' is end note 169, located on page 421. End notes are numbered independently by chapter.

A **Note on Historical Names**: During the period under study the development of the modern surname was ongoing. The use of surnames varied by country and social class, with a number of other naming conventions still in common use. The following rules will help the reader locate indexed persons.

Those people with *descriptive titles* are indexed under their first name: 'Jacob the Scribe' is under J, 'Karen, the wife of the Weaver' is under K. Persons with a *geographic identification* are under their first names: 'Håkon in Gulskog' is under H, 'Nils in Hallbo' is under N. Persons with a *patronymic* name are listed as if the patronym is a surname: 'Anne Knutsdatter' is under K, 'Lucas Jacobsen' is under J. Persons with *surnames* are listed by those surnames: 'Agnes Sampson' is under S, 'Mayken Karrebrouck' under K.

mark 258, 259, 357, 359; devil's pact 257, 258, 259, 357; witches' gathering 258, 324; witch-pricking 258); interrogation (confession 257; denial of witchcraft 259, 260; judicial officials present 257; jury 257; leading questions 260; *maleficium* to demonology transition 263; shadow questions 259; torture or threat of 257, 259, 264, 357; transportation for 256–7; turning point 259, 260, 261); interrogator, voice of 263; law, voice of 263–4; *maleficium* 257–8, 262, 263, 343, 350; narrative structures (delegation of voice 260; demonological narrative 259, 263; duration 259, 260; mood 259; order 259); orality (additive sentence structure 260; cause-and-effect 260–1; exaggeration 259, 260; oral transmission 259, 261; repetition 260; scribe, voice of 264); voice (cooperative 260; direct speech 258; indirect speech 258, 259; personal narrative 260; voices of others 262; witnesses, voices of 262–3)
Anderson, Håkon (bailiff) 257
Anderson, Patrick (Scotland) 109
Ankarloo, Bengt 24, 28, 252, 253, 254, 280
Anna, the wife of Hans the Smith 129, 131
Anna, the wife of Jens 130
Anna, the wife of Niels 129, 130, 132
Anna in Åkersvik 278
Anne, the wife of Jesper 114
Annieson, Jonet (witness) 159
Anten, Konrad v. (executive officer, Lübeck Chapter) 93, 394n177
Antwerp (Spanish Netherlands) 15
Apps, Lara 22
Århus district (Denmark) 121
Arild, Thomas (father of Berthel Thomasen) 128
Arildsen, Kosmos (husband of Tora Cosmassis, Court of Appeal Judge) 218, 221, 418n66
Arras (Spanish Netherlands) 31
Ashby William (English ambassador to Scotland) 108, 109–10, 110
Åstrand, Björn 23
Atcheson, Isabel: case (accusation 199; background 199; court decision 207; Jacobean Witchcraft Act of 1604 204, 206; outcome unknown 202, 208; weakness of case 207); interrogation (denial of witchcraft 202, 204, 206, 353; expansive response to questions 201–2; leading questions 206; questions

and responses, complete list of 201; shadow questions 202); interrogator, voice of 206–7; law, voice of 207–8; *maleficium* (blood, drawing of 200–1; cause-and-effect fallacy 342; charms 202; malevolent witchcraft 200); narrative structure (colloquial speech 204; duration 345; oral discourse 204; scribe, voice of 201, 208); voice (indirect speech 204; outspoken 204; resistance 204); witchcraft (persecution, decline in 205; shared belief in 201; witnesses, voices of 205–6); *see also* Simpson, Jane
Atcheson, Ralph (husband of Isabel) 199
Augustin I (Saxony) 107

Backe, Peder (police officer) 227
Balfour, David (commissioner of judiciary) 173
Ballvollen (witches' gathering, Vardø, Norway) 27, 334
Balsvik, Randi Rønning 323
Baltic Sea 289
Bara (witches' gathering, Scotland) 149, 153
Barliehill (witches' gathering, Scotland) 174
Baroja, Julio Caro 328
Barry, Jonathan 24, 27, 184
Båtsman, Olof (husband of witness) 276
Bavaria (Germany) 26
Behringer, Wolfgang 23, 25, 26
Beictspeigel (questionnaire) 70
Bengstsen, Mats (father of Gertrud Matsdotter) 294
Bengtsdotter, Karin 257, 258, 259, 263
Beniaume, Jaene (witchcraft victim) 56
Bergen (Norway): flight, witches 366, 376n106; Knutsdatter, Anne 212, 218, 219, 221, 225, 248, 249; Lyderhorn 333, 334; Olsdatter, Gundelle 238; Pedersdatter, Anne 27–8; witchcraft persecution 214
Bergenheim, Åsa 21, 28
Bergenhus district (Hordaland) 214
Bergenhus Fortress (Norway) 219
Beyer, Absalon Pedersen (Magister and castle minister, husband of Anne Pedersdatter) 418n78
biblical law (Sweden) 255
Bille, Sten (messenger, Denmark) 108
Binsfeld, Peter (Bishop of Trier) 15
Birkelund, Merete 21, 26, 126
Bisset, James (husband of Jonet Annieson, witchcraft victim) 159, 162–3, 166
Bissett, Helene (witchcraft victim) 158